ARBITRATION (SCOTLAND) ACT 2010

ARBITRATION (SCOTLAND) ACT 2010

Professor Fraser Davidson
University of Stirling
Hew R. Dundas, FCIArb, Chartered Arbitrator
International Arbitrator, Mediator & Expert Determiner
David Bartos, FCIArb, Advocate
Terra Firma Chambers

W. GREEN  THOMSON REUTERS

Published in 2010 by
Thomson Reuters (Legal) Limited
(Registered in England and Wales,
Company No 1679046.
Registered office and address for service
100 Avenue Road, Swiss Cottage,
London, NW3 3PF) trading as W. Green

ISBN 978-0-414-01772-6

A catalogue record for this title is available
from the British Library

All rights reserved. UK statutory material used in this publication is acknowledged as Crown Copyright. No part of this publication may be reproduced or transmitted, in any form or by any means, electronic, mechanical, photocopying, recording or otherwise, or stored in any retrieval system of any nature, without prior written permission of the copyright holder and the publisher, application for which should be made to the publisher, except for permitted fair dealing under the Copyright, Designs and Patents Act 1988, or in accordance with the terms of a licence issued by the Copyright Licensing Agency in respect of photocopying and/or reprographic reproduction. Full acknowledgement of publisher and source must be given. Material is contained in this publication for which publishing permission has been sought, and for which copyright is acknowledged. Permission to reproduce such material cannot be granted by the publishers and application must be made to the copyright holders.

No natural forests were destroyed to make this product; only farmed timber was used and replanted.

© 2010 Thomson Reuters (Legal) Limited

Thomson Reuters and the Thomson Reuters Logo
are trademarks of Thomson Reuters.

FOREWORD

The passage of the Arbitration (Scotland) Act 2010 by our devolved administration, often preoccupied as it has been with many other significant priorities, is a fine example of the high value to be gained for our society from close collaboration between practitioners and legislators. From the first meeting of the small steering group in the early 1990s, to the date of Royal Assent, it has been the dream of many enthusiasts to see in Scotland a coherent and enforceable code for dispute resolution outside the court. The 1999 and 2007 Scottish Arbitration Codes were steps along the way, though lacking any legislative backing. Now the dream has been realised, thanks to the opportunity that our own Parliament has given for home grown ideas. Our legal system has done well to survive the Treaty of Union and three centuries in a United Kingdom, with all its pressures for legal conformity. Opting for a distinctive Scottish solution for arbitration that resists the traditional approach flowing from the pervasive Anglicisation of our common law has been a much more difficult task.

The responsive and determined encouragement of our senior politicians in government and in Committee, the spectacular and imaginative approach of our civil servants, and the informed contributions of practitioners, have all enabled our legislature to create an Act of considerable domestic and international significance for the 21st century. Used well, it has the capability to make a great difference to our economic and public life.

At home, the potential exists to turn dispute resolution in all its forms away from the familiar tedium of courts, lawyers and their inevitable costs and delays, to a cleaner, swifter, more private and more economical process, using skilled people from all walks of life. In the field of international disputes, it is now commonly accepted across the world that arbitration has become the single most important form of dispute resolution. It is the only system of dispute resolution that leads to binding, readily enforceable decisions between countries and corporate of different nationalities. International arbitration is a recognised legal discipline, regulated by a sophisticated web of conventions and national and institutional rules. There are arbitral institutions in every country and the subject is widely taught. There is a huge and very valuable amount of activity in this field, and the areas of its application are fast expanding. Construction and maritime, insurance and reinsurance, commodities, aviation and interstate commercial transactions of all kinds have been joined by sports arbitration, intellectual property issues, and, perhaps most significantly, by investor-state arbitration. Now all of these can happen in Scotland, with confidence.

In starting from scratch, adaptation of the UNCITRAL Model Law, per se, (like Bermuda and New Zealand) or adoption of our southern neighbours' 1996 Act were both "easy" options for a nation feeling its way. For a range of carefully researched reasons, Scotland decided upon its own solution, and has devised an Act and rules of its own design, incorporating and developing not only the Model Law itself, with all its clearly focused attributes and many advantages drawn from enormous experience, but also embracing the key features of the 1996 Act, seen over 14 years to have worked so well in England and Wales.

With the world's jurisprudence available to the draftsman, he has been able to include a number of key features not seen elsewhere, tackling difficult areas like confidentiality of process from a standing start. Scotland has thus found itself causing a ripple in the restless and growing world of global arbitration regulation.

Arbitration (Scotland) Act 2010

This first commentary on the Act of 2010 by Professor Fraser Davidson, Mr Hew Dundas and Mr David Bartos shines a bright light on the intricate, yet elegant, provisions of a powerful and articulate code. The work is easy to understand and easy to use. By the clear exposition of principle, yet drawing on the vast body of available precedent and teaching, it enables us to call on the developed skills and practice of the entire world, taking Scotland's aspirations for this vital commercial activity forward by a giant leap. There is no ready parallel in the world today. All three authors must be warmly congratulated for the giving of their time and experience, and for the speed and diligence they have applied to a work which will turn out to be indispensable to practitioners, men and women of business, teachers, students, and indeed to all those with an interest in private and public law.

For all of them, I suggest that political Scotland, the arbitral community and these distinguished authors have clearly shown the way forward. As a result this Act is the best it can be. We should be most grateful for this work.

John Campbell QC
President, Chartered Institute of Arbitrators in 2009

CONTENTS

	Page
Foreword	v
Table of Cases	ix
Table of Statutes	xxix
Table of Scottish Statutes	xxxiii
Table of Abbreviations	xxxix
Introduction	1
Arbitration (Scotland) Act 2010	7
Schedule 1: Scottish Arbitration Rules	102
Schedule 2: Repeals	336
Index	337

TABLE OF CASES

A v B (Costs) [2007] EWHC 54 (Comm); [2007] 1 All E.R. (Comm) 633; [2007] 1 Lloyd's Rep. 358; [2007] 2 C.L.C. 203; [2007] Bus. L.R. D59 24
A v B (No.2). *See* A v B (Costs)
A v B [2006] EWHC 2006 (Comm); [2007] 1 All E.R. (Comm) 591; [2007] 1 Lloyd's Rep. 237; [2007] 2 C.L.C. 157 18
A Sanderson & Son v Armour & Co Ltd; sub nom. Sanderson & Son v Armour & Co Ltd, 1922 S.C. (H.L.) 117; 1922 S.L.T. 285 HL 22, 30
AAMCO Transmissions Inc v Kunz [1996] A.D.R.L.J. 32 CA (Saskatchewan) 70
AB Gotaverken v General NationalMaritime Transport Co (1981) VI YCA 237 Sup Ct (Sweden) 71
ABB Lummus Global Ltd v Keppel Fels Ltd (formerly Far East Levingston Shipbuilding Ltd) [1999] 2 Lloyd's Rep. 24 QBD (Comm Ct) 29, 147
ABN Amro Bank Canada v Krupp Mak Maschinenbau GmbH [1997] A.D.R.L.J. 34 .... 34, 35
ACD Tridon Inc v Tridon Australia Pty Ltd (2004) XIX YCA 533 37
AI Trade Finance v Bulgarian Trade Bank (case 1881-99) Unreported October 27, 2000 Sup Ct 167
AOOT Kalmneft v Glencore International AG. *See* Kalmneft JSC v Glencore International AG
ASM Shipping Ltd of India v TTMI Ltd of England (The Amer Energy); Amer Energy, The [2009] 1 Lloyd's Rep. 293[2009] 1 Lloyd's Rep. 293 QBD (Comm Ct) 42
ASM Shipping Ltd of India v TTMI Ltd of England [2005] EWHC 2238 (Comm); [2006] 2 All E.R. (Comm) 122; [2006] 1 Lloyd's Rep. 375; [2006] 1 C.L.C. 656 .... 118, 123, 128, 129, 162, 325
AT&T Corp v Saudi Cable Co [2000] 2 All E.R. (Comm) 625; [2000] 2 Lloyd's Rep. 127; [2000] C.L.C. 1309; [2000] B.L.R. 293 CA (Civ Div) 129, 159
Aasma v American Steamship Owners Mutual Protection and Indemnity (2003) XXVIII YCA 1140 Dis Ct (US) 71
Aberdeen City Council v Bredero Aberdeen Centre Ltd, 1998 S.C. 269; 1997 G.W.D. 38-1924 IH (1 Div) 261
Aberdeen Railway Co v Blaikie Bothers (1853) 15 D. (HL) 20 242
Abu Dhabi Investment Co v H Clarkson & Co Ltd [2006] EWHC 1252 (Comm); [2006] 2 Lloyd's Rep. 381 36
Agnew v Scott Lithgow Ltd (No.2), 2003 S.C. 448; 2003 S.C.L.R. 426; 2003 G.W.D. 13-443 325
Agrimex Ltd v Tradigrain SA [2003] EWHC 1656 (Comm); [2003] 2 Lloyd's Rep. 537; (2003) 153 N.L.J. 1121 .... 192, 264
Agro Industries (P) Ltd v Texuna International Ltd [1994] 1 H.K.L.R. 89 75
Air India Ltd v Caribjet Inc [2002] 2 All E.R. (Comm) 76; [2002] 1 Lloyd's Rep. 314 QBD (Comm Ct) 79
Al Haddad Bros Enterprises v M/S Agapi (1987) XII YCA 549 .... 67, 68
Al-Hadha Trading Co v Tradigrain SA [2002] 2 Lloyd's Rep. 512 QBD (Mer Ct) 255, 270
Al-Naimi (t/a Buildmaster Construction Services) v Islamic Press Agency Inc; sub nom. Al-Naimi (t/a Buildmaster Construction Services) v Islamic Press Services Inc [2000] 1 Lloyd's Rep. 522; [2000] C.L.C. 647; [2000] B.L.R. 150; (2000) 2 T.C.L.R. 499; 70 Con. L.R. 21 CA (Civ Div) 31, 148
Albon (t/a NA Carriage Co) v Naza Motor Trading Sdn Bhd [2007] EWHC 1879 (Ch); [2007] 2 Lloyd's Rep. 420 .... 33, 35
Ali Shipping Corp v Shipyard Trogir [1999] 1 W.L.R. 314; [1998] 2 All E.R. 136; [1998] 1 Lloyd's Rep. 643; [1998] C.L.C. 566 CA (Civ Div) 51, 52, 167, 169, 170, 171, 172, 173
Allianz SpA (formerly Riunione Adriatica di Sicurta SpA) v West Tankers Inc (C-185/07); Front Comor, The; sub nom. West Tankers Inc v Allianz SpA (formerly Riunione Adriatica di Sicurta SpA) (C-185/07) [2009] 1 A.C. 1138; [2009] 3 W.L.R. 696; [2009] All E.R. (EC) 491; [2009] 1 All E.R. (Comm) 435; [2009] 1 Lloyd's Rep. 413; [2009] 1 C.L.C. 96; [2009] C.E.C. 619; [2009] I.L.Pr. 20; 2009 A.M.C. 2847 19

Table of Cases

Amec Building Ltd v Cadmus Investment Co Ltd [1997] C.L.Y. 262 246
Amec Civil Engineering Ltd v Secretary of State for Transport [2005] EWCA Civ 291; [2005] 1 W.L.R. 2339; [2005] B.L.R. 227; 101 Con. L.R. 26; (2005) 21 Const. L.J. 640; [2005] 12 E.G. 219 (C.S.); (2005) 102(20) L.S.G. 30 15
American Oil Co v Libya (1981) 20 I.L.M. 893 63
Anderson v Gibb, 1993 S.L.T. 726 OH 229
Anderson v Wood (1821) 1 S. 31 39
Antclizo Shipping Corp v Food Corp of India (The Antclizo); Antclizo, The (No.2) [1991] 2 Lloyd's Rep. 485 QBD (Comm Ct) 246
Apis AS v Fantazia Kereskedelmi KFT (No.1) [2001] 1 All E.R. (Comm) 348 QBD (Comm Ct) 43
Apollo Engineering Ltd v James Scott Ltd, 2008 S.L.T. 472; [2009] CSIH 39; 2009 S.C. 525 IH (Ex Div) 257, 282
Arab Business Consortium International Finance & Investment Co v Banque Franco-Tunisienne [1996] 1 Lloyd's Rep. 485 QBD (Comm Ct) 79
Arab National Bank v El-Abdali [2004] EWHC 2381 (Comm); [2005] 1 Lloyd's Rep. 541 48
Arenson v Casson Beckman Rutley & Co; sub nom. Arenson v Arenson [1977] A.C. 405; [1975] 3 W.L.R. 815; [1975] 3 All E.R. 901; [1976] 1 Lloyd's Rep. 179; (1975) 119 S.J. 810 HL 14
Ascot Commodities NV v Olam International Ltd [2002] C.L.C. 277 ...... 303, 310, 311
Ashville Investments Ltd v Elmer Contractors Ltd; sub nom. Elmer Contractors Ltd v Ashville Investments Ltd [1989] Q.B. 488; [1988] 3 W.L.R. 867; [1988] 2 All E.R. 577; [1988] 2 Lloyd's Rep. 73 (Note); 37 B.L.R. 55; 10 Con. L.R. 72; (1987) 3 Const. L.J. 193; (1988) 132 S.J. 1553CA (Civ Div) 245
Associated Electric & Gas Insurance Services Ltd v European Reinsurance Co of Zurich [2003] UKPC 11; [2003] 1 W.L.R. 1041; [2003] 1 All E.R. (Comm) 253; [2003] 2 C.L.C. 340; (2003) 100(11) L.S.G. 31; (2003) 147 S.J.L.B. 148 .... 39, 49, 50, 51, 169, 171
Athletic Union of Constantinople (AEK) v National Basketball Association [2002] 1 All E.R. (Comm) 70; [2002] 1 Lloyd's Rep. 305 QBD (Comm Ct) 150, 151, 325
Atlanska Plovidba v Consignaciones Asturianas SA (The Lapad); Lapad, The [2004] EWHC 1273 (Admlty); [2004] 2 Lloyd's Rep. 109; [2004] 2 C.L.C. 886 ..... 105, 107
Atlantic Lines & Navigation Co Inc v Italmare SpA (The Apollon); Apollon, The [1985] 1 Lloyd's Rep. 597 QBD (Comm Ct) 255
Azov Shipping Co v Baltic Shipping Co (No.1) [1999] 1 All E.R. 476; [1999] 1 Lloyd's Rep. 68; [1998] C.L.C. 1240 QBD (Comm Ct) 147, 148, 292
Azov Shipping Co v Baltic Shipping Co (No.2) [1999] 1 All E.R. (Comm.) 716; [1999] 2 Lloyd's Rep. 39; [1999] C.L.C. 624 QBD (Comm Ct) 317

BHPB Freight Pty Ltd v Cosco Oceania Chartering Pty Ltd [2008] F.C.A. 551 ... 32
BLCT (13096) Ltd v J Sainsbury Plc [2003] EWCA Civ 884; [2004] 1 C.L.C. 24; [2004] 2 P. & C.R. 3; (2003) 147 S.J.L.B. 815 .... 12, 310
BMBF (No.12) Ltd v Harland & Wolff Shipbuilding & Heavy Industries Ltd [2001] EWCA Civ 862; [2001] 2 All E.R. (Comm) 385; [2001] 2 Lloyd's Rep. 227; [2001] C.L.C. 1552 259
BP Chemicals Ltd v Kingdom Engineering (Fife) Ltd [1994] 2 Lloyd's Rep. 373; 69 B.L.R. 113; 38 Con. L.R. 14; (1994) 10 Const. L.J. 116 QBD 246
Babanaft International Co SA v Avanti Petroleum Inc (The Oltenia); Oltenia, The; sub nom. Babanaft International Co SA v Avant Petroleum Inc [1982] 1 W.L.R. 871; [1982] 3 All E.R. 244; [1982] 2 Lloyd's Rep. 99; [1982] Com. L.R. 104; [1983] E.C.C. 365; (1982) 79 L.S.G. 953; (1982) 126 S.J. 361 CA (Civ Div) 215
Babcock Rosyth Defence Ltd v Grootcon (UK) Ltd, 1998 S.L.T. 1143; 1997 G.W.D. 19-864 OH 21
Baillie v Pollock (1829) 7 S. 619 43
Baird's Trustees v Baird & Co (1877) 4 R. 1005 248
Baker Marine (Nigeria) Ltd v Chevron (Nigeria) Ltd, 191 F.3d 194 (1999) 73
Bakwin and Erie International Trading Co v Sothebys Unreported 2005 35
Baleares, The. See Geogas SA v Trammo Gas Ltd (The Baleares)

Table of Cases

Bandwidth Shipping Corp v Intaari (A Firm) (The Magdalena Oldendorff); Magdalena Oldendorff, The [2007] EWCA Civ 998; [2008] Bus. L.R. 702; [2008] 1 All E.R. (Comm) 1015; [2008] 1 Lloyd's Rep. 7; [2007] 2 C.L.C. 537 297
Bank Mellat v GAA Development Construction Co Ltd [1988] 2 Lloyd's Rep. 44; [1988] F.T.L.R. 409 QBD (Comm Ct) 249
Bargues Agro Industrie SA v Young Pecan Ltd (2005) XXX YCA 499 CA (Paris) ... 66
Bay Hotel and Resort Ltd v Cavalier Construction Co Ltd [2001] UKPC 34 ... 189, 253, 254
Belgravia Property Co Ltd v S&R (London) Ltd [2001] C.L.C. 1626; [2001] B.L.R. 424; 93 Con. L.R. 59; (2003) 19 Const. L.J. 36 QBD (T&CC) 154
Benaim (UK) Ltd v Davies Middleton & Davies Ltd (No.2) [2005] EWHC 1370 (TCC); 102 Con. L.R. 1255 .... 296, 297, 299
Bermuda Court of Appeal in Sojuzneftexport v Joc Oil Ltd (1990) XV YCA 384 62
Bernuth Lines Ltd v High Seas Shipping Ltd (The Eastern Navigator); Eastern Navigator, The [2005] EWHC 3020 (Comm); [2006] 1 All E.R. (Comm) 359; [2006] 1 Lloyd's Rep. 537; [2006] 1 C.L.C. 403; [2006] C.I.L.L. 2343; (2006) 156 N.L.J. 64 .... 103, 292, 332
Birkett v James [1978] A.C. 297; [1977] 3 W.L.R. 38; [1977] 2 All E.R. 801; (1977) 121 S.J. 444 HL 202, 203
Birse Construction Ltd v Cooperative Wholesale Society Ltd (1997) 84 B.L.R. 58 39
Blair v Gibb (1738) Mor. 664 263
Bonnor v Balfour Kilpatrick Ltd, 1974 S.C. 223; 1975 S.L.T. (Notes) 3 IH (1 Div) ... 305
Bottiglieri di Navigazione SpA v Cosco Qingdao Ocean Shipping Co (The Bunga Saga Lima); Bunga Saga Lima, The [2005] EWHC 244 (Comm); [2005] 2 Lloyd's Rep. 1 309
Boyd & Forrest (A Firm) v Glasgow & South Western Railway Co (No.1), 1912 S.C. (H.L.) 93; 1912 1 S.L.T. 476 HL 301
Bradford v McLeod, 1986 S.L.T. 244; 1985 S.C.C.R. 379; [1986] Crim. L.R. 690 HCJ 160
Braes of Doune Wind Farm (Scotland) Ltd v Alfred McAlpine Business Services Ltd [2008] EWHC 426 (TCC); [2008] 2 All E.R. (Comm) 493; [2008] 1 Lloyd's Rep. 608; [2008] 1 C.L.C. 487; [2008] B.L.R. 321; [2008] Bus. L.R. D137 ...... 18, 19, 29, 188, 309
Bremen v Zapata Off-Shore Co, 407 U.S. 1 (1972) 35
Bremer Handelsgesellschaft mbH v Westzucker GmbH (No.2); sub nom. Bunge GmbH v Westzucker GmbH [1981] 2 Lloyd's Rep. 130; [1981] Com. L.R. 179 CA (Civ Div) 254
Bremner v Elder (1875) 2 R. (HL) 136 108
Brown v EE Caledonia Ltd, 1993 G.W.D. 24-1478 93
Brown v Hamilton DC, 1983 S.C. (H.L.) 1; 1983 S.L.T. 397; (1983) 133 N.L.J. 63 IIL 46
Bulbank 2000 Sup Ct (Sweden) 167, 172
Bulgarian Foreign Trade Bank Ltd v Al Trade Finance Inc (2001) XXVI YCA 291 Sup Ct (Swedish) 24
Bulk & Metal Transport (UK) LLP v Voc Bulk Ultra Handymax Pool LLC (Voc Gallant); Voc Gallant, The [2009] EWHC 288 (Comm); [2009] 2 All E.R. (Comm) 377; [2009] 1 Lloyd's Rep. 418 106
Bunge SA v ADM do Brasil Ltda [2009] EWHC 845 (Comm); [2009] 2 Lloyd's Rep. 175; [2009] 1 C.L.C. 608 209
Burt v Kirkcaldy [1965] 1 W.L.R. 474; [1965] 1 All E.R. 741; (1965) 129 J.P. 190; (1965) 109 S.J. 33 QBD 332
Butera v Pagnan (1979) IV YCA 296 Sup Ct (Italy) 72

C v D [2007] EWCA Civ 1282; [2008] Bus. L.R. 843; [2008] 1 All E.R. (Comm) 1001; [2008] 1 Lloyd's Rep. 239; [2008] C.P. Rep. 11; [2007] 2 C.L.C. 930; 116 Con. L.R. 230 .... 24, 29, 39
CGU International Insurance Plc v AstraZeneca Insurance Co Ltd (Permission to Appeal); sub nom. AstraZeneca Insurance Co Ltd v CGU International Insurance Plc (Permission to Appeal) [2006] EWCA Civ 1340; [2007] Bus. L.R. 162; [2007] 1

Table of Cases

All E.R. (Comm) 501; [2007] 1 Lloyd's Rep. 142; [2007] C.P. Rep. 4; [2006] 2 C.L.C. 441; [2006] H.R.L.R. 43; 311
CMA CGM SA v Beteiligungs KG MS Northern Pioneer Schiffahrtsgesellschaft mbH & Co [2002] EWCA Civ 1878; [2003] 1 W.L.R. 1015; [2003] 3 All E.R. 330; [2003] 1 All E.R. (Comm) 204; [2003] 1 Lloyd's Rep. 212; [2003] 1 C.L.C. 141; (2003) 100(9) L.S.G. 28 ..... 308, 309
COMITAS v SOVAG (1983) VIII YCA 366 72
Caledonian Railway Co v Lockhart (1860) 22 D. (HL) 8 192
Calvan Consolidated Oil & Gas Co Ltd v Manning (1958) 16 D.L.R. (2d) 27 15
Campbell v Mirror Group Newspapers Ltd; sub nom. Campbell v MGN Ltd [2004] UKHL 22; [2004] 2 A.C. 457; [2004] 2 W.L.R. 1232; [2004] 2 All E.R. 995; [2004] E.M.L.R. 15; [2004] H.R.L.R. 24; [2004] U.K.H.R.R. 648; 16 B.H.R.C. 500; (2004) 101(21) L.S.G. 36; (2004) 154 N.L.J. 733; (2004) 148 S.J.L.B. 572 173
Cane v Hegeman-Harris Co Ltd [1993] 4 All E.R. 68 CA 245
Caparo Group Ltd v Fagor Arrasate Sociedad Cooperative [2000] A.D.R.L.J. 254 ... 48
Capital & Counties Plc v Hawa [1991] 2 E.G.L.R. 133; [1991] 46 E.G. 163 Ch D 178
Cargill International SA Antigua (Geneva Branch) v Sociedad Iberica de Molturacion SA [1998] 1 Lloyd's Rep. 489 ..... 249, 253
Cargill SRL (Milan) (formerly Cargill SpA) v P Kadinopoulos SA [1992] 1 Lloyd's Rep. 1 HL 200, 201
Carnegie v Nature Conservancy Council, 1992 S.L.T. 342 OH 283, 284
Carter (t/a Michael Carter Partnership) v Harold Simpson Associates (Architects) Ltd [2004] UKPC 29; [2005] 1 W.L.R. 919; [2004] 2 Lloyd's Rep. 512; [2004] 2 C.L.C. 1053; (2004) 101(27) L.S.G. 29; (2004) 148 S.J.L.B. 759 320
Carters (Merchants) Ltd v Ferraro (1979) IV YCA 275 CA (Naples) 66
Cetelem SA v Roust Holdings Ltd [2005] EWCA Civ 618; [2005] 1 W.L.R. 3555; [2005] 4 All E.R. 52; [2005] 2 All E.R. (Comm) 203; [2005] 2 Lloyd's Rep. 494; [2005] 1 C.L.C. 821 ..... 171, 233
Channel Tunnel Group Ltd v Balfour Beatty Construction Ltd; France Manche SA v Balfour Beatty Construction Ltd [1993] A.C. 334; [1993] 2 W.L.R. 262; [1993] 1 All E.R. 664; [1993] 1 Lloyd's Rep. 291; 61 B.L.R. 1; 32 Con. L.R. 1; [1993] I.L.Pr. 607; (1993) 137 S.J.L.B. 36; [1993] N.P.C. 8 HL 24, 32, 34
Charles M Willie & Co (Shipping) Ltd v Ocean Laser Shipping Ltd (The Smaro); George Roussos Sons SA v Charles M Willie & Co (Shipping) Ltd [1999] 1 Lloyd's Rep. 225; [1999] C.L.C. 301 QBD (Comm Ct) 200, 260
Checkpoint Ltd v Strathclyde Pension Fund [2003] EWCA Civ 84; [2003] L. & T.R. 22; [2003] 1 E.G.L.R. 1; [2003] 14 E.G. 124; [2003] 8 E.G. 128 (C.S.); (2003) 100(12) L.S.G. 29; (2003) 147 S.J.L.B. 233; [2003] N.P.C. 23 296
Chimimport Plc v G D'Alesio SAS (The Paula D'Alesio); Paula D'Alesio, The [1994] 2 Lloyd's Rep. 366; [1994] C.L.C. 459 QBD (Comm Ct) 147
China Agribusiness Development Corp v Balli Trading [1998] 2 Lloyd's Rep. 76; [1997] C.L.C. 1437 QBD (Comm Ct) 60, 67
China Merchant Heavy Industry Co Ltd v JGC Corp (2003) XXVIII YCA 267 CA (HK) 37
China Nanhai Oil Joint Service Corp v Gee Tai Holdings Ltd [1995] A.D.R.L.J. 127 ..... 60, 67
China Resources Metal Ltd v Anada Non-Ferrous Metals Ltd [1994] H.K.C. 526 35
Chromalloy Aeroservices Inc v Arab Republic of Egypt, 939 F.Supp. 907 (1996) Dis Ct (US) 73
City of Moscow v Bankers Trust Co. *See* Department of Economic Policy and Development of the City of Moscow v Bankers Trust Co
Clark v Stirling (1839) 1 D. 955 232
Classic Maritime Inc v Lion Diversified Holdings bhd [2009] EWHC 1142 (Comm); [2010] 1 Lloyd's Rep. 59 31
Coal Authority v Trustees of the Nostell Trust [2005] EWHC 154 (TCC) 308, 310
Collins (Contractors) Ltd v Baltic Quay Management (1994) Ltd [2004] EWCA Civ 1757; [2005] B.L.R. 63; [2005] T.C.L.R. 3; 99 Con. L.R. 1; (2005) 102(5) L.S.G. 26 15
Cominco France SA v Soquiber SL (1983) VIII YCA 408 Sup Ct (Spain) 65

Table of Cases

Commerce & Industry Insurance Co (Canada) v Lloyd's Underwriters; sub nom. Viking Insurance Co v Rossdale [2002] 1 W.L.R. 1323; [2002] 2 All E.R. (Comm) 204; [2002] 1 Lloyd's Rep. 219; [2002] C.L.C. 26 QBD (Comm Ct) 220
Commerzbank AG v Large, 1977 S.C. 375; 1977 S.L.T. 219 IH (1 Div) 242
Commonwealth of Australia v Cockatoo Dockyard Pty Ltd (1995) 36 N.S.W.L.R. 662 52
Compagnie d'Armement Maritime SA v Compania Tunisienne de Navigation SA. *See* Compagnie Tunisienne de Navigation SA v Compagnie d'Armement Maritime SA
Compagnie de Saint Gobain-Pont a Mousson v Fertilizer Corp of India Ltd (1976) I YCA 184 72
Compagnie des Bauxites de Guinee v Hammermills Inc (1993) XVIII YCA 566 Dis Ct (US) 67
Compagnie Tunisienne de Navigation SA v Compagnie d'Armement Maritime SA; sub nom. Compagnie d'Armement Maritime SA v Compagnie Tunisienne de Navigation SA [1971] A.C. 572; [1970] 3 W.L.R. 389; [1970] 3 All E.R. 71; [1970] 2 Lloyd's Rep. 99; (1970) (1970) 114 S.J. 618 HL 238
Compania Sud-Americana De Vapores SA v Nippon Yusen Kaisha; Nippon Yusen Kaisha v Compania Sud-Americana De Vapores SA [2009] EWHC 1606 (Comm) 297
Conder Structures v Kvaerner Construction Ltd [1999] A.D.R.L.J. 305 127
Corcoran v Adra Insurance Company Ltd (1989) XIV YCA 733 37
Corcoran v AIG Multi-line Syndicate Inc (1990) XV YCA 586 63
Corcoran v Ardra Insurance Co Ltd (1991) XVI YCA 663 63
Corporacion Transnacional de Inversiones SA de CV v STET International SpA (2000) O.R. 414 59
Corvetina Technology Ltd v Clough Engineering Ltd [2004] N.S.W.S.C. 700 76
Craig's Trustee v Lord Malloch (1900) 2 F. 541 39
Crudens, Applicants; sub nom. Crudens Ltd, Petitioners, 1971 S.C. 64 220
Czech Republic v CME Unreported May 15, 2003 CA (Sweden) 250

DDT Trucks of North America Ltd v DDT Holdings Ltd [2007] EWHC 1542 (Comm); [2007] 2 Lloyd's Rep. 213 302
Dalimpex v Janicki [2003] 172 O.A.C. 321 36
Dallah Real Estate & Tourism Holding Co v Pakistan; sub nom. Dallah Real Estate & Tourism Holding Co v Ministry of Religious Affairs [2009] EWCA Civ 755; [2010] 2 W.L.R. 805; [2010] Bus. L.R. 384; [2010] 1 All E.R. 592; [2010] 1 Lloyd's Rep. 119; [2009] 2 C.L.C. 84; [2010] B.L.R. 1; 125 Con. L.R. 37; [2009] 30 E.G. 67 (C.S.) 64
Dalmia Dairy Industries v National Bank of Pakistan [1978] 2 Lloyd's Rep. 223; (1977) 121 S.J. 442 CA (Civ Div) 77
Dalmine SpA v M & M Sheet Metal Forming Machinery (1999) XXIV YCA 709 Sup Ct (Italy) 62
Damond Lock Grabowski v Laing Investments (Bracknell) Ltd, 60 B.L.R. 112 127
Danae Air Transport SA v Air Canada [2000] 1 W.L.R. 395; [2000] 2 All E.R. 649; [1999] 2 All E.R. (Comm) 943; [1999] 2 Lloyd's Rep. 547; [2000] C.P. Rep. 25; [1999] C.L.C. 1859; (1999) 96(32) L.S.G. 31; [1999] N.P.C. 108 CA (Civ Div) 272
Dardana Ltd v Yukos Oil Co (No.1); sub nom. Petroalliance Services Co Ltd v Yukos Oil Co; Yukos Oil Co v Dardana Ltd [2002] EWCA Civ 543; [2002] 1 All E.R. (Comm) 819; [2002] 2 Lloyd's Rep. 326; [2002] C.L.C. 1120 .... 60, 79, 80, 81
Dardana Ltd v Yukos Oil Co (No.2) [2002] 2 Lloyd's Rep. 261 QBD (Comm Ct) ... 80
David Wilson Homes Ltd v Survey Services Ltd (In Liquidation) [2001] EWCA Civ 34; [2001] 1 All E.R. (Comm) 449; [2001] B.L.R. 267; (2001) 3 T.C.L.R. 13; 80 Con. L.R. 8 14
De Cubber v Belgium (A/86); sub nom. De Cubber v Belgium (9186/80) (1985) 7 E.H.R.R. 236 ECtHR 160
Deko Scotland Ltd v Edinburgh Royal Joint Venture, 2003 S.L.T. 727; 2003 G.W.D. 13-396 OH 279
Demco Investments & Commercial SA v SE Banken Forsakring Holding AB [2005] EWHC 1398 (Comm); [2005] 2 Lloyd's Rep. 650 .... 178, 308, 309
Department of Economic Policy and Development of the City of Moscow v Bankers Trust Co; sub nom. Department of Economics, Policy and Development of the City

Table of Cases

of Moscow v Bankers Trust Co; Moscow City Council v Bankers Trust Co [2004]
EWCA Civ 314; [2005] Q.B. 207; [2004] 3 W.L.R. 533; [2004] 4 All E.R. 746; [2004]
2 All E.R. (Comm) 193; [2004] 2 Lloyd's Rep. 179; [2004] 1 C.L.C. 1099; [2004]
B.L.R. 229; (2004) 148 S.J.L.B. 389 .... 51, 168, 169, 172
Dermajaya Properties Sdn Bhd v Premium Properties Sdn Bhd (2002) 2 S.L.R. 164 H Ct
(Singapore) 96
Deutsche Schachtbau- und Tiefbohrgesellschaft mbH v Ras Al-Khaimah National Oil
Co; Deutsche Schachtbau- und Tiefbohrgesellschaft mbH v Ras Al-Khaimah
National Oil Co (Garnishee Proceedings); Deutsche Schachtbau- und Tiefbohrge-
sellschaft mbH v Shell International Petroleum Co Ltd (Nos.1 and 2); sub nom.
DST v Rakoil [1990] 1 A.C. 295; [1988] 3 W.L.R. 230; [1988] 2 All E.R. 833; [1988] 2
Lloyd's Rep. 293; (1988) 85(28) L.S.G. 45 HL 24, 63, 69
Director General of Fair Trading v Proprietary Association of Great Britain. *See*
Medicaments and Related Classes of Goods (No.2), Re
Director General of Fair Trading v Proprietary Association of Great Britain; sub nom.
Medicaments and Related Classes of Goods (No.2), Re [2001] 1 W.L.R. 700; [2001]
U.K.C.L.R. 550; [2001] I.C.R. 564; [2001] H.R.L.R. 17; [2001] U.K.H.R.R. 429;
(2001) 3 L.G.L.R. 32; (2001) 98(7) L.S.G. 40; (2001) 151 N.L.J. 17; (2001) 145
S.J.L.B. 29 CA (Civ Div) 119, 160
Discain Project Services Ltd v Opecprime Developments Ltd [2001] EWHC 450
(TCC) 144
Dodwell & Co (Australia) Pty v Moss Security (1994) XIX YCA 615 37
Dolling-Baker v Merrett [1990] 1 W.L.R. 1205; [1991] 2 All E.R. 890; (1990) 134 S.J. 806
CA (Civ Div) 166, 167, 168, 169, 170
Double K Oil Products 1996 Ltd v Neste Oil Oyj [2009] EWHC 3380 (Comm); [2010] 1
Lloyd's Rep. 141; (2010) 160 N.L.J. 68 QBD (Comm Ct) 302
Drummond v Bell-Irving; sub nom. Drummond v Peel's Trustees, 1929 S.C. 484; 1929
S.L.T. 450 IH 227
Dubois & Vanderwalle v Boots Frites BV (1999) XXIV YCA 640 CA (Paris) 69
Duffy (John) v Normand, 1995 S.L.T. 1264; 1995 S.C.C.R. 538 HCJ (Appeal) 332
Dupont Scandinavia AB v Coastal (Bermuda) Ltd (1990) XV YCA 378 CA
(Bermuda) 36
Durham CC v Darlington BC [2003] EWHC 2598 (Admin); [2004] B.L.G.R. 311; [2003]
N.P.C. 136; 246
Dutco (Pvt) Ltd v Dajen (Pvt) Ltd [1997] 2 Zimbabwe L.R. 199 72
Dykes v Roy (1869) 7 M. 357 250

ECONERG Ltd v National Electricity Company AD (2000) XXV YCA 678 Sup Ct
(Bulgarian) 81
ERDC Construction Ltd v HM Love & Co (No.2), 1996 S.C. 523; 1997 S.L.T. 175; 1996
S.C.L.R. 886 IH (1 Div) 92, 210, 211, 212, 213
Eagle Star Insurance Co Ltd v Yuval Insurance Co Ltd [1978] 1 Lloyd's Rep. 357 CA
(Civ Div) 33
Eastern Navigator, The. *See* Bernuth Lines Ltd v High Seas Shipping Ltd (The Eastern
Navigator)
Easy Rider, The. *See* Tame Shipping Ltd v Easy Navigation Ltd (The Easy Rider)
Ecoswiss China Time Ltd v Bennetton International [1999] 2 All E.R. (Comm) 44 78
Edinburgh and Glasgow Railway v Hill (1840) 2 D. 468 259
Edwards (Inspector of Taxes) v Bairstow; Edwards (Inspector of Taxes) v Harrison
[1956] A.C. 14; [1955] 3 W.L.R. 410; [1955] 3 All E.R. 48; 48 R. & I.T. 534; 36 T.C.
207; (1955) 34 A.T.C. 198; [1955] T.R. 209; (1955) 99 S.J. 558 HL 176, 178, 179, 211
Egypt v SPP Ltd (1985) X YCA 113 63
Elektrim SA v Vivendi Universal SA [2007] EWHC 11 (Comm); [2007] 2 All E.R.
(Comm) 365; [2007] 1 Lloyd's Rep. 693; [2007] 1 C.L.C. 16; [2007] Bus. L.R.
D69 302
Elektrim SA v Vivendi Universal SA [2007] EWHC 571 (Comm); [2007] 2 Lloyd's Rep.
8; [2007] 1 C.L.C. 227 171
Emmott v Michael Wilson & Partners Ltd; Michael Wilson & Partners Ltd v Emmott
[2009] EWHC 1 (Comm); [2009] Bus. L.R. 723; [2009] 2 All E.R. (Comm) 856;
[2009] 1 Lloyd's Rep. 233 226

Table of Cases

Emmott v Michael Wilson & Partners Ltd. *See* Michael Wilson & Partners Ltd v Emmott
Essex CC v Premier Recycling Ltd [2006] EWHC 3594 (TCC); [2007] B.L.R. 233 304
Esso Australia Resources Ltd v Plowman (1995) 128 A.L.R. 391 .... 52, 167
Esso v Plowman (1995) 128 A.L.R. 391 H Ct (Aus) 167, 172, 173
Ethiopia v Baruch Foster Corp (1977) II YCA 252 81
Etri Fans Ltd v NMB (UK) Ltd [1987] 1 W.L.R. 1110; [1987] 2 All E.R. 763; [1987] 2 Lloyd's Rep. 565; [1987] F.S.R. 389; (1987) 84 L.S.G. 2457; (1987) 131 S.J. 1063 CA (Civ Div) 31
Europcar Italia SpA v Maiellano Tours International Inc, 156 F.3d 310 (1998) CA (US) 79
European Grain & Shipping Ltd v Johnston [1983] Q.B. 520; [1983] 2 W.L.R. 241; [1982] 3 All E.R. 989; [1982] 2 Lloyd's Rep. 550; [1982] Com. L.R. 246; [1984] E.C.C. 219; (1982) 126 S.J. 783 CA (Civ Div) 249
Everglade Maritime Inc v Schiffahrtsgesellschaft Detlef von Appen GmbH (The Maria); Maria, The [1993] Q.B. 780; [1993] 3 W.L.R. 176; [1993] 3 All E.R. 748; [1993] 2 Lloyd's Rep. 168 CA (Civ Div) 177
Excelsior Film TV Srl v UGC-PH (1999) XXIV YCA 643 Ct of First Instance (France) 77
Exmar BV v National Iranian Tanker Co (The Trade Fortitude); Trade Fortitude, The [1992] 1 Lloyd's Rep. 169 QBD (Comm Ct) 260

F&G Sykes (Wessex) Ltd v Fine Fare Ltd [1967] 1 Lloyd's Rep. 53 CA 15
FCLG Enterprises v Golden Margarine Ltd [2004] O.J. 3804 260
FIAT SpA v Suriname (1998) XXIII YCA 880 Dis Ct (US) 78
Fairlie Yacht Slip v Lumsden, 1977 S.L.T. (Notes) 41 IH (1 Div) 92, 261
Far Eastern Shipping Co v AKP Sovcomflot [1995] 1 Lloyd's Rep. 520 QBD (Comm Ct) 79
Fashion Ribbon Co Inc v Iberband SL (2005) XXX YCA 627 Sup Ct (Spain) 66
Federal Insurance Co v Transamerica Occidental Life Insurance Co; Transamerica Occidental Life Insurance Co v Federal Insurance Co [1999] 2 All E.R. (Comm) 138; [1999] 2 Lloyd's Rep. 286; [1999] C.L.C. 1406; (1999) 149 N.L.J. 1037 QBD (Comm Ct) 12
Feeney v Fife Coal Co, 1918 S.C. 197 283
Fence Gate Ltd v NEL Construction Ltd [2001] 82 Con. L.R. 41 QBD (T&T Ct) 176, 179
Fertilizer Corp of India v IDI Management Inc (1982) VII YCA 382 Dis Ct (US) ... 71, 72
Fidelity Management SA v Myriad International Holdings BV [2005] EWHC 1193 (Comm); [2005] 2 All E.R. (Comm) 312; [2005] 2 Lloyd's Rep. 508 299
Fincantieri-Cantieri Navali Italiani SpA v M (1995) XX YCA 76 Federal Tribunal (Switzerland) 94
Fincantieri-Cantieri Navali Italiani SpA v Ministry of Defence of Iraq (1996) XXI YCA 594 CA (Genoa) 93
Finelvet AG v Vinava Shipping Co Ltd (The Chrysalis); Chrysalis, The [1983] 1 W.L.R. 1469; [1983] 2 All E.R. 658; [1983] 1 Lloyd's Rep. 503; [1983] Com. L.R. 126; (1983) 80 L.S.G. 2684; (1983) 127 S.J. 680 QBF 254
Fiona Trust & Holding Corp v Privalov; sub nom. Premium Nafta Products Ltd v Fili Shipping Co Ltd [2007] EWCA Civ 20; [2007] Bus. L.R. 686; [2007] 1 All E.R. (Comm) 891; [2007] 2 Lloyd's Rep. 267; [2007] 1 C.L.C. 144; (2007) 23 Const. L.J. 307; (2007) 104(6) L.S.G. 33 103
Fiona Trust & Holding Corp v Privalov; sub nom. Premium Nafta Products Ltd v Fili Shipping Co Ltd [2007] UKHL 40; [2007] Bus. L.R. 1719; [2007] 4 All E.R. 951; [2007] 2 All E.R. (Comm) 1053; [2008] 1 Lloyd's Rep. 254; [2007] 2 C.L.C. 553; 114 Con. L.R. 69; [2007] C.I.L.L. 2528; (2007) 104(42) L.S.G. 34; (2007) 151 S.J.L.B. 1364 .... 22, 245
Fisher v Colquhoun (1844) 6 D. 1286 88
Fleming v Gemmill, 1908 S.C. 340; (1907) 15 S.L.T. 691 IH (1 Div) 276
Flight Training International Inc v International Fire Training Equipment Ltd [2004] EWHC 721 (Comm); [2004] 2 All E.R. (Comm) 568 14

xv

Table of Cases

Food Corp of India v Marastro Cia Naviera SA (The Trade Fortitude) (No.1); Food Corp of India v Marastro Cia Naviera SA (The Trade Fortitude) (No.2); Trade Fortitude, The (No.1); Trade Fortitude, The (No.2) [1987] 1 W.L.R. 134; [1986] 2 All E.R. 500; [1986] 2 Lloyd's Rep. 209; (1986) 83 L.S.G. 2919; (1986) 136 N.L.J. 607; (1986) 130 S.J. 649 CA (Civ Div) 270
Food Services of America Inc v Pan Pacific Specialities Ltd (2004) XXIX YCA 581 Sup Ct (BC) 69
Fougerolle SA v Syrian Ministry of Defence (1995) XX YCA 515 63
Fowler v Merrill Lynch Pierce and Smith Inc (1985) X YCA 499 37
Fraser v Pattie (1847) 9 D. 303 227
Fraser v Wright (1838) 16 S. 1049 263
Fuga AG v Bunge AG [1975] 2 Lloyd's Rep. 192 QBD (Comm Ct) 270
Fun Sang Trading Ltd v Kai Sun Sea Products & Food Co Ltd [1992] A.D.R.L.J. 93 .... 31, 146, 147

G SpA v V SpA (1993) XVIII YCA 143 93
GWL Kersten & Co BV v Societe Commerciale Raoul-Duval & Cie (1994) XIX YCA 708 CA (Amsterdam) 67
Galloway Water Power Co v Carmichael, 1937 S.C. 135; 1937 S.L.T. 188 IH (2 Div) 229, 236
Gannet Shipping Ltd v Eastrade Commodities Inc; Eastrade Commodities Inc v Gannet Shipping Ltd [2002] 1 All E.R. (Comm) 297; [2002] 1 Lloyd's Rep. 713; [2002] C.L.C. 365 QBD (Comm Ct) 273, 297
Gater Assets Ltd v Nak Naftogaz Ukrainiy [2007] EWCA Civ 988; [2008] Bus. L.R. 388; [2008] 1 All E.R. (Comm) 209; [2007] 2 Lloyd's Rep. 588; [2008] C.P. Rep. 4; [2007] 2 C.L.C. 567 80
Gater Assets Ltd v Nak Naftogaz Ukrainiy [2008] EWHC 1108 (Comm); [2009] Bus. L.R. 396; [2009] 1 All E.R. (Comm) 667; [2008] 2 Lloyd's Rep. 295 76
Gatoil v National Iranian Oil Co (1993) Revue de l'Arbitrage 281 35
Gbangbola v Smith & Sherriff Ltd [1998] 3 All E.R. 730; (1999) 1 T.C.L.R. 136 QBD (T&CC) 39, 272
Generica Ltd v Pharmaceuticals Basics Inc, 125 F.3d 1123 (1997) CA (US) 66
Genoa Court of Appeal in Della Sanara Kustvaart v Fallimento Cap Giovanni Coppola Srl (1992) XVII YCA 542 35
Geogas SA v Trammo Gas Ltd (The Baleares); Baleares, The [1993] 1 Lloyd's Rep. 215 CA (Civ Div) 177, 178
George Cohen Sons & Co Ltd v Jamieson & Paterso, 1963 S.C. 289; 1963 S.L.T. 35 OH 227
Glidepath BV v Thompson [2005] EWHC 818 (Comm); [2005] 2 All E.R. (Comm) 833; [2005] 2 Lloyd's Rep. 549; [2005] 1 C.L.C. 1090 .... 168, 169
Goodwins, Jardine & Co v Brand (1905) 7 F. 995 21
Grampian RC v John G McGregor (Contractors) Ltd, 1994 S.L.T. 133 IH (1 Div) ... 282
Gray v Brown (1833) 11 S. 353 .... 231, 243
Groundshire v VHE Construction [2001] B.L.R. 395 QBD (T&CC) 126, 271
Grovit v Doctor [1997] 1 W.L.R. 640; [1997] 2 All E.R. 417; [1997] C.L.C. 1038; (1997) 94(20) L.S.G. 37; (1997) 147 N.L.J. 633; (1997) 141 S.J.L.B. 107 HL 202
Grow Biz International v DLT Holdings Inc (2005) XXX YCA 450 67
Guandong New Technology Import and Export Corp v Chiu Sing (1993) XVIII YCA 385 H Ct (HK) 65
Guardcliffe Properties Ltd v City & St James [2003] EWHC 215 (Ch); [2003] 2 E.G.L.R. 16; [2003] 25 E.G. 143; (2003) 147 S.J.L.B. 693 179
Guns 'n' Roses Missouri Storm Inc v Productions Musicales Donald K Donald Inc (1994) 114 D.L.R. (4th) 441 37

HOK Sport Ltd (formerly Lobb Partnership Ltd) v Aintree Racecourse Co Ltd [2002] EWHC 3094 (TCC); [2003] B.L.R. 155; 86 Con. L.R. 165; [2003] Lloyd's Rep. P.N. 148 .... 137, 214
Hackwood Ltd v Areen Design Services Ltd [2005] EWHC 2322 (TCC); (2006) 22 Const. L.J. 68 48
Haendler v Paczy. See Paczy v Haendler & Natermann GmbH (No.2); Halfdan Grieg & Co A/S v Sterling Coal & Navigation Corp (The Lysland); Lysland, The [1973] Q.B.

Table of Cases

843; [1973] 2 W.L.R. 904; [1973] 2 All E.R. 1073; [1973] 1 Lloyd's Rep. 296; (1973) 117 S.J. 415 CA (Civ Div) 211

Halki Shipping Corp v Sopex Oils Ltd (The Halki); Halki, The [1998] 1 W.L.R. 726; [1998] 2 All E.R. 23; [1998] 1 Lloyd's Rep. 465; [1998] C.L.C. 583; (1998) 142 S.J.L.B. 44; [1998] N.P.C. 4 CA (Civ Div) 12, 15

Halvanon Insurance Co Ltd v Companhia de Seguros do Estado de Sao Paolo [1995] L.R.L.R 403 37

Hamlyn v Talisker Distillery Co (1894) 21 R. (HL) 21 .... 32, 83, 300, 301

Harbour Assurance Co (UK) Ltd v Kansa General International Insurance Co Ltd [1993] Q.B. 701; [1993] 3 W.L.R. 42; [1993] 3 All E.R. 897; [1993] 1 Lloyd's Rep. 455 CA (Civ Div) 22

Hassneh Insurance Co of Israel v Stuart J Mew [1993] 2 Lloyd's Rep. 243 QBD (Comm Ct) 167, 169, 170

Hauschildt v Denmark (A/154) (1990) 12 E.H.R.R. 266 ECtHR 160

Hayter v Nelson & Home Insurance Co [1990] 2 Lloyd's Rep. 265; 23 Con. L.R. 88 QBD (Comm Ct) 15, 34

Hebei Import & Export Corp v Politek Engineering Co Ltd (1998) XXIV YCA 652 CA (HK) 65, 77

Heifer International Inc v Christiansen [2007] EWHC 3015 (TCC); [2008] 2 All E.R. (Comm) 831; [2008] Bus. L.R. D49 6

Henderson v Maclellan (1874) 1 R. 920 232

Henry Boot Construction Ltd v Alstom Combined Cycles Ltd [2005] EWCA Civ 814; [2005] 1 W.L.R. 3850; [2005] 3 All E.R. 832; [2005] 2 C.L.C. 63; [2005] B.L.R. 437; 101 Con. L.R. 52; (2005) 102(30) L.S.G. 28 88

Henry v Hepburn (1835) 13 S. 361 39

Highland Railway Co v Mitchell (1868) 6 M. 896 219

Hill v Council of the Law Society of Scotland, 2000 S.C. 582; 2000 S.L.T. 1389; 2000 G.W.D. 26-1001 IH (Ex Div) 243

Himpurna California Energy Ltd v PT (Persero) Perusahaan Listruik Negara (2000) XXV YCA 13 94,125

Hip Hing Construction Co Ltd v Hope Lee Iron Work Co [2002] 633 H.K.C.U. 1 ... 36

Hiscox Underwriting Ltd v Dickson Manchester & Co Ltd [2004] EWHC 479 (Comm); [2004] 1 All E.R. (Comm) 753; [2004] 2 Lloyd's Rep. 438 13

Hiscox v Outhwaite (No.1) [1992] 1 A.C. 562; [1991] 3 W.L.R. 297; [1991] 3 All E.R. 641; [1991] 2 Lloyd's Rep. 435 HL 57, 189, 256, 257

Hober, Kraus ND Melis v Soyak International Construction & Investment Inc, Mealey's International Arbitration Report, Vol.24 No.3 (March, 2009) 264

Holburn v Buchanan (1915) 31 Sh. Ct Rep. 178 39

Holland House Property Investments Ltd v Crabbe [2008] CSIH 40; 2008 S.C. 619; 2008 S.L.T. 777; 2008 S.C.L.R. 633; 2008 G.W.D. 23-367 14

Holmes v Nursing and Midwifery Council [2009] CSIH 82; 2010 G.W.D. 9-147 315

Home & Overseas Insurance Co v Mentor Insurance Co (UK) [1990] 1 W.L.R. 153; [1989] 3 All E.R. 74; [1989] 1 Lloyd's Rep. 473; (1989) 86(7) L.S.G. 36; (1989) 133 S.J. 44 CA (Civ Div) 237, 238

Home of Homes Ltd v Hammersmith and Fulham LBC [2003] EWHC 807 (TCC); 92 Con. L.R. 48 272

Home Office v Harman; sub nom. Harman v Home Office [1983] 1 A.C. 280; [1982] 2 W.L.R. 338; [1982] 1 All E.R. 532; (1982) 126 S.J. 136 HL 170

Hrvatska Elektroprivreda dd v the Republic of Slovenia (ICSID case no.ARBl05124) ... 195

Hume v Nursing and Midwifery Council, 2007 S.C. 644 315

Hussmann (Europe) Ltd v Al Ameen Development & Trade Co; sub nom. Hussman (Europe) Ltd v Al Ameen Development & Trade Co [2000] 2 Lloyd's Rep. 83; [2000] C.L.C. 1243 QBD (Comm Ct) 147, 150, 194, 198, 255, 277, 292, 297, 299

Huyton SA v Jakil SpA [1999] 2 Lloyd's Rep. 83; [1998] C.L.C. 937 CA (Civ Div) ... 319

III ZR 33/00, April 9, 2009 the Sup Ct (Germany) 36

IPCO (Nigeria) Ltd v Nigerian National Petroleum Corp [2005] EWHC 726 (Comm); [2005] 2 Lloyd's Rep. 326; [2005] 1 C.L.C. 613 .... 60, 79, 80

IPCO (Nigeria) Ltd v Nigerian National Petroleum Corp; sub nom. Nigerian National Petroleum Corp v IPCO (Nigeria) Ltd [2008] EWCA Civ 1157; [2009] Bus. L.R.

Table of Cases

545; [2009] 1 All E.R. (Comm) 611; [2009] 1 Lloyd's Rep. 89; [2008] 2 C.L.C. 550; [2009] B.L.R. 71 .... 42, 56, 58, 79
Inco Europe Ltd v First Choice Distribution [1999] 1 W.L.R. 270; [1999] 1 All E.R. 820; [1999] C.L.C. 165; (1999) 1 T.C.L.R. 169; (1998) 95(41) L.S.G. 45; (1998) 142 S.J.L.B. 269 CA (Civ Div) 34
Insurance Co v Lloyd's Syndicate [1995] 1 Lloyd's Rep. 272; [1994] C.L.C. 1303; [1995] 4 Re. L.R. 37 QBD(Comm Ct) 167, 169
Inter-Arab Investment Guarantee Corp v Banque Arabe et Internationale d'Investissements (2001) XXVI YCA 207 Cour de Cassation 64
Inter-Arab Investment Guarantee Corp v Banque Arabe et Internationale d'Investissements (1997) XXII YCA 643 Ct of First Instance (Brussels) 66
Inter-Arab Investment Guarantee Corp v Banque Arabe et Internationale d'Investissements (1999) XXIV YCA 603 69
International Civil Aviation Organisation v Tripal Systems Ltd (1998) XXIII YCA 226 Sup Ct (Quebec) 148
International Investor KCSC v Sanghi Polyesters Ltd (2005) XXX YCA 577 H Ct (India) 64
International Petroleum Refining & Supply Sdad v Elpis Finance SA (The Faith); Faith, The [1993] 2 Lloyd's Rep. 408 QBD(Comm Ct) 262
International Standard Electric Corp v Bridas Sociedad Anonima Petrolera (1992) XVII YCA 639 Dis Ct (US) 73
Inverclyde (Mearns) Housing Society Ltd v Lawrence Construction Co Ltd, 1989 S.L.T. 815; 1989 S.C.L.R. 486 OH 33, 34
Inverurie Town Council v Sorrie, 1956 S.C. 175; 1956 S.L.T. (Notes) 17 IH (2 Div) ... 231
Iran Aircraft Ind v Avco Corp (1993) XVIII YCA 599 CA (US) 67

JA Payne Limited v GAJ Construction [1999] CILL 1521 177
JSC Surgutneftegaz v Harvard College, 2005 WL 1863676 Dis Ct (US) 93
JSC Zestafoni G Nikoladze Ferroalloy Plant v Ronly Holdings Ltd [2004] EWHC 245 (Comm); [2004] 2 Lloyd's Rep. 335; [2004] 1 C.L.C. 1146 .... 147, 292
JT Mackley & Co Ltd v Gosport Marina Ltd [2002] EWHC 1315 (TCC); [2002] B.L.R. 367; [2002] T.C.L.R. 26 .... 146, 156
James Lazenby & Co v McNicholas Construction Co Ltd [1995] 1 W.L.R. 615; [1995] 3 All E.R. 820; [1995] 2 Lloyd's Rep. 30 QBD (Comm Ct) 200, 201, 203
Japan Line Ltd v Aggeliki Charis Compania Maritima SA (The Angelic Grace); Angelic Grace, The (Arbitrators: Misconduct); sub nom. Japan Line Ltd v Davies and Potter [1980] 1 Lloyd's Rep. 288; (1979) 123 S.J. 487 CA (Civ Div) 259
Javor v Francoeur (2004) XXIX YCA 596 81
Jean Charbonneau v Les Industries AC Davie Inc Unreported March 14, 1989 Sup Ct (Quebec) 34
Johannesburg Municipal Council v D Stewart & Co (1902) Ltd; sub nom. Municipal Council of Johannesburg v Stewart & Co (1902) Ltd, 1909 S.C. (H.L.) 53; 1909 2 S.L.T. 313 HL 22
John G McGregor (Contractors) Ltd v Grampian RC (No.2), 1991 S.L.T. 136 IH (2 Div) 246
John Nimmo & Son Ltd, Petitioners (1905) 8 F. 173; (1905) 13 S.L.T. 539 IH (1 Div) 220
John v Rees [1969] 2 All E.R. 27 163
Joseph Muller AG v Bergesen (1986) IX YCA 437 67

K Trading v Bayerische Motoren Werke AG (2005) XXX YCA 568 CA (Barvarian) 69
Kajo-Erzeugnisse Essenzen GmbH v DO Zdravilisce Radenska (1995) XX YCA 1051 73
Kalmneft JSC v Glencore International AG; sub nom. AOOT Kalmneft v Glencore International AG [2002] 1 All E.R. 76; [2001] 2 All E.R. (Comm) 577; [2002] 1 Lloyd's Rep. 128; [2001] C.L.C. 1805 QBD (Comm Ct) 152, 291, 315
Kanoria v Guinness [2006] EWCA Civ 222; [2006] 2 All E.R. (Comm) 413; [2006] 1 Lloyd's Rep. 701 .... 60, 61, 67
Karaha Bodas Co LLC v Perusahaan Pertambangan Minyak Dan Gas Bumi Negara-Pertamina (2003) XXVIII YCA 752 .... 60, 61, 66, 70

Table of Cases

Karaha Bodas Co LLC v Perusahaan Pertambangan Minyak Dan Gas Bumi Negara-Pertamina [2003] 380 H.K.C.U. 1 7
Kastner v Jason; Sherman v Kastner [2004] EWCA Civ 1599; [2005] 1 Lloyd's Rep. 397; (2004) 148 S.J.L.B. 1436; [2004] N.P.C. 181 .... 243, 258
Kazakhstan v Istil Group Inc; sub nom. Kazakhstan v Istil Group Ltd [2007] EWCA Civ 471; [2008] Bus. L.R. 878; [2008] 1 All E.R. (Comm) 88; [2007] 2 Lloyd's Rep. 548 .... 293, 304, 311
Kersa Holding Co v Infancourtage (1996) XXI YCA 617 CA (Luxembourg) 71
Kid v Bunyan (1842) 5 D. 193 223
Kintore (Earl of) v Union Bank of Scotland (1863) 4 Macq. 465 92

LG CALTEX GAS CO LTD v CHINA NATIONAL PETROLEUM CORP; CONTIGROUP COMPANIES INC (FORMERLY CONTINENTAL GRAIN CO) v CHINA PETROLEUM TECHNOLOGY & DEVELOPMENT CORP [2001] EWCA Civ 788; [2001] 1 W.L.R. 1892; [2001] 4 All E.R. 875; [2001] 2 All E.R. (Comm) 97; [2001] C.L.C. 1392; [2001] B.L.R. 325; (2001) 3 T.C.L.R. 22; (2001) 98(25) L.S.G. 46; (2001) 145 S.J.L.B. 142 .... 12, 153
LKT Industrial Berhad (Malaysia) v Chun [2004] N.S.W.S.C. 820 65
La Societe National des Hydrocarbures v Shaheen National Resources Inc, 585 F.Supp. 57 (1983) 64
Laboratories Grossman v Forest Laboratories, 295 N.Y. Supp. (2d) 756 (1985) 35
Lafarge (Aggregates) Ltd v Newham LBC [2005] EWHC 1337 (Comm); [2005] 2 Lloyd's Rep. 577 148
Laminoires-Trefileries-Cableries de Lens SA v Southwire Co, 484 F. Supp. 1065 (1981) CA (US) 66, 75
Lapad, The. See Easy Rider, The. See Tame Shipping Ltd v Easy Navigation Ltd (The Easy Rider)
Law v Chartered Institute of Patent Agents [1919] 2 Ch. 276 Ch D 160
Leach (Stanley Hugh) v Haringey LBC, The Times, March 23, 1977 260
Ledee v Ceramiche Ragno (1984) IX YCA 471 CA (US) 94
Ledee v Ceramiche Ragno, 684 F.2d 184 (1981) 187 CA (US) 35
Lesotho Highlands Development Authority v Impregilo SpA [2005] UKHL 43; [2006] 1 A.C. 221; [2005] 3 W.L.R. 129; [2005] 3 All E.R. 789; [2005] 2 All E.R. (Comm) 265; [2005] 2 Lloyd's Rep. 310; [2005] 2 C.L.C. 1; [2005] B.L.R. 351; 101 Con. L.R. 1; [2005] 27 E.G. 220 (C.S.); (2005) 155 N.L.J. 1046 .... 70, 242, 248, 298, 299
Lobb Partnership Ltd v Aintree Racecourse Co Ltd [2000] C.L.C. 431; [2000] B.L.R. 65; 69 Con. L.R. 79 QBD (Comm Ct) 147
Locabail (UK) Ltd v Bayfield Properties Ltd (Leave to Appeal); R. v Bristol Betting and Gaming Licensing Committee Ex p. O'Callaghan; Williams v Inspector of Taxes; Timmins v Gormley; Locabail (UK) Ltd v Waldorf Investment Corp (Leave to Appeal) [2000] Q.B. 451; [2000] 2 W.L.R. 870; [2000] 1 All E.R. 65; [2000] I.R.L.R. 96; [2000] H.R.L.R. 290; [2000] U.K.H.R.R. 300; 7 B.H.R.C. 583; (1999) 149 N.L.J. 1793; [1999] N.P.C. 143 CA (Civ Div) 129, 160
London and Leeds Estates Ltd v Paribas Ltd [1995] 1 E.G.L.R. 102; [1995] 02 E.G. 134 QBD 52, 169, 170
London Central and Suburban Developments Ltd v Banger [1999] A.D.R.L.J. 119 ... 33
Lonrho Ltd v Shell Petroleum Co Ltd (No.2) [1982] A.C. 173; [1981] 3 W.L.R. 33; [1981] 2 All E.R. 456; (1981) 125 S.J. 429 HL 36
Lord Advocate v Scotsman Publications Ltd [1990] 1 A.C. 812; [1989] 3 W.L.R. 358; [1989] 2 All E.R. 852; 1989 S.C. (H.L.) 122; 1989 S.L.T. 705; [1989] 1 F.S.R. 580; (1989) 86(38) L.S.G. 32; (1989) 139 N.L.J. 971 HL 173
Lovell Partnerships (Northern) Ltd v AW Construction Plc, 81 B.L.R. 83 QBD (Comm Ct) 126
Lovelock (EJR) v Exportles [1968] 1 Lloyd's Rep. 163 CA (Civ Div) 35
Lowndes v The Earl of Stamford and Warrington, 118 E.R. 160; (1852) 18 Q.B. 425 QB 37
Lucille, The [1983] 1 Lloyd's Law Reports 387 177
Lucky-Goldstar International (HK) Ltd v Ng Moo Kee Engineering Ltd [1994] A.D.R.L.J. 49 35
Luzon Hydro Corp v Transfield Philippines Inc [2004] S.G.H.C. 204; [2004] 4 S.L.R. 705 .... 193, 194, 197, 198
Lyle v Falconer (1842) 5 D. 236 .... 257, 259

Table of Cases

McArdle v J&R Howie Ltd, 1927 S.C. 779; 1927 S.L.T. 521 IH (2 Div) 282
MacBryde v Macrae's Executors (1748) Mor. 657 269
McCallum v Robertson (1825) 4 S. 66 250
McCallum v Robertson (1826) 2 W. & S. 344 261
MacDonald Estates Plc v National Car Parks Ltd, 2010 S.L.T. 36; 2009 G.W.D. 38-639 IH (Ex Div) 15
McDonald Estates v National Car Parks Ltd. *See* MacDonald Estates Plc v National Car Parks Ltd
Macepark (Whittlebury) Ltd v Sargeant Unreported July 18, 2002 Ch 245
McFeetridge v Stewarts & Lloyds Ltd, 1913 S.C. 773; 1913 1 S.L.T. 325 IH (2 Div) 62
Macintyre Bros (A Firm) v Smith, 1913 S.C. 129; 1913 1 S.L.T. 148 IH (Ex Div) 276
McKenzie v Aberdeen and Inverness Junction Railway Co (1866) 4 M. 810 269
Mackley & Co Ltd v Gosport Marina Ltd. *See* JT Mackley & Co Ltd v Gosport Marina Ltd
McLaren v Aikman, 1939 S.C. 222; 1939 S.L.T. 267 IH (2 Div) 250
McMillan v Free Church of Scotland (1862) 24 D. 1282 320
McQuater v Fergusson, 1911 S.C. 640; 1911 1 S.L.T. 295 IH (1 Div) 274
Magill v Weeks [2001] UKHL 67; [2002] 2 A.C. 357; [2002] 2 W.L.R. 37; [2002] 1 All E.R. 465; [2002] H.R.L.R. 16; [2002] H.L.R. 16; [2002] B.L.G.R. 51; (2001) 151 N.L.J. 1886; [2001] N.P.C. 184 .... 119, 128, 160
Malden Mills Inc (US) v Hilaturas Lourdes SA (1979) IV YCA 302 65
Mangistaumunaigaz Oil Production Association v United World Trade Inc (1999) XXIV YCA 808 Dis Ct (US) 66
Mangistaumunaigaz Oil Production Association v United World Trading Inc [1995] 1 Lloyd's Rep. 617 QBD (Comm Ct) 147
Manufacturer v Exclusive Distributor (2004) XIX YCA 687 Sup Ct (Germany) 75
Margulead Ltd v Exide Technologies [2004] EWHC 1019 (Comm); [2004] 2 All E.R. (Comm) 727; [2005] 1 Lloyd's Rep. 324 .... 131, 163, 296
Masinimport v Scottish Mechanical Light Industries Ltd, 1976 S.C. 102; 1976 S.L.T. 245 OH 76
Matermaco SA v PPM Cranes Inc (2000) XXV YCA 653 Comm Ct (Brussels) 24, 93
Maule v Maule (1816) 4 Dow 363 266
Michael Wilson & Partners Ltd v Emmott; sub nom. Emmott v Michael Wilson & Partners Ltd [2008] EWCA Civ 184; [2008] Bus. L.R. 1361; [2008] 2 All E.R. (Comm) 193; [2008] 1 Lloyd's Rep. 616; [2008] C.P. Rep. 26; [2008] B.L.R. 515 .... 52, 167
Midgulf International Ltd v Groupe Chimiche Tunisien 2009] EWHC 963 (Comm); [2009] 2 Lloyd's Rep. 411; [2009] 1 C.L.C. 984 19
Mikuta v William Baird & Co Ltd, 1916 S.C. 194; 1915 2 S.L.T. 396 IH (1 Div) 284
Millar (David Cameron) v Dickson; Marshall v Ritchie; Tracey v Heywood; Payne v Heywood; Stewart v Heywood [2001] UKPC D 4; [2002] 1 W.L.R. 1615; [2002] 3 All E.R. 1041; 2002 S.C. (P.C.) 30; 2001 S.L.T. 988; 2001 S.C.C.R. 741; [2001] H.R.L.R. 59; [2001] U.K.H.R.R. 999; 2001 G.W.D. 26-1015 160
Miller Construction Ltd v James Moore Earthmoving; sub nom. James Moore Earthmoving v Miller Construction Ltd [2001] EWCA Civ 654; [2001] 2 All E.R. (Comm) 598; [2001] B.L.R. 322 .... 126, 130
Minerals and Metals Trading Corp of India Ltd v Encounter Bay Shipping Co Ltd (The Samos Glory) (No.2) [1988] 1 Lloyd's Rep. 51 260
Minermet SpA Milan v Luckyfield Shipping Corp SA [2004] EWHC 729 (Comm); [2004] 2 Lloyd's Rep. 348; [2004] 2 C.L.C. 421 148
Ministere Tunisien de l'Equipment v Bec Freres (1997) XXII YCA 682 CA (Paris) ... 62
Ministry of Defence of the Republic of Iran v Cubic Defense Systems Inc, 29 F.Supp. 2d 1168 (1998) Dis Ct (US) 70
Minmetals Germany GmbH v Ferco Steel Ltd [1999] 1 All E.R. (Comm.) 315; [1999] C.L.C. 647 .... 60, 66, 70, 77
Mitchell-Gill v Buchan, 1921 S.C. 390; 1921 1 S.L.T. 197 IH (1 Div) 215
Mitsubishi Corp v Castletown Navigation (The Castle Alpha); Castle Alpha, The [1989] 2 Lloyd's Rep. 383 QBD (Comm Ct) 238
Mitsubishi Motors Corp v Soler Chrysler-Plymouth Inc, 473 U.S. 614 (1985) Sup Ct (US) 94

Table of Cases

Molino e Pacifico Ponte San Giovanni Spa v Anrde & Cie SA (1983)VIII YCA 378 Sup Ct (italic) 37
Monegasque de Reassurance SAM v NAK Naftogart of Ukraine, 311 F.3d 488 (2002) 61
Montan, The. *See* Mutual Shipping Corp of New York v Bayshore Shipping Co of Monrovia (The Montan)
Montgomerie v Carrick (1848) 10 D. 1387 39
Mowbray v Dickson (1848) 10 D. 1102 192
Municipal Council of Johannesburg v Stewart & Co (1902) Ltd. *See* Johannesburg Municipal Council v D Stewart & Co (1902) Ltd
Municipalite de Khoms El Megreb v Societe Dalico, 1994 Revue de l'Arbitrage 116 ... 24
Murphy v Farme Coal Co Ltd, 1918 S.C. 659; 1918 2 S.L.T. 8 IH (2 Div) 284
Mutual Shipping Corp of New York v Bayshore Shipping Co of Monrovia (The Montan); Montan, The [1985] 1 W.L.R. 625; [1985] 1 All E.R. 520; [1985] 1 Lloyd's Rep. 189; (1985) 82 L.S.G. 1329; (1985) 129 S.J. 219 CA (Civ Div) 270
Mylcrist Builders Ltd v Buck [2008] EWHC 2172 (TCC); [2009] 2 All E.R. (Comm) 259; [2008] B.L.R. 611; [2008] C.I.L.L. 2624; (2008) 105(39) L.S.G. 22; (2008) 152(38) S.J.L.B. 29 .... 6, 164

NANJING CEREALS, OILS AND FOODSTUS IMPORT AND EXPORT CORP V LUCKMATE COMMODITIES TRADING LTD (1999) XXI YCA 542 Sup Ct (HK) 66
Nasmyth v Magistrates of Glasgow (1777) 5 Br. Supp. 427 269
National Development Co v Khashoggi (1993) XVIII YCA 506 Dis Ct (New York) ... 66
National Thermal Power Corp v The Singer Co (1993) XVIII YCA 403 Sup Ct (India) 24
Naviera Amazonica Peruana SA v Compania Internacional de Seguros de Peru [1988] 1 Lloyd's Rep. 116; [1988] 1 F.T.L.R. 100 CA (Civ Div) 24, 29, 189
Navigation Somanar Inc v Algoma Steamships Ltd (1994) XIX YCA 256 Sup Ct (Quebec) 254
Nema, The. *See* Pioneer Shipping Ltd v BTP Tioxide Ltd (The Nema) (No.2)
Newfield Construction Ltd v Tomlinson [2004] EWHC 3051 (TCC); 97 Con. L.R. 148 .... 296, 298
Nigerian National Petroleum Corp v IPCO (Nigeria) Ltd. *See* IPCO (Nigeria) Ltd v Nigerian National Petroleum Corp
Norbrook Laboratories Ltd v Tank [2006] EWHC 1055 (Comm); [2006] 2 Lloyd's Rep. 485; [2006] B.L.R. 412 .... 127, 183, 297
Norsk Hydro ASA v State Property Fund of Ukraine [2002] EWHC 2120 (Admin); [2009] Bus. L.R. 558 58
North Range Shipping Ltd v Seatrans Shipping Corp (The Western Triumph); Western Triumph, The [2002] EWCA Civ 405; [2002] 1 W.L.R. 2397; [2002] 4 All E.R. 390; [2002] 2 All E.R. (Comm) 193; [2002] 2 Lloyd's Rep. 1; [2002] C.L.C. 992; (2002) 99(20) L.S.G. 31 311
Norwest Holst Ltd v Carfin Developments Ltd [2008] CSOH 138; [2009] B.L.R. 167; 2008 G.W.D. 33-493 OH 15

OTM v HYDRANAUTICS [1981] 2 Lloyd's Rep. 211 QBD (Comm Ct) 35
O'Donoghue v Enterprise Inns Plc [2008] EWHC 2273 (Ch); [2009] 1 P. & C.R. 14; [2008] N.P.C. 103 185
O'Neill v Giffnock Collieries Ltd, 1924 S.C. 376; 1924 S.L.T. 325 IH (2 Div) 282
Omnibridge Consulting Ltd v Clearsprings (Management) Ltd [2004] EWHC 2276 (Comm) 270, 297
Omnium de Traitement et de Valorisation SA v Hilmarton Ltd [1999] 2 All E.R. (Comm) 146; [1999] 2 Lloyd's Rep. 222 QBD (Comm Ct) 76
Orion Compania Espanola de Seguros v Belfort Maatschappij voor Algemene Verzekgringeen [1962] 2 Lloyd's Rep. 257 QBD (Comm Ct) 237
Osuuskunta METEX Anderlag VS v Turkiye Electric Kurumu Genel Mudurlugu General Directorate (1997) XXII YCA 807 CA (Ankara) 69
Overseas Cosmos Inc v NR Vessel Corp (1998) XXIII YCA 1096 Dis Ct (New York) 66
Overseas Union Insurance v AA Mutual International Insurance [1988] 2 Lloyd's Rep. 63; [1988] F.T.L.R. 421 QBD (Comm Ct) 34

Table of Cases

Owerri Commercial Inc v Dielle Srl (1994) XIX YCA 703 H Ct (Hague) 24
Owners of the Bamburi v Compton (The Bamburi); Bamburi, The [1982] 1 Lloyd's Rep.
  312; [1982] Com. L.R. 31 87

PACZY V HAENDLER & NATERMANN GMBH (No.2) [1981] 1 Lloyd's Rep. 302; [1981] Com.
  L.R. 12; [1981] F.S.R. 250 CA (Civ Div) 36
Paklito Investment Ltd v Klockner (East Asia) Ltd [1995] A.D.R.L.J. 127 H Ct
  (HK) 67
Pan Liberty Navigation Co Ltd v World Link (HK) Resources Ltd (2005) B.C.C.A.
  206 81
Panchaud Freres SA v Pagnan (R) & Fratelli [1974] 1 Lloyd's Rep. 394 CA (Civ
  Div) 246
Pancommerce SA v Veecheema BV [1983] 2 Lloyd's Rep. 304; [1983] Com. L.R. 230 CA
  (Civ Div) 270
Parochial Board of Greenock v Coghill (1878) 5 R. 732 15
Parsons & Whittemore Overseas Co Inc Societe Generale de l'Industrie du Papier
  (RAKTA), 508 F.2d 969 (2nd Cir. 1974) 61, 71, 75
Parsons & Whittemore Overseas Co Inc v Societe Generale de l'Industrie du Papier
  (RAKTA) (1976) I YCA 205 CA (US) 66
Pasrederiet m/v Jytte Dania v Mas SA (1989) XIV YCA 704 Sup Ct (Spain) 66
Patel (Jitendra) v Patel (Dilesh) [2000] Q.B. 551; [1999] 3 W.L.R. 322; [1999] 1 All E.R.
  (Comm.) 923; [1999] B.L.R. 227; 65 Con. L.R. 140; (1999) 15 Const. L.J. 484; (1999)
  143 S.J.L.B. 134 CA (Civ Div) 33, 34
Paterson v Sanderson (1829) 7 S. 616 279
Patrick v McCall (1867) 4 S.L.R. 12 269
Peterson Farms Inc v C&M Farming Ltd (Payment into Court) [2003] EWHC 2298
  (Comm); [2004] 1 Lloyd's Rep. 614 318
Peterson Farms Inc v C&M Farming Ltd; sub nom. Petersen Farms Inc v C&M
  Farming Ltd [2004] EWHC 121 (Comm); [2004] 1 Lloyd's Rep. 603; [2004] N.P.C.
  13 239
Peterson v Ayre (1855) 15 C.B. 724 249
Pierreux NV v Transportmaschinen Handelshaus GmbH (1997) XXII YCA 631 36
Piersack v Belgium (A/53) (1983) 5 E.H.R.R. 169 ECtHR 160
Pioneer Shipping Ltd v BTP Tioxide Ltd (The Nema) (No.2); BTP Tioxide Ltd v
  Armada Marine SA; Nema, The (No.2); sub nom. BTP Tioxide Ltd v Pioneer
  Shipping Ltd [1982] A.C. 724; [1981] 3 W.L.R. 292; [1981] 2 All E.R. 1030; [1981] 2
  Lloyd's Rep. 239; [1981] Com. L.R. 197; (1981) 125 S.J. 542 HL 176, 179
Pirtek (UK) Ltd v Deanswood Ltd [2005] EWHC 2301 (Comm); [2005] 2 Lloyd's Rep.
  728 248
Pollich v Heatley (No.2), 1910 S.C. 469; (1910) 1 S.L.T.203 IH (1 Div) 270, 281, 282
Porter v Magill; Phillips v Magill; England v Magill; Hartley v Magill; Weeks v Magill;
  sub nom. Magill v Porter
Positive Software Solutions, Inc v New Century Mortgage Corp, 337 F.Supp. 2d 862
  (N.D. Tex. 2004), affirmed 436 F.3d 495 (5th Cir. 2006), rehearing en banc granted,
  449 F.3d 616 (5th Cir. 2006), revised 476 F.3d 278 (5th Cir. 2007) (en banc), cert.
  den. 551 U.S. 1114 (2007) 120
Premium Nafta Products Ltd v Fili Shipping Co Ltd. *See* Fiona Trust & Holding Corp v
  Privalov
President of India v La Pintada Compania Navigacion SA (The La Pintada); La Pintada,
  The (No.1) [1985] A.C. 104; [1984] 3 W.L.R. 10; [1984] 2 All E.R. 773; [1984] 2
  Lloyd's Rep. 9; [1984] C.I.L.L. 110; (1984) 81 L.S.G. 1999; (1984) 128 S.J. 414 ... 243
Primetrade AG v Ythan Ltd; Ythan, The [2005] EWHC 2399 (Comm); [2006] 1 All E.R.
  367; [2006] 1 All E.R. (Comm) 157; [2006] 1 Lloyd's Rep. 457; [2005] 2 C.L.C.
  911 .... 151, 325
Protech Projects Construction (Pty) Ltd v Al-Kharafi & Sons; Mohammed Abdul-
  mohsin Al-Kharafi & Sons WLL v Big Dig Construction (Proprietary) Ltd (In
  Liquidation) [2005] EWHC 2165 (Comm); [2005] 2 Lloyd's Rep. 779 302
Pullar v United Kingdom (22399/93) 1996 S.C.C.R. 755; (1996) 22 E.H.R.R. 391
  ECtHR 160

QUINTETTE COAL LTD V NIPPON STEEL CORP (1993) XVIII YCA 159 CA (BC) 94

Table of Cases

R. v Bow Street Metropolitan Stipendiary Magistrate Ex p. Pinochet Ugarte (No.2); sub nom. Pinochet Ugarte (No.2), Re; R. v Evans Ex p. Pinochet Ugarte (No.2); R. v Bartle Ex p. Pinochet Ugarte (No.2) [2000] 1 A.C. 119; [1999] 2 W.L.R. 272; [1999] 1 All E.R. 577; 6 B.H.R.C. 1; (1999) 11 Admin. L.R. 57; (1999) 96(6) L.S.G. 33; (1999) 149 N.L.J. 88 HL 160
R. v Gough (Robert) [1993] A.C. 646; [1993] 2 W.L.R. 883; [1993] 2 All E.R. 724; (1993) 97 Cr. App. R. 188; (1993) 157 J.P. 612; [1993] Crim. L.R. 886; (1993) 157 J.P.N. 394; (1993) 143 N.L.J. 775; (1993) 137 S.J.L.B. 168 HL 160, 161
R. v Warrington Crown Court Ex p. RBNB. *See* R. (on the application of RBNB) v Warrington Crown Court
R. (on the application of Anufrijeva) v Secretary of State for the Home Department [2003] UKHL 36; [2004] 1 A.C. 604; [2003] 3 W.L.R. 252; [2003] 3 All E.R. 827; [2003] H.R.L.R. 31; [2003] Imm. A.R. 570; [2003] I.N.L.R. 521; (2003) 100(33) L.S.G. 29; 314
R. (on the application of RBNB) v Warrington Crown Court; sub nom. R. v Warrington Crown Court Ex p. RBNB [2001] 1 W.L.R. 2239; [2001] 2 All E.R. 851; [2002] B.C.C. 210; (2000) 164 J.P. 644; (2000) 150 N.L.J. 1492 CA (Civ Div) 177
R v V [2008] EWHC 1531 (Comm); [2009] 1 Lloyd's Rep. 97; 119 Con. L.R. 73 76
R SA v A Ltd (2001) XXVI YCA 863 82
RC Pillar & Sons v Edwards [2002] C.I.L.L. 1799 .... 272, 273
Ransohoff v Burrell (1897) 21 R. 284 147
Ratnam v Cumarasamy [1965] 1 W.L.R. 8; [1964] 3 All E.R. 933; (1964) 108 S.J. 1028 PC (Malaysia) 151
Recyclers of Australia Pty Ltd v Hettinga Equipment Inc (2000) 175 A.L.R. 725 Fed Ct (Aus) 24
Rederi Aktiebolaget Sally v Srl Termarea (1979) IV YCA 294 CA (Florence) 68
Rena K, The; Rena K, The [1979] Q.B. 377; [1978] 3 W.L.R. 431; [1979] 1 All E.R. 397; [1978] 1 Lloyd's Rep. 545; (1978) 122 S.J. 315 QBD (Admlty Ct) 36
Resort Condominiums International Inc v Bolwell (1994) XX YCA 628 Sup Ct (Queensland) 56, 72
Rhone Mediterranee v Achille Lauro, 712 F.2d 50 (1983) 35, 36
Riley v Kingsley Underwriting Agencies, 969 F.2d 953 (1992) 35
Rio Algom Ltd v Sammi Steel Co (1991) 47 C.P.C. 251 147
Robertson v Cheynes (1847) 9 D. 599 39
Rosseel NV v Oriental Commercial & Shipping Co (UK) Ltd [1991] 2 Lloyd's Rep. 625 QBD (Comm Ct) 61, 72
Roussel- UCLAF v G D Searle & Co Ltd [1978] 1 Lloyd's Rep. 225 33
Royal Bank of Scotland Plc v Theobald Unreported January 10, 2007 EAT 325
Russell v Russell (1880) (1880) L.R. 14 Ch. D. 471 Ch D 167
Rustal Trading Ltd v Gill & Duffus SA [2000] 1 Lloyd's Rep. 14; [2000] C.L.C. 231 QBD (Comm Ct) 129
Rutherford v Licences and General Insurance Co Ltd, 1934 S.L.T. 31 OH 39

SEEE v Yugoslavia (1986) XI YCA 491 CA (Appeal) 68
SL Sethia Liners v Naviagro Maritime Corp (The Kostas Melas); Kostas Melas, The [1981] 1 Lloyd's Rep. 18; [1980] Com. L.R. 3 QBD (Comm Ct) 260
SODIME v Schuurmans & Van Ginneken BV (1996) XXI YCA 607 Sup Ct (Italy) ... 81
SPP (Middle East) Ltd v Egypt (1985) X YCA 487 Dis Ct (Amsterdam) 72, 82
Samos Glory, The (No.2) Minerals and Metals Trading Corp of India Ltd v Encounter Bay Shipping Co Ltd (The Samos Glory) (No.2); Samos Glory, The (No.2) [1988] 1 Lloyd's Rep. 51 260
Sanderson v Armour, A Sanderson & Son v Armour & Co Ltd 22
Schreter v Gasmac Inc (1992) 89 D.L.R. (4th) 365 72
Science Research Council v Nasse; Leyland Cars (BL Cars Ltd) v Vyas; Science Research Council v Nass; sub nom. Nasse v Science Research Council; Vyas v Leyland Cars [1980] A.C. 1028; [1979] 3 W.L.R. 762; [1979] 3 All E.R. 673; [1979] I.C.R. 921; [1979] I.R.L.R. 465; (1979) 123 S.J. 768 HL 168
Scott Lithgow Ltd v Secretary of State for Defence, 1988 S.L.T. 697 IH (1 Div) 88
Scott v Avery, 10 E.R. 1121; (1856) 5 H.L. Cas. 811 HL 37
Sea Traders SA v Participaciones, Proyectos y Estudios SA (1996) XXI YCA 676 ... 81

Table of Cases

Seabridge Shipping AB v AC Orssleff's Eftf's A/S; sub nom. Seabridge Shipping AB v AC Orsleff's EFTS A/S [2000] 1 All E.R. (Comm) 415; [1999] 2 Lloyd's Rep. 685; [2000] C.L.C. 656 QBD (Comm Ct) 104
Seawest Industries Inc, Re (1995) XX YCA 811 Dis Ct (US) 37
Secretary of State for the Environment v Reed International [1994] 1 E.G.L.R. 22; [1994] 06 E.G. 137 179
Sesostris v Transportes Navales, 727 F.Supp. 737 (1989) Dis Ct (US) 65
Shamil Bank of Bahrain EC v Beximco Pharmaceuticals Ltd (No.1); sub nom. Beximco Pharmaceuticals Ltd v Shamil Bank of Bahrain EC [2004] EWCA Civ 19; [2004] 1 W.L.R. 1784; [2004] 4 All E.R. 1072; [2004] 2 All E.R. (Comm) 312; [2004] 2 Lloyd's Rep. 1; [2004] 1 C.L.C. 216; (2004) 101(8) L.S.G. 29 239
Shashoua v Sharma [2009] EWHC 957 (Comm); [2009] 2 All E.R. (Comm) 477; [2009] 2 Lloyd's Rep. 376; [2009] 1 C.L.C. 716 19
Shell Egypt West Manzala GmbH v Dana Gas Egypt Ltd (formerly Centurion Petroleum Corp) [2009] EWHC 2097 (Comm); [2010] 1 Lloyd's Rep. 109; [2009] 2 C.L.C. 481; 127 Con. L.R. 27 304
Shepherd v Elliot (1896) 23 R. 695 283
Shin-Etsu Chemical Co v Aksh Opticfibre Ltd (2006) XXXI YCA 747 Sup Ct (India) 31
Siemens AG and BKMI Industrienlagen GmbH v Dutco Construction Co January 7, 1992 (1992) 1 Bull Civ Cass. Civ. 1ere (France) 115
Simpson v Strachan (1736) Mor. 17007 269
Sinclair v Woods of Winchester Ltd [2005] EWHC 1631 (QB); 102 Con. L.R. 127 ... 130, 185, 315
Sinclair v Woods of Winchester Ltd [2006] EWHC 3003 (TCC); 109 Con. L.R. 14 ... 272
Small Business Ltd v Big Multinational Plc 195
Smits Leslie v Roach [2006] H.C.A. 36 159
Socadec SA v Pan Afric Inpex Co Ltd [2003] EWHC 2086 (QB) 43
Societe Arabe des Engrais Phosphates v Gemanco Srl (1997) XXII YCA 737 Sup Ct (Italy) 62
Societe Tunisienne d'Electricitee et de Gaz v Societe Entrepose (1978) III YCA 283 .. 62
Societe Van Hopplymus v Societe Coherent Inc (1997) XXII YCA 637 Comm Ct (Brussels) 93
Soinco SACI v Novokuznetsk Aluminium Plant (No.1) [1998] 2 Lloyd's Rep. 337; [1998] C.L.C. 730 76
Sojuzneftexport v Joc Oil Ltd (1990) XV YCA 384 CA (Bermuda) 70, 71
Sokofl Star Shipping Co Inc v GPVO Technopromexport (1998) XXIII YCA 742 Dis Ct (Moscow) 62
Soleh Boneh International v Uganda and National Housing Corp [1993] 2 Lloyd's Rep. 208 CA (Civ Div) 79, 318
Soleimany v Soleimany [1999] Q.B. 785; [1998] 3 W.L.R. 811; [1999] 3 All E.R. 847; [1998] C.L.C. 779 .... 75, 76, 301
South Tyneside MBC v Wickes Building Supplies Ltd [2004] EWHC 2428 (Comm); [2004] N.P.C. 164 169
Star Shipping AG v China National Foreign Trade Transportation Corp (The Star Texas); Star Texas, The [1993] 2 Lloyd's Rep. 445 CA (Civ Div) 35
Star Texas, The. See Star Shipping AG v China National Foreign Trade Transportation Corp (The Star Texas)
Starlight Shipping Co v Tai Ping Insurance Co Ltd (Hubei Branch); Alexandros T, The [2007] EWHC 1893 (Comm); [2008] 1 All E.R. (Comm) 593; [2008] 1 Lloyd's Rep. 230; [2007] 2 C.L.C. 440 171
Steel Authority of India Ltd v Hind Metals Inc; Hind Metals Inc v Sail International Ltd; Hind Metals inc v Steel Authority of India Ltd [1984] 1 Lloyd's Rep. 405; (1984) 134 N.L.J. 204 QBD (Comm Ct) 24
Stinnes Interoil GmbH v A Halcoussis & Co (The Yanxilas); Yanxilas, The [1982] 2 Lloyd's Rep. 445 QBD (Comm Ct) 250
Studd v Cook (1883) 10 R. (HL) 53 227
Success International Inc v Environmental Export International of Canada Inc (1995) 23 O.R. (3d) 137 35
Succula & Pomona Shipping Co Ltd v Harland & Wolff Ltd [1980] 2 Lloyd's Rep. 381 QBD (Comm Ct) 131

Table of Cases

Sumitomo Heavy Industries v Oil and Natural Gas Commission [1994] 1 Lloyd's Rep. 45 QBD (Comm Ct) 147

Svenska Handelsbanken v India Charge Chrome Ltd (1996) XXI YCA 557 Sup Ct (India) 37

Svenska Petroleum Exploration AB v Lithuania (No.1) [2005] EWHC 9 (Comm); [2005] 1 All E.R. (Comm) 515, [2005] 1 Lloyd's Rep. 515 .... 58, 60

Svenska Petroleum Exploration AB v Lithuania (No.2) [2006] EWCA Civ 1529; [2007] Q.B. 886; [2007] 2 W.L.R. 876; [2007] 1 All E.R. (Comm) 909; [2007] 1 Lloyd's Rep. 193; [2006] 2 C.L.C. 797 63

Syria v SIMER (1983) VIII YCA 386 78

TAG WEALTH MANAGEMENT V WEST [2008] EWHC 1466 (Comm); [2008] 2 Lloyd's Rep. 699 .... 203, 204

Tame Shipping Ltd v Easy Navigation Ltd (The Easy Rider); Easy Rider, The [2004] EWHC 1862 (Comm); [2004] 2 All E.R. (Comm) 521; [2004] 2 Lloyd's Rep. 626; [2004] 2 C.L.C. 1155 .... 255, 316

Taylor Woodrow Construction (Scotland) Ltd v Sears Investment Trust Ltd (No.2), 1992 S.L.T. 609 OH 257, 259

Taylor Woodrow Construction Ltd v RMD Kwikform Ltd [2008] EWHC 825 (TCC); [2009] Bus. L.R. 292; [2009] 1 All E.R. (Comm) 770; [2008] 2 Lloyd's Rep. 345; [2008] 1 C.L.C. 793; [2008] B.L.R. 383; 118 Con. L.R. 57 106

Taylor Woodrow Holdings Ltd v Barnes & Elliott Ltd [2006] EWHC 1693 (TCC); [2006] 2 All E.R. (Comm) 735; [2006] B.L.R. 377; 110 Con. L.R. 169; [2006] C.I.L.L. 2375 .... 211, 213

Television New Zealand Ltd v Langley Productions Ltd [2000] N.Z.L.R. 250 50

The Bremer Vulkan (Bremer Vulkan Schiffbau und Maschinenfabrik v South India Shipping Corp Ltd [1981] A.C. 909 203

Thomson v Earl of Galloway (Expenses), 1919 S.C. 611; 1919 2 S.L.T. 80 IH (2 Div) 213, 235

Thyssen Canada Ltd v Mariana Maritima SA [2000] 3 F.C. 398 Fed CA (Can) 94

Thyssen Canada Ltd v Mariana Maritime SA [2005] EWHC 219 (Comm); [2005] 1 Lloyd's Rep. 640 315

Tianhjin Medicine and Health Products Import and Export Corp v JA Moeller (Hong Kong) Ltd [1994] 1 H.K.C. 545 35

Tiong Huat Rubber Factory Bhd v Wah Chang International Co Ltd (1992) XVII YCA 516 70

Tongyuan (USA) International Trading Group v Uni-Clan Ltd (2001) XXVI YCA 886 .... 61, 68

Tongyuan (USA) International Trading Group v Uni-Clan Ltd Unreported January 19, 2001 QB 299

Torch Offshore LLC v Cable Shipping Inc [2004] EWHC 787 (Comm); [2004] 2 All E.R. (Comm) 365; [2004] 2 Lloyd's Rep. 446; [2004] 2 C.L.C. 433 .... 271, 314

Tournier v National Provincial and Union Bank of England [1924] 1 K.B. 461 CA ... 51, 170, 171

Tracomin SA v Sudan Oil Seeds (No.1) [1983] 1 W.L.R. 1026; [1983] 3 All E.R. 137; [1983] 2 Lloyd's Rep. 384; [1983] Com. L.R. 269; [1984] E.C.C. 165 CA (Civ Div) 19

Trade Fortitude, The. See Food Corp of India v Marastro Cia Naviera SA (The Trade Fortitude) (No.1)

Trans Trust SPRL v Danubian Trading Co Ltd [1952] 2 Q.B. 297; [1952] 1 All E.R. 970; [1952] 1 Lloyd's Rep. 348; [1952] 1 T.L.R. 1066; (1952) 96 S.J. 312 CA 260

Trans World Film SpA v Film Polski Import and Export of Films (1993) XVIII YCA 433 Sup Ct (Italy) 65

Transocean Shipping Agency (P) Ltd v Black Sea Shipping (1998) XXIII YCA 713 Sup Ct (India) 77

Traube v Perelman, Unreported July 25, 2001 Ch D 37

Trayfoot v Lock [1957] 1 W.L.R. 351; [1957] 1 All E.R. 423; (1957) 101 S.J. 171 CA ... 176

Tresor Public v Galakis, 1966 Revue de l'Arbitrage 99 Cour de Cassation 62

Tuyuti, The; Tuyuti, The [1984] Q.B. 838; [1984] 3 W.L.R. 231; [1984] 2 All E.R. 545; [1984] 2 Lloyd's Rep. 51; (1984) 81 L.S.G. 1362; (1984) 128 S.J. 498 CA (Civ Div) 32

Table of Cases

UNICHIPS FINANZIARIA SpA v GESNOUIN (1994) XIX YCA 658 CA (Paris) 64
Union de Cooperativas Agricolas Epis-Centre v La Palentina SA (2002) XXVII YCA
533 64
Union of India v McDonnell Douglas Corp [1993] 2 Lloyd's Rep. 48 QBD (Comm
Ct) 23, 24
United Mexican States v Karpa [2005] 74 O.R. 3d 180 CA (Ontario) 75
United Steelworkers of America v Enterprise Wheel & Car Corp, 363 U.S. 593 (1960) 253

VA MARITIMA ZOROSA SA v SESOSTRIS [1984] 1 Lloyd's Rep. 161 23
Vale do Rio doce Navegacao SA v Shanghai Bao Steel Ocean Shipping Co Ltd (t/a Bao
Steel Ocean Shipping Co); sub nom. Vale do Rio doce Navegacao SA v Shanghai
Bao Steel Ocean Shipping Co Ltd (t/a Baosteel Ocean Shipping Co) [2000] 2
All E.R. (Comm) 70; [2000] 2 Lloyd's Rep. 1; [2000] C.L.C. 1200 QBD (Comm
Ct) 13, 157
Van der Giessen-de Noord Shipbuilding Division BV v Imtech Marine & Offshore BV
[2008] EWHC 2904 (Comm); [2009] 1 Lloyd's Rep. 273 .... 297, 299
Vee Networks Ltd v Econet Wireless International Ltd [2004] EWHC 2909 (Comm);
[2005] 1 All E.R. (Comm) 303; [2005] 1 Lloyd's Rep. 192 .... 147, 292
Vertex Data Science Ltd v Powergen Retail Ltd [2006] 2 Lloyd's Rep. 11 36

W&S v BB Unreported June 8, 2001 TCC 133, 142, 164, 267
WAC Ltd v Whillock, 1989 S.C. 397; 1990 S.L.T. 213; 1990 S.C.L.R. 193 IH (2
Div) 232
Walker v Rome; sub nom. Walker v Rowe [1999] 2 All E.R. (Comm) 961; [2000] 1
Lloyd's Rep. 116; [2000] C.L.C. 265 QBD (Comm Ct) 12, 42
Ward v Walker, 1920 S.C. 80; 1920 1 S.L.T. 2 IH (1 Div) 226
Wealands v CLC Contractors Ltd; sub nom. Wealand v CLC Contractors Ltd [2000] 1
All E.R. (Comm) 30; [1999] 2 Lloyd's Rep. 739; [1999] C.L.C. 1821; [1999] B.L.R.
401; (2000) 2 T.C.L.R. 367; 74 Con. L.R. 1 243
Webb v The Queen (1994) 181 C.L.R. 41 160
Weinstein International Corp v Nagtegaal NV (1980) V YCA 269 81
Weldon Plant Ltd v Commission for the New Towns [2001] 1 All E.R. (Comm) 264;
[2000] B.L.R. 496; (2000) 2 T.C.L.R. 785; 77 Con. L.R. 1 QBD (T&CC) 252
Welex AG v Rosa Maritime Ltd (The Epsilon Rosa) (No.2); Epsilon Rosa, The (No.2)
[2003] EWCA Civ 938; [2003] 2 Lloyd's Rep. 509; [2003] 2 C.L.C. 207 243
West v Secretary of State for Scotland; sub nom. West v Scottish Prison Service, 1992
S.C. 385; 1992 S.L.T. 636; 1992 S.C.L.R. 504 IH (1 Div) 46
Westacre Investments Inc v Jugoimport SPDR Holding Co Ltd [2000] Q.B. 288; [1999] 3
W.L.R. 811; [1999] 3 All E.R. 864; [1999] 1 All E.R. (Comm) 865; [1999] 2 Lloyd's
Rep. 65; [1999] C.L.C. 1176; [1999] B.L.R. 279 CA (Civ Div) 75, 76, 302
Westdeutsche Landesbank Girozentrale v Islington LBC; Kleinwort Benson Ltd v
Sandwell BC; sub nom. Islington LBC v Westdeutsche Landesbank Girozentrale
[1996] A.C. 669; [1996] 2 W.L.R. 802; [1996] 2 All E.R. 961; [1996] 5 Bank. L.R. 341;
[1996] C.L.C. 990; 95 L.G.R. 1; (1996) 160 J.P. Rep. 1130; (1996) 146 N.L.J. 877;
(1996) 140 S.J.L.B. 136 HL 248
Westland Helicopters Ltd v Al-Hejailan [2004] EWHC 1625 (Comm); [2004] 2 Lloyd's
Rep. 523 248
Whatley v Ardrossan Harbour Co (1893) 1 S.L.T. 382 IH (1 Div) 39
Whatlings (Foundations) Ltd v Shanks & McEwan (Contractors) Ltd, 1989 S.C. 253;
1989 S.L.T. 857; 1989 S.C.L.R. 552 IH (1 Div) 242
Willcock v Pickfords Removals [1979] 1 Lloyd's Rep. 244 CA (Civ Div) 31, 147
William Co v Chiu Kong Agency Ltd [1995] 2 H.K.L.R. 139 35
Wilson v Keen Unreported June 25, 1991 CA 89
Wm Dixon Ltd v Jones, Heard & Ingram (1884) 11 R. 739 108
Wood v Adcock (1852) 7 Ex. 468 241
World Trade Corp Ltd v C Czarnikow Sugar Ltd [2004] EWHC 2332 (Comm); [2004] 2
All E.R. (Comm) 813; [2005] 1 Lloyd's Rep. 422 .... 271, 298

XL INSURANCE LTD V OWENS CORNING [2001] 1 All E.R. (Comm) 530; [2000] 2 Lloyd's
Rep. 500; [2001] C.P. Rep. 22; [2001] C.L.C. 914 .... 24, 64

Table of Cases

Youell v La Reunion Aerienne [2009] EWCA Civ 175; [2009] Bus. L.R. 1504; [2009] 2 All E.R. (Comm) 1071; [2009] 1 Lloyd's Rep. 586; [2009] C.P. Rep. 28; [2009] 1 C.L.C. 336 19
Younger v Caledonian Railway Co (1847) 10 D. 133 .... 278, 279, 280
Yukos Oil Ltd v Dardana Ltd. *See* Dardana Ltd v Yukos Oil Co (No.1)

Zealander v Laing Homes Ltd (2000) 2 T.C.L.R. 724 6
Zheijiang Province Garment Import and Export Co v Siemssen & Co (Hong Kong) Trading Ltd [1993] A.D.R.L.J. 183 H Ct (HK) 72

Bavarian Court of Appeal (2002) XXVII YCA 445 65
Swiss court (1979) IV YCA 30 65
Schleswig Court of Appeal (2004) XXIX YCA 687 65
Cologne Court of Appeal (1979) IV YCA 258 65
Dutch Supreme Court (1976) I YCA 195 68
Hamburg Court of Appeal (2000) XXV YCA 714 71
German Supreme Court (2004) XXIX YCA 700 77
Austrian Supreme Court (1977) I YCA 232 80
Rostock Court of Appeal (2000) XXV YCA 717 81
German Supreme Court in (2001) XXVI YCA 771 81
(1994) XIX YCA 700 Italy 81
ICC case 5946 (1991) XVI YCA 97 242
Decision of June 4, 1992 BGHZ 118 242

TABLE OF STATUTES

1843 Evidence by Commission Act
(6 & 7 Vict. c.82) 219, 220
1868 Titles to Land Consolidation
(Scotland) Act (31 & 32
Vict. c.101)
  s.155 230
  s.159 337
1894 Arbitration (Scotland) Act (57 &
58 Vict. c.13) 1, 5, 91, 100, 336
1895 Court of Session Consignations
(Scotland) Act (58 & 59
Vict. c.19) 317, 319
1907 Sheriff Courts (Scotland) Act
(7 Edw. 7 c.51)
  s.6 .... 216, 221, 232, 234
1924 Conveyancing (Scotland) Act
1924 (14 & 15 Geo. 5 c.27)
  s.46 91
1947 Crown Proceedings Act (c.44)
  s.21 .... 243, 244
  s.43 243
1950 Arbitration Act (c.27) ... 1, 6, 44, 68,
176, 200, 203, 336
  Pt I 6
  Pt II 6, 44, 91, 100
  s.4 33
  s.9(1) 68
  s.11 87
  s.13A 201, 203
  s.14 260
  s.15 244
  s.16 38
  s.17 .... 269, 270
  s.19 262
  s.26 41
  s.30 98
  s.31 53
1966 Arbitration (International
Investment Disputes) Act
(c.41) 5
1970 Administration of Justice Act
(c.31)
  s.4 .... 87, 88
1971 Sheriff Courts (Scotland) Act
(c.58)
  s.6 88
1972 Administration of Justice
(Scotland) Act (c.59) 336
  s.1 .... 229, 236
  s.3 .... 1, 5, 92, 100, 101, 210, 211,
212, 261, 305, 336
    (1) 101
1973 Prescription and Limitation
(Scotland) Act (c.52) 85
  s.1(1) 84
    (5) 84
  s.2 84
  s.3 84

  s.4 85
    (2)(c) 84
    (3) 84
    (4) 84
  ss.6–8 85
  s.9 85
    (3) 85
  s.17 85
  s.18 85
  s.18A 85
  s.18B 85
  s.19D 85
  s.22A 85
1975 Arbitration Act (c.3) ... 5, 31, 34, 35,
36, 55, 73, 82, 92, 100, 257,
300, 336
  s.1 .... 30, 31, 32, 34, 36
    (1) 33
  s.3(2) 58
  s.4 80
  s.5 59
    (1) 61
    (d) 69
    (f) 71, 72
    (2)(a) 61
    (b) 63
    (c) 64
    (e) 67
    (3) 74, 75
    (4) 78
    (5) 78, 79
  s.6 82
  s.7(2) 57
  Evidence (Proceedings in Other
Jurisdictions) Act (c.34) ... 220
  Industry Act (c.68)
  Sch.3 para.18 54
1977 Unfair Contract Terms Act
(c.50)
  s.27(2) 238
    (3) 238
1978 Interpretation Act (c.30)
  s.7 .... 332, **333**
  Sch.1 .... 218, 223
  State Immunity Act (c.33)
  s.9(1) 63
1979 Arbitration Act (c.42) 178, 179,
200, 213, 215
  s.1(2) 179
    (4) 308
  s.5 206
1980 Law Reform (Miscellaneous
Provisions) (Scotland) Act
(c.55) 89, 336
  s.17 .... 87, 88, 92, 336
1981 Supreme Court Act (c.54)
  s.16 311
  s.37 171

xxix

1982	Civil Jurisdiction and Judgments Act (c.27)	
	s.18	44
	s.21(1)(a)	221, 234
	s.32	19
	Sch.6	44
	Sch.8	221, 234
1985	Law Reform (Miscellaneous Provisions) (Scotland) Act (c.73)	
	s.8	245
1987	Debtors (Scotland) Act (c.18)	
	s.15D	234
	s.15E(2)	230
	s.15F(3)	230
	s.15G	228, 230
	s.15K	230
	s.15L	231
	Consumer Protection Act (c.43)	85
1988	Civil Evidence (Scotland) Act (c.32)	
	s.9	176, 187
	Court of Session Act (c.36)	311
	s.10	233
	s.18	311
	s.40	293, 303, 311
	s.47(2)	233
1991	Coal Mining Subsidence Act (c.45)	
	s.19	309
1990	Contracts (Applicable Law) Act (c.36)	238
	Law Reform (Miscellaneous Provisions) (Scotland) Act (c.40)	2, 336
	s.66	2, 4, 28, 90, 92, 100, 336
	(4)	3, 100, 101
	Sch.7	2, 28, 90, 92, 100, 336
	Courts and Legal Services Act (c.41)	
	s.99	87
	s.102	201, 203
1992	Trade Union and Labour Relations (Consolidation) Act (c.52)	
	s.212A	93
1995	Requirements of Writing (Scotland) Act (c.7)	
	s.1(1)	21
	(2)	21
	s.6	44
	Merchant Shipping Act (c.21)	
	ss.95–97	54
1996	Employment Rights Act (c.18)	
	s.203	93
	Arbitration Act (c.23)	1, 2, 3, 4, 5, 12, 13, 13, 14, 16, 19, 22, 23, 26, 27, 29, 32, 33, 34, 36, 40, 45, 54, 55, 73, 88, 93, 95, 99, 105, 108, 110, 111, 112, 118, 122, 129, 135, 145, 149, 150, 151, 152, 153, 154, 156, 157, 159, 162, 173, 178, 179, 188, 193, 197, 200, 206, 226, 237, 240, 243, 248, 250, 251, 252, 253, 255, 257, 259, 261, 264, 265, 268, 271, 272, 273, 277, 300, 311, 314
	Pt I	13, 17
	s.1	11, 12
	(a)	184
	(c)	12, 13, 122
	s.2	188
	(1)	17
	(2)	189
	(3)	16, 189
	(4)	189
	s.3	17, 57, 188
	(a)	17
	(b)	17
	(c)	17
	s.4	27
	(1)	26
	(3)	28
	(5)	18, 29
	s.5	56, 57
	(1)	21
	(2)–(6)	21
	s.6	35
	(2)	20
	s.7	22
	s.8	54
	s.9	30, 32, 36, 40, 146
	(1)	31
	(2)	30
	(3)	32, 33
	ss.9–11	189
	s.12	54
	s.14	104, 105
	(4)	104, 106
	s.16(5)(b)	112
	s.17	112
	s.18	116
	s.21(4)	111
	s.24	122, 126, 128, 130, 131, 183, 185
	(1)(d)	268
	s.25	135, 140
	(2)	140
	(5)	140
	s.28	264
	(5)	277
	s.30	27, 56
	(1)	146
	(a)	147
	(2)	146
	s.31	149
	(4)	152
	(5)	157
	s.32	96, 155, 156, 157, 165
	(2)	156
	(a)	156
	(3)	156

Table of Statutes

(4)	157
s.33	183, 185, 195, 203
(1)(a)	128
s.34(1)	175
(2)(a)	180
(b)	187
(d)	182
(e)	183
(f)	178, 179
(h)	185
s.36	196
s.37	197
(1)(b)	194, 198
(2)	198
s.38(4)	199
(5)	199
s.39	258, 259
s.40(1)	165
(2)	165
s.41	165
(3)	200, 203, 204
(5)	127, 206, 207
(7)	207
s.42	207, 208
s.43	189
s.44	189
(2)(e)	171
(4)	225
s.45	165, 168, 211
(2)(b)(i)	213
s.46(1)(b)	237
(2)	238
(3)	239
s.47	260
s.48	241, 243
(1)	243
(5)(b)	244
s.49	246, 248
(3)(a)	246
(5)	246
(6)	248
s.51	266
(2)	267
s.52	249
(5)	251, 252
s.53	256, 257
s.54(1)	252
(2)	252
s.56	262
(2)	263
(4)	265
(5)	263, 264
(7)	265
s.57	255, 269
(3)	270, 271
(5)	273
s.58	38
(1)	39
(2)	40
s.63(4)	278
(5)	280
s.65	287, 288
s.66	41, 42, 189
(3)	43
(4)	44
s.67	239
s.68	128, 130, 131, 17, 185, 192, 204, 296
(2)	128
(a)	185, 203, 204
(b)	298
(d)	203, 204
(g)	300
s.69	168, 179, 203, 204, 304, 308, 309
(1)	177
(2)(b)	177
(3)(c)	178, 179
s.70(2)	255
(4)	254, 255, 316
(7)	318
s.72	47, 48
s.73	151, 325
s.79	273
s.81(1)	105
s.82(1)	95, 96
(2)	32, 95
s.84(2)	99
s.85(2)	14
ss.89–91	6, 164
s.90	6
s.93	87
(1)(2)	88
s.94(2)	54
(3)	53, 54
ss.94–97	53
s.95(1)	53
(2)	54
s.96	177
(1)	176
(2)	148
(b)	176
(3)	54
s.97	54
s.98(1)	55
s.100(2)(a)	56
(b)	57
(3)	57
(4)	56
ss.100–104	5, 55
s.101(1)	58
s.102	80
s.103	59
(1)	61
(2)(a)	61
(b)	63
(c)	64
(d)	69
(e)	67
(5)	78, 79
s.106	98
Sch.1	5, 26

Table of Statutes

para.78	5	s.9(1)	311
para.79	5	Scotland Act (c.46)	162
Sch.2	88, 89	s.29(2)(b)	6
para.2(1)	89	s.104	6
1998 Human Rights Act (c.42)	159	Sch.5 para.7(1)	6

TABLE OF SCOTTISH STATUTES

2000 Adults with Incapacity (Scotland) Act (asp 4)
    s.1(6) 141
2002 Debt Arrangement and Attachment (Scotland) Act (asp 17)
    s.9C 234
    s.9D(2) 228
    s.9E(3) 228
    s.9G 228
    s.9M 228
    s.9N 228
2007 Bankruptcy and Diligence etc. (Scotland) Act (asp 3)
    s.149 230
2010 Arbitration (Scotland) Act (asp 1) 1, 2, 3, 4, 6, 12, 13, 16, 17, 20, 31, 33, 34, 44, 53, 54, 55, 56, 57, 61, 73, 88, 95, 96, 99, 100, 101, 152, 256, 257, 266, 268, 270
    s.1 .... **11**, 117, 162, 164, 221, 308, 313, 317
      (a) 122, 134, 137, 140, 144, 152, 157, 159, 181, 185, 186, 187, 191, 195, 204, 205, 206, 207
      (c) 13, 116, 134, 140
    s.2 ... **13**, 23, 25, 27, 41, 53, 102, 107, 110, 111, 121, 324, 326, 327, 328, 329, 330, 335
      (1) 11, 13, 16, 20, 21, 23, 25, 26, 27, 30, 38, 41, 45, 47, 49, 53, 55, 59, 84, 87, 89, 91, 92, 97, 145, 149, 153, 154, 155, 175, 187, 189, 191, 194, 195, 198, 199, 200, 205, 206, 208, 210, 211, 215, 217, 219, 224, 225, 236, 242, 246, 249, 257, 259, 261, 262, 265, 269, 274, 275, 278, 281, 284, 287, 289, 304, 307, 313, 319, 320, 322, 323, 324, 326, 327, 328, 329, 330, 334
      (2) 11, 15, 16, 20, 23, 25, 26, 27, 30, 41, 45, 47, 49, 53, 55, 59, 84, 89, 91, 97, 145, 146, 153, 155, 208, 246, 259, 265, 274
      (3) 16
    s.3 .... **16**, 18, 180, 251, 256
      (1)(a) 17, 18
        (b) 18
      (2) 19
    s.4 .... **20**, 21, 22, 23, 26, 27, 30, 47, 53, 56, 59, 80, 102, 107, 108, 110, 112, 116, 117, 121, 124, 126, 132, 133, 135, 139, 143, 144, 145, 206, 215, 216, 290, 294, 297, 324

    s.5 .... **21**, 22, 145, 290, 313, 328, 329, 330, 335
      (3) 22
    s.6 .... **22**, 25, 84
    s.7 .... 16, **25**, 26, 27, 38, 45, 47, 53, 55, 84, 86, 89, 249, 251, 265
    s.8 .... **25**, 108, 110, 117, 121, 126, 132, 133, 135, 139, 158, 165, 175, 276, 281, 294, 328, 330, 334, 335
      (2) 175
      (4)(b) 253
    s.9 .... **27**, 102, 107, 110, 112, 116, 121, 124, 143, 144, 158, 187, 190, 191, 195, 197, 198, 199, 200, 205, 206, 209, 278, 287, 289, 304, 327, 329, 334
      (1) 25, 27, 334, 335
      (2) 27, 46
      (3) 27, 28, 46, 108, 331
        (b) 331
      (4) 28
        (a) 28, 46, 237
        (b) 18, 20, 28, 29, 145
    s.10 ... 17, **29**, 30, 38, 42, 50, 92, 145, 146
      (1)(a) 30
        (b) 32
        (c) 32
        (d) 32, 33
        (e) 31, 34
      (2) 37
      (3) 17, 37
    s.11 .... **38**, 39
      (1) 38, 39
      (2) 40, 42, 245
      (3) 38, 40
      (4) 40
    s.12 ...... **41**, 43, 44, 46, 48, 82, 83, 91
      (1) 41, 44, 58, 83
      (2) 42, 43, 151
      (3) 43, 151
      (4) 43
      (5) 43, 44, 82, 83
      (6) 17, 44
        (b) 82
      (7)(a) 44
        (b) 44
      (8) 44
    s.13 .... 13, 44, **45**, 46, 50
      (1) 45
        (b) 212, 226
      (2) 46
      (3) 46
      (4) 28, 46
    s.14 .... **47**, 48, 149
      (1) 47
        (a)–(c) 47

Table of Scottish Statutes

(2)	48
s.15	**48**, 50
(1)	49
(2)	51
(a)	51
(b)	52
(c)	52
(d)	52
(3)	52
s.16	20, **52**, 58
(1)	30, 47, 53, 55, 145, 335
(2)	37, 53
(3)	54
(4)	17, 54
(5)	54
(6)	54
ss.16–20	5
s.17	**55**
(a)	55
(b)	55
s.18	44, **56**, 57, 59, 80, 82
(1)	56, 82
(2)	57, 256
(3)	57
ss.18–21	56
ss.18–22	44, 55, 92
s.19	49, 56, **57**, 80
(1)	58
(2)	58
ss.19–21	44, 50
s.20	44, **58**, 59, 61, 80, 83, 225
(1)	61
(2)	59, 60, 61, 69
(a)	61
(b)	63, 70, 74, 94
(c)	64
(d)	66, 67
(3)	59, 60, 61, 69
(a)	69
(b)	69, 71, 78
(c)	71
(d)	67, 71, 72, 80
(4)	59, 61, 74
(a)	74
(b)	64, 74
(5)	78
(6)	43, 78
(a)	72, 78
(b)	79, 318
(7)	72, 80
s.21	**80**, 83
(1)	80
(a)	81
(b)	58, 81
(2)	82
s.22	44, 56, **82**, 116, 125, 190, 274, 275, 322
s.23	**83**
(1)	84
(2)	84
(3)	85

(4)	85
(5)	85
(6)	85
s.24	**86**, 335
(1)(a)	159
(b)	300
(c)	185
(d)	184
(2)	86, 101, 116
s.25	**86**, 89, 153, 165
(1)	88
(2)	89
(3)	89
s.26	**89**, 26, 300
(1)	108
(2)	90
s.27	**90**, 91
s.28	**91**, 165, 302
s.29	**91**
s.30	**92**, 147
(2)	146
s.31	32, 45, **95**, 274
(1)	11, 16, 19, 20, 21, 23, 25, 26, 27, 28, 30, 38, 41, 45, 47, 48, 50, 52, 53, 55, 56, 58, 59, 80, 82, 84, 86, 87, 89, 91, 92, 95, 96, 97, 102, 107, 108, 110, 112, 116, 117, 121, 124, 126, 132, 133, 135, 139, 143, 144, 145, 149, 153, 154, 155, 156, 200, 208, 210, 212, 215, 217, 218, 224, 236, 242, 246, 249, 257, 259, 261, 262, 265, 269, 274, 275, 278, 281, 284, 287, 289, 294, 304, 307, 313, 319, 320, 322, 323, 324, 326, 327, 328, 329, 330, 334, 335
(2)	11, 16, 23, 25, 26, 27, 30, 38, 41, 45, 47, 48, 53, 55, 59, 84, 96, 97, 112, 116, 149, 153, 154, 155, 156, 210, 212, 215, 217, 218, 224, 236, 242, 249, 261, 262, 265, 269, 275, 278, 281, 284, 287, 289, 294, 304, 307, 313, 324, 326, 327, 328, 329, 330
s.32	**96**
(1)	96
(2)	96
s.33	**97**, 185
(1)(a)	159, 184
(2)	184
s.34	**97**
(2)(f)	177
s.35	**98**
s.36	**98**, 102
(1)	99
(2)	100
(3)	100, 101
(4)	101
(5)	101

Table of Scottish Statutes

(6)	101
(7)	101
(8)	101, 210, 305
(9)	100, 102
s.37	**102**
Sch.1	29, **102**
Pt 1	**102**
Pt 2	103, **145**
Pt 3	**158**
Pt 4	**174**
Pt 5	49, **210**
Pt 6	**236**
Pt 7	**273**
Pt 8	42, 49, 91, 268, **289**, 295
Pt 9	**320**
r.1	84, 85, 99, **102**, 226, 232
r.2	91, **107**
(e)	126
rr.2–7	143, 290
r.3	108, 112, 192, 328
r.4	26, **109**, 112, 139, 141, 142, 223, 325
(a)	141
r.5	**110**
r.6	107, **111**, 112, 114, 122, 143, 216
(b)	113, 114, 125, 190
r.7	26, 27, 50, 86, 92, 107, 112, 114, **115**, 116, 143, 149, 157, 190, 216, 274, 275, 322
(1)	116
(2)	26
(6)	116, 117
(7)	116
r.8	**117**, 128, 162, 327
(2)	118, 327
r.9	**120**, 122, 139, 141, 143, 144
r.10	47, 118, **121**, 122, 136, 137, 139, 141, 142
(1)	122
(2)	122, 123, 126, 131, 302, 327
(3)	123
(4)	123, 124
r.11	**124**, 136, 139, 141, 142
(1)	125
(2)	125
r.12	50, 122, 123, **125**, 126, 132, 136, 137, 139, 141, 142, 164, 268
(a)	113, 126, 129, 162, 327
(b)	126, 131, 163
(c)	126, 131, 137, 163, 302
(d)	123, 126, 131, 302
(e)	126, 131, 175
r.13	50, 122, **132**, 140, 141, 142
r.14	**133**, 140
(1)	134
(2)	134
(3)	134
r.15	**135**, 136, 139, 140, 142
(1)	131, 136, 137, 138
(2)	138, 322
r.16	135, 136, **139**, 140
(1)	140, 141, 142, 322, 327
(2)	136, 142
r.17	**142**, 143
(1)	143
(2)	143
(3)	144
r.18	**144**
(1)	195
r.19	22, 25, 27, 107, **145**, 146, 290, 291
(a)	31, 146
(a)–(c)	146
(b)	148
(c)	148
rr.19–23	94, 103
r.20	47, 107, **148**, 149, 150, 291, 297, 325
(1)	149, 50
(2)	149, 157
(3)	151, 266
(4)	152, 291
r.21	46, 146, **152**, 153, 291
(1)	153, 266
(2)	154
(3)	154, 291
r.22	46, 149, **154**, 155, 157, 211, 291, 297
r.23	26, **155**, 206, 211, 213
(1)	113, 155
(2)	155, 156
(3)	157
(4)	158, 291
r.24	117, 122, 129, 137, **158**, 183, 204, 207, 213, 218, 223, 235, 236, 278, 279, 287, 288, 297, 316, 334
(1)	18, 117, 134, 136, 137, 140, 144, 152, 157, 158, 158, 162, 162, 164, 181, 186, 187, 191, 195, 205, 260, 261, 302, 325, 327
(2)	131, 164, 206
r.25	122, 137, 142, 144, **165**, 181, 191
(a)	191
r.26	4, 50, 51, **166**, 172, 182, 209
r.27	**173**
(1)	173
(2)	174
r.28	165, **174**, 175, 288
(1)	175, 176
(2)	180, 181, 183, 185, 186, 187, 221

Table of Scottish Statutes

r.29 .... 16, 18, 180, **187**, 189
r.30 .... 18, **189**, 190, 250, 329
    (1) 190
    (2) 111, 190
r.31 .... **190**, 221
    (1) 191
    (2) 191
r.32 .... 109, **191**, 192
    (1) 265
    (2) 265
r.33 .... **194**, 195, 196
r.34 .... 138, **196**, 197, 298
r.35 .... **198**, 221, 226
r.36 .... **199**
r.37 .... **199**, 200, 205, 216, 266
    (1) 96, 200
    (2) 204
rr.37–39 165
r.38 .... 200, **205**, 216
    (a) 206
    (a)(i) 205
r.39 .... **205**, 207, 208, 216
    (1) 207
    (2) 207, 208
r.40 .... 101, **208**, 209, 210
r.41 .... 92, 101, **210**, 212, 226, 274, 305
    (1) 211
rr.41–42 92
rr.41–45 226
r.42 .... 26, **212**
    (1) 213
    (2) 211, 213, 214, 238
    (3) 215
    (4) 215
r.43 .... 54, **215**, 216, 217
r.44 .... 26, **216**
    (1)–(3) 217
    (2) 217
    (5) 218
r.45 .... 16, **218**, 219, 221, 229
    (1) 220, 221, 286
    (2) 222, 286
    (3) 223
    (4) 223
r.46 ... 16, 199, **223**, 225, 229, 233, 234, 235, 236, 247
    (1) 207, 225, 226, 227, 228, 229, 230, 231, 233, 234, 258
    (2) 207, 225, 232, 234, 258
    (3) 226, 228, 229, 230, 235
    (4) 229, 236
r.47 .... 20, **236**, 237, 238, 239, 240, 305
    (1) 238, 240
    (2) 240
    (3) 240, 241
r.48 .... 27, **241**, 251

    (1) 241
    (2) 242, 297, 299
r.49 .... 241, **242**, 243, 244, 248, 258
    (a) 243
    (b) 231, 233, 243
    (c) 244, 245
    (d) 243
    (d) 91
r.50 .... 27, **245**, 247, 248, 251
    (1) 246, 247
    (2) 247
    (3) 247
    (4) 246, 247
    (5) 248
r.51 ...... 18, 40, **249**, 250, 253, 256
    (1) 249, 260
    (2) 251, 253, 254, 255, 257, 262, 268, 305, 316
    (3) 252, 253, 256, 262, 314
r.52 .... 57, 189, **256**
r.53 ..... 27, 40, 231, 243, 255, **257**, 258, 259, 260, 313, 335
    (2) 40
r.54 .... 27, 255, **259**, 282, 335
    (1) 259
    (2) 259
    (3) 260
r.55 .... **260**, 261
r.56 .... **262**, 263, 264, 265
    (1) 262
    (2) 263, 264
    (3) 265
    (4) 265, 268
r.57 .... 222, **265**, 268
    (1) 265, 266, 282
    (2) 266
    (3) 266, 271
    (4) .. 253, 266, 267, 268, 316
    (5) 268
r.58 .... 42, 255, 261, 262, 266, **268**, 269, 271, 272, 276, 290, 295, 299, 314
    (1) 252, 260, 270, 271, 277
    (2) 263, 271
    (3) 271
    (4) 251, 271, 314
    (5) 272
    (6) 251, 272, 273
    (7) 273
    (8) 273
r.59 .... 134, 138, 139, 213, 218, 235, 263, **273**, 274, 278, 281, 284, 286, 287, 289, 335
    (c) 274
r.60 .... 139, 263, 264, **275**, 276, 277, 284
    (1) 276, 279, 284
    (2) 263, 276

Table of Scottish Statutes

(3) 277	(6) 310
(4) 277	(7) 308, 310
(5) 264, 277	(8) 308, 310
r.61 .... 274, **277**, 278, 281, 282, 288, 335	(9) 293, 304, 311
(1) 278, 279	(10) 293, 304, 311
(2) 278, 279	(11) 293, 304, 311
(3) 164, 279, 280	(12) 311
r.62 .... 213, 263, 274, 278, **281**, 282, 299	r.71 .... 95, 266, 272, **312**, 313, 316
(1) 277, 282	(1) 313
(2) 283	(2) 48, 146, 255, 290, 295, 299, 306, 313
(3) 277, 284	(3) 259, 288, 314
(4) 284	(4) 262, 272, 290, 295, 306, 307, 314, 315, 316
r.63 .... **284**, 285	(5) 304, 306, 311, 314, 315
r.64 .... 228, 234, 286, 317	(6) 314, 315
(1) 287	(7) 299, 315
(2) 234, 287	(8) 254, 316
rr.64–66 274	(9) 43, 54, 317
r.65 .... **287**, 288	(10) 317
r.66 .... 266, 282, **288**, 289	(10)–(12) 306
(2) 126, 299, 302	(11) 317
r.67 ...... 28, 46, 94, 101, 107, 149, 151, 152, 153, 154, 254, 261, **289**, 290, 291, 292, 295, 297, 305, 313, 325	(12) 292, 317, 318
	r.72 .... 303, 311, **319**
	(1) 303, 311
	r.73 .... 127, 135, 139, 140, 141, 142, 249, 316, **320**
(1) 291, 313	(1) 321
(2) 292	(2) 141, 316, 321
(3) 292, 293	rr.73–75 14
(4)–(6) 293	r.74 .... **322**
rr.67–69 .... 248, 272	(1) 323
rr.67–72 295	(2) 323
r.68 ... 28, 164, 205, 215, 223, 226, 236, 238, 240, 251, 268, 270, 282, 283, 290, **293**, 295, 299, 300, 301, 305, 313	r.75 .... 198, **323**
	r.76 ... 43, 140, 151, 153, 291, **323**, 324, 325, 326
(1) 295, 313, 316, 319, 323, 325	(1) 324
(2) 116, 132, 162, 162, 162, 175, 248, 249, 270, 271, 272, 281, 282, 295, 296, 297, 298, 299, 300, 301, 302, 303	(2) 291, 324, 325, 326
	r.77 .... **326**, 335
	r.78 .... **327**
	r.79 .... 141, 142, **327**
	r.80 .... 54, **328**
(3) 271, 300, 303	(2) 328
(4) 303, 327	r.81 .... **328**, 329
(5) 303	r.80 328
(6) 303	(2) 328
(7) 303	r.82 .... 111, 263, **329**
(8) 303	r.83 .... 102, 103, 124, 125, 135, 139, 256, 262, 266, 273, 313, 314, 331, 333, 334
r.69 ..... 28, 92, 101, 213, 215, 226, 239, 240, 242, 261, 281, 282, 295, 300, **304**, 305, 307, 313	(1) 331
(1) 304, 306, 307, 313, 319, 323	(2) 331
	(3) 332, 333
(2) 253, 260, 290	(4) 331
r.70 ... 26, 290, 295, 304, 305, **306**, 307, 319	(5) 252, 273, 332, 333
	(6) 333, 334
(2) 306, 307	(7) 331
(3) 306, 308, 309	r.84 .... 314, **334**, 335
(4) 306, 307	(b) 335
(5) 310	Sch.2 .... **336**

TABLE OF ABBREVIATIONS

Act or 2010 Act	Arbitration (Scotland) Act 2010 (asp 1) (January 5, 2010)
Bill or 2009 Bill	Arbitration (Scotland) Bill 2009, laid before the Scottish Parliament on January 30, 2009 and finally passed on November 18, 2009
1695 Articles	Articles of Regulation 1695
1894 Act	Arbitration (Scotland) Act 1894 (57 and 58 Vict. c.13) (July 3, 1894)
1950 Act	Arbitration Act 1950 (14 Geo 6, c.27); repealed (as regards England & Wales and Northern Ireland but not Scotland) by the 1996 Act; repealed as regards Scotland by the 2010 Act;
1966 Act	Arbitration (International Investment Disputes) Act 1966 (c.41); the 1966 Act implemented the International Convention on the Settlement of Investment Disputes between States and Nationals of Other States ("ICSID"; the "Washington Convention"); the 1966 Act applies in each of England & Wales, Scotland and Northern Ireland and is not affected by the 1996 Act or the 2010 Act
1972 Act	Administration of Justice (Scotland) Act 1972 (c.59)
1975 Act	Arbitration Act 1975 (c.3); the 1975 Act implemented the New York Convention into the law of England & Wales, Scotland and Northern Ireland but was repealed, insofar as regards England & Wales and Northern Ireland, by the 1996 Act; repealed as regards Scotland by the 2010 Act
1979 Act	Arbitration Act 1979 (c.42); this made a number of important changes to the 1950 Act but did not recodify the law; not applicable in Scotland
1990 Act	Law Reform (Miscellaneous Provisions) (Scotland) Act 1990 (c.40)
1996 Act	Arbitration Act 1996 (c.23); the 1996 Act applies in full in England & Wales and in Northern Ireland but only ss.89–91 (dealing with consumer arbitration) applied (and continues to apply) in Scotland
AAA	American Arbitration Association
ABA	American Bar Association
ABA Code	The Code of Ethics for Arbitrators in Commercial Disputes Approved by the American Bar Association House of Delegates on February 9, 2004, approved by the Executive Committee of the Board of Directors of the AAA.

Table of Abbreviations

CIArb	Chartered Institute of Arbitrators, a worldwide organisation with > 12,000 members in > 105 countries
Chartered Arbitrator	the highest level of qualification in the CIArb, broadly analogous to QC
CIArb Code of Ethics	CIArb *Code of Professional and Ethical Conduct* (October 2009)
CIArb Practice Guidelines	CIArb Practice Guidelines, available at: *http://www.ciarb.org/information-and-resources/practice-guidelines-and-protocols/list-of-guidelines-and-protocols/* [Accessed March 17, 2010]
CIArb Protocols	CIArb Protocols, available at: *http://www.ciarb.org/information-and-resources/practice-guidelines-and-protocols/list-of-guidelines-and-protocols/* [Accessed March 17, 2010]
CIArb Scottish Rules	CIArb Scottish Short Form Rules dated March 1, 2010, intended for use (if the parties so agree) in consumer and smaller value arbitrations
DAC	Departmental Advisory Committee on Arbitration Law; it produced a Report (February 1996) and a Supplementary Report (January 1997) on the Arbitration Act 1996, both of which are considered highly persuasive in interpreting the 1996 Act
Dervaird Bill	the Arbitration (Scotland) Bill 2002, a privately-drafted Bill prepared by a joint working group of the CIArb, SCIA and RICS
Dervaird Committee	The Scottish Advisory Committee on Arbitration Law chaired by Lord Dervaird—it produced a *Report to the Lord Advocate on the UNCITRAL Model Law* (1989), *The Operation of Arbitration in Scotland in light of the UNCITRAL Model Law* (1990), and a *Report on Legislation for Domestic Arbitration in Scotland* (1996).
ECHR	European Convention on Human Rights
FCIArb/MCIArb/ACIArb	Fellow/Member/Associate of the CIArb
HGCRA	Housing Grants, Construction and Regeneration Act 1996 (colloquially known as the "Construction Act") of which ss.107–113 provides for adjudication of disputes in the UK construction industry; it applies (separately) in each of England & Wales, Scotland and Northern Ireland
IBA	International Bar Association
IBA Conflict Guidelines	*IBA Guidelines on Conflicts of Interest in International Arbitration* (approved on May 22, 2004 by the Council of the IBA)

Table of Abbreviations

IBA Evidence Rules	*IBA Rules on the Taking of Evidence in International Commercial Arbitration*, adopted by a Resolution of the IBA Council on June 1, 1999
ICC	International Chamber of Commerce
ICC Rules	[ICC] Rules of Arbitration (in force January 1, 1998)
ICC Expertise Rules	[ICC] Rules for Expertise (in force January 1, 2003)
ICSID	International Centre for the Settlement of Investment Disputes, established under the Washington Convention
LCIA	London Court of International Arbitration
LCIA Rules	LCIA Arbitration Rules (effective January 1, 1998)
Model Law	UNCITRAL Model Law on International Commercial Arbitration; United Nations document A/40/17, Annex I, dated December 1, 1985 as adopted by the UN by General Assembly Resolution 40/72 on December 11, 1985 and as amended by General Assembly Resolution 61/33 dated December 4, 2006
New York Convention	Convention on the Recognition and Enforcement of Foreign Arbitral Awards done in New York on June 10, 1958; the Convention came into force on June 7, 1959
PCA	Permanent Court of Arbitration, based at The Hague, Netherlands; established by treaty in 1899, it is an intergovernmental organisation providing a variety of dispute resolution services to the international community
RCS	Act of Sederunt (Rules of the Court of Session 1994) 1994 (SI 1994/1443) Sch.2 (as amended)
RICS	Royal Institution of Chartered Surveyors
SAC99	Scottish Arbitration Code 1999
SAC05	Scottish Arbitration Code 2005
SAC07	Scottish Arbitration Code 2007
SASAR	Act of Sederunt (Summary Applications, Statutory Applications and Appeals etc. Rules) 1999 (SI 1999/929) (as amended)
SCC	Arbitration Institute of the Stockholm Chamber of Commerce
SCC Rules	Arbitration Rules of the SCC, adopted by the SCC and in force from April 1, 1999
Swiss Rules	Swiss Rules of International Arbitration (January 2004)

Table of Abbreviations

SCIA	Scottish Council for International Arbitration
SIAC	Singapore International Arbitration Centre
UN	the United Nations
UNCITRAL	the United Nations Commission on International Trade Law, an arm of the United Nations based in Vienna
UNCITRAL Rules	the Arbitration Rules of UNCITRAL adopted by UN General Assembly Resolution 31/98 on December 15, 1976
Washington Convention	International Convention on the Settlement of Investment Disputes between States and Nationals of Other States, done in Washington DC on March 18, 1965

INTRODUCTION

The Arbitration (Scotland) Act 2010 represents the most significant step in the history of the Scots law of arbitration, witnessing a move from a regime mainly based on common law to one mainly based on statute. Its importance therefore cannot be overestimated. Its immediate genesis lies in the production by the Scottish Government of a draft Bill in June 2008. This was followed by an extensive consultation exercise as a result of which the draft underwent significant revision and expansion, a process which continued throughout its journey through the legislative process. What has emerged is a fairly comprehensive, modern arbitration statute. Although debate may still arise regarding the meaning of certain provisions and as to whether particular provisions represent the most appropriate approach to given issues, there is no doubt that the Act puts the Scots law of arbitration on a sound footing, providing effective support for the arbitral process, and remedying the inadequacies and lacunae of the previous law.

Historical background

As indicated in the previous paragraph, the Scots law of arbitration was mainly based on common law. Although it had been built up over the course of several centuries, it could hardly be described as a dynamic system. Thus on a number of important issues it provided little or no guidance, while in other areas the law was obscure and uncertain. Indeed at certain points where the law was clear, the answers which it provided were not always helpful and sometimes bordered on the dysfunctional. At the same time, also over the course of several centuries, a number of fragments of legislation had appeared dealing with particular issues, usually not in an entirely satisfactory way. While most of the ancient statutes had been repealed or simply fallen into disuse prior to the passing of the 2010 Act, legislation dating back as far as 1695 was still operative. Thus art.25 of the Articles of Regulation 1695 sought to lay down grounds for the reduction of an arbitral award which were intended to be exclusive. This provision was expressed in archaic and somewhat opaque language, which was not entirely elucidated by subsequent judicial pronouncements thereon.

This was followed nearly 200 years later by the Arbitration (Scotland) Act 1894. Despite its name, this was not a comprehensive measure along the lines of the Arbitration Acts of 1950 and 1996 in England. Rather, containing only seven sections, it sought to deal with the unfortunate common law rule that an arbitration agreement which did not name an arbiter was invalid, as well as creating procedures for court appointment of arbiters (and oversmen) when contractual appointment procedures had failed. Even in this however, the Act was not comprehensive, dealing with only a limited number of situations. Thus, as subsequent case law revealed, there were many situations where the breakdown of contractual appointment procedures would leave the parties without recourse.

Mention should also be made of s.3 of the Administration of Justice (Scotland) Act 1972. Despite no domestic support ever having been expressed for such a development, this sought to introduce the stated case procedure into the Scots law of arbitration. It is very likely that one of the aims of the provision was the creation of a right of appeal against an arbitral award on a point of law, but because of a drafting mishap the section failed to achieve this objective. It was widely believed that s.3 was employed by parties simply to delay and obstruct the arbitral process, and its repeal was advocated by many including the judiciary.

The Model Law and its influence

The above account of course misses what was potentially the most significant piece of legislation in the pre-2010 history of the Scots Law of arbitration—s.66 and Sch.7 of the Law Reform (Miscellaneous Provisions) (Scotland) Act 1990, which introduced the UNCITRAL Model Law on International Commercial Arbitration into Scotland. The Model Law arose out of a meeting in 1978 between the African-Asian Legal Consultative Committee of the United Nations Commission on International Trade Law (UNCITRAL), the International Council on Commercial Arbitration and the International Chamber of Commerce ("ICC") which concluded that "it would be in the interest of international commercial arbitration if UNCITRAL would initiate steps leading to the establishment of uniform standards of arbitral procedure", and that the preparation of a model law on arbitration would be "the most appropriate way to achieve the desired uniformity" (see *Note by the Secretariat: further work in respect of international commercial arbitration*, UN A/CN.9/169, para.6, found at *http://www.uncitral.org*). A Model Law was thus designed by UNCITRAL, the process taking several years and a number of drafts, and involving many states and a number of international organisations. The final version of the Model Law was promulgated in 1985 and was given force in Scotland (in a slightly amended form) by the 1990 Act, following the recommendations of the Scottish Advisory Committee on Arbitration Law's, *Report to the Lord Advocate on the UNCITRAL Model Law* (Edinburgh: Scottish Courts Administration, 1989). Unfortunately, the opportunity was not taken at that stage to deal with the deficiencies of the Scots law of arbitration, which law provided the wider context in which the Model Law required to operate.

The Model Law had already been adopted by a significant number of jurisdictions when Scotland followed suit in 1990, and since then it has been adopted in many more. Moreover, most states which had been traditionally seen as major centres for arbitration were prompted to reform their arbitration law in the wake of the Model Law, and, given that the Model Law aimed to capture best practice in the law of international commercial arbitration, there was considerable congruence between it and these new regimes. The most remarkable conversion to the Model Law is of course England which had begun by rejecting the adoption of the Model Law on the basis that it did not offer a regime which was superior to that which then operated in England, and ended up engaging in the wholesale reform of its law of arbitration through the Arbitration Act 1996, which had followed, "wherever possible the structure, language and spirit of the Model Law".

The Model Law therefore has been one of the great success stories of international commercial law. Not only does it continue to be adopted in increasing numbers of countries around the world and used as a template by jurisdictions such as England, but even those states which choose not to follow the Model Law when reforming their arbitration law, e.g. Sweden in 1999, tend explicitly to acknowledge that they have kept its provisions in mind during the process of reform.

Given the stature and influence of the Model Law then, it is one of the most striking features of the 2010 Act that it appears to discard the Model Law. However, appearances are misleading in this instance, in that while the exact form of the Model Law is not retained, practically almost all the principles which underpin the Model Law are to be found in the Act. There are a variety of reasons for this approach. It was quite awkward to have separate systems which governed international commercial arbitrations and other arbitrations, as was the case after Scotland adopted the Model Law,

Introduction

albeit that parties to other types of arbitration could invoke the application of the Model Law under s.66(4) of the Law Reform (Miscellaneous Provisions) (Scotland) Act 1990. One possible answer to that would have been to follow the example of a number of other states and apply the Model Law to all forms of arbitration. A limitation of that approach would have been that the Model Law was a partial law, which only dealt with those issues on which the various drafting parties could reach general agreement. Thus a number of issues were not addressed by the Model Law, either because they proved too controversial, or because it was felt that they could be more appropriately dealt with by domestic law. The Model Law then was designed to operate within the context of an existing domestic arbitration regime, which, given the deficiencies of Scots arbitration law, was rather unfortunate. One way of dealing with that difficulty would have been to have drafted a comprehensive arbitration statute which addressed the problems of Scots arbitration law while incorporating the Model Law. Examples of this approach can be found (e.g. in Singapore, New Zealand and Ireland), but these examples testify to the difficulty of constructing such legislation in an elegant manner, and to the fact that the provisions of the Model Law tend to contrast awkwardly with the other provisions. This is because the Model Law does not resemble a standard statute. In several places it clearly bears the hallmarks of being drafted by a large international committee, and being obliged to employ terminology which would resonate in a variety of legal cultures. Often its provisions appear more like those which might be expected to appear in the types of codes which are familiar in civilian jurisdictions, and of course the full meaning of certain provisions could only be understood by reading them in light of the extensive *travaux preparatoires* generated during the drafting process. The fact remains that the arbitration statutes in the jurisdictions mentioned are not uniform and can only be understood by studying both the Model Law and the additional provisions very closely.

It can be understood then why it was decided to follow the English example and draft a comprehensive modern arbitration statute which would be an entirely new beginning. Of course, given that not just the approach of the Arbitration Act 1996 but a number of the ideas of that Act are borrowed by the 2010 Act, and given that the 1996 Act explicitly adopts the Model Law as a template in those areas the Model Law addresses, those who know the Model Law will find much that is familiar in the 2010 Act, even if Scotland can no longer formally be called a Model Law jurisdiction. Whether that will ultimately prove a disadvantage may never be known. Certainly, as far as domestic arbitration is concerned, it is preferable to have an Act which is considerably more comprehensive than the Model Law and drafted in terms which will be familiar to domestic users. Thus it is only in respect of international arbitration that it will matter whether Scotland no longer operates the Model Law. That may be the price to be paid for greater elegance and brevity.

It had been suggested during the consultation process that the adoption of the Model Law had failed to attract significant numbers of international arbitrations to Scotland. Some took issue with that view, and even if it were true, it is impossible to say whether Scotland would have been rather more attractive as an arbitral forum had it swiftly followed its adoption of the Model Law by addressing the deficiencies of the domestic regime within which the Model Law had to operate. It cannot be doubted that it would hardly be calculated to inspire confidence in those who might have considered Scotland as a potential arbitral forum to learn that the law in those areas not addressed by the Model law was often obscure or even defective.

Nor can it have helped that Scotland did not update the Model Law in line with the reforms achieved by UNCITRAL in 2006. In that context, one interesting feature of the Act may be observed. Section 26 allows the Scottish Ministers to modify any provision of the Act in consequence of any amendment made to the Model Law. This provision would of course have been particularly appropriate had Scotland retained the Model Law, and it may be regretted that no similar provision was incorporated in s.66 of the Law Reform (Miscellaneous Provisions) (Scotland) Act 1990 when Scotland first adopted the Model Law. Its appearance when Scotland seems to be repealing the Model Law might be thought to be remarkable. However, the provision reinforces the view that the Government considers that the Act retains the spirit of the Model Law, and that Scotland is determined to remain in the forefront of improvements to the legislation governing international arbitration.

The road to reform

Much emphasis has been laid above on the deficiencies of the Scots law of arbitration. However it would be unfair to suggest that those involved in seeking to develop the law have been unaware of its deficiencies. The Scottish Advisory Committee on Arbitration Law highlighted the weaknesses of domestic arbitration law in 1990 in their report *The Operation of Arbitration in Scotland in light of the UNCITRAL Model Law* (Edinburgh: Scottish Courts Administration, 1990). Its 1996 consultation paper, *Report to the Lord Advocate on Legislation for Domestic Arbitration in Scotland* (Edinburgh: Scottish Courts Administration, 1996) then contained a draft Arbitration Bill. If that measure had been enacted, it would certainly have wrought a considerable improvement in the law, albeit that there were suggestions that it could have gone further than it did. However, the appearance of radical, modern arbitration legislation in a variety of other jurisdictions, in particular the Arbitration Act 1996 in England, then inspired a number of private parties (chiefly the Scottish Branch of the Chartered Institute of Arbitrators ("CIArb") and the Scottish Council for International Arbitration under the chairmanship of Lord Dervaird who had chaired the Scottish Advisory Committee on Arbitration Law) to produce a much more ambitious and wide-ranging Arbitration Bill in 2002. Yet the then Scottish Executive failed to implement that Bill. Legislative reform of arbitration in Scotland thus seemed unlikely until both the current Government and the Labour Party adopted in 2007 the manifesto goal of encouraging arbitration in Scotland. A draft Arbitration (Scotland) Bill and accompanying consultation document was thus produced in June 2008, and was followed by a lengthy consultation process. The original Bill drew heavily on the 2002 Bill (and thus, like that Bill, on the Model Law and the 1996 Act), but covered a number of matters not addressed in that Bill. Some but not all of these provisions survived the consultation process and appear in the 2010 Act. The consultation document also sought to canvass opinion on whether certain matters not addressed in the Bill should be the subject of a provision. In the end, most of these matters were not addressed by the Act. However, one issue—confidentiality—is now the subject of a specific statutory provision—see the commentary to r.26 below.

The approach of the Act

A detailed analysis of the provisions of the Act appears below. However, certain features of the Act are worthy of separate comment. Thus although it is suggested above that much of the Act will strike a chord with those who

Introduction

are familiar with the Arbitration Act 1996 and the Model Law, there is at least one aspect of the Act which is unique. Its main substance is divided into the Act proper (consisting of 37 sections) and Sch.1, which contains the 84 Scottish Arbitration Rules. The reason why this most unusual approach has been followed is perhaps hinted at by the fact that those provisions regarding the conduct of the arbitral process are consigned to the rules. The accompanying policy memorandum indeed states (para.78) that the, "intention is that the rules will guide the parties and the arbitrator through various stages of the arbitral process". The drafters appear to believe that it is more user friendly for those provisions which will govern how the arbitration is carried on to take the form of rules like the many sets of institutional rules which are available in both domestic and international arbitration for parties to invoke by means of agreement to govern their arbitration, and in fact the policy memorandum continues (para.79) that they can be compared with such institutional rules. The advantage of this is probably that parties can decide whether they would prefer institutional rules to govern their arbitration rather than those Scottish Arbitration Rules which are default rules (i.e. open to being excluded, modified or replaced by the parties). The policy memorandum adds that some consultees were pleased that, "arbitrators would not have to search for the rules in the middle of the legalese of the main body of the legislation". To that it might be rejoined that the same effect could easily have been achieved by dividing up the legislation into a number of discrete parts, that arbitrators may have to take account of certain provisions of the Act proper as well as the rules, and that numerous examples of "legalese" can be found in the rules.

It may be that experience will prove the hopes the drafters have for the legislative structure to be well founded. On the other hand, it seems curious that the bulk of the actual law of arbitration is found in the rules, while a number of relatively inconsequential provisions appear in the Bill, and some may think that framing the law of arbitration in the same way as institutional rules diminishes its stature. There is also scope for confusion in the fact that the alternative title of the Scottish Arbitration Code—a set of rules developed by the Scottish Branch of the Chartered Institute of Arbitrators—is the Scottish Arbitration Rules. This will probably change, since the code is almost certain to be revised to take account of the Act.

The relationship of the Act to other legislation

A word or two might be said regarding how the Act relates to other legislation, since it is not entirely the case that those who wish to understand Scots arbitration law need look only to the 2010 Act. The Act disapplies art.25 of the Articles of Regulation 1695 in relation to arbitration and sweeps away both the Arbitration (Scotland) Act 1894 and s.3 of the Administration of Justice (Scotland) Act 1972 (the stated case procedure). Nonetheless, other legislation remains intact or is re-enacted by the Act—the legislation which gives effect to international treaties on arbitration ratified by the UK. Thus the Arbitration (International Investment Disputes) Act 1966, which gives effect to the 1965 Washington Convention on the Settlement of Investment Disputes between States and Nationals of other States, continues to operate. By contrast, the Arbitration Act 1975 which gave effect to the 1958 New York Convention for the Recognition and Enforcement of Foreign Arbitral Awards is repealed and its provisions re-enacted in ss.16–20 of the 2010 Act. In this the Act follows the example of the Arbitration Act 1996, which had repealed the 1975 Act as regards

England (but not Scotland) and reproduced its provisions in ss.100–104 of the later Act.

Mention should also be made of ss.89–91 of the Arbitration Act 1996, currently the only sections of that Act which apply in Scotland. These subject consumer arbitration agreements to the Unfair Terms in Consumer Contracts Regulations 1999 (SI 1999/2083), even though those regulations and their 1994 predecessors already applied to such agreements. More importantly, they also provide that an arbitration agreement will be automatically unfair and thus not bind the consumer where the amount sought to be recovered does not exceed £5,000 (Unfair Arbitration Agreements (Specified Amounts) Order 1999 (SI 1999/2167)). Thus even if such an agreement is not automatically unfair because the sum sought exceeds those limits, it may be found to be unfair as a result of the application of the fairness test under the regulations. This was indeed the outcome in *Zealander v Laing Homes Ltd* (2000) 2 T.C.L.R. 724; and *Mylcrist Builders Ltd v Buck* [2009] 2 All E.R. (Comm) 259; where the court felt that the arbitration clause was financially disadvantageous to the consumer, and that its impact would not have been apparent to a layperson. While ordinarily under these regulations a consumer requires to be a natural person acting for non-business purposes, s.90 of the 1996 Act makes it clear that a consumer may be a legal person. So a company which contracts for non-business purposes can challenge the fairness of an arbitration clause in that contract. Such was the case in *Heifer International Inc v Christiansen* [2008] 2 All E.R. (Comm) 831; where the company bought a residential property for an individual employee, albeit that the clause was held not to be unfair in that instance. It is the intention of the Government to make an order under s.104 of the Scotland Act 1998 in order to disapply ss.89–91 in Scotland and to recast those provisions, suitably amended, as sections of the 2010 Act (*SP Official Report*, col.216267 (November 18, 2009)). It is understood that this will not happen until after the commencement date of the Act.

One curious feature is the repeal of the Arbitration Act 1950. While that measure was primarily intended to regulate English arbitration law, Pt II of the Act gives effect to the 1927 Geneva Convention for the Execution of Foreign Arbitral Awards and thus was extended to Scotland. Whereas Pt I of the 1950 Act was repealed by the Arbitration Act 1996, Pt II was not. After the 2010 Act, Pt II of the 1950 Act now no longer applies in Scotland, but continues to apply in England. Admittedly, the Geneva Convention is now primarily of historical interest, having been effectively supplanted by the New York Convention, and the policy memorandum indeed observes (para.119) that every contracting state to the earlier Convention has ratified the later. Nonetheless, the UK remains bound to give effect to the earlier Convention and there seems to be no reason why Scotland alone should feel able to repeal the provisions giving effect to that obligation. It may indeed be noted that under the terms of the Scotland Act 1998 s.29(2)(b) and Sch.5 para.7(1) the Scottish Parliament probably lacks competence to legislate contrary to the terms of Treaty provisions. Given that the UK remains bound by the Geneva Convention, the repeal of Pt II of the 1950 Act is therefore arguably of no effect.

The law is stated as at May 1, 2010, although references to some later material have been added.

ARBITRATION (SCOTLAND) ACT 2010

(asp 1)

CONTENTS

Introductory

1. Founding principles
2. Key terms
3. Seat of arbitration

Arbitration agreements

4. Arbitration agreement
5. Separability
6. Law governing arbitration agreement

Scottish Arbitration Rules

7. Scottish Arbitration Rules
8. Mandatory rules
9. Default rules

Suspension of legal proceedings

10. Suspension of legal proceedings

Enforcing and challenging arbitral awards etc.

11. Arbitral award to be final and binding on parties
12. Enforcement of arbitral awards
13. Court intervention in arbitrations
14. Persons who take no part in arbitral proceedings
15. Anonymity in legal proceedings

Statutory arbitration

16. Statutory arbitration: special provisions
17. Power to adapt enactments providing for statutory arbitration

Recognition and enforcement of New York Convention awards

18. New York Convention awards
19. Recognition and enforcement of New York Convention awards
20. Refusal of recognition or enforcement

Arbitration (Scotland) Act 2010

21. Evidence to be produced when seeking recognition or enforcement
22. Saving for other bases of recognition or enforcement

Supplementary

23. Prescription and limitation
24. Arbitral appointments referee
25. Power of judge to act as arbitrator or umpire
26. Amendments to UNCITRAL Model Law or Rules or New York Convention
27. Amendment of Conveyancing (Scotland) Act 1924 (c. 27)
28. Articles of Regulation 1695
29. Repeals
30. Arbitrability of disputes

Final provisions

31. Interpretation
32. Ancillary provision
33. Orders
34. Crown application
35. Commencement
36. Transitional provisions
37. Short title

SCHEDULE 1—SCOTTISH ARBITRATION RULES

PART 1

COMMENCEMENT AND CONSTITUTION OF TRIBUNAL ETC.

Rule 1. Commencement of arbitration D
Rule 2. Appointment of tribunal D
Rule 3. Arbitrator to be an individual M
Rule 4. Eligibility to act as arbitrator M
Rule 5. Number of arbitrators D
Rule 6. Method of appointment D
Rule 7. Failure of appointment procedure M
Rule 8. Duty to disclose any conflict of interests M
Rule 9. Arbitrator's tenure D
Rule 10. Challenge to appointment of arbitrator D
Rule 11. Removal of arbitrator by parties D
Rule 12. Removal of arbitrator by court M
Rule 13. Dismissal of tribunal by court M
Rule 14. Removal and dismissal by court: supplementary M
Rule 15. Resignation of arbitrator M
Rule 16. Liability etc. of arbitrator when tenure ends M
Rule 17. Reconstitution of tribunal D
Rule 18. Arbitrators nominated in arbitration agreements D

PART 2

JURISDICTION OF TRIBUNAL

Rule 19. Power of tribunal to rule on own jurisdiction M

Rule 20. Objections to tribunal's jurisdiction M
Rule 21. Appeal against tribunal's ruling on jurisdictional objection M
Rule 22. Referral of point of jurisdiction D
Rule 23. Jurisdiction referral: procedure etc. M

Part 3

General duties

Rule 24. General duty of the tribunal M
Rule 25. General duty of the parties M
Rule 26. Confidentiality D
Rule 27. Tribunal deliberations D

Part 4

Arbitral proceedings

Rule 28. Procedure and evidence D
Rule 29. Place of arbitration D
Rule 30. Tribunal decisions D
Rule 31. Tribunal directions D
Rule 32. Power to appoint clerk, agents or employees etc. D
Rule 33. Party representatives D
Rule 34. Experts D
Rule 35. Powers relating to property D
Rule 36. Oaths or affirmations D
Rule 37. Failure to submit claim or defence timeously D
Rule 38. Failure to attend hearing or provide evidence D
Rule 39. Failure to comply with tribunal direction or arbitration agreement D
Rule 40. Consolidation of proceedings D

Part 5

Powers of court in relation to arbitral proceedings

Rule 41. Referral of point of law D
Rule 42. Point of law referral: procedure etc. M
Rule 43. Variation of time limits set by parties D
Rule 44. Time limit variation: procedure etc. M
Rule 45. Court's power to order attendance of witnesses and disclosure of evidence M
Rule 46. Court's other powers in relation to arbitration D

Part 6

Awards

Rule 47. Rules applicable to the substance of the dispute D
Rule 48. Power to award payment and damages M
Rule 49. Other remedies available to tribunal D
Rule 50. Interest M
Rule 51. Form of award D
Rule 52. Award treated as made in Scotland D

Rule 53. Provisional awards D
Rule 54. Part awards M
Rule 55. Draft awards D
Rule 56. Power to withhold award on non-payment of fees or expenses M
Rule 57. Arbitration to end on last award or early settlement D
Rule 58. Correcting an award D

Part 7

Arbitration expenses

Rule 59. Arbitration expenses D
Rule 60. Arbitrators' fees and expenses M
Rule 61. Recoverable arbitration expenses D
Rule 62. Liability for recoverable arbitration expenses D
Rule 63. Ban on pre-dispute agreements about liability for arbitration expenses M
Rule 64. Security for expenses D
Rule 65. Limitation of recoverable arbitration expenses D
Rule 66. Awards on recoverable arbitration expenses D

Part 8

Challenging awards

Rule 67. Challenging an award: substantive jurisdiction M
Rule 68. Challenging an award: serious irregularity M
Rule 69. Challenging an award: legal error D
Rule 70. Legal error appeals: procedure etc. M
Rule 71. Challenging an award: supplementary M
Rule 72. Reconsideration by tribunal M

Part 9

Miscellaneous

Rule 73. Immunity of tribunal etc. M
Rule 74. Immunity of appointing arbitral institution etc. M
Rule 75. Immunity of experts, witnesses and legal representatives M
Rule 76. Loss of right to object M
Rule 77. Independence of arbitrator M
Rule 78. Consideration where arbitrator judged not to be impartial and independent D
Rule 79. Death of arbitrator M
Rule 80. Death of party D
Rule 81. Unfair treatment D
Rule 82. Rules applicable to umpires M
Rule 83. Formal communications D
Rule 84. Periods of time D

Index

SCHEDULE 2—REPEALS

Arbitration (Scotland) Act 2010 (s.1)

The Bill for this Act of the Scottish Parliament was passed by the Parliament on 18th November 2009 and received Royal Assent on 5th January 2010
An Act of the Scottish Parliament to make provision about arbitration.

Introductory

Founding principles

1. The founding principles of this Act are—
   (a) that the object of arbitration is to resolve disputes fairly, impartially and without unnecessary delay or expense,
   (b) that parties should be free to agree how to resolve disputes subject only to such safeguards as are necessary in the public interest,
   (c) that the court should not intervene in an arbitration except as provided by this Act.

Anyone construing this Act must have regard to the founding principles when doing so.

DEFINITIONS
"arbitration": ss.2(1), (2), 31(1)
"court": s.31(1)
"party": ss.2(1), 31(1), (2)

COMMENTARY
The inspiration of this provision is clearly the "general principles" to be found in s.1 of the 1996 Act. The drafters of that Act were persuaded to include the statement of general principles therein partly because of a "significant number of submissions" which called for this, and partly because they saw the value in such an exercise, given the fact that the Act marked the dawn of a new approach to arbitration in England—see the Departmental Advisory Committee on Arbitration Law, *Report on the Arbitration Bill* (1996), paras 18–22 (hereafter "the DAC Report"). It was thought important to stress the principle of party autonomy, which lies at the heart of practically all modern arbitration regimes. Equally, it was seen as useful to emphasise the principle of limited court intervention, since England had begun to acquire an international reputation for allowing too extensive a degree of court intervention, threatening the attractiveness of England as a major forum for international arbitration. Given that Scotland has never been a significant forum for international arbitration, some might question whether Scotland needs such a statement of principles. Yet given that this is the first ever general statute on arbitration in Scotland, a statute which effects significant changes in the law, it is surely useful to advertise to both domestic users and the wider world the key principles on which it is based.

The consultation paper had asked in Q.1 whether these founding principles should be ranked. It can be seen that any temptation to do so has been resisted. This is surely sensible. The principles are of great generality, and indeed carry within them their own qualifications. It would be very difficult to say in the abstract that any one of them must always have precedence over the others. Much depends on the context. More importantly, the principles underpin most of the Scottish Arbitration Rules, and the appropriate balance between the principles is struck in particular contexts by the detailed provisions of the rules.

The principles are to be borne in mind by anyone seeking to interpret or apply the Act—arbitrators, parties and judges. However, it cannot be said that s.1 creates any actual rights or duties, albeit that the principles are echoed in the substantive provisions of the Act. The point of stating these principles in s.1 is mainly symbolic, but not exclusively so, since courts in England have on occasion found s.1 of the 1996 Act useful in indicating the approach they should take to particular questions, e.g. whether the court or tribunal should determine whether a dispute exists between the parties (see Henry L.J. in *Halki Shipping Corp v Sopex Oils Ltd* [1998] 1 W.L.R. 726 at 750), the extent to which the parties might override the provisions of the Act (see Rix J. in *Federal Insurance Co v Transamerica Occidental Life Insurance Co* [1999] 2 Lloyd's Rep. 286 at 290), the extent of court control of the arbitral process (see Aikens J. in *Walker v Rome* [2000] 1 Lloyd's Rep. 116 at 121), the extent to which the parties might empower the tribunal to rule on its own jurisdiction (see Lord Phillips M.R. in *LG Caltex Gas Co Ltd v China National Petroleum Co* [2001] 1 W.L.R. 1892 at [49]), and whether the court might refuse an oral hearing to a party seeking to appeal against an award (see Arden L.J. in *BLCT (13096) Ltd v J Sainsbury Plc* [2004] 1 C.L.C. 24 at [43]).

Subsection (a)

Object of arbitration: It is impossible to argue that arbitration should aim to do other than seek to resolve disputes fairly and impartially, and a number of specific rules seek to achieve that object. Rather more interesting is that arbitration should have as its object the avoidance of unnecessary delay and expense. This is the phraseology employed by the 1996 Act. An earlier version of the 2010 Act was sufficiently bold to speak of disputes being resolved "quickly", rather than "without unnecessary delay". The problem of that formulation is that that certain disputes may be too complex to be resolved "quickly", and it is sensible that the 1996 Act has been followed here. Looked at from a practical point of view, it might be hoped that the reference to avoiding delay and expense should give tribunals the confidence to manage proceedings expeditiously and to refuse to indulge the excesses of parties.

Subsection (b)

Party autonomy: This stresses the importance of party autonomy, which is at the root of all modern arbitration legislation across the world including the Model Law (see DAC Report, para.19). It is useful to advertise this fact, and the principle receives practical expression in the fact that the majority of rules under the Act are default rules, which may be excluded or varied by the parties. Of course party autonomy cannot be insisted upon if this would mean that fairness or justice is denied. Accordingly, a number of rules are mandatory.

Subsection (c)

Limited court intervention: Another key aspect of modern arbitration legislation is that court intervention in the arbitral process is limited to the extent laid down by that legislation. Thus the principle is expressed in art.5 of the Model Law and echoed in the 1996 Act s.1(c). The drafters of the Model Law were driven by the fact that the Model Law was originally designed to be adopted in jurisdictions which had no great profile as arbitral forums, or which indeed had a reputation for inappropriate court intervention in the arbitral process. Thus the drafters wished to signal that such intervention was to be limited to that laid down by the Model Law (see

Report of the UNCITRAL on the work of its 18th session, UN A/40/17, paras 61–63). The drafters of the 1996 Act were sensitive to the fact that internationally English courts were regarded as having a tendency to intervene in arbitrations more than was appropriate (DAC Report, para.21). Thus the Act was intended to signal a departure from the traditional English approach. The background of the 2010 Act is rather different, but s.1(c) is nonetheless welcome, first, because it articulates a key principle, and secondly, because it might indeed help curb any tendency towards intervention on the part of the Scots courts, for example exercise of the Court of Session's inherent supervisory jurisdiction over inferior tribunals—see the commentary to s.13 below.

An interesting contrast exists between the respective ss.1(c) of the 1996 and 2010 Acts. The former states that *"in matters governed by this Part* [our emphasis] the court should not intervene except as provided by this Part", thus conceding that the court may yet have a role to play as regards matters not governed by that Part. It has been held that courts in England have general supervisory jurisdiction as regards matters not covered by Pt I of the 1996 Act—*Hiscox Underwriting Ltd v Dickson Manchester & Co* [2004] 2 Lloyd's Rep. 438. In similar fashion art.5 of the Model Law speaks of limited court intervention, "in matters governed by this Law". Yet s.1(c) of the 2010 Act seems to exclude the court from supervision of the arbitral process except where the Act so provides. That might seem to run the risk that a court might not be able to intervene where it might seem appropriate to do so as regards any matter not addressed by the Act, and comprehensive as the Act is, it does not deal with every issue which might arise in the context of arbitral proceedings. Nonetheless, as s.1 articulates principles rather than binding rules, a court would probably feel free to assert jurisdiction in such a situation. Both versions of s.1(c) state that the court "should" not intervene. The use of this word, as opposed to the word "shall", which is employed in art.5 of the Model Law, has been interpreted in England as indicating that court intervention is not entirely precluded, even when the statute suggests otherwise—see *Vale do Rio Doce Navegacos SA v Shanghai Bao Steel Ocean Shipping Co Ltd* [2000] 2 All E.R. (Comm) 70.

Key terms

2.—(1) In this Act, unless the contrary intention appears—
"arbitration" includes—
    (a) domestic arbitration,
    (b) arbitration between parties residing, or carrying on business, anywhere in the United Kingdom, and
    (c) international arbitration,
"arbitrator" means a sole arbitrator or a member of a tribunal,
"dispute" includes—
    (a) any refusal to accept a claim, and
    (b) any other difference (whether contractual or not),
"party" means a party to an arbitration,
"rules" means the Scottish Arbitration Rules (see section 7), and
"tribunal" means a sole arbitrator or panel of arbitrators.

(2) References in this Act to "an arbitration", "the arbitration" or "arbitrations" are references to a particular arbitration process or, as the case may be, to particular arbitration processes.

(3) References in this Act to a tribunal conducting an arbitration are references to the tribunal doing anything in relation to the arbitration, including—
 (a) making a decision about procedure or evidence, and
 (b) making an award.

COMMENTARY

This is a curious section, since although both the consultation paper and policy memorandum (at paras 7 and 64 respectively) indicate that it sets out "the main definitions", it does not really essay any definitions and is comprised mainly of statements of the obvious.

Subsection (1)

Arbitration: Very wisely the provision has avoided seeking to define the concept of arbitration. Most national laws and international conventions follow this line, while the DAC Report (para.18) suggested that any attempt to do so in the Arbitration Act 1996 would be fraught with difficulties and would serve no useful purpose.

The consultation paper (at Q.2) had asked whether the Act needed to distinguish between arbitration and valuation. The context of this question (para.8) was that the House of Lords in England has suggested that valuers are not entitled to immunity in negligence, which at common law might be available to arbitrators (see *Arenson v Casson Beckman Rutley & Co* [1977] A.C. 405). In the end this idea has, sensibly, not been pursued even in the context of arbitral immunity (see rr.73–75). It would have been a daunting task to draw a statutory distinction between arbitration and valuation. The distinction between arbitration and valuation, or indeed arbitration and certification or other forms of expert determination is not always clear. A process which could be described as arbitration in one context might not be so regarded in another context (compare *David Wilson Homes Ltd v Survey Services Ltd* [2001] B.L.R. 267 with *Flight Training International v International Fire Training Equipment Ltd* [2004] EWHC 721 (Comm), and see *Holland House Property Investments Ltd v Crabbe*, 2008 S.L.T. 777 and *McDonald Estates v National Car Parks Ltd*, 2009 GWD 38-639.). The policy memorandum (para.65) notes that the, "view was expressed quite strongly that the Bill should not extend to valuations and expert determination", continuing that, "the Bill follows this policy". However, while such processes are not mentioned by the Act, it is submitted that they are not invariably excluded from the scope of the Act. Rather, the Act has (correctly) followed the example of the Arbitration Act 1996 in leaving it to the courts to determine in the circumstances of each case whether the process with which they are concerned amounts to arbitration.

Arbitration is expressed to include domestic and international arbitration. These terms are not defined, but the fact that arbitration also includes arbitration between parties in the different parts of the UK suggests that it is believed that domestic arbitration involves Scottish parties, while international arbitration involves at least one party from outwith the UK. This approach can be contrasted with the careful definition of domestic arbitration under s.85(2) of the Arbitration Act 1996 and the very elaborate definition of international arbitration under art.1(3), (4) of the Model Law, (under which it would be possible for certain arbitrations between Scottish parties to be regarded as international). Nonetheless, the failure to define these concepts is probably of little importance, as under the Act nothing turns on the distinction between domestic and international arbitration, the key to applicability of the Act being the juridical seat of the arbitration under s.3.

Dispute: There is English authority to the effect that "difference" is a term of potentially wider meaning than "dispute", so that by indicating that a "dispute" includes a "difference", the Act probably allows tribunals to be authorised to fill in gaps in contracts and to deal with failures to agree. Thus in *F & G Sykes (Wessex) Ltd v Fine Fare Ltd* [1967] 1 Lloyd's Rep. 53, where a clause indicated that any difference as to the meaning, effect or performance of an agreement should be referred to arbitration, the arbitrator was held to be allowed to decide how many goods should be supplied under the contract where the contract had not dealt with this point and the parties could not reach agreement thereon. There is no authority in Scots law as to whether this is an appropriate role for a tribunal. On one view it is not, as gap-filling is not truly an adjudicative process. The alternative view would say that this is too narrow and conservative an approach, and that parties should be permitted to empower tribunals in this way, as is possible in England and elsewhere (see, e.g. *Calvan Consolidated Oil & Gas Co Ltd v Manning* (1958) 16 D.L.R. (2d) 27). However, it is doubtful whether the Act would allow the parties to authorise a tribunal actually to alter the terms of the parties' contract to reflect changing circumstances, as is contemplated in certain other jurisdictions.

In England it has been held that a dispute exists where it is clear that one party is refusing to entertain the other's claim, and this idea no doubt inspires the other leg of the definition of that term (see explanatory notes para.21). It of course largely depends on the circumstances as to whether a party can actually be taken to refuse a claim (see the guidance given by Jackson J. in *Amec Civil Engineering Ltd v Secretary of State for Transport* [2005] 1 W.L.R. 2339 at [68], approved by the Court of Appeal in *Collins v Baltic Quay Management (1994) Ltd* [2005] 1 B.L.R. 63). English case law also suggests that a dispute exists between the parties even if it is clear that a party has no real basis for making a claim or no arguable defence (see *Halki Shipping Corp v Sopex Oils Ltd* [1998] 1 W.L.R. 726). As Saville J. notes in *Hayter v Nelson* [1990] 2 Lloyd's Rep. 265 at 268:

"Because one man can be said to be indisputably right and the other indisputably wrong does not ... entail that there was never therefore any dispute between them."

By contrast there is authority in Scots law that if there is already an answer to the question between the parties, there is no dispute and the arbitral proceedings may be interdicted (see, e.g. Lord President Inglis in *Parochial Board of Greenock v Coghill* (1878) 5 R. 732 at 734–735, and most recently *Norwest Holst Ltd v Carfin Developments Ltd* [2009] 1 B.L.R. 167). Perhaps this line will not be maintained and there is an argument that it should not be in light of s.1(b).

Other terms: Whether the "definitions" of the terms "arbitrator", "party", "rules" and "tribunal" serve any useful purpose is open to question, but they may serve to avoid doubt.

Subsection (2)

The meaning and purpose of this provision are far from clear and no guidance is provided in either the explanatory notes or the policy memorandum.

Subsection (3)

This perhaps serves slightly more purpose than subs.(2) above, in that it makes the (possibly obvious) point that the conduct of the proceedings encompasses the making of the award.

Seat of arbitration

3.—(1) An arbitration is "seated in Scotland" if—
   (a) Scotland is designated as the juridical seat of the arbitration—
      (i) by the parties,
      (ii) by any third party to whom the parties give power to so designate, or
      (iii) where the parties fail to designate or so authorise a third party, by the tribunal, or
   (b) in the absence of any such designation, the court determines that Scotland is to be the juridical seat of the arbitration.

(2) The fact that an arbitration is seated in Scotland does not affect the substantive law to be used to decide the dispute.

DEFINITIONS
   "arbitration": ss.2(1), (2), 31(1)
   "court": s.31(1)
   "dispute": ss.2(1), 31(1)
   "party": ss.2(1), 31(1), (2)
   "tribunal": ss.2(1), 31(1)

COMMENTARY
While this provision might at first glance appear strange to domestic users, modern international arbitration law is quite familiar with the ideas that the juridical seat of an arbitration determines the applicability of a particular national law, and that the juridical seat is not necessarily the same place as the physical location of the arbitral proceedings, which proceedings indeed may be held in more than one state. Thus r.29 indicates that the tribunal may meet anywhere it chooses, in or outwith Scotland. The idea of the juridical seat is particularly useful in terms of supplying a governing law for arbitrations which are peripatetic, or which have no obvious location, as in the case of online arbitrations. It is recognised by the New York Convention and well established in national legislation, being central to both the 1996 Act and the Model Law, so that the 2010 Act in adopting the concept is simply bringing Scotland into line with contemporary thinking.

The effect of the provision is probably that if parties designate Scotland as the seat of the arbitration, the provisions of the Arbitration (Scotland) Act 2010, including of course the Scottish Arbitration Rules, would apply to that arbitration, even if it has no connection with Scotland, and even if none of the proceedings are held in Scotland. The corollary of that is of course that if two Scottish parties hold arbitral proceedings in Scotland, but have designated England as the seat of the arbitration, that arbitration would not be governed by the 2010 Act but by the 1996 Act. The word "probably" is used because the 2010 Act is not entirely clear on the consequences of the arbitration being seated in Scotland. It is plain enough that the Scottish Arbitration Rules only apply when the arbitration is seated in Scotland (see s.7 below), and this of course means that certain of the supportive powers of the court—see rr.45 and 46 below—cannot be exercised in support of non-Scottish arbitrations—contrast s.2(3) of the 1996 Act. However what is the position regarding the provisons of the actual Act? There is nothing equivalent to s.2(1) of the 1996 Act, which indicates that the provisions of Pt I of that Act only apply to an arbitration seated in England and Wales or

Northern Ireland. However, it is expressly stated that certain provisions are to apply even though an arbitration is not seated in Scotland, i.e. s.10, requiring that court proceedings be sisted where a valid arbitration agreement is cited (see s.10(3) below); and s.12 dealing with the enforcement of awards (see s.12(6) below). The fact that the drafters felt the need to make this plain suggests that it would otherwise be presumed that the provisions of the Act would only apply if an arbitration was seated in Scotland.

Accordingly, it is submitted that the logic of the Act's approach is that, apart from the provisions mentioned, the Act and rules do not apply if Scotland is not the seat of the arbitration. Accordingly, if for example, the parties were to designate England as the seat of the arbitration, but agreed that the procedural law were that of Scotland, the 2010 Act and Rules would only apply as a matter of contract, and in particular the parties could not call on the assistance of the Scottish courts.

It should also be borne in mind that under s.16(4) all statutory arbitrations are seated in Scotland.

Subsection (1)(a)

Scotland is designated as the seat: As under s.3(a) of the 1996 Act, the agreement of the parties is the primary determinant of where the seat might be. Alternatively, as under s.3(b) of the 1996 Act, the parties may entrust that designation to a third party. It must be presumed that a third party here would include an institution. Thus if the parties have agreed to arbitrate under the ICC Rules but have not agreed on a seat, art.14 indicates that the ICC Court will determine the place (seat) of arbitration. This example also serves to illustrate that while the parties may explicitly empower a third party to designate the seat, they may also do so implicitly by adopting arbitral rules which confer that power. It must be assumed that the power in question may also be withdrawn. Thus if the parties, having so empowered a third party, then agree on a different arbitral seat, that agreement will prevail.

If the parties do not agree on the seat, nor authorise a third party to determine the seat, then the tribunal is automatically entitled to do so. This contrasts with s.3(c) of the 1996 Act under which the tribunal may only designate the seat if authorised to do so by the parties. In this the Act is much closer to art.20(1) of the Model Law than the 1996 Act s.3. This is one of these curious provisions under which the tribunal is effectively invited to haul itself up by its own bootstraps, since the tribunal only has the power to designate Scotland as the seat under s.3(1)(a)(iii), but that provision, like most of the Act, only applies if Scotland is already the seat. In any event, a decision by the tribunal that Scotland should be the seat is validated by s.3(1)(a)(iii). Again, while the provision does not seem to contemplate the parties entrusting this decision to the tribunal, whether explicitly or by arbitrating under rules which do just that (see, e.g. art.9 of the Scottish Arbitration Code and art.16.1. of the UNCITRAL Arbitration Rules), this is surely only an academic issue, since if such a choice were not permitted by the Act, the decision would devolve on the tribunal in any case.

The question also arises whether designation by the parties might be implied. If, for example, an arbitration is to be held under a contract between two French parties, that contract being governed by French law and concerning an entirely French subject matter, then the parties may see no reason to agree explicitly that the seat of the arbitration is France. Would this amount to an implied designation, or would it be open to the tribunal to designate Scotland as the seat in terms of s.3(1)(a)(iii)? This of course would only be a practical problem if the parties were unable to agree that they would not accept this designation. It is suggested that where Scottish parties simply commence arbitral proceedings in Scotland that may usually be taken as an implied agreement regarding the juridical seat. Again, while as under s.9(4)(b) of the 2010 Act, s.4(5) of the 1996 Act allows the parties to an arbitration seated in England to apply a foreign procedural law to govern issues not covered by mandatory provisions of that Act, the English courts have taken the view that an agreement that an arbitration is to be governed by a particular procedural law yields a strong inference that it is agreed that the state in question should also be the seat (see *A v B* [2007] 1 Lloyd's Rep. 237).

Where the decision devolves on the tribunal in terms of s.3(1)(a)(iii) it is not afforded any guidance as to what considerations it should take into account in determining what the seat is to be, whereas under art.20(1) of the Model Law it must have, "regard to the circumstances of the case, including the convenience of the parties". However, the tribunal's seemingly absolute discretion under s.3 might have to take into account its duty to treat the parties fairly under r.24(1)(b) and to conduct the arbitration without incurring unnecessary expense under r.24(1)(c)(ii). Arguably, the tribunal would be failing in at least the latter duty if it chose Scotland as the seat of the arbitration when the parties came from South America, although it should also be remembered that the proceedings need not physically take place in Scotland—see r.29 below.

There is also the question of the stage at which the seat might be designated. Presumably designation could happen at any time, perhaps even after the award was made, although difficulties might then arise since, unless the parties have agreed otherwise, r.51 provides that the award must state the seat of the arbitration. However, as a practical matter one would expect a tribunal, if no designation had already been made, to seek to establish the seat as early as possible, since it would wish to know what constraints the procedural law—in this case Scots law—imposed on it.

Subsection (1)(b)

Court decides on the seat: If no designation is made by the parties, a third party empowered by the parties to do so, or by the arbitral tribunal, then the question of what the seat is to be devolves on the court. It might be thought that this is an unlikely scenario, since if the parties do not designate the seat, then the tribunal surely will, and indeed the framers of the Model Law made no provision for what might happen if the tribunal did not do so. Yet such an eventuality is not impossible, since if the tribunal has more than one member they may prove unable to agree on a seat. This is true notwithstanding that the view of the majority will prevail under r.30, as no majority view may exist. In that case, presumably any party or the tribunal might apply to the court to decide the issue, albeit that the Act is silent on how the matter might come before the court. The court may also have a role in the case of an invalid designation, e.g. where an institution or individual has sought to designate Scotland or another jurisdiction as the seat, but is found not to have the authorisation of both parties. Equally, a seeming designation may be ambiguous. In *Braes of Doune Wind Farm (Scotland) Ltd v Alfred McAlpine Business Services Ltd* [2008] 1 Lloyd's Rep. 608, the seat of an arbitration was stated to be Glasgow. However, because of a variety of factors—the agreement between the parties expressed itself to be subject to English law and invoked certain provisions of the 1996 Act, any arbitration was said to be subject to the Construction Industry Model Arbitration Rules

("CIMAR"), which only apply where England is the seat and which also invoke the 1996 Act, the agreement further stated that the English courts had exclusive jurisdiction to settle any dispute—it was held that the inevitable conclusion was that the parties had intended England to be the juridical seat. The court decided that Glasgow was intended to be the physical seat, in the sense of the geographical location of any proceedings, albeit that the arbitral proceedings were actually conducted in Edinburgh.

In this context, the "court" can be any court—see s.31(1) below. Could this include a court outside Scotland, so that if a foreign court decides that Scotland is the seat, then the Act and the rules will govern that arbitration? This is probably not what is intended.

Of course, it may be that, as in *Braes of Doune Wind Farm (Scotland) Ltd v Alfred McAlpine Business Services Ltd* [2008] 1 Lloyd's Rep. 608, a foreign court decides that Scotland is not to be the seat of the arbitration. To what extent would that prevent a disgruntled party inviting a Scots court to decide that Scotland should be the seat of the arbitration? Under art.27 of Council Regulation 44/2001 on jurisdiction and the recognition and enforcement of judgments in civil and commercial matters [2001] OJ L12/1 and art.21 of the Lugano Convention on jurisdiction and the enforcement of judgments in civil and commercial matters 1988 within the EU and EFTA areas a court first seised of a dispute has jurisdiction over it. While art.1(4) of both those measures indicates that they are not applicable to arbitration, the view might be taken that judgments which relate to the correct interpretation of the parties' agreement does not fall within that exception and so should be recognised (see *Allianz SpA v West Tankers Inc (The Front Comor)* [2009] 1 Lloyd's Rep. 413 ECJ; *Youelle v La Reunion Aerienne* [2009] 1 Lloyd's Rep. 586 CA). As regards a judgment of a court outside those areas, the Civil Jurisdiction and Judgments Act 1982 s.32 indicates that it should not be recognised if there was an arbitration agreement and the person against whom judgment is given did not raise the foreign proceedings nor agree to them or otherwise submit to the jurisdiction of the court (see *Tracomin SA v Sudan Oil Seeds Ltd* [1983] 1 W.L.R. 1026). Section 19 of the 1982 Act provides that a judgment from another part of the UK is not to be refused recognition solely on the grounds that the court was not competent under Scots private international law rules.

When the English courts believe that a dispute is most closely connected to England, so that they should most appropriately rule on the issue of the seat, they have certainly been prepared to issue injunctions restraining parties from seeking to ask foreign courts to rule on the matter. While the decision in *The Front Comor* [2009] 1 Lloyd's Rep. 413 prevents them issuing such injunctions as regards proceedings with the EU and EFTA areas, they have continued to issue injunctions to restrain proceedings outwith those areas (see, e.g. *Shashoua v Sharma* [2009] EWHC 957 (Comm); *Midgulf International Ltd v Group Chimiche Tunisien* [2009] EWHC 963 (Comm)). There is no recorded instance of a Scots court behaving in a similar way

Subsection (2)

Seat does not affect law governing the substance of the dispute: Various laws may have relevance to the arbitral proceedings—the law governing the contract between the parties, the law governing the arbitration agreement, the law governing the arbitral procedure, the law governing the substance of the dispute, not to mention the law or laws governing the capacity of the parties. All of these laws may be the same, but some or all may be different, especially in international arbitrations. This provision therefore makes the point that the fact that Scotland is the seat of the arbitration does not mean that Scots law will govern the substance of the dispute—see r.47 below. The fact that Scotland is the seat means only that the procedural law of the arbitration will be governed by Scots law in the shape of the 2010 Act including the Scottish Arbitration Rules and presumably the common law in areas not addressed by the Act or rules. Indeed, by virtue of s.9(4)(b) a foreign law can even apply to the arbitral procedure if the parties agree that it should supplant the default provisions of the Scottish Arbitration Rules.

Arbitration agreements

Arbitration agreement

4. An "arbitration agreement" is an agreement to submit a present or future dispute to arbitration (including any agreement which provides for arbitration in accordance with arbitration provisions contained in a separate document).

DEFINITIONS
"arbitration": ss.2(1), (2), 31(1)
"dispute": ss.2(1), 31(1)

COMMENTARY
Section 4 points out that an arbitration agreement may be an agreement to submit an existing dispute to arbitration or an agreement that the parties will submit any dispute which arises between them in the future to arbitration, typically an arbitration clause. In its original incarnation the provision stated that in a statutory arbitration the enactment providing for a dispute to be submitted to arbitration was also an arbitration agreement. Sensibly, this has been omitted, and statutory arbitrations are now dealt with in s.16.

Arbitration agreement incorporated: The reference to, "any agreement which provides for arbitration in accordance with arbitration provisions contained in a separate document" is clearly an attempt to make clear that an arbitration agreement includes an arbitration agreement incorporated by reference. This might arise where, for example, parties agree to be bound by the terms of a contract which is standard in a particular industry, which agreement contains an arbitration clause. This dimension did not appear in the original version of the Bill, and its addition is helpful, since it advertises to users the possibility of incorporation by reference. What it does not do is provide any guidance as to when incorporation by reference might occur. However, this is also true of s.6(2) of the 1996 Act and art.7(2) of the Model Law, both of which deal with the matter. The framers of those provisions believed that it would be difficult to draft an intelligible statutory rule which would indicate when incorporation by reference might occur, so that it might be more sensible to leave such matters to the courts (see DAC Report, para.42; *Report of the Working Group on International Contract practices on the work of its seventh session*, UN A/CN.9/246, para.9). Different legal systems take differing approaches to this issue, with some reluctant to contemplate the possibility of incorporation by reference unless it is made explicit that the parties intend to adopt not only the major terms of the other contract, but also the arbitration clause (see *Report of the Working Group on International Contract practices on the work of its fourth session*, UN A/CN.9/232, para.44).The Scots courts have never gone so far, but neither are they always persuaded that in every instance of incorporation of the terms of another contract by reference the parties must have intended to be bound by an arbitration clause in the contract (see, e.g. Lord President Dunedin in *Goodwins, Jardine & Co v Brand* (1905) 7 F. 995 at 1000). Lord Hamilton in *Babcock Rosyth Defence Ltd v Grootcon (United Kingdom) Ltd*, 1998 S.L.T. 1143 at 1150, has indeed remarked that, "the Scottish courts have regarded arbitration clauses as in a special position in relation to incorporation", and it might be opined that our courts have been rather more conservative than those in England in this respect. There would appear to be no reason why this should change following the passage of the Act.

Oral agreements: The consultation paper at Q.3. asked whether oral agreements should be recognised as valid arbitration agreements. Given the significance of the fact that the parties are giving up the right to litigate and to reduce the scope for argument as to whether such an agreement has been entered into, both s.5(1) of the 1996 Act and art.7(2) of the Model Law adopt the approach that arbitration agreements must be in writing. It is not that oral agreements are invalid, but rather that such arbitrations are governed by the common law rather than those pieces of legislation. In the end, it has clearly been decided that this issue should not be addressed by the 2010 Act. The policy memorandum suggests (para.71) that this means that oral arbitration agreements will be governed by the Act. In reality of course the silence of the Act on this point means that this question depends on whether oral arbitration agreements are otherwise valid. Since they do not appear in the list of agreements which require to be in writing in terms of s.1(1), (2) of the Requirements of Writing (Scotland) Act 1995, it must be assumed that they are, although there may be an argument that arbitration agreements which could affect rights relating to land might have to be. Oral arbitration agreements will be extremely rare in any case (but see para.73 of the policy memorandum).

Writing: It might be added that both s.5(2)—(6) of the 1996 Act and art.7(2) of the Model Law in making it clear that "writing" comprehends any form of record of the agreement and indeed certain situations in which the parties have acted as if they have an arbitration agreement. It is by no means clear whether, at least as regards the latter situation, Scots law would regard an arbitration agreement as existing at all. In this regard the Act is out of step with the modern approach. It is therefore a pity that the Act did not indicate that arbitration agreements could be in writing or any other form, before going on to adopt the more extended definition of writing.

Finally, it might be noted that s.4 adds nothing to the law, being essentially a restatement of the common law position. Nonetheless, it is useful in making such matters clear, especially for potential users who are not familiar with the Scottish system.

Separability

5.—(1) An arbitration agreement which forms (or was intended to form) part only of an agreement is to be treated as a distinct agreement.

(2) An arbitration agreement is not void, voidable or otherwise unenforceable only because the agreement of which it forms part is void, voidable or otherwise unenforceable.

(3) A dispute about the validity of an agreement which includes an arbitration agreement may be arbitrated in accordance with that arbitration agreement.

DEFINITIONS
"arbitration agreement": ss.4, 31(1)

"dispute": ss.2(1), 31(1)

COMMENTARY

This section adopts the principle of separability, which is well established in most major arbitration regimes, including the 1996 Act and the Model Law.

There is usually no difficulty in parties agreeing to arbitrate a dispute as to the meaning of their contract. But suppose the parties have entered into a contract which contains an arbitration clause and a dispute then arises as to the validity of that contract. Is it the case that the invalidity of the contract necessitates the invalidity of the arbitration clause, thus depriving the arbitral tribunal of jurisdiction to hear the dispute? Common law authority would tend to support that proposition (see, e.g. *Municipal Council of Johannesburg v D Stewart & Co*, 1909 S.C. (HL) 53; *Sanderson v Armour*, 1909 S.C. (HL) 117). While it might be hoped that the courts would nowadays prefer to follow more modern authority (e.g. *Harbour Assurance Ltd v Kansa Ltd* [1993] Q.B. 701) which would favour the view that an arbitration clause is an agreement distinct from the contract of which it forms part, so that the invalidity of the latter does not necessitate the invalidity of the former, it is useful to see this explicitly established by statute. Indeed s.5(3) is helpfully more explicit than either s.7 of the 1996 Act or art.16 of the Model Law in explicitly providing that a dispute concerning the validity of the main agreement may be arbitrated. Whereas the latter provision arguably confused matters by conflating this principle with the admittedly connected principle of competence-competence, the Act follows the example of the 1996 Act (see DAC Report, para.43) by expressing the principles in separate provisions, albeit that the latter principle is to be found in the rules—r.19—rather than the Act proper.

While both the 1996 Act and the Model Law adopt a concept of separability which would allow the arbitral tribunal to rule on disputes as to whether the underlying contract actually existed (see Lord Hoffmann in *Premium Nafta Products Ltd v Fili Shipping Ltd* [2008] 1 Lloyd's Rep. 254 at [7], [12]), s.5(3) does not seem to be so extensive. It may also be noted that despite s.7 of the 1996 Act, the English courts do not consider an arbitrator as having jurisdiction in cases where the underlying contract is affected by "palpable" illegality. Waller L.J. opines in *Soleimany v Soleimany* [1999] Q.B. 785 at 797:

> "There may be illegal or immoral dealings which are ... incapable of being arbitrated because an agreement to arbitrate them would be illegal or contrary to public policy."

It may be that the Scottish courts would construe s.5 in a similar light.

Finally, as under art.16 of the Model Law, but unlike s.7 of the 1996 Act, the parties cannot agree to disapply this principle. There can be no doubt that the principle of separability is very useful, and one cannot imagine why the parties should wish to contract out of it. However, if that is their wish, it is not obvious why the Act should deny them this opportunity.

Law governing arbitration agreement

6. Where—
   (a) the parties to an arbitration agreement agree that an arbitration under that agreement is to be seated in Scotland, but
   (b) the arbitration agreement does not specify the law which is to govern it,

then, unless the parties otherwise agree, the arbitration agreement is to be governed by Scots law.

DEFINITIONS
 "arbitration": ss.2(1), (2), 31(1)
 "arbitration agreement": ss.4, 31(1)
 "party": ss.2(1), 31(1), (2)
 "seated in Scotland": ss.2, 31(1)

COMMENTARY
This was a provision which was introduced into the Act at a late stage—as part of the stage 2 amendments. It is noteworthy also for being the only provision outside of Sch.1 which is not mandatory. The thrust of the provision is that if the parties choose Scotland as the seat of their arbitration but do not specify the law governing the arbitration agreement, then the governing law will be Scots law. However, the parties may agree to the contrary. Such agreement will usually arise after the conclusion of the arbitration agreement, as and when the parties decide that, despite agreeing on Scotland as the seat, they would prefer a law other than that of Scotland to govern the arbitration agreement. Nonetheless, it is always possible for the arbitration agreement to designate Scotland as the seat but to declare that Scots law will not govern the agreement, leaving that issue to be decided in the traditional way. Given that the provision refers to the *arbitration* agreement not specifying the governing law thereof, it must be assumed that if a contract containing an arbitration clause features a provision designating the law which is to govern the main agreement, that will not amount to a choice of law regarding the arbitration agreement. Accordingly, the selection of Scotland as the seat will lead to the application of Scots law to the arbitration agreement in such a case. It is thought that institutional rules will play no role in this context, since the only set of rules which features a choice of law provision is art.6 of the London Maritime Arbitrators Association ("LMAA") Terms which lay down the default rule that London is the seat of the arbitration and English law governs the agreement to arbitrate.

This is an issue which is addressed by neither the 1996 Act nor the Model Law—at least not directly. Indeed, it is rarely directly addressed by arbitration statutes. The Swiss Private International Law Act 1987 art.178(2) and the Spanish Arbitration Act art.9(6) both provide that the arbitration agreement will be regarded as valid if it conforms with the law by the parties, or the law governing the main agreement, or Swiss/Spanish law, but that is a long way removed from an actual choice of law provision. The only actual choice of law provision of which the authors are aware is s.48 of the Swedish Arbitration Act 1999, which indicates that international arbitration agreements shall be governed, in the absence of an express choice, by the law of the arbitral forum.

Up till now, outside of Sweden, if the question of which law governed the arbitration agreement arose, it would be for the courts to determine. Sometimes that was a straightforward issue, since the parties would have made an express choice of law. In the absence of such an express choice the traditional approach was to assume that the arbitration agreement was governed by the system of law which governed the main contract between the parties (see *V A Maritima Zorosa SA v Sesostris* [1984] 1 Lloyd's Rep. 161; and Saville J. in *Union of India v McDonnell Douglas Corp* [1993] 2 Lloyd's Rep. 48 at 50), unless there were factors pointing towards some other system of law (see, e.g. *Naviera Amazonica Peruans SA v Cia Inter-*

nacional de Seguros del Peru [1988] 1 Lloyd's Rep. 116 CA). That might sometimes lead to the conclusion that the law of the forum will prevail, since in the absence of an express choice of governing law, the designation of an arbitral forum can be regarded as an implied choice of the law governing the main contract (see Hobhouse J. in *Steel Authority of India v Hind Metals Inc* [1984] 1 Lloyd's Rep. 405 at 409). Of course in such cases it was still generally assumed that the law governing the main contract would also govern the arbitration agreement, and Lord Mustill in *Channel Tunnel Group Ltd v Balfour Beatty Construction Ltd* [1993] A.C. 334 at 357 thought that the law governing the contract between the parties would differ from that governing the arbitration agreement only "exceptionally". There is authority to the same effect from both other common law jurisdictions (see *National Thermal Power Corp v The Singer Co* (1993) XVIII YCA 403 at 406–407 Indian Supreme Court; *Recyclers of Australia Pty Ltd v Hettinga Equipment Inc* (2000) 175 A.L.R. 725 Australian Federal Court) and civil law jurisdictions (see *Owerri Commercial Inc v Dielle Srl* (1994) XIX YCA 703 at 706 Hague High Court).

Nonetheless, it has long been acknowledged that an arbitration clause is effectively a self-contained contract—a fact underlined by the principle of separability—which might well be governed by a law different from the law governing the main contract (see Donaldson M.R. in *Deutsche Schaachtbau v Shell Petroleum International Co Ltd* [1990] 1 A.C. 295 at 309G). Thus in recent years in England the view has gained strength that since the law relating to the arbitral proceedings and the law governing the arbitration agreement are not easily divisible, it makes sense that the choice of a particular forum is an implied choice not only of the former law but also the latter (see Toulson J. in *XL Insurance Ltd v Owens Corning* [2000] 2 Lloyd's Rep. 500 at 507; see also *A v B (No.2)* [2007] 1 Lloyd's Rep. 358). So in *C v D* [2008] 1 Lloyd's Rep. 239 at [22], Longmore L.J. opines that:

> "... if there is no express law of the arbitration agreement, the law with which the agreement has its closest and most real connection is more likely to be the law of the seat of the arbitration than the law of the underlying contract."

Courts elsewhere have also taken such an approach (e.g. *Ledee v Ceramich Ragno*, 684 F.2d 184 (1982); *Matermaco SA v PPM Cranes Inc* (2000) XXV YCA 653 Brussels Commercial Court; *Bulgarian Foreign Trade Bank Ltd v Al Trade Finance Inc* (2001) XXVI YCA 291 Swedish Supreme Court; compare the approach of the Cour de Cassation which considers that the scope and validity of international arbitration agreements depends only on the intention of the parties, divorced from any national law—*Municipalite de Khoms El Megreb v Societe Dalico*, 1994 Revue de l'Arbitrage 116 at 117).

Indirect support for the view that the law of the forum should be the default choice of law to govern the arbitration agreement is also provided by art.V(1)(b)of the New York Convention which indicates that it is a ground for refusing enforcement of an arbitral award that the arbitration agreement is invalid under the law chosen by the parties, or, in the absence of any indication thereon, under the law of the place where the award was made. This is echoed by art.36(1)(a)(i) of the Model Law (and by art.VI(2) of the European Convention on International Commercial Arbitration to which the UK is not a party). Moreover, given that the grounds for setting an award aside under the Model Law were deliberately aligned with the grounds for refusing enforcement under the Convention, art.34(2)(a)(i) of the version of Model Law adopted in Scotland stated that an award might be set aside if it was invalid under the law to which the parties subjected it, or in the absence of any indication thereon, if it was invalid under Scots law.

Section 6 thus adopts the approach taken by such cases as *C v D* [2008] 1 Lloyd's Rep. 239. It affords useful guidance not only for courts but for arbitral tribunals, who will often require to be aware of the law governing the arbitration agreement when performing such functions as ruling on their own jurisdiction in terms of r.19. The provision only applies where the parties have agreed that the arbitration is to be seated in Scotland. Thus it does not apply where Scotland is designated as the seat by a third party, by the arbitral tribunal or by the court. This is no doubt inspired by the idea that while a choice of forum by the parties might amount to an implied choice of law, it is not possible to infer such an implied choice if the parties have not chosen the forum. However, it might be pointed out that while s.6 is inspired by cases in which the court is looking to discern an implied choice of law, the provision is ultimately a statutory rule, and thus not subject to the same restrictions as the courts in this context. Thus it might be wondered whether there might have been merit in s.6 applying however the forum was designated, since it will often become necessary to determine the governing law, and a universal rule to apply in the absence of agreement of the parties could have proved quite useful.

Scottish Arbitration Rules

Scottish Arbitration Rules

7. The Scottish Arbitration Rules set out in schedule 1 are to govern every arbitration seated in Scotland (unless, in the case of a default rule, the parties otherwise agree).

DEFINITIONS
 "arbitration": ss.2(1), (2), 31(1)
 "default rule": ss.9(1), 31(1)
 "party": ss.2(1), 31(1), (2)
 "seated in Scotland": ss.2, 31(1)

COMMENTARY
As indicated in the introduction to this commentary, the structure of the Act is strikingly unusual in dividing its main substance into the Act proper and Sch.1, which contains the 84 Scottish Arbitration Rules. That introduction also considers the juridical basis of the application of these rules. Suffice to say here then, that, prima facie, every arbitration seated in Scotland is to be governed by these rules, although as will be seen presently, the parties may contract out of certain of them.

Mandatory rules

8. The following rules, called "mandatory rules", cannot be modified or disapplied (by an arbitration agreement, by any other agreement between the parties or by any other means) in relation to any arbitration seated in Scotland—
 rule 3 (arbitrator to be an individual)
 rule 4 (eligibility to act as an arbitrator)
 rule 7 (failure of appointment procedure)
 rule 8 (duty to disclose any conflict of interests)
 rules 12 to 16 (removal or resignation of arbitrator or dismissal of tribunal)
 rules 19 to 21 and 23 (jurisdiction of tribunal)
 rules 24 and 25 (general duties of tribunal and parties)

rule 42 (point of law referral: procedure etc.)
rule 44 (time limit variation: procedure etc.)
rule 45 (securing attendance of witnesses and disclosure of evidence)
rule 48 (power to award payment and damages)
rule 50 (interest)
rule 54 (part awards)
rule 56 (power to withhold award if fees or expenses not paid)
rule 60 (arbitrators' fees and expenses)
rule 63 (ban on pre-dispute agreements about liability for arbitration expenses)
rules 67, 68, 70, 71 and 72 (challenging awards)
rules 73 to 75 (immunity)
rule 76 (loss of right to object)
rule 77 (independence of arbitrator)
rule 79 (death of arbitrator)
rule 82 (rules applicable to umpires)

DEFINITIONS
"arbitration": ss.2(1), (2), 31(1)
"arbitration agreement": ss.4, 31(1)
"arbitrator": ss.2(1), 31(1)
"dispute": ss.2(1), 31(1)
"party": ss.2(1), 31(1), (2)
"rules": ss.7, 31(1)
"seated in Scotland": ss.2, 31(1)
"tribunal": ss.2(1), 31(1)

COMMENTARY
Certain of the rules are mandatory rules of law, which apply irrespective of the will of the parties, and the Act sensibly follows s.4(1) and Sch.1 of the 1996 Act in stipulating which of the Scottish Arbitration Rules to be found in Sch.1 are mandatory and thus (by omission) which can be disapplied or varied by the agreement of the parties. The status of each rule is indicated by the appearance alongside it of the letter "D" (default) or "M" (mandatory). That approach is of course subject to the limitation that, unlike provisions in the 1996 Act, a rule cannot be mandatory only in part. That has led to certain of the original rules having to be split into two separate rules, one default and the other mandatory, when it has been realised that that the objectives of the Act could not be achieved if the rule were wholly default. This meant the creation of rr.23, 42, 44 and 70. It should be noted, however, that one provision has slipped through the net. Although r.7 is designated as mandatory r.7(2) is clearly default in form. The explanatory notes (para.29) observe that failure to conduct the proceedings in accordance with mandatory rules may make the arbitrator liable to removal and any award open to challenge.

The question of which rules should be mandatory is very much a matter of policy, and each individual would probably have a different opinion as to which rules should be mandatory. The policy memorandum notes (para.85) that an attempt has been made to keep mandatory rules to a minimum, while reference is also made to ensuring, "the fairness and impartiality of the process" (para.82), and the smooth and efficient running of the arbitration, as well as reducing the prospect of delay (para.83). However, at stage 2 several rules which were originally default were rendered mandatory—rr. 4, 7, 48, 50 and 54—while r.53 (power to make provisional awards) was dropped from the list of mandatory rules. It may also be observed that while r.19 (power of tribunal to rule on own jurisdiction) is mandatory, the corresponding provision of the 1996 Act (s.30) is not.

Default rules

9.—(1) The non-mandatory rules are called the "default rules".

(2) A default rule applies in relation to an arbitration seated in Scotland only in so far as the parties have not agreed to modify or disapply that rule (or any part of it) in relation to that arbitration.

(3) Parties may so agree—
    (a) in the arbitration agreement, or
    (b) by any other means at any time before or after the arbitration begins.

(4) Parties are to be treated as having agreed to modify or disapply a default rule—
    (a) if or to the extent that the rule is inconsistent with or disapplied by—
        (i) the arbitration agreement,
        (ii) any arbitration rules or other document (for example, the UNCITRAL Model Law, the UNCITRAL Arbitration Rules or other institutional rules) which the parties agree are to govern the arbitration, or
        (iii) anything done with the agreement of the parties, or
    (b) if they choose a law other than Scots law as the applicable law in respect of the rule's subject matter.

This subsection does not affect the generality of subsections (2) and (3).

DEFINITIONS
"arbitration": ss.2(1), (2), 31(1)
"arbitration agreement": ss.4, 31(1)
"arbitrator": ss.2(1), 31(1)
"party": ss.2(1), 31(1), (2)
"rules": ss.7, 31(1)
"seated in Scotland": ss.2, 31(1)
"UNCITRAL Arbitration Rules": s.31(1)

COMMENTARY

Subsections (1) and (2)

The majority of the rules are default rules, which may be modified or disapplied, whether in whole or in part, by the agreement of the parties. This ensures maximum party autonomy and flexibility. On the other hand, the default rules ensure a ready made procedural framework on which the parties can rely if they so choose, or indeed on which they can fall back if they prove unable to agree how to proceed (see policy memorandum, paras 86–88).

Subsection (3)

When rules may be modified or disapplied: Section 9(3) goes further than s.4 of the 1996 Act in making it plain that the parties may reach agreement to modify or disapply any non-mandatory rules even after the arbitration has begun. Moreover, while any such agreement under the 1996 Act would require to be in writing, under s.9(3) there is no need for the agreement to take any particular form. However, s.9(3) contemplates express agreement. Implicit modification or disapplication arises under s.9(4).

Subsection (4)(a)(i)

How rules may be modified or disapplied: The arbitration agreement need not explicitly exclude particular default rules. If, for example, it specifies a method of appointing the tribunal which is at odds with r.6, that rule will be excluded to the extent that it is inconsistent with the agreement.

Subsection (4)(a)(ii)

Arbitration rules: This provision to some degree echoes s.4(3) of the 1996 Act. A number of sets of arbitration rules have been developed to govern domestic and/or international arbitration or arbitrations dealing with particular types of dispute, or within given industries. Most of these rules are very comprehensive, and if adopted by the parties would cover most if not all of the matters dealt with by the default rules. The Act makes it clear that if the parties agree that such rules should apply, they will prevail over the default rules to the extent that the latter are inconsistent with the chosen rules. Of course the chosen rules will have no effect to the extent that they are inconsistent with any mandatory rule. For example, if the parties arbitrate under the ICC Rules, art.28.6., which excludes recourse to the court, will validly exclude a challenge on the basis of error of law, since r.69 is a default rule, but cannot exclude challenges on the basis of serious procedural irregularity or lack of jurisdiction, since rr.67 and 68 are mandatory. The provision takes the interesting step of citing the UNCITRAL Arbitration Rules as an example of a set of institutional rules—interesting in the fact that an example is thought necessary, and also that the UNCITRAL Rules rather than domestic arbitration rules are chosen. This reflects the underlying policy drive to emphasise that the Act is friendly to international arbitrations.

At stage 2 there was added a reference to the default rules being inconsistent with another document such as the UNCITRAL Model Law. This is clearly a concession to the body of opinion which argued against the replacement of the Model Law by the new legislative regime. The parties could always achieve this effect under s.9(4)(b) (which allows the parties to disapply the default rules by choosing a foreign procedural law) by choosing a foreign procedural law based on the Model Law, albeit that it would then be uncertain whether the Scots courts would be prepared to support that arbitration—see s.13(4) below. However, s.9(4)(a)(ii) would equally allow them to choose the Model Law as promulgated by and amended by UNCITRAL rather than the version which operates in a particular legal system. Indeed they might choose the version of the Model Law which was specially adapted for use in Scotland by the (now repealed) s.66 and Sch.7 of the Law Reform (Miscellaneous Provisions) (Scotland) Act 1990. It will be an interesting question of interpretation to determine which of these versions is intended if parties simply invoke the Model Law. Section 31(1) makes it clear that any reference to the Model Law *within the Act* should be taken to refer to the former version, but that is not necessarily a guide to contractual intention.

Subsection (4)(a)(iii)

What this provision probably has in mind is that parties may entrust certain decisions regarding the organisation and conduct of the arbitral process to the arbitral tribunal itself or to an administering authority such as the London Court of International Arbitration. It therefore serves to make clear that anything done by such tribunal or authority is done with the agreement of the parties and this is capable of modifying or disapplying default rules.

Subsection (4)(b)

Invoking a foreign procedural law: Like s.4(5) of the 1996 Act, this provision indicates that agreement to disapply non-mandatory rules may take the form of invoking a law other than the law of Scotland. Thus if the parties agree that Scotland should be the seat of the arbitration, but that French law should govern the arbitration, French law will prevail over the default rules but not the mandatory rules of Sch.1, while should French law fail to deal with any matter covered by a default rule, that rule will apply. It is important to be aware that what we are talking about here is procedural law. A choice of French law to govern the substance of the dispute will not exclude any default rules (see *C v D* [2007] 2 Lloyd's Rep. 367). Of course, to choose to arbitrate in Scotland but under a foreign procedural law creates all sorts of possibilities for mishaps and confusion. For example, if court intervention is sought, in most cases a foreign court will decline to become involved in an arbitration seated outwith its jurisdiction (see *Naviera Amazonica Peruans SA v Cia Internacional de Seguros del Peru* [1988] 1 Lloyd's Rep. 116 at 120), while it is by no means certain that the Scottish courts will be willing to act as contemplated by that foreign procedural law. Thus it is not surprising that English experience suggests that the courts will strive to interpret the parties' agreement as not making this election (see, e.g. *ABB Lummus Global Ltd v Keppel Fels Ltd* [1999] 2 Lloyd's Rep. 24), while the reader may recall the example *Braes of Doune Wind Farm (Scotland) Ltd v Alfred McAlpine Business Services Ltd* [2008] 1 Lloyd's Rep. 608, where an arbitration agreement which indicated that Glasgow was to be the seat of the arbitration, but that the 1996 Act was to apply to the proceedings, was interpreted as meaning that England was the true seat of the arbitration with Scotland only the location of the proceedings.

Suspension of legal proceedings

Suspension of legal proceedings

10.—(1) The court must, on an application by a party to legal proceedings concerning any matter under dispute, sist those proceedings in so far as they concern that matter if—
  (a) an arbitration agreement provides that a dispute on the matter is to be resolved by arbitration (immediately or after the exhaustion of other dispute resolution procedures),
  (b) the applicant is a party to the arbitration agreement (or is claiming through or under such a party),
  (c) notice of the application has been given to the other parties to the legal proceedings,
  (d) the applicant has not—
    (i) taken any step in the legal proceedings to answer any substantive claim against the applicant, or
    (ii) otherwise acted since bringing the legal proceedings in a manner indicating a desire to have the dispute resolved by the legal proceedings rather than by arbitration, and
  (e) nothing has caused the court to be satisfied that the arbitration agreement concerned is void, inoperative or incapable of being performed.

(2) Any provision in an arbitration agreement which prevents the bringing of the legal proceedings is void in relation to any proceedings which the court refuses to sist.

This subsection does not apply to statutory arbitrations.

(3) This section applies regardless of whether the arbitration concerned is to be seated in Scotland.

DEFINITIONS
"arbitration": ss.2(1), (2), 31(1)
"arbitration agreement": ss.4, 31(1)
"court": s.31(1)
"dispute": ss.2(1), 31(1)
"party": ss.2(1), 31(1), (2)
"statutory arbitrations": ss.16(1), 31(1)

COMMENTARY
While this provision was not included in the original draft Bill, some sort of provision of this kind was clearly necessary, given that it was always intended to repeal the Arbitration Act 1975, s.1 of which gives effect to art.II of the 1958 New York Convention on the Recognition and Enforcement of Foreign Arbitral Awards, so that if the provision were not replaced, there would have been a breach of the UK's treaty obligations. Indeed, given that the Scottish Parliament does not have competence to legislate contrary to those obligations, the repeal of s.1 of the Arbitration Act 1975 would arguably have been ineffective in the absence of a provision such as s.10.

It was formerly the case that s.1 of the 1975 Act would oblige the court to sist (stay) legal proceedings if a party to an agreement to arbitrate abroad applied for it to do so. It was also the case in relation to domestic arbitration that the court was obliged to sist if a party pointed to a binding arbitration agreement (see Lord Dunedin in *Sanderson v Armour*, 1922 S.C. (HL) 117 at 126). Section 10 seeks to place the matter on a statutory footing as regards both domestic and non-domestic arbitration agreements, much as s.9 of the 1996 Act does in England. The common law is thus supplanted. There are distinct similarities between s.9 of the 1996 Act and s.10, which is hardly surprising given that they are both intended to replace s.1 of the 1975 Act. Again, the provision carries distinct echoes of art.8 of the Model Law, but once more this is unsurprising, given that the ultimate inspiration for both is art.II of the New York Convention.

Subsection (1)(a)

Applying for a sist: As under the 1996 Act, the court is, subject to a variety of conditions, obliged to sist any legal proceedings, if it is satisfied that it has been agreed that the matter under dispute is to be settled by arbitration. It is presumably for the party making the application to satisfy the court in this regard. It can be seen that proceedings may only be sisted in part if other aspects of the proceedings concern issues which are not the subject of an arbitration agreement. As under s.9(2) of the 1996 Act, a sist must be granted whether or not arbitration is to occur after other dispute resolution procedures. Thus a court must grant a stay if a party can point to an arbitration agreement, or, for example, to an agreement which insists that a dispute must be referred to mediation and then to arbitration if no settlement is reached.

Party to legal proceedings: It can also be seen that the applicant must be a party to the legal proceedings concerned. This condition was not present in the original version of the Bill, but was sensibly added at stage 2. Section 9(1) of the 1996 Act insists that the applicant must be a party, "against whom legal proceedings have been brought". This would seem to prevent a party to the arbitration agreement who is not otherwise a party to the proceedings to seek to be joined as a party in order to request a stay, while the 2010 Act would not seem to prevent that. Yet such a step was prevented in the admittedly slightly different context of s.1 of the 1975 Act, Woolf L.J., delivering the judgment of the Court of Appeal in *Etri Fans Ltd v NMB (United Kingdom) Ltd* [1987] 2 All E.R. 763, opining (at 767d–e):

"It is not the intention of the [Act] that those who have not been sued should be able to take advantage of the provision ... by applying to become parties to the proceedings ... purely for the purposes of obtaining a stay of an action which has been commenced, not against them, but another party who either did not have or did not wish to avail himself of the right to seek a stay."

The omission of the qualifying words found in s.9(1) of the 1996 Act would, nonetheless, allow the party who initiated the proceedings to seek a sist, and this is quite deliberate. Among the reasons why it should be open to that party to seek a sist the Government in its explanatory memorandum to the stage 2 amendments lists the fact that, having raised an action, he then realises that there is an arbitration agreement and decides that arbitration would lead to a quicker resolution of the dispute.

Arbitration agreement: Suppose a party denies that there is an arbitration agreement? The view of Roskill L.J. in *Willcock v Pickfords Removals Ltd* [1979] 1 Lloyd's Rep. 244 at 246, a decision under the 1975 Act, was that:

"As long as there is a dispute whether there is not an arbitration agreement, it cannot be said that there is an arbitration agreement as defined [by] ... the 1975 Act. Accordingly the provisions of s.1 are not complied with."

However, the 2010 Act seems to presuppose that it is for the arbitral tribunal, at least in the first instance, to rule on its own jurisdiction, and indeed r.19(a), a mandatory provision, indicates that the tribunal may rule on, "whether there is a valid arbitration agreement". Moreover, in the context of the Model Law, the conceptual scheme of which is similar in this regard, certain courts have indeed insisted that it is for the tribunal rather than the court to examine this question (see Kaplan J. in *Fun Sang Trading Ltd v Kai Sun Sea Products & Food Co Ltd* [1992] A.D.R.L.J. 93 at 101; and the Indian Supreme Court in *Shin-Etsu Chemical Co v Aksh Opticfibre Ltd* (2006) XXXI YCA 747). On the other hand, the court seems to be invited to consider the validity of the arbitration agreement under s.10(1)(e), so that it would be strange if it felt unable to consider whether there was such an agreement in the first place. It may also be suggested that if the issue is raised before the arbitral tribunal is created, a court is particularly likely to be willing to address the matter.

Certainly, the English courts continue to take the view that, since they are required to determine whether the conditions for the grant of a stay are met, it must be for them to decide whether an arbitration agreement exists and whether the dispute falls within its scope, perhaps except where it seems fairly certain that an agreement does exist and extends to the dispute in question (see, e.g. *Al-Naimi v Islamic Press Agency* [2000] 1 Lloyd's Rep. 522; *Classic Maritime Inc v Lion Diversified Holdings bhd* [2009] EWHC 1142 (Comm)). The same approach seems to be taken to the issue of who is to deal with questions of invalidity (see *O'Callaghan v Coral Racing Ltd*, *The Times*, November 26, 1998). If an agreement does exist, then a sist should be granted even though the agreement was entered into after the proceedings commenced (see Robert Goff L.J. in *The Tuyuti* [1984] 2 All E.R. 545 at 555).

Where should an application be made? It is not clear to which court the application should be made. Section 31 defines "court" in this context as meaning any court, but it would seem to make sense that the application should be made to the court in which the legal proceedings are being heard, as is clearly the case under s.9 of the 1996 Act. What if the legal proceedings are not being held in a court, but a tribunal, such as an employment tribunal?

Effect of sist: Article 8 of the Model Law sees the court in such a context actually referring the parties to arbitration, but that would not be the effect of a sist, which merely suspends the judicial proceedings (see Lord Watson in *Hamlyn & Co v Talisker Distillery* (1894) 21 R. (H.L.) 21 at 25 and 27; *Channel Tunnel Group Ltd v Balfour Beatty Construction Ltd* [1993] A.C. 334, per Lord Mustill at 345H–346A). This might seem to run contrary to the terms of art.II(3) of the 1958 New York Convention, which do appear to require that the parties be referred to arbitration. However, there is an argument that such is not the intention of the Convention, which fact is clear from reading the original French version of art.II(3) (see Claude Reymond, "The Channel Tunnel Case and the Law of International Arbitration" (1993) 109 L.Q.R. 337).

Subsection (1)(b)

The applicant must also be a party to the arbitration agreement. Thus, as under the 1996 Act, a party to the legal proceedings who is not a party to the arbitration agreement cannot seek a sist (see *BHPB Freight Pty Ltd v Cosco Oceania Chartering Pty Ltd* [2008] F.C.A. 551). Alternatively, the applicant may be an individual who is claiming under or through a party to the arbitration agreement. This was the position under s.1 of the 1975 Act (see also s.82(2) of the 1996 Act), but this wording was inexplicably omitted from the original version of the Bill. Happily, it was restored at stage 2.

Subsection (1)(c)

Notice of the application must be given to the other parties to the legal proceedings. Under Rules of the Court of Session ("RCS") 1994 (SI 1994/1443) r.23.11 any motion is only competent if intimated to the other party. Presumably, an application cannot be granted if notice has not been given.

Subsection (1)(d)(i)

The court need not grant a sist if the applicant has taken any step in the proceedings to answer the substantive claim against him. This formulation is drawn from s.9(3) of the 1996 Act. Article 8 of the Model Law as originally promulgated would have allowed a party to request a sist, "not later than when submitting his first statement on the substance of the dispute". However, the Model Law as adopted in Scotland allowed a party to request a sist, "at any time before the pleadings in the action [were] finalised", a rather more liberal approach which gives effect to the view of the Scottish Advisory Committee on Arbitration Law (*Report to the Lord Advocate on the UNCITRAL Model Law*, 1989, para.3.13) that the provision should conform more closely, "to existing Scottish practice". That practice was perhaps not as uniform as might be supposed, since while at common law it was agreed that a sist could be sought until a party had waived his right to arbitrate, it was not entirely clear how far proceedings could be allowed to proceed before that result was reached (see Fraser P. Davidson, *Arbitration* (Edinburgh: W. Green, 2000), para.7.19). Finally, s.1(1) of the (now repealed) Arbitration Act 1975, which sought to give effect to the New York Convention indicated that a party who sought a sist in respect of a non-domestic arbitration agreement had to do so before delivering any pleadings or taking any other step in the proceedings. It was clear that a purely defensive act by a defender could not amount to a "step" (see *Roussel-UCLAF v G D Searle & Co Ltd* [1978] 1 Lloyd's Rep. 225), and in *Eagle Star Insurance Co Ltd v Yuval Insurance Co Ltd* [1978] 1 Lloyd's Rep. 357 at 361, Lord Denning M.R. suggested that a "step" must be one which, "impliedly affirms the correctness of the proceedings".

This provision seems less liberal than any of these measures, in that any step to contest the claim may preclude a sist being granted. There is considerable authority on this point under s.9(3) of the 1996 Act. Considerations of space prevent a detailed analysis of the case law, but it seems clear that taking any step, however minor, beyond simply acknowledging the proceedings tends to lead to the right to a stay being forfeited (see, e.g. *London Central and Suburban Developments Ltd v Banger* [1999] A.D.R.L.J. 119), unless the party at the same time asserts that right (see *Patel v Patel* [1999] 1 All E.R. (Comm) 923). Given that the general thrust of the 2010 Act is towards supporting arbitration, with both party autonomy and limited court intervention being laid down as founding principles, it seems a pity that a party who has agreed that a dispute should be determined by arbitration should be able to lose the right to arbitrate so easily. The Act has probably moved the law in the wrong direction in this respect. That being said, the approach of s.10 is to direct that the court *must* grant a sist if certain conditions are met. It does not actually provide that the court may not grant a sist if those conditions are not met, and it might be the case that the court will feel able to exercise a discretion here. It is certainly the case that the English courts assert such a discretion (*Albon v Naza Motor Trading SDN BHD* [2007] 2 Lloyd's Rep. 420).

It may be added that the original version of the Bill would have demanded that the applicant must have taken any appropriate procedural step to acknowledge the proceedings. This wording is drawn from s.9(3) of the 1996 Act, which was designed to improve upon the wording of s.4 of the Arbitration Act 1950 under which the taking of any step in legal proceedings, even simply acknowledging them, precluded a party seeking a stay. Its usefulness in a Scottish context was doubtful, and its omission from the Act must be applauded.

Subsection (1)(d)(ii)

The applicant must not have acted since bringing the legal proceedings in a manner which indicates a desire to have the dispute resolved by litigation rather than arbitration. This provision was added at stage 2. It has no counterpart in either the 1996 Act or the Model Law and is decidedly peculiar. It must be assumed that the legal proceedings referred to are the application for a sist rather than the proceedings sought to be sisted. How might a party behave in a way which indicated a desire to have the dispute resolved by litigation? The explanatory memorandum to the stage 2 amendments suggest that the intention is to reflect the decision in *Inverclyde (Mearns) Housing Ltd v Lawrence Construction Co Ltd*, 1989 S.L.T. 815. That case is one of many which recognise that there may be implied waiver of the right to arbitrate—in that instance by significant delay in applying for a sist. There is case law in England which suggests that a party may be estopped from seeking a sist (stay) if he has insisted that he does not intend to arbitrate (see *Patel v Patel* [1999] 1 All E.R (Comm) 923). However, this does not seem to fall within the scope of the present provision unless such behaviour has arisen since the proceedings were initiated.

Subsection (1)(e)

This is slightly curiously worded. Under the 1996 Act the court is not to stay proceedings if satisfied of such matters, whereas a Scots court must sist if nothing causes it to be so satisfied.

The provision allows the court to decline to sist if it is satisfied that the arbitration agreement is, "void, inoperative or incapable of being performed". The 1975 Act s.1 also allowed the court to decline to sist if it was satisfied that there was, "not in fact any dispute between the parties with regard to the matter agreed to be referred". However, the English courts had tended to urge caution as regards being too ready to remove cases from arbitrators (see, e.g. Saville J. in *Hayter v Nelson* [1990] 2 Lloyd's Rep. 265 at 268), while the DAC Report (para.55) had observed that the extra ground did not appear in the New York Convention and was confusing and unnecessary. The ground was thus omitted from the 1996 Act, and the 2010 Act seems to have followed suit. The meaning of each of the terms, "void, inoperative or incapable of being performed" is individually considered below. Yet it should be borne in mind that the Convention was not drafted with the terminological exactitude of a British statute and employs expressions which require to make sense in a variety of languages. Thus it has been held that the three grounds tend to overlap (see, e.g. *Jean Charbonneau v Les Industries AC Davie Inc* Unreported March 14, 1989 Supreme Court of Quebec), and should be read together.

As regards the burden of proof in relation to the court being "satisfied" Evans J. in *Overseas Union Insurance Ltd v AA Mutual Insurance Ltd* [1988] 2 Lloyd's Rep. 63 at 70 states that:

"Once the applicant has proved the existence of what appears to be a relevant arbitration agreement, then the burden shifts to the opposing party to prove that the agreement is in fact null and void, etc."

Accordingly, even if there is some evidence suggesting that the agreement is invalid, should the party in question fail to discharge the burden of proof, then the court cannot be satisfied as required by the legislation, and a sist must be granted (see Hobhouse L.J. in *Inco Europe Ltd v First Choice Distribution Ltd* [1999] 1 W.L.R. 270 at 280D). It is suggested that the wording employed by the 2010 Act points even more strongly towards the burden lying on the party who is resisting a sist.

Governing law: Which law should the court apply in order to determine whether an arbitration agreement is "void", etc.? This might not always be a straightforward question where a non-domestic arbitration agreement is involved. Yet in the context of the Arbitration Act 1975 there is House of Lords authority (Lord Mustill in *Channel Tunnel Group Ltd v Balfour Beatty Construction Ltd* [1983] A.C. 334 at 358) to the effect that a court should apply domestic law to that question. This of course means Scots law in the context of the Act. There must however be an argument that it is more logical to apply the proper law of the contract to this question (see *ABN Amro Bank Canada v Krupp Mak Maschinenbau GmbH* [1997] A.D.R.L.J. 37). The Paris Court of Appeal in *Gatoil v National Iranian Oil Co* (1993) Revue de l'Arbitrage 281, even suggested that validity should be assessed not according to any national law but, "solely in light of the requirements of international public policy". This has proved rather too bold an approach

for some (e.g. the Genoa Court of Appeal in *Della Sanara Kustvaart v Fallimento Cap Giovanni Coppola Srl* (1992) XVII YCA 542). However, echoes of that approach are to be found in the statement of the US Court of Appeals in *Ledee v Ceramiche Ragno*, 684 F.2d 184 (1981) at 187:
"The goal of the Convention ... was to encourage the recognition and enforcement of commercial arbitration agreements in international contracts and to unify the standards by which agreements to arbitrate are observed ... in signatory countries. The parochial interests of ... any state cannot be the measure of how the 'null and void' clause is interpreted.... . Rather, the clause must be interpreted to encompass only those situations—such as fraud, mistake, duress and waiver—that can be applied neutrally on an international scale."

Void: The Convention and the 1975 Act both refer to the agreement being null and void, as indeed does s.9 of the 1996 Act, but it must be assumed that the omission of the former term makes no difference, since the French version simply refers to the agreement being *caduque*, and the Spanish version, *nulo*. There is authority in England that, since the court has to consider whether there is a valid arbitration agreement in order to determine whether the conditions for a stay are met, this category cannot mean to address agreements which are void ab initio, but must be directed towards agreements which were initially valid, but have since become void (*Albon v Naza Motor Trading SDN BHD* [2007] 2 Lloyd's Rep. 420; relying on *Rhone Mediterranee v Achille Lauro*, 712 F.2d 50 (1983)). There is also authority pointing to the opposite conclusion (e.g. *OTM Ltd v Hydranautics* [1981] 2 Lloyd's Rep. 211). It might be suggested that it matters little which view is correct, since the result in either case must be that a sist is refused.

The English courts have held void agreements obtained by duress (*Bakwin and Erie International Trading Co v Sothebys* Unreported 2005), or which contain a floating choice of procedural law (*The Star Texas* [1993] 2 Lloyd's Rep. 445; but compare *Bremen v Zapata Off-Shore Co*, 407 U.S. 1 (1972)). There is also considerable international case law under both the Convention and the Model Law. So courts outside the UK have held that an agreement is not void simply because the means for carrying it out have failed, as where a designated appointing institution does not exist (*Lucky-Goldstar International (HK) Ltd v Ng Moo Kee Engineering Ltd* [1994] A.D.R.L.J. 49; see also *Laboratories Grossman v Forest Laboratories*, 295 N.Y. Supp. (2d) 756 (1985)). Nor is an agreement void for uncertainty where it is based on mutual error (*China Resources Metal Ltd v Anada Non-Ferrous Metals Ltd* [1994] H.K.C. 526), nor where it suggests that a dispute "may" be referred to arbitration (*Tianhjin Medicine and Health Products Import and Export Corp v JA Moeller (Hong Kong) Ltd* [1994] 1 H.K.C. 545), or even that the matter may be decided by litigation or arbitration (*William Co v Chiu Kong Agency Ltd* [1995] 2 H.K.L.R. 139; but compare *Lovelock v Exportles Ltd* [1968] 1 Lloyd's Rep. 163), since there is a valid arbitration agreement as soon as a party elects to arbitrate. An agreement has been held void, however, where one of the parties clearly lacked capacity (*Success International Inc v Environmental Export International of Canada Inc* (1995) 23 O.R. (3d) 137), or was induced to agree by fraud (*Riley v Kingsley Underwriting Agencies*, 969 F.2d 953 (1992)).

Incapable of being performed: The idea that the agreement may be incapable of being performed seems to suggest that the agreement is entirely valid but faces some sort of practical impossibility. Thus in *Dupont Scandinavia AB v Coastal (Bermuda) Ltd* (1990) XV YCA 378 at 383, the Court of Appeal of Bermuda suggests that it arises where performance is impossible even if both parties are willing to perform. The English cases suggest that an agreement is not incapable of being performed merely because it is suggested that a party lacks the financial resources to meet any award (see *The Rena K* [1979] Q.B. 377), or to participate in the arbitration (see *Haendler v Paczy* [1981] 1 Lloyd's Rep. 302). Nor is an agreement incapable of being performed simply because several parties are in dispute and the arbitration will not settle all the relevant issues (see *Lonrho v Shell Petroleum* [1981] 2 All E.R. 456). However, stays have been refused on this ground on the basis that the remedy sought is not within the power of the arbitral tribunal to grant (*Vertex Data Science Ltd v Powergen Retail Ltd* [2006] 2 Lloyd's Rep. 11), and, rather more controversially, where the courts of the system which governed the contract would not have regarded the agreement as excluding the right to litigate (*Abu Dhabi Investment Co v H Clarkson & Co Ltd* [2006] 2 Lloyd's Rep. 381).

Elsewhere, it has been held that an agreement is not incapable of being performed merely because it may not be performed immediately (see *Hip Hing Construction Co Ltd v Hope Lee Iron Work Co* [2002] 633 H.K.C.U. 1, where arbitration could not be commenced until the completion of the contract works), or because there are doubts about the enforceability of the award (*Rhone Mediterranee v Achille Lauro*, 712 F.2d 50 (1983)). But a sist has been denied on this basis where the nominated arbitration institution no longer exists (*Pierreux NV v Transportmaschinen Handelshaus GmbH* (1997) XXII YCA 631), although sometimes a court will still grant a sist in such cases (see, e.g. *Dalimpex v Janicki* [2003] 172 O.A.C. 321). In a German case (III ZR 33/00, April 9, 2009) the Supreme Court found that an agreement was incapable of being performed because one party would have been unable to pay the costs of the arbitration had it lost. This seems extremely dubious.

Inoperative: At one point the Bill referred to the agreement being "unenforceable" rather than "inoperative", despite the latter term being employed by the New York Convention and the 1975 Act (and the 1996 Act in England). This was mildly alarming, since the terms are hardly synonymous. Gloag, *The Law of Contract*, 2nd edn (Edinburgh: W. Green, 1929), p.14, states that the former term:

"... has no special or technical meaning, but is most commonly applied to cases whereby under the terms of a statute, a particular agreement cannot be directly enforced, but may be productive of rights to the one party against the other."

By contrast, "inoperative" seems to denote an agreement which was initially invalid, but which for some reason no longer carries legal force (see Max Bonnell, "When is an Arbitration Agreement 'Inoperative'?" (2008) 11 Int. A.L.R. 111). If the terms had indeed carried a different meaning then s.9 would have failed properly to give effect to the New York Convention, and since the Scottish Parliament lacks competence to legislate contrary to the UK's treaty obligations, the repeal of s.1 of the 1975 Act might have been ineffective. This unhappy outcome might have been avoided by purposive interpretation of the provision, and in many instances where an agreement has been held to be inoperative it would have been just as easy to say the arbitration agreement was unenforceable. However, as will be seen, that outcome might not be so easily achieved in certain other cases. Accordingly, it is something of a relief that the drafters decided to persist with this rather puzzling departure from the language of the Convention.

An arbitration agreement has been held to be inoperative where the subject matter of the dispute was not permitted to be settled by arbitration under the governing law (see *Aguna v Smith Industries* (1983) VIII YCA 360), where it allowed a party to elect either to arbitrate or to bring proceedings before a US regulatory authority and the latter choice had clearly been made (*Fowler v Merrill Lynch Pierce and Smith Inc* (1985) X YCA 499; but compare *China Merchant Heavy Industry Co Ltd v JGC Corp* (2003) XXVIII YCA 267 Hong Kong Court of Appeal), where a party has rescinded it in response to a repudiatory breach (*Traube v Perelman*, Unreported July 25, 2001 Chancery Division), where parties have waived the right to arbitrate (see, e.g. *ACD Tridon Inc v Tridon Australia Pty Ltd* (2004) XIX YCA 533), where a party is estopped (personally barred) from seeking to arbitrate (*Halvanon Insurance Co Ltd v Companhia de Seguros do Estado de Sao Paolo* [1995] L.R.L.R 403), where the agreement has been impliedly revoked (*Corcoran v Adra Insurance Company Ltd* (1989) XIV YCA 733), and where the pursuer is obviously not a party to it (*Guns 'n' Roses Missouri Storm Inc v Productions Musicales Donald K Donald Inc* (1994) 114 D.L.R. (4th) 441). It has been said, however, that a, "party arguing that another party has waived a contractual right to arbitration bears a heavy burden of proof" (by a US District Court in *Re Seawest Industries Inc* (1995) XX YCA 811 at 812).

But an arbitration agreement is not inoperative simply because arbitration may be inconvenient or expensive (*Dodwell & Co (Australia) Pty v Moss Security* (1994) XIX YCA 615 at 618), or may produce an unenforceable award (*Molino e Pacifico Ponte San Giovanni Spa v Anrde & Cie SA* (1983) VIII YCA 378 Italian Supreme Court), or may lead to multiple proceedings (*Svenska Handelsbanken v India Charge Chrome Ltd* (1996) XXI YCA 557 at 566 Indian Supreme Court).

Subsection (2)

Scott v Avery clauses: An arbitration agreement might not merely insist that a dispute be determined by arbitration. It might actually prohibit the determination of the dispute by legal proceedings. Where a party has lost the right to insist on arbitration, such a clause might have the effect of preventing effective determination of the dispute. In such circumstances the clause might well be held unenforceable as against public policy (see *Lowndes v Earl of Stamford and Warrington* (1852) 18 Q.B. 425), but this provision removes any doubt in the matter by rendering such a clause void where the proceedings are not sisted. The provision is in some respects similar to s.9(5) of the 1996 Act, which deals with so-called *Scott v Avery* clauses (see *Scott v Avery* (1856) 5 HL Cas. 811; and the DAC Report, para.57), but is not so narrowly drawn.

The provision indicates that it does not apply to statutory arbitrations. This is because s.16(2) provides that any reference to the arbitration agreement shall in the case of statutory arbitrations be taken to be a reference to the relevant enactment. Consequently, were it not for this saving, subs.(2) could conceivably be interpreted as nullifying any provision in such enactments which insisted that certain disputes could only be resolved via arbitration.

Subsection (3)

Sisting for non-Scots arbitrations: The section applies whether or not the arbitration is seated in Scotland. So if a party who applies for a sist can point to an agreement that the dispute be arbitrated in England, then a sist must still be granted. The same would be true if the agreement provided that the dispute should be arbitrated in France. In this latter case of course, s.10 would be implementing the UK's obligation to give effect to art.II of the New York Convention. It is submitted that the wording would mean that the section should apply even if the seat of the arbitration was yet to be determined, or indeed even if the agreement indicated that the arbitration was not to have a seat. Provided the other requirements of s.10 were met, the court in such cases would still be obliged to suspend proceedings.

Enforcing and challenging arbitral awards etc.

Arbitral award to be final and binding on parties

11.—(1) A tribunal's award is final and binding on the parties and any person claiming through or under them (but does not of itself bind any third party).

(2) In particular, an award ordering the rectification or reduction of a deed or other document is of no effect in so far as it would adversely affect the interests of any third party acting in good faith.

(3) This section does not affect the right of any person to challenge the award—
    (a) under Part 8 of the Scottish Arbitration Rules, or
    (b) by any available arbitral process of appeal or review.

(4) This section does not apply in relation to a provisional award (see rule 53), such an award not being final and being binding only—
    (a) to the extent specified in the award, or
    (b) until it is superseded by a subsequent award.

DEFINITIONS
"party": ss.2(1), 31(1), (2)
"rules": ss.7, 31(1)
"tribunal": ss.2(1), 31(1)

COMMENTARY
Somewhat surprisingly, this provision, which articulates principles which are central to arbitration was at one point part of the rules and even more remarkably a default rule, although it could hardly be supposed that the parties through their agreement could disturb the fundamental principle that an award may not affect the rights of third parties.

Subsection (1)

The award binds the parties: Subject to s.11(3), an award, including a part award, is final and binding on the parties. This is essentially the position at common law, and might be taken to be axiomatic, but there may be merit in making this explicit, especially as regards awards which may be sought to be enforced outside the UK, since it is a ground for refusing enforcement of an award under art.V(1)(e) of the New York Convention that an award has not yet become binding. There is no equivalent provision in the Model Law, although art.32(2) of the UNCITRAL Arbitration Rules is in similar terms. The provision is clearly inspired (at least in part) by s.58 of the 1996 Act, which in turn was based on s.16 of the 1950 Act. Unlike s.58 it is mandatory in form, so that an agreement that an award will only become binding when promulgated by some institution or third party, or indeed will not have binding effect at all will itself be of no effect.

The finality of an award means that the issues which it addresses are res judicata and cannot be revisited by either of the parties or indeed the arbitrator. In the context of s.58(1) of the 1996 Act H.H. Judge Lloyd QC noted in *Gbangola v Smith and Sheriff Ltd* [1998] 3 All E.R. 730 at 738 that an award, "is as binding on the arbitrator as much as the parties". The Privy

Council has held that under English law there is an implied obligation on the parties to honour the award (*Associated Electric and Gas Insurance Services Ltd v European Reinsurance Company of Zurich* [2003] 1 W.L.R. 1041). On this basis the High Court has been prepared to issue injunctions to restrain applications to challenge an award in foreign courts (see *C v D* [2007] EWHC 1541 (Comm)). It is submitted that in light of the mandatory nature of s.11, it is not open to the parties to agree to ignore the award so as to open up the possibility of either litigation or fresh arbitral proceedings.

Award binds persons claiming through parties: The award binds not only parties but persons claiming through or under parties. That might include successors in title (*Holburn v Buchanan* (1915) 31 Sh. Ct Rep. 178), successors under contracts such as leases (see Lord Mackenzie in *Montgomerie v Carrick* (1848) 10 D. 1387 at 1388) and statutory successors such as trustees in sequestration (*Craig's Trustee v Lord Malloch* (1900) 2 F. 541), the assignee of a party (*Henry v Hepburn* (1835) 13 S. 361; *Whatley v Ardrossan Harbour Co* (1893) 1 S.L.T. 382), including judicial assignees such as a person injured by an insolvent insured who looks to arrest the proceeds of an insurance policy in the hands of the company (as in *Rutherford v Licences and General Insurance Co Ltd* 1934 S.L.T. 31), or the heir of a deceased party (*Robertson v Cheynes* (1847) 9 D. 599). There is also authority that a cautioner (guarantor) is bound by an award against a principal debtor (*Anderson v Wood* (1821) 1 S. 31). The rules of certain trade associations (e.g. Grain and Feed Trade Association ("GAFTA") Arbitration Rules r.7.1.) indicate that in certain circumstances where there is a string of contracts for the sale of goods, any dispute regarding the quality or condition of the goods shall be settled by an arbitration between the first seller and last buyer, and all intermediate parties will be bound by the award. Yet that result only occurs as a result of that special agreement, and the rights of intermediate parties do not really derive from other parties. The same is true of construction contracts which allow contractors to arbitrate on behalf of subcontractors (see Phillips L.J. in *Birse Construction Ltd v Co-operative Wholesale Society Ltd* (1997) 84 B.L.R. 58 at 71). It might be added that an entirely different range of individuals might be seen as claiming through or under parties if the parties choose a law other than that of Scotland to govern this issue.

The award does not bind third parties: Section 11(1) differs from s.58(1) of the 1996 Act in that it makes clear that the award does not bind third parties. This is again axiomatic. The jurisdiction of an arbitral tribunal is created by an agreement between two private parties and cannot extend beyond those limits. Interestingly enough, the DAC Report, para.263 having noted the suggestion that the "other side" of s.58(1) be spelt out, "i.e. whatever the parties may or may not agree, the award is of no substantive or evidential effect against anyone who is neither a party nor claiming through or under a party", concluded (para.264):

"Such a provision would, of course, have to be mandatory. It would have to confine itself to the cases exclusively concerned with the laws of this country, for otherwise it could impinge on other applicable laws which have a different rule. Even where the situation was wholly domestic, it would have to deal with all those cases (e.g. insurers) who are not parties to the arbitration but whose rights and obligations may well be affected by awards (agreed or otherwise) in one way or another. In our view it would be very difficult to construct an acceptable provision and we are not persuaded it is needed."

Subsection (2)

It is noted above that it is a fundamental principle of arbitration that, since the foundation of the tribunal's jurisdiction is the agreement to arbitrate, only the rights of the parties to the proceedings may be determined, while the rights of third parties cannot be affected. Section 11(2) seems to go further as it seems to imply that a third party who, for example, has in good faith acted on the basis on an unreduced or unrectified document cannot be prejudiced. However, it is unclear how this provision is intended to work, and nothing similar to it appears in the 1996 Act. Is the provision perhaps to be taken into account by a court should litigation subsequently ensue? Section 11(2) can be contrasted with the extremely detailed provisions which seek to protect the interests of third parties when a court is asked to rectify a document (see s.9 of the Law Reform (Miscellaneous Provisions) (Scotland) Act 1985 and the discussion thereof in Fraser P. Davidson, *Evidence* (Edinburgh: W. Green, 2007), paras 6.90–6.91).

Subsection (3)

To some extent echoing s.58(2) of the 1996 Act, this points out that the finality and binding nature of an award is qualified by the availability of any process of arbitral appeal or review, and by the rights of appeal under the Act. Certain arbitral rules permit institutional scrutiny of an award, e.g. the ICC Rules, while others, like the International Centre for Settlement of Investment Disputes ("ICSID") Rules, permit a full annulment appeal to a different arbitral tribunal. The reference to the rights of challenge in Pt 8 not applying in every case no doubt has in mind the fact that the right to challenge an award on the basis of error of law does not apply where the applicable law is not Scots law, nor where the award is not required to be reasoned, nor where that right has otherwise been excluded by the parties.

Subsection (4)

Effect of provisional award: A provisional award is an award which deals with a particular issue or set of issues on an interim basis. The power to make such awards is conferred by r.53, and this provision was indeed originally r.53(2). Presumably, it was decided that it made more sense to move it to the body of the Act to become part of a provision dealing with the effect of awards. Such awards are indeed not designed to be final. Yet what is meant by saying that the award is binding only to the extent specified in the award? Perhaps it is contemplated that the award might grant a certain form of relief only for a period set out in the award, even if by that stage it has not been superseded by another award. The reference to a subsequent award rather than final award suggests that such an award may be overtaken by a later provisional award. Rule 51 makes it clear that the final award must make reference to any provisional award. Thus any payment which the final award orders must take account of any payment already ordered, and indeed if it finds for the defender must order the repayment of any sum paid under a provisional award.

Enforcement of arbitral awards

12.—(1) The court may, on an application by any party, order that a tribunal's award may be enforced as if it were an extract registered decree bearing a warrant for execution granted by the court.

(2) No such order may be made if the court is satisfied that the award is the subject of—

(a) an appeal under Part 8 of the Scottish Arbitration Rules,
(b) an arbitral process of appeal or review, or
(c) a process of correction under rule 58 of the Scottish Arbitration Rules,

which has not been finally determined.

(3) No such order may be made if the court is satisfied that the tribunal which made the award did not have jurisdiction to do so (and the court may restrict the extent of its order if satisfied that the tribunal did not have jurisdiction to make a part of the award).

(4) But a party may not object on the ground that the tribunal did not have jurisdiction if the party has lost the right to raise that objection by virtue of the Scottish Arbitration Rules (see rule 76).

(5) Unless the parties otherwise agree, a tribunal's award may be registered for execution in the Books of Council and Session or in the sheriff court books (provided that the arbitration agreement is itself so registered).

(6) This section applies regardless of whether the arbitration concerned was seated in Scotland.

(7) Nothing in this section or in section 13 affects any other right to rely on or enforce an award in pursuance of—
(a) sections 19 to 21, or
(b) any other enactment or rule of law.

(8) In this section, "court" means the sheriff or the Court of Session.

DEFINITIONS
"arbitration": ss.2(1), (2), 31(1)
"court": s.31(1)
"party": ss.2(1), 31(1), (2)
"seated in Scotland": ss.2, 31(1)
"tribunal": ss.2(1), 31(1)

COMMENTARY

This is another provision which did not appear in the original Bill. It seems to have been inspired by s.66 of the 1996 Act, which was in turn based on s.26 of the Arbitration Act 1950, although the provision has obviously been adapted to make sense in Scotland.

Subsection (1)

Application to enforce: On application by a party the court may order that an award is to be enforced as if it were a court decree, i.e. by doing diligence upon it without further warrant (see explanatory notes, para.37). It may be that rules of court will be promulgated detailing the procedure to be followed if this is to happen as is the case in relation to awards made in Scotland under the Model Law (RCS r.62.58). The current rules demand such things as the presentation of the original arbitration agreement and the authenticated original award.

Court discretion: As will be seen, there are situations in which the court is prohibited from enforcing the award. Otherwise, the use of the word "may" gives the court discretion to enforce the award, and it may thus decline to do so. Cases where the court might decline to enforce the award might include the situation where the award deals with issues which are not arbitrable, or where it appears to be illegal or otherwise to offend against public policy (see DAC Report, para.273).

Authority under s.66 of the 1996 Act indicates that it is the award as it stands which can be ordered to be enforced, and the court at this stage has no power to correct it or otherwise remedy deficiencies (see, e.g. *Walker v Rome* [1999] 2 All E.R. (Comm) 961). However, such authority also suggests that it is open to the court to enforce an award in part (*ASM Shipping Ltd of India v TTMI Ltd* [2009] 1 Lloyd's Rep. 293; see also *Nigerian National Petroleum Corp v IPCO (Nigeria) Ltd* [2008] EWCA Civ 1157, and the commentary by Hew R. Dundas at (2008) 74 *Arbitration* 330 and (2009) 75 *Arbitration* 126), and the Scots courts might also decide that this is within their discretion. There would appear to be no need for the party seeking enforcement to notify the other party of the proceedings, although rules of court may be brought forward to deal with this issue.

Setting aside by exception not contemplated: Finally, it should be noted that it no longer seems open for a party to respond to an action to enforce an award by seeking to have it reduced by exception (*ope exceptionis*), an option available at common law (see Davidson, *Arbitration*, 2000, paras 18.01–18.02). This possibility is not contemplated by s.10, while s.11(2) explicitly rules out any means of challenging an award except as provided for by Pt 8 of the rules. This would also seem to rule out a party raising a petition for suspension of an award. However, a court will surely be able to exercise its discretion not to enforce an award if challenge proceedings are pending.

Subsection (2)

Award not to be enforced where subject to appeal, review or correction: In a number of situations the court cannot enforce an award. One of these is addressed by the following subsection. The others fall under subs.(2) which was introduced at stage 2. Thus the award may not be enforced where the court is satisfied that the award is:
- the subject of an appeal to the Outer House under any of the grounds laid down by Pt 8 of the rules (lack of jurisdiction, serious irregularity, legal error);
- the subject of an arbitral process of appeal or review, e.g. an appeal to a second arbitral tribunal or other body;
- the subject of an application to have the award corrected by the tribunal under r.58;

and that process has not been determined. It must be presumed that it is for the other party to satisfy the court under any of these grounds, although this should be fairly straightforward, since an award is either subject to an ongoing process of appeal, etc. or it is not. Accordingly, this subsection will not apply if the party resisting enforcement suggests that he is merely contemplating such a course of action. In such a situation, the court would not be disabled from enforcing the award, but would surely have a discretion to decline to do so if it thought that the objecting party would take such action and would stand a good chance of success.

It might be noted that in England under the relevant rules of court the court is not prevented from enforcing an award in the circumstances contemplated by this subsection, the matter falling within its general discretion Thus where the award is being challenged by the other party, whether before the courts or under a process of arbitral review, the English courts may or may not stay enforcement until the outcome is known, but in deciding whether to do so will take into account the apparent strength of the case against the award and the potential implications of the stay, including the possibility that ultimate enforcement might be prejudiced as a result of the losing party hiding his assets (see *Apis AS v Fantazia Kereskedelmi KFT* [2001] 1 All E.R. (Comm) 348; *Socadec SA v Pan Afric Inpex Co Ltd* [2003]

EWHC 2086 (QB)). Under subs.(2) the court has no power to enforce even where it seems clear that the party who has challenged the award has no prospect of success and has only raised the challenge to give himself a breathing space, during which time he can take action to defeat the ultimate enforcement of the award.

In this context it may also be noted that under s.20(6) if a party is looking to enforce a New York Convention award which is the subject of challenge proceedings, the court is specifically empowered to adjourn the enforcement proceedings, and (on the application of the party seeking enforcement) to order the other party to provide suitable security. It is a pity that similar powers are not expressly conferred in the context of s.12, especially as it is unlikely that the court will regard itself as having inherent power to order security. The omission is doubly striking given that the Outer House is given the power under r.71(9) to order that an appellant provide security for the expenses of an appeal.

Subsection (3)

Award not to be enforced where tribunal lacked jurisdiction: Another situation where the court has no discretion and must decline to make the order is where it is satisfied that the tribunal lacked jurisdiction to make the award. Once again, it is surely contemplated that the other party must satisfy the court on this issue. Thus that party may seek to show that in terms of the arbitration agreement the tribunal had no jurisdiction or exceeded its jurisdiction, or indeed that the tribunal lacked jurisdiction because of the invalidity of the arbitration agreement. It may also be appreciated that the court may order enforcement of only part of the award where that part is within the tribunal's jurisdiction and the remainder is not. This provision is based on s.66(3) of the 1996 Act.

Subsection (4)

Loss of right to raise jurisdictional objection: However, a party may not wait until the stage of enforcement before raising the issue of jurisdiction. Rule 76 articulates the general principle that a party who participates in an arbitration without raising an objection at the appropriate stage may not thereafter complain about the issue in question. Thus a party who goes through the arbitral process believing that the tribunal lacks jurisdiction or is exceeding its jurisdiction, but who does not articulate that belief, cannot then seek to resist enforcement on that basis. It is of course a different matter if the party has refused to engage in the proceedings, or if the party had no idea that the tribunal would exceed its jurisdiction until the appearance of the award.

Subsection (5)

Registration for execution: At common law if the arbitration agreement is registered for execution in the books of a sheriff court or the Books of Council and Session, then provided the parties agree (see *Baillie v Pollock* (1829) 7 S. 619), the award may also be so registered. This will then allow summary diligence to be done on the award. The Act removes the need for both parties to consent to registration, and instead allows either party to register an award for execution unless they have agreed that this should not happen. The Requirements of Writing Act 1995 s.6 indicates that it is not competent to register a document for execution unless the document has self-proving status. Is that provision impliedly disapplied with regard to arbitral awards by subs.(5)? Even if that is the case, it does not appear to be disapplied with regard to arbitration agreements.

The law regarding registration simply for preservation does not appear to be affected by subs.(5).

Subsection (6)

Scope of application: This makes it clear that enforcement may be granted in respect of awards made outside Scotland. As is pointed out below, most awards made outside the UK will fall within the New York Convention and will thus be subject to the enforcement regime established by ss.19–21. However, s.22 makes it possible for a party seeking enforcement of a Convention award to take advantage of any more favourable right of enforcement, so that a party to such an award who cannot obtain enforcement because one of the grounds for resisting enforcement under s.18 is established, might appear to be entitled to seek enforcement under s.12. Nonetheless, even though the only ground for refusing enforcement under s.12 is lack or excess of jurisdiction, the discretion which the court appears to have under s.12(1) might be exercised in favour of not enforcing an award if a ground for resisting enforcement under s.20 is established. One cannot imagine that a Scots court would be happy to enforce an award which, for example, had been set aside in the arbitral seat.

It might be added that foreign awards which are not Convention awards might hitherto have been enforced under arts 35–36 of the Model Law. The repeal of the Model Law precludes that possibility.

Would this provision allow for the enforcement under s.12 of an arbitral award which claimed to have no seat? Its wording would seem to allow for such a possibility.

Subsection (7)(a)

Other bases of enforcement: Neither this section or s.13 affect the right to seek enforcement of awards under the New York Convention, which are subject to their own regime (see ss.18–22). Almost every award made outside the UK will fall within the Convention, with Taiwanese awards being the most likely exception in practice. Section 66(4) of the 1996 Act adopts the same approach to awards subject to the Geneva Convention in terms of Pt II of the Arbitration Act 1950. Since the 2010 Act purports to repeal the 1950 Act, this reference is omitted. The question whether the Scottish Parliament can effectively repeal that Act is addressed above.

Subsection (7)(b)

Awards made elsewhere in the UK are previously subject to the Civil Jurisdiction and Judgments Act 1982 s.18 and Sch.6, while certain foreign awards are subject to specific statutory enforcement regimes.

Subsection (8)

The section applies irrespective of whether it is sought to enforce an award in the Court of Session or the sheriff court.

Court intervention in arbitrations

13.—(1) Legal proceedings are competent in respect of—
   (a) a tribunal's award, or

Arbitration (Scotland) Act 2010 (s.13)

    (b) any other act or omission by a tribunal when conducting an arbitration,
only as provided for in the Scottish Arbitration Rules (in so far as they apply to that arbitration) or in any other provision of this Act.
  (2) In particular, a tribunal's award is not subject to review or appeal in any legal proceedings except as provided for in Part 8 of the Scottish Arbitration Rules.
  (3) It is not competent for a party to raise the question of a tribunal's jurisdiction with the court except—
    (a) where objecting to an order being made under section 12, or
    (b) as provided for in the Scottish Arbitration Rules (see rules 21, 22 and 67).
  (4) Where the parties agree that the UNCITRAL Model Law is to apply to an arbitration, articles 6 and 11(2) to (5) of that Law are to have the force of law in Scotland in relation to that arbitration (as if article 6 specified the Court of Session and any sheriff court having jurisdiction).

DEFINITIONS
  "arbitration": ss.2(1), (2), 31(1)
  "court": s.31(1)
  "party": ss.2(1), 31(1), (2)
  "rules": ss.7, 31(1)
  "tribunal": ss.2(1), 31(1)

COMMENTARY
This is yet another provision which did not appear in the original Bill. There is nothing quite like it in the 1996 Act, but there are similarities with art.5 of the Model Law which baldly states: "In matters governed by this Law, no court shall intervene except where so provided by this Law."

Section 13 is clearly rather more detailed. Section 31 indicates that in this context, "court" means any court, thus guarding against the possibility that a court other than the sheriff court or Outer House might seek to assert some sort of jurisdiction over the arbitration.

Subsection (1)

By indicating that proceedings are only competent as contemplated by the Act as regards the award or anything done or not done by the tribunal, the possibility is left open that the court might have a role not contemplated by the Act in other areas, e.g. the creation of the arbitral tribunal or the relationship between the arbitrators and the parties. In the areas covered by subs.(1), by not employing a saving phrase such as, "in matters governed by this Law", the Act seemingly prevents the court from intervening even as regards matters not addressed by the Act. It is hoped that the understandable zeal to limit court intervention does not prevent the court from assisting should difficulties arise because the framers of the Act have inadvertently failed to provide for every eventuality. That being said, it appears to be the view of the Government that intervention and support are different things, so that, "common law powers of the court to support arbitration are preserved, and are not struck at by [this section]" (explanatory memorandum to stage 2 amendments).

Subsection (2)

  Court intervention regarding awards: The Act takes particular care to emphasise that the award may only be challenged in the way and on the grounds it prescribes. There is perhaps merit in making this clear since Lord President Hope suggested in *West v Secretary of State for Scotland*, 1992 S.L.T. 636 at 644 that a party might appeal to the inherent supervisory jurisdiction which the Court of Session exercises over all inferior tribunals:

> "... in order to insist on standards of rationality and fairness of procedure in addition to what might have been expressly required by the statute [concerned]".

The Court of Session has traditionally been reluctant to accept that the jurisdiction has been excluded, Lord Fraser asserting in *Brown v Hamilton District Council*, 1983 S.L.T. 397 at 414 that it exists, "even in cases where appeal is expressly excluded by statute". It is to be hoped that the jurisdiction has been effectively excluded by s.13 (see explanatory notes, para.42).

Subsection (3)

Court intervention regarding jurisdiction: The Act also stresses that the tribunal's jurisdiction cannot be challenged except as it contemplates: under r.21 when a party appeals against the tribunal's own jurisdictional ruling; under r.22 when the issue of jurisdiction has been referred to the Outer House; under r.67 when the award is challenged on the basis of lack of jurisdiction; and under s.12 when the award is sought to be enforced. It has been seen above, however, that a court may effectively determine an issue of jurisdiction when ruling on the validity of the arbitration agreement.

Subsection (4)

This subsection was added at stage 2. It was seen earlier how default (but not mandatory) rules could be overridden by the parties in terms of s.9(2), (3), and how s.9(4)(a)(ii) was amended to make it clear that one of the ways of doing so would be through the invocation of the Model Law. It was noted that one of the difficulties attendant upon the invocation of a foreign procedural law was that courts in the foreign jurisdiction would almost certainly decline to become involved in supporting the arbitration. Invoking the Model Law would create a slightly different problem in that, unless the Model Law is linked to a specific legal system, it is not clear which courts are being addressed by its provisions. A simple solution to that issue would be to assume that the jurisdiction of the ordinary civil courts is being invoked, and that view might be assisted if parties choose explicitly to invoke the version of the Model Law which was adopted in Scotland. This of course is premised on the assumption that the courts can be required to act as laid down in the Model Law, simply because the parties agree that they should. This assumption is probably sound, since it rather defeats the purpose of having default rules if the courts may decline to act as agreed by the parties on the basis that this is different to what is laid down in the original rule. However, this provision prefers to put such matters beyond doubt by indicating that if the parties do invoke the Model Law, then it is a rule of law that the court which under art.6 is to exercise functions under various other provisions is to be the Court of Session or any sheriff court having jurisdiction. This echoes the version of art.6 which was originally adopted in Scotland. The provisions under which the court is to act are arts 11(2)–(5), which deal with appointment of arbitrators and the role of the court where agreed procedures break down. Thus where the Model Law is invoked, if the parties cannot reach agreement as to the membership of the tribunal, appointment will not be made by an arbitral appointments referee under r.7, but by the court under art.11(4).

It may be added that art.6 also speaks of the court exercising functions under arts 13(3) (appeal against tribunal's decision on challenge), 14 (removal of arbitrator who fails to or cannot act), 16(3) (appeal against tribunal's decision on jurisdiction), 34(2) (challenging an award) and 35 and 36 (recognition and enforcement of awards). The reason why no reference is made to these provisions is that the matters concerned are all the subject of mandatory provisions of the Act so that there is no room for the Model Law to apply in such contexts.

Persons who take no part in arbitral proceedings

14.—(1) A person alleged to be a party to an arbitration but who takes no part in the arbitration may, by court proceedings, question—
  (a) whether there is a valid arbitration agreement (or, in the case of a statutory arbitration, whether the enactment providing for arbitration applies to the dispute),
  (b) whether the tribunal is properly constituted, or
  (c) what matters have been submitted to arbitration in accordance with the arbitration agreement,
and the court may determine such a question by making such declaration, or by granting such interdict or other remedy, as it thinks appropriate.

(2) Such a person has the same right as a party who participates in the arbitration to appeal against any award made in the arbitration under rule 67 or 68 (jurisdictional and serious irregularity appeals) and rule 71(2) does not apply to such an appeal.

DEFINITIONS
  "arbitration": ss.2(1), (2), 31(1)
  "arbitration agreement": ss.4, 31(1)
  "court": s.31(1)
  "dispute": ss.2(1), 31(1)
  "party": ss.2(1), 31(1), (2)
  "rules": ss.7, 31(1)
  "statutory arbitrations": ss.16(1), 31(1)
  "tribunal": ss.2(1), 31(1)

COMMENTARY
Again, this provision did not appear in the original version of the Bill. It is essentially a Scottish version of s.72 of the 1996 Act, and deals with a situation not properly addressed by the Model Law.

Subsection (1)

An individual who is sought to be made a party to arbitral proceedings, but who contests the tribunal's jurisdiction may obviously participate in those proceedings in the sense of challenging the tribunal or its jurisdiction under rr.10 or 20. However, the Act recognises a second possibility—that a party may simply refuse to have anything to do with the proceedings. Under art.25 of the Model Law such a course of action would mean that the party risked having an enforceable arbitral award made against him, but under the Act such a party has a right not to participate in the proceedings and instead may ask the court to consider the questions mentioned in s.14(1)(a)–(c). This position has the merit that a person who contends that the tribunal has no jurisdiction is not effectively forced to participate in arbitral proceedings in order to defend his position (see DAC Report, para.295).

Under s.72 of the 1996 Act it is for the applicant to specify the relief sought, but under s.14 the court may determine the appropriate relief. A declaration as to the correct legal position may be the usual remedy, but there may be situations where it may be appropriate for the court to interdict the arbitrator(s) and the other party from proceeding. Authorities under s.72 have indicated that the provision is only operative when the arbitration has its seat in England (see *Arab National Bank v El Sharif Saoud Bin Masoud Bin Haza'a El-Abdali* [2005] 1 Lloyd's Rep. 541), and that a party who reacts to an attempt to instigate arbitral proceedings by simply questioning their propriety is not to be regarded as taking part in those proceedings (*Caparo Group Ltd v Fagor Arrasate Sociedad Cooperative* [2000] A.D.R.L.J. 254). Of course, once a party reaches the stage of actually taking part in arbitral proceedings, then it is no longer possible for him to seek relief under s.14, and if he has questions relating to the jurisdiction or constitution of the tribunal, he should follow the procedures laid down by the Scottish Arbitration Rules. Finally, if the court rules against a party making a s.14 application, as where it confirms that the tribunal does indeed have the jurisdiction claimed of it, the party would be foolish to continue to refuse to participate in the proceedings, since the tribunal would be entitled to make an award on the basis of the evidence before it. (In *Hackwood v Areen Design Services Ltd* [2005] EWHC 2322 (TCC) the court rejected the absurd contention that a party who sought relief under s.72 was not entitled to take part in subsequent arbitral proceedings if the court ruled against him.)

Subsection (2)

If an award has actually been made, a party who has taken no part in arbitral proceedings retains the right to challenge it on the basis that tribunal lacked jurisdiction or that there was serious irregularity in the proceedings, e.g. that the tribunal was improperly constituted. In this situation the requirement under r.71(2) that a party must first exhaust any available arbitral appeal or review before coming to court does not apply. If the party's objection is jurisdictional, then rather than challenge the award, he might look to resist its enforcement under s.12.

Anonymity in legal proceedings

15.—(1) A party to any civil proceedings relating to an arbitration (other than proceedings under section 12) may apply to the court for an order prohibiting the disclosure of the identity of a party to the arbitration in any report of the proceedings.
(2) On such an application, the court must grant the order unless satisfied that disclosure—
    (a) is required—
        (i) for the proper performance of the discloser's public functions, or
        (ii) in order to enable any public body or office-holder to perform public functions properly,
    (b) can reasonably be considered as being needed to protect a party's lawful interests,
    (c) would be in the public interest, or
    (d) would be necessary in the interests of justice.
(3) The court's determination of an application for an order is final.

DEFINITIONS
"arbitration": ss.2(1), (2), 31(1)
"court": s.31(1)
"party": ss.2(1), 31(1), (2)

COMMENTARY

This provision did not appear in the original draft Bill, and the version which appears here is significantly different to that which was first laid before the Scottish Parliament. The latter version would have been unique, and would have prima facie outlawed any disclosure of the identity of a party to arbitral proceedings, even by the court itself, whether or not this was desired by either party. The most obvious sort of report might have been a law report, or perhaps a press report. However giving the word "report" its ordinary English meaning, any account of the proceedings, even if oral, even if given only to a single individual, would have been caught. The prohibition would then have been subject to a series of exceptions of rather uncertain content, so that it would have been difficult for any individual to ascertain precisely when he might have been entitled to disclose the identity of a party. A party who wrongly disclosed would then have been regarded as in breach of an obligation of confidence. How significant a deterrent that would have been is open to doubt. Anyone who sought to raise an action on that basis would have had to show loss before damages could be awarded, and it must surely be exceedingly rare that loss will follow simply from the disclosure of a party's identity. It is thus a matter of some relief that the provision was recast as it now appears, although certain reservations regarding it might still be expressed.

Subsection (1)

Instead of imposing a blanket prohibition, the provision now places the burden on a party to civil proceedings to apply to the court for an order prohibiting disclosure of the identity of a party to the proceedings in any report of the proceedings. It will presumably be reinforced by rules of court which ensure that all such proceedings are held in private. It might be imagined that a party would ordinarily apply for an order preventing the disclosure of his own identity, but he might equally seek to prevent the disclosure of the identity of the other party where such disclosure might effectively reveal his own identity. The order will prohibit disclosure of such identity in *any* report of the proceedings. The point regarding the meaning of this term made in the previous paragraph is equally valid here. However giving the word "report" its ordinary English meaning, if an order is made, any account of the proceedings, even if oral, even if given only to a single individual, would be prohibited. Perhaps, despite the words of the section, the courts will assert a discretion to restrict such orders to certain types of report.

Civil proceedings: The provision addresses only civil proceedings. Thus if an arbitration leads to criminal proceedings, e.g. as regards an attempt to bribe an arbitrator, such an order may not be sought. When do civil proceedings relate to an arbitration? Clearly that would be the case where a court is invited to exercise its powers under Pt 5 of the rules, or where an award is under challenge in terms of Pt 8, or where a court is invited to enforce an award under s.19, in this case whether or not it decides to enforce an award (but see *Associated Electric & Gas Insurance Services Ltd v European Reinsurance Co of Zurich* [2003] 1 All E.R. (Comm) 253 PC; *Television New Zealand Ltd v Langley Productions Ltd* [2000] N.Z.L.R. 250). The same must presumably be true where the court is involved in appointing an arbitrator under r.7 or removing an arbitrator under r.12, or dismissing the tribunal under r.13, or in deciding on a jurisdictional objection under r.21— even if it decides that the tribunal does not have jurisdiction. But suppose a court has to make a decision under r.16 on an arbitrator's entitlements or liabilities when his tenure ends, or a party seeks to sue an arbitrator in respect of something done in bad faith. Do such proceedings fall within s.15? It must be assumed that they do, since the object is the protection of the identity of the parties to the arbitration. What if a party responds to an action being raised against him by pleading the existence of an arbitration agreement and asking that the proceedings be sisted? The same argument as above must presumably apply. But suppose the court refuses a sist because it finds that there is no arbitration agreement, or that the agreement is incapable of being performed. It could be said that there is no arbitration in such cases so that s.15 cannot apply. In support of that view, it might be said that parties to litigation cannot normally claim anonymity and a party should not be able to throw a cloak of anonymity over the proceedings simply by pleading a non-existent arbitration agreement. The counter argument is that the policy of s.15 is best served by granting anonymity in any proceedings which involve arbitration in any way. It may be added that under s.31(1), "court", in this context means any court.

It will be noted that anonymity may not be sought where an application is made to enforce an award under s.10. The rationale for this exclusion articulated in the explanatory notes to stage 2 amendments is that, "a party who is not complying with an arbitral award should not be able to hide behind the confidentiality rule". The conflation of anonymity and confidentiality is discussed below, but the more immediate point is that it may not only be the party against whom enforcement is sought who might seek anonymity and the provision would prevent either party making an application. The Government also seems to assume that the party against whom enforcement is sought will invariably be acting reprehensibly, whereas it may be that he has a cast-iron defence against enforcement. It is also curious that this exclusion applies where enforcement is sought under this section but not when enforcement is sought under ss.19–21.

There is an obvious relationship between this provision and the statutory obligation of confidentiality created by r.26. The policy memorandum (para.93) indeed seems to regard anonymity as an aspect of confidentiality, noting that matters in dispute may be commercially sensitive. However, while confidentiality and anonymity are obviously closely related, they are not the same thing, and it is possible for a report to reveal commercially sensitive information without compromising anonymity. Indeed, the explanatory notes (para.46), while also speaking of confidentiality, state that s.13, "only covers the parties' identities and not the other contents of any court judgment".

If it is otherwise learned that certain persons are involved in arbitral proceedings, then that may be reported. This seems slightly strange given that it is the fact that the parties are arbitrating rather than the fact that they are litigating which lies at the heart of s.15. There may have been merit in dealing with this matter through the extension of the obligation under r.26. This would have had the advantage that the concentration would have been on confidential information rather than the identity of the parties, while the obligation need not have been confined to court proceedings.

It is noteworthy that in England such matters are dealt with via rules of court. The presumption is that applications to determine a preliminary point of law or to set aside an award on the basis of error of law will be heard in public, while all other arbitration claims will be heard in private, although the court has discretion to hold any hearing in public or private and thus may be persuaded by either party to hold a hearing in private (CPR r.62.10). Any judgment is then presumed to be a public document, although the English courts have asserted an inherent power to decline to publish, albeit that they will only exercise that power if a party makes a persuasive case against publication. They have made it clear that non-publication is very much the exception, and will only be assented to where publication will reveal sensitive information (see Mance L.J. in *Department of Economics Policy and Development of the City of Moscow v Bankers Trust Co* [2005] Q.B. 207 at [38]). If anyone should thereafter reveal such sensitive information, the matter can be dealt with by the well developed English common law rules regarding confidentiality. It might be suggested that the English approach is appropriately sensible, practical and flexible and might have afforded a preferable template for Scotland to follow.

Subsection (2)

Exceptions: At stage 2 the court, in deciding whether to grant the order, was required to have regard to a variety of considerations which might favour disclosure, but the explanatory notes to stage 2 amendments stated that there was, "a presumption in favour of granting the application". It can be seen that the provision now goes further and obliges the court to make the order unless the court is satisfied that disclosure meets any one of a number of exceptions. Is it is for the party seeking disclosure (who may not be a party to the arbitration) to satisfy the court regarding such matters? Perhaps not, since there may not be a party seeking disclosure at that point.

At first glance it is difficult to discern what the legislature has in mind in relation to certain of these exceptions. The answer is perhaps that it has nothing particular in mind at all, since in line with the Act's tendency to conflate anonymity and confidentiality, these exceptions have been chosen in order to align the provision as far as possible with the exceptions to the obligation of confidentiality under r.26. Thus it is sometimes difficult to guess at their scope in this context

Subsection (2)(a)

Public functions: Leading on from what is said immediately above, this is exactly the sort of exception which might make sense in the context of confidentiality, but is rather opaque in meaning in the present context. Indeed, it arguably does not make sense in the context of confidentiality either. The rule as regards confidentiality essentially attempts to codify English case law on the issue. The exception in question appears to address situations where there is a public duty to disclose. This is drawn from the attempts by Potter L.J. in *Ali Shipping Corp v Shipyard Trogir* [1998] 2 All E.R. 136 at 147–148 to devise a list of exceptions based on the exceptions to the banker's duty of confidentiality elaborated by Bankes L.J. in *Tournier v National Provincial and Union Bank of England* [1924] 1 K.B. 461 at 472–473, an approach which has been the subject of criticism by Lord Hobhouse in *Associated Electric and Gas Insurance Services Ltd v European Reinsurance Company of Zurich* [2003] 1 W.L.R. 1041 at [20]. It is clear how the exception operates in a banking context, less clear as regards confidentiality in an arbitral context, while it is difficult to think of an example in the context of anonymity.

Subsection (2)(b)

Lawful interests: When might disclosure of a party's identity in a report be necessary in order to protect the discloser's lawful interests? It is much easier to think of examples of situations where this exception might apply in the context of confidentiality. However, one example which might operate in the current context is where the fact that a company has succeeded in an arbitration against a named party has to be revealed in order to defend its share price or reassure its shareholders.

Subsection (2)(c)

Public interest: The English courts have been unclear whether there is a public interest exception to the principle of confidentiality which is separate from the interests of justice exception (compare Potter L.J. in *Ali Shipping Corp v Shipyard Trogir* [1998] 2 All E.R. 136 at 148 with Lawrence Collins L.J. and Carnwath L.J in *Emmott v Michael Wilson & Partners Ltd* [2008] 1 Lloyd's Rep. 616 at [99], [100], [134]), although such an exception has been mooted by the Australian courts (see *Esso Australia Resources v Plowman* (1995) 128 A.L.R. 391; *Commonwealth of Australia v Cockatoo Dockyard Pty Ltd* (1995) 36 N.S.W.L.R. 662). But when might disclosure of a party's identity be in the public interest? It might perhaps be in the public interest to reveal that a party which has failed in a challenge of an award of £500 million against it is a publicly quoted construction company, even if such revelation is very damaging to the company.

Subsection (2)(d)

Interests of justice: Again there are examples where it is clearly in the interests of justice that the principle of confidentiality should not be maintained, such as where a witness gives evidence which is materially different to that which he gave in an earlier arbitration (see Mance J. in *London and Leeds Estates Ltd v Paribas Ltd (No.2)* [1995] 1 E.G.L.R. 102 at 109). But in what circumstances may disclosure of a party's identity be in the interests of justice?

Subsection (3)

The ruling of the court on this matter is not subject to appeal. The court in this context means any court rather than merely the sheriff court or Outer House—see s.31(1). Presumably, this means that a party would be expected to apply to the appropriate court. Thus if the matter is the subject of proceedings before the Inner House, the application should be made to that court.

Statutory arbitration

Statutory arbitration: special provisions

16.—(1) "Statutory arbitration" is arbitration pursuant to an enactment which provides for a dispute to be submitted to arbitration.

(2) References in the Scottish Arbitration Rules (or in any other provision of this Act) to an arbitration agreement are, in the case of a statutory arbitration, references to the enactment which provides for a dispute to be resolved by arbitration.

(3) None of the Scottish Arbitration Rules (or other provisions of this Act) apply to a statutory arbitration if or to the extent that they are

excluded by, or are inconsistent with, any provision made by virtue of any other enactment relating to the arbitration.

(4) Every statutory arbitration is to be taken to be seated in Scotland.

(5) The following rules do not apply in relation to statutory arbitration—
    rule 43 (extension of time limits)
    rule 71(9) (power to declare provision of arbitration agreement void)
    rule 80 (death of party)

(6) Despite rule 40, parties to a statutory arbitration may not agree to—
  (a) consolidate the arbitration with another arbitration,
  (b) hold concurrent hearings, or
  (c) authorise the tribunal to order such consolidation or the holding of concurrent hearings,

unless the arbitrations or hearings are to be conducted under the same enactment.

DEFINITIONS
    "arbitration": ss.2(1), (2), 31(1)
    "arbitration agreement": ss.4, 31(1)
    "dispute": ss.2(1), 31(1)
    "party": ss.2(1), 31(1), (2)
    "rules": ss.7, 31(1)
    "seated in Scotland": ss.2, 31(1)
    "tribunal": ss.2(1), 31(1)

COMMENTARY

The Act looks to extend its provisions to statutory arbitrations where those provisions might appropriately apply to such arbitrations. Much the same ground is covered by ss.94–97 of the 1996 Act (previously by s.31 of the 1950 Act).

Subsection (1)

A wide variety of statutes indicate that certain types of dispute should be determined via arbitration. These arbitrations are thus statutory arbitrations. Section 94(3) of the 1996 Act makes it clear that an enactment embraces subordinate legislation, while the 2010 Act does not. Section 94(1) indicates that the principle applies to both existing and future enactments, and that must surely be the effect of s.16 even though the 2010 Act does not make this explicit.

Subsection (2)

The Act is clearly designed to apply to consensual arbitrations. Accordingly, in order to ensure that the Act (including the rules) applies to statutory arbitrations, it is necessary to treat the relevant statute as if it were an arbitration agreement. Indeed, while s.95(1) of the 1996 Act deems the statute to be such an agreement and the parties to any arbitration under the statute to be parties to that agreement, s.16(2) deals with the issue more simply.

Subsection (3)

This echoes s.94(2) of the 1996 Act, save that s.94(2) does not include the phrase, "relating to the arbitration". It is not thought that the difference is significant, since if any statutory provision seems to embrace a particular form of statutory arbitration it should be taken to apply to it, whether or not the provision mentions that type of arbitration or even mentions arbitration at all. What subs.(3) has in mind is that certain types of statutory arbitration are subject to their own statutory codes which would either partly or wholly embrace the matters dealt with by the rules. The provisions specific to these types of arbitration will continue to apply to them rather than the rules.

Subsection (4)

The key to the application of the Act is that Scotland is the seat of the arbitration. Like s.95(2) of the 1996 Act, this provision ensures that all statutory arbitration is to be regarded as seated in Scotland, so that it is not possible for the parties to argue that, because they have agreed that the seat is elsewhere, the provisions of the Act do not apply. The explanatory notes (para.49), however, point out that this, "is subject to conflict of law rules (for instance on the interaction with the equivalent section 95(2) of the Arbitration Act 1996 for the other jurisdictions of the UK)." It is submitted that where the statute concerned applies exclusively within Scotland then any agreement that the arbitration should be held outside the jurisdiction should be regarded as void. Many statutes, of course, apply throughout Great Britain or the UK, so that the issue might arise as to whether the 1996 Act or 2010 Act applies. Often that issue will be determined by the location of the subject matter of the dispute (see, e.g. Merchant Shipping Act 1995 ss.95–97), while other statutes themselves specify the criteria which will determine whether arbitration is to be Scottish (see, e.g. Industry Act 1975 Sch.3 para.18).

Subsection (5)

Rule 43, like s.79 of the 1996 Act, allows any party to apply to the court to extend contractually agreed time limits, while r.80, like s.8 of the 1996 Act, provides that the arbitration agreement is not discharged by the death of a party. Like s.97 of the 1996 Act, subs.(5) disapplies these rules in relation to statutory arbitration, presumably because they only make sense when there is an actual rather than deemed agreement. In the same way, r.71(9), which has no counterpart in the 1996 Act, and which provides for the Outer House when setting aside an award to render void any provision in arbitration agreement which would prevent the resolution of the dispute by legal proceedings, is also disapplied.

Subsection (6)

Like s.96(3) of the 1996 Act, this makes it clear that in the statutory context the power to agree to the consolidation of other proceedings or to the holding of concurrent hearings only applies to proceedings held under the same enactment, thus avoiding the potential difficulties of the consolidation of proceedings held under inconsistent statutory codes or indeed of the consolidation of statutory and consensual arbitrations.

Power to adapt enactments providing for statutory arbitration

17. Ministers may by order—
  (a) modify any of the Scottish Arbitration Rules, or any other provisions of this Act, in so far as they apply to statutory arbitrations (or to particular statutory arbitrations),

(b) make such modifications of enactments which provide for disputes to be submitted to arbitration as they consider appropriate in consequence of, or in order to give full effect to, any of the Scottish Arbitration Rules or any other provisions of this Act.

DEFINITIONS
"arbitration": ss.2(1), (2), 31(1)
"dispute": ss.2(1), 31(1)
"Ministers": s.31(1)
"party": ss.2(1), 31(1), (2)
"rules": ss.7, 31(1)
"statutory arbitrations": ss.16(1), 31(1)

COMMENTARY

Section (a)

This provision allowing the modification of any provision of the Act in relation to statutory arbitrations or particular statutory arbitrations, is the equivalent of s.98(1) of the 1996 Act, albeit that the latter provision also confers power to exclude any provision of that Act in relation to statutory arbitrations. No orders have as yet been made under the 1996 Act.

Section (b)

This power to modify other enactments to give full effect to the 2010 Act is not similar to anything in the 1996 Act, and seems rather bold. It is of course beyond the competence of the Scottish Parliament to empower Ministers to modify an enactment of the UK Parliament.

Recognition and enforcement of New York Convention awards

COMMENTARY

In 1975 the UK became a party to the 1958 New York Convention for the Recognition and Enforcement of Foreign Arbitral Awards, a convention created by the United Nations, prompted by the ICC, which Convention ensures the international recognition of arbitration agreements (see s.10 above) and more importantly the recognition and enforcement in contracting states of arbitral awards made in other states. It originally gave effect to the Convention within the UK via the Arbitration Act 1975. The Arbitration Act 1996 repealed the 1975 Act as regards England and re-enacted its provisions in ss.100–104. Meanwhile the 1975 Act remained in force in Scotland. The 2010 Act now follows the example of the 1996 Act by repealing the 1975 Act as regards Scotland and re-enacting its provisions with certain modifications in ss.18–22. This is obviously sensible as it is important to have as many as possible of the statutory provisions bearing on arbitration contained within a single, comprehensive arbitration statute. Sections 18–22 are rather different to the rest of the Act in that they do not address arbitral proceedings where Scotland is the seat of the arbitration, but rather the recognition and/or enforcement in Scotland of arbitral awards made outwith the UK. How often such awards require to be recognised or enforced in Scotland is not known, but the dearth of case law on the subject might tend to suggest that it is not a common occurrence. While ss.18 and 19 speak of the New York Convention, one must refer to the definition section, s.31(1), to ascertain that it is indeed the above Convention which is contemplated—contrast s.100(4) of the 1996 Act.

New York Convention awards

18.—(1) A "Convention award" is an award made in pursuance of a written arbitration agreement in the territory of a state (other than the United Kingdom) which is a party to the New York Convention.

(2) An award is to be treated for the purposes of this section as having been made at the seat of the arbitration.

(3) A declaration by Her Majesty by Order in Council that a state is a party to the Convention (or is a party in respect of any territory) is conclusive evidence of that fact.

DEFINITIONS
"arbitration agreement": ss.4, 31(1)
"New York Convention": s.31(1)

COMMENTARY

Subsection (1)

Convention awards: Sections 18–21 provide for the recognition and enforcement in Scotland of arbitral awards made in other states which are parties to the Convention—hence the idea of a "Convention award". This does not mean that foreign awards which are not Convention awards may not be enforced in Scotland—see s.22—but they cannot be enforced under the regime created by ss.18–21. This restriction, known as the reciprocity reservation, is sanctioned by art.I(3) of the Convention, and a large number of contracting states have adopted it. Almost 150 states are parties to the Convention, including practically every significant trading nation. Article I(3) also allows contracting states to apply the Convention only to legal relationships which are considered commercial—the commercial reservation. While some 45 states have adopted this reservation, the UK is not among them. It seems clear that while under the law of certain states procedural and jurisdictional rulings and the like may take the form of awards (see, e.g. s.30 of the 1996 Act), the Convention is aimed at the recognition and enforcement of final awards in the sense of an award which deals conclusively with a substantive issue between the parties. Thus part awards can be enforced under the Convention (see *Resort Condominiums International Inc v Bolwell* (1994) XX YCA 628; *Nigerian National Petroleum Corp v IPCO (Nigeria) Ltd* [2008] EWCA Civ 1157).

In pursuance of a written arbitration agreement: It is also made clear that Convention awards can only be made, "in pursuance of a written arbitration agreement". This echoes s.102(2)(a) of the 1996 Act. However, while an agreement in writing is particularly widely defined by s.5 of the 1996 Act, following the example of art.7(2) of the Model Law, the 2010 Act does not offer any definition. For that one must refer to the Scotland Act 1998 (Transitory and Transitional Provisions) (Publication and Interpretation etc. of Acts of the Scottish Parliament) Order 1999 (SI 1999/1379), by virtue of para.6(2) and Sch.2 of which, "writing includes any means of representing or reproducing words in a visible form". Although this is not how writing is defined in art.II(2) of the Convention, it is no doubt sufficiently widely defined to accord with Convention obligations. Nonetheless, the definition is not as wide as s.5 of the 1996 Act under which there is a written arbitration agreement where the agreement is made by an exchange of communications in writing, where it is evidenced in writing, where the parties agree otherwise than in writing to an agreement in writing, e.g. an oral agreement to a standard form contract which contains an arbitration clause, and where there is an exchange of submissions in legal or arbitral proceedings where the existence of a non-written arbitration agreement is alleged by one party and not denied by the other. It is also provided that the idea of writing includes an agreement being recorded by any means. Even if a wide, purposive interpretation is given to the idea of a written arbitration agreement under the 2010 Act, it can hardly embrace all of the above situations. This might lead to the suspect result that, while the UK is a party to the Convention, certain awards might be enforced in England which are not enforceable in Scotland or at least not enforceable under the regime laid down by s.18.

Subsection (2)

Award made at seat of arbitration: This follows the line of s.100(2)(b) of the 1996 Act in making it clear that an award is to be regarded as made at the seat of the arbitration. This negates the effect of the remarkable decision of the House of Lords in *Hiscox v Outhwaite* [1992] 1 A.C. 562 that an award in an arbitration between two English parties, conducted in London by an English arbitrator under English substantive and procedural law, was to be treated as a French award because the arbitrator indicated that he had signed it while in Paris. The question of where an arbitrator (or the last arbitrator to sign) happens to be when he signs the award is now irrelevant—see also the discussion of r.52. The idea of the seat of the arbitration appears in s.3 which determines when Scotland is to be treated as the seat of the arbitration, and it can be inferred from that that the seat is the juridical location of the arbitration, which may not be the same as its physical location. However, there is nothing in the 2010 Act equivalent to s.3 of the 1996 Act actually defining that concept and indicating how the seat is to be determined.

Subsection (3)

This, like s.100(3) of the 1996 Act, represents an advance on s.7(2) of the 1975 Act by recognising the possibility, contemplated by art.IX of the Convention, that a state may be a party to the Convention in respect of a specified territory. This is probably of little practical moment, as no state is a party to the Convention only in respect of a specified territory. That being said, there are several examples of territories which are parties to the Convention separately from the states of which they form part, e.g. Hong Kong.

Recognition and enforcement of New York Convention awards

19.—(1) A Convention award is to be recognised as binding on the persons as between whom it was made (and may accordingly be relied on by those persons in any legal proceedings in Scotland).

(2) The court may order that a Convention award may be enforced as if it were an extract registered decree bearing a warrant for execution granted by the court.

DEFINITIONS
 "Convention award": ss.16, 31(1)
 "court": s.31(1)

COMMENTARY

Subsection (1)

Recognition: This provides for the recognition of a Convention award. It derives from s.3(2) of the 1975 Act, which used to say that the award could be, "relied on ... by way of defence, set off or otherwise in any legal proceedings" in the UK. Section 101(1) of the 1996 Act is still in similar terms. Even though s.19(1) is not in these terms, the wider wording gives an indication of what its effect might be. Thus if litigation is sought to be commenced in Scotland, the award can be used to support a plea of res judicata. In one case decided in England it was held that an award might be recognised as barring litigation, but not be enforced, since appeal proceedings remained open in the place where the award was made (*Svenska Petroleum Exploration AB v Republic of Lithuania* [2005] 1 Lloyd's Rep. 515). The award may also justify a plea of compensation, so that if one party is suing the other for, say £1 million, the respondent can point out that he is due £500,000 from the other under an arbitral award. It has also been held in England that it is possible to seek a declaration that an award is binding (*Irvani v Irvani* [2000] 1 Lloyd's Rep. 412).

Subsection (2)

Enforcement: The same procedure as applies under s.12(1) to the enforcement of an award made in Scotland is made available to enforce a Convention award. The term "may" is employed, since a party may be able to establish a defence to enforcement under s.20. It should also be remembered that the award binds only the parties between whom it was made. Thus it is not possible to enforce it against a person alleged to be the principal of the other party (*Norsk Hydro ASA v State Property Fund of Ukraine* [2002] EWHC 2120 (Admin)). Any such issue of agency, representation or joinder should be dealt with in the arbitral proceedings rather than the stage of enforcement. Problems can exist where individuals have been joined as parties, due to the requirement that a copy of the arbitration agreement is supplied—see the commentary to s.21(1)(b) below. In *IPCO (Nigeria) Ltd v Nigerian National Petroleum Corp (No.2)* [2009] 1 Lloyd's Rep. 89 CA the court granted partial enforcement where the award was being contested in the seat, but certain sums were undoubtedly due to the claimant.

Refusal of recognition or enforcement

20.—(1) Recognition or enforcement of a Convention award may be refused only in accordance with this section.

(2) Recognition or enforcement of a Convention award may be refused if the person against whom it is invoked proves—
    (a) that a party was under some incapacity under the law applicable to the party,
    (b) that the arbitration agreement was invalid under the law which the parties agree should govern it (or, failing any indication of that law, under the law of the country where the award was made),
    (c) that the person—
        (i) was not given proper notice of the arbitral process or of the appointment of the tribunal, or
        (ii) was otherwise unable to present the person's case,
    (d) that the tribunal was constituted, or the arbitration was conducted, otherwise than in accordance with—
        (i) the agreement of the parties, or

(ii) failing such agreement, the law of the country where the arbitration took place.

(3) Recognition or enforcement of a Convention award may also be refused if the person against whom it is invoked proves that the award—
   (a) deals with a dispute not contemplated by or not falling within the submission to arbitration,
   (b) contains decisions on matters beyond the scope of that submission,
   (c) is not yet binding on the person, or
   (d) has been set aside or suspended by a competent authority.

(4) Recognition or enforcement of a Convention award may also be refused if—
   (a) the award relates to a matter which is not capable of being settled by arbitration, or
   (b) to do so would be contrary to public policy.

(5) A Convention award containing decisions on matters not submitted to arbitration may be recognised or enforced to the extent that it contains decisions on matters which were so submitted which are separable from decisions on matters not so submitted.

(6) The court before which a Convention award is sought to be relied on may, if an application for the setting aside or suspension of the award is made to a competent authority—
   (a) sist the decision on recognition or enforcement of the award,
   (b) on the application of the party claiming recognition or enforcement, order the other party to give suitable security.

(7) In this section "competent authority" means a person who has authority to set aside or suspend the Convention award concerned in the country in which (or under the law of which) the Convention award concerned was made.

DEFINITIONS
   "arbitration": ss.2(1), (2), 31(1)
   "arbitration agreement": ss.4, 31(1)
   "Convention award": ss.18, 31(1)
   "court": s.31(1)
   "dispute": ss.2(1), 31(1)
   "party": ss.2(1), 31(1), (2)
   "tribunal": ss.2(1), 31(1)

COMMENTARY
A court faced with a request for recognition or enforcement is not bound to grant it in all cases. There are situations where it will be appropriate to decline recognition or enforcement and these are addressed by s.20, which is an updated version of s.5 of the 1975 Act, which in turn is based on arts V and VI of the Convention (see also s.103 of the 1996 Act). The grounds on which recognition or enforcement may be denied fall into two categories. The first category, which appears in subss.(2) and (3), consists of grounds which have to be established by the party resisting recognition or enforcement. It is thus clear that that party bears the burden of proof (see *Corporacion Transnacional de Inversiones SA de CV v STET International SpA* (2000) O.R. 414), by contrast to the position taken by the Geneva Convention. The second category, which appears in subs.(4), consists of two grounds which merely have to be seen by the court to exist. Thus even if a party seems to have no defence to an application to enforce an award, or if a tendered defence under subss.(2) or (3) is found to have no substance, should the court find, for example, that the award deals with a matter which

may not be arbitrated under the law of Scotland, then it will almost certainly refuse enforcement, whether or not the issue is raised by any party.

The primary aim of the Convention is to ensure the enforcement of arbitral awards, rather than to find grounds upon which enforcement may be denied. It is acknowledged to have a pro-enforcement bias (see Gross J. in *IPCO (Nigeria) Ltd v Nigerian National Petroleum Corp* [2005] 2 Lloyd's Rep. 326 at 328). Thus it can be seen that the grounds below afford a basis on which the recognition or enforcement of an award "may" be denied, allowing for the possibility that an award might yet be enforced even if a ground is made out. As Kaplan J. notes in the Hong Kong Supreme Court in *China Nanhai Oil Joint Service Corp v Gee Tai Holdings Ltd* [1995] A.D.R.L.J. 127 at 132:

> "Even if a ground of opposition is proved, there is still a residual discretion left in the enforcing court to enforce nonetheless. This shows that the grounds of opposition are not to be inflexibly applied. The residual discretion enables the enforcing court to achieve a just result in all the circumstances."

Thus, as will be seen below, examples abound of situations where the award has been enforced despite the establishing of a seeming defence. This might arise where, for example, although a ground might technically exist, it is not regarded as having sufficient substance to prevent enforcement. It also seems to be recognised that the doctrine of personal bar or estoppel may be invoked to prevent a party relying on a ground of which he must have been aware throughout most of the arbitral proceedings, but which he chose not to raise before the stage of enforcement. So Kaplan J. observes in *China Nanhai Oil* [1995] A.D.R.L.J. 127 (at 131):

> "If the doctrine of estoppel can apply to arguments of the written form of the arbitration agreement ... then I fail to see why it cannot also apply to the grounds ... in Article V. It strikes me as quite unfair for a party to appreciate that there might be something wrong with the composition of the tribunal yet not to make any formal submission whatsoever to the tribunal about its own jurisdiction ... and then to proceed to fight the case on its merits and then two years after the award to attempt to nullify the whole proceedings".

In similar fashion courts are often reluctant to deny enforcement on the basis of an issue which might have been raised before the courts of the seat, but which was not (see *Minmetals Germany GmbH v Ferco Steel Ltd* [1999] 1 All E.R. (Comm) 315; *Svenska Petroleum AB v Lithuania* [2005] 1 Lloyd's Rep. 515). Thus Longmore J. opines in *China Agribusiness Development Corp v Balli Trading* [1998] 2 Lloyd's Rep. 76 at 80 (see also *Karaha Bodas Co LLC v Perusahaan Pertambangan Minyak Dan Gas Bumi Negara-Pertamina* (2003) XXVIII YCA 752):

> "A party who, only at the door of the enforcing court, dreams up a reason for suggesting that a Convention award should not be enforced is unlikely to have the Court's sympathy exercised in his favour."

It should however be mentioned that the English Court of Appeal has in recent years made it plain that the discretion to enforce despite a ground being made out should not be exercised lightly, so that if a party establishes substantial grounds of objection the court should decline to enforce the award unless estoppel appears to have arisen (see *Yukos Oil Ltd v Dardana Ltd* [2002] 2 Lloyd's Rep. 326; *Kanoria v Guinness* [2006] 1 Lloyd's Rep. 701). Moreover the above-mentioned approach tends only to be adopted in relation to the grounds mentioned in subss.(2) and (3), which largely deal with issues which are particular to the parties or the arbitral proceedings in question. The grounds which appear in sub.(4) are entirely more fundamental, lying at the heart of Scots law. Thus it is practically inconceivable that a Scots court would, for example, enforce an award on an issue which may not be arbitrated under the law of Scotland.

Subsection (1)

Exclusive grounds for refusing recognition or enforcement: It seems fairly clear from the text of art.V of the Convention that recognition or enforcement may only be refused on the basis of the grounds laid down by art.V, and that contracting states may not seek to add to these. This principle has also been widely accepted in Convention jurisprudence (see e.g. *Parsons & Whittemore Overseas Co Inc Societe Generale de l'Industrie du Papier (RAKTA)*, 508 F.2d 969 (2nd Cir. 1974); *Karaha Bodas Co LLC v Perusahaan Pertambangan Minyak Dan Gas Bumi Negara-Pertamina* (2003) XXVIII YCA 752). However, from time to time a court will decide that the grounds laid down by art.V are not exclusive, as where the US second circuit in *Monegasque de Reassurance SAM v NAK Naftogart of Ukraine*, 311 F.3d 488 (2002) refused to enforce a Russian award on the basis of *forum non conveniens*. It is thus useful to establish that recognition or enforcement may only be refused as contemplated by s.20, even if this leads to peculiar results, such as a court being obliged to hold that it has no discretion to decline to enforce an award against a party who has no assets in the UK (*Rosseel NV v Oriental Commercial Shipping Co Ltd* [1991] 2 Lloyd's Rep. 625). Both s.5(1) of the 1975 Act, which this provision replaces, and s.103(1) of the 1996 Act are in slightly different terms, indicating that enforcement, "of a Convention award shall not be refused except in the cases mentioned in this section". However, the effect must presumably be identical. It might also be added that as a practical matter enforcement might not be granted where it is not clear what the award has ordered (see *Tongyuan (USA) International Trading Group v Uni-Clan Ltd* (2001) XXVI YCA 886).

Subsection (2)

Defences to recognition or enforcement: This subsection allows the court to refuse recognition or enforcement if the party resisting recognition or enforcement can establish any one or more of a number of grounds.

Subsection (2)(a)

Incapacity: This re-enacts in slightly different terms s.5(2)(a) of the 1975 Act (see also s.103(2)(a) of the 1996 Act). Article V(1)(a) of the Convention speaks of the parties to the arbitration agreement being, "under the law applicable to them, under some incapacity", but there is no doubt that the wording of the 2010 Act translates the intended meaning more accurately, since it was certainly not envisaged that *both* parties had to lack capacity before the provision was triggered, while the capacity of each party may be governed by a different law.

What is the law which governs the capacity of a party? The wording of art.V(1)(a) was criticised by the framers of the Model Law, since:

"... they appeared to contain a conflict of law rule which in fact was either incomplete or misleading in that the rule might be understood as referring to the law of the nationality, domicile or residence of the parties" (*Report of the UNCITRAL on the work of its eighteenth session*, UN A/40/17, para.280).

Yet the framers of the Model Law offered no practical solution to this problem, and nor does the current provision. It is thus necessary to have reference to Scots conflict of law rules to determine the issue, and these would point to capacity being determined by the law governing the contract between the parties (*McFeetridge v Stewart & Lloyds*, 1913 S.C. 773; but see the thinking of the drafters of the Convention on this issue at *Summary Record of the 24th meeting of the United Nations Conference on International Commercial Arbitration*, UN E/CONF.26/SR.24, para.7).

However, difficult issues may arise in relation to corporate entities and public bodies, the capacity of which might be regarded as determined by the law of the state in which they were incorporated or created. Thus there have been cases where an award has been refused enforcement because the act of entering into the agreement was ultra vires a corporate party (compare the approaches of the German Supreme Court in (1999) XXIV YCA 928; and the Bermuda Court of Appeal in *Sojuzneftexport v Joc Oil Ltd* (1990) XV YCA 384), or because such a party was not properly incorporated (see *Sokofl Star Shipping Co Inc v GPVO Technopromexport* (1998) XXIII YCA 742 Moscow District Court). A number of awards have also been denied enforcement on this ground on the basis that the individual seeking to bind the corporation to the arbitration agreement lacked the power or authority to do so (see, e.g. the Italian Supreme Court in *Dalmine SpA v M & M Sheet Metal Forming Machinery* (1999) XXIV YCA 709). It is suggested that this is a matter affecting the validity of the arbitration agreement or the jurisdiction of the tribunal and not an issue of capacity at all, and this is the view of the Cour de Cassation in *Tresor Public v Galakis*, 1966 *Revue de l'Arbitrage* 99. There is no UK authority on the issue, but then there is no UK authority on any aspect of art.V(1)(a).

As far as public bodies are concerned, it is sometimes the case that such a body will claim that it has no capacity to arbitrate under the law of the state which created it, or that such capacity is dependent on receiving certain official approval or permission, which has not been obtained in the case in question. Certain states (e.g. Spain, Switzerland) have enacted legislation preventing such bodies relying on their own law to seek to evade their obligations under arbitral awards where they freely agreed to arbitrate in the first place, but the UK is not among them. Nonetheless, certain courts have taken the view that by agreeing to arbitrate such bodies have impliedly waived the right to rely on the issue of capacity. Thus the Italian Supreme Court opines in *Societe Arabe des Engrais Phosphates v Gemanco Srl* (1997) XXII YCA 737 at 742:

> "Under the law applicable to international commercial arbitration, which necessarily governs the arbitration clause in the present case, legal persons of public law may ... undoubtedly agree to arbitration, independent of domestic prohibitions, by expressing their consent."

And other courts held that while such restrictions may be pleaded in domestic arbitrations, they may not be insisted upon to prevent the enforcement of awards in international arbitration (see the decision of a Tunisian court in *Societe Tunisienne d'Electricitee et de Gaz v Societe Entrepose* (1978) III YCA 283; and the Paris Court of Appeal in *Ministere Tunisien de l'Equipment v Bec Freres* (1997) XXII YCA 682). The alternative approach is that the failure to follow the steps dictated by law leads to a fundamental incapacity preventing the enforcement of the award. Such was the view taken by a Syrian court in *Fougerolle SA v Syrian Ministry of Defence* (1995) XX YCA 515 in denying enforcement of an award when the Ministry of Defence had entered into an arbitration agreement without obtaining the requisite administrative approval, although the ultimate basis for refusing enforcement in that case was contravention of public policy. It is submitted that this approach should not be preferred by the Scots courts should the issue ever arise.

Although this is perhaps not, strictly speaking, an issue of capacity, it may be noted that state entities may sometimes seek to invoke the doctrine of state or sovereign immunity to resist enforcement of arbitral awards. This has sometimes been done successfully (e.g. *Egypt v SPP Ltd* (1985) X YCA 113), while on other occasions courts have taken the view that an arbitration agreement operates as a waiver of immunity (e.g. *American Oil Co v Libya* (1981) 20 I.L.M. 893). In Scotland the position is governed by State Immunity Act 1978 s.9(1) which indicates that a state which agrees to arbitrate is not immune as respects proceedings in the courts of the United Kingdom which relate to the arbitration (see, e.g. *Svenska Peroleum AB v Republic of Lithuania (No.2)* [2006] 1 Lloyd's Rep. 181).

It seems clear from the case law that, subject to such issues as waiver, the party seeking to resist enforcement may found on his own incapacity or that of the other party. Indeed, the wording of the provision would seem to allow him to found on the incapacity of any party to the arbitration agreement, whether or not they are party to enforcement proceedings, or indeed participated in the arbitration. There is no authority on this point, and it must be doubted whether a court would see this as a bar to enforcement.

There remains the issue of when the issue of incapacity should be judged. By using the term "was", the provision seems to invite the interpretation that the relevant point should be the date of entering into the arbitration agreement, so that incapacity arising after that point is irrelevant, and that is the view taken by one New York decision (*Corcoran v AIG Multi-line Syndicate Inc* (1990) XV YCA 586). However a later decision from the same jurisdiction insists that supervening incapacity is a good ground for refusing enforcement (*Corcoran v Ardra Insurance Co Ltd* (1991) XVI YCA 663).

Subsection (2)(b)

Arbitration agreement invalid: This re-enacts s.5(2)(b) of the 1975 Act (see also s.103(2)(b) of the 1996 Act), and is based on the second part of art.V(1)(a) of the Convention. A party can seek to resist enforcement if he can establish that the arbitration agreement was invalid under the agreed governing law, or in the absence thereof under the law of the seat. The law of the seat therefore only becomes of importance if there is no indication of the governing law. The parties may, of course, have explicitly chosen the law to govern the arbitration agreement. If they have not, then the fact that the parties have chosen a particular law to govern the contract between them has in the past been regarded as an implied choice of the law governing the arbitration agreement, in the absence of strong indications to the contrary. For example in *Deutsche Schachtbau v Shell Petroleum International Co Ltd* [1990] 1 A.C. 295, although the contract was governed by English law, the House of Lords decided that the circumstances suggested that the parties must have intended that the arbitration agreement be governed by Swiss law. Increasingly, however, the English courts have held that the choice of a particular arbitral seat amounts to an implied choice of the law of that state to govern the arbitration agreement, even though the contract between the parties is explicitly subject to a different law (see, e.g. *XL Insurance Ltd v Owens Corning* [2000] 2 Lloyd's Rep. 500). That approach was recently followed in *Dallah Real Estate and Tourism Holding Co v Pakistan* [2009] EWCA Civ 755; where the Court of Appeal held that Aikens J. had correctly applied French law to the issue of the validity of the arbitration agreement, since the proceedings were held in Paris. Since French law suggested that Pakistan was not a party to the agreement, it could not be valid, so that the award—an ICC award—was denied enforcement. While, as will be seen below, English courts are often unimpressed by grounds being raised as a basis for resisting enforcement which could have been pleaded as a ground for setting the award aside before the courts of the seat, in this case the Court of Appeal agreed with Aikens J. that it was appropriate in this case to raise the issue at the stage of enforcement. Aikens J. had earlier ([2000] 2 Lloyd's Rep. 535) held that the arbitration agreement here was the agreement that disputes be referred to arbitration, whether in the form of an arbitration clause or otherwise, rather than the submission to arbitration.

Subsection (2)(c)

Party not able to present case: A party can seek to resist enforcement if he can establish that he was not given proper notice of the arbitral process or the appointment of the tribunal or was otherwise unable to present his case. This largely re-enacts s.5(2)(c) of the 1975 Act (see also s.103(2)(c) of the 1996 Act), and is based on art.V(1)(b) of the Convention. Both those measures refer to the arbitral proceedings rather than the arbitral process. The latter term is perhaps employed to make it clear that a party might complain about given proper notice of parts of the arbitral process which occur before the "proceedings" are under way, e.g. the appointment of the tribunal. It is not appropriate to found on this ground if what is involved is essentially an attack of the correctness of the award (see, e.g. *Inter-Arab Investment Guarantee Corp v Banque Arabe et Internationale d'Investissements* (2001) XXVI YCA 207 Cour de Cassation). It is also clear that the principle of waiver of objection may apply in this context if the enforcing court considers that the party opposing enforcement might appropriately have raised the matter before the tribunal and/or a court of the seat but failed to do so (see, e.g. *La Societe National des Hydrocarbures v Shaheen National Resources Inc*, 585 F.Supp. 57 (1983)). When the matter has been raised before a court of the seat and the award has been upheld, the authorities are divided as to whether the issue can be raised again at the enforcement stage. The Paris Court of Appeal in *Unichips Finanziaria SpA v Gesnouin* (1994) XIX YCA 658, insists that it can, while the Indian High Court in *International Investor KCSC v Sanghi Polyesters Ltd* (2005) XXX YCA 577, suggests that the matter should be regarded as res judicata.

Relationship with public policy: It has been judicially noted that there has been a growing tendency to raise the question as to whether a party was allowed properly to present his case as an issue of public policy under art.V(2)(b)—see s.20(4)(b) below. That is generally regarded as acceptable, since the enforcement of an award where a party has been denied the benefit of due process or the rules of natural justice would be regarded as contrary to public policy in most jurisdictions. The Spanish Supreme Court has indeed described due process as, "procedural public policy" in *Union de Cooperativas Agricolas Epis-Centre v La Palentina SA* (2002) XXVII YCA 533 at 538. However, there may be a tactical advantage in raising such a matter under the public policy ground, since ordinarily a party who founds on this ground does not bear the burden of proof, by contrast to the position had he raised the matter under art.V(1)(b). This led Mason J. in the Hong Kong Court of Appeal in *Hebei Import & Export Corp v Politek Engineering Co Ltd* (1998) XXIV YCA 652 at 667, to suggest that a party who raises as a matter of public policy a specific issue which might appropriately fall under art.V(1)(b) might still appropriately bear the burden of proof.

Lack of notice: As regards lack of notice, in *Sesostris v Transportes Navales*, 727 F.Supp. 737 (1989) a US District Court denied enforcement when the first proper notice a party received of the proceedings was the award, an earlier indication that proceedings had commenced, "in Madrid, Spain" being insufficient. And the Bavarian Court of Appeal (2002) XXVII YCA 445, took the view that when a party's address is different from that laid down in the contract, there should be a genuine attempt to discover its business or mailing address. If that is done, then notice sent to its last known address will be sufficient. But if, as in the case in question, no such attempt is made, then notice is not properly sent and the award should be denied enforcement. However, if proper notice is given, the fact that the relevant notice employed the wrong name will not suffice to prevent enforcement if the party in question received it and should have realised that it referred to him (*LKT Industrial Berhad (Malaysia) v Chun* [2004] N.S.W.S.C. 820). And if notice is served, it will not avail a party simply to seek to reject the notice (see *Cominco France SA v Soquiber SL* (1983) VIII YCA 408 Spanish Supreme Court). The burden of proof lies on the party seeking to contend that the means of providing notice were unsuitable (*Trans World Film SpA v Film Polski Import and Export of Films* (1993) XVIII YCA 433 Italian Supreme Court), while it has been held that if it is clear that a party was not prejudiced despite receiving seemingly inadequate notice—as where it is unable to submit a defence in any case—enforcement will not be denied (see *Guandong New Technology Import and Export Corp v Chiu Sing* (1993) XVIII YCA 385 Hong Kong High Court).

The idea that "proper" notice must be given implies that sufficient time must be given for the party to respond to the notice. Yet this can sometimes be consistent with fairly tight time limits being imposed in relation to certain aspects of the process. Thus the Swiss courts (see (1979) IV YCA 309) ultimately enforced a Dutch award where the tribunal had refused to extend a seven day time limit envisaged in the applicable arbitral rules for a party to appoint its arbitrator. It is also clear that the concept of proper notice is not necessarily dependent on the standard procedural formalities of the enforcing state. Thus in *Malden Mills Inc (US) v Hilaturas Lourdes SA* (1979) IV YCA 302, the Mexican Court of Appeal overturned a first instance decision that the service of notices in accordance with the Rules of the American Arbitration Association, by which the parties had agreed to be bound, did not amount to proper notice since it did not adhere to what was required by Mexican law. More dubiously, the Schleswig Court of Appeal ((2004) XXIX YCA 687) has indicated that even when a party can establish that it was denied the right to present its case, it must establish that it had a case to present before enforcement could be denied.

Enforcement may also be refused under this provision where the identity of the arbitrators is not known to the parties. This occurred when, under the rules of a commodity trade association, parties were allowed to veto names from a list of potential arbitrators put forward by the association, but were not permitted to know the eventual composition of the tribunal, lest they should seek to influence its members. The award was only signed by the chairman. The Cologne Court of Appeal ((1979) IV YCA 258) declined to enforce the award.

Inability to present case: In terms of not being able to present one's case, the fact that a party chooses not to present his case—as where he declines to participate in the proceedings altogether (e.g. *Pasrederiet m/v Jytte Dania v Mas SA* (1989) XIV YCA 704 Spanish Supreme Court), or fails to submit evidence (e.g. *Nanjing Cereals, Oils and Foodstuffs Import and Export Corp v Luckmate Commodities Trading Ltd* (1999) XXI YCA 542 Hong Kong

Supreme Court)—or not to present it as fully as possible (see, e.g. *Inter-Arab Investment Guarantee Corp v Banque Arabe et Internationale d'Investissements* (1997) XXII YCA 643 Brussels Court of First Instance), does not mean that he was unable to present his case. As Colman J. notes in *Minmetals Germany GmbH v Ferco Steel Ltd* [1999] 1 All E.R. (Comm) 315 at 318:

> "Inability to present a case .... contemplates at least that the enforcee has been prevented from presenting his case by matters outside his control.... Where, however, the enforcee has, due to matters within his control, not provided himself with the means of taking advantage of an opportunity to present his case, he does not ... bring himself within that exception."

So in *Mangistaumunaigaz Oil Production Association v United World Trade Inc* (1999) XXIV YCA 808 at 810, a US District Court described as "empty" an argument that a party could not present its case because it could not afford to do so, while arguments based on language difficulties, either in terms of a failure of the arbitrator to comprehend the proceedings (see *Bargues Agro Industrie SA v Young Pecan Ltd* (2005) XXX YCA 499 Paris Court of Appeal), or in terms of the problems which the applicable language had caused the party in question (see *Fashion Ribbon Co Inc v Iberband SL* (2005) XXX YCA 627 Spanish Supreme Court), have also received short shrift. Nor does a party's fear of arrest at the seat mean that he was unable to present his case (see *National Development Co v Khashoggi* (1993) XVIII YCA 506 New York District Court).

Moreover, if a party is aggrieved about the way in which he was allowed to present his case, that will usually not prevent enforcement, since the tribunal is usually regarded as the master of the procedure and of what evidence is or is not relevant (see, e.g. *Laminoires-Trefileries-Cableries de Lens SA v Southwire Co*, 484 F.Supp. 1065 (1981) US Court of Appeals), and is not necessarily expected to follow the sorts of procedures one would see in court (see, e.g. *Generica Ltd v Pharmaceuticals Basics Inc*, 125 F.3d 1123 (1997) US Court of Appeals). The tribunal in particular is generally entitled to decide whether requests for adjournments and the like are justified (*Parsons & Whittemore Overseas Co Inc v Societe Generale de l'Industrie du Papier (RAKTA)* (1976) I YCA 205 US Court of Appeals), and to set time limits in relation to such matters as the presentation of evidence as long as these are not unreasonably short (see *Carters (Merchants) Ltd v Ferraro* (1979) IV YCA 275 Naples Court of Appeal). It also appears that the tribunal may decide whether oral hearings are required (see *Overseas Cosmos Inc v NR Vessel Corp* (1998) XXIII YCA 1096 New York District Court), although the law of the seat may also bear on this issue—see s.20(2)(d) below. The party seeking to resist enforcement will face a particularly daunting task if what was done was proper in terms of the procedural law of the seat (see *Karaha Bodas Co LLC v Perusahaan Pertambangan Minyak Dan Gas Bumi Negara-Pertamina* (2003) XXVIII YCA 752). As was said in *Parsons & Whittemore Overseas Co Inc* (1976) I YCA 205 (at 215): "The Convention essentially sanctions the forum state's notions of due process."

To succeed under this ground then, an applicant will generally have to show that the tribunal proceeded on the basis of evidence that he had no opportunity to counter, whether because he was not made aware of that evidence (see, e.g. *Kanoria v Guinness* [2006] EWCA Civ 222), or was not permitted to challenge it (see *Paklito Investment Ltd v Klockner (East Asia) Ltd* [1995] A.D.R.L.J. 127 High Court of Hong Kong). This might happen where the tribunal considers evidence tendered by one party but not made available to the other (see, e.g. *GWL Kersten & Co BV v Societe Commerciale Raoul-Duval & Cie* (1994) XIX YCA 708 Amsterdam Court of Appeal). The same result has followed when the tribunal has misled the party as to the type of evidence required (*Iran Aircraft Ind v Avco Corp* (1993) XVIII YCA 599 US Court of Appeals).

Subsection (2)(d)

Arbitration improperly conducted: A party can seek to resist enforcement if he can establish that the tribunal was constituted or the arbitration conducted contrary to the agreement of the parties or, if the agreement did not address those issues, contrary to the law of the seat. This re-enacts s.5(2)(e) of the 1975 Act (see also s.103(2)(e) of the 1996 Act), and is based on art.V(1)(d) of the Convention, although the phraseology of those provisions is slightly different. The logic of the provision is clear. The enforcing court must first look to see whether the parties have reached agreement on the issues concerned, and only if they have not, need it concern itself with the law of the seat. However, this creates a potential practical problem. If the agreement of the parties runs contrary to mandatory provisions of the law of the seat, a tribunal which follows the former runs the risk that a court of the seat may choose to set the award aside if invited to do so by a party. Under art.V(1)(d) of the Convention and s.20(3)(d) of the Act, the fact that this court has set the award aside is itself a ground for refusing enforcement. Such situations will undoubtedly be rare, but where they arise a tribunal is presented with a dilemma, since whichever path it chooses to follow it opens up the possibility that the award might be refused enforcement. However, there seems to be a tendency on the part of enforcing courts to exercise their discretion in favour of enforcing awards. On certain occasions this means enforcing an award when what has been done is in accordance with the law of the seat, albeit running contrary to what the parties agreed (see, e.g. *Al Haddad Bros Enterprises v M/S Agapi* (1987) XII YCA 549), while on others it means enforcing an award when the tribunal followed the will of the parties even though it conflicted with mandatory norms of the law of the seat (see, e.g. *Joseph Muller AG v Bergesen* (1986) IX YCA 437).

As always, the burden of proof lies on the party resisting enforcement (see e.g. *Grow Biz International v DLT Holdings Inc* (2005) XXX YCA 450 at 457), while once more the principle of waiver might operate in this context. Courts are often unimpressed where this issue is raised for the first time at the stage of enforcement, when it could easily have been raised before either the tribunal or a court of the seat (see Longmore J. in *China Agribusiness Development Corp v Balli Trading* [1998] 2 Lloyd's Rep. 76 at 80). So in *China Nanhai Oil Joint Service Corp v Gee Tai Holdings Ltd* [1995] A.D.R.L.J. 127 (see Kaplan J. at 132) the Hong Kong Supreme Court was happy to enforce an award even though the arbitrators were not chosen from the list agreed by the parties, since the party in question had gone through the entire arbitral process without once voicing this objection.

Nor, waiver aside, is it every procedural breach which will lead to refusal of enforcement. Thus a US District Court opined in *Compagnie des Bauxites de Guinee v Hammermills Inc* (1993) XVIII YCA 566 at 571:

> "The Court does not believe that Article V(1)(d) was intended to permit courts to police every procedural ruling by the arbitrator, and to refuse to enforce the award if any procedural violation is found. Such an interpretation would directly conflict with the 'pro-enforcement bias' of the Convention and its intention to remove obstacles to confirmation of arbitral awards. The Court believes that a more appropriate standard

of review would be to refuse to enforce an award based on a procedural violation only if such violation worked substantial prejudice to the complaining party."

So in *Tongyuan (USA) International Trading Group v Uni-Clan Ltd* (2001) XXVI YCA 886, Moore-Bick J. did not see the fact that an arbitration had been held in Beijing rather than in Shanghai or Shenzen as stipulated in the arbitration clause as providing grounds for refusing enforcement. That case also emphasises the fact that it will be difficult for a party to persuade a court that he was prejudiced by an irregularity when he opted not to participate in the arbitral proceedings.

Tribunal not in agreed form: Cases where enforcement has been refused on the basis that the tribunal did not take the form agreed by the parties include *Rederi Aktiebolaget Sally v Srl Termarea* (1979) IV YCA 294 Florence Court of Appeal, where in a London arbitration the party-appointed arbitrators had decided the issue without bothering to appoint a third arbitrator as indicated by the arbitration agreement. This course of action was sanctioned by the now repealed s.9(1) of the Arbitration Act 1950, so that this is a rare instance of a court in this instance regarding the agreement of the parties as overriding the law of the seat. However, where a party declines to act as contemplated by the agreement, so that the tribunal cannot be constituted as agreed, enforcing courts tend to take the view that it is proper for the other party to fall back on the law of the seat. That was what occurred in *Al Haddad Bros Enterprises v M/S Agapi* (1987) XII YCA 549 where a party appointed arbitrator was asked to serve as sole arbitrator when the other party failed to nominate an arbitrator, this being acceptable in terms of the Arbitration Act 1950. A US District Court was prepared to enforce the award, noting (at 551) that:

"The Convention allows recognition of an award, which although not in accord with the parties' agreement, complied with the law of the country where the arbitration occurred."

It is also the case that the courts of certain jurisdictions have been happy to enforce arbitral awards where the composition of the tribunal was as had been agreed by the parties, even though that composition contravened mandatory rules of the law of the seat (see *SEEE v Yugoslavia* (1986) XI YCA 491 Rouen Court of Appeal; but the same award had been earlier denied enforcement by the Dutch Supreme Court (1976) I YCA 195).

One situation where one might expect the plea to arise is where two or more arbitrations have been compulsorily consolidated, a power historically asserted by the courts in certain jurisdictions and conferred on them by legislation in others. In such situations the tribunal is very clearly not composed in the way agreed by at least certain of the parties. The counter argument is that by agreeing to arbitrate in such jurisdictions the parties have impliedly accepted this possibility. So far there has been no decision on this issue under the Convention.

Procedural irregularity: As regards the position where it is alleged that there has been procedural irregularity, it is often difficult to find consistency in the authorities. Thus while the Paris Court of Appeal in *Dubois & Vanderwalle v Boots Frites BV* (1999) XXIV YCA 640, refused to enforce an award where the tribunal failed to observe an agreed time limit for making it, the Bavarian Court of Appeal in *K Trading v Bayerische Motoren Werke AG* (2005) XXX YCA 568, enforced an award in the same circumstances, opining (at 572–573):

"In order to prevent the setting aside of an award on purely formal grounds and the carrying out of a new arbitration necessarily leading to the same result as the annulled arbitral award ... a distinction must be made between essential and nonessential procedural defects ... even if such distinction is not made in the text of Article V(1)(d) of the Convention ... A procedural defect is deemed essential to the arbitral award when it is causal to it ... or when the arbitral tribunal would have decided differently had it not been for the procedural violation."

A similar approach is seen in *Food Services of America Inc v Pan Pacific Specialities Ltd* (2004) XXIX YCA 581, where the Supreme Court of British Columbia enforced an award even though it did not contain reasons as stipulated by the International Arbitration Rules of the American Arbitration Asssocaition ("AAA"), which had been invoked by the parties. The court stated (at 587) that the failure to give reasons had not affected the fairness of the hearing or the decision-making process. It is of course the case that such a failure would render an award subject to being set aside by the courts of the seat in many jurisdictions, which would itself afford a basis for refusing enforcement.

Finally, in *Inter-Arab Investment Guarantee Corp v Banque Arabe et Internationale d'Investissements* (1999) XXIV YCA 603, a Belgian court rejected an objection that the tribunal had improperly acted as *amiables compositeurs* on the basis that the tribunal had in fact done no such thing. However, the interesting aspect is that the court clearly felt that the question of the powers the tribunal has to decide the dispute was a matter of procedure rather than of substantive law, thus allowing a challenge to enforcement to be considered in the first place. By analogy, the question of whether the tribunal has applied the appropriate substantive law to the dispute might also permit a challenge to enforcement. And in *Osuuskunta METEX Anderlag VS v Turkiye Electric Kurumu Genel Mudurlugu General Directorate* (1997) XXII YCA 807, the Ankara Court of Appeal held that an award might be denied enforcement on the basis of the tribunal's erroneous choice of procedural law.

Subsection (3)

This subsection contains a number of grounds for resisting enforcement which relate to the award. Like those in subs.(2), they appear in art.V(1) of the Convention.

Subsection (3)(a)

Lack of jurisdiction: This and subs.(3)(b) together replace s.5(1)(d) of the 1975 Act and seek to give effect to art.V(1)(c)of the Convention. Section s.5(1)(d) of the 1975 Act employed the term "difference" rather than "dispute", as indeed does s.103(2)(d) of the 1996 Act, but this is probably not material.

As usual, the burden of proof lies on the party resisting enforcement (see Donaldson M.R. in *Deutsche Schachtbau und Tiefbohrgesellschaft v Ras Al Khaimah National Oil Co* [1987] 2 Lloyd's Rep. 522 at 529), while it has even been said that there is a presumption that the tribunal has acted within the scope of its authority (by the Bermuda Court of Appeal in *Sojuzneftexport v Joc Oil Ltd* (1990) XV YCA 384 at 390). The House of Lords has confirmed that art.V(1)(c) is to be construed narrowly (see Lord Steyn in *Lesotho Highlands Authority v Impregilo SpA* [2006] 1 A.C. 221 at [30]). Matters of procedural impropriety, such as where the tribunal relies on evidence not placed before it, do not fall under it (*Minmetals Germany GmbH v Ferco Steel Ltd* [1999] 1 All E.R. (Comm) 315). Nor does failure to apply the chosen law to the substance of the dispute (*Karaha Bodas Co LLC v Per-*

usahaan Pertambangan Minyak Dan Gas Bumi Negara-Pertamina (2003) XXVIII YCA 752), even if the argument is that the tribunal has improperly applied a-national norms to the subject matter of the dispute. Thus in *Ministry of Defence of the Republic of Iran v Cubic Defense Systems, Inc*, 29 F.Supp. 2d 1168 (1998) at 1173 a US District Court opined that an arbitral tribunal's:

> "... reference to an application of the UNIDROIT Principles (i.e. the Principles of International Commercial Contracts) and principles of good faith and fair dealing do not violate Article V(1)(c). The Tribunal applied these principles to differences falling within the terms of the submission to arbitration and therefore the Award does not violate Article V(1)(c)."

It seems then that if the tribunal has been asked to deal with the matter, a complaint about how it does so may not be raised under art.V(1)(c).

A party then can resist enforcement of an award if he can prove that it deals with a dispute not contemplated by or not falling within the scope of the submission to arbitration. This ground is sometimes known as *extra petita* and arises when the tribunal deals with an issue it was not asked to address. One very fundamental respect in which the tribunal may lack jurisdiction is where it is alleged that there is no valid arbitration agreement. However, this would be a plea to be raised under s.20(2)(b), giving effect to art.V(1)(a) of the Convention. There have indeed been cases where it has been pleaded that there is no valid arbitration agreement, but that if there is then the tribunal has exercised powers not conferred by that agreement. The courts have tended to react by indicating that it is appropriate to deal first with the former question, and then only if the decision is made that there is a valid arbitration agreement will they proceed to deal with the issue of jurisdiction (see (1979) IV YCA 305 Hague Court of First Instance).

An example of an award being denied enforcement under this head is the case of *Tiong Huat Rubber Factory Bhd v Wah Chang International Co Ltd* (1992) XVII YCA 516, where under the contract for the supply of rubber it was provided that all disputes regarding, "the quality or condition of rubber or other dispute" should be settled by arbitration. The contract also provided that payment was to be made via a letter of credit, and when this was not provided the seller went to arbitration and obtained an award in his favour. The buyer sought to resist enforcement on the basis that the contract only provided for the arbitration of disputes relating to the quality, etc. of the rubber. The High Court of Hong Kong took the view that it could not be imagined that the arbitration clause intended to exclude claims for payment from its scope, but the Court of Appeal agreed with the buyer and held that the matter did indeed lie outwith the tribunal's jurisdiction. And in *AAMCO Transmissions Inc v Kunz* [1996] A.D.R.L.J. 32, the Court of Appeal of Saskatchewan held that where an arbitration clause was a standard form contract, its terms should be construed *contra proferentem* when seeking to decide what matters lay within its scope.

Such decisions are rare however, and most of the time this defence fails. This is mainly due to the fact that the tribunal is usually regarded as best placed to determine the scope of the arbitration agreement and the law which governs that issue (see, e.g. *Sojuzneftexport v Joc Oil Ltd* (1990) XV YCA 384). As the US Court of Appeals states in *Parsons & Whittemore Overseas Co Inc v Societe Generale de l'Industrie du Papier (RAKTA)*, 508 F.2d. 969 (2nd Cir. 1974) at 976–977:

"Although the Convention recognises that an award may not be enforced where predicated on a subject matter outside the arbitrator's jurisdiction, it does not sanction second-guessing the arbitrator's construction of the parties' agreement."

Subsection (3)(b)

Excess of jurisdiction: A party can also resist enforcement of an award if he can prove that it contains decisions on matters beyond the scope of the submission to arbitration. This ground is sometimes known as *ultra petita* and arises when the tribunal in dealing with the issues it was asked to address exceeds the scope of its jurisdiction. However, as above, courts are generally reluctant to question a tribunal's view as to the scope of their jurisdiction. Thus instances abound where enforcement has been granted despite the tribunal awarding remedies not claimed by a party (e.g. price reductions, *AB Gotaverken v General National Maritime Transport Co* (1981) VI YCA 237 Swedish Supreme Court; interest, (2000) XXV YCA 714 Hamburg Court of Appeal; and expenses, *Aasma v American Steamship Owners Mutual Protection and Indemnity* (2003) XXVIII YCA 1140 US District Court), or which even appear to be expressly excluded by the agreement of the parties (see *Fertilizer Corp of India v IDI Management Inc* (1982) VII YCA 382 US District Court—damages for consequential loss).

Moreover, it is not a good ground for resisting enforcement under the Convention that an award fails to exhaust the submission. As the Luxembourg Court of Appeal points out in *Kersa Holding Co v Infancourtage* (1996) XXI YCA 617 at 625:

"This ground even if established, could not hinder the enforcement of the awards, as an *infra petita* decision is not sanctioned by the New York Convention."

Subsection (3)(c)

Award not yet binding: This and subs.(3)(d) together replace s.5(1)(f) of the 1975 Act and seek to give effect to art.V(1)(e) of the Convention. A court may refuse enforcement if the party resisting enforcement can show that the award is not yet binding on him. Under the Geneva Convention enforcement might be resisted if a party could show that the award was not "final". That invited the interpretation that enforcement might be denied if there was a possibility that the award might be open to challenge, or if the law of the seat required some further formality before an award was fully enforceable. The use of the term "binding" was deliberately chosen to avoid such an interpretation (see *Summary Record of the 17th meeting of the United Nations Conference on International Commercial Arbitration*, UN E/CONF.26/SR.17). Thus the Swedish Supreme Court notes in *AB Gotaverken v General National Maritime Transport Co* (1981) VI YCA 237 at 240:

"The possibility of an action for setting aside the award shall not mean that the award is considered as not being binding ... A case in which a foreign award is not binding is when its merits are open to appeal ... The choice of the term binding was [intended] to avoid the necessity of a double *exequatur*, or the need for the party relying on the award to prove that the award is enforceable according to the authorities of the country in which it was rendered."

Generally then, awards are binding as soon as they are made (see *SPP (Middle East) Ltd v Egypt* (1985) X YCA 487 District Court of Amsterdam) and have been enforced even though some formality is missing which would be necessary to make them enforceable in the seat (*Resort Condominiums International Inc v Bolwell* (1994) XX YCA 628 Supreme Court of Queensland), e.g. confirmation by (*Fertilizer Corp of India v IDI Management Inc* (1982) VII YCA 382 US District Court) or deposit with (*Compagnie de Saint Gobain-Pont a Mousson v Fertilizer Corp of India Ltd* (1976) I YCA 184) a court of the seat. And where a court confirms an award, it remains an award enforceable under the Convention. It is not converted into a judgment (*Schreter v Gasmac Inc* (1992) 89 D.L.R. (4th) 365). Nonetheless, in *Rosseel NV v Oriental Commercial Shipping Co Ltd* [1991] 2 Lloyd's Rep. 625 at 628, Steyn J. suggests that an award cannot be considered binding if the parties agreed that it could not be enforced without authorisation from a particular court. On the other hand, the High Court of Hong Kong in *Zheijiang Province Garment Import and Export Co v Siemssen & Co (Hong Kong) Trading Ltd* [1993] A.D.R.L.J. 183, per Kaplan J. at 187, took the view that an award is still binding although a party argues that a condition precedent to its operation has not been fulfilled. The fact that an award has ceased to be binding is not specified as a ground for refusing enforcement, yet where the parties agreed to ignore an award and arbitrated the matter anew, reaching a different result, enforcement was refused (*Dutco (Pvt) Ltd v Dajen (Pvt) Ltd* [1997] 2 Zimbabwe L.R. 199).

The *Gotaverken* dicta, however, suggest that an award is not binding if it can be challenged on the merits. The parties may provide for such a mechanism themselves, and will do so implicitly if they arbitrate under certain arbitral rules. Alternatively, the law of the seat may allow an award to be challenged on the basis of an error of law. An award which may not be issued until it has undergone some form of scrutiny, such as that by the ICC Court under art.27 of the ICC Rules, does not fall to be regarded as an award at all until that process is complete.

It should also be mentioned that while an award may be enforced although there is a possibility it may be challenged, the fact that it is actually being challenged may cause a court to take a different attitude to enforcement—see the commentary to s.20(6)(a) below.

The issue of whether "awards" made via informal dispute resolution processes such the Italian *arbitrato irrituale* are binding is perhaps not for discussion in this context, since the real issue is whether such awards are to be recognised under the Convention at all. The Italian Supreme Court in *Butera v Pagnan* (1979) IV YCA 296, says yes, while the German Supreme Court in *COMITAS v SOVAG* (1983) VIII YCA 366, says no.

Subsection (3)(d)

Award set aside: This replaces s.5(1)(f) of the 1975 Act and seeks to give effect to the second ground under art.V(1)(e) of the Convention. A court may refuse enforcement if the party resisting enforcement can show that the award has been set aside by a competent authority. Section 20(7) seeks to define the term "competent authority" as a "person" who has the authority to set aside or suspend the award in the country in which (or under the law of which) the award was made. No attempt is made to define that term under the 1975 and 1996 Acts, or indeed the Convention itself. All the authority under the Convention suggests that a competent authority means a court. By using the term "person", the 2010 Act invites the interpretation that an award might be refused enforcement because it has been "set aside" by an individual or institution which is contractually empowered to do so. It is doubtful whether this is what was intended by the drafters of the Convention, and since the emphasis of the Convention is on ensuring the enforcement of foreign arbitral awards, subject only to the limited exceptions it lays down, any attempt to extend the grounds on which enforcement may be denied is arguably inept. That being said, an award which has been set aside under some sort of contractual appeal process is presumably to be regarded as a nullity.

The general thrust of the provision is that enforcement may be denied if the award has been set aside at the seat of arbitration. The reference to an award being made under a different law than that of the seat seems to relate to the possibility that one might arbitrate in State A under the procedural law of State B, and that might give the courts of State B jurisdiction to seek to set the award aside. In practice, however, only the law of the seat seems to be recognised. That of course means that the setting aside of an award by any other court is not a ground for denying enforcement. Thus in *Karaha Bodas Co LLC v Perusahaan Pertambangan Minyak Dan Gas Bumi Negara-Pertamina* [2003] 380 H.K.C.U. 1, an award made in Switzerland was set aside in Indonesia on the basis that the contract was governed by Indonesian law. The High Court of Hong Kong did not see this as a basis for refusing enforcement.

Certain Conventions (e.g. the 1961 Geneva Convention—to which the UK is not a party) only characterise the setting aside of an award in the seat as a ground for resisting enforcement if the award is set aside on certain limited grounds, so that the award should not be denied enforcement if it is set aside on any other ground. Thus the Austrian Supreme Court in *Kajo-Erzeugnisse Essenzen GmbH v DO Zdravilisce Radenska* (1995) XX YCA 1051, enforced an award set aside in Slovenia on the basis of contravention of public policy, since that was not a ground recognised by the Convention. In the context of the New York Convention a US District Court observed in *International Standard Electric Corp v Bridas Sociedad Anonima Petrolera* (1992) XVII YCA 639 at 645:

> "Article V(1)(e) refers exclusively to procedural and not substantive law, and more precisely the regimen of arbitral procedural law under which the arbitration was conducted."

However, there is not otherwise any restriction on the grounds upon which an award may be set aside.

It should not be supposed, however, that an award set aside by the courts of the seat will never be enforced. As will be seen later, the fact that it cannot be enforced under the New York Convention is no bar to it being enforced under any other applicable Convention or any other rule of law. More importantly, however, it is not unknown for courts to exercise their discretion under the New York Convention in favour of enforcing such awards. Thus in *Chromalloy Aeroservices Inc v Arab Republic of Egypt*, 939 F.Supp. 907 (1996) a US District Court enforced an award which an Egyptian Court had set aside because it believed that the tribunal had applied the wrong substantive law. However, while countries like France routinely enforce awards set aside by the courts of the seat, *Chromalloy* is rather untypical of the US approach (see, e.g. *Baker Marine (Nigeria) Ltd v Chevron (Nigeria) Ltd*, 191 F.3d 194 (1999) at 197) and courts are generally reluctant to enforce such awards. On one view, it is in line with the pro-enforcement bias of the Convention that awards, especially international awards where the parties may have no real connection with the seat, should not be denied enforcement because of some peculiarity of the law of the seat. The alternative view is that such awards only gain legal force because they are part of the legal fabric of the law of the seat, so that they are in effect deprived of legal authority if set aside at the seat. Even if one does not accept this argument, however, it is suggested that Scots courts should be slow to enforce awards set aside at the seat, given that the Convention seems to contemplate the courts of the seat having this power.

Subsection (4)

The final two grounds on which recognition or enforcement may be refused are of a quite different character to those which have gone before. The previous grounds were largely particular to the parties, their agreement or the arbitral proceedings. The grounds addressed by this subsection deal essentially with arbitral awards which a Scottish court should not consider enforcing. This is reflected in the fact that while in relation to the previous grounds the party resisting enforcement had to establish the existence of the ground in question, no such burden is imposed under subs.(4). Thus if a Scottish court recognises that an award deals with a matter which is not arbitrable in Scotland, it should refuse to enforce it even if that plea is not raised by any party. Of course, a party may make such a plea and may in certain situations even be practically compelled to tender evidence to establish that the ground exists, e.g. when it is contended that to enforce the award would be contrary to public policy due to the way in which the award was allegedly procured.

Subsection (4)(a)

Matter not arbitrable under Scots law: Recognition or enforcement may be refused when the award relates to a matter which is not capable of being settled by arbitration. This and subs.(4)(b) replace s.5(3) of the 1975 Act, and the provision seeks to give effect to art.V(2)(a) of the Convention. The Convention makes it clear that arbitrability is to be judged according to the law of the place of enforcement, and while the current provision, like s.5(3) of the 1975 Act, omits that reference, it is the only sensible way to interpret the provision. The fact that a dispute is not arbitrable in terms of the law governing the substance of the dispute or the law of the seat may of course have consequences, since in the former situation enforcement might be resisted under s.20(2)(b), while in the latter situation the award might be set aside in the seat so that enforcement might be resisted under s.20(3)(d). However in the current context the question is whether the dispute is arbitrable under Scots law.

The question of arbitrability is discussed in relation to s.30. Suffice it to say here then, that there are relatively few matters which are not arbitrable under Scots law. Since arbitrability is in one sense a dimension of public policy there may sometimes be an overlap between this and the following ground.

Subsection (4)(b)

Public policy: Recognition or enforcement may be refused when to do so would be contrary to public policy. This provision seeks to give effect to art.V(2)(b) of the Convention. Once again, the Convention makes it clear that the public policy referred to is that of the place of enforcement, and while the current provision, like s.5(3) of the 1975 Act, omits that reference, this is how the English courts have interpreted the provision. It may be observed that courts in certain jurisdictions have decided that where only part of an award offends against public policy, the remainder of the award might be enforced if it is properly separable (see *Laminoires-Trefileries-Cableries de Lens SA v Southwire Co*, 484 F.Supp. 1065 (1981); *Agro Industries (P) Ltd v Texuna International Ltd* [1994] 1 H.K.L.R. 89).

International public policy: It has long been clear that there is a tendency to treat foreign awards differently than the court would treat a domestic award in this context. As the US Court of Appeals notes in *Parsons & Whittemore Overseas Co Inc v Societe Generale de l'Industrie du Papier (RAKTA)*, 508 F.2d 969 (2nd Cir. 1974) at 973):
 "Enforcement should only be denied on the basis of public policy where enforcement would violate the forum state's most basic notions of morality and justice."
This approach is often described on the basis that an award must run contrary to international public policy for enforcement to be denied. Some states indeed have enshrined the idea of international public policy in legislation (see, e.g. the French Code of Civil Procedure art.1502). While the Swiss Federal Tribunal speaks of "a universal conception of public policy, under which an award will be incompatible with public policy if it is contrary to the fundamental moral or legal principles recognised in all civilised countries" (1996) XXI YCA 172, as the *Parsons* quotation suggests, the concept does not properly relate to a core of public policy which is uniform in every state, but to each individual state's fundamental concepts of justice (numerous examples might be cited but see, e.g. the German Supreme Court in *Manufacturer v Exclusive Distributor* (2004) XIX YCA 687 at 696; and Armstrong J.A. in the Ontario Court of Appeal in *United Mexican States v Karpa* [2005] 74 O.R. 3d 180 at [116]). Such a doctrine also seems to be recognised by the English courts. In *Westacre Investments Inc v Jugiimport-SPDR Holding Co Ltd* [1998] 2 Lloyd's Rep. 65 at 74, Waller L.J. noted that:
 "... while there are some rules of public policy which if infringed will lead to non-enforcement whatever their proper law and wherever their place of performance,"
other rules did not fall into that category. Thus whereas an award relating to a contract, "for the purchase of influence" would not be enforceable on public policy grounds if the award were domestic, it was not so fundamentally repugnant to English law's notions of justice that it offended against international public policy. He added that even if an award offended against the domestic public policy of the forum state, it could still be enforced if it did not contravene the English standard of international public policy.
 It is suggested that if the English courts have embraced the idea of international public policy in interpreting legislation which gives effect to the UK's treaty obligations, the Scots courts could hardly do otherwise.
Illegality: While public policy is clearly an extremely broad concept, certain broad headings may be identified. Thus the fundamental immorality or illegality of the contract between the parties may preclude the enforcement of an award. So Waller L.J. pronounces in *Soleimany v Soleimany* [1998] 3 W.L.R. 811 at 821G that:
 "There may be illegal or immoral dealings which are, from an English law perspective, incapable of being arbitrated, because an agreement to arbitrate them would itself be ... contrary to public policy."
This was a case decided at common law, but in the context of the Convention, Colman J. notes in *Westacre Investments Inc v Jugiimport-SPDR Holding Co Ltd* [1998] 2 Lloyd's Rep. 111 at 127, that if a contract was:
 "... indisputably illegal at common law, the award would not be enforced for it would be contrary to public policy that the arbitrator should be able to ignore palpable and indisputable illegality."
That being said, it is increasingly commonplace for jurisdictions to permit arbitrators themselves to rule, at least in the first instance, on the issue of

illegality under the related principles of separability and competence-competence. Thus Colman J. in *Westacre Investments* observed that in such a situation the court would have to consider whether the illegality was of such a nature for it to be in line with public policy to allow it to be considered in an arbitration. If such was the case, and the arbitrator had decided that the contract was not illegal then (contrast the view of Waller L.J. in *Soleimany* [1998] 3 W.L.R. 811 at 821D–G):

> "... the enforcement court would have to consider whether the public policy against the enforcement of illegal contracts outweighed the countervailing public policy in support of the finality of awards."

Colman J. concluded (*Westacre Investments* [1998] 2 Lloyd's Rep. 111 at 131) that:

> "... an English court would give predominant weight to the public policy of sustaining the parties' agreement to submit the particular issue of illegality and initial invalidity to arbitration rather than of sustaining the non-enforcement of contracts illegal at common law."

A similar view was expressed regarding allegations that the contract had been illegally procured, e.g. by bribery (*Westacre Investments* [1998] 2 Lloyd's Rep. 111 at 129, the decision was upheld by a majority of the Court of Appeal at [1999] 1 All E.R. (Comm) 865; but contrast *Corvetina Technology Ltd v Clough Engineering Ltd* [2004] N.S.W.S.C. 700). Thus as long as a contract is not blatantly illegal, the fact that an arbitrator has treated it as legal in his award will count heavily against the award being refused enforcement.

It is also the case that enforcement is commonly granted even if the contract between the parties is admittedly illegal in the place of performance, and indeed even if it has been judicially declared to be so, as long as it is not illegal under the law chosen by the parties to govern the contract (*Omnium SA v Hilmarton Ltd* [1998] 2 Lloyd's Rep. 222; *R v V* [2008] EWHC 1531 (Comm)). As Waller L.J. states in *Soinco Saci v Novokuznetsk Aluminium Plant* [1998] 2 Lloyd's Rep. 337 at 340:

> "[I]t is the award with which the English Court is concerned and not the underlying contract. The question of illegality having been raised and dealt with by the arbitrators, and there being no requirement as a result to perform some act which English law would regard as illegal or contrary to the recognised morals of this country, the public policy is if anything in favour of abiding by the terms of the Convention and enforcing the award."

Improperly obtained awards: Public policy is often seen as being bound up with the substance of an award, but the phrase is the translation of the French *ordre public*, which undoubtedly has a procedural dimension (see Nadelmann and Von Mehren, "Equivalences in Treaties in the Conflicts Fields" (1966) 15 Am. J.Comp. L. 195). Consequently, where it is suggested that the award had been improperly obtained, e.g. on the basis of perjury or fraud, enforcement may be resisted on the grounds of public policy (see Lord Keith in *Masimport v SMLI Ltd*, 1976 S.C. 102 at 109; *Gater Assets Ltd v Nak Naftogaz Ukrainiy (No.2)* [2008] 2 Lloyd's Rep. 295). However the court will wish to know why the award has not been challenged in the forum. Moreover, if such a challenge has already failed, enforcement is unlikely to be denied. As Colman J. points out in *Westacre Investments* [1998] 2 Lloyd's Rep. 111 at 139:

"Where a party to a foreign New York Convention award alleges at the enforcement stage that it has been obtained by perjured evidence that party will not normally be permitted to adduce in the English courts additional evidence to make good that allegation unless it is established that:
(i) the evidence sought to be adduced is of sufficient cogency and weight to be likely to have materially influenced the arbitrators' conclusion had it been advanced at the hearing and,
(ii) the evidence was not available or reasonably obtainable either,
(a) at the time of the hearing of the arbitration; or
(b) at such time as would have enabled the party concerned to have adduced it in the Court of supervisory jurisdiction to support an application to reverse the award if such procedure were available.
Where the additional evidence has already been deployed before the Court of supervisory jurisdiction for the purpose of an application for the setting aside of the award but the application has failed, the public policy of finality would normally require that the English Courts should not permit further evidence to be adduced at the enforcement stage."

As regards bias on the part of an arbitrator, the potential for bias is not enough. An enforcing court will wish to know why the aggrieved party did not challenge an apparently biased arbitrator at the appropriate time (see *Hebei Import and Export Corp v Polytek Engineering Co Ltd* (1999) XXIV YCA 652 Hong Kong Court of Final Appeal). Moreover in (2004) XXIX YCA 700 at 704, the German Supreme Court has opined that:

"... the participation of a biased arbitrator must have had a concrete impact on the arbitration ... It must be proven that the biased arbitrator was prejudiced against a party and that this prejudice influenced the decision."

For examples of cases where enforcement has been refused see the decision of a French Court of First Instance in *Exceslsior Film TV Srl v UGC-PH* (1999) XXIV YCA 643; and the decision of the Indian Supreme Court in *Transocean Shipping Agency (P) Ltd v Black Sea Shipping* (1998) XXIII YCA 713.

Procedural irregularity: It might be expected that enforcement might be denied on the basis of public policy when the arbitration had been conducted in flagrant breach of the rules of natural justice. However, deference must be paid to the procedural rules of the forum, to the tribunal's right to conduct the proceedings, and to the fact that arbitral proceedings cannot be expected to be conducted with the same level of formality as court proceedings (see Kerr J. in *Dalmia Dairy Industries Ltd v National Bank of Pakistan* [1978] 2 Lloyd's Rep. 223 at 270). It is also the case that any such challenge might be expected to be made under art.V(1)(b) of the Convention. Moreover, Colman J. in *Minmetals Germany GmbH v Ferco Steel Ltd* [1999] 1 All E.R. (Comm) 315 insisted that the English courts would be unlikely to consider denying enforcement where the enforcee has unreasonably failed to invoke the supervisory jurisdiction of the courts of the forum, or a fortiori where such a court has declined to set aside the award (see also the decision of the Hong King Court of Final appeal in *Hebei Import and Export Corp v Polytek Engineering Co Ltd* (1999) XXIV YCA 652). Accordingly, while it remains a theoretical possibility that enforcement might be denied because of how the arbitration was conducted, there is no English case where this has actually happened.

Breach of EU law: The European Court of Justice pointed out in *Ecoswiss China Time Ltd v Bennetton International* [1999] 2 All E.R. (Comm) 44, that any agreement or decision which infringed a fundamental provision of EU law, such as art.81 relating to unfair competition, was automatically void. It seems therefore to follow that any award which does so should be refused enforcement on grounds of public policy. However the High Court of Bavaria has adopted the approach that it does not itself have to consider the agreement of the parties in order to decide whether it is anti-competitive. It is enough that the tribunal appears to have considered the issue—see decision of August 25, 2004 reported in (2006) *Cahiers de l'Arbitrage* 441.

Subsection (5)

Partial enforcement: This replaces s.5(4) of the 1975 Act, giving effect to a proviso to art.V(1)(c) of the Convention. Thus the context in which it operates is s.20(3)(b). If the award only partly exceeds a tribunal's jurisdiction, then the court may enforce the remainder of the award. The author of the main commentary on the Convention suggests that a court should only exercise this discretion when the excess of authority, "is of a very incidental nature and the refusal of enforcement would lead to unjustified hardship for the party seeking enforcement" (Albert Jan van den Berg, *The New York Arbitration Convention of 1958: Towards a Uniform Judicial Interpretation* (Boston: Kluwer Law and Taxation, 1981), p.319). However, this would seem to run counter to the general thrust of the Convention, and such limited case law as exists on this issue would not seem to support such an approach. An example of the provision in action is provided by *Syria v SIMER* (1983) VIII YCA 386, where a contract provided that non-technical disputes should be settled by local arbitration, while technical disputes should be referred to ICC arbitration. A series of issues were referred to local arbitration and an award made. In enforcement proceedings the Court of Appeal of Trento held that some of the issues which the award purported to determine were technical and thus only granted enforcement of that part of the award which addressed non-technical issues. Another example is the decision of a US District Court in *FIAT SpA v Suriname* (1998) XXIII YCA 880, that an award made against a party to the arbitration agreement and someone who was not a party could only be enforced against the former.

Subsection (6)

This echoes s.5(5) of the 1975 Act, which echoes art.VI of the Convention (see also s.103(5) of the 1996 Act).

Subsection (6)(a)

Sisting decision on recognition or enforcement: Since it is a ground for refusing enforcement that the award has been set aside by a court of the forum, it makes sense that a Scots court which has been asked to enforce an award should be able to sist (i.e. stay/adjourn) its decision pending the outcome of setting aside proceedings. It follows that the court does not have this power if setting aside proceedings are in train elsewhere. Nor, given that the provision speaks of an application having been made, does it have this power if the party resisting enforcement indicates that it is contemplating embarking on such proceedings. It seems that the court can exercise this power on an application by the party resisting enforcement or on its own motion, although in the latter case it would of course have to be made aware of the setting aside proceedings. The Court of Appeal in England in *Yukos Oil Ltd v Dardana Ltd* [2002] 1 Lloyd's Rep. 326, held that it is not open to the party seeking enforcement to apply for a stay under this provision.

It might be thought that, where the conditions for the application of this subsection are met, a sist will be routinely granted in order to avoid the possibility of inconsistency (see, e.g. *Europcar Italia SpA v Maiellano Tours International Inc*, 156 F.3d 310 (1998) US Court of Appeals at 317). However, it frequently happens that an award is enforced despite the fact that such proceedings are ongoing (see W. Michael Tupman, "Staying Enforcement of Arbitral Awards under the New York Convention" (1987) 3 Arbitration Int. 209). This may be because it is thought that the proceedings have been raised simply as a device to delay enforcement, or that they have no reasonable prospect of success, or that the grounds on which the award might be set aside are not such as should prevent its enforcement. In *IPCO (Nigeria) Ltd v Nigerian National Petroleum Corp* [2005] 2 Lloyd's Rep. 326, when an English court considered that a certain sum awarded was certainly due, but that there was an arguable case that the remainder of the award might be set aside in the seat, it ordered partial enforcement, staying the proceedings in respect of the remaining sum. The English courts have also held that it is possible to reconsider a decision on staying enforcement proceedings if it can be shown that circumstances have changed (see *IPCO (Nigeria) Ltd v Nigerian National Petroleum Corp (No.2)* [2008] EWHC 797 (Comm)).

The Convention does not speak about the adjournment of enforcement proceedings except in this context, and its logic might seem to be that such proceedings should not be sisted except on this basis. From time to time the English courts have asserted a general discretion to stay enforcement proceedings (see *Far Eastern Shipping Co v AKP Sovconflot* [1995] 1 Lloyd's Rep. 520; *Air India v Caribjet Inc* [2002] 1 Lloyd's Rep. 314; but compare *Arab Business Consortium International Finance & Investment Co v Banque Franco-Tunisienne* [1995] 1 Lloyd's Rep. 485), but it is suggested that the Scots courts should not follow them in this regard.

Subsection (6)(b)

Ordering the provision of security: In both art.VI of the Convention and s.5(5) of the 1975 Act as well as s.103(5) of the 1996 Act the question of security and adjournment are treated together. The separation of these provisions seems to raise the possibility that security might be ordered to be provided even if immediate enforcement were granted, but that is not the intention (see *Yukos Oil Ltd v Dardana Ltd* [2002] 1 Lloyd's Rep. 326). If the court does decide to adjourn enforcement proceedings pending the outcome of setting aside proceedings, then there may be an enhanced risk that the ultimate enforceability of the award may be imperilled. This may be because the enforcee may seek to thwart enforcement, whether by moving its assets out of Scotland or otherwise, but may also arise in other ways, e.g. the continuing deterioration of the enforcee's financial situation. Accordingly the party seeking enforcement may ask the court to order the other party to provide security for the enforcement of the award.

As to how this power should be exercised, Staughton L.J., delivering the judgment of the Court of Appeal in *Soleh Boneh International Ltd v Uganda* [1993] 2 Lloyd's Rep. 208 at 212, offers the following guidance:

"If the award is manifestly invalid, there should be an adjournment and no order for security; if it is manifestly valid, there should be either an order for immediate enforcement, or else an order for substantial security. In between there will be various degrees of plausibility in the argument for invalidity; and the Judge must be guided by his preliminary conclusion on the point.

... [T]he court must consider the ease or difficulty of enforcement of the award, and whether it will be rendered more difficult, for example, by movement of assets or by improvident trading, if enforcement is delayed. If that is likely to occur, the case for security is stronger; if, on the other hand, there are and always will be insufficient assets within the jurisdiction, the case for security must necessarily be weakened."

It has also been suggested that the fact that the party resisting enforcement has been unduly dilatory in raising setting aside proceedings enhances the case for ordering security (*Yukos Oil Ltd v Dardana Ltd* [2002] 1 Lloyd's Rep. 326). The amount for which security should be ordered lies at the discretion of the court, taking into account all the circumstances (see *IPCO (Nigeria) Ltd v Nigerian National Petroleum Corp* [2005] 2 Lloyd's Rep. 326). Where the proceedings are adjourned, the English courts have asserted a power to order the party seeking enforcement to provide security for the cost of the enforcement proceedings, on the basis that the party might seek to abandon the proceedings if the award is in fact set aside in the seat (*Dardana Ltd v Yukos Oil Ltd (No.2)* [2002] 2 Lloyd's Rep. 261). However, it would appear that they will not otherwise order that party to provide security (*Gater Assets Ltd v Nak Naftogaz Ukrainiy* [2007] EWCA Civ 988).

Subsection (7)

This is discussed in the context of s.20(3)(d), above.

Evidence to be produced when seeking recognition or enforcement

21.—(1) A person seeking recognition or enforcement of a Convention award must produce—
  (a) the duly authenticated original award (or a duly certified copy of it), and
  (b) the original arbitration agreement (or a duly certified copy of it).

(2) Such a person must also produce a translation of any award or agreement which is in a language other than English (certified by an official or sworn translator or by a diplomatic or consular agent).

DEFINITIONS
"arbitration agreement": ss.4, 31(1)
"Convention award": ss.18, 31(1)

COMMENTARY

This section echoes s.4 of the 1975 Act, which in turn echoes art.IV of the Convention. It is in almost identical terms to s.102 of the 1996 Act, and logically might be better appearing before s.20. Unless a party can produce the documentation required, the court may not recognise or enforce the award under s.19, although that does not preclude the court finding some other basis on which to recognise or enforce the award.

Who should perform the authentication or certification demanded by s.21(1)? The Austrian Supreme Court ((1977) I YCA 232), has pointed out that the Convention does not make it clear whether it should be done in terms of the law of the seat or that of the enforcing state, opining that either would usually be acceptable, but recommending the latter. The Italian Supreme Court in *SODIME v Schuurmans & Van Ginneken BV* (1996) XXI YCA 607 was adamant that it is the law of the seat which prevails, while the Bulgarian Supreme Court in *ECONERG Ltd v National Electricity Company AD* (2000) XXV YCA 678 insisted that the requirements of the seat and the enforcing state must both be satisfied. It is difficult to say any of these approaches is more correct that any other, since while art.4(1) of the Geneva Convention had insisted that these issues be determined by the law of the seat, the drafters of the New York Convention had deliberately omitted this requirement in order to confer discretion on the enforcing court (see van den Berg, *The New York Arbitration Convention of 1958*, 1981, p.252). Nonetheless, if the issue ever arose in Scotland, it is to be hoped that the courts would favour the position adopted by the Austrian Supreme Court. It may be added that art.III of the Convention directs that an enforcing state must not impose conditions on recognition and enforcement which are substantially more onerous than those imposed on parties seeking recognition or enforcement of domestic awards.

Subsection (1)(a)

Duly authenticated original award: A party must produce the duly authenticated original award or a duly certified copy, and courts in various jurisdictions have declined to enforce an award where this has not been done (see, e.g. *Weinstein International Corp v Nagtegaal NV* (1980) V YCA 269 (Holland); (1994) XIX YCA 700 (Italy)). Yet this is a curable defect in that enforcement will be granted if the party returns to the court with the proper document (see *Sea Traders SA v Participaciones, Proyectos y Estudios SA* (1996) XXI YCA 676 (Spain)). Where the document seems to have been tendered, the onus will then lie on the party disputing authenticity. The German Supreme Court in (2001) XXVI YCA 771 at 773 has observed that it, "would be a hollow formality to require that the claimant prove the existence and authenticity of the arbitral award, whose copy is supplied."

This also seems to be the approach taken by the English Court of Appeal (*Yukos Oil Ltd v Dardana Ltd* [2002] 1 Lloyd's Rep. 326). Authentication means that the signatures of the arbitrators are confirmed as genuine, while certification means that a copy is attested as a true copy of the original (see van den Berg, *The New York Arbitration Convention of 1958*, 1981, p.648). It follows that if a duly certified copy of the award is produced, then there is no need to prove that the signatures thereon are genuine (see (2000) XXV YCA 717 Rostock Court of Appeal).

Subsection (1)(b)

Original arbitration agreement: A party must also produce the original arbitration agreement or a duly certified copy. Again, while a party who produces the award but not the agreement cannot be granted enforcement, this can be cured if he returns to the court with the agreement at a later stage (see *Ethiopia v Baruch Foster Corp* (1977) II YCA 252). This requirement has sometimes caused difficulties where parties have been joined to arbitral proceedings (see, e.g. *Javor v Francoeur* (2004) XXIX YCA 596), although on other occasions courts have been willing to treat a party as the representative or alter ego of the party to the agreement (see, e.g. *Pan Liberty Navigation Co Ltd v World Link (HK) Resources Ltd* (2005) B.C.C.A. 206).

Subsection (2)

Translation: If the award or agreement is not in English, the party seeking recognition or enforcement must also produce a translation thereof certified by an official or sworn translator or by a diplomatic or consular agent. This means that the translation can be conducted by anyone, as long as it is appropriately certified. Again, this certification can be carried out in terms of either the law of the seat or the place of enforcement (see van den Berg,

The New York Arbitration Convention of 1958, 1981, pp.259–262). Even though this appears to be a mandatory requirement, an Amsterdam court in *SPP (Middle East) Ltd v Egypt* (1985) X YCA 487 enforced an untranslated award because it was in English and understood by the court. Rather more surprisingly, in *R SA v A Ltd* (2001) XXVI YCA 863 a court in Geneva recognised an award rendered in the Chinese language since no reason had been advanced why it should not be recognised.

Postscript—the Model Law

Finally, a word should be said about the repeal of the Model Law in this context. The Model Law also deals with the recognition and enforcement of arbitral awards (in arts 35 and 36). However, since art1(1) of the Model Law states that it is, "subject to any agreement in force between this State and any other State or States", foreign arbitral awards would tend to be enforced under the 1975 Act, giving effect to the New York Convention. Yet whereas under both the 1975 Act and s.18(1) of the current Act one can only seek enforcement of an award which is made in another state which is a party to the New York Convention, art.35(1) of the Model Law provides for the recognition and enforcement of an arbitral award, "irrespective of the country in which it was made". In other words, arts 35 and 36 provide a framework for the recognition and enforcement of arbitral awards made in those countries which have not yet adhered to the New York Convention (see *Report of the UNCITRAL on the work of its eighteenth session*, UN A/40/17, para.309). The repeal of the Model Law removes this possibility, so that such awards, if not subject to any other enforcement convention, must seek enforcement under s.12. It used also to be the case that enforcement could be sought at common law (see Davidson, *Arbitration*, 2000, para.19.54). Is this now precluded? The logic of the Act might suggest that enforcement should be sought under s.12 if it is not to be sought under ss.19–21, since s.12(5) makes it plain that the section applies whether or not the arbitration is seated in Scotland. Yet s.12(6)(b) continues that the section does not affect the right to enforce the award under, "any other enactment or rule of law". The only sensible construction of that provision is that the right to seek enforcement at common law is preserved.

Saving for other bases of recognition or enforcement

22. Nothing in sections 19 to 21 affects any other right to rely on or enforce a Convention award in pursuance of any other enactment or rule of law.

DEFINITIONS
"Convention award": ss.18, 31(1)

COMMENTARY
This replaces s.6 of the 1975 Act, and gives effect to art.VII(1) of the Convention. If it would be more straightforward to enforce a Convention award at common law, or under another treaty or under another set of statutory provisions, then that is permissible. So a party might seek to enforce an award at common law which would not be enforceable under s.18 because he was unable to meet the requirements of s.21 (see *Hamlyn & Co v Talisker Distillery* (1894) 21 R. (HL) 21). It must be doubted, however, whether a party could seek to enforce an award at common law where enforcement was refused under s.20, since it is submitted Scots law would generally accept those grounds for resisting enforcement. Could a party seek

to rely on s.12 as a basis for enforcement? There seems to be no reason why he could not, since, as noted above, s.12(5) makes it clear that the section applies to foreign as well as domestic awards. There might indeed be an advantage in doing so, since s.12 only appears to contemplate one ground for resisting enforcement—lack of jurisdiction. Still, since s.12(1) gives courts a discretion whether or not to enforce an award, that advantage may be more apparent than real.

Supplementary

Prescription and limitation

23.—(1) The Prescription and Limitation (Scotland) Act 1973 (c. 52) is amended as follows.
  (2) In section 4 (positive prescription: interruption)—
    (a) in subsection (2)(b), after "Scotland" insert "in respect of which an arbitrator (or panel of arbitrators) has been appointed",
    (b) in subsection (3)(a), for the words from "and" to "served" substitute ", the date when the arbitration begins",
    (c) for subsection (4) substitute—
    "(4) An arbitration begins for the purposes of this section—
      (a) when the parties to the arbitration agree that it begins, or
      (b) in the absence of such agreement, in accordance with rule 1 of the Scottish Arbitration Rules (see section 7 of, and schedule 1 to, the Arbitration (Scotland) Act 2010 (asp 1)).".
  (3) In section 9 (negative prescription: interruption)—
    (a) in subsection (3), for the words from "and" to "served" substitute "the date when the arbitration begins",
    (b) in subsection (4), for "preliminary notice" substitute "the date when the arbitration begins".
  (4) After section 19C, insert—
  "19D Interruption of limitation period: arbitration
  (1) Any period during which an arbitration is ongoing in relation to a matter is to be disregarded in any computation of the period specified in section 17(2), 18(2), 18A(1) or 18B(2) of this Act in relation to that matter.
    (2) In this section, "arbitration" means—
      (a) any arbitration in Scotland,
      (b) any arbitration in a country other than Scotland, being an arbitration an award in which would be enforceable in Scotland.".
  (5) In section 22A(4), for the words from "and" to "served" substitute "the date when the arbitration begins (within the meaning of section 4(4) of this Act)".
  (6) After section 22C, insert—
  "22CA Interruption of limitation period for 1987 Act actions: arbitration
  (1) Any period during which an arbitration is ongoing in relation to a matter is to be disregarded in any computation of the period specified in section 22B(2) or 22C(2) of this Act in relation to that matter.
    (2) In this section, "arbitration" means—
      (a) any arbitration in Scotland,
      (b) any arbitration in a country other than Scotland, being an arbitration an award in which would be enforceable in Scotland.".

DEFINITIONS
"arbitration": ss.2(1), (2), 31(1)
"party": ss.2(1), 31(1), (2)

COMMENTARY

Subsection (1)

Effect of Act on prescription and limitation: Positive prescription sees someone who has registered title to an interest in land and has enjoyed that right openly, peaceably and without judicial interruption for 10 years (in certain cases 20 years—Prescription and Limitation (Scotland) Act 1973 ss.1(5), 2, 3) having that title rendered unchallengeable, subject to certain exceptions (see s.1(1)). Negative prescription deals with the process whereby rights are extinguished as a result of no attempt being made to enforce them for a period of five years (s.6; the period is 20 years in some cases, s.7). Both positive and negative prescription is interrupted by arbitration and s.23 simply looks to align the date of interruption with the date of commencement of arbitration provided for by r.1 of the Scottish Arbitration Rules. While negative prescription extinguishes rights, limitation simply prevents an action of damages for personal injury being raised once three years has elapsed after the injury was sustained. The right to claim damages itself is not extinguished and thus recourse to arbitration is not prevented. The Act does not seek to change that situation, but allows the limitation period to be interrupted by the commencement of an arbitration, that interruption to continue for as long as the arbitration is ongoing (see explanatory notes, para.64).

Subsection (2)

Interruption of period of positive prescription: Section 4(3) of the Prescription and Limitation (Scotland) Act 1973 currently indicates that in relation to positive prescription the date of a judicial interruption shall be taken to be:

"(a) where the claim has been made in an arbitration and the nature of the claim has been stated in a preliminary notice, the date when that preliminary notice was served;

(b) in any other case the date when the claim was made."

The date of a judicial interruption as regards any arbitration seated in Scotland will now be the date when the arbitration begins. As regards arbitrations seated elsewhere, the date of a judicial interruption will continue to be the date when the claim was made. In terms of s.4(2)(c) of the 1973 Act, arbitral proceedings held outside Scotland amount to a judicial interruption if the award would be enforceable in Scotland, and foreign (including English) awards are readily enforceable here.

When does an arbitration begin? Section 4(4) of the 1973 Act, which currently defines the term "preliminary notice", will now indicate that an arbitration will begin either when the parties so agree, or, in default of agreement, as indicated by r.1 of the Scottish Arbitration Rules, i.e. when one party gives the other notice submitting a dispute to arbitration in accordance with their arbitration agreement. However, this is now subject to the qualification as regards arbitrations seated in Scotland that an arbitral tribunal must ultimately be appointed for the period to be interrupted.

Subsection (3)

Interruption of period of negative prescription: Under ss.6–8 of the 1973 Act the making of a "relevant claim" interrupts the running of the period of negative prescription—either five or 20 years. A relevant claim means a claim made by or on behalf of the creditor for implement of the obligation in appropriate proceedings. Appropriate proceedings include any arbitration in Scotland or an arbitration seated elsewhere if the award would be enforceable in Scotland. At the moment s.9(3) of that Act states that where the nature of the claim has been stated in a preliminary notice, the date when the notice was served shall be treated as the date when the claim was made. Section 9(3) will now indicate that the date when the arbitration begins shall be treated as the date when the claim was made. Section 9(4) will then make it clear that the date when the arbitration begins has the same meaning as under s.4 (see previous paragraph). This makes sense as regards as regards arbitrations seated in Scotland, but not as regards arbitrations seated elsewhere, since they are not subject to r.1 of the Scottish Arbitration Rules. It is hoped that if the issue arises in practice courts will take a pragmatic approach and simply look to when the relevant claim was made, rather than asking when the arbitration begins.

Subsection (4)

Limitation period: The 1973 Act imposes a three year period for the bringing of various actions, after which time limitation applies and court action is no longer competent—s.17, damages or solatium in respect of personal injury; s.18, damages in respect of personal injury leading to death; s.18A, damages in respect of defamation; s.18B, damages in respect of harassment. Currently recourse to arbitration does not interrupt the limitation period, but the Act inserts s.19D which provides that an arbitration will have this effect for as long as the arbitration is ongoing. It can be seen that the arbitration in question need not be seated in Scotland if the award would be enforceable in Scotland.

Subsection (5)

Interruption of period of negative prescription—Consumer Protection Act: Under s.22A of the 1973 Act the period of negative prescription in relation to an obligation to make reparation for damage caused by a defect in a product in terms of the Consumer Protection Act 1987 is 10 years. As ever, the raising of a relevant claim in an arbitration interrupts the running of that period, and subs.(5) simply brings the issue of when a claim is raised in line with the position under s.9 (see the commentary to subs.(3) above).

Subsection (6)

Limitation period—Consumer Protection Act: This simply makes it clear that, like subs.(4) above recourse to arbitration will interrupt the limitation period for as long as the arbitration is ongoing—this time in the context of actions brought under the Consumer Protection Act 1987.

Arbitral appointments referee

24.—(1) Ministers may, by order, authorise persons or types of person who may act as an arbitral appointments referee for the purposes of the Scottish Arbitration Rules.

(2) Ministers must, when making such an order, have regard to the desirability of ensuring that arbitral appointments referees—
(a) have experience relevant to making arbitral appointments, and
(b) are able to provide training, and to operate disciplinary procedures, designed to ensure that arbitrators conduct themselves appropriately.
(3) Despite subsection (2)(b), an arbitral appointments referee is not obliged to appoint arbitrators in respect of whom the referee provides training or operates disciplinary procedures.

DEFINITIONS
"arbitral appointments referee": s.31(1)
"Ministers": s.31(1)
"rules": ss.7, 31(1)

COMMENTARY
One of the striking features of the Act is that under r.7 the default position when procedures for appointing arbitrators fail is that any appointment is to be made not by the court, as is traditional, but by an arbitral appointments referee, a concept not known to any other legal system. It can be seen that Ministers are empowered to authorise persons so to act. In terms of the Scotland Act 1998 (Transitory and Transitional Provisions) (Publication and Interpretation etc. of Acts of the Scottish Parliament) Order 1999 (SI 1999/1379) para.6(2) and Schedule a person would include a body of persons and it is envisaged that the chair of bodies such as the "Chartered Institute of Arbitrators, the Scottish Council on International Arbitration, and the Royal Institute of Chartered Surveyors" might act on their behalf (see policy memorandum, para.109). The policy memorandum, para.112, noted widespread support for this concept in the consultation exercise and, in response to those consultees who argued that the court should continue to appoint, pointed out that in practice the court will usually refer any such application to a body like the Chartered institute of Arbitrators in any case. The law is therefore simply reflecting practical reality. It also suggested (para.111) that any body, e.g. the Law Society of Scotland, which can satisfy the requirements of s.24(2) might apply to be an arbitral appointments referee. Those requirements are a track record of past appointments, plus an ability to provide appropriate training and operate suitable disciplinary procedures, both designed to ensure that arbitrators conduct themselves appropriately. It must be wondered whether all the bodies mentioned above could satisfy those criteria, especially in respect of disciplinary procedures. The consultation paper at para.39 mentioned a further criterion—that the body had regularly to assess the procedures of arbitrators. That criterion does not appear in s.24, presumably because it was realised that no body, save perhaps the Chartered Institute of Arbitrators, could meet it.

Power of judge to act as arbitrator or umpire

25.—(1) A judge may act as an arbitrator or umpire only where—
(a) the dispute being arbitrated appears to the judge to be of commercial character, and
(b) the Lord President, having considered the state of Court of Session business, has authorised the judge to so act.

(2) A fee of such amount as Ministers may by order prescribe is payable in the Court of Session for the services of a judge acting as an arbitrator or umpire.

(3) Any jurisdiction exercisable by the Outer House under the Scottish Arbitration Rules (or any other provision of this Act) in relation to—
    (a) a judge acting as a sole arbitrator or umpire, or
    (b) a tribunal which the judge forms part of,
is to be exercisable instead by the Inner House (and the Inner House's decision on any matter is final).

(4) In this section—
"judge" means a judge of the Court of Session, and
"Lord President" means the Lord President of the Court of Session.

DEFINITIONS
"arbitrator": ss.2(1), 31(1)
"dispute": ss.2(1), 31(1)
"Inner House": s.31(1)
"Outer House": s.31(1)
"tribunal": ss.2(1), 31(1)

COMMENTARY

This largely re-enacts s.17 of the Law Reform (Miscellaneous Provisions) (Scotland) Act 1980 by virtue of which it is already possible for a judge of the Court of Session who considers that a dispute is of a commercial character to accept appointment as an arbitrator, as long as the Lord President authorises her/him so to act.

It may appear strange that sitting judges should sit as arbitrators and the concept is unknown in some jurisdictions, and indeed prohibited in others, but it is certainly known in England where it is currently authorised by s.93 of the 1996 Act and was previously authorised by s.4 of the Administration of Justice Act 1970 and s.99 of the Courts and Legal Services Act 1990 (and before that by s.11 of the Arbitration Act 1950.)

Why might parties consider appointing a judge as arbitrator? In England there appear to be five main reasons:
    (i) simple economics: a judge of the Technology and Construction Court in England costs under £2,000 per day as arbitrator and the use of the courtroom is free;
    (ii) particular expertise: Technology and Construction Court judges are expert in dealing with construction cases, particularly large, complex ones. Indeed Technology and Construction Court judges actively seek appointments as arbitrator. It is understood that approximately 15–20 cases a year are heard by Technology and Construction Court judge-arbitrators;
    (iii) where the key to the arbitration is a particular point of law and the judge chosen is a noted authority in that area of law. For example, Sir Christopher Staughton, while a sitting judge, sat as sole arbitrator in *Oweners of the Bamburi v Compton (The Bamburi)*. The case concerned the question whether a vessel trapped in the Shatt-al-Arab waterway during the 1979 Iraq/Iran war was a constructive total loss for the purposes of the applicable insurance policy. Many other vessels were similarly trapped and Sir Christopher's award, containing an elegant and comprehensive restatement of the law, was considered sufficiently important to be published at [1982] 1 Lloyd's Rep. 312, thus providing authoritative guidance on the issue;

(iv) national security, where a judge is preferred to a "civilian" arbitrator on such grounds;
(v) the fact that, by virtue of Sch.2 of the 1996 Act, a number of powers that are normally only exercisable by the court can be exercised by a judge-arbitrator, while any appeal against the award would be heard by the Court of Appeal, rather limiting the risk of an appeal.

As is discussed more fully below, not all of these reasons would have resonance in Scotland. Currently, there appears to be no recourse to judge-arbitrators, and the policy memorandum, para.115, notes that in light of pressures on the Court of Session there is at present no scope for a judge to be used in this way. It continues that this may change as a result of the recommendations following the Scottish Civil Courts Review (*Report of the Scottish Civil Courts Review* (Scottish Civil Courts Review, 2009), so that the possibility of recourse to a judge-arbitrator was retained in the Act. While those recommendations, if implemented, may reduce some of the pressure on the Court of Session, this may prove a rather optimistic view.

The last known recourse to a judge-arbitrator in Scotland was in 1986 when Lord Jauncey (then a Court of Session judge) sat as sole arbiter pursuant to s.17 of the 1980 Act in an arbitration which eventually saw him stating a case for the opinion of the Court of Session on two issues. He was upheld on one issue but not the other in *Scott Lithgow Ltd v Secretary of State for Defence*, 1988 S.L.T. 697. However, the House of Lords (1989 S.L.T. 236) ultimately upheld him on neither issue. There has only been one recorded challenge to a judge-arbitrator's award under the 1996 Act—*Henry Boot Construction Ltd v Alstom Combined Cycles Ltd* [2005] EWCA Civ 814.

Subsection (1)

When a judge may act as an arbitrator: This is the equivalent of s.93(1)–(2) of the 1996 Act by virtue of which a judge can only act if the Lord Chief Justice has informed her/him that he can be made available. Under the 2010 Act the Lord President must authorise her/him to act. However under both Acts, subject to this authorisation, it is for the judge in question to decide whether she/he wishes to act. Under the 2010 Act a judge must consider a dispute to be of a commercial character in order to be able to act. That condition need not apply under the 1996 Act (compare Administration of Justice Act 1970 s.4), but only a Commercial Court judge or a Technology and Construction Court judge is allowed to act as a judge-arbitrator under that Act, although the DAC Report, para.390 (see also paras 341–343) recommended that all judges should be allowed so to act. Under the 1996 Act a judge may only act as a sole arbitrator or umpire, whereas under the 2010 Act a judge-arbitrator may also be a member of an arbitral tribunal. Whether it would be sensible for the Lord President to authorise scarce judicial resources to be deployed in this way is open to question, and it might be guessed that few judges would be prepared to act except as a sole arbitrator, since the point of having a judge-arbitrator is otherwise largely lost.

In this context it might be noted that the terms of the Sheriff Courts (Scotland) Act 1971 s.6 would appear to preclude a sheriff or sheriff principal accepting appointment as an arbitrator. There is venerable authority which suggests that a judge of the Court of Session may accept appointment as an arbitrator (*Fisher v Colquhoun* (1844) 6 D. 1286). The use of the word "only" in subs.(1) might seem to preclude such appointment except as directed by s.25. However, it might be argued that the provision deals with the appointment of judges qua public officials as arbitrators and does not prevent a judge accepting appointment in her/his capacity as an individual. This is likely to remain a purely theoretical issue.

In England an application that a judge should sit simultaneously as both judge and arbitrator was rejected on the basis that an individual cannot discharge both functions at the same time (*Wilson v Keen* Unreported June 25, 1991 CA).

Subsection (2)

As under the 1980 Act, a charge will be made for the services of a judge. If the previous model is followed that will amount to a fee on appointment plus a daily rate—see the Appointment of Judges as Arbiters (Fees) Order 1993 (SI 1993/3125).

Subsection (3)

Most of the powers exercisable by the court under the rules are invested in the Outer House. It would be highly inappropriate for certain powers, e.g. in relation to appeals, to be exercisable by an Outer House judge when the arbitrator is her/himself a Senator of the College of Justice, so that jurisdiction is invested in the Inner House, whose decision is final.

This provision is the equivalent of Sch.2 para.2(1) of the 1996 Act where references to the High Court are generally treated as reference to the Court of Appeal in cases of judge-arbitrators. However, Sch.2 then goes on to enumerate the various powers which are ordinarily exercisable by the court, but which may be exercised by a judge-arbitrator. There is nothing like this in s.25, which is unfortunate, as all such powers must be exercised by the Inner House. It is not evident, for example, why the power to summon witnesses cannot be entrusted to the judge-arbitrator, rather than wasting the valuable time of the Inner House on such matters.

Amendments to UNCITRAL Model Law or Rules or New York Convention

26.—(1) Ministers may by order modify—
  (a) the Scottish Arbitration Rules,
  (b) any other provision of this Act, or
  (c) any enactment which provides for disputes to be resolved by arbitration,
in such manner as they consider appropriate in consequence of any amendment made to the UNCITRAL Model Law, the UNCITRAL Arbitration Rules or the New York Convention.

(2) Before making such an order, Ministers must consult such persons appearing to them to have an interest in the law of arbitration as they think fit.

DEFINITIONS
  "arbitration": ss.2(1), (2), 31(1)
  "dispute": ss.2(1), 31(1)
  "Ministers": s.31(1)
  "New York Convention": s.31(1)
  "rules": ss.7, 31(1)
  "UNCITRAL Arbitration Rules ": s.31(1)
  "UNCITRAL Model Law": s.31(1)

COMMENTARY

This section allows the Scottish Ministers, subject to affirmative procedure in the Scottish Parliament, to modify the Act or any other statutory provision to reflect changes in the Model Law, the New York Convention, or the UNCITRAL Arbitration Rules. This is a particularly noteworthy provision. The New York Convention is now rather venerable, and there have been calls for certain of its provisions to be updated (see Bockstiegel, "Future Perspectives" in Emmanuel Gaillard and Domenico Di Pietro (eds), *Enforcement of Arbitral Agreements and International Arbitral Awards* (London: Cameron May, 2008)). It is therefore possible (albeit unlikely) that it may be amended at some point in the future, and one might expect that the UK would ultimately ratify any amended version. Section 26 treats any such ratification as certain or indeed as irrelevant in conferring this power. It is doubtful whether this lies within the legislative competence of the Scottish Parliament. No corresponding provision is to be found in the 1996 Act, it being contemplated that the provisions of that Act which deal with the New York Convention should only be amended by primary legislation.

When Scotland adopted the Model Law, there was no power conferred by s.66 of the Law Reform (Miscellaneous Provisions) Scotland Act 1990 to amend the version of the Model Law which applied in Scotland under Sch.7 of that Act. The Model Law was indeed amended by UNCITRAL in 2006, and no attempt was made by the Scottish Parliament to amend Sch.7. It is thus particularly striking that the Act which repeals the Model Law in Scotland should confer a power to amend its provisions to take account of future changes in the Model Law. The policy memorandum, para.117, comments that this will permit Scots arbitration law to keep up-to-date with international arbitral practice, and that Scotland will have an arbitration law which is based on Model Law principles. More remarkable still is the power, added at stage 2, to alter the legislation to reflect amendments in the UNCITRAL Arbitration Rules, since the rules have no legislative status. Yet they are undoubtedly the source of good arbitration practice, and indeed many of them are the inspiration behind key provisions of the Model Law. More importantly, they are much more dynamic than the Model Law. Thus this step goes even further in helping Scotland keep up to date with modern arbitral practice, and the international arbitration community may regard Scotland as having stolen a march on the rest of the world in this respect.

Subsection (2)

This subsection was also added at stage 2 to meet concerns expressed during the consultation process. It was always going to be the case that the Scottish Ministers would consult key stakeholders rather than amending the legislation without reference to the views of others. Indeed, in practice any amendment is likely to arise as a result of lobbying from interested parties. However, the legislation now imposes an actual duty to consult. Ministers must consult such persons appearing to have an interest in arbitration as they think fit, which gives some degree of protection against challenges from marginal groups who believe they should have been consulted.

Amendment of Conveyancing (Scotland) Act 1924 (c. 27)

27. In section 46 of the Conveyancing (Scotland) Act 1924—
    (a) in subsection (2), for "This section" substitute "Subsection (1)", and
    (b) after subsection (2) insert—

"(3) Where—
(a) an arbitral award orders the reduction of a deed or other document recorded in the Register of Sasines (or forming a midcouple or link of title in a title recorded in that Register), and
(b) the court orders that the award may be enforced in accordance with section 12 of the Arbitration (Scotland) Act 2010 (asp 1),
subsection (1) applies to the arbitral award as it applies to a decree of reduction of a deed recorded in the Register of Sasines.".

DEFINITIONS
"court": s.31(1)

COMMENTARY
Section 46 of the above Act provides for the recording in the Register of Sasines of the extract of a court decree reducing or rectifying a deed or other document registered in that register. Under r.49(d) of the Scottish Arbitration Rules, unless the parties have agreed otherwise, the arbitral tribunal itself has the power to reduce or rectify a deed or other document, and its award may then be enforced by the court under s.12. Section 27 then permits the award to be recorded in the Register of Sasines. Such an award is of no effect in so far as it would adversely affect the interests of any third party acting in good faith (s.12).

Articles of Regulation 1695

28. The 25th Act of the Articles of Regulation 1695 does not apply in relation to arbitration.

DEFINITIONS
"arbitration": ss.2(1), 2(2), 31(1)

COMMENTARY
The 25th Act of the Articles of Regulation provides that the Court of Session will not reduce a "decreet arbitral" unless on the grounds of, "corruption, bribery of falsehood to be alleged against the judges arbitrators". This provision is now disapplied in relation to arbitration, and the exclusive grounds for challenging awards are now laid down in Pt 8 of the Scottish Arbitration Rules. The removal of this archaic and confusingly expressed provision is to be commended.

Repeals

29. The repeals of the enactments specified in column 1 of schedule 2 have effect to the extent specified in column 2.

COMMENTARY
A number of other statutes and statutory provisions are repealed. The repeal of Pt II of the Arbitration Act 1950 is discussed in the Introduction. Also repealed are:
- The Arbitration (Scotland) Act 1894. This disapplied the common law rule whereby an arbitration agreement was invalid unless it named an arbitrator. See now r.2 below. It also laid down procedures whereby the court could appoint an arbitrator or oversman (umpire) where conventional appointments procedures failed. However, the court could act only in a limited range of circum-

stances, and in a variety of situations was powerless to assist the parties (see the commentary to r.7 below). Rule 7 now contains a much more comprehensive set of provisions to deal with failure of appointments procedures.
- The Administration of Justice (Scotland) Act 1972 s.3. This section introduced the notorious stated case procedure into Scotland on the model of the old English special case procedure. There had been no particular call for this to happen from within Scotland, and the provision was even then widely regarded as an unnecessary and unwelcome English transplant (see Hunter, "Stated Cases in Contractual Arbitration in Scotland" (1972) 17 J.L.S.S. 168). It was, moreover, a provision which, due to inept drafting, failed in one of its main objectives of permitting appeals against arbitral awards on questions of law (see Lord President Emslie in *Fairlie Yacht Slip v Lumsden*, 1977 S.L.T. (Notes) 41 at 42). Repeal of s.3 was advocated by the Scottish Advisory Committee on Arbitration Law at para.5.22 of its *Report on Legislation for Domestic Arbitration in Scotland*, 1996, and the stated case procedure was roundly criticised by Lord President Hope in *ERDC Construction Ltd v H M Love & Co (No.2)*, 1997 S.L.T. 175 at 178. The policy memorandum, para.121, echoes these views, noting also that its costs are a matter of concern, since it involves reference to the Inner House, and that it has, "caused parties to view arbitration in Scotland as a process where delays occur frequently, since it is thought to be too easy to identify possibly spurious points of law for referral, thus delaying the arbitral process". It should be observed however, that under rr.41–42 there is to be a rather more limited procedure for referring questions of law for the opinion of the Outer House, while r.69 creates a right of appeal against an award on the basis of legal error in certain circumstances. Both rr.41 and 69 are default rules.
- The Arbitration Act 1975. This gave effect to the New York Convention, and is now replaced by ss.10 and 18–22 of the 2010 Act.
- The Law Reform (Miscellaneous Provisions) (Scotland) Act 1980 s.17. This allows a judge of the Court of Session to accept appointment as an arbitrator. It is re-enacted by s.25.
- The Law Reform (Miscellaneous Provisions) (Scotland) Act 1990 s.66 and Sch.7. This gave effect to the Model Law in Scotland.

Arbitrability of disputes

30. Nothing in this Act makes any dispute capable of being arbitrated if, because of its subject-matter, it would not otherwise be capable of being arbitrated.

DEFINITIONS
"dispute": ss.2(1), 31(1)

COMMENTARY
Like art.1(5) of the Model Law, the section makes it clear that the Act does not render any dispute capable of being arbitrated, if it was not previously capable of being arbitrated. There is probably no need for this provision, since nothing in the Act or rules is capable of leading to the opposite conclusion, but it probably does no harm to state this. There is no corresponding provision in the 1996 Act. The provision does not actually

indicate which disputes are or are not arbitrable. In some jurisdictions provisions list the matters which may not be referred to arbitration (see, e.g. French Civil Code art.2060). In others legislation provides that matters which are of a pecuniary nature (e.g. Swiss Private International Law Act art.177(1)) or are capable of being settled by the parties may be arbitrated, while it is increasingly common to combine these two criteria (as in the Austrian Arbitration Law art.582(1)).

The idea of what can be settled by agreement also lies at the heart of the Scots law of arbitrability. As regards domestic arbitration, the 18th century statement of the institutional writer, Lord Bankton (*Institute* I, 23, 17), still represents the law: "Whatever can be transacted may be determined by arbitrament ...".

Thus while matters of status or criminal liability cannot be settled by arbitration, the civil consequences of an alleged fraud may be so referred (*Earl of Kintore v Union Bank of Scotland* (1863) 4 Macq. 465), as may the question of who counts as a dependant of a deceased individual for the purposes of a contractual compensation scheme (*Brown v EE Caledonia Ltd*, 1993 G.W.D. 24-1478). Equally, while an arbitrator may not wind up a company, he may be empowered to dissolve a partnership (*Hackston v Hackston*, 1956 S.L.T. (Notes) 38), since the latter result can be achieved by agreement. And while an arbitrator cannot create property rights, he can decide a dispute between two parties as to whether one has infringed the other's property rights. In certain states employment disputes are not arbitrable. In Scotland most disputes relating to statutory employment rights must be referred to an employment tribunal, and by virtue of the Employment Rights Act 1996 s.203 parties may not contract otherwise, thus effectively outlawing agreements to arbitrate such disputes. However, the Trade Union and Labour Relations (Consolidation) Act 1992 s.212A also allowed the Advisory, Conciliation and Arbitration Service to create a mechanism whereby unfair dismissal claims disputes may be referred to arbitration (see ACAS Arbitration Scheme (Great Britain) Order 2004 (SI 2004/753)). Since disputes arising out of employment contracts may be referred to the ordinary courts, they must be assumed to be arbitrable.

If the issue of arbitrability arose in relation to an international arbitration which chose Scotland as its seat, what law would decide the issue (see Bernadini, "The Problem of Arbitrability" in Gaillard and Di Pietro (eds), *Enforcement of Arbitral Agreements and International Arbitral Awards*, 2008)? The most straightforward and perhaps the most appealing answer is that Scots law deals with the matter. This is the approach taken in a variety of jurisdictions (see *Matermaco SA v PPM Cranes Inc* (2000) XXV YCA 673 (Belgium); *G SpA v V SpA* (1993) XVIII YCA 143 (Switzerland)). Thus in *Fincantieri-Cantieri Navali Italiani SpA v Ministry of Defence of Iraq* (1996) XXI YCA 594 at 599 the Court of Appeal of Genoa insisted that:

"... when an objection for foreign arbitration is raised ... the arbitrability of the dispute must be ascertained according to Italian law, as ... the court ... can only deny jurisdiction on the basis of its own legal system. This also corresponds to the principles expressed in Articles II and V of the New York Convention."

However, alternative approaches see the matter as being governed by the law which governs the arbitration agreement (see *Societe Van Hopplymus v Societe Coherent Inc* (1997) XXII YCA 637 Brussels Commercial Court), or the law chosen to apply to the substance of the dispute (*JSC Surgutneftegaz v Harvard College*, 2005 WL 1863676 US District Court), should that be different, and there is an argument that a tribunal should decline jurisdiction if the dispute is not arbitrable under any of these laws (see Bernard Hanotiau, "What Law Governs the Issue of Arbitrability?" (1996) 12 Arbitration Int. 391).

It will be interesting to see whether, if a tribunal does not decline jurisdiction, inarbitrability would be regarded as a jurisdictional objection in terms of challenging the tribunal's jurisdiction under rr.19–23, or in terms of challenging the award under r.67. Instances exist in other jurisdictions where courts have declined to entertain claims that a dispute is not arbitrable in terms of a foreign governing law (see *Ledee v Ceramiche Ragno* (1984) IX YCA 471 US Court of Appeals; and *Thyssen Canada Ltd v Mariana Maritima SA* [2000] 3 F.C. 398 Canadian Federal Court of Appeal) and one might hope that even if a Scottish court were to accept that some foreign law were to apply to the issue of arbitrability, it would not countenance overly restrictive approaches to that issue, such as that exhibited in *Himpurna California Energy Ltd v PT (Persero) Perusahaan Listruik Negara* (2000) XXV YCA 13, where an Indonesian court ruled that issues regarding the termination of contract were not arbitrable. There is furthermore an argument that in international arbitration the forum state should seek to be more accommodating and should not automatically apply domestic standards of arbitrability. As the British Columbia Court of Appeal observes in *Quintette Coal Ltd v Nippon Steel Corp* (1993) XVIII YCA 159 at 161 (see also the US Supreme Court in *Mitsubishi Motors Corp v Soler Chrysler-Plymouth, Inc*, 473 U.S. 614 (1985) at 639), "it will be necessary for courts to subordinate domestic notions of arbitrability to the international policy favouring commercial arbitration".

It is also the case that in certain states particular sorts of bodies may not arbitrate, or require special authorisation to do so, or require special authorisation to arbitrate certain types of disputes. This may be more a matter of capacity rather than arbitrability, but is treated as an issue of arbitrability (subjective rather than objective arbitrability) in certain jurisdictions (see, e.g. the Swiss Private International Law Act art.177(2), and the approach of the Swiss Federal Tribunal in *Fincantieri-Cantieri navali italiani SpA v M* (1995) XX YCA 76).

It should also be pointed out that when the stage of enforcing an award is reached, a court is entitled to decline to enforce an award under art.V(2)(a) of the New York Convention on the basis that the dispute in question is not arbitrable under the law of that state. Thus, if a party knows that any award will ultimately have to be enforced against the other party by the courts of State X, and their dispute is not arbitrable under the law of State X, practically it does not really matter that the dispute is arbitrable under Scots law or any other of the governing laws. It might be added that despite the statement above that it will usually not be relevant whether the dispute in question is arbitrable under Scots law as the law governing the arbitral procedure, a court is entitled to decline to enforce an award under art.V(1)(a) of the New York Convention if, failing any indication of the law chosen to govern the arbitration agreement, it was not valid under the law of the country where the award was made. It will doubtless be very rare that there is no indication of the law chosen to govern the arbitration agreement, but should such a case arise, the fact that the dispute was not arbitrable under Scots law would arguably render that agreement invalid, and provide grounds for resisting the enforcement of an award made in Scotland. See the commentary to s.20(2)(b) above.

Final provisions

Interpretation

31.—(1) In this Act, unless the contrary intention appears—
"arbitral appointments referee" means a person authorised under section 24,
"arbitration" has the meaning given by section 2,
"arbitration agreement" has the meaning given by section 4,
"arbitrator" has the meaning given by section 2,
"claim" includes counterclaim,
"Convention award" has the meaning given by section 18,
"court" means the Outer House or the sheriff (except in sections 1, 3, 10, 13 and 15, where it means any court),
"default rule" has the meaning given by section 9(1),
"dispute" has the meaning given by section 2,
"Inner House" means the Inner House of the Court of Session,
"mandatory rule" has the meaning given by section 8,
"Ministers" means the Scottish Ministers,
"New York Convention" means the Convention on the Recognition and Enforcement of Foreign Arbitral Awards adopted by the United Nations Conference on International Commercial Arbitration on 10 June 1958,
"Outer House" means the Outer House of the Court of Session,
"party" is to be construed in accordance with section 2 and subsection (2) below,
"rule" means one of the Scottish Arbitration Rules,
"Scottish Arbitration Rules" means the rules set out in schedule 1,
"seated in Scotland" has the meaning given by section 3,
"statutory arbitration" has the meaning given by section 16(1),
"tribunal" has the meaning given by section 2,
"UNCITRAL Arbitration Rules" means the arbitration rules adopted by UNCITRAL on 28 April 1976, and
"UNCITRAL Model Law" means the UNCITRAL Model Law on International Commercial Arbitration as adopted by the United Nations Commission on International Trade Law on 21 June 1985 (as amended in 2006).

(2) This Act applies in relation to arbitrations and disputes between three or more parties as it applies in relation to arbitrations and disputes between two parties (with references to both parties being read in such cases as references to all the parties).

COMMENTARY

Subsection (1)

Relatively little need be said about this provision, since it is mainly straightforward. It must be assumed that these rules of interpretation apply to the rules as well as the Act proper, especially since terms such as "claim" appear in the rules but not elsewhere in the Act. It might also be pointed out that, despite the impression conveyed, not all of the terms mentioned are actually defined in the provisions to which the subsection makes reference.

A number of terms are defined in the 1996 Act which are not mentioned in s.31(1). Thus s.82(1) of the earlier Act defines what is meant by "available arbitral process", a phrase which the 2010 Act employs in r.71. And s.82(2) also makes it clear that reference to a party to an arbitration agreement, "include any person claiming under or through a party", a matter on which the 2010 Act is silent. Other terms are not defined or explained by s.31(1), but in individual rules, as is made plain by the index of such terms in Sch.1—"arbitration expenses, recoverable arbitration expenses" and "independent". The 1996 Act s.82(1) indicates that a claimant includes a counterclaimant, whereas s.31(1) follows art.2(k) of the Model Law in stating that a claim includes a counterclaim. Section 31(1) suggests that these rules of interpretation should be applied, "unless the contrary intention appears". Article 2(k) of the Model Law may provide useful guidance as to when a claim might not embrace a counterclaim, since it states explicitly that this is not the case in relation to the provision which empowers the tribunal to terminate the arbitration where a party delays unnecessarily in submitting or pursuing a claim (see r.37(1)).

Subsection (2)

This provision reflects the fact that although normally an arbitration will involve two parties, multi-party arbitration is not uncommon. The provision ensures that where a section or rule speaks of a party taking certain action in relation to, "the other party", it is to be interpreted as if it means all other parties. Equally where a section or rule speaks of "either" party being entitled to take certain action, it is to be interpreted as if it means "any" party.

Ancillary provision

32.—(1) Ministers may by order make any supplementary, incidental, consequential, transitional, transitory or saving provision which they consider appropriate for the purposes of, or in connection with, or for the purposes of giving full effect to, any provision of this Act.

(2) Such an order may modify any enactment, instrument or document.

DEFINITIONS
"Ministers": s.31(1)

COMMENTARY

Subsection (1)

The Scottish Ministers may make any order they consider necessary to give full effect to any provision of the Act. This is clearly a saving provision should it transpire that, whether because of unfortunate drafting, unanticipated judicial interpretation or otherwise, any provision of the Act is found to fall short of its intended effect. It is not a provision which allows Ministers to fill gaps in the Act, or to add provisions which might later be deemed desirable. There is nothing comparable to s.32 in either the 1996 Act or the Model Law. In *Dermajaya Properties Sdn Bhd v Premium Properties Sdn Bhd* (2002) 2 S.L.R. 164, the Singapore High Court surprisingly treated as ineffective the parties' agreement that the UNCITRAL Arbitration Rules should be applied rather than the default provisions of the Singapore Arbitration Act. This was rectified by primary legislation, but if a similar situation arose in Scotland, it could be addressed under s.32.

Subsection (2)

Such an order may go so far as to modify any enactment, including primary legislation and indeed the Act itself.

Orders

33.—(1) Any power of Ministers to make orders under this Act—
  (a) is exercisable by statutory instrument, and
  (b) includes power to make—
    (i) any supplementary, incidental, consequential, transitional, transitory or saving provision which Ministers consider appropriate,
    (ii) different provision for different purposes.

(2) A statutory instrument containing such an order (or an Order in Council made under section 18) is subject to annulment in pursuance of a resolution of the Scottish Parliament.

This subsection does not apply—
  (a) to orders made under section 35(2) (commencement orders), or
  (b) where subsection (3) makes contrary provision.

(3) An order—
  (a) under section 17 or 32 which adds to, replaces or omits any text in this or any other Act,
  (b) under section 26, or
  (c) under section 36(4),

may be made only if a draft of the statutory instrument containing the order has been laid before, and approved by resolution of, the Scottish Parliament.

DEFINITIONS
"Ministers": s.31(1)

COMMENTARY

Any orders made by the Scottish Ministers will take the form of statutory instrument. These are to be promulgated using the negative procedure, whereby the statutory instrument will stand unless annulled by a resolution of the Scottish Parliament. The exceptions are any order which brings a provision into force, or amends primary legislation, or which seeks to bring the Act into line with future amendments of the Model Law or the New York Convention, or which seeks to remove the right of parties to arbitration agreements made before the commencement of the Act to opt out of the Act. Any such order would require to be approved by a positive resolution of the Scottish Parliament.

Crown application

34.—(1) This Act binds the Crown.

(2) Her Majesty may be represented in any arbitration to which she is a party otherwise than in right of the Crown by such person as she may appoint in writing under the Royal Sign Manual.

(3) The Prince and Steward of Scotland may be represented in any arbitration to which he is a party by such person as he may appoint.

(4) References in this Act to a party to an arbitration are, where subsection (2) or (3) applies, to be read as references to the appointed representative.

DEFINITIONS
"arbitration": ss.2(1), (2), 31(1)
"party": ss.2(1), 31(1), (2)

COMMENTARY

This provision is the equivalent of s.106 of the 1996 Act, which in turn largely re-enacts s.30 of the 1950 Act. It makes it clear not only that the Crown may be a party to an arbitration, but also that the Queen or Prince Charles may equally be a party to an arbitration in their personal capacities, and may be represented therein by such person as she or he may appoint. The Act applies to the Crown or to any such representative as it would apply to any other party

Commencement

35.—(1) The following provisions come into force on Royal Assent—
section 2
sections 31 to 34
this section
section 37

(2) Other provisions come into force on the day Ministers by order appoint.

COMMENTARY

All of the important provisions of the Act require to be brought into effect by ministerial order. Only the ancillary and definitional provisions come into effect on the day of the Royal Assent (January 5, 2010).

Transitional provisions

36.—(1) This Act does not apply to an arbitration begun before commencement.

(2) This Act otherwise applies to an arbitration agreement whether made on, before or after commencement.

(3) Despite subsection (2), this Act does not apply to an arbitration arising under an arbitration agreement (other than an enactment) made before commencement if the parties agree that this Act is not to apply to that arbitration.

(4) Ministers may by order specify any day falling at least 5 years after commencement as the day on which subsection (3) is to cease to have effect.

(5) Before making such an order, Ministers must consult such persons appearing to them to have an interest in the law of arbitration as they think fit.

(6) Any reference to an arbiter in an arbitration agreement made before commencement is to be treated as being a reference to an arbitrator.

(7) Any reference in an enactment to a decree arbitral is to be treated for the purposes of section 12 as being a reference to a tribunal's award.

(8) An express provision in an arbitration agreement made before commencement which disapplies section 3 of the Administration of Justice (Scotland) Act 1972 (c. 59) in relation to an arbitration arising under that agreement is, unless the parties otherwise agree, to be treated as being an agreement to disapply rules 41 and 69 in relation to such an arbitration.

(9) In this section, "commencement" means the day on which this section comes into force.

COMMENTARY

This was another section added at stage 2. It is undoubtedly a necessary section, since the lack of transitional provisions was a serious deficiency. However, the Act has approached the matter in an interesting way, which represents a compromise between two opposing points of view. Inevitably, whenever a new arbitration regime is introduced, there will at that point be a number of arbitrations which are already under way under the previous regime. Many of these could no doubt continue without difficulty under the new legislative framework, but others will have been set up to operate by reference to the old law. There is no easy way to distinguish between the two categories, so that a blanket rule is required, and the only sensible approach is to provide that existing arbitrations will continue to operate under the former regime. This is the approach which successive Arbitration Acts, including the 1996 Act (see DAC, *Supplementary Report on the Arbitration Act 1996* (Stationery Office, 1996), paras 70–74), have taken in England since at least 1889 and this is indeed the approach the 2010 Act adopts.

There then arises the matter of how one should treat arbitrations which begin after the commencement of the Act, but under arbitration agreements which were entered into prior to that commencement. One approach is to take the view that parties to these agreements contemplated arbitrating under the old law so that the new law should only apply to arbitrations under agreements entered into after the date of commencement. The downside of this approach is that it perpetuates the existence of parallel regimes. Of course the operation of transitional provisions renders parallel regimes inevitable, in that the old law will apply to existing arbitrations in any case. However, while arbitral proceedings may drag on for years, it is difficult to envisage there being much need to have recourse to the old law after about a decade following commencement. By contrast, arbitration clauses in long term contracts may be in existence for many years before being invoked. The DAC (DAC Report, para.315) gives the example of such a clause in a 999 year lease between two organisations, noting that to cater for such situations the old law may have to operate alongside the new law "indefinitely". Thus the traditional English approach has been to provide that the new law will apply to any arbitrations which begin after the commencement of the Act—see s.84(2) of the 1996 Act. It might also be added that if the legislature has decided that the law is in need of reform, then it seems appropriate that parties to all arbitrations which occur after the measure is passed should obtain the benefit of the new provisions—an argument which applies with particular force to the 2010 Act.

A third alternative is to assume that the later system will ordinarily prevail, but to allow the parties to opt for the old law to apply. This would have the advantage that arguments regarding disappointed expectations would have less force. The main disadvantage is that once again this creates the possibility that parallel regimes will operate indefinitely. Accordingly, the 2010 Act, while pursuing this alternative, also empowers Ministers (no earlier than five years after commencement) to remove this option from the parties. This looks rather peculiar, but is probably the most sensible way to address the problem if the drafters did not feel sufficiently bold simply to follow the English example.

Subsection (1)

This seems straightforward, but when does an arbitration begin? Rule 1 provides an answer, but if the Act does not apply to an arbitration, can courts, parties and arbitral tribunals be guided by r.1? Rule 1 is also a default rule, so the parties can agree when an arbitration is regarded as commencing. Would such an agreement be effective in terms of s.36(1)? Perhaps it is best to take a commonsense approach to the issue. Article 21 of the Model Law indicates that unless the parties agree otherwise arbitral proceedings are to be seen as commencing when a request made by a party for a dispute to be referred to arbitration is received by the other party. In arbitrations governed by Model Law this provision should arguably prevail, but there is a certain circularity to this argument since the Model Law, being part of the superseded regime, would only apply if the arbitration began before commencement. And when is commencement? See subs.(9) below.

An arbitration begun before commencement is subject to the previous law of arbitration. This of course means the common law plus the various statutory fragments—art.25 of the Articles of Regulation 1695, the Arbitration (Scotland) Act 1894 and the stated case procedure under s.3 of the Administration of Justice (Scotland) Act 1972. Would foreign awards made in such arbitrations be enforced under Pt II of the Arbitration Act 1950 and the Arbitration Act 1975? Of course if the arbitration was an international commercial arbitration seated in Scotland, then it will be governed by the Model Law as laid out in s.66 and Sch.7 of the Law Reform (Miscellaneous Provisions) Scotland Act 1990. The same will be true if the parties to an arbitration which is not an international commercial arbitration contract into the terms of the Model Law as permitted by s.66(4) of that Act.

It may be noted that the parties to such an arbitration do not have the option to invoke the application of the Act.

Subsection (2)

As noted in the introduction to this section, if the arbitration has not itself begun at the date of commencement, then it does not matter when the arbitration agreement was entered into. Even if it were entered into 100 or more years previously, any arbitration under it is subject to the 2010 Act. Obviously the Act also governs all future arbitration agreements. However, this is subject to subs.(3).

Subsection (3)

If the arbitration has not itself begun at the date of commencement, but the arbitration agreement was nonetheless made before commencement, then while the assumption will be that any arbitration under that agreement will be governed by the Act, the parties may agree that the Act is not to apply. This will then mean that the previous law will apply. It seems to be envisaged that the Act must be entirely excluded. It does not appear possible for the parties to choose to be governed partly by the Act while invoking aspects of the previous regime, although in many cases the parties can achieve a similar result by replacing default provisions of the Act with contractual provisions similar to the old law, e.g. by invoking the Model Law. Presumably, the exclusion of the Act would have to be fairly explicit. Thus if the parties agreed that the arbitration was to be governed by the Model Law, the assumption would be that the parties were accepting the operation of the Act, but using their power to exclude default rules by applying some other set of rules. However, if the parties agreed that the arbitration was to be governed by the law as it stood prior to the passage of the 2010 Act, that would surely amount to an exclusion. It would be more difficult to assess the parties' intentions in situations where they simply invoked provisions which were not compatible with the Act, e.g. the stated case procedure under s.3 of the Administration of Justice (Scotland) Act 1972. Would that be taken to be an attempt to exclude the Act, or simply an ineffective agreement?

Obviously, we are speaking here of agreements made after the advent of the Act. No agreement made in ignorance of the Act could be taken to exclude it. But consider an arbitration clause in a contract made several years ago, which stipulates that any dispute shall be referred to arbitration and that such arbitration will be governed by the Model Law. When the parties entered into that agreement, they would have believed that they were invoking the provisions of the Model Law to replace pre-existing Scots common law and statute as allowed by s.66(4) of the Law Reform (Miscellaneous Provisions) Scotland Act 1990. After the Act such an agreement would serve rather to replace the default rules of the Act with different rules. The effect of the clause is thus rather different. Should it still be enforced? Presumably so.

Subsection (4)

Parties may not be permitted to contract out of the Act indefinitely. Ministers have power to deprive subs.(3) of effect. Presumably, any such order would have to make clear its effect. For example, arbitrations which were already being carried out under the old law as a result of the agreement of the parties would continue to be subject to that law. Equally, no agreement to exclude the Act made from that point on could be effective. But what of existing arbitration clauses which sought to disapply the Act, but which had not come into force? It would surely be sensible to deprive these of effect, otherwise the problem of parallel regimes could once again be around indefinitely.

The order could not be made earlier than five years after commencement. This would give those who are wedded to the old law a significant period to see how the new regime operates and for that regime to prove its superiority. Potentially, the order might never be made so that Scotland might operate forever with parallel regimes, but it is surely much more likely that an order will be made as soon as the five year period has elapsed.

Subsection (5)

Once more the Ministers must consult as envisaged by s.24(2). Such consultation may of course reveal that adherents of the old order are not yet won over, but that would presumably not prevent an order being made.

Subsections (6) and (7)

Arbitrators have traditionally been known as arbiters in Scotland and are so designated in both contracts and legislation. Similarly statute tends to speak of decrees (or decreets) arbitral when referring to an award. It is extremely unlikely that such references would have been interpreted otherwise under the new regime, but these provisions remove any doubt.

Subsection (8)

The parties were entitled to contract out of the stated case procedure under s.3 of the Administration of Justice (Scotland) Act 1972—s.3(1)—and many contracts routinely did so. There are two default rules under the Act which occupy the same broad territory as s.3—the power of a party to refer a point of law to the court under r.41 and the power to challenge an award on the basis of legal error under r.69. But for this provision, a court which was invited to consider the effect of an exclusion of s.3 in the context of the 2010 Act would have faced a difficult task. Presumably, it could not have interpreted such an exclusion as effectively contracting out of quite different provisions in a later statute. The Act, however, operates on the assumption that if the parties had decided they did not want the stated case procedure, they will similarly reject rr.40 and 67. It is doubtful whether that assumption would be well founded in every case, but this provision at least has the merit of clarity. Parties who decide they do want the benefit of these rules may so agree. If only one party takes this view, then he is to be disappointed.

Subsection (9)

Several subsections speak of commencement. It is made clear that this is not the date when the Act receives the Royal Assent (i.e. January 5, 2010), but the date when s.36 itself comes into force. Thus the Act commences on that date no matter when individual provisions are brought into force. It is to be hoped that the date of commencement is the same date as that when the substantive provisions are all brought into force.

Short title

37. This Act is called the Arbitration (Scotland) Act 2010.

SCHEDULE 1

SCOTTISH ARBITRATION RULES

(introduced by section 7)

Mandatory rules are marked "**M**".
Default rules are marked "**D**".

PART 1

COMMENCEMENT AND CONSTITUTION OF TRIBUNAL ETC.

Rule 1: Commencement of arbitration **D**

1. An arbitration begins when a party to an arbitration agreement (or any person claiming through or under such a party) gives the other party notice submitting a dispute to arbitration in accordance with the agreement.

DEFINITIONS
 "arbitration": ss.2, 31(1)
 "arbitration agreement": ss.4, 31(1)
 "dispute": ss.2, 31(1)
 "notice": r.83

STATUS
 This is a default rule so it is open to the parties to modify it, agree something different or disapply it completely (see s.9).
 All sets of arbitral rules known to the authors contain an equivalent provision; see below.

MODEL LAW
 Article 21 "Commencement of arbitral proceedings" provides that:
  "Unless otherwise agreed by the parties, the arbitral proceedings in respect of a particular dispute commence on the date on which a request for that dispute to be referred to arbitration is received by the respondent."
It will be noted that this refers to "receipt" by the respondent but the Model Law provides no definition of what "receipt" requires, inter alia because

practice varies around the world (see below regarding rules applicable in litigation).

COMMENTARY

Introduction

The principle is straightforward, i.e. that an arbitration is commenced by a notice of arbitration, but practical difficulties have arisen in deciding what constitutes a valid notice, particularly where the purported notice appears to be conditional on some other event occurring or when it is not expressed with legal precision.

In addition, there is a critical threshold question of whether or not there is any arbitration agreement at all and this will be addressed under Pt 2 (rr.19–23) below. For the present, "a party to an arbitration agreement" should, in practical terms, be interpreted as, "a party *believing itself to be party* to an arbitration agreement".

The giving/receipt of notice

This is a default rule so it is open to the parties to agree some different approach to the important question of what constitutes a notice of arbitration and when it is received and by whom, sufficient to determine the date of commencement. Typically art.1 of the Scottish Arbitration Code 2007 ("SAC 07") provides in some detail for what must be included in such notice as do (inter alia) art.3 of the UNCITRAL Rules, art.1 of the LCIA Rules and art.4 of the ICC Rules.

The various sets of rules differ in who is to be the recipient of the notice; the rules of institutions which administer arbitrations normally require that the notice to be sent to the institution and the date of receipt thereat is the date of commencement (LCIA Rules art.1.2; ICC Rules art.4(2)).

Where there is no administering institution (e.g. as in SAC 07 and UNCITRAL Rules), the notice will normally be sent to the other party and the date of receipt thereby becomes the date of commencement. This can, of course, give rise to practical difficulties in establishing what constitutes "receipt" and the matter of delivery of contractual notices is normally provided elsewhere in the contract containing the arbitration agreement (the "main contract" or "container contract"). Absent such contractual notice provisions, general principles apply and, in the normal course of events, and particularly where the claimant (or its legal advisers) is relatively sophisticated and/or experienced, the time of commencement is clearly established from a clearly-drafted notice, e.g. along the lines of "we hereby serve notice that ...".

Absent clear contractual notice provisions, r.83, common sense and commercial practice must prevail; see the commentary to r.83 below. Recent English jurisprudence (e.g. *Fiona Trust & Holding Corp v Yuri Privalov* [2007] EWCA Civ 20, per Longmore L.J. at [17] with concurring support in the House of Lords at [2007] UKHL 40, e.g. Lord Hoffmann at [6]–[8], [13]) has stressed that arbitration is primarily for commercial businessmen. Typically, in *Bernuth Lines Ltd v High Seas Shipping Ltd (The Eastern Navigator)* [2005] EWHC 3020 (Comm); [2006] 1 Lloyd's Rep. 537, Christopher Clarke J. dismissed a challenge to an arbitral award where the entire arbitration had been conducted by email (the final award was also sent by courier) including the service of the notice of arbitration. The judge said this (at [28]):

"I do not regard the provisions of CPR Part 6 as an appropriate benchmark by which to judge whether or not service by e-mail is effective in the context of an arbitration. The CPR cater for litigants of all kinds from major corporations represented by the most accomplished firms of solicitors to individuals represented by more modest firms and those who are not represented at all. By contrast arbitrations are usually conducted by businessmen represented by, or with ready access to, lawyers. Section 76(3), when providing that a notice could be served on a person by any effective means was, in my judgment, purposely wide. It contemplates that any means of service will suffice provided that it is a recognised means of communication effective to deliver the document to the party to whom it is sent at his address for the purpose of that means of communication (eg post, fax or e-mail). *There is no reason why, in this context, delivery of a document by e-mail — a method habitually used by businessmen, lawyers and civil servants — should be regarded as essentially different from communication by post, fax or telex*" (authors' emphasis added).

It is submitted that this is, in general, the correct, modern approach, consistent with one of the objectives of arbitration being to appeal to, and be useable by, business people.

What is a valid notice?

Problems can arise where the intentions of the party serving the notice or alleged notice are unclear, particularly when the intention to proceed to arbitration can be read as conditional on some other event occurring, e.g. the expiry of a time period, or is a mere threat of arbitration. This issue has arisen in several English cases of which three are particularly relevant.

In *Seabridge Shipping AB v AC Orssleff's Eftf's A/S (The MV Fjellvang)* [1999] 2 Lloyd's Rep. 685, two relevant issues arose for determination by Thomas J.: had the charterers' notice, given just before the expiry of the applicable one year time limit, satisfied the requirements of s.14 of the Arbitration Act 1996? If not, could an arbitration be commenced in a manner other than that expressly permitted by s.14? The purported notice, a fax by the charterers to an LMAA arbitrator, Mr O, (cc the owners), said, inter alia:

> "Pursuant to the arbitration agreement charterers are to appoint their arbitrator and we would be grateful if you could indicate your acceptance of your appointment as charterers' arbitrator in this reference.
>
> Would owners who read in copy please indicate if they are prepared to accept you [as] sole arbitrator, alternatively, attend to the appointment of their arbitrator within 7 days of this fax, failing which charterers will seek to have you appointed as sole arbitrator."

The following day the arbitrator confirmed by telephone his acceptance of the appointment and the charterers replied by fax (cc the owners) stating:

> "We refer to your today's telephone conversation with our [Mr A] when you confirmed your appointment as arbitrator on behalf of [charterers]."

The owners did not respond to either fax and charterers then took steps to have Mr O appointed sole arbitrator. Several weeks later the owners challenged the validity of Mr O's appointment and he decided that the purported notice had not been valid. The issue before the court was whether the fax had complied with s.14(4) of the 1996 Act which provided:

"Where the arbitrator or arbitrators are to be appointed by the parties, arbitral proceedings are commenced in respect of the matter where one party serves on the other party or parties notice in writing requiring him or them to appoint an arbitrator or to agree to the appointment of an arbitrator in respect of that matter".

The owners accepted that the words, "would owners . . .", required them to appoint an arbitrator, or to agree to Mr O's appointment but contended that the fax was not a proper notice because it was not addressed to them but merely copied to them. The judge considered:

". . . that section 14 should be interpreted broadly and flexibly and that a strict and technical approach to this section had no place in the scheme of the 1996 Act. Notices are given by international traders and businessmen who often use shorthand expressions, or ways of doing things, which are objectively clear in giving notice to the other party of a reference and of the requirement to appoint an arbitrator."

In the judge's view the charterers' notice was objectively clear, requiring the owners to appoint an arbitrator or to agree the appointment of Mr O and it was sent by an effective means and received by owners.

The second issue addressed by Thomas J. was whether an arbitration could be commenced in a manner other than that expressly permitted by s.14. The charterers had argued in the alternative that the arbitration had been commenced on the day when Mr O had accepted the appointment and when the owners had been given notice thereof. This argument, however, involved the contention that s.14 was not a complete code for the commencement of arbitration proceedings and that it was permissible to commence an arbitration in another manner (see s.81(1) of the 1996 Act; see also Professor Robert Merkin, *Arbitration Law* (London: Informa, 1991), para.11.5). Thomas J. considered that in cases where a party had given an objectively clear notice it was likely that these would be met by a construction of s.14 which was broad enough to include an implied request to appoint an arbitrator. If there were circumstances which could not properly be met in this way, then the question must remain open as to whether an arbitration could be commenced in a way not expressly set out in s.14. While it was not necessary for the judge to decide that question, he considered that given the fact that the 1996 Act was intended for use by laymen and was written in "user-friendly language" capable of application by international traders and businessmen, it was difficult to see why it should have been intended that methods for commencing an arbitration other than those set out in s.14 were to be permitted. The section was very clearly expressed, easy to follow and apply, and provided for certainty and, from it, the requirements of the law of England and Wales were readily ascertainable without resort to pre-Act authorities. Since, in the judge's view, the section should be construed broadly, it was difficult to envisage an apparent justification for providing for other means outside the Act which would only make for complexity and uncertainty and diminish the easy ascertainability of the law of arbitration where the Act, as in this case, expressly dealt with this subject matter.

Similarly, in *Atlanska Plovidba v Consignaciones Asturianas SA (The Lapad)* [2004] EWHC 1273 (Comm); [2004] 2 Lloyd's Rep. 109, Moore-Bick J. stated at [17]:

"Arbitration is widely used by commercial parties, often acting without the benefit of legal advice, and there are good reasons, therefore, for concentrating on the substance of their communications rather than the form. *If a notice of arbitration is to be effective, it must identify the dispute to which it relates with sufficient particularity and must also make it clear that the person giving it is intending to refer the dispute to arbitration, not merely threatening to do so if his demands are not met.* Apart from that, however, I see no need for any further requirements. Whether any particular document meets those requirements will depend on its terms which must be understood in the context in which it was written. The weight of authority supports a broad and flexible approach to this question" (authors' emphasis added).

In *Bulk & Metal Transport (UK) LLP v VOC Bulk Ultra Handymax Pool LLC (The VOC Gallant)* [2009] EWHC 288 (Comm) a similar issue arose and H.H. Judge Mackie QC (sitting as a Deputy Judge of the High Court) quoted with approval from the skeleton argument of counsel for the charterers, stating that it was common ground that:

"(1) A broad and flexible approach must be adopted with respect to the effect of s.14(4).
(2) The requirements of that section will be satisfied provided that it is objectively clear that a communication is intended to refer a dispute to arbitration and to require the necessary steps in that regard to be taken. In that regard the communication must be viewed in its context and not taken in isolation.
(3) A communication will satisfy that test if, by its wording (construed in a matter which is not unduly strict, scrutinous, technical, legalistic or formulaic, and which focuses upon its substance rather than its form) that intention is objectively express or implied.
(4) That intention will be implied from a communication which simply demonstrates that an arbitration clause is being invoked, or which intimates that a dispute is to be submitted to arbitration or that an arbitration is to be resorted to, or which states to the effect that 'I demand the right to have this dispute decided by arbitration as we agreed and require your co-operation in bringing about' or 'I require the difference between us to be submitted to arbitration' or 'unless you are prepared to make proposals for settlement, you must take this letter as requiring you to appoint your arbitrators'.
(5) A communication which makes the invocation of the arbitration clause conditional upon the failure to accept an offer of settlement will also suffice, provided that the time of commencement is made clear (by way of a time limit for acceptance of any proposal). Thus, a communication to the effect of 'Unless you are prepared to settle the matter amicably, we must ask you to agree to the appointment of an arbitrator' will suffice to commence proceedings as from the expiry of the stated time limit for acceptance."

His Honour Judge Mackie QC made a separate but important point: it was important not to confuse commencing arbitration under s.14(4) with taking a step towards constituting the tribunal.

In contrast to these three decisions, in distinguishable circumstances Ramsey J. reached a different conclusion in *Taylor Woodrow Construction v RMD Kwikform Ltd* [2008] EWHC 825 (TCC) in which solicitors for Taylor Woodrow had written as follows:

"We have tried to avoid the need to litigate, but our approaches have been rebuffed. We therefore enclose a draft Particulars of Claim, which will be served in due course. Kindly advise us [concerning communications] ... [TW]'s Standard Conditions of Sub-Contract were incorporated into the contract and Paragraph 26 provides that disputes should be referred to Arbitration. Please confirm whether you wish to rely on Paragraph 26 and insist on proceedings by way of arbitration, or would be agreeable to the matter being litigated."

Ramsey J. agreed with RMD's submission that that letter was not objectively clear in giving notice to the other party of a reference to arbitration and of the requirement to appoint an arbitrator, rather that it gave notice that TW was preparing to litigate and was seeking to find out whether RMD would insist on arbitration. The emphasised passage in *The Lapad* [2004] 2 Lloyd's Rep. 109 was applicable: the notice, "must also make it clear that the person giving it is intending to refer the dispute to arbitration, not merely threatening to do so if his demands are not met."

The case raised a separate issue which can arise in practice: Taylor Woodrow had applied to the President of the CIArb for the appointment of an arbitrator and he had duly made one, in the full knowledge of RMD's objections. Ramsey J. (wholly correctly) set that appointment aside: where did that leave the appointment system? As a general rule (on a worldwide basis, e.g. see Model Law art.16) it is for the arbitrator(s), not the appointing body or person, to become involved in, and decide, issues of jurisdiction subject to any available rights of challenge (refer rr.19, 20, 67). Irrespective of whether the appointing body is an administering one with a full time secretariat (e.g. ICC, LCIA, SIAC et al) or a non-administering appointing body (e.g. CIArb, LMAA), the correct response to such circumstances is to appoint and leave the arbitrator(s) to deal with the jurisdictional issue.

Summarising, we submit that the English jurisprudence in this area offers Scotland persuasive assistance, inter alia giving a wide construction of any notice of arbitration and applying commercial common sense in strong preference to over-attention to form requirements.

Rule 2: Appointment of tribunal **D**

2. An arbitration agreement need not appoint (or provide for appointment of) the tribunal, but if it does so provide it may—
   (a) specify who is to form the tribunal,
   (b) require the parties to appoint the tribunal,
   (c) permit another person to appoint the tribunal, or
   (d) provide for the tribunal to be appointed in any other way.

DEFINITIONS
"arbitration agreement": ss.4, 31(1)
"tribunal": ss.2, 31(1)

STATUS
This is a default rule so it is open to the parties to modify it, agree something different or disapply it completely (see s.9).

MODEL LAW
There is no equivalent of r.2 in the Model Law.

COMMENTARY
Rules 6 and 7 below provide a mechanism for appointing the arbitrator, absent any contrary agreement by the parties. It is expected that the majority of such contrary agreements will be in the form of the parties' agreement, normally incorporated in their arbitration agreement by reference to a set of rules such as SAC 07 (whose art.3 addresses these matters); the UNCITRAL (arts 5–8), ICC Rules (art.9), LCIA Rules (art.5) and Swiss Rules (arts 5–8) contain equivalent provisions.

It may appear that r.2 is otiose but the draftsman appears to have considered it important, given that these rules are to be user-friendly in the context of commercial and individual parties, to set out the main options at the outset for the benefit of commercial parties perhaps unfamiliar with the various options.

Rule 3: Arbitrator to be an individual **M**

3. Only an individual may act as an arbitrator.

DEFINITIONS
"arbitrator": ss.4, 31(1)

STATUS
This is a mandatory rule so the parties cannot disapply or vary it (see s.8).

MODEL LAW
There is no equivalent of r.3 in the Model Law.

COMMENTARY
To some this rule may appear otiose but it is in fact necessary since under the common law it was competent to appoint an unincorporated body as arbiter (*Bremner v Elder* (1875) 2 R. (HL) 136) or a firm (*Wm Dixon Ltd v Jones, Heard & Ingram* (1884) 11 R. 739) and that possibility had to be eliminated.

The question of whether or not an arbitrator can be a legal person, whether corporate entity, partnership or otherwise, proves a surprisingly difficult one to answer as a worldwide survey by one of the authors in late 2009 demonstrated.

The Model Law provides at art.11(1) that, "No person shall be precluded by reason of his nationality from acting as an arbitrator, unless otherwise agreed by the parties", and that might appear strong support for the proposition that the arbitrator must be an individual. That proposition fails, however, since art.3(1)(a) provides that, "any written communication is deemed to have been received if it is delivered to the addressee personally or if it is delivered at his place of business, habitual residence or mailing address ...", and it is clear from that reference that "person" includes legal persons. Further, in Malaysia (which has adopted the Model Law in its Arbitration Act 2005), the Interpretation Acts 1948 and 1967 state that "person" includes a body of persons, corporate or unincorporate. That approach is common in common law countries and not only provides no support for the proposition that an arbitrator must be an individual, but in fact points in the other direction.

The 1996 Act is no clearer on the issue either since claimant is referred to as "person" or "he", e.g. at s.9(3):

"An application may not be made by a person before taking the appropriate procedural step (if any) to acknowledge the legal proceedings against him or after he has taken any step in those proceedings to answer the substantive claim."

However, s.26(1) provides that, "[t]he authority of an arbitrator is personal and ceases on his death", and we submit that that has the same effect as r.3 since a legal person cannot "die".

The English law position is further complicated by the fact that, in expert determination, it is common for a body corporate (e.g. an accounting or quantity surveying partnership, or limited liability partnership, or a materials testing laboratory, i.e. a limited company) to be the expert determiner.

If that is acceptable in expert determination, it is far from obvious why it should be unacceptable in principle in arbitration.

Surprisingly, few of the leading English law texts even consider the issue at all: Sir Michael J. Mustill and Stewart C. Boyd, *The Law and Practice of Commercial Arbitration in England*, 2nd edn (London: Butterworths, 1989)), state at p.247:

"... the person appointed as arbitrator must be a natural person. A limited company, possessing only corporate personality, cannot validly be appointed [fn.]. Nor can a group of people, such as a partnership firm, be nominated to act as an arbitrator."

Footnote: "We can cite no authority for this proposition, but it must surely be correct."

In some states in the USA, a law firm, i.e. a limited liability partnership, can be appointed arbitrator but in practice it will nominate one partner to fulfil the role but there appears to be no express statutory or other requirement to that effect.

The position in civil law jurisdictions varies between (a) the crystal clarity of the French Civil Code which at art.1451 expressly requires that the arbitrator be an individual; (b) the equally clear position in Italy, where Corte de Cassazione case law provides that an arbitration agreement providing for a corporate entity as arbitrator is void (case no.123365 (November 1999); ditto case no.258717 (August 1962)); and (c) the lack of precision in Belgium where para.1680 of the Code of Civil Procedure provides that:

"[A]nyone who has the capacity to conclude a contract, can be an arbitrator, with the exception of minors, persons who have a legal tutor, and those who have lost their right to vote."

Since legal persons can conclude contracts, one might conclude that they can also be arbitrators. However, since paras 1687 and 1688 refer to the death of an arbitrator it appears that the legislators had probably only natural persons in mind.

More confusingly still, in Germany there appears to be not only no applicable statute or case law but there is conflicting academic authority on the point. The leading English-language commentary, K. Böckstiegel, S. Kröll and P. Nacimiento (eds), *Arbitration in Germany*, 1st edn (Kluwer, 2007) formulates in its annotation 9 to para.1035 Zivilprozeßordnung (corresponding to art.11 of the Model Law) as follows: "... only natural persons can be arbitrators. If a legal person is specified in the arbitration agreement as being responsible for the arbitration, it is to be ascertained by interpretation which natural person according to the law, statute or the intention of the parties is meant".

However, K.H. Schwab and G. Walter, *Schiedsgerichtsbarkeit*, 7th edn (Munich: CHBeck, 2005), at Ch.9, note 1, argue that, since there is no rule in German law which would regulate this question, both natural and legal persons can be arbitrators.

In conclusion, therefore, while few jurisdictions address this surprisingly complicated issue head on, Scotland has.

The concept of personal appointment has a second and important implication in that arbitrators may be obliged to carry out their main duties and fulfil their main responsibilities themselves; see the commentary to r.32 below.

Rule 4: Eligibility to act as arbitrator **M**

4. An individual is ineligible to act as an arbitrator if the individual is—

(a) aged under 16, or
(b) an incapable adult (within the meaning of section 1(6) of the Adults with Incapacity (Scotland) Act 2000 (asp 4)).

DEFINITIONS
"arbitrator": ss.4, 31(1)

STATUS
This is a mandatory rule so the parties cannot disapply or vary it (see s.8).

MODEL LAW
There is no equivalent of r.4 in the Model Law.

COMMENTARY
The as-published draft Bill (January 30, 2009) had this as a default rule so that it would have been open to the parties to agree that a minor or an incapable adult should be their arbitrator but the draftsman was persuaded by the CIArb that no acceptable circumstance could exist in a Scottish-seated arbitration where parties might do so.

Further, if a party had sought to enforce any award so made abroad under the New York Convention 1958, we submit that art.V(2)(b) (the public policy exception) would have proved a major, possibly insuperable, hurdle.

Rule 5: Number of arbitrators **D**

5. Where there is no agreement as to the number of arbitrators, the tribunal is to consist of a sole arbitrator.

DEFINITIONS
"arbitrator": ss.4, 31(1)
"tribunal": ss.2, 31(1)

STATUS
This is a default rule so it is open to the parties to modify it, agree something different or disapply it completely (see s.9).

MODEL LAW
Article 10 provides for a default to a tribunal of three in accordance with international practice.

COMMENTARY
Since this is a default rule, the parties may agree otherwise; in domestic arbitrations a sole arbitrator is the norm (a main reason being to limit costs) while in international arbitrations a tribunal of three is almost always chosen. SAC 07 defaults to a sole arbitrator as does the 1996 Act while the LCIA Rules remain flexible and the ICC Rules art.8(2) default to a sole arbitrator, "save where it appears to the Court that the dispute is such as to warrant three arbitrators". The UNCITRAL Rules (refer art.5) default to a tribunal of three. The Swiss Rules (art.6.1) empower the chambers to decide taking account of all relevant circumstances, with a slight push towards a sole arbitrator (art.6.2).

In international arbitration, the almost invariable choice is three for the following reasons: (a) to allow each party to select one, thereby giving effect to the "party autonomy" principle; (b) to achieve a constructive and balanced mix of some or all of nationalities, skill sets, professional disciplines and languages; (c) the key role played by tribunal deliberations in the decision-making process where discussion of key issues can lead to a fuller understanding of them. In addition, in some cases, e.g. large ones, the tribunal workload, particularly drafting the award, can helpfully be shared between the three arbitrators. It is sometimes asserted that three person tribunals are an unnecessary expense but an ICC study showed that approximately only 16 per cent of the costs of arbitration were the costs of the tribunal (plus ICC 2 per cent, parties' legal and other costs 82 per cent) (an earlier ICC study had reported 12 per cent/8 per cent/80 per cent).

There are some classes of London arbitration which proceed with two arbitrators and an umpire (formerly "oversman" in Scotland); concerning umpires, see below under r.30(2)(b)(ii) and r.82. The LMAA Terms (r.8) provide that the two arbitrators may proceed with the preliminary stages of the reference, deferring the appointment of the third until a later date.

> "If the tribunal is to consist of three arbitrators: ... (b) the two so appointed may at any time thereafter appoint a third arbitrator so long as they do so before any substantive hearing or forthwith if they cannot agree on any matter relating to the arbitration, and if the two said arbitrators do not appoint a third within 10 working days of one calling upon the other to do so, the President shall, on the application of either arbitrator or of a party, appoint the third arbitrator ...".

However, the 1996 Act is, in our view, inaccurately drafted in this regard. The underlying concept is that (and this in fact occurs in many circumstances in practice) of the arbitration proceeding until the point where the two arbitrators fail to agree on the substantive decision at which point the umpire steps in and makes the decision; however, that is not what s.21(4) of the 1996 Act provides:

> "Decisions, orders and awards shall be made by the other arbitrators unless and until *they cannot agree on a matter* relating to the arbitration.
>
> In that event they shall forthwith give notice in writing to the parties and the umpire, whereupon the umpire shall replace them as the tribunal with power to make decisions, orders and awards as if he were sole arbitrator" (emphasis added).

A disagreement on some minor matter, e.g. a procedural one such as whether to allow 7, 14, 21 or 28 days for replies (or even on something as minor as the timing of the lunch break) triggers the replacement of the two arbitrators by the umpire for the entirety of the arbitration.

Rule 6: Method of appointment **D**

6. The tribunal is to be appointed as follows—
   (a) where there is to be a sole arbitrator, the parties must appoint an eligible individual jointly (and must do so within 28 days of either party requesting the other to do so),
   (b) where there is to be a tribunal consisting of two or more arbitrators—
       (i) each party must appoint an eligible individual as an arbitrator (and must do so within 28 days of the other party requesting it to do so), and
       (ii) where more arbitrators are to be appointed, the arbitrators appointed by the parties must appoint eligible individuals as the remaining arbitrators.

DEFINITIONS
"arbitrator": ss.4, 31(1)
"eligible": r.4
"individual": r.3
"party": ss.4, 31(1), (2)
"tribunal": ss.2, 31(1)

STATUS
This is a default rule so it is open to the parties to modify it, agree something different or disapply it completely (see s.9).

MODEL LAW
Article 11 provides a similar mechanism, including that the two arbitrators appoint the third (see below). The Model Law also provides (on an opt-otherwise basis) that nationality shall not be a bar to appointment.

COMMENTARY
Since this is a default rule, the parties may agree a different procedure, e.g. as provided by art.3 of SAC 07. The appointment here is to be made by the parties, not by any appointing body; in contrast, all LCIA appointments are made by the LCIA Court (refer art.5.5 of the LCIA Rules) even where a party has purported to nominate an arbitrator (the LCIA will, of course, take careful account of any party's stated preference).

Section 17 of the 1996 Act provides that, absent contrary agreement of the parties, where each of them is to appoint an arbitrator and one party refuses or fails timeously to do so, the other party may, having complied with applicable procedural requirements, convert its arbitrator into a sole arbitrator. There is no equivalent in r.6 and r.7 will apply in the event of such refusal or failure.

Article 6 of the UNCITRAL Rules takes a different course, requiring one of the parties to propose both (i) the names of prospective sole arbitrators; and (ii) if no appointing authority has been agreed upon by the parties, the name or names of one or more institutions or persons, one of whom would serve as appointing authority. If within 30 days after receipt by a party of such a proposal the parties have not reached agreement on the choice of a sole arbitrator, he/she shall be appointed by the appointing authority agreed upon. If no appointing authority has been agreed upon, or if the appointing authority agreed upon refuses to act or fails to appoint the arbitrator within 60 days of the receipt of a party's request therefor, either party may request the Secretary General of the PCA to designate an appointing authority. Such appointing authority may be an institution or an individual. It is important to note that the Secretary General does not appoint any arbitrator and, other than said designating, plays no role in any such arbitration.

In many instances in practice, the parties' relationship will be such that they will not agree anything in this regard in which case r.7 will apply.

Conventionally, the third arbitrator, whether chosen by the two co-arbitrators or by the administering institution, shall chair the tribunal—refer art.7.1 of the UNCITRAL Rules, art.5.6 of the LCIA Rules and art.8.4 of the ICC Rules; in any event, a chairman is appointed whereas r.6(b) does not so provide; in the view of the authors, this is a curious and unnecessary lacuna. However, the 1996 Act suffers from the same lacuna, since s.16(5)(b) which appears to solve the problem is a non-mandatory rule and could be disapplied by the parties without any replacement.

Party-appointed arbitrators ("PAAs")

In the circumstances of r.6(b)(i), the PAAs are obliged to be wholly neutral in relation to the parties, r.23(1)(a) requiring all the arbitrators impartiality and independence (refer also para.7.1 of the CIArb Code of Ethics) and r.12(a) providing for an application to the court to remove an arbitrator who fails to be both impartial and independent. While in some US domestic arbitrations the PAAs may, by prior agreement, be partisan (refer to Canon X of the ABA Code), this is not the case elsewhere; it is a reasonably popular misconception that the PAA owes some obligation to his/her appointor (but see below regarding appointment of the third arbitrator).

A party's choice of its PAA is a very important stage in the process, arguably even critically so, but it can be a difficult task with attendant complications. In an article by Doak Bishop and Lucy Reed, "Practical Guidelines for Interviewing, Selecting and Challenging Party-appointed Arbitrators in International Commercial Arbitration" (1998) 14 Arbitration Int. 395), the authors state

> "The ability to appoint one of the decision-makers is a defining aspect of the arbitral system and provides a powerful instrument when used wisely by a party. It is also a truism that a party will strive to select an arbitrator who has some inclination or predisposition to favour that party's side of the case such as by sharing the appointing party's legal or cultural background or by holding doctrinal views that, fortuitously, coincide with a party's case. Provided the arbitrator does not 'allow this shared outlook to override his conscience and professional judgment' (Redfern & Hunter) this need carry no suggestion of disqualifying partiality. This is a natural and unexceptional aspect of the party appointment system in international arbitration. There is a distinction to be drawn, however, between a general sympathy or predisposition and a positive bias or prejudice. Bias in favour of, or prejudice against, the party or its case encompasses a willingness to decide a case in favour of the appointing party regardless of the merits or without critical examination of the merits."

The PAA, while remaining impartial and independent, has a vital contribution to play in the effective conduct of the proceedings and the determination of the merits of the case, not because the PAA advocates his/her appointing party's case but because the two PAAs (i) choose the third, presiding, arbitrator (see below), and (ii) play a role in ensuring that both parties' cases are given appropriate consideration during the procedural stages of the arbitration and when the merits are discussed.

Interviewing of prospective arbitrators

Given the right of each party to choose its PAA, it is generally accepted internationally that a party need not make such choice based solely on CVs, websites or word-of-mouth recommendations since these might not give a complete picture of the appointee. It is therefore common practice, in some jurisdictions but not in others, that the appointor interviews a list of prospective PAAs prior to making the appointment. Such a practice undoubtedly carries certain risks but practical experience shows that a comprehensive interview can be conducted without jeopardising the PAA's neutrality, independence or impartiality.

In *Law and Practice of International Commercial Arbitration*, 4th edn (London: Sweet & Maxwell, 2004), Professors Alan Redfern and Martin Hunter state at para.4-50:

"However, it is hard to perceive the practice [i.e. of interviews] as being objectionable in principle, provided that it is not done in a secretive way and that the scope of the discussion is appropriately restricted."

Certain information must in any event be disclosed by the prospective appointor before the arbitrator can contemplate accepting the appointment: the names of the parties in the dispute and any third parties involved must be disclosed in order for the arbitrator to assess his position with regard to conflicts and it may be necessary for the prospective appointor to disclose the names of other *dramatis personae*. Some information about the nature of the dispute must be disclosed: for example, there is a substantial difference between expertise in building (i) offshore oil and gas production platforms, (ii) LNG carriers and (iii) petrochemical refineries although all three might be seen as "oil and gas construction". It is also reasonable that the location of the project be disclosed since the conduct of business varies in different parts of the world and the US business environment is not the same as that in South Asia, West Africa or England.

The CIArb has published a practice guideline on "The Interviewing of Prospective Arbitrators" which explains and delineates the interview process including the danger and the no-go areas (available at *http://www.ciarb.org/information-and-resources/practice-guidelines-and-protocols/list-of-guidelines-and-protocols* [Accessed February 19, 2010]).

Appointment of third or additional arbitrators gives rise to some practical difficulties concerning the role of the parties in this part of the process. On the one hand, the arbitration "belongs to the parties" and the principle of party autonomy would appear to require that the parties are involved in the selection of a third arbitrator; on the other hand, r.6(b)(ii) requires that the two PAAs select the third. Article 3.6 of SAC 07 also requires the two PAAs to appoint the third, failing which the Chairman, CIArb Scottish Branch will make the appointment; art.7 of the UNCITRAL Rules is the same save that the PCA-related default mechanism outlined above in respect of art.6 applies.

Questions therefore arise as to (i) how to balance these conflicting requirements and (ii) to what extent, and how, the parties can become involved in the selection process. It is standard practice that the third arbitrator should not be appointed without the consent of (or, at least, not over the objection of) the parties but practice varies as to (i) whether the parties should be given a shortlist of prospective third arbitrators or be given a single name, (ii) whether the parties agree a shortlist between themselves and present this to the two PAAs for consideration and (iii) whether there can be any consultation between the parties and their respective PAAs concerning the appointment. It is generally accepted that such consultation is permissible (subject to obvious limits) and that this is an exception to the general rule prohibiting communication between each party and its PAA.

The CIArb Practice Guideline (refer above) also addresses the question of the parties' interviewing prospective third arbitrators. A suggestion has been made to the relevant CIArb committee that the guideline should be extended to cover the foregoing issues relating to selection of a third arbitrator.

Multi-party arbitrations

Rules 6 and 7 provide for multi-party arbitrations involving more than two parties. This is clear from the definition of "party". Rule 6, read with r.7, ensures equality between parties in such a multi-party arbitration and that the situation in *Siemens AG and BKMI Industrienlagen GmbH v Dutco*

Construction Co, French Cass. Civ. 1ere, January 7, 1992 (1992) 1 Bull Civ. is avoided.

In *Dutco* there was a contract with two parties on one side (B and S) and one party (D) on the other side. The contract provided for disputes to be resolved by a tribunal of three arbitrators and under the then ICC Rules. The ICC Rules contemplated that there would be no more than three arbitrators in the tribunal but that parties would each appoint an arbitrator and that the third arbitrator would be appointed by the ICC Court failing agreement between the parties. When D sought to claim in an arbitration against B and S, the latter parties did not agree on a joint arbitrator. The ICC requested B and S to make a joint nomination which they did under protest. B and S then applied to the tribunal objecting to its jurisdiction. The tribunal made a provisional award finding it to have jurisdiction which was eventually successfully set aside by the French Cour de Cassation on the grounds that the tribunal had not been properly constituted because the ICC's intervention was contrary to French public policy that there should be equality between the parties in the appointment of the tribunal.

Rule 7: Failure of appointment procedure **M**

7.—(1) This rule applies where a tribunal (or any arbitrator who is to form part of a tribunal) is not, or cannot be, appointed in accordance with—
   (a) any appointment procedure set out in the arbitration agreement (or otherwise agreed between the parties), or
   (b) rule 6.

(2) Unless the parties otherwise agree, either party may refer the matter to an arbitral appointments referee.

(3) The referring party must give notice of the reference to the other party.

(4) That other party may object to the reference within 7 days of notice of reference being given by making an objection to—
   (a) the referring party, and
   (b) the arbitral appointments referee.

(5) If—
   (a) no such objection is made within that 7 day period, or
   (b) the other party waives the right to object before the end of that period,
the arbitral appointments referee may make the necessary appointment.

(6) Where—
   (a) a party objects to the arbitral appointments referee making an appointment,
   (b) an arbitral appointments referee fails to make an appointment within 21 days of the matter being referred, or
   (c) the parties agree not to refer the matter to an arbitral appointments referee,
the court may, on an application by any party, make the necessary appointment.

(7) The court's decision on whom to appoint is final.

(8) Before making an appointment under this rule, the arbitral appointments referee or, as the case may be, the court must have regard to—
   (a) the nature and subject-matter of the dispute,
   (b) the terms of the arbitration agreement (including, in particular, any terms relating to appointment of arbitrators), and
   (c) the skills, qualifications, knowledge and experience which would make an individual suitable to determine the dispute.

(9) Where an arbitral appointments referee or the court makes an appointment under this rule, the arbitration agreement has effect as if it required that appointment.

DEFINITIONS
"arbitrator": ss.4, 31(1)
"arbitration agreement": ss.4, 31(1)
"arbitral appointments referee": s.22
"court": s.31(1)
"party": ss.2, 31(1), (2)

STATUS
This is a mandatory rule so the parties cannot disapply or vary it (see s.8).

MODEL LAW
Article 11 provides a similar mechanism; rr.7(6) and 7(7) substantially replicate Model Law art.11(5).

COMMENTARY
Section 18 of the 1996 Act provides that, absent contrary agreement of the parties, in the event of any failure in the appointment process, any party to the arbitration agreement may (upon notice to the other parties) apply to the court to rectify that failure by exercise its powers under the section. The Scottish draftsmen took the view that (i) the court is not in the business of, and has little experience of, either appointing arbitrators or rectifying failures in the appointment process; and (ii) s.1(c) of this Act (reflecting art.5 of the Model Law) seeks to minimise the involvement of the court in the arbitral process. In consequence, as envisaged by arts 6 and 11(3) of the Model Law, an arbitral appointments referee ("AAR") will, at first instance, deal with such matters although there is a right of appeal to the court. Such right of appeal is grounded, inter alia, in the possibility that the parties each want a different AAR.

To put this in context, it is understood that the Commercial Court in England makes fewer than 10 appointments per annum; the CIArb makes 2,000–2,500, the RICS 8,000–12,000 and several other UK-based bodies more than 1,000. Such bodies not only have detailed appointment processes and procedures but also specialised departments handling them, e.g. with the administration of the CIArb's appointment processes being dealt with by a wholly-owned subsidiary whose sole business is making appointments and administering arbitration schemes.

The view was also taken by the draftsmen that in the great majority of commercial contracts provision would have been made for an appointing institution and that it would be a rare or exceptional case which would require application of r.7.

It should be noted that if an AAR acts outwith its powers then any subsequent award may be rendered appealable under r.68(2)(d)

Rule 7(1)
While the full eligibility criteria for AARs have yet to be published (but see s.24(2) of the Act; note that this effectively excludes the concept of an individual acting as AAR whereas the Secretary General of the PCA does from time to time designate an individual as appointing authority), it is expected that the several well-known existing institutions which routinely

make arbitral appointments will qualify as, and will apply to become, AARs, e.g. the CIArb, RICS, Law Society of Scotland, Faculty of Advocates and the Institute of Civil Engineers.

Rule 7(6)

The issue here is the selection of an arbitrator who is obliged to be both impartial and independent (see r.24(1)(a) below) and it therefore follows that there must be an early close to argument over the appointment so there is no right of appeal

Rule 8: Duty to disclose any conflict of interests **M**

8.—(1) This rule applies to—
  (a) arbitrators, and
  (b) individuals who have been asked to be an arbitrator but who have not yet been appointed.
(2) An individual to whom this rule applies must, without delay disclose—
  (a) to the parties, and
  (b) in the case of an individual not yet appointed as an arbitrator, to any arbitral appointments referee, other third party or court considering whether to appoint the individual as an arbitrator,
any circumstances known to the individual (or which become known to the individual before the arbitration ends) which might reasonably be considered relevant when considering whether the individual is impartial and independent.

DEFINITIONS
"arbitrator": ss.4, 31(1)
Note that neither "impartial" nor "independent" is defined in the Act (nor in the Model Law).

STATUS
This is a mandatory rule so the parties cannot disapply or vary it (see s.8).

MODEL LAW
Article 12(1) is in equivalent terms.

COMMENTARY
The necessity for arbitrators to be impartial and independent is fundamental, as is recognised in s.1 of this Act: "The founding principles of this Act are: (a) that the object of arbitration is to resolve disputes fairly [and] impartially ..."; and in r.24(1)(a).

These provisions are consistent with art.6(1) of the European Convention on Human Rights ("ECHR"):

"In the determination of his civil rights and obligations ... everyone is entitled to a fair ... hearing within a reasonable time by an independent and impartial tribunal established by law."

The various issues arising from this fundamental principle are addressed below under r.24, in particular the questions of what is impartiality and what is independence.

The key principle underlying r.8 is that each party is entitled to know all "relevant" facts of an arbitrator's involvement with one or other of them so that it can either choose another arbitrator or can challenge one already appointed (see r.10 below); for the parties to be put in a state of knowledge, there must be disclosure.

Article 12(1) of the Model Law, art.9 of the UNCITRAL Rules and art.4.4 of SAC 07 contain language to the same effect as r.8, particularly as regards disclosure (note that the 1996 Act addresses neither disclosure nor independence). The Model Law provides that:

"When a person is approached in connection with his possible appointment as an arbitrator, he shall disclose any circumstances likely to give rise to justifiable doubts as to his impartiality or independence. An arbitrator, from the time of his appointment and throughout the arbitral proceedings, shall without delay disclose any such circumstances to the parties unless they have already been informed of them by him." (Article 9 of the UNCITRAL Rules is substantially identical.)

Similarly, the CIArb's Code of Ethics provides in Pt 2 that:

"3.1 Both before and throughout the dispute resolution process, a member shall disclose all interests, relationships and matters likely to affect the member's independence or impartiality or which might reasonably be perceived as likely to do so.

3.2 Where a member is or becomes aware that he or she is incapable of maintaining the required degree of independence or impartiality, the member shall promptly take such steps as may be required in the circumstances, which may include resignation or withdrawal from the process."

The disclosure obligation is expressly made a continuing one (r.8(2)).

The difficult questions here, and these are major ones, include:
  (i) how does an arbitrator (or prospective arbitrator) determine what is "relevant" in order to effect disclosure?
  (ii) who determines what is relevant?
  (iii) to what extent is the arbitrator obliged to search for disclosable facts?
  (iv) how do individuals disclosing facts do so on a common basis?

What is relevant?

As regards the first question, there are no UK, or Scottish, standards in this regard and domestic arbitrators have to rely on the CIArb's Code of Ethics, Pt 2, para.3.1 above (and equivalent obligations contained in the respective ethical codes of similar institutions) and extensive coverage of the issue in (non-Scottish) case law.

However, valuable assistance is available from the International Bar Assocation ("IBA"), *IBA Guidelines on Conflicts of Interest in International Arbitration* (International Bar Assocation, 2004) which, although not universally accepted either in England (e.g. they were summarily dismissed by Morison J. in *ASM Shipping Ltd of India v TTMI Ltd of England* [2005] EWHC 2238 (Comm) at [39(4)], a judgment regarded by many commentators as controversial, even wrong) or internationally, have attracted widespread support as being the best current solution to the difficult problem of trying to establish standards

The IBA Guidelines class conflicts of interest into three categories, red, orange and green, where (i) red ones are serious and normally require the arbitrator to decline the appointment (e.g. the arbitrator owns a significant shareholding in one of the parties); (ii) orange ones require disclosure (e.g. the arbitrator has within the past three years served as counsel in a case against one of the parties or an affiliate of one of the parties in an unrelated matter) but do not normally require the arbitrator to decline; and (iii) green ones are minor matters which do not require disclosure (e.g. the arbitrator has a relationship with another arbitrator or with the counsel for one of the parties through membership in the same professional association or social organisation or the arbitrator and counsel for one of the parties or another arbitrator have previously served together as arbitrators or as co-counsel).

The IBA Guidelines take the view that unnecessary disclosure sometimes raises an incorrect implication in the minds of the parties that the disclosed circumstances would affect the arbitrator's impartiality or independence. Excessive disclosures can thus unnecessarily undermine the parties' confidence in the process.

Despite lacking unanimous international acceptance, the IBA Guidelines are the most comprehensive, and most balanced, guidelines available and provide a well-tried baseline against which to measure disclosure.

Who determines what is relevant?

This is, perhaps, the "easiest" of the four questions to answer: in the definitive English case *Porter v Magill* [2001] UKHL 67 it was finally decided that the determiner is to be a "fair-minded, informed observer" as identified by Lord Phillips of Worth Matravers M.R. in the judgment in *Re Medicaments and Related Classes of Goods (No.2)* [2001] 1 W.L.R. 700 at 726H–727C [85]:

> "When the Strasbourg jurisprudence is taken into account, we believe that a modest adjustment of the test in *R v Gough* is called for, which makes it plain that it is, in effect, no different from the test applied in most of the Commonwealth and in Scotland. The court must first ascertain all the circumstances which have a bearing on the suggestion that the judge was biased. It must then ask whether those circumstances would lead a *fair-minded and informed observer* to conclude that there was a real possibility, or a real danger, the two being the same, that the tribunal was biased" (authors' emphasis added).

This passage was cited with approval by Lord Hope in *Porter* at [102].

Extent of obligation to search for disclosable facts

This question is also not fully addressed in literature, standards or guidelines, except by the ABA (see below). It is clearly implicit that the arbitrator must make a reasonable endeavour to ascertain such facts and, for example, law firms' standard anti-conflict systems in place for their legal advisory work will reveal conflicts which might affect a solicitor considering an arbitral appointment. Sole practitioner arbitrators can, for example, run a search of their laptop easily and quickly.

Common basis for disclosure

This question is in part covered by the discussion above but where each arbitrator makes his/her own decision concerning disclosure, no system can regulate to such a high degree of precision. This gives rise to a consequent and very difficult practical question: if there are two shortlisted arbitrators and both possess the same factual matrix but one discloses certain facts and the other does not, what then ensues? These and related questions have been, and continue to be, hotly debated, particularly recently in the USA with the "Draft Arbitrator Disclosure Guidelines" promulgated by the ABA's Dispute Resolution Subcommittee (these are considered further below).

Some US courts have taken disclosure to an extraordinary level, e.g. as in *Positive Software v New Century*[1] where the arbitrator, S, had, seven years previously, been a partner in a law firm (LF1) which had handled part of a multi-company six lawsuit litigation involving a large corporate group, Intel, (which had no relation to the present parties). Intel was represented by seven separate law firms and a total of 34 attorneys. Upon losing in the arbitration, Positive Software conducted a detailed investigation of S's background and discovered that, seven years earlier, he and his former law firm LF1 had represented the same party as New Century's law firm (LF2) in the present arbitration and one of the latter's attorneys in the arbitration, C, had been involved in the earlier litigation. C had participated in representing Intel in three of its lawsuits from August 1991 until July 1992, although her name remained on the pleadings in one of the cases until June 1993. In September 1992, S along with 12 other attorneys from LF1 had entered an appearance in two of the three cases on which C had worked. Although their names appeared together on pleadings, S and C never attended or participated in any meetings, telephone calls, hearings, depositions, or trials together.

On these facts the District Court vacated the arbitrator's award for his failure to disclose the "prior professional relationship"; this decision was subsequently upheld by the five judge Fifth Circuit Court of Appeals but, thereafter the full 16 judge court sat "en banc" and overruled the earlier decision 11–5, concluding that the Federal Arbitration Act ("FAA") did not mandate the extreme remedy of vacatur for non-disclosure of a trivial past association.

The ABA's proposed disclosure checklist (as at May 2009, this had been "parked" following a wave of heavy criticism) required, inter alia, that the arbitrator should investigate and disclose common membership in professional groups and committees, common membership in a church, social group, country club, etc. attendance at the same college or graduate school, that one of the counsel, co-arbitrators or party representatives is an "acquaintance" or a "neighbour", and that the arbitrator has had a, "life interest pertinent to the matter." It is submitted that, as a matter of English law and of the IBA Guidelines, this is a wholly unnecessary imposition. It is submitted, further, that the ABA's excessive approach has no place whatsoever in Scotland.

Rule 9: Arbitrator's tenure **D**

9. An arbitrator's tenure ends if—
    (a) the arbitrator becomes ineligible to act as an arbitrator (see rule 4),
    (b) the tribunal revokes the arbitrator's appointment (see rule 10),
    (c) the arbitrator is removed by the parties, a third party or the Outer House (see rules 11 and 12),

---

[1] Refer to the "en banc" decision *Positive Software Solutions, Inc v New Century Mortgage Corp*, 476 F.3d 278 (5th Cir. 2007) (en banc), cert. den. 551 U.S. 1114 (2007); the initial Fifth Circuit Court of Appeals decision was *Positive Software Solutions, Inc v New Century Mortgage Corp*, 436 F.3d 495 (5th Cir. 2006), rehearing en banc granted, 449 F.3d 616 (5th Cir. 2006), revised 476 F.3d 278 (5th Cir. 2007) (en banc), cert. den. 551 U.S. 1114 (2007); the District Court decision was *Positive Software Solutions, Inc v New Century Mortgage Corp*, 337 F.Supp. 2d 862 (N.D. Tex. 2004), affirmed 436 F.3d 495 (5th Cir. 2006), rehearing en banc granted, 449 F.3d 616 (5th Cir. 2006), revised 476 F.3d 278 (5th Cir. 2007) (en banc), cert. den. 551 U.S. 1114 (2007).

(d) the Outer House dismisses the tribunal of which the arbitrator forms part (see rule 13), or
(e) the arbitrator resigns (see rule 15) or dies (see rule 79).

DEFINITIONS
"arbitrator": ss.4, 31(1)

STATUS
This is a default rule so it is open to the parties to modify it, agree something different or disapply it completely (see s.9).

MODEL LAW
There is no equivalent in the Model Law; see next paragraph.

COMMENTARY
This rule does no more than collect together, for ease of reference, the various relevant circumstances which are addressed individually under the respective rules.

Rule 10: Challenge to appointment of arbitrator **D**

10.—(1) A party may object to the tribunal about the appointment of an arbitrator.
(2) An objection is competent only if—
  (a) it is made on the ground that the arbitrator—
    (i) is not impartial and independent,
    (ii) has not treated the parties fairly, or
    (iii) does not have a qualification which the parties agreed (before the arbitrator's appointment) that the arbitrator must have,
  (b) it states the facts on which it is based,
  (c) it is made within 14 days of the objector becoming aware of those facts, and
  (d) notice of it is given to the other party.
(3) The tribunal may deal with an objection by confirming or revoking the appointment.
(4) If the tribunal fails to make a decision within 14 days of a competent objection being made, the appointment is revoked.

DEFINITIONS
"arbitrator": ss.4, 31(1)
"tribunal": ss.2, 31(1)
Note that neither "impartial" nor "independent" is defined in the Act (nor in the Model Law) but see the commentary to r.24 below.

STATUS
This is a default rule so it is open to the parties to modify it, agree something different or disapply it completely (see s.9).

MODEL LAW
Articles 12 and 13 have substantially the same effect as r.10; the Model Law's challenge procedure (but not the grounds) is also open to contrary agreement by the parties (art.13(1)).

COMMENTARY
Model Law art.12 allows no variation by the parties but r.10 does through being a default rule.

A challenge may be made at any time prior to the arbitrator's tenure ending; see r.9.

Compliance with r.10 (if applicable) is a necessary prerequisite to the court's becoming involved pursuant to rr.12 and 13 (see below); see r.14(1)(b)(i).

Rule 10(1)

This gives a right to object which is not the same as a right to remove. This is in contrast to the very different world of jury trial-based systems widespread in the USA, e.g. Florida, where the parties can strike out, e.g. three members of the proposed jury without showing cause. This is mirrored in US arbitration practice (e.g. AAA and Financial Industry Regulatory Authority ("FINRA")) where the parties are presented with lists of, e.g. 10 ranked arbitrators and can strike out whomsoever they wish without needing to show cause; the highest-ranked remaining arbitrators form the tribunal; if all 10 names are struck out, then either (i) another 10 names are produced and so on, or (ii) the institution will appoint the arbitrators, i.e. the parties will have ceded control of the appointment process.

The challenge is to be made to the tribunal. United Kingdom and international practice varies in this regard; s.24 of the 1996 Act provides that the challenge is made to the court (this Act has sought to minimise the involvement of the court (see s.1(c)) even in comparison to the 1996 Act) but SAC 07 has the more imaginative mechanism of an appeal to a panel specially established by the Chairman, CIArb Scottish Branch, and that panel's decision is final. However, SAC 07 places the entirety of this appeal panel in the hands of the chairman with no rights of objection or appeal elsewhere, opening the door to potential ECHR art.6 arguments.

The UNCITRAL Rules provide for the appointing authority to determine the challenge or, if there was no such authority, the PCA-based mechanism considered at r.6 above applies, whereas the LCIA Rules (refer art.10.4) and ICC Rules (refer art.11) provide for the respective courts to determine the challenge and, under the Swiss Rules (art.11), a special committee of the chambers is the determiner. Interestingly, the LCIA now publishes its decisions on challenges whereas, in contrast, the ICC does not.

Natural justice requires that the challenged arbitrator be given the opportunity to respond; this is implicit in r.10 since the tribunal deals with the challenge. Neither the LCIA Rules nor the Swiss Rules expressly provide for the arbitrator to be given the opportunity to respond but the ICC Rules (art.11(3)) do; absent express such provision, there must be an implied one pursuant to ECHR art.6.

As a general rule, unmeritorious challenges to arbitrators are to be discouraged since otherwise a party might use the challenge procedure to delay or even derail the arbitral proceedings and this is not acceptable and cannot be tolerated (inter alia s.1(a) and rr.24 and 25 apply).

Rule 10(2)(a)

The list is exhaustive; there is no provision for groundless objection (in contrast to the very different world of those US jury-based systems where challenge without cause is permitted). The LCIA and the Swiss Rules limit the scope for challenge in a manner similar to r.10 but, anomalously, the ICC Rules do not place any limit on the grounds of challenge, art.11(1) stating: "A challenge of an arbitrator, whether for alleged lack of independence or otherwise, shall be made ...".

Rule 10(2)(a)(iii)

A far from uncommon scenario in recruitment is to discover, after the employment commences, that the employee has claimed qualifications which he/she does not in fact possess and, e.g. professorships have been achieved on the basis of deliberate inclusion of false information in CVs. Separate from the implications of any code of ethics (e.g. the CIArb's Code of Ethics at Pt 2, rr.1, 4.1 and 4.2 will establish a prima facie charge of professional misconduct in such circumstances), an arbitrator in such circumstances is open to immediate challenge. However, a relatively common scenario is where the arbitrator is appointed by agreement based on his/her (accurate) CV but, later, one of the parties (looking for a ground of challenge) discovers that she/she is not precisely what they thought he/she was, e.g. a Professor of Civil Engineering, appointed as arbitrator on that ground, might in fact prove not to be a Chartered Civil Engineer as stated in the arbitration agreement; alternatively, a brilliant young QC might be appointed as arbitrator where many arbitration agreements refer to a barrister/advocate of not less than 15 years' call. In many such cases r.10(2)(c) will operate so as to extinguish the challenge.

See also r.12(d) below.

Rule 10(2)(b)

This refers to "facts" as opposed to allegations but in practice it will often be difficult, even impossible, to distinguish them.

Rule 10(2)(c)

The time limit is deliberately short in order to limit the derailing of the arbitration by the objection.

Rule 10(3)

The tribunal is not obliged to deal with the challenge but see r.10(4) below for the consequences of not doing so.

As in the Model Law art.13(2), the challenge is heard first by the tribunal, irrespective of whether the tribunal is of one or three arbitrators. If one, then while it might appear that that arbitrator is being made a judge in his/her own cause, r.12 (a mandatory rule) below gives the challenger a right of application to the court. In any event, an important practical requirement for an arbitrator is to maintain the trust and the confidence of the parties so, should that be lost by reason of whatever ground gave rise to the challenge, the arbitrator might well, in a finely-balanced circumstance, choose to resign (e.g. as happened in *ASM Shipping Ltd of India v TTMI Ltd of England* [2005] EWHC 2238 (Comm)), or revoke his/her own appointment rather than continue in a negative (or hostile) atmosphere. In *ASM Shipping Ltd v Harris* [2007] EWHC 1513 (Comm) there was a secondary challenge to the two remaining arbitrators on the ground that they had become "infected" by the perceived bias on the part of the now-resigned third arbitrator. Very properly, this absurd challenge was robustly dismissed by Andrew Smith J.

Where the challenge is to one member of a tribunal of three, there is no requirement for the challenged arbitrator to stand aside from determining the challenge but many arbitrators will choose to do so in practice—"no man shall be a judge in his own cause".

Rule 10(4)

The time limit is deliberately short in order (i) not to permit the arbitration to be derailed by the objection and (ii) to force the tribunal to an early decision, failing which the challenge will be successful.

Rule 11: Removal of arbitrator by parties **D**

11.—(1) An arbitrator may be removed—
 (a) by the parties acting jointly, or
 (b) by any third party to whom the parties give power to remove an arbitrator.
(2) A removal is effected by notifying the arbitrator.

DEFINITIONS
 "arbitrator": ss.4, 31(1)
 "notification": r.83

STATUS

This is a default rule so it is open to the parties to modify it, agree something different or disapply it completely (see s.9).

MODEL LAW

The Model Law has no direct equivalent of r.11 but art.14 deals with the circumstances where the arbitrator(s) fail, or are unable, to act in which event the parties may jointly remove him/her/them.

COMMENTARY

Arbitration is a consensual process so it is logical that the parties can agree both (a) whether or not to adopt r.11 at all and, if so, (b) whether and when to operate it. Circumstances do arise, albeit in the UK very rarely, where an arbitrator has lost the confidence of the parties, for whatever reason, and they jointly agree to remove him/her.

Whereas in most circumstances the principles of natural justice would apply so that the arbitrator would be given the opportunity to make representations, in this circumstance such principles are irrelevant—the parties want rid of him/her and, despite his/her fulfilling a judicial function, he/she is, in one sense, merely a contracted service provider and such contract may be summarily terminated. The consequences for the arbitrator's fees and expenses are dealt with under r.16. In addition, the parties will, in practice, have to consider the impact on their own legal and other expenses consequent on removing the arbitrator, particularly if he/she is a sole arbitrator.

If the arbitration agreement calls for a three person tribunal, the question then arises of whether, and if so how, to replace the arbitrator; in agreeing to remove the arbitrator, the parties may (and should) agree on this or, alternatively, the applicable institutional rules may cover the point. Under the ICC Rules art.12(5) the court may decide, but only if the removal is after the close of proceedings, that the two remaining arbitrators continue as a truncated tribunal; the LCIA Rules have no equivalent provision. Both LCIA Rules (art.11(1)) and ICC Rules (art.12(4)) give the institution the discretion whether or not to follow the same appointment process as originally; if they do not, r.6(b) (or agreed alternative) applies to appoint a replacement arbitrator.

The question may arise as to whether the truncated two person tribunal can continue with the arbitration pending replacement of the removed arbitrator; these rules make no such provision expressly but if the arbitration agreement calls for a three person tribunal, a two person one is evidently not in accordance with that agreement but the agreement to remove one of the arbitrators is arguably a variation to the original arbitration agreement.

A different issue of a truncated tribunal arose in an arbitration *Himpurna California Energy Ltd v PT (Persero) Perusahaan Listruik Negara* (2000) XXV YCA 13 (PLN was a state owned electricity utility that supplied electricity to the Indonesian public). This was an ad hoc arbitration under UNCITRAL Rules concerning the cancellation of a power plant construction project and the tribunal, sitting in Jakarta, was injuncted by the Indonesian Courts (at the instigation of the Indonesian government) with a fine of US$1 million/day if they continued with the arbitration. The tribunal immediately relocated to The Hague to continue proceedings but, on arrival at Schiphol Airport, the Indonesian arbitrator was "met" by staff from the Indonesian Embassy and "escorted away", never (so far as concerned the arbitration) to be seen again. The other two arbitrators continued on a truncated basis and rendered a final award (in Himpurna's favour).

Rule 11(1)

This mirrors s.23(3) of the 1996 Act but SAC 07 has no comparable provision.

Rule 11(1)(b)

Absent express agreement by the parties, no arbitral appointment referee (see s.22) can act here and the reference will in practice be to an administering institution such as the LCIA or ICC where the institution's court plays a central role. Typically, the LCIA Rules (art.10) and the ICC Rules (art.12(2): "An arbitrator shall also be replaced on the Court's own initiative when it decides that he is prevented *de jure* or *de facto* from fulfilling his functions, or that he is not fulfilling his functions in accordance with the Rules or within the prescribed time limits") provide that the respective court may revoke his/her appointment, or remove, an arbitrator. There is no difference in practice here between revocation and removal.

Rule 11(2)

The notification must be in writing and for the method of notification see r.83.

Rule 12: Removal of arbitrator by court **M**

12. The Outer House may remove an arbitrator if satisfied on the application by any party—
 (a) that the arbitrator is not impartial and independent,
 (b) that the arbitrator has not treated the parties fairly,
 (c) that the arbitrator is incapable of acting as an arbitrator in the arbitration (or that there are justifiable doubts about the arbitrator's ability to so act),
 (d) that the arbitrator does not have a qualification which the parties agreed (before the arbitrator's appointment) that the arbitrator must have,
 (e) that substantial injustice has been or will be caused to that party because the arbitrator has failed to conduct the arbitration in accordance with—

(i) the arbitration agreement,
(ii) these rules (in so far as they apply), or
(iii) any other agreement by the parties relating to conduct of the arbitration.

DEFINITIONS
"arbitrator": ss.4, 31(1)
"Outer House": s.31(1)
Note that none of "impartial", "independent" or "substantial injustice" is defined in the Act (nor in the Model Law) but see the commentary to r.24 below.

STATUS
This is a mandatory rule so the parties cannot disapply or vary it (see s.8).

MODEL LAW
The Model Law has no direct equivalent of r.12 but art.13(3) provides for such an application to the court but only after there has been an unsuccessful challenge lodged with the tribunal.

COMMENTARY
This list is exhaustive in that no other grounds for such removal are competent.

Rules 12(a), (b) and (d) replicate r.10(2)(a)(i)–(iii) but r.12(c) and (e) are "new" in this Act. Rule 12(c) replicates s.24(1)(c) of the 1996 Act and r.2(e) mirrors r.66(2)(a) on challenging the award.

None of SAC 07, UNCITRAL, LCIA or ICC Rules cover the issues addressed in r.12 since such institutional rules, being agreements between parties, cannot affect the functioning of the court system.

There have been relatively few removals under s.24 of the 1996 Act, those that have occurred being anomalous cases; this experience matches that of the CIArb which sees a very small number of professional misconduct cases each year and most are dismissed, the majority being no more than an attack on the arbitrator by a disgruntled loser. Most of the English cases covering s.24 feature removal applications being rejected.

Circumstances may arise where the court has to consider whether to remove the arbitrator or remit the matter in question back to him/her for reconsideration; in *James Moore Earthmoving v Miller Construction Ltd* [2001] EWCA Civ 654; [2001] 2 All E.R. (Comm) 598, the Court of Appeal said:

> "The question whether an arbitrator should be removed or the matter remitted to an arbitrator in the case of misconduct may well depend upon the answer to the objective question formulated by Mance LJ in *Lovell Partnerships Northern Limited v A W Construction PLC* (1996) 81 BLR 83, 99, namely: '... whether a reasonable person would no longer have confidence in the present arbitrator's ability to come to a fair and balanced conclusion on the issues if remitted.'"

The removal of an arbitrator was described by H.H. Judge Bowsher QC (in *Groundshire v VHE Construction* [2001] B.L.R. 395) as a "most serious step" which would only be ordered if the arbitrator's misconduct was so serious that, in the judge's words, he could not be trusted, "to complete the arbitration fairly and properly even with the benefit of an examination of his conduct by the parties and their representatives and guidance from the court ... ." Further, the mere fact that one party has lost confidence in an arbitrator will not without evidence of real and substantial injustice lead to an order removing the arbitrator (*Conder Structures v Kvaerner Construction Ltd* [1999] A.D.R.L.J. 305).

A pre-1996 example of a case where the arbitrator was removed for misconduct is *Damond Lock Grabowski v Laing Investments (Bracknell) Ltd*, 60 B.L.R. 112, where even the party resisting the application to remove him described him as, "eccentric, autocratic and obsessive". The judge concluded:

"Looking at the whole sorry history of the matter, it seems to me clear that the arbitrator has unquestionably pointed the finger at the Applicants and repeatedly accused them, in my judgment unfairly, of deliberate delay. Above all, he has not paid proper heed to their objections and has insisted that the hearing must start on the day he ordered, when they cannot be in a position to conduct their case properly. In my judgment he must be removed. I therefore grant the order asked in paragraph 1 of the notice of motion."

Post-1996 there have been very few successful removal applications in the English courts but two merit mention.

First, in *W and S v BB* Unreported June 8, 2001, TCC the arbitrator was removed inter alia because he appeared either to have had no comprehension of how to conduct the case, a £60,000 dispute concerning building works at a residential property, or had otherwise wholly lost control of it. Although the case had reached only the conclusion of the claimants' evidence, the arbitrator had issued 19 directions orders and had spent 170 hours on it; in consequence, the parties had, of course, incurred substantial legal and other costs far out of proportion to the sums in dispute. Further he had issued a directions order which sought to impose on the parties certain matters that they should incorporate in a proposed settlement agreement. Further, he issued a purported peremptory order which (i) failed to follow s.41(5) and (ii) sought to secure 100 per cent of his fees from each party. In removing him, the judge said this:

"Not only that, but the terms of the two sets of directions to which I have referred, demonstrate to my satisfaction that [the arbitrator] has a pitifully inadequate comprehension of the nature of his function as arbitrator, what powers he has and what is the appropriate way in which to exercise these powers. He seems to have no conception of the fact that these powers are to be exercised in accordance with law, or what the relevant principles of law are.

That fact on its own means that if the arbitration proceeds with [him] as the arbitrator, it is likely that substantial injustice will be caused to the claimants, because it is likely that [he] will continue to demonstrate that wholly inadequate grasp of the nature of his functions and powers to which I have referred."

This (and other similar comment by the judge) appears to be the harshest criticism on record in any English case.

This case also raised a serious issue concerning the extent of an arbitrator's liability from suit; this is discussed under r.73 below.

In *Norbrook Laboratories Ltd v Tank* [2006] EWHC 1055 (Comm), the arbitrator, an engineer, inter alia contacted witnesses directly and contacted one of the parties to the arbitration directly, bypassing its solicitors. He was removed on the grounds (i) that circumstances existed that had given rise to justifiable doubts as to his impartiality, (ii) that he had failed properly to have conducted the proceedings, including in particular a failure to have acted in accordance with s.33(1)(a) of the 1996 Act and had conducted the proceedings in such a manner as to have amounted to a serious irregularity under s.68(2) of the Act. Colman J. concluded (emphasis added):

"153. I am not persuaded that the Arbitrator has by his conduct demonstrated any all-pervading bias or want of impartiality against Norbrook on the grounds relied upon. He has been attempting to impose an orderly and economical procedure on the parties in an effort to achieve a relatively speedy award. ... Further, with one exception, those procedural irregularities in the course of the reference to which I have referred have not caused substantial injustice to either party ... *Although I am satisfied that a more experienced Arbitrator would probably have avoided some, if not all, of those irregularities, it is important to keep firmly in mind that, particularly where, as here, the parties have agreed to the appointment of a sole Arbitrator because of his technical skill and knowledge, his procedural responses to a case involving relatively complicated evidence might not necessarily reflect the kind of management regime that would be imposed by a Queen's Counsel fulfilling that function* (authors' emphasis added).

154. However, I take a very different view of the Arbitrator's direct contact with the witnesses. For the reasons given ... above I have come to the conclusion that by the Arbitrator's conduct in that respect he has or may have been exposed to information about the operation of the plant or the pre-contract laboratory testing which consciously or unconsciously could have influenced him in his decision under Rule 16.3 and which might well influence him in his future conduct of the reference and in particular his final award.

155. To this risk his stated determination to put matters 'out of his mind' is, as *Porter v. McGill*, supra, shows, no answer. The essential attribute of objective impartiality is not to be achieved by subjective self-discipline.

156. In the event, I have no doubt that the fair minded and informed observer, having considered all the facts in this case relating to contact with the three witnesses would conclude that there was a real possibility that the tribunal was biased. The consequence of this conclusion is that the Second Decision cannot stand and must be set aside under s.68, there having been a serious irregularity which has caused substantial injustice. Further, although I am quite sure that the Arbitrator is admirably qualified to resolve the technical issues between the parties, the fact remains that his impartiality has been apparently impaired. The fair-minded and informed observer would entertain great reservations as to whether the Arbitrator's judgment had been affected by what he had been told by at least one of the potential witnesses. Accordingly, although the removal of the Arbitrator at this stage in the proceedings would involve the parties in considerable additional expense in the further prosecution of this arbitration, I have reluctantly come to the conclusion that this is the correct course. Consequently, an order will be made under s.24 of the 1996 Act that the Arbitrator be removed. I shall hear such representations as the parties may wish to advance ancillary to s.24, in particular with regard to s.24(4) of the 1996 Act."

In *ASM Shipping Ltd of India v TTMI Ltd of England* [2005] EWHC 2238 (Comm) (see r.8) ASM had taken up an award and had, it was held, thereby waived its right to object to the chairman of the tribunal so he was not removed but the judge made it clear that he should have been. The judgment was heavily criticised (see, inter alia [2006] 72 *Arbitration* 104) as misapplying the law to the facts.

In brief, ASM (the owners) and TTMI (the charterers) were engaged in a London arbitration arising out of a charterparty where Mr X QC was appointed chairman of the tribunal. The owners' principal witness was Mr

M, a shipbroker. In a wholly separate (but relatively recent) arbitration (the "other arbitration") between entirely unrelated parties, M had been a key witness for one of the parties and TTMI's solicitors in the present case, WH, had represented the other side and, for a short time and in respect of one preliminary issue only (which was settled), X had been instructed by WH and had drafted certain disclosure applications. Summarising a long story, X had had a brief and peripheral involvement in the other arbitration in respect of which M, so the latter alleged (but these allegations were never substantiated), had been the target of an attack by WH. X had no recollection of meeting M and had not conducted any part of any hearing or other proceeding involving M. M was not even a party to the present arbitration, merely a witness.

The law is clear—the test for apparent bias is as formulated by Lord Hope in Porter v Magill [2001] UKHL 67 at [103]:

"The question is whether the fair-minded and informed observer, having considered the facts, would conclude that there was a real possibility that the Tribunal was biased."

Based on M's unsubstantiated allegations and a connection between X and M which can, at best, be described as tenuous, the judge concluded: "In my view, given the facts and conclusions I have stated, Mr X QC should not continue to act in this matter." In reaching this conclusion, the judge appears to have accepted M's allegations without substantiation, dismissing X's clear counter-statements concerning the other arbitration made after consultation of his papers. In effect M and his perceptions, however spurious, have been substituted for those of the FMIO. Further, the decision in *ASM Shipping Ltd* is wholly incompatible with that in *Rustal Trading Ltd v Gill & Duffus SA* [2000] 1 Lloyd's Rep. 14, which has stood the test of time and has never been criticised or dissented from.

Rule 12(a)

See discussion of "impartial" and "independence" under the mandatory r.24; in particular, whereas the 1996 Act expressly refers to "justifiable doubts", it is clear that the jurisprudence implies such a concept into the definition.

In *AT&T Corp v Saudi Cable Co* [2000] 1 Lloyd's Rep 22 the applicant sought to remove the chairman of an ICC tribunal, a distinguished Canadian QC, on the basis of his possessing a small number of shares in, and being a non-executive director of, Nortel which was a competitor of AT&T and which had been the disappointed bidder for a major telecoms contract with Saudi Cable which contract was the subject matter of the present arbitration. The Court of Appeal upheld Longmore J.'s rejection of the application, the arbitrator's connection with the parties and the contract being too remote.

The well known *Locabail* cases (*Locabail (UK) Ltd v Bayfield Properties Ltd* [2000] 1 All E.R. 65) were not arbitration cases but the same principles apply. They were five conjoined applications including:

  (i) the applicant had complained to an industrial tribunal of racial discrimination by her former employers and the tribunal's chairman had disclosed during the hearing that he had been employed, many years previously, for a short period by the same employers;
  (ii) the applicant was refused renewal of a bookmakers' licence and, following his failing to have entered and served the proceedings within the prescribed period, he applied for an extension of time;

the judge refused the application but subsequently learnt from a newspaper article that the bookmakers were tenants of premises let to them by a company owned by the judge's family in which he held shares and a non-executive directorship; the judge stated that he was not involved in the management of the company, that until reading the article he had been unaware that the bookmakers were its tenants and that the rent payable for the single shop let to them represented approximately four per cent of the company's total receivable rent.

These applications were dismissed

In *James Moore Earthmoving v Miller Construction Ltd* ([2001] EWCA Civ 654; [2001] 2 All E.R. (Comm) 598; the first instance case was reported at [2001] B.L.R. 10) the Court of Appeal set aside the first instance judge's removal of an arbitrator for misconduct. The judge had held that the way in which the arbitrator had dealt with one key issue in the arbitration had amounted to misconduct and that the matter had been so serious that only his removal was appropriate. The judge had reached those conclusions by holding (i) that the question was whether, in the light of what had occurred, a reasonable person would no longer have confidence in the arbitrator's ability to come to a fair and balanced conclusion if the matter were remitted, and (ii) that Miller could rely upon misconduct, which did not cause prejudice to it but which did or may have caused prejudice to Moore, even though Moore had made no complaint about the way in which the arbitrator dealt with the key issue. The court held that the evidence had not supported a finding of misconduct, either on the basis found by the judge or on the different ground originally advanced by Miller.

In *Sinclair v Woods of Winchester Ltd* [2005] EWHC 1631 (QB) the claimants sought to remove the arbitrator in a dispute over a £300,000 domestic housebuilding project. They contended that there had been a number of serious irregularities in the arbitrator's conduct of the arbitration which had caused them substantial injustice including that he had failed (i) to have conducted the arbitration properly both before and during one hearing and (ii) in his award to have addressed all the issues put to him or have dealt with the issues clearly and unambiguously. They applied (a) under s.68 of the 1996 Act for the award to be set aside and (b) under s.24 for the removal of the arbitrator since the irregularities had been so serious and the injustice so substantial. H.H. Judge Coulson, QC dealt trenchantly with the claimants' application:

"41. The Claimants contend that the arbitrator was wrong to [have issued] the peremptory order of 24th March 2004 requiring them to serve a statement of case ...

42. ... [A]s part of an application under sections 24 or 68 of the 1996 Act, this complaint can fairly be categorised as risible. First, it is clear from the arbitrator's letter of 2nd January 2004 that from the outset he expected the Claimants 'to quantify their claim concurrently with the preparation of their Statement of Case.' The arbitrator's understanding was based on the fact that the Claimants had promised to do just that. ... Thirdly, it is plain that the Claimants were in delay, even at this early stage, in complying with the arbitrator's orders because they had not provided all the documentation they relied on to accompany the pleading.

43. In those circumstances it was entirely appropriate for the arbitrator on 24th March 2004 to issue an order in peremptory terms to get the Claimants to do in April what they had promised to do by early February, namely to provide a quantified claim document

together with all documents relied on. There was therefore not only no serious irregularity, there was instead an entirely appropriate order. ...

45. [Counsel for the claimants] said that he really relied on the order as 'evidence of the arbitrator's inability to control the course of the arbitration'. In my judgment the order demonstrates precisely the opposite: an arbitrator having to come to grips, not for the last time, with Claimants who were not prepared to do what they said they would do.

46. This purported criticism of the arbitrator is therefore rejected. Not only was it a hopeless point, but it also revealed another all-pervasive feature of the Claimants' application before me, namely a tendency to attack the arbitrator for an underlying situation, in this case delay, for which, on analysis, they themselves were responsible."

This case typifies the many robust rejections of s.24 and s.68 applications.

Rule 12(b)

This derives from the mandatory r.24(2), the concept being of the arbitrator being unfair on both parties; to be unfair on one is to fail the impartiality test.

Rule 12(c)

In *Succula & Pomona Shipping Co Ltd v Harland & Wolff Ltd* [1980] 2 Lloyd's Rep. 381 Mustill J. said:
"No doubt [the words 'refuses to act' and 'incapable of acting'] embrace situations where the refusal or the incapacity is not life-long. But the disability must be serious enough to put the arbitrator out of action altogether, so far as the arbitration is concerned."
See below under r.15(1)(d).

Rule 12(d)

See the commentary to r.10(2)(a)(iii).

Rule 12(e)

This is necessarily qualified by reference to "substantial injustice" otherwise any minor complaint could trigger a removal application.

In *Margulead Ltd v Exide Technologies* [2004] EWHC 1019 (Comm); [2005] 1 Lloyd's Rep. 324 (this was a challenge under s.68 of the 1996 Act, not a removal application, but the point is the same), Margulead claimed that the sole arbitrator had failed to permit its counsel to reply orally to closing submissions by counsel for Exide, i.e. the latter (as respondent in the arbitration) would have the last word. However, the arbitrator had made it clear in advance that that was to be his proposed course of action and Margulead had accepted that at the time. Further, although it is conventional practice in common law courts that the claimant has the last word (since he must prove his claim), this is by no means an absolute rule in English, let alone international, arbitration. Colman J. held, inter alia, that there had been no substantial injustice. "Substantial injustice" is considered in the commentary on r.68(2).

Rule 13: Dismissal of tribunal by court **M**

13. The Outer House may dismiss the tribunal if satisfied on the application by a party that substantial injustice has been or will be caused to that party because the tribunal has failed to conduct the arbitration in accordance with—
    (a) the arbitration agreement,
    (b) these rules (in so far as they apply), or
    (c) any other agreement by the parties relating to conduct of the arbitration.

DEFINITIONS
"arbitration agreement": ss.4, 31(1)
"arbitrator": ss.4, 31(1)
"Outer House": s.31(1)
Note that "substantial injustice" is not defined in the Act (nor in the Model Law).

STATUS
This is a mandatory rule so the parties cannot disapply or vary it (see s.8).

MODEL LAW
The Model Law has no direct equivalent of r.13 but art.13(3) provides for such an application to the court but only after there has been an unsuccessful challenge lodged with the tribunal.

COMMENTARY
This list is exhaustive in that no other grounds for such removal are competent.

None of SAC 07, UNCITRAL, LCIA or ICC Rules cover the issues addressed in Rule 12 since such institutional rules, being agreements between parties, cannot affect the functioning of the court system.

Rule 13 empowers the Court to dismiss the entire tribunal as opposed to removing a single arbitrator.

The controversial decision in *ASM Shipping Ltd of India v TTMI Ltd of England* [2005] EWHC 2238 (Comm) is discussed above under r.12, where the judge held that the chairman of a three person tribunal should have been removed, or should have recused himself, for apparent bias but ASM had, by taking up an award, lost its right to object to that arbitrator. The arbitrator subsequently resigned. ASM then sought (see *ASM Shipping Ltd v Harris* [2007] EWHC 1513 (Comm)) to remove the other two arbitrators on the ground that, "circumstances exist[ed] that give rise to justifiable doubts about [their] impartiality"; however, it was made clear that no suggestion had been made that either continuing arbitrator had been guilty of any sort of improper or unprofessional conduct or was to be the subject of any such criticism—in brief, it was alleged that they must have been infected by their departed colleague's alleged bias.

The judge was unable to accept that there was an invariable rule, or it was necessarily the case, that where one member of a tribunal was tainted by apparent bias the whole tribunal was affected second-hand by apparent bias, and therefore should recuse themselves, or should be excluded, from the proceedings. Further, any objection to the two arbitrators continuing with the reference because M (see above) would be a witness would not be on the basis of any involvement that they themselves had had with M, but could only be made on the basis that there was a risk that they would be other than impartial because they have been influenced by discussions that they had with the departed chairman. The judge considered this suggestion to be fanciful. ASM's application was dismissed.

Rule 14· Removal and dismissal by court: supplementary **M**

14.—(1) The Outer House may remove an arbitrator, or dismiss the tribunal, only if—
    (a) the arbitrator or, as the case may be, tribunal has been—
        (i) notified of the application for removal or dismissal, and
        (ii) given the opportunity to make representations, and
    (b) the Outer House is satisfied—
        (i) that any recourse available under rule 10 has been exhausted, and
        (ii) that any available recourse to a third party who the parties have agreed is to have power to remove an arbitrator (or dismiss the tribunal) has been exhausted.

(2) A decision of the Outer House under rule 12 or 13 is final.

(3) The tribunal may continue with the arbitration pending the Outer House's decision under rule 12 or 13.

DEFINITIONS
    "arbitration agreement": ss.4, 31(1)
    "arbitrator": ss.4, 31(1)
    "Outer House": s.31(1)
    Note that "substantial injustice" is not defined in the Act (nor in the Model Law).

STATUS
    This is a mandatory rule so the parties cannot disapply or vary it (see s.8).

MODEL LAW
    The Model Law has no direct equivalent of r.14.

COMMENTARY
    This is an expression of a simple, yet fundamental, rule of natural justice.
    It is, however, open to question whether the arbitrator in *W and S v BB* Unreported June 8, 2001 TCC (see above) enjoyed the benefits of natural justice, appearing without legal representation in the court hearing the application to remove him and where the judge failed to address the question of arbitrator immunity.
    The application for removal of an arbitrator or dismissal of a tribunal is made to the Outer House by petition in the style contained in Form 14.4 of the Rules of the Court of Session 1994 (RCS rr.14.2(h), 14.4). The requirements for the petition are set out in r.14.4 of the RCS together with the need to:
        (i) aver why the order of removal or dismissal is necessary;
        (ii) aver the circumstances in which the prerequisites for an application in rr.12 or 13 are satisfied;
        (iii) aver the satisfaction of the requirements in r.14(1)(b);
        (iv) aver the reasons why the usual period of 21 days for answers should be dispensed with (if that is necessary);
        (v) require service or intimation on the other parties to the arbitration, and members of the tribunal.

If a shorter period of notice is required, then this should also be craved in the petition.

Together with the petition the applicant should lodge with the Court of Session:
> (i) as a production, any written arbitration agreement in which or other agreement or other document by virtue of which, the time limit is imposed;
> (ii) the written statements of case and defence in the arbitration (the pleadings);
> (iii) the bundle of court documents known as the process (see RCS rr.4.3, 4.4).

Inventories of any supporting productions should be intimated to the other parties, including the members of the tribunal, on whom the petition is served.

On the lodging of the above, the court will automatically make a first order for service on the other party or parties to the arbitration, and the members of the tribunal and anyone else who has an interest to allow such persons to lodge answers opposing the petition if they wish within 21 days (RCS r.14.5). Therefore it is advised that if a shorter period is required a motion for that shorter period should be enrolled (RCS r.14.6(2)). The period for answers should be sufficient to enable the arbitrator or tribunal concerned to make representations in their answers.

After the end of the period for answers, whether answers have been lodged or not, the petitioner should enrol a motion to have the court determine the petition, with or without a hearing as may be appropriate in the circumstances. If answers have been lodged there will have to be a hearing.

The expenses of the application will not be included in the "arbitration expenses" (see the commentary to r.59 below) but will fall to be dealt with by the court rather than the tribunal.

Rule 14(1)(b)

Note that (i) r.10 is a default rule and (ii) there may be no reference to any third party in the arbitration agreement so r.14(1)(b) may not apply.

Rule 14(2)

This reflects a key policy underlying this Act of minimising the involvement of the Court; see s.1(c), reflecting art.5 of the Model Law.

Rule 14(3)

This can give rise to difficult considerations in practice; on the one hand, the arbitrator or tribunal is obliged to proceed without unnecessary delay (refer s.1(a) and mandatory r.24(1)(c)(i)) but, on the other hand, if one member of a tribunal is removed or the sole arbitrator/entire tribunal is dismissed, the question of the ongoing proceedings has to be considered, in particular to what extent the existing proceedings have to be repeated (at worst the entire arbitration started again ab initio) at consequent additional expense (s.1(a) and r.24(1)(c)(ii)). At its simplest, proceedings should not be halted merely because a challenge has been made, otherwise a party might seek to derail the arbitration by making a series of unmeritorious challenges.

The arbitrators will have to weigh all relevant factors very carefully but, as a very general indication, the "if in doubt" policy is to proceed inter alia because the English experience shows that only a small minority of challenges are successful.

Rule 15: Resignation of arbitrator **M**

15.—(1) An arbitrator may resign (by giving notice of resignation to the parties and any other arbitrators) if—
    (a) the parties consent to the resignation,
    (b) the arbitrator has a contractual right to resign in the circumstances,
    (c) the arbitrator's appointment is challenged under rule 10 or 12,
    (d) the parties disapply or modify rule 34(1) (expert opinions) after the arbitrator is appointed, or
    (e) the Outer House has authorised the resignation.
(2) The Outer House may authorise a resignation only if satisfied, on an application by the arbitrator, that it is reasonable for the arbitrator to resign.
(3) The Outer House's determination of an application for resignation is final.

DEFINITIONS
"arbitrator": ss.4, 31(1)
"Outer House": s.31(1)
"notice": r.83

STATUS
This is a mandatory rule so the parties cannot disapply or vary it (see s.8).

MODEL LAW
The Model Law has no direct equivalent of r.15 but addresses part of it in art.14.

COMMENTARY
Rules 15 and 16 are very closely related to r.73 (immunity of the tribunal) since, absent the significant effect on immunity, these provisions covering resignation might appear merely administrative. In fact, they are quite the opposite, creating very significant potential for an arbitrator to incur crippling liability

Rule 15(1)

One anomaly in the 1996 Act is that it provides (at s.25) for the consequences of resignation but nowhere provides for the act or process of resignation itself. Interestingly, this matter is not addressed by Robert Merkin and Louis Flannery, *Arbitration Act 1996*, 4th edn so it may be that it was considered self-evident that there existed a right to resign. This Act not only puts the matter beyond doubt, it does so on a mandatory basis. Rule 16 (below, also mandatory) addresses the consequences of resignation.

Viewed purely as a matter of contract, in accepting an appointment the arbitrator has contracted (a tripartite contract) to provide a service to the parties and is therefore bound to do so, subject to the applicable provisions of the law of contract, e.g. concerning rescission, termination, etc. However, the matter cannot be determined solely by the law of contract since other considerations apply, in particular the ECHR art.6 right of the parties to have civil disputes resolved (art.6(1) states: "In the determination of his civil rights and obligations ... everyone is entitled to a fair ... hearing within a reasonable time by an independent and impartial tribunal established by law

...") in an appropriate manner so the arbitrator is in a different position to that of a plumber who fails or refuses to carry out a repair.

The DAC Report said this:

"111. In theory it could be said that an arbitrator cannot unilaterally resign if this conflicts with the express or implied terms of his engagement. However, as a matter of practical politics an arbitrator who refuses to go on cannot be made to do so, though of course he may incur a liability for breach of his agreement to act. ...

115. ... [T]he arbitrator may (reasonably) not be prepared to adopt a procedure agreed by the parties (i.e. under Clause 34) during the course of an arbitration, taking the view that his duty under Clause 33 conflicts with their suggestions (the relationship between the duty of arbitrators in Clause 33 and the freedom of the parties in Clause 34, is discussed in more detail below). Again, an arbitration may drag on for far longer than could reasonably have been expected when the appointment was accepted, resulting in an unfair burden on the arbitrator. In circumstances where the Court was persuaded that it was reasonable for the arbitrator to resign, it seems only right that the Court should be able to grant appropriate relief."

There are numerous other circumstances where it might be appropriate for an arbitrator to resign, including the grounds addressed by rr.10, 11 (challenge/removal by the parties) and 12 (removal by the court) above. Further, application of the mandatory r.24(1)(c) may oblige the arbitrator to resign forthwith rather than prolong the matter at additional expense (this is considered further under r.16 below).

The following comments on r.15 reflect the fact that there are two separate, albeit closely related, issues for consideration: first, can or should the arbitrator be released from his/her obligations and responsibilities and, second, if so, what consequences should follow?

Note that r.16(2) envisages an arbitrator resigning otherwise than in accordance with r.15; this is discussed below.

Rule 15(1)(a)

Given the tripartite relationship between the arbitrator and the parties, and given the fundamental principle of party autonomy, i.e. that the arbitration "belongs" to the parties, it is self-evident that if they consent to the resignation, the arbitrator can be released from his obligations (subject, of course, to the provisions of r.16 below).

While the rule places no limitations on the circumstances in which the parties might grant such consent and, while their decision whether or not to grant it might be affected by how r.16 might apply, we submit that there is a presumption (rebuttable) derived from r.24(1)(c) that there must be a genuine and valid reason for resigning, not merely that the arbitrator is too busy or wishes to take an extended vacation.

It is likely that in practice the institutional rules agreed by the parties, whether in their arbitration agreement or subsequently, will provide the necessary consent.

Rule 15(1)(b)

If the parties' agreement with the arbitrator provides for resignation in certain circumstances, then the arbitrator has a contractual right to resign (subject, of course, to the provisions of r.16 below). There is, arguably, an overlap with r.15(1)(a) in that such contractual provisions constitute advance consent.

The agreement referred to here is likely to be found in the institutional rules agreed by the parties, whether in their arbitration agreement or subsequently.

Rule 15(1)(c)

Faced with a challenge to the arbitrator under rr.10 or 12, and taking appropriate account of r.24(1)(c) he/she may choose to resign rather than prolonging the matter (subject, of course, to the provisions of r.16 below). This is a matter for that individual's judgment and often involves striking a difficult balance, even before r.16 is considered.

As a general rule, unmeritorious challenges to arbitrators are to be discouraged since otherwise a party might use the challenge procedure to delay or even derail the arbitral proceedings and this is not acceptable and cannot be tolerated (inter alia s.1(a) and rr.24 and 25 apply); it follows that for an arbitrator to resign in a knee-jerk response to any challenge cannot be acceptable either. Conversely, if the challenge is well founded, e.g. a conflict of interest, then for the arbitrator to "prolong the agony" by resisting breaches his/her obligations under s.1(a) and r. 24(1)(c).

Rule 15(1)(d)

This is necessary because the arbitrator might otherwise be forced into a position of deciding matters over which he/she has no professional competence, a circumstance in contradiction to that envisaged by r.12(c) where an arbitrator may be removed if he/she is incapable of acting. In the r.12 context, "incapable" is usually taken to mean "wholly unable to", e.g. by reason of a serious or debilitating medical condition; we submit that inviting an arbitrator to determine matters over which he/she has no professional competence is also "incapability". To expect an arbitrator to make a quasi-judicial decision in such circumstances is clearly unfair on that individual but, perhaps more importantly, is to undermine the entire process.

While it has hitherto been the practice in Scotland for non-lawyer arbitrators to rely on outside legal advice on legal issues, in England and internationally arbitrators are, in general, expected to deal with all the issues before them; if they have doubts about their capability to accept the appointment, they should not do so. Anecdotal evidence in London suggests that the taking of external legal advice by arbitrators is rare whereas the taking by legally-qualified arbitrators of expert advice on welding, concrete, sub-sea oilfield equipment, etc. is commonplace.

In *HOK Sport Ltd v Aintree Racecourse Co Ltd* [2003] B.L.R. 156 a non-lawyer arbitrator was "sandwiched" between apparently conflicting House of Lords decisions, the later of which was decided after the close of proceedings in the arbitration; H.H. Judge Thornton QC said this (at [64])

> "In formulating this summary, I have not taken into account ... nor Lord Lloyd's suggestion in *Aneco* [the later decision], at paragraph 13, that *South Australia* is no more than an example of a special class of case where the scope of the defendant's duty is confined to the giving of specific information ... nor the other views ... which question some or all of the *South Australia* principles. These opinions provide indications of the direction in which the law in this area and in this jurisdiction may develop or be pinned back but they cannot be taken by a judge sitting at first instance, albeit as a judge on appeal from the award of an arbitrator, as representing the currently applicable law for a tribunal sitting in England and Wales."

There was no suggestion in the appeal that the non-lawyer arbitrator had been out of his depth or had failed to engage adequately with the legal issues

It is, however, possible (even relatively common) that the complexion of a case changes over time so what starts as a dispute over issue X becomes transmuted (e.g. after submissions of statement of claim and of defence) into a dispute over issue Y and it may well be that the arbitrator is eminently qualified and experienced to deal with issue X but is less so with issue Y and therefore might require expert advice as envisaged by r.34.

Rule 15(1)(e)

The application for authorisation to resign is made to the Outer House by petition in the style contained in Form 14.4 of the Rules of the Court of Session 1994 (RCS rr.14.2(h), 14.4). The requirements for the petition are set out in r.14.4 of the RCS together with the need to:
 (i) aver why it is reasonable that his resignation should be authorised;
 (ii) require service or intimation on the parties to the arbitration, and any other members of the tribunal.
If a shorter period of notice is required, then this should also be craved in the petition and supported by averments in the petition.

Together with the petition the applicant should lodge with the Court of Session:
 (i) as a production, any written arbitration agreement in which or other agreement or other document by virtue of which, the time limit is imposed;
 (ii) the written statements of case and defence in the arbitration (the pleadings);
 (iii) the bundle of court documents known as the process (see RCS rr.4.3, 4.4).
Inventories of any supporting productions should be intimated to the other parties, including the members of the tribunal, on whom the petition is served.

On the lodging of the above, the court will automatically make a first order for service on the party or parties to the arbitration, any other members of the tribunal and anyone else who has an interest to allow such persons to lodge answers opposing the petition if they wish within 21 days (RCS r.14.5). Therefore it is advised that if a shorter period is required a motion for that shorter period should be enrolled (RCS r.14.6(2)).

After the end of the period for answers, whether answers have been lodged or not, the petitioner should enrol a motion to have the court determine the petition, with or without a hearing as may be appropriate in the circumstances. If answers have been lodged there will have to be a hearing.

The expenses of the application will not be included in the "arbitration expenses" (see the commentary to r.59 below) but will fall to be dealt with by the court rather than the tribunal.

Rule 15(2)

If the Outer House receives an application by the arbitrator, it follows that none of the requirements in r.15(1)(a)–(d) will have been met; in particular it follows that one or both of the parties has refused or declined to accept the resignation. This gives rise to three principal considerations:
 (i) if neither party accepts the resignation then the authors submit that the Court must be loth, and must find exceptional circumstances, to authorise it; one obvious possibility is where the parties agree on

some procedural matter(s) which the arbitrator finds wholly unacceptable but that is a rare occurrence since it is difficult to envisage circumstances where the difference of views as to procedure is sufficient to trigger resignation;
(ii) if one party accepts the resignation but the other does not, there is a significant practical difficulty in that whatever decision is made will upset one of the parties; however, if the arbitrator is not permitted to resign, the party willing to accept his/her resignation will be compelled to continue the arbitration with an arbitrator it wishes taken off the case. Conversely, if the court authorises the resignation, the replacement arbitrator will, prima facie, be unacceptable to neither party which might well prove the lesser of two evils;
(iii) the effect of r.16 will inevitably be critical.

Rule 16: Liability etc. of arbitrator when tenure ends **M**

16.—(1) Where an arbitrator's tenure ends, the Outer House may, on an application by any party or the arbitrator concerned, make such order as it thinks fit—
  (a) about the arbitrator's entitlement (if any) to fees and expenses,
  (b) about the repaying of fees or expenses already paid to the arbitrator,
  (c) where the arbitrator has resigned, about the arbitrator's liability in respect of acting as an arbitrator.
(2) The Outer House must, when considering whether to make an order in relation to an arbitrator who has resigned, have particular regard to whether the resignation was made in accordance with rule 15.
(3) The Outer House's determination of an application for an order is final.

DEFINITIONS
  "arbitrator": ss.4, 31(1)
  "fees and expenses": rr.59, 60
  "notice": r.83
  "Outer House": s.31(1)
  "resigned": r.15
  "tenure": r.9

STATUS
This is a mandatory rule so the parties cannot disapply or vary it (see s.8).

MODEL LAW
The Model Law makes no provision for the consequences of an arbitrator's tenure ceasing.

COMMENTARY
As with r.15, r.16 is closely related to r.73 (immunity of tribunal).
As stated above, r.9 is a summary of the five ways an arbitrator's tenure can end: (a) the arbitrator becomes ineligible to act as an arbitrator (r.4); (b) the tribunal revokes the arbitrator's appointment (r.10); (c) the arbitrator is removed by the parties, a third party or by the Outer House (rr.11, 12); (d) the Outer House dismisses the tribunal of which the arbitrator forms part (see r.13); or (e) the arbitrator resigns (see r.15) or dies (see r.76).

There is a general principle (applicable in most (but not all) common law jurisdictions but in few civil law ones) that the arbitrator is immune from suit by the parties but this immunity is restricted in certain circumstances; see r.73 (mandatory) below which provides an exclusion in respect of r.16(1)(c). It should be noted that that sub-rule is very much wider than r.16(1)(a) and (b) which are concerned only with the arbitrator's fees and expenses.

Consider the position part-way through an arbitration where, for one of the five reasons stated above, the arbitrator's tenure ends. The parties will, at that point, have expended time and resources, possibly significant, in pursuing the case but, in effect, will have to start again, at least in part, with consequent inevitable delay and additional costs. Given the provisions of s.1(a) and r.24(1)(c), it follows that the arbitrator may incur liability accordingly. Of course, much of the documentary materials could be reused and taken over by a replacement arbitrator but even with a full transcript, the hearing would be wasted. In any event, there will be inevitable costs as the replacement arbitrator is brought up-to-speed and there will also inevitably be some delay.

The quantum of delay and additional costs will differ according to when the tenure ends; in broad terms, if that end is immediately after appointment of the arbitrator, then it is likely that there will in fact be minimal delay and little, if any, additional costs. Conversely, the worst point would likely be after the close of proceedings (including a hearing) but before the arbitrator starts to draft his/her award; in such a case, the delay and additional costs could both be significant.

It should be noted that r.16 differs from the equivalent s.25 of the 1996 Act in two key regards:
  (i) s.25(2) obliges the court to respect any agreement between the arbitrator and the parties concerning the consequences of his/her resignation (the July 1995 Bill included a provision allowing the court to reopen any such agreement but this was deleted following consultation) but r.16 does not;
  (ii) s.25(5) of the 1996 Act contemplates an appeal against the court's order but r.16 allows no such appeal.

We question both differences: as regards (i), we do not believe it appropriate that the court has the power to interfere with the parties' agreement, even if it may choose not to do so. As regards (ii), while a policy driver underlying this Act is the limiting of the grounds of appeal to the court (see s.1(c)), an issue of natural justice arises in that the arbitrator's livelihood, even solvency (consider a major arbitration where the parties have racked up substantial costs of which £1,000,000 will be wasted as a consequence of the arbitrator's resignation; if he/she is made liable for that amount, he/she could well face bankruptcy) may be at stake in a context where he/she has no avenue for appeal. We submit that this falls foul of both art.6(1) ECHR and of art.1 of the First Protocol thereto.

Rule 16 provides no express right for the arbitrator to be heard in respect of the court's consideration of the question of his/her liability thereunder but such right, and the right to be represented, is given by art.6(1) ECHR and associated jurisprudence.

The application under r.16 is made, "where an arbitrator's tenure ends". If there is no ongoing court procedure at that point, then the application will have to be made by petition along the lines described in the commentary on r.14. If the arbitrator's tenure is ended by the court, then there may be scope for a party to that court process making the application by note in that process under RCS r.15.2. It is suggested that an application by note would

Arbitration (Scotland) Act 2010 (r.16)

give the arbitrator sufficient notice in relation to what may be an order against him with severe consequences.

The arbitrator has no right of appeal.

The five legs of r.9 have different implications so, for the purposes of this r.16, it is therefore necessary to consider the five separately:

Rule 4: Rule 4(a) cannot apply in r.9 so the only possibility is that, at some date subsequent to the date of appointment, the arbitrator becomes an incapable adult (as defined by s.1(6) of the Adults with Incapacity (Scotland) Act 2000). In general (there could conceivably be exceptions) the court can be expected to apply r.16(1)(a) and (b) to adjust the arbitrator's fees and expenses to the actual amounts earned up to the date of end of tenure.

So far as any wider liability is concerned, the court has no power to make any order, e.g. one which limits the arbitrator's liability, and the question of liability then falls to be determined under r.73 under which, absent bad faith, the arbitrator is immune. It is very difficult to envisage a realistic scenario where the circumstances provided for by s.1(6) of the 2000 Act could arise as a consequence of bad faith on the part of the arbitrator.

These comments apply equally to the circumstances of r.79.

Rule 10: As for r.4, adjustment of fees and expenses to the actual amounts earned is logical in principle save that the relevant end date might well be an earlier one than the date the arbitrator's tenure ends, e.g. the date upon which the events or circumstances which led to the revocation occurred or commenced. It would be unreasonable for the arbitrator to be remunerated during a period when his/her conduct of the arbitration merited, and ultimately led to, revocation.

So far as any wider liability is concerned, the court has no power to make any order, e.g. one which limits the arbitrator's liability and the question of liability then falls to be determined under r.73 under which, absent bad faith, the arbitrator is immune.

These comments apply equally to the circumstances of rr.11, 12 and 13.

Rule 15: As for r.4, adjustment of fees and expenses to the actual amounts earned is logical in principle save that the relevant end date will normally be the date the arbitrator's resignation is submitted. It would be unreasonable for the arbitrator to be remunerated thereafter, e.g. while the consequences of the resignation were being addressed.

So far as any wider liability is concerned, immunity under r.73 is excluded (r.73(2) states: "This rule does not apply: ... (b) to any liability arising from an arbitrator's resignation (but see rule 16(1)(c))") and liability therefore falls to be dealt with solely under r.16(1)(c) and the court has the power to make an order, e.g. one which limits the arbitrator's liability. The court will examine the reason(s) for the arbitrator's resignation: there is a substantial difference between, e.g. the position of an arbitrator who resigns to take up a more lucrative alternative arbitral appointment and the position of an arbitrator who genuinely finds the approach of the parties to the proceedings unacceptable, e.g.

through breach of their obligations under r.25. Although r.73 is excluded in favour of r.16(1)(c), the principle of good faith cannot be discarded and must be taken into account.

Rule 16(1)(a)

See above in respect of rr.4, 10, 11, 12, 13 and 79.

Rule 16(1)(b)

This is a natural and necessary corollary to r.16(1)(a) covering, for example, the standard practice of the arbitrator taking in deposits by way of security against future fees but having to refund the parties to the extent that fees have not been earned. It is self-evident that the arbitrator should not profit from the cessation of his/her tenure.

The taking of such security may not presently be common in Scotland but is standard practice elsewhere. Typically, the CIArb's Practice Guideline No.3 ("Guidelines for Arbitrators as to How to Formulate their Terms of Remuneration") states at para.5.6.2:

> "The most appropriate form of security may be a cash sum to be lodged with a stakeholder, such as the arbitrators' solicitor(s), or in a special deposit account at the arbitrators' bank(s), on terms that it may be drawn upon on the arbitrators' signatures alone. The Institute provides facilities for the holding of cash security."

Rule 16(1)(c)

See above with reference to r.15. Absent any such order by the Outer House, the arbitrator's liability is unlimited.

As stated (above under r.12; below under r.73), in *W and S v BB* Unreported June 8, 2001 TCC the arbitrator was removed by the court and his fees reduced from £17,000 to £10,000 and, in addition, he was also made liable for all of the costs of two court hearings concerning his removal, estimated to be approximately £15,000, i.e. he ended the entire case £5,000 out of pocket despite having spent substantial time on it. While we have questioned this decision (see commentary on rr.12, 73), it does indicate that the arbitrator's liability could exceed the amount of his fees.

Rule 16(2)

As commented above, this rule is not exhaustive of the matters the court should consider. However, the question of whether or not the resignation was made in accordance with r.15 envisages the possibility that it was not but r.15 is, we submit, exhaustive of the grounds for resignation so it follows that this r.16(2) is otiose.

Rule 17: Reconstitution of tribunal **D**

17.—(1) Where an arbitrator's tenure ends, the tribunal must be reconstituted—
    (a) in accordance with the procedure used to constitute the original tribunal, or
    (b) where that procedure fails, in accordance with rules 6 and 7.

(2) It is for the reconstituted tribunal to decide the extent, if any, to which previous proceedings (including any award made, appointment by or other act done by the previous tribunal) should stand.

(3) The reconstituted tribunal's decision does not affect a party's right to object or appeal on any ground which arose before the tribunal made its decision.

DEFINITIONS
"arbitration agreement": ss.4, 31(1)
"arbitrator": ss.4, 31(1)
"tenure": r.9

STATUS
This is a default rule so it is open to the parties to modify it, agree something different or disapply it completely (see s.9).

MODEL LAW
The Model Law makes no equivalent provision.

COMMENTARY
Although this is a default rule, it is inconceivable that the parties should agree to disapply it in its entirety without any alternative. Typically, LCIA art.11 places the responsibility for replacing the arbitrator(s) on the LCIA Court.

Rule 17(1)

If the parties have agreed to arbitrate then, absent clear agreement to the contrary, they are under a binding contractual obligation to do so therefore the tribunal must, as a matter of law, be reconstituted. Section 9 denies (with exceptions) each party (individually) access to the court in respect of the substance of the dispute.

Rule 17(1)(a)

This is wholly logical since the procedure forms part of a binding contractual obligation irrespective of whether rr.2–7 apply or some alternative rules apply. In contrast, LCIA art.11 gives the court discretion as to whether to follow the original procedure or not.

Rule 17(1)(b)

This is also wholly logical; however, an apparent anomaly arises in that if the parties have both (a) either agreed alternatives to, or have wholly disapplied, rr.6 and/or 7 and (b) have agreed, e.g. by failing to vary or disapply it, that r.17 shall apply, then they are forced back in to rr.6 and 7 which they had previously agreed not to apply. The anomaly resolves itself in that agreeing to apply r.17 brings with it the agreement to apply rr.6 and 7 in the specified circumstances.

Rule 17(2)

This rule purports to gives a new tribunal wide discretion but that discretion is far less wide than first appears. While we might conceivably envisage the new tribunal starting the arbitration from the very beginning, s.1(a) and rr.24(1)(c) and 25 reflect, in this context, simple common sense in that the new tribunal must endeavour to make the transition as near to seamless as is practicable and, therefore, to re-use as much of what had gone before as possible.

In practice, this will normally mean re-using all written submissions, correspondence, expert reports and the like but more difficulty arises in respect of (a) witnesses and (b) oral argument:
- (i) If witnesses are not examined/cross-examined and reliance placed solely on witness statements, it is likely that these can be re-used but if there had been any actual appearance by witnesses there is no substitute, not even a full transcript, for their physical examination since their demeanour, particularly in responding to cross-examination or tribunal questioning, may be fundamental to assessing their credibility.
- (ii) While oral argument can be transcribed, practical experience shows that such is not fully sufficient to appreciate the strengths of the oral presentations, the interplay between opposing counsel often being a key factor.

Concerning assessment of credibility, in *Discain Project Services Ltd v Opecprime Developments Ltd* [2001] EWHC 450 (TCC), H.H. Judge Seymour QC said (at [50]):

"As was obvious, Mr X's evidence was extremely economical as an account of what had actually happened to the extent of being positively misleading. *Mr X was not, in my judgment, a very proficient purveyor of untruths.* His tactic to deal with the unwelcome experience of cross-examination was to give his evidence quite unnecessarily loudly. He was virtually shouting. No explanation for such behaviour was offered or emerged" (authors' emphasis added).

No transcript can capture this degree of "flavour" of a witness.

Rule 17(3)

This is, we submit, self-evident.

Rule 18: Arbitrators nominated in arbitration agreements **D**

18. Any provision in an arbitration agreement which specifies who is to be an arbitrator ceases to have effect in relation to an arbitration when the specified individual's tenure as an arbitrator for that arbitration ends.

DEFINITIONS
"arbitration agreement": ss.4, 31(1)
"arbitrator": ss.4, 31(1)
"tenure": r.9

STATUS
This is a default rule so it is open to the parties to modify it, agree something different or disapply it completely (see s.9).

MODEL LAW
The Model Law makes no equivalent provision.

COMMENTARY
This is, we submit, self-evident.

Part 2

Jurisdiction of tribunal

Rule 19: Power of tribunal to rule on own jurisdiction **M**

19. The tribunal may rule on—
 (a) whether there is a valid arbitration agreement (or, in the case of a statutory arbitration, whether the enactment providing for arbitration applies to the dispute),
 (b) whether the tribunal is properly constituted, and
 (c) what matters have been submitted to arbitration in accordance with the arbitration agreement.

DEFINITIONS
 "arbitration": ss.2(1), (2), 31(1)
 "arbitration agreement": ss.4, 31(1)
 "statutory arbitration": ss.16(1), 31(1)
 "tribunal": ss.2(1), 31(1)

COMMENTARY

The power of an arbitral tribunal to rule on questions relating to its jurisdiction is central to any modern arbitration regime. While an arbitrator could probably rule on his own jurisdiction at common law (see Davidson, *Arbitration*, 2000, para.11.01), the explicit recognition of this principle in r.19 is helpful. The power is certainly to be found in art.16 of the Model Law, which conflates it with the, admittedly related, principle of separability. The 2010 Act is to be commended for following the example of the 1996 Act in expressing these principles in different provisions. (Separability is covered in s.5.) Yet whereas the 1996 Act allows the parties to contract out of the principles, r.19 and s.5 follow the lead of the Model Law in making them mandatory. This is curious in a measure which explicitly espouses the philosophy of party autonomy, and while the principle of "competence-competence" is undoubtedly extremely convenient, it is surely not so fundamental as to have to be forced on the parties, whatever their views. The policy memorandum, para.136, notes that discussions with stakeholders suggests that r.19 introduces, "an important new power for arbitrators which will save a great deal of time and therefore expense". That is surely correct, but is still not a strong argument for rendering the power mandatory, since it is arguably for the parties to decide whether they want to save that time and expense. The policy memorandum, para.135, also observes that the current system, "may result in unnecessary referrals to the courts", and this may be the real reason for making the provision mandatory. Since the rule is mandatory, it cannot be ousted by the parties purporting under s.9(4)(b) to choose a foreign procedural law, which does not recognise the principle of "competence-competence", to govern the arbitration.

There is obviously a relationship between this rule and s.10, which demands that a court must sist legal proceedings if a party can show that the dispute is covered by an arbitration agreement, unless the court is satisfied that the arbitration agreement is void, unenforceable or incapable of being performed. The commentary to s.10 noted that this principle is a key feature of the Act and because party autonomy and limited court intervention are among the guiding principles on which the Act is based, it might be thought that if there is at least an arguable case than an arbitration agreement exists, the court should sist any proceedings and let the arbitral tribunal determine questions relating to whether the agreement exists and whether it is rendered void, etc. by any factor. It should be observed that this is certainly the approach adopted by at least some courts in considering the interaction of arts 8 and 16 of the Model Law (see Kaplan J. in the Hong Kong case of *Fung Sang Trading Ltd v Kai Sun Sea Products & Food Co Ltd* [1992] A.D.R.L.J. 93 at 101). But the commentary also acknowledged that the English courts in interpreting s.9 of the 1996 Act, which is worded in similar fashion to s.10 of the 2010 Act, have taken the view that since they are required to determine whether the conditions for the grant of a stay (sist) are met, it must be for them to decide whether an arbitration agreement exists and whether the dispute falls within its scope, perhaps except where it seems fairly certain that an agreement does exist and extends to the dispute in question (see, e.g. *Al-Naimi v Islamic Press Agency Inc* [2000] 1 Lloyd's Rep. 522). Thus despite the terms of r.19, the arbitral tribunal may be precluded from ruling on its own jurisdiction if a court rules that the arbitration agreement is void in terms of s.10.

Section 30(2) of the 1996 Act indicates that a jurisdictional ruling may be challenged by any available arbitral process of review. Thus if the parties are arbitrating under a set of arbitration rules which allows a party to appeal to a further arbitral tribunal or the governing body of an arbitral institution against a jurisdictional ruling, that is permitted by s.30(2). There is nothing equivalent to s.30(2) in the 2010 Act, and since r.19 is mandatory, any agreement as to further arbitral review might appear to be void. Yet it might alternatively be argued that merely because the Act provides for the tribunal to review its own jurisdiction, and for that decision to be subject to review by the court, it is not inconsistent with those provisions that the parties might agree that a process of arbitral review be built into the arrangements as a precursor to any appeal. In other words, just because the Act does not explicitly acknowledge a process of arbitral review, does not mean that it is prohibited. That interpretation is perhaps bolstered by the fact that r.71(2) indicates that an appeal against an award, including a jurisdictional appeal is only available after the exhaustion of any available arbitral process of review. Standing against that interpretation is the fact that the period for appeal to the court against a jurisdictional ruling under r.21 hardly seems to afford scope for further arbitral review.

The rule goes on to consider exactly what issues of jurisdiction the tribunal may rule upon in r.19(a)–(c), and here it clearly derives its inspiration from s.30(1) of the 1996 Act rather than the Model Law. That provision seems to indicate that the matters mentioned in r.19(a)–(c) comprehend what is meant by the tribunal determining its own jurisdiction, so that any other jurisdictional matters might not lie within the competence of the tribunal to determine. Although rather differently phrased, r.19 might be open to the same interpretation. Thus it is interesting to note that the English courts have taken the view that it makes sense in terms of the approach taken by the 1996 Act that all jurisdictional issues should be dealt with by the arbitrator, even if not squarely within the categories featured in r.19(a)–(c). Thus in *Mackley & Co Ltd v Gosport Marina Ltd* [2002] B.L.R. 367 it was held that it was for the tribunal to decide whether a procedural step which was necessary to trigger the arbitral process had been taken.

Rule 19(a)

Valid arbitration agreement: The tribunal may rule on the question of whether there is a valid arbitration agreement. This would include deciding whether the agreement is undermined by the invalidity of the main contract, and whether a party is no longer bound by the arbitration agreement because it has been abandoned (see *Chimimport Plc v G D'Alesio SAS (The Paola d'Alesio)* [1994] 2 Lloyd's Rep. 366), or the other party has acted so as to repudiate it (see *ABB Lummus Global Ltd v Keppel Fels Ltd* [1999] 2 Lloyd's Rep. 24). One would not expect the invalidity of the main agreement to render the arbitration clause invalid, given that the Act embraces the principle of separability, but the English courts have suggested that if the main agreement is so fundamentally void as to be incapable of legal recognition, an arbitration clause cannot be allowed to have a separate existence (*O'Callaghan v Coral Racing Ltd, The Times*, November 26, 1998). Yet except in such rare cases the invalidity of the main agreement will have no effect on the validity of the arbitration clause, so that the arbitral tribunal will have jurisdiction to rule as to whether the main agreement is or is not valid and to determine the dispute accordingly (*Vee Networks Ltd v Econet Wireless Ltd* [2005] 1 Lloyd's Rep. 192).

Article 16 of the Model Law speaks of the tribunal dealing with objections as to the "existence" of the arbitration agreement, and in certain jurisdictions that has been interpreted as meaning that the tribunal rather than the court should determine the question of jurisdiction even where a party contends that he never entered into the agreement in the first place (see Kaplan J. in the Hong Kong case of *Fung Sang Trading Ltd v Kai Sun Sea Products & Food Co Ltd* [1992] A.D.R.L.J. 93 at 101; and Henry J. in *Rio Algom Ltd v Sammi Steel Co* (1991) 47 C.P.C. 251 at 256 (Ontario)). Whether s.30(1)(a) of the 1996 Act extends so far is doubtful. An arbitrator would certainly not have this jurisdiction under Scots common law (see Lord Moncrieff in *Ransohoff v Burrell* (1897) 21 R. 284 at 297). That being said, if the issue was whether an arbitration clause has been incorporated from another agreement, then the tribunal would almost certainly have jurisdiction (see *Willcock v Pickfords Removals Ltd* [1979] 1 Lloyd's Rep. 244).

Arbitral tribunals can be expected to rule on such matters as whether an alleged agreement is sufficiently certain to be binding (*Mangistaumunaigaz Oil Production Association v United World Trading Inc* [1995] 1 Lloyd's Rep. 617), whether an individual can properly be regarded to be a party to it (*Hussmann (Europe) Ltd v Al Ameen Development Trade Co* [2000] 2 Lloyd's Rep. 83), whether its terms in fact oblige the parties to arbitrate (*Lobb Partnership Ltd v Aintree Racecourse Ltd* [2000] B.L.R. 65), whether the agreement has been frustrated (*Sumitomo Heavy Industries Ltd v Oil and Natural Gas Commission* [1994] 2 Lloyd's Rep. 45), and whether the conditions for the operation of an arbitration clause have been met (*Sonatrach Petroleum Corp (BVI) v Ferrell International Ltd* [2002] 1 All E.R. (Comm) 627).

There is also the question of the law the tribunal should apply to the question of validity. That should normally be the law applicable to the contract, which of course may not be Scots law (see *JSC Zestafoni G Nikoladze Ferroalloy Plant v Ronly Holdings Ltd* [2004] 2 Lloyd's Rep. 335). However, if it is asserted that the agreement is invalid because a party lacked capacity, some other law might govern that issue. Equally, if the dispute is not arbitrable under Scots law, a tribunal might feel obliged to rule that the agreement is not valid, even though it might be arbitrable under the law governing the agreement (see the commentary to s.30 above). There might be those who argue that issues such as arbitrability should not be for the tribunal to determine, but the English courts seem to favour the tribunal having jurisdiction in such cases (see *Azov Shipping Co v Baltic Shipping Co*

(No.3) [1999] 1 Lloyd's Rep. 68; a similar approach has been taken under the Model Law—*International Civil Aviation Organisation v Tripal Systems Ltd* (1998) XXIII YCA 226 Supreme Court of Quebec).

The rule continues that in the case of a statutory arbitration the tribunal may rule on whether the relevant enactment applies to the dispute, in this respect echoing s.96(2) of the 1996 Act. It would obviously have been entirely inappropriate for the tribunal to have been empowered to consider whether an enactment was actually valid.

Rule 19(b)

Whether tribunal properly constituted: The tribunal may rule as to whether it has been properly constituted. This would obviously include issues such as whether each arbitrator has been validly appointed, and whether the tribunal takes the shape agreed by the parties, or stipulated by rules, contractual or statutory, which might apply in default of agreement. In *Minermet SpA Milan v Luckyfield Shipping Corp* [2004] 2 Lloyd's Rep. 348, while the arbitration clause provided that each party should appoint an arbitrator and that the two arbitrators should then appoint a third, it continued that if a party did not appoint an arbitrator within 14 days of being notified that the other party had appointed an arbitrator, the single arbitrator could then proceed with the reference alone. The latter scenario duly unfolded and the arbitrator ruled that that he had jurisdiction to determine the dispute.

Rule 19(c)

Extent of jurisdiction: This empowers the tribunal to determine the extent of its jurisdiction, including the scope of the arbitration clause and whether the particular dispute falls within that scope (see *Al Naimi v Islamic Press Agency Inc* [2000] 1 Lloyd's Rep. 522). However, it also empowers it to decide whether certain issues have been laid before it in the way required by the arbitration agreement (*Lafarge (Aggregates) Ltd v London Borough of Newham* [2005] 2 Lloyd's Rep. 577).

Rule 20: Objections to tribunal's jurisdiction **M**

20.—(1) Any party may object to the tribunal on the ground that the tribunal does not have, or has exceeded, its jurisdiction in relation to any matter.

(2) An objection must be made—
    (a) before, or as soon as is reasonably practicable after, the matter to which the objection relates is first raised in the arbitration, or
    (b) where the tribunal considers that circumstances justify a later objection, by such later time as it may allow,
but, in any case, an objection may not be made after the tribunal makes its last award.

(3) If the tribunal upholds an objection it must—
    (a) end the arbitration in so far as it relates to a matter over which the tribunal has ruled it does not have jurisdiction, and
    (b) set aside any provisional or part award already made in so far as the award relates to such a matter.

(4) The tribunal may—
    (a) rule on an objection independently from dealing with the subject-matter of the dispute, or

(b) delay ruling on an objection until it makes its award on the merits of the dispute (and include its ruling in that award),

but, where the parties agree which of these courses the tribunal should take, the tribunal must proceed accordingly.

DEFINITIONS

"arbitration": ss.2(1), (2), 31(1)
"dispute": ss.2(1), 31(1)
"party": ss.2(1), 31(1), (2)
"tribunal": ss.2(1), 31(1)

COMMENTARY

Rule 20(1)

Raised by party: While it would arguably be possible for a tribunal to rule on jurisdictional matters of its own volition, almost invariably it will do so when a party raises the issue. Thus, as under s.31 of the 1996 Act and art.16(2) of the Model Law, the Act provides that a party may raise a jurisdictional objection, whether by claiming that the arbitral tribunal has no jurisdiction over a particular issue or that it has exceeded its jurisdiction. It should be borne in mind that it may be possible for a point of jurisdiction instead to be referred to the Outer House under r.22 (see the commentary on that rule below).

Rule 20(2)

When objection must be made: An objection must be made before or as soon as is reasonably practicable after the matter is first raised in the arbitration. What appears to be contemplated by this provision is that if a party believes from the outset that the tribunal lacks jurisdiction altogether, or may exceed its jurisdiction, then that objection should be made almost immediately. However, if it only becomes evident that a tribunal proposes to exceed its jurisdiction during the course of the proceedings, then an objection must be made as soon as reasonably practicable thereafter.

This provision carries echoes of s.31 of the 1996 Act and art.16(2) of the Model Law. Both of those provisions make a distinction between an initial objection to jurisdiction and a later plea that it is exceeding its jurisdiction. Under s.31(1) the former type of objection must be raised not later than the time the party in question takes the first step in the proceedings to contest the merits of any matter in relation to which he challenges the tribunal's jurisdiction. Under art.16(2) such an objection must be raised not later than the submission of the statement of defence. The DAC (DAC Report, para.140) deliberately avoided the use of such language in the 1996 Act, "since this might give the impression, which we are anxious to dispel, that every arbitration requires some formal pleading or the like". Both provisions also indicate that a party is not precluded from raising such an objection by the fact that he has appointed or participated in the appointment of an arbitrator. That statement is not to be found in r.20, but it is to be hoped that is how the matter will be approached. It is of course perfectly possible in terms of r.7 for the tribunal to be appointed without the participation of a dissenting party. Equally, under s.14 a party who denies that the tribunal has jurisdiction and who thus refuses to participate in the proceedings may still challenge any award under r.67. However, given that the Act embraces the principle of competence-competence, a party might feel that his interests are best protected by co-operating in the establishment of the tribunal with a view to asking it to rule that it has no jurisdiction. It would be absurd if such a step was regarded as barring a jurisdictional challenge.

As regards when an objection might be regarded as having been made, since r.20(1) speaks of a party objecting "to the tribunal", it may be suggested that anything done before the tribunal is constituted does not count as an objection. Thus a communication with another party in which a party contests whether the parties are bound to arbitrate would not amount to an objection in terms of r.20, even if the members of the tribunal were aware of it. Indeed, if the parties were to approach an individual, asking him whether he would accept an appointment as a sole arbitrator, and indicating that one of them believed that the tribunal would lack jurisdiction, that would not count as an objection either. Once the tribunal is constituted, the objection should be raised no later than the point at which the tribunal first addresses the issue of the substance of what it is to decide. It can of course be raised earlier. Thus as soon as the tribunal is constituted a party might ask it to address the question of its jurisdiction, while the matter could also be raised in a preliminary meeting designed to address procedural rather than substantive matters, or during discussions between a party and the tribunal (see *Athletic Union of Constantinople v National Basketball Association* [2002] 1 Lloyd's Rep. 305).

The above analysis would apply equally to the situation where a party denies that the tribunal has any jurisdiction whatsoever, and the situation where it is claimed from the outset that it is being asked to exceed its jurisdiction. In such situations the idea that a party may raise an objection as soon as is reasonably practicable after the matter is first raised in the arbitration seems strange. If the objection was clear from the outset, why should a party not have to raise it, *at the very latest*, when the issue is first considered in the arbitration. This peculiarity derives from the attempt to take the same approach to initial objections and objections which emerge when it appears that the tribunal might exceed its jurisdiction. The approach of the 1996 Act and Model Law in differentiating between these two situations may be more sensible in this context. Obviously, in the case where it only becomes apparent that the tribunal might exceed its jurisdiction when the proceedings are under way, such as where the other party in its submission raises such matters or where the tribunal itself proposes to examine evidence beyond the scope of its authority (see *Report of the UNCITRAL on the work of its eighteenth session*, UN A/40/17, para.155), it makes perfect sense to say that a party must raise this objection as soon as is reasonably practicable after the ground of objection emerges. So in *Hussmann (Europe) Ltd v Al Ameen Development Trade Co* [2002] 2 Lloyd's Rep. 83 it was held to be appropriate to raise an objection on the first day of the substantive hearing, since it only became clear at that point that the tribunal intended to treat an assignee of a party to the original contract as a party to the proceedings.

It can also be seen that the tribunal may permit a later objection, if it is satisfied that circumstances so justify it. The provision then suggests that the objection may be made by such later time as the tribunal may allow. In practice, it will be rare for a tribunal to specify a time by which such later objections may be made. Rather, it will be a case of the tribunal deciding whether to entertain a late objection by one of the parties.

It would appear to be the case that a tribunal may not entertain a late objection if it does not believe the circumstances justify it. Can the tribunal's decision on whether a late objection should be entertained be reviewed by the court? It is probably the case that it is not open to the court to review a decision that a late objection should be considered, even if there was no justification for the tribunal doing so (but see *Ratnam v Cumarasamy* [1965] 1 W.L.R. 8). Nor does it appear that the court is entitled to review the exercise of the tribunal's discretion not to entertain a late objection. But suppose a party's complaint is that it raised an objection timeously, but that the tribunal refused to entertain the objection on the basis that it was not made timeously. Surely it is not intended that the tribunal should have the exclusive right to determine whether an objection is timeous? It is suggested that the court should be entitled to review this question.

It is vital that an objection should be made timeously, since although lack or excess of jurisdiction is a ground of challenging an award under r.67, it is made clear by r.76 that a party may lose its right to challenge an award if it fails to raise an objection timeously (see the commentary on that rule below). In other words, a party who is aware of a jurisdictional objection, but chooses not to raise it and instead lets the arbitration proceed, may not then challenge the award on the basis of lack of jurisdiction. Equally, while lack or excess of jurisdiction is a ground of refusing to enforce an award (in whole or in part) under s.12(2), s.12(3) makes it clear that the right to contest enforcement on this ground may be lost by virtue of r.76. The position is similar under s.73 of the 1996 Act, and in that context it has been held that even if a party has raised a jurisdictional objection at an appropriate point, he may not challenge the award on the basis of a new jurisdictional issue which he had failed to raise at an appropriate point (*Athletic Union of Constantinople v National Basketball Association* [2002] 1 Lloyd's Rep. 305). On the other hand, in *Primetrade AG v Ythan Ltd (The Ythan)* [2006] 1 Lloyd's Rep. 457, Aikens J. held that a party was not barred from challenging an award under the 1996 Act where a rather similar challenge had been raised before the arbitrator, even though the grounds of challenge in court were slightly different and rather broader. It might be added that the Model Law is entirely unclear as to the effect on the power to mount a jurisdictional challenge to an award of a failure to object (see Fraser P. Davidson, *International Commercial Arbitration, Scotland and the UNCITRAL Model Law* (Edinburgh: W. Green, 1991) paras 5.6–5.8), and the 2010 Act thus represents a considerable advance over the Model Law in this respect.

It can be seen that a jurisdictional objection may not be made once the final award has been made. A party's recourse is then to challenge the award under r.67. That party may of course be barred from doing so by r.76 if the objection is not timeous, but it is possible for the fact that the tribunal has exceeded its jurisdiction only to become evident when the final award it made, and in those circumstances the award could be challenged.

Rule 20(3)

Effect of upholding an objection: Where a tribunal upholds an objection it must set aside any provisional or part award in so far as it exceeds its jurisdiction and must end the arbitration in so far as it relates to a matter over which it lacks jurisdiction. There is no counterpart of this provision in either the 1996 Act or the Model Law. It seems to be contemplated that the arbitration might continue in so far as it addresses matters which lie within the tribunal's jurisdiction, and this concept of a part-termination seems rather obscure. There may be more merit in terminating the arbitration where jurisdiction is lacking completely in that it makes clear that the tribunal is functus. It is also arguable that any part or provisional award is automatically a nullity once the tribunal rules that it has no jurisdiction, but again it might be useful for the tribunal formally to set such awards aside, since it then becomes clear what the effect of the jurisdictional ruling has been. Again, it seems to be contemplated that such awards might only be set aside in part, and this seems to hold more possibility for confusion.

Rule 20(4)

How tribunal may rule on objection: This provision did not appear in the original version of the Bill and is a welcome addition. As under s.31(4) of the 1996 Act and art.16(3) of the Model Law, the tribunal may rule on a jurisdictional objection either separately or as part of its award on the merits. However, as under the 1996 Act, but unlike the Model Law, the tribunal must defer to the agreement of the parties on this issue. Disposing of the matter as part of an award on the merits has obvious attractions when the tribunal has to deal with such an objection when on the threshold of making an award, and the DAC Report, para.146 points out that, "in some cases it may be simply impracticable to rule on jurisdiction before determining merits". The framers of the Model Law also felt that the tribunal should have this discretion since it would allow it to continue the proceedings where it believed that the raising of an objection was without merit and being employed merely as a delaying tactic (see *Report of the UNCITRAL on the work of its eighteenth session*, UN A/40/17, para.155). It would appear that it would be very difficult to challenge the exercise of the tribunal's discretion in this context (see *AOOT Kalmneft v Glencore International AG* [2001] 2 All E.R. (Comm) 577). In exercising that discretion the tribunal will obviously have regard to the fact that one of the objects of arbitration in terms of s.1(a) is to resolve disputes without unnecessary delay or expense and indeed to its duty under r.24(1)(c) to conduct the arbitration without unnecessary delay or expense.

Where a separate ruling is issued, a party may appeal against it under r.21. Where it is made as part of the award on the merits, a party who disagreed with the ruling would challenge the award under r.67. The 2010 Act follows the lead of the Model Law in categorising a separate decision on jurisdiction as a ruling. By contrast, such a decision under the 1996 Act would take the form of an award on that issue. The DAC Report, para.142 opined that it was, "unnecessary to introduce the new concept of a preliminary ruling which is somehow different from an award", continuing that this had, "the advantage that awards on jurisdiction will have the benefit of those provisions on awards generally and, if appropriate, may be enforced in the same way as any other award." This leads to the question of what the status of a jurisdictional ruling might be if it is not an award. What form should it take, if any? Does it have to contain reasons? If the tribunal rules that it has no jurisdiction, is it permitted make an award as to expenses? Might all these issues be rendered irrelevant if the tribunal itself casts the ruling in the form of an award?

Rule 21: Appeal against tribunal's ruling on jurisdictional objection **M**

21.—(1) A party may, no later than 14 days after the tribunal's decision on an objection under rule 20, appeal to the Outer House against the decision.

(2) The tribunal may continue with the arbitration pending determination of the appeal.

(3) The Outer House's decision on the appeal is final.

DEFINITIONS
   "arbitration": ss.2(1), (2), 31(1)
   "Outer House": s.31(1)
   "party": ss.2(1), 31(1), (2)
   "tribunal": ss.2(1), 31(1)

COMMENTARY
   This is a fairly straightforward provision. While it was a default rule in the original version of the Bill, it is now mandatory. Its previous status as a default rule would not have meant that the parties could have excluded the possibility of judicial review of the tribunal's decision as to jurisdiction, but rather that a party's only recourse would have been to challenge the award on jurisdictional grounds under r.67. That still leaves the question of whether a party who disagrees with the tribunal's ruling on jurisdiction, but who neglects to appeal under r.21, would still be entitled to raise that same jurisdictional point in challenging the award under r.67. It is submitted that the answer, would be yes, since r.76 would not appear to bar such a challenge.

Rule 21(1)

   Period for appeal: A party has 14 days from the tribunal's ruling on an objection to appeal to the Outer House. (If the tribunal consists of or contains a Court of Session judge, then the appeal would be to the Inner House—see s.25 above). It remains to be seen whether this right of appeal would include a right to appeal against a tribunal's decision that it cannot entertain a jurisdictional objection because it was not timeously raised. In the context of the 1996 Act it seems unclear whether there can be an appeal against a tribunal's ruling that it lacks jurisdiction (see *LG Caltex Gas Co Ltd v China National Petroleum Co* [2001] 1 W.L.R. 1892). However, r.21(1) appears to be phrased to allow an appeal against a decision that the tribunal has no jurisdiction just as much as a decision that it has jurisdiction. Here it can be observed that art.16(3) of the Model Law, which r.21 resembles in several respects, would only have allowed an appeal against a decision that the tribunal has jurisdiction, since it was felt inappropriate to compel arbitrators who had ruled that they lacked jurisdiction to continue (see *Report of the UNCITRAL on the work of its eighteenth session*, UN A/40/17, para.163). However, it appeared to the Dervaird Committee that if parties thereafter resorted to litigation, one of them might raise the issue of the arbitration agreement and the court might rule that it was binding, so that the parties would have to arbitrate after all (see joint consultative document, Departmental Advisory Committee on Arbitration Law and Scottish Advisory Committee on Arbitration Law, *The UNCITRAL Model Law on International Commercial Arbitration* (1987), p.57). During the process of drafting the Model Law the UK raised a similar point, but the (surely erroneous) response was that in such a case the arbitration agreement could no longer be invoked by the court (see *Summary Record of the 316th meeting of the United Nations Conference on International Commercial Arbitration*, UN A/CN.9/SR.316, paras 16–19). Thus it was felt more sensible to provide for a more immediate means of referring such matters to the court, so that the version of art.16(3) which was adopted in Scotland permitted appeals on any jurisdictional ruling. The wording of r.21(1) seems very similar in this respect.
   The period within which an appeal might be brought is very tight—14 days after the tribunal's decision. The aim is clearly to prevent this process

delaying the proceedings unduly, but it might be noted that the corresponding period under art.16(3) of the Model Law is 30 days, which was itself regarded as a demanding time limit. Fourteen days may prove rather taxing for participants in an international arbitration seated in Scotland, since during that period a party who may be located at the other side of the world has to digest the implications of the tribunal's decision, decide whether to appeal, frame an appeal, and instruct Scottish counsel.

Rule 21(2)

As under art.16(3) the tribunal may continue the proceedings pending the determination of the appeal. That article actually empowers the tribunal to make an award. Rule 21(2) does not indicate whether the tribunal may go so far, but neither does it preclude such a step. It is suggested that such a course of action would lie within the tribunal's discretion, albeit that if the court then decided that it had no jurisdiction or had exceeded its jurisdiction, the award would be vitiated to that extent.

Rule 21(3)

In order that the matter should be dealt with expeditiously, and the tribunal should not have to proceed against the background of the possibility that the arbitration may be undermined by a further appeal or appeals, the Outer House's decision on the issue is declared to be final. It would seem to make sense that it would be inappropriate for a party who has made an unsuccessful appeal to seek to raise a jurisdictional appeal against the award under r.67, unless the ground of challenge is quite different, since the matter would be *res judicata*. However, if that is correct, it means that there is a degree of inconsistency in the Act's approach to the matter. This is because if a jurisdictional appeal is raised against the award under r.67 the decision of the Outer House may in certain limited circumstances be subject to a further appeal to the Inner House—a course of action which does not lie under r.21(3). Such an inconsistency does not arise under the 1996 Act, since the tribunal's decision on jurisdiction will always take the form of an award, and be subject to challenge under s.67, just like a final award.

Rule 22: Referral of point of jurisdiction **D**

22. The Outer House may, on an application by any party, determine any question as to the tribunal's jurisdiction.

DEFINITIONS
  "Outer House": s.31(1)
  "party": ss.2(1), 31(1), (2)
  "tribunal": ss.2(1), 31(1)

COMMENTARY
A party may seek to refer a jurisdictional question to the Outer House, subject to the conditions laid down in the next section. This provision did not appear in the original Bill, but was added when consultees indicated that such a power could be useful (policy memorandum, para.139). Sometimes a difficult and/or important issue of jurisdiction will arise, in relation to which any tribunal ruling is bound to be challenged by the losing party (see, e.g. *Belgravia Property Co Ltd v S & R (London) Ltd* [2001] B.L.R. 424). In such circumstances it is sensible that it should be possible to bypass the tribunal and go straight to the court for a jurisdictional ruling. The provision is

obviously inspired by s.32 of the 1996 Act, but while s.32 is for the most part mandatory, r.22 may be disapplied by the parties either expressly or by adopting institutional rules which restrict recourse to the courts. Nor does it require the party to give notice of this step to the other party or parties as s.32 does. There is no corresponding provision in the Model Law.

Rule 23: Jurisdiction referral: procedure etc. **M**

23.—(1) This rule applies only where an application is made under rule 22.
(2) Such an application is valid only if—
   (a) the parties have agreed that it may be made, or
   (b) the tribunal has consented to it being made and the court is satisfied—
      (i) that determining the question is likely to produce substantial savings in expenses,
      (ii) that the application was made without delay, and
      (iii) that there is a good reason why the question should be determined by the court.
(3) The tribunal may continue with the arbitration pending determination of an application.
(4) The Outer House's determination of the question is final (as is any decision by the Outer House as to whether an application is valid).

DEFINITIONS
"arbitration": ss.2(1), (2), 31(1)
"Outer House": s.31(1)
"party": ss.2(1), 31(1), (2)
"tribunal": ss.2(1), 31(1)

COMMENTARY

Rule 23(1)

Rule 23 was previously part of r.22. However, at a late stage it was decided that while it should be open to the parties to exclude such recourse to the courts, if such recourse had not been excluded the parties should not be entitled to alter the basis on which a point should be referred. Since the Act operates on the basis that a rule is entirely default or entirely mandatory, there was no alternative to detaching the procedural aspects of r.22 and expressing them as this separate, mandatory rule.

It is pointed out in s.32 of the 1996 Act that a party may lose his right to raise a jurisdictional objection, the implication being that if a party had failed to raise such an objection at an appropriate stage, it would not be possible to make a reference to the court under s.32. There is no reference in r.23 to that right being lost. Nonetheless, if a party sought to raise a jurisdictional issue too late in the proceedings, the tribunal would presumably not consent to the reference being made, and even if it did the court would presumably not be satisfied that the application had been made without delay, as required by r.23(2)(b)(ii). The other alternative is that the application is made with the consent of the other party, and here the court need not be satisfied on any point. Of course, one would expect that the other party would decline to consent to the application when the party making it had lost his right to raise a jurisdictional objection, but consent might be unwittingly given when the consenting party was ignorant of or had misunderstood the legal position. Where that is the case, it would appear that the court should rule on the jurisdictional point.

Rule 23(2)

Conditions for valid application: While a party is able to make such an application, the court may only grant it if either of two conditions has been met. The first is that the other party has agreed to it being made. Where there are more than two parties to the arbitration, all other parties must agree. (That is the effect of s.31(1), (2).) Under s.32(2)(a) of the 1996 Act such agreement would have to be given in writing. This is not a requirement of r.23(2)(a) so that if written agreement is not obtained, it would be enough if agreement were signified during the course of the proceedings.

If the agreement of the other party or parties cannot be obtained, then the party making the application must obtain the consent of the tribunal, and the court must be satisfied on each of three points:

- that determining the question is likely to produce substantial savings in expenses;
- that the application has been made without delay;
- that there is a good reason why the question should be determined by the court.

The provision is silent as to the burden of proof, and it may be that the court will decide whether it is satisfied on the above points without reference to that concept. That being said, the court is unlikely to be satisfied on any of the points in the absence of some sort of evidence and argument. In this context it might be observed that, while the provision mirrors almost exactly s.32(2) of the 1996 Act, there is nothing equivalent to s.32(3), which requires the party making the application to explain why the matter should be decided by the court.

The obvious sort of situation where the court would be satisfied on the above matters is where a party makes an immediate jurisdictional objection which raises a point in relation to which the determination of the tribunal is practically certain to be appealed by the losing party, so that much time and expense would be saved if the court considered the matter at a preliminary stage rather than as an appeal from a tribunal decision. It might nonetheless be noted that in relation to the identical provisions of s.32(2) of the 1996 Act the DAC Report, para.147 was clearly of the view that in most cases it would still be most appropriate for a tribunal to consider its own jurisdiction in the first instance, and "anticipated that the Courts will take care to prevent this exceptional provision from becoming the normal route for challenging jurisdiction".

In terms of the above scheme, if the tribunal is not prepared to give consent to the application, then it would appear that the court may not rule on the issue. However, in *Mackley & Co Ltd v Gosport Marina Ltd* [2002] B.L.R. 367 a party contested whether a necessary precondition for the operation of the arbitration clause had been met. Neither the other party nor the tribunal were prepared to agree that the matter should be referred to the court under s.32 of the 1996 Act, but the party contesting jurisdiction successfully applied to the court for a declaration that the precondition had not been met. In some ways this case is exceptional, since there was some doubt as to whether the particular jurisdictional issue fell within the competence of the tribunal to determine under the particular scheme of the 1996 Act. The judge (H.H. Judge Seymour QC) also pointed out at para.31 that courts:

> "... should not customarily be troubled with disputes as to the validity of a reference to arbitration. Any question between parties as to the validity of a reference should in the first instance, at least, be determined by the arbitral tribunal."

Nonetheless, despite the 1996 Act embracing the principle of competence-competence and directing that the court should not intervene in an arbitration except where permitted by the Act, the court asserted this residual discretion to rule on jurisdiction.

It is hoped that the Scottish courts do not follow suit. Yet if a party denies that he is bound by an arbitration clause, and thus refuses to accede in the creation of the tribunal, the court may under r.7 be asked to make the necessary appointment (unless an arbitral appointments referee is asked to do so). Once the tribunal is appointed, the party in question would probably ask that the question of jurisdiction be referred to the court under r.22. If neither the other party nor the tribunal were prepared to consent to this referral, he would then no doubt require the tribunal to consider the jurisdictional objection, and then appeal against its ruling if it decided that it had jurisdiction. There must be a temptation on the part of a court which is asked to make an appointment (unless perhaps it is the sheriff court) to rule on the jurisdictional issue in order to avoid the waste of time and money involved if it did not do so. Even so, the logic of the Act is that in such circumstances it would still be the tribunal rather than the court which should deal with matters of jurisdiction in the first instance (see *Vale do Rio Doce Navegacos SA v Shanghai Bao Steel Ocean Shipping Co Ltd* [2000] 2 All E.R. (Comm) 70).

Rule 23(3)

Tribunal discretion to continue proceedings: As under s.32(4) of the 1996 Act, the tribunal may continue the proceedings pending the determination of the application. The 1996 Act goes so far as to empower the tribunal to make an award during this period. As with r.20(2), r.23(3) does not indicate whether the tribunal has this power, but does not preclude such a step. It is once more suggested that such a course of action would lie within the tribunal's discretion, albeit that if the court then decided that it had no jurisdiction or had exceeded its jurisdiction, the award would be vitiated to that extent. It will probably be the case that if a point of jurisdiction is seen as being sufficiently doubtful to justify seeking a referral, the tribunal will be less inclined to continue the proceedings, far less make an award, while the decision is pending, unless it is possible for the proceedings to continue without reference to the disputed point. In deciding on the best course of action the tribunal will obviously have regard to the fact that one of the objects of arbitration in terms of s.1(a) is to resolve disputes without unnecessary delay or expense and indeed to its duty under r.24(1)(c) to conduct the arbitration without unnecessary delay or expense.

When this subrule was part of r.22, the default status of that rule would surely have meant that the parties could agree that the tribunal should not be permitted to continue the arbitration in these circumstances. Now that the subrule is part of a mandatory provision, the power cannot be excluded by the parties. It is perhaps ironic that while s.32 is primarily mandatory, s.32(4) indicates that the tribunal's power to continue is subject to the contrary agreement of the parties.

Under s.31(5) of the 1996 Act the tribunal is allowed to stay the proceedings pending the determination of an application under s.32, and must stay them if the parties so agree. There is no similar provision in the rules, but it is submitted that any such provision would be otiose, since a discretion to continue the proceedings is equally a discretion not to continue. Again, s.1(a) and r.24(1)(c) will be relevant in this context.

Rule 23(4)

Decision of Outer House final: As in relation to the Outer House's disposal of an appeal against a tribunal's jurisdictional ruling, the Outer House's decision is final. Once more it is submitted that a party who has unsuccessfully contested jurisdiction at this stage may not raise a jurisdictional appeal against the award under r.67, unless the ground of challenge is quite different, since the matter would be res judicata. Once again, this also leads to inconsistency in the Act's approach to the matter, as if a jurisdictional appeal is raised against the award under r.67 the decision of the Outer House may in certain limited circumstances be subject to a further appeal to the Inner House—a course of action which does not lie under r.23(4). Under s.32(6) of the 1996 Act an appeal will lie, but only if the court gives leave, which can only be given if the court considers that the question involves a point of law which is of general importance or is one which for some other special reason should be considered by the Court of Appeal. It will also be seen that the Outer House's decision is final as regards the question whether an application is validly made, such as where it is contested whether the application was indeed made without delay. Such a question could be the subject of an appeal under s.32(5) of the 1996 Act, albeit only if the court gives leave. The rules once more take a firmer line than the 1996 Act in this context.

PART 3

GENERAL DUTIES

Rule 24: General duty of the tribunal **M**

24.—(1) The tribunal must—
  (a) be impartial and independent,
  (b) treat the parties fairly, and
  (c) conduct the arbitration—
    (i) without unnecessary delay, and
    (ii) without incurring unnecessary expense.
(2) Treating the parties fairly includes giving each party a reasonable opportunity to put its case and to deal with the other party's case.

DEFINITIONS

Neither "impartial" nor "independent" is defined in the Act (nor in the Model Law).

STATUS

This is a mandatory rule so it is not open to the parties to agree anything else or to disapply it completely (see s.8). It is difficult to conceive of a rule which is any more fundamental to and central to the arbitral process.

MODEL LAW

There is no direct equivalent of r.24 in the Model Law, save that r.24(1)(b) is very similar to art.18 (equal treatment of parties): "The parties shall be treated with equality and each party shall be given a full opportunity of presenting his case."

As discussed above (see r.8) art.12(1) of the Model Law provides that:

"When a person is approached in connection with his possible appointment as an arbitrator, he shall disclose any circumstances likely to give rise to justifiable doubts as to his impartiality or independence. An arbitrator, from the time of his appointment and throughout the arbitral proceedings, shall without delay disclose any such circumstances to the parties unless they have already been informed of them by him."

COMMENTARY

Rule 24(1)(a)

Section 1 provides that, "The founding principles of this Act are: (a) that the object of arbitration is to resolve disputes impartially ...". The necessity for arbitrators to be both impartial and independent is fundamental as is also recognised in r.24(1)(a). This is consistent with art.6(1) of the ECHR, which provides that:
"In the determination of his civil rights and obligations ... everyone is entitled to a fair ... hearing within a reasonable time by an independent and impartial tribunal established by law."
In the view both of the drafters of the Act and of the present authors the two-part requirement (impartial and independent) is axiomatic; the same view is common, almost universal around the world, including many non-ECHR jurisdictions. England and Wales (see below at p.161) represent the major difference here, but we should bear in mind that the 1996 Act predates the Human Rights Act 1998; however, the difficult question then arises as to what constitutes "independence" and whether it is an absolute term or whether any de minimis considerations apply.

The 1996 Act does not include such language but achieves substantially the same end by less direct means (refer ss.1(a), 24(1)(a), 33(1)(a)); further, the 1996 Act does not address independence at all (see below at p.161).

In *AT&T Corp v Saudi Cable Co* [2000] 2 Lloyd's Rep. 127 CA; [2000] EWCA Civ 154, the applicant sought to remove the chairman of an ICC tribunal, a distinguished Canadian QC, on the basis of his possessing a small number of shares in, and being a non-executive director of, Nortel which was a competitor of AT&T and which had been the disappointed bidder for a major telecoms contract with Saudi Cable which contract was the subject matter of the present arbitration. The Court of Appeal upheld Longmore J.'s rejection of the application, the arbitrator's connection with the parties and the contract being too remote. What made this case of particular interest was that the arbitrator also owned a small shareholding in AT&T, the complainant.

In contrast, in *Smits Leslie v Roach* [2006] H.C.A. 36 (Australia), a judge declined to recuse himself in circumstances where, if Smits Leslie, a law firm, had won its action (optimistic at best and, in fact, it lost) to recover fees from Roach, the latter would have had grounds for action in professional negligence, albeit close to hopeless, against another law firm F. F could only attract liability at all if both cases went massively against the odds and, assuming (optimistically) that each of the two cases stood a 10 per cent chance of success, the odds against F were then 100:1. A partner in F would therefore be at risk, on a probabilistic basis, for $A.85 less any insurance recovery. The chairman of partners in F was the brother of the judge. While five judges in the High Court of Australia (the Supreme Court, despite its anomalous name), expressing obiter views, considered the connection too remote (even before putting numbers into the discussion), the sixth, Kirby J., in a powerful and widely-admired judgment, rejected such an approach

Arbitration (Scotland) Act 2010

and, effectively, rejected any consideration of applying a de minimis threshold.

Impartiality is closely associated with bias, the question of which is a perennial. So far as the law is concerned, the leading case on bias (following a long line of such cases) is *Porter v Magill* [2001] UKHL 67 in which Lord Hope said:

"100. The 'reasonable likelihood' and 'real danger' tests which Lord Goff described in *R v Gough* have been criticised by the High Court of Australia on the ground that they tend to emphasise the court's view of the facts and to place inadequate emphasis on the public perception of the irregular incident: *Webb v The Queen* (1994) 181 CLR 41, 50 per Mason CJ and McHugh J. There is an uneasy tension between these tests and that which was adopted in Scotland by the High Court of Justiciary in *Bradford v McLeod*, 1986 SLT 244. Following Eve J's reference in *Law v Chartered Institute of Patent Agents* [1919] 2 Ch 276 (which was not referred to in *R v Gough*), the High Court of Justiciary adopted a test which looked at the question whether there was suspicion of bias through the eyes of the reasonable man who was aware of the circumstances: see also *Millar v Dickson*, 2001 SLT 988, 1002L–1003B. This approach, which has been described as 'the reasonable apprehension of bias' test, is in line with that adopted in most common law jurisdictions. It is also in line with that which the Strasbourg court has adopted, which looks at the question whether there was a risk of bias objectively in the light of the circumstances which the court has identified: *Piersack v Belgium* (1982) 5 EHRR 169, 179–180, paras 30–31; *De Cubber v Belgium* (1984) 7 EHRR 236, 246, para 30; *Pullar v United Kingdom* (1996) 22 EHRR 391, 402–403, para 30. In *Hauschildt v Denmark* (1989) 12 EHRR 266, 279, para 48 the court also observed that, in considering whether there was a legitimate reason to fear that a judge lacks impartiality, the standpoint of the accused is important but not decisive: 'What is decisive is whether this fear can be held objectively justified.'

101. The English courts have been reluctant, for obvious reasons, to depart from the test which Lord Goff of Chieveley so carefully formulated in *R v Gough*. In *R v Bow Street Metropolitan Stipendiary Magistrate, Ex p Pinochet Ugarte (No 2)* [2000] 1 AC 119, 136A–C Lord Browne-Wilkinson said that it was unnecessary in that case to determine whether it needed to be reviewed in the light of subsequent decisions in Canada, New Zealand and Australia. I said, at p 142F–G, that, although the tests in Scotland and England were described differently, their application was likely in practice to lead to results that were so similar as to be indistinguishable. The Court of Appeal, having examined the question whether the 'real danger' test might lead to a different result from that which the informed observer would reach on the same facts, concluded in *Locabail (UK) Ltd v Bayfield Properties Ltd* [2000] QB 451, 477 that in the overwhelming majority of cases the application of the two tests would lead to the same outcome.

102. In my opinion however it is now possible to set this debate to rest. The Court of Appeal took the opportunity in *In re Medicaments and Related Classes of Goods (No 2)* [2001] 1 WLR 700 to reconsider the whole question. Lord Phillips of Worth Matravers MR, giving the judgment of the court, observed, at p 711 A–B, that the precise test to be applied when determining whether a decision should be set aside on account of bias had given rise to difficulty, reflected in judicial decisions that had appeared in conflict, and that the attempt to resolve that

conflict in *R v Gough* had not commanded universal approval. At p 711B–C he said that, as the alternative test had been thought to be more closely in line with Strasbourg jurisprudence which since 2 October 2000 the English courts were required to take into account, the occasion should now be taken to review *R v Gough* to see whether the test it lays down is, indeed, in conflict with Strasbourg jurisprudence. Having conducted that review he summarised the court's conclusions, at pp726H–727C:

'85 When the Strasbourg jurisprudence is taken into account, we believe that a modest adjustment of the test in *R v Gough* is called for, which makes it plain that it is, in effect, no different from the test applied in most of the Commonwealth and in Scotland. The court must first ascertain all the circumstances which have a bearing on the suggestion that the judge was biased. It must then ask whether those circumstances would lead a fair-minded and informed observer to conclude that there was a real possibility, or a real danger, the two being the same, that the tribunal was biased.'

103. I respectfully suggest that your Lordships should now approve the modest adjustment of the test in *R v Gough* set out in that paragraph. It expresses in clear and simple language a test which is in harmony with the objective test which the Strasbourg court applies when it is considering whether the circumstances give rise to a reasonable apprehension of bias. It removes any possible conflict with the test which is now applied in most Commonwealth countries and in Scotland. I would however delete from it the reference to 'a real danger'. Those words no longer serve a useful purpose here, and they are not used in the jurisprudence of the Strasbourg court. The question is whether the fair-minded and informed observer, having considered the facts, would conclude that there was a real possibility that the tribunal was biased."

While the matter of bias is worth an entire book on its own, we content ourselves with this clear statement of the law.

To return to the English view of the requirement for (or lack of) independence (to repeat, pre direct application of the ECHR via the Human Rights Act 1998), the DAC Report (1995) stated:

"101. The Model Law (Article 12) specifies justifiable doubts as to the independence (as well as impartiality) of an arbitrator as grounds for his removal. We have considered this carefully, but despite efforts to do so, no-one has persuaded us that, in consensual arbitrations, this is either required or desirable. It seems to us that lack of independence, unless it gives rise to justifiable doubts about the impartiality of the arbitrator, is of no significance. The latter is, of course, the first of our grounds for removal. If lack of independence were to be included, then this could only be justified if it covered cases where the lack of independence did not give rise to justifiable doubts about impartiality, for otherwise there would be no point including lack of independence as a separate ground.

102. We can see no good reason for including 'non-partiality' lack of independence as a ground for removal and good reasons for not doing so. We do not follow what is meant to be covered by a lack of independence which does not lead to the appearance of partiality. Furthermore, the inclusion of independence would give rise to endless arguments, as it has, for example, in Sweden and the United States, where almost any connection (however remote) has been put forward to

challenge the 'independence' of an arbitrator. For example, it is often the case that one member of a barristers' Chambers appears as counsel before an arbitrator who comes from the same Chambers. Is that to be regarded, without more, as a lack of independence justifying the removal of the arbitrator? We are quite certain that this would not be the case in English law. Indeed the Chairman has so decided in a case in Chambers in the Commercial Court. We would also draw attention to the article 'Barristers' Independence and Disclosure' by Kendall in (1992) 8 Arb. Int. 287. We would further note in passing that even the oath taken by those appointed to the International Court of Justice; and indeed to our own High Court, refers only to impartiality.

103. Further, there may well be situations in which parties desire their arbitrators to have familiarity with a specific field, rather than being entirely independent.

104. We should emphasise that we intend to lose nothing of significance by omitting reference to independence. Lack of this quality may well give rise to justifiable doubts about impartiality, which is covered, but if it does not then we cannot at present see anything of significance that we have omitted by not using this term."

In Scotland post-ECHR (via the Scotland Act 1998), we see no justification for omitting "independence" even if it may give rise to difficulties in practice. Since the 1996 Act entered into force a great deal of work has been done on conflicts of interest (see discussion under r.8) and, other than in the USA (particularly in California), there is broad consensus, whether or not following the IBA Conflict Guidelines, which, although not universally accepted either in England (e.g. they were summarily dismissed by Morison J. in *ASM Shipping Ltd of India v TTMI Ltd of England* [2005] EWHC 2238 (Comm) at [39](4), a judgment regarded by many commentators as controversial, even wrong) or internationally, have attracted widespread support as being the best current solution to the difficult problem of trying to establish standards.

Rule 68(2)(g) allows for a serious irregularity appeal if the tribunal fails the "impartial and independent" test but requires the challenger to show substantial injustice as well.

See also the commentary to r.12(a) above.

Rule 24(1)(b)

Section 1 of the Act provides that: "The founding principles of this Act are: (a) that the object of arbitration is to resolve disputes fairly ...". This is axiomatic since it goes deep into the roots of natural justice.

Model Law art.18 provides the basic principle that the parties shall be treated with equality and each party shall be given a "full" opportunity of presenting his case. Supplementing this fundamental principle, art.24(1) provides that, absent contrary agreement by the parties, there shall be oral hearings at an appropriate stage and art.24(3) provides for all documents to be copied equally to each party.

What is "fairness"?

Fairness is like the proverbial elephant—very difficult to define but you know it when you see it. It is a broad concept and should not be interpreted too literally—the fact that counsel for one party addressed the tribunal for 90 minutes and his opponent for 89 is wholly irrelevant. If one party is permitted by the tribunal to be represented by a QC and the other denied even an advocate, then we have unfairness. Megarry V.C. famously said:

"It may be that there are some who would decry the importance which the courts attach to the observance of the rules of natural justice. 'When something is obvious', they may say, 'why force everybody to go through the tiresome waste of time involved in framing charges and giving an opportunity to be heard? The result is obvious from the start.' Those who take this view do not, I think, do themselves justice. As everybody who has anything to do with the law well knows, the path of the law is strewn with examples of open and shut cases which, somehow, were not; of unanswerable charges which, in the event, were completely answered; of inexplicable conduct which was fully explained; of fixed and unalterable determinations that, by discussion, suffered a change. Nor are those with any knowledge of human nature who pause to think for a moment likely to underestimate the feelings of resentment of those who find that a decision against them has been made without their being offered any opportunity to influence the course of events" (*John v Rees* [1969] 2 All E.R. 274 at 309).

Rule 68(2)(h) allows for a serious irregularity appeal if the tribunal fails the fairness test but requires the challenger to show substantial injustice as well. This will filter out the great majority of minor complaints made, in practice, by disgruntled losers.

Typically, in *Margulead Ltd v Exide Technologies* [2004] EWHC 1019 (Comm), a challenge under s.68 of the 1996 Act, Margulead claimed that the sole arbitrator had failed to permit its counsel to reply orally to closing submissions by counsel for Exide, i.e. the latter (as respondent in the arbitration) had had the last word. However, the arbitrator had made it clear in advance that that was to be his proposed course of action and Margulead had accepted that at the time. Further, although it may be conventional practice in common law courts that the claimant has the last word (since it must prove his claim), this is by no means an absolute rule in English, let alone international, arbitration. Colman J. held, inter alia, that there had been no substantial injustice.

In a private arbitration conducted by one of the authors, one of the parties was very late in lodging a written submission just before the final half-day hearing for closing oral submissions, causing real scheduling difficulties for the other side; this was redressed by the time in the closing hearing being split one and a half/two and a half hours, later adjusted (by agreement of the parties) to three quarters/two and a quarter hours. Curiously, the counsel with the longer allowance overran it and his opponent addressed the arbitrator for just over a half an hour. The arbitrator found the shorter address much more persuasive.

See also the commentary to r.12(b) above.

Rule 24(1)(c)(i)

Section 1 of the Act provides that: "The founding principles of this Act are: (a) that the object of arbitration is to resolve disputes ... without unnecessary delay ...".

Rule 68(2) does not expressly refer to delay (as it does to impartiality, independence and fairness) but delay can still constitute a serious irregularity via r.68(2)(a), "the tribunal failing to conduct the arbitration in accordance with ... (ii) these rules (in so far as they apply) ...", or r.68(2)(i), "... there being justifiable doubts about an arbitrator's ability to so act". As above, the substantial injustice test must be met by the challenger.

See also the commentary to r.12(c) above.

There is often a difficult balance to be struck in practice between the time schedule and fairness, e.g. where a party asserts that it needs 90 days to prepare its submission, not the 30 allowed in the agreed rules. In the past, arbitrators tended to give in to the parties, whether because of fear of an unfairness challenge or otherwise, but in practice now (outside Scotland) arbitrators are taking a more proactive and robust approach and are driving cases forward—active case management is the "name of the modern game". In a recent case (non-arbitration) in the English courts, the judge cut the time allowances requested by the parties by between 40 and 60 per cent and they merely buckled down to work within the shorter timescale. At a seminar in London, that judge made it clear that any application to him complaining of an arbitrator shortening time scales in the interests of efficient case management would likely receive a distinctly negative response.

Rule 24(1)(c)(ii)

Section 1 of the Act provides that: "The founding principles of this Act are: (a) that the object of arbitration is to resolve disputes ... without unnecessary ... expense ...".

In contrast to r.24(1)(c)(i), there is no clear direct or indirect entry into rr.68 or 12 in the context of breach of this obligation and it is rare for a tribunal to be responsible, even in part, for high levels of expense, the fault here almost always being with the parties and their advisers. One such case is *W and S v BB* Unreported June 8, 2001 TCC (see above under r.12 and see below under r.73).

There are limits as to what a tribunal can achieve to control costs in the sense that if a party wishes to instruct 12 advocates, six law firms and 10 experts, that is for that party to decide. However, the arbitrator has two ways of minimising the effect of this, first by efficient case management so as to limit the usefulness of the excess manpower, and secondly, by being robust in awarding expenses; see r.61(3) so, in this example, recoverability should be restricted.

Rule 24(2)

The Model Law at art.18 states that "The parties shall be treated with equality and each party shall be given a full opportunity of presenting his case." See the commentary to r.24(1)(b), above.

There is one particular class of circumstances where "treating fairly" presents real difficulties in practice, arbitrations involving consumers and parties with significant differences of resources; these can raise difficult issues of jurisdiction and of case management.

In the remainder of this section we ignore the provisions of the Unfair Terms in Consumer Contracts Regulations 1999 (SI 1999/2083) which are substantially replicated (and therefore duplicated) in ss.89–91 of the 1996 Act which do apply in Scotland (the only part of that Act which does). The 1999 Regulations are the successor to the Unfair Terms in Consumer Contracts Regulations 1994 (SI 1994/3159) which implemented Council Directive 93/13/EEC on unfair terms in consumer contracts [1993] OJ L95/29, with the effect of creating a presumption that pre-dispute arbitration clauses in consumer contracts are unfair and, therefore, invalid. For a useful survey of the law in this area see *Mylcrist Builders v Buck* [2008] EWHC 2172 (TCC) which is considered in Hew R. Dundas, "Recent Developments in English Arbitration Law: Arbitrations Involving Consumers" (2009) 75 *Arbitration* 115.

Returning to the main theme, the difficulties spring from circumstances where one party, e.g. an individual or a small business, may have difficulties affording professional help in presenting their claims and their case generally. The arbitrator has to decide how much help he/she can give without compromising either his/her neutrality or his/her appearance of neutrality. Where there are significant differences of resources, the arbitrator's primary duty is to do justice in the case and he/she must do this while ensuring that he shows no bias in favour of any party. He can achieve this by asking questions and suggesting amendments to claims and the way in which a case is presented where this is necessary to achieve the primary objective.

The CIArb's Practice Guideline no.17, "Guideline on Arbitrations Involving Consumers and Parties with Significant Differences Of Resources", provides detailed guidance in this difficult area; see *http://www.ciarb.org/information-and-resources/practice-guidelines-and-protocols/list-of-guidelines-and-protocols/* [Accessed February 21, 2010].

Rule 25: General duty of the parties **M**

25. The parties must ensure that the arbitration is conducted—
 (a) without unnecessary delay, and
 (b) without incurring unnecessary expense.

DEFINITIONS
None.

STATUS
This is a mandatory rule so it is not open to the parties to agree anything else or to disapply it completely (see s.8).

MODEL LAW
There is no equivalent provision in the Model Law.

COMMENTARY
This rule mirrors s.40(1) of the 1996 Act but the latter is augmented by s.40(2) providing that:
 "This includes (a) complying without delay with any determination of the tribunal as to procedural or evidential matters, or with any order or directions of the tribunal, and (b) where appropriate, taking without delay any necessary steps to obtain a decision of the court on a preliminary question of jurisdiction or law (see sections 32 and 45)."
There are two major difficulties in practice: first, applying the axiom that arbitration is a consensual process, if the parties have agreed on some course of action either by agreeing some alternative to r.28 (a default rule) or by agreeing some deviation therefrom, then the tribunal has to overcome substantial, even insuperable difficulty in seeking to change that agreement. Secondly, there is no immediate sanction available to force or persuade a party to comply with its r.25 obligation; however, there are other provisions in the Act or in the rules, e.g. establishing time limits or providing limits on recoverability of expenses, which will at least go part way to ensuring compliance.

Section 41 of the 1996 Act provides, absent contrary agreement by the parties, a procedural structure giving the tribunal certain powers in the event that a party breaches its obligation under s.40(1). See rr.37–39 for the equivalent.

Rule 26: Confidentiality **D**

26.—(1) Disclosure by the tribunal, any arbitrator or a party of confidential information relating to the arbitration is to be actionable as a breach of an obligation of confidence unless the disclosure—
- (a) is authorised, expressly or impliedly, by the parties (or can reasonably be considered as having been so authorised),
- (b) is required by the tribunal or is otherwise made to assist or enable the tribunal to conduct the arbitration,
- (c) is required—
  - (i) in order to comply with any enactment or rule of law,
  - (ii) for the proper performance of the discloser's public functions, or
  - (iii) in order to enable any public body or office-holder to perform public functions properly,
- (d) can reasonably be considered as being needed to protect a party's lawful interests,
- (e) is in the public interest,
- (f) is necessary in the interests of justice, or
- (g) is made in circumstances in which the discloser would have absolute privilege had the disclosed information been defamatory.

(2) The tribunal and the parties must take reasonable steps to prevent unauthorised disclosure of confidential information by any third party involved in the conduct of the arbitration.

(3) The tribunal must, at the outset of the arbitration, inform the parties of the obligations which this rule imposes on them.

(4) "Confidential information", in relation to an arbitration, means any information relating to—
- (a) the dispute,
- (b) the arbitral proceedings,
- (c) the award, or
- (d) any civil proceedings relating to the arbitration in respect of which an order has been granted under section 15 of this Act,

which is not, and has never been, in the public domain.

DEFINITIONS
None.

STATUS
This is a default rule so it is open to the parties to modify it, agree something different or disapply it completely (see s.9).

MODEL LAW
There is no equivalent in the Model Law.

COMMENTARY
For at least the 120 years to 1995 the arbitral world had existed in the belief that arbitral proceedings were both private and confidential; although there were (until 1990) no authorities specifically in point, there was clear evidence of strong judicial support for this proposition, as Sir Patrick Neill QC (as he then was) showed in his 1995 Bernstein Lecture (published at (1996) 62 *Arbitration* 1), with an erudite and comprehensive historical survey dating back to the 17th century. The first English case directly in point was *Dolling-Baker v Merrett* [1990] 1 W.L.R. 1205 CA, in which the Court of Appeal recognised the existence of a confidentiality obligation arising out

of the very nature of arbitration, binding the parties thereto and preventing them from voluntarily disclosing or using materials from the arbitration outside it.

This decision certainly appeared unremarkable at the time since it appeared, at least in England, to reflect in formal terms what had been the status quo for more than 120 years. However, a major international reconsideration began in 1995 with the decision in the High Court of Australia in *Esso Australia Resources Ltd v Plowman* (1995) 128 A.L.R. 391 (note that the High Court is the Supreme Court of Australia; the case was an appeal from the Supreme Court of Victoria) where, on a three to two majority, it was held that there was no inherent confidentiality (as distinct from privacy) in respect of arbitral proceedings in Australia. This decision was seen by some as cataclysmic, threatening the very foundations of the principles of arbitration but, in his 1995 Bernstein Lecture, Sir Patrick Neill QC meticulously analysed the Australian judgments in critical terms and concluded that while, as the Chief Justice had stated (at 400), *Esso* reflected the Australian position, its arguments had no effect on English law; in particular, it clearly turned on its own facts, not least a strong "freedom of information" theme and on the rather surprising expert evidence that details of arbitrations in Victoria were common knowledge. Sir Patrick's opinion was essentially upheld by the Court of Appeal in *Ali Shipping Corp v Shipyard Trogir* [1999] 1 W.L.R. 314, in 1998 where the previous line of English jurisprudence (*Dolling-Baker* [1990] 1 W.L.R. 1205, *Hassneh Insurance Co of Israel v Mew* [1993] 2 Lloyd's Rep. 243, *Insurance Co v Lloyds Syndicate* [1995] 1 Lloyd's Rep. 272) was confirmed.

In 2000 the Swedish Supreme Court reached a conclusion in *Bulbank* effectively concurring with that in *Esso v Plowman* (1995) 128 A.L.R. 391, i.e. that there was no implied term of confidentiality in Swedish law (*AI Trade Finance v Bulgarian Trade Bank* (case 1881-99) Unreported October 27, 2000 Supreme Court), a decision widely considered to represent civil law thinking on the matter.

So far as English law is concerned, the leading (and, in all likelihood, definitive) judgment is that in *Emmott v Michael Wilson & Partners Ltd* [2008] EWCA Civ 184 (Carnwath, Thomas and Lawrence Collins L.JJ.) in the Court of Appeal which not only refined and redefined the law but also developed it since this appeal raised questions of considerable practical importance relating to confidentiality in national and international arbitration. The article Hew R. Dundas, "Confidentiality in English Arbitration: The Final Word?" (2008) 74 *Arbitration* 458, gives a detailed exposition of this case which is central to r.26.

Per Lawrence Collins L.J., who gave the leading judgment, the uncontroversial starting point was that, in English law, arbitration was a private process, e.g. in *Russell v Russell* (1880) 14 Ch.D. 471 at 474, Sir George Jessel M.R. had said:

"As a rule, persons enter into [arbitration] contracts with the express view of keeping their quarrels from the public eyes, and of avoiding that discussion in public, which must be a painful one, and which might be an injury even to the successful party to the litigation, and most surely would be to the unsuccessful."

Parties who arbitrated in England expected that the hearing would be in private and that was an important advantage for commercial people as compared with litigation in court (Lawrence Collins L.J.'s view here is borne out in the 2006 and 2008 Queen Mary University of London/PriceWaterhouseCoopers studies of the attitudes of commercial users to arbitration, where confidentiality ranked second to enforceability as the principal reason for choosing arbitration.)

The privacy of arbitration was underlined by CPR r.62.10(3)(b), which provides that, subject to the power of the court to order that an arbitration claim may be heard in public or in private, all arbitration claims will be heard in private except hearings pursuant to ss.45 or 69 of the 1996 Act appeal where the converse applies. The default position is that the parties' desire for confidentiality and privacy outweighs the public interest in a public hearing: (*Department of Economic Policy and Development of the City of Moscow and the Government of Moscow v Bankers Trust Co* [2004] EWCA Civ 314). Furthermore, CPR PD 62.5.1 provides that an arbitration application may be inspected only with the permission of the court (*Glidepath BV v Thompson* [2005] EWHC 818 (Comm); [2005] 2 Lloyd's Rep. 549). The privacy of arbitration is almost universally recognised by institutional rules (including LCIA Rules art.19(4); ICC Rules art.21(3); World Intellectual Property Organisation ("WIPO") Rules art.53(c); UNCITRAL Rules art.25(4)) as is the confidentiality of the award itself (LCIA Rules, art.30(1), (3); ICC Rules art.28(2); WIPO Rules, art.75; UNCITRAL Rules art.32(5)).

In the last 20 years or so the English courts have had to consider, in several different contexts, the consequences of the privacy of the arbitral process and the scope of the obligation of confidentiality. It is apparent that the English jurisprudence on this subject (as distinct from the confidentiality of awards, which is much discussed in other countries) is much richer than that of any other important arbitration centre, and that it constitutes a major contribution to the development of the law of international arbitration (see ICC, *Report on Confidentiality as a purported obligation of the parties in arbitration* (ICC, 2002); *Fouchard, Gaillard and Goldman on International Commercial Arbitration*, edited by Emmanual Gaillard and John Savage, (London: Kluwer Law International, 1999), at para.1412; Julian D.M. Lew, Loukas A. Mistelis and Stefan M. Kröll, *Comparative International Commercial Arbitration* (London: Kluwer, 2003), at paras 24-99 to 24-104). However, only a minority of the major arbitration centres had rules dealing expressly with the confidentiality of material generated in arbitrations (see LCIA Rules art.30(1); Swiss Rules art.43(1)); WIPO Rules arts 52, 73; see also the UNCITRAL, *Notes on Organizing Arbitral Proceedings* (UNCITRAL, 1996) at para.31).

In reviewing the authorities, Lawrence Collins L.J. noted that it was not always easy to distinguish confidentiality from privacy and that it was also important to bear in mind the context of the decisions because quite different considerations might apply in different contexts.

First, a party to litigation in the courts could seek discovery or disclosure of documents generated in an arbitration. Confidentiality of documents was, of course, not in itself a reason for withholding disclosure, but the court will compel disclosure only if it considered it necessary for the fair disposal of the case (*Science Research Council v Nassé* [1980] A.C. 1028). In *Dolling-Baker* [1990] 1 W.L.R. 1205, Parker L.J. had said (at 1213):

"It must be perfectly apparent that, for example, the fact that a document is used in an arbitration does not *confer* on it any confidentiality or privilege which can be availed of in subsequent proceedings. If it is a relevant document, its relevance remains. But that the obligation exists in some form appears to me to be abundantly apparent. It is not a question of immunity or public interest. It is a question of an implied obligation arising out of the nature of arbitration itself. When a question arises as to production of documents or indeed discovery by list or affidavit, the court must, it appears to me, have regard to the existence of the implied obligation, whatever its precise limits may be. If it is satisfied that despite the implied obligation, disclosure and inspection is necessary for the fair disposal of the action, that consideration must prevail. But in reaching a conclusion, the court should consider, amongst other things, whether there are other and possibly less costly ways of obtaining the information which is sought which do not involve any breach of the implied undertaking."

Secondly, confidentiality was no absolute bar in cases where a party to an arbitration may seek the assistance of the court to obtain, through a witness summons, material deployed in another arbitration (*London and Leeds Estates Ltd v Paribas Ltd (No.2)* [1995] 1 E.G.L.R. 102 and *Council of the Borough of South Tyneside v Wickes Building Suppliers Ltd* [2004] EWHC 2428 (Comm)). In such cases the court will take into account the strong policy in favour of confidentiality in arbitration.

Thirdly, issues may arise about the disclosure of documents on the court file relating to an arbitration (*Glidepath BV v Thompson* [2005] EWHC 818 (Comm)) or whether the judgment of a court given in relation to an arbitration should be published (*City of Moscow v Bankers Trust Co* [2004] EWCA Civ 314). Here the privacy of arbitration will be an important, but not a decisive, factor.

In each of these three circumstances the court will exercise a discretion in which privacy or confidentiality is an important factor in the balance.

Fourthly (and most relevant to the present case), a party to an arbitration may have an interest (commercial or otherwise) in disclosing documents generated in an arbitration (including the award itself) to third parties (*Hassneh Insurance Co of Israel v Mew* [1993] 2 Lloyd's Rep. 243; *Insurance Co v Lloyd's Syndicate* [1995] 1 Lloyd's Rep. 272; *Ali Shipping Corp v Shipyard Trogir* [1999] 1 W.L.R. 314; *Associated Electric and Gas Insurance Services Ltd v European Reinsurance Co of Zurich* [2000] UKPC 11; [2003] 1 W.L.R. 1041) and the other party to the arbitration may seek to restrain disclosure by injunction.

Three legal concepts or categories have been in play in these cases. The first is privacy, in the sense that because arbitration is private that privacy would be violated by the publication or dissemination of documents deployed in the arbitration. The second is confidentiality in the sense where it is used to refer to inherent confidentiality in the information in documents, such as trade secrets or other confidential information generated or deployed in an arbitration. The third is confidentiality in the sense of an implied agreement that documents disclosed or generated in arbitration can only be used for the purposes of the arbitration. The distinction between the second and third cases may be illustrated by the example of the relevant documents in the arbitration (such as the defence) not containing anything in themselves which is confidential but nevertheless the parties are under an obligation not to use it for any purpose other than the arbitration, and that obligation is described in the authorities as an obligation of confidence. Some of the authorities treat privacy and confidentiality as equivalent: *London and Leeds Estates Ltd v Paribas Ltd (No.2)* [1995] 1 E.G.L.R. 102 at 109; *Hassneh Insurance Co of Israel v Mew* [1993] 2 Lloyd's Rep. 243 at 246–247; others draw a distinction between privacy and confidentiality, e.g. *Dolling-Baker* [1990] 1 W.L.R. 1205 at 1213–1214. In *Ali Shipping Corp v Shipyard Trogir* [1999] 1 W.L.R. 314, Potter L.J. said at 326 that, "the obligation of confidentiality ... arises as an essential corollary of the privacy of arbitration proceedings."

What has emerged from the recent authorities in England is that there is, separate from confidentiality in that sense, an implied obligation (arising out of the nature of arbitration itself) on both parties not to disclose or use for any other purpose any documents prepared for and used in the arbitration, or disclosed or produced in the course of the arbitration, or transcripts or notes of the evidence in the arbitration or the award, and not to disclose in any other way what evidence has been given by any witness in the arbitration, save with the consent of the other party, or pursuant to an order or leave of the court. That obligation is not limited to documents which contain material which is confidential, such as trade secrets and it does not arise as a matter of business efficacy, but is implied as a matter of law (*Ali Shipping Corp v Shipyard Trogir* [1999] 1 W.L.R. 314 at 326, disapproving *Hassneh Insurance Co of Israel v Mew* [1993] 2 Lloyd's Rep. 243 on this point). The formulation of the implied obligation in arbitration is plainly influenced by the English rule in court proceedings (CPR r. 31.22; for the history thereof see *Home Office v Harman* [1983] 1 A.C. 280) that a party to whom a document has been disclosed may use the document only for the purpose of the proceedings in which it is disclosed. Breach of this rule of court is a contempt, but the court has a power to give permission for the document to be used, particularly when it is in the public interest; of course, this is inapplicable in arbitration.

There are, of course, limits and exceptions to the confidentiality obligation: an award may fall to be enforced, or challenged, in a court and the existence and details of an arbitration claim may need to be disclosed to insurers or to shareholders or to regulatory authorities. What, then, are the limits of the obligation to use documents in an arbitration only for the purposes of that arbitration? Two preliminary points should be stressed: (i) the applicable institutional rules may provide an answer; (ii) it is particularly important that what has been said about the possible exceptions to confidentiality must be read in context. Consider two examples: first, if a court decides in the context of a witness summons (as it did in *London and Leeds Estates Ltd v Paribas Ltd (No.2)* [1995] 1 E.G.L.R. 102) that the "public interest" may outweigh the confidentiality of arbitration documents, it does not necessarily follow that a party may voluntarily disclose documents to third parties on the ground that it is in "the public interest"; secondly, the court has no general or unlimited jurisdiction to consider whether an exception to confidentiality existed and was applicable.

The principles of banking confidentiality have played a key role in the development of exceptions to the basic rule of confidentiality in arbitration, e.g. Bankes L.J. had said in *Tournier v National Provincial and Union Bank of England* [1924] 1 K.B. 461 CA:

"In my opinion it is necessary in a case like the present to direct the jury what are the limits and what are the qualifications of the contractual duty of secrecy implied in the relation of banker and customer. There appears to be no authority on the point. On principle I think that the qualifications can be classified under four heads: (a) where disclosure is under compulsion by law; (b) where there is a duty to the public to disclose; (c) where the interests of the bank require disclosure; (d) where the disclosure is made by the express or implied consent of the customer."

It is clear that the exceptions (especially the cases of "duty to the public" and "interests of the bank") are potentially very wide indeed. The application to arbitration of these banking principles started in *Dolling-Baker* [1990] 1 W.L.R. 1205, continued in *Hassneh Insurance Co of Israel v Mew* [1993] 2 Lloyd's Rep. 243 and culminated in *Ali Shipping Corp v Shipyard*

Trogir [1999] 1 W.L.R. 314, where Potter L.J. formulated a series of exceptions closely modelled on *Tournier*. However, in *Associated Electric & Gas Insurance Services Ltd v European Reinsurance Company of Zurich* [2003] 1 All E.R. (Comm) 253 the Privy Council expressed reservations about this approach, inter alia because it ran the risk of failing to distinguish between different types of confidentiality which attached to different types of document or to documents which have been obtained in different ways and because it elided privacy and confidentiality; generalisations and the formulation of detailed implied terms were inappropriate.

In summary, English case law of the last 20 years has established that there is an obligation, implied by law and arising out of the very nature of arbitration, on both parties not to disclose or use for any other purpose any documents prepared for and used in the arbitration, or disclosed or produced in the course of the arbitration, or transcripts or notes of the evidence in the arbitration or the award, and not to disclose in any other way what evidence has been given by any witness in the arbitration. The obligation is not limited to commercially confidential information in the traditional sense.

This is in reality a substantive rule of arbitration law reached through the device of an implied term but this approach has led to difficulties of formulation and reliance (perhaps, over-reliance) on the banking principles in *Tournier*. The content of the obligation may depend on the context in which it arises and on the nature of the information or documents at issue and the limits of that obligation are still in the process of development on a case-by-case basis. On the authorities as they now stand, the principal cases in which disclosure will be permissible are these: (i) where there is consent, express or implied; (ii) where there is an order, or leave of the court (but that does not mean that the court has a general discretion to lift the obligation of confidentiality); (iii) where it is reasonably necessary for the protection of the legitimate interests of an arbitrating party; and (iv) where the interests of justice require disclosure, and also (perhaps) where the public interest requires disclosure.

In his judgment, Lawrence Collins L.J. addressed a different matter, expressing the tentative view that, because the confidentiality obligation had developed as an implied term of the arbitration agreement, any dispute as to its scope would fall within the scope of the arbitration agreement but since the respondent had not sought a stay on that ground he did not think it necessary to explore it further. The question is who (at least at first instance) should deal with issues of confidentiality, the tribunal or the court? The answer must be the former; Thomas L.J. broadly agreed with Lawrence Collins L.J. but Carnwath L.J. declined to express any view.

It was also necessary to explore the questions either whether the court would have an inherent jurisdiction in relation to these matters or whether Supreme Court Act 1981 s.37 or s.44(2)(e) of the 1996 Act might have a role to play (see *Cetelem SA v Roust Holdings Ltd* [2005] EWCA Civ 618; [2005] 1 W.L.R. 3555 at [74]; *Elektrim SA v Vivendi Universal SA (No.2)* [2007] 2 Lloyd's Rep. 8 at [67]–[79]; *Starlight Shipping Co v Tai Ping Insurance Co Ltd* [2007] EWHC 1893 (Comm) at [18]–[19]).

There is, of course, one apparently simple route for the parties to an arbitration to adopt if they wish to clarify what part of the arbitral proceedings (and, in practice, most importantly the documents generated in the arbitration) are to be confidential as opposed to merely the proceedings being private and that is to agree specific confidentiality provisions, either by choice of law or in contract or in selecting the rules to govern the arbitration. Both Australian and Swedish law will recognise and enforce an express contractual confidentiality obligation, the *Esso v Plowman* (1995) 128 A.L.R. 391 and *Bulbank* decisions rejecting the proposition (enshrined in English law—see p.167 above) that such an obligation is an implied term of an arbitration agreement but not rejecting such an obligation per se.

While the Model Law is silent as regards confidentiality, New Zealand, in adopting it, has augmented it (at considerable length) by a specific statutory confidentiality provision. Among the major international arbitration institutions, only the LCIA has an express confidentiality provision in its rules whereas the ICC, AAA and others are generally silent, typically including confidentiality obligations binding the tribunal but with none binding the parties. LCIA r.30.1 states:

"Unless the parties expressly agree in writing to the contrary, the parties undertake as a general principle to keep confidential all awards in their arbitration, together with all materials in the proceedings created for the purpose of the arbitration and all other documents produced by another party in the proceedings not otherwise in the public domain—save and to the extent that disclosure may be required of a party by legal duty, to protect or pursue a legal right or to enforce or challenge an award in bona fide legal proceedings before a state court or other judicial authority."

Practical considerations

There are two main practical difficulties in enforcing any confidentiality obligation, whether expressly set out in an arbitration agreement or incorporated in the agreed set of rules. First, breaches are normally discovered too late to take any action (your arbitration is headline news in today's tabloids) and, secondly, it is normally impossible to prove any loss and, even if it is, quantification will normally be very difficult. In discussions of the draft Bill, it was suggested that these were near insuperable obstacles to any such obligation and it was queried whether r.26 had any purpose. There are a number of responses to this: (i) the Scottish business community's response to the consultation process overwhelmingly endorsed the principle of having a confidentiality obligation; (ii) the two Queen Mary University of London/PriceWaterhouseCoopers studies confirmed that the international market place also so endorsed; (iii) the drafters considered that, facing a clear obligation, the overwhelming majority of parties would comply with it; (iv) neither LCIA Rules r.30.1 nor the implied term in English law had given rise to any significant difficulties over the years, the *City of Moscow v Bankers Trust Co* [2004] EWCA Civ 314 case showing that a confidentiality obligation could work; (v) the Bill would give parties a tool which they could use as they saw fit and to the extent that they could so far as the courts would allow.

The position in Scotland under the common law

Like so much of pre-2010 arbitration law in Scotland, it was unclear to what extent there was any confidentiality in arbitration. It has generally been accepted that, if a case arose, the judiciary would give close consideration to the views of their English brethren.

The issue of confidentiality was one of the many which the Scots common law of arbitration had never had to address. It is almost certainly the case that the Scots courts would have regarded privacy as an essential characteristic of arbitration. Whether they would then have agreed with the English view that a requirement of privacy is essentially meaningless unless it is combined with an obligation of confidentiality (see e.g. Potter L.J. in *Ali*

Shipping Corp v Shipyard Trogir [1998] 2 All E.R. 136 at 146g), or the view expressed elsewhere that privacy usually tends towards practical confidentiality but does not imply an obligation of confidentiality (see Mason C.J. in the Australian High Court—*Esso v Plowman* (1995) 128 A.L.R. 391), is less certain. However, the Scots courts have followed English law in holding that a third party is subject to a duty of confidence in relation to information which he knows was originally communicated in confidence (see *Lord Advocate v Scotsman Publications Ltd*, 1988 S.L.T. 490, affirmed 1989 S.C. (HL) 122). The test in England is now that the person ought to know that the information is fairly and reasonably to be regarded as confidential—*Campbell v Mirror Group Newspapers Ltd* [2004] A.C. 457— and it is anticipated that the Scots courts would accept that refinement). This might tend towards the conclusion that the Scottish judiciary would have tended to look to England for a lead on confidentiality in the arbitral process. Yet the issue is now rendered academic by the appearance of this detailed statutory provision, except of course as regards those arbitrations where the parties have opted to contract into the pre-Act law.

Rule 27: Tribunal deliberations **D**

27.—(1) The tribunal's deliberations may be undertaken in private and accordingly need not be disclosed to the parties.

(2) But, where an arbitrator fails to participate in any of the tribunal's deliberations, the tribunal must disclose that fact (and the extent of the failure) to the parties.

DEFINITIONS
None.

STATUS
This is a default rule so it is open to the parties to modify it, agree something different or disapply it completely (see s.9).

MODEL LAW
There is no equivalent in the Model Law.

COMMENTARY
This may appear a curious rule, albeit one which is intuitively obvious, since there is no equivalent either in the 1996 Act or in the ICC Rules but there is in the LCIA Rules (see below). The policy memorandum published with the Bill on January 30, 2009 stated as follows (at para.158):

"Although the parties will normally receive the tribunal's reasons for an award as part of that award, they should not be entitled to know what the deliberations of the tribunal are prior to the award, which should be confidential to its members (unless of course the tribunal shows the parties a draft award prior to issuing the final award). This is the policy behind rule 27. The only exception to this is that it may be necessary to disclose an arbitrator's refusal to participate in the arbitration."

Rule 27(1)

While intuitively obvious, it is perhaps less than straightforward to pin down the reasons, the main one being the concern that if the tribunal was obliged to deliberate "in public" (in the sense of the involvement of the parties, not in the sense of "live on TV"), the process would run a serious risk of contamination, in several regards: (i) by the loss of the arbitrators' freedom to express themselves fully which they can do with each other in private but not in a hearing room full of party representatives and advisers; (ii) party-appointed arbitrators might sense pressure from their respective appointing party or might be tempted to "play to the gallery"; (iii) all three arbitrators might feel concern that whatever they might say or write in deliberating might lead to challenge to the award or, worse still, some challenge to them individually, e.g. on grounds of perceived bias; and (iv) judges normally deliberate in private.

LCIA Rules r.30.2 states:

"The deliberations of the Arbitral Tribunal are likewise confidential to its members, save and to the extent that disclosure of an arbitrator's refusal to participate in the arbitration is required of the other members of the Arbitral Tribunal under Articles 10, 12 and 26."

See r.27(2) below concerning LCIA Rules r.12.

Rule 27(2)

There is no equivalent in this Act of LCIA Rules r.12.1 which states:

"If any arbitrator on a three-member Arbitral Tribunal refuses or persistently fails to participate in its deliberations, the two other arbitrators shall have the power, *upon their written notice of such refusal or failure to the LCIA Court, the parties and the third arbitrator*, to continue the arbitration (including the making of any decision, ruling or award), notwithstanding the absence of the third arbitrator" (emphasis added).

LCIA Rules r.12 goes on to deal with the two consequent options, either the tribunal continues as a truncated one or it stops the arbitration; in either case, this is a matter of very great significance hence the necessity for written notice.

Part 4

Arbitral proceedings

Rule 28: Procedure and evidence **D**

28.—(1) It is for the tribunal to determine—
    (a) the procedure to be followed in the arbitration, and
    (b) the admissibility, relevance, materiality and weight of any evidence.

(2) In particular, the tribunal may determine—
    (a) when and where the arbitration is to be conducted,
    (b) whether parties are to submit claims or defences and, if so, when they should do so and the extent to which claims or defences may be amended,
    (c) whether any documents or other evidence should be disclosed by or to any party and, if so, when such disclosures are to be made and to whom copies of disclosed documents and information are to be given,
    (d) whether any and, if so, what questions are to be put to and answered by the parties,
    (e) whether and, if so, to what extent the tribunal should take the initiative in ascertaining the facts and the law,
    (f) the extent to which the arbitration is to proceed by way of—
        (i) hearings for the questioning of parties,

(ii) written or oral argument,
(iii) presentation or inspection of documents or other evidence, or
(iv) submission of documents or other evidence,
(g) the language to be used in the arbitration (and whether a party is to supply translations of any document or other evidence),
(h) whether to apply rules of evidence used in legal proceedings or any other rules of evidence.

DEFINITIONS
"arbitration": s.2(1)
"tribunal": s.2(1)

STATUS
This is a default rule so it is open to the parties to modify it, agree something different or disapply it completely (see s.9).
All sets of arbitral rules known to the authors contain equivalent provisions.

MODEL LAW
Articles 19–24 are similar in principle but marginally less detailed.

COMMENTARY
It is a universal feature of modern arbitration laws around the world that the tribunal is (or, at least, should be) the masters of procedure so that it can select procedural rules, techniques and processes appropriate to the case in hand. Conversely, the principle of party autonomy applies here so the parties are included in this decision-making process but to a limited degree inter alia bearing in mind that they have almost no such involvement in litigation.

If the parties agree to apply r.28, the language might appear at first sight to give the tribunal total control so that the option available to the parties is an all-or-nothing one; however s.8(2) of the Act makes it clear that the parties may agree to modify or disapply any rule or any part of it.

Note that s.34(1) of the 1996 Act provides that, "[i]t shall be for the tribunal to decide all procedural and evidential matters, subject to the right of the parties to agree any matter", prima facie a marginally weaker form of language but the distinction (if any) is, the authors submit, of no consequence.

The procedure has a greater significance over and above the day-to-day management of proceedings since once fixed, whether by agreement or by determination, a failure by the tribunal to follow the procedure opens up a potential removal application under r.12(e) and its counterpart, challenge to any subsequent award under r.68(2)(a).

Similarly, the procedure must, axiomatically, comply with all the mandatory rules in the Act (see s.8).

Rule 28(1)

This rule tracks the Model Law language closely and establishes the key principles; a key factor is that rules of court, etc. do not apply; while the *White Book* (the Civil Procedure Rules) still finds its way into arbitration hearing rooms, the English judiciary appear finally to have defeated the many attempts to introduce the main part of the *White Book* (excepting Pts 35 and 62) into arbitration applications.

Rule 28(1)(a)

Reference to "the procedure" is to be taken as to being to "all or any part of" the procedure; see s.9(2).

Rule 28(1)(b)

It was unclear under the common law to what extent, if at all, issues relating to evidence were governed by rules of court and associate judicial decisions. In particular, there was an apparent contradiction between (a) the proposition that that an award could not be reduced solely on the grounds that the arbiter had relied on evidence which would have been excluded in court, and (b) s.9 of the the Civil Evidence (Scotland) Act 1988 which appears to imply that court rules are or may be applicable in arbitrations.

The question of the tribunal determining the weight to be given to evidence can, absent the express provisions of the rule, prove problematic. English authority under the 1950 Act provided that any evident failure by the tribunal to give the "correct" weight to evidence would amount to misconduct where the measure of correctness was by reference to what the court would have done in like circumstances (see *Trayfoot v Lock* [1957] 1 All E.R. 423). Post-1996 authority has repeatedly stressed that the courts are not to impose their analyses on tribunals, i.e. that the latter are not to be second-guessed.

However, a spanner was thrown into the works by the decision of H.H. Judge Thornton QC in *Fence Gate Ltd v NEL Construction Ltd*, 82 Con. L.R. 42 that a finding of fact for which there was no evidence or other supporting material could give rise to an appealable question of law ("legal error appeal" in Scotland). The judge said this (the footnotes are his except where stated otherwise):

"41. What is more problematic is whether an appeal can arise when it is contended that there was no basis for, or evidence to support, critical findings of fact. This question was always, prior to the abolition of the case stated procedure, characterised as raising a question of law. Nowadays, it is important to consider carefully the context in which the question arises as to whether or not a finding of fact was based on any evidence. This context can include cases where the relevant finding was of primary fact where it is said that there was no supporting evidence or that the evidence was misunderstood or wrongly believed. Alternatively, the finding may have been an inference that it is said was erroneously drawn from the primary facts or was one involving the application of the facts to a relevant statutory or contractual label such as: 'an adventure in the nature of trade' or 'frustration' [fn.: See *Edwards v Bairstow* [1956] A.C. 14, (HL) and *The "Nema"* [1982] AC 724, (HL) at page 738 per Lord Diplock]. Finally, the finding of fact may have been made as part of the exercise of a discretion as opposed to the determination of an issue arising as part of the substantive dispute. It is also necessary to consider the procedural context in which the question can arise. This can include, in an arbitration context, an appeal under section 69(1) of the Act or an application for leave to appeal under section 69(2)(b) of the Act. In other contexts, the question can arise as part of the judicial consideration of a case that has been stated by magistrates or special commissioners of income tax, as part of an appeal from a judicial discretionary decision or as part of a judicial review hearing.

42. There is no reason why, in an appropriate case, it should not still be possible in an appeal under section 69 of the Act to raise as a question of law the question of whether or not there was any evidence to support a material finding of fact even though an arbitrator is no longer bound by strict rules of evidence [fn.: Section 34(2)(f) of the Act provides that it shall be for the tribunal to decide all procedural and evidential matters including whether to apply strict rules of evidence (or any other rules) as to the admissibility, relevance or weight or any material sought to be tendered on any matters of fact or opinion.] This is because an arbitrator is bound to decide the dispute in accordance with the law chosen by the parties as being applicable. In a domestic dispute, the governing law will usually be the law of England and Wales which does not allow a decision as to a party's rights or obligations to be made where there is no evidence to support that decision [fn.: For a recent example of this principle being applied (in a successful judicial review of an appeal decision of the Crown Court on appeal from Licensing Justices) see *R v Warrington Crown Court, ex parte RBNB (a company)* [2001] 2 All ER 851 at paragraph 39.] The relaxation of the strict rules of evidence in arbitrations is a procedural provision which would not justify a finding which decides a dispute and which is not based on any supporting evidence at all.

43. Three decisions were brought to my attention where it was questioned whether an appeal can still be brought under section 69(1) of the Act on this ground. These were *The "Baleares"* [authors' fn.: [1993] 1 Lloyd's Rep. 215], *How Engineering Services Ltd v Lindner Ceilings Floors Partitions Plc* and *JA Payne Limited v GAJ Construction and another* [fn.: ibid.; [1999] CILL 1521, 24 June 1999, Dyson J, TCC, TCC website; Unreported, 16 March 2001; Judge Gilliland QC, Manchester Mercantile List.] These cases show that where the suggested appeal is one attacking a primary finding of fact on the basis of there being no evidence to support it or where an application for leave to appeal is being mounted under section 69(2)(b) of the Act, the decision of the arbitrator will almost invariably be accepted and may not usually be challenged. The parties have entrusted fact-finding functions to the arbitrator and the parties' autonomy must be respected by the court. However, where the finding is one of mixed law and fact [fn.: See *The "Lucille"* [1983] 1 Lloyd's Law Reports 387, Bingham J at page 393 affirmed on appeal [1984] 1 Lloyd's Law Reports 245, (CA)] or where the suggested error is that the arbitrator's discretionary decision erroneously took into account facts which should not have been taken into account [fn.: *Everglade Maritime Inc v Schiffahrtsgesellschaft Detlef on Apen m.b.h., The "Maria"*, ibid.], a question of law can still arise in the context of an arbitration appeal.

44. I conclude that if it can be shown that there was no evidence of any kind to support an arbitrator's finding, including an absence of evidence admissible by virtue of the relaxation of the strict rules of evidence, at least where the finding amounted to the taking into account of factors that should not have been taken into account, or was a mixed finding of fact and law or was part of the exercise of a discretion whose consequent exercise led to an error of principle, an absence of supporting evidence can give rise to a question of law. However, even if the arbitrator's finding was susceptible to an appeal, a court should give full weight to that finding since the arbitrator is the person whom the parties have chosen as the final determiner of fact.

Only if that finding is nonetheless both material and clearly lacking any factual basis should a court consider allowing an appeal on the resulting question of law."

In *Demco Investments & Commercial SA v SE Banken Forsakring Holding AB* [2005] EWHC 1398 (Comm); [2005] 2 Lloyd's Rep. 650, Cooke J. said this:

"35. With regard to the second supposed question of law in relation to the evidence required to find a mis-sale, the problem with the *Edwards v Bairstow* approach is that the terms of s.69 (3)(c) of the 1996 Arbitration Act has changed the position from that which previously obtained. Leave to appeal is only to be given if the Court is satisfied '*that on the basis of the findings of fact in the Award*' the decision of the Tribunal on the question of law which arises out of the Award is obviously wrong or, if the question is one of general public importance, is at least open to serious doubt. There is no room for any appeal under s.69 against the findings of fact in the Award itself since these have to be accepted for the purpose of any application for permission to appeal.

36. The legislative intent behind the form of words used in the Act was made clear in the DAC Report of 1996 at paragraph 286 (iii) in the following words:

'There have been attempts, both before and after the enactment of the Arbitration Act 1979, to dress up questions of fact as questions of law and by that means to seek an appeal on the Tribunal's decision on the facts. Generally, these attempts have been resisted by the Courts but to make the position clear, we propose to state expressly that consideration by the Court of the suggested question of law is made on the basis of the findings of fact in the award.'

37. Furthermore, section 34 (2)(f) of the 1996 Act, under the heading of 'Procedural and Evidential Matters' provides that it is for the Tribunal to decide all procedural and evidential matters which include '*whether to apply strict rules of evidence (or any other rules) as to the admissibility, relevance or weight of any material (oral, written or other) sought to be tendered on any matters of fact or opinion and the time, manner and form in which such material should be exchanged and presented*.' Although there is no suggestion that the Arbitrators made any specific ruling in relation to relaxation of rules of evidence, and there is some insistence in the award on the need for convincing evidence if gross negligence is to be found, the DAC Report at paragraph 170 throws light on the provision in stating that '*Clause 34 (2)(f) helps to put an end to any arguments that it is a question of law whether there is material to support a fact*'.

38. In *The Baleares* [1993] 1 Lloyd's Report 215 at page 232 column 1, Steyn LJ stated that an appeal on the *Edwards v Bairstow* principle did not constitute an appeal on a point of law under the Arbitration Act of 1979. Whilst there was some debate about this position under the 1979 Act because of the decision of Millett J in *Capital & Counties PLC v Hawa* [1991] 2 EGLR 133, in my judgment it is clear from the terms of the 1996 Act itself that there is no room for an appeal on this basis under that Act.

39. The leading text books on Arbitration are unanimous in saying that it is not open to a party to an arbitration to appeal on the basis that the question whether the Tribunal was right to find a fact on the basis of the evidential material before it is a question of law. The parties have chosen the tribunal which is to decide the facts and its conclusions cannot be questioned.

40. Mustill and Boyd on Commercial Arbitration 2nd ed., 2001 Companion states at p. 357:
'The guidelines for granting leave to appeal derived from the decision in the House of Lords in *The Nema* [1981] 2 Lloyd's Reports 239 are now set out in the Act itself: subs.69(3)(c). They are that (i) the decision of the tribunal is at least open to serious doubt: subs.69(3)(c). This must be demonstrated on the basis of findings of fact in the award: one effect of this is that it is now clearly impossible to challenge the findings of fact in an award on the ground that there was no evidence to support them. (Even under the old law this kind of challenge was strongly discouraged ...'.

41. Russell on Arbitration 22nd ed. At pp. 394–395 states:
'The tribunal's findings of fact are conclusive ... the parties will not be allowed to circumvent the rule that the tribunal's findings of fact are conclusive by alleging that they are inconsistent, or that they constitute a serious irregularity, or an excess of jurisdiction, or on the basis that there was insufficient evidence to support the findings in question. Consequently, the argument that it is a question of law whether there is material to support a finding of fact is no longer available. (This is a consequence of s.34 (2)(f) of the Arbitration Act 1996 (see the DAC report Para. 170).'

42. Merkin on Arbitration Law, 2004 deals with the position in more detail at Paras. 15.42 to 15.44 and 21.9 to 21.11. In essence, he states that, whilst it is now clear that an award cannot be challenged on the basis that there was insufficient evidence to support the arbitrator's factual findings, it may be possible to challenge it on the basis that there was no evidence at all (which could not be alleged in this case, where it is said that the evidence there was did not justify the inferences drawn).

43. I have been referred to *Guardcliffe Properties Limited v City & St James* [2003] 2 EGLR 16 in which Etherton J expressed the view, *obiter*, that an error of law within the *Edwards v Bairstow* principle could be an error of law under s.69 of the 1996 Act. He relied upon the earlier decision of Millett J and considered a decision of Evans Lombe J in *Secretary of State for the Environment v Reed International* [1994] 1 EGLR 22 as decided *per incuriam,* in ignorance of Millett J's decision. I regret that I am unable to agree with him and respectfully note that the point does not appear to have been argued before him by reference to the opening words of s 69(3) (c), nor to the wording of the DAC report. The learned judge did not have, in the event, to consider the scope of s.69 because the challenge under section 68 succeeded, but he drew no distinction between the 1979 Act and the 1996 Act, whereas the terms of section 1(2) of the earlier Act do not include the words to which I have drawn attention with which s.69 (3)(c) commences. For the same reasons I disagree with the decision of HH Judge Thornton QC in *Fence Gate Ltd v NEL Construction Ltd* [2001] 82 Con LR 41.

44. Under the terms of the 1996 Act therefore Steyn LJ's dictum in relation to Arbitrations under the 1979 Arbitration Act, with which Neill LJ was impressed, without agreeing, takes full force and effect.

45. In the same decision, Steyn LJ, at page 228 said:
'The Arbitrators are the masters of the facts. On an appeal the Court must decide any question of law arising from an Award on the basis of a full and unqualified acceptance of the findings of facts of the Arbitrators. It is irrelevant whether the Court considers those findings of fact to be right or wrong. It also does not matter

how obvious a mistake by the Arbitrators on the issues of fact might be, or what the scale of the financial consequences of the mistake of fact might be. That is of course an unsurprising position. After all, the very reason why parties conclude an arbitration agreement is because they do not wish to litigate in the Courts. Parties who submit their disputes to arbitration bind themselves by agreement to honour the Arbitrator's Award on the facts. The principle of party autonomy decrees that a Court ought never to question the Arbitrator's findings of fact.'"

Rule 28(2)

"May" is an odd choice of language here since the matters itemised will have to be determined, whether by the tribunal, the parties or the realities of the case, in any event.

In an arbitration without a pre-agreed set of applicable rules, it will be necessary in practice to work through these and other items and most professional arbitrators have their own extensive checklist. One of the authors was sole arbitrator in a highly complex arbitration in England with senior (i.e. QC) and junior counsel and a large team of solicitors on each side (one of the QCs was elevated to the Bench shortly afterwards). The parties had agreed the procedural details and presented a draft procedural order for the arbitrator's approval; his response was "what about ...", and he listed a further 14 items, some significant, the parties' lawyers had overlooked.

Rule 28(2)(a)

See s.3 and r.29; see also art.20 of the Model Law and s.34(2)(a) of the 1996 Act.

Rule 28(2)(b)

Refer art.23 of the Model Law.

The authors submit that this should refer to, "written claims ..." since, absent the submission of any claim at all, the arbitration cannot proceed.

Modern arbitration outwith Scotland has (with a few exceptions) moved far away from the court-based style of submissions and pleadings, e.g. as too often used in Scottish arbitrations. A typical modern procedural order states:

"Claim & Defence
Submissions in the form of comprehensive statements, including all relevant facts, evidence (including witness statements if applicable), citations and all documents relied upon shall be served by one Party on the other (copied to the Arbitrator) as follows:
[schedule of dates]"

The intention is that each of the claimant and respondent has "one shot" (with, where appropriate, a single reply each) so that the process of exchanging claim and defence is completed quickly (e.g. LCIA Rules r.15 gives a maximum of 120 days), without the continual, time consuming (and expensive) adjustment derived from the process in the Scottish courts and too often replicated in arbitration in Scotland.

In smaller arbitrations, it is always possible (and may be expeditious) to limit the size of submissions of claim and defence; too often substantial time and money is wasted preparing vast bundles of documentation which is never referred to or otherwise used.

Arbitration (Scotland) Act 2010 (r.28)

While it is axiomatic that parties have the opportunity to respond to their opponent's case, this does not mean continual rounds of rebuttal. Typically, the defence will respond to the claim and may introduce a counterclaim then the claimant will respond (i) to the defence and (ii) to the counterclaim. Response (i) should be limited to responding to the points made in the defence and should not introduce any new claim or arguments; ditto response (ii). The respondent will then respond only to the response to counterclaim. In some forms of arbitration, e.g. rent review, the parties conventionally make simultaneous submissions and, e.g. 20 working days later, simultaneous responses. There are no fixed rules, save that the process must be efficient (see s.1(a) and rr.24(1)(c), 25 above) by terminating quickly.

See s.34(2)(c) of the 1996 Act.

Rule 28(2)(c)

This rule gives the tribunal very wide powers and, in practice, the parties may well agree a narrower scope to prevent disclosure becoming a vast and expensive copy of US-style litigation practices. It is important to remember that disclosure is very much an American/English process, not mirrored (at least to the same degree) in non-American/English common law jurisdictions and considered almost alien in civil law jurisdictions.

Fortunately, an excellent and widely-used compromise has been reached in the *IBA Evidence Rules*, which also serve as a useful and recommended approach in domestic arbitration. The *IBA Evidence Rules* provide as follows:

"Article 3 Documents

1. [dealt with under r.28(2)(b) above]

2. Within the time ordered by the Arbitral Tribunal, any Party may submit to the Arbitral Tribunal a Request to Produce.

3. A Request to Produce shall contain:
   (a) (i) a description of a requested document sufficient to identify it, or (ii) a description in sufficient detail (including subject matter) of a narrow and specific requested category of documents that are reasonably believed to exist;
   (b) a description of how the documents requested are relevant and material to the outcome of the case; and
   (c) a statement that the documents requested are not in the possession, custody or control of the requesting Party, and of the reason why that Party assumes the documents requested to be in the possession, custody or control of the other Party.

4. Within the time ordered by the Arbitral Tribunal, the Party to whom the Request to Produce is addressed shall produce to the Arbitral Tribunal and to the other Parties all the documents requested in its possession, custody or control as to which no objection is made.

5. If the Party to whom the Request to Produce is addressed has objections to some or all of the documents requested, it shall state them in writing to the Arbitral Tribunal within the time ordered by the Arbitral Tribunal. The reasons for such objections shall be any of those set forth in Article 9.2.

6. The Arbitral Tribunal shall, in consultation with the Parties and in timely fashion, consider the Request to Produce and the objections. The Arbitral Tribunal may order the Party to whom such Request is addressed to produce to the Arbitral Tribunal and to the other Parties those requested documents in its possession, custody or control as to which the Arbitral Tribunal determines that (i) the issues that the

requesting Party wishes to prove are relevant and material to the outcome of the case, and (ii) none of the reasons for objection set forth in Article 9.2 apply.

7. In exceptional circumstances, if the propriety of an objection can only be determined by review of the document, the Arbitral Tribunal may determine that it should not review the document. In that event, the Arbitral Tribunal may, after consultation with the Parties, appoint an independent and impartial expert, bound to confidentiality, to review any such document and to report on the objection. To the extent that the objection is upheld by the Arbitral Tribunal, the expert shall not disclose to the Arbitral Tribunal and to the other Parties the contents of the document reviewed.

8. If a Party wishes to obtain the production of documents from a person or organization who is not a Party to the arbitration and from whom the Party cannot obtain the documents on its own, the Party may, within the time ordered by the Arbitral Tribunal, ask it to take whatever steps are legally available to obtain the requested documents. The Party shall identify the documents in sufficient detail and state why such documents are relevant and material to the outcome of the case. The Arbitral Tribunal shall decide on this request and shall take the necessary steps if in its discretion it determines that the documents would be relevant and material.

9. The Arbitral Tribunal, at any time before the arbitration is concluded, may request a Party to produce to the Arbitral Tribunal and to the other Parties any documents that it believes to be relevant and material to the outcome of the case. A Party may object to such a request based on any of the reasons set forth in Article 9.2. If a Party raises such an objection, the Arbitral Tribunal shall decide whether to order the production of such documents based upon the considerations set forth in Article 3.6 and, if the Arbitral Tribunal considers it appropriate, through the use of the procedures set forth in Article 3.7.

10. Within the time ordered by the Arbitral Tribunal, the Parties may submit to the Arbitral Tribunal and to the other Parties any additional documents which they believe have become relevant and material as a consequence of the issues raised in documents, Witness Statements or Expert Reports submitted or produced by another Party or in other submissions of the Parties.

11. If copies are submitted or produced, they must conform fully to the originals. At the request of the Arbitral Tribunal, any original must be presented for inspection.

12. All documents produced by a Party pursuant to the IBA Rules of Evidence (or by a non-Party pursuant to Article 3.8) shall be kept confidential by the Arbitral Tribunal and by the other Parties, and they shall be used only in connection with the arbitration. The Arbitral Tribunal may issue orders to set forth the terms of this confidentiality. This requirement is without prejudice to all other obligations of confidentiality in arbitration."

It should be noted that all such documents produced are covered by r.26 (confidentiality), provided that the parties have not agreed to disapply that rule.

See s.34(2)(d) of the 1996 Act.

Rule 28(2)(d)

It is submitted that this is self-explanatory; further the rule is widely drawn and covers the parties questioning of each other (including, of course, their respective witnesses, whether of fact or of opinion) and the questioning of the parties by the tribunal (see also r.28(2)(e)).

Common and civil law cultures differ in their approach to cross-examination of witnesses, this being a central component of the Anglo-American approach to litigation but not much relied on (or even frowned upon) in civil law jurisdictions.

See s.34(2)(e) of the 1996 Act.

Rule 28(2)(e)

This was at one time considered controversial since it was perceived as a foreign (civil law) practice with no place in Scots (or English) law.

The DAC Report addressed certain concerns as follows:

> "172. ... Once again it seems to us that provided the tribunal in exercising its powers follows its simple duty as set out in Clause 33 (and subsection (2) of this Clause tells the tribunal that this is what they must do) then in suitable cases an inquisitorial approach to all or some of the matters involved may well be the best way of proceeding. Clause 33, however, remains a control, such that, for example, if an arbitrator takes the initiative in procuring evidence, he must give all parties a reasonable opportunity of commenting on it."

This argument applies equally under this Act since r.24 and s.33 of the 1996 Act are based on common ground.

In some civil law jurisdictions, e.g. Germany and Switzerland, the tribunal drives the proceedings and leads the questioning of witnesses with counsel contributing as and when necessary or appropriate, quite unlike the traditional Anglo-Saxon style. Further, some leading international arbitrators favour a more open style which can become close to a discussion. Whether or not such an approach appeals in Scotland remains to be seen but it certainly offers a greater flexibility than the formal court-style alternation of submissions by counsel; the authors are confident that Scottish arbitrators will embrace this and other new approaches and avoid being trapped in the mire of pre-2010 arbitration practices derived from litigation.

The inquisitorial approach has to be adopted with restraint; it is not a licence for the arbitrator to assume the role of Chief Detective. In *Norbrook Laboratories Ltd v Tank* [2006] EWHC 1055 (Comm), the arbitrator, Mr Tank, took it upon himself to contact three potential witness directly and for this and other reasons he was removed under s.24 of the 1996 Act (one of the tiny handful of s.24 removals under that Act).

Colman J. said:

> "138. There is however a further matter of procedural management which is of a more serious nature. That began to occur before 22 September 2004. It involved the Arbitrator making direct unilateral contact with three witnesses as described in paragraph 84 above. The Arbitrator explained his contact with Ms Mountford, Mr Colussi and Mr Hendrix in the passages in his first witness statement quoted at paragraph 78 above. His reference to Rule 7 is clearly to 7(e). That Rule provides:
>
>> 'whether and to what extent the Arbitrator should himself take the initiative in ascertaining the facts and the law, and to rely upon his own knowledge and expertise to such extent as he thinks fit. I interpreted this to give me wide powers to ascertain the facts by

speaking to witnesses including in this case, Matthew Forde, particularly as I considered that non-payment would lead to the arbitration coming to a close if Moulson Chemplant so chose and this could potentially disadvantage Norbrook.'

139. That rule certainly provides a power to the Arbitrator to ascertain by his own initiative primary facts relevant to the substantive issues. That is to say he can cause to be injected into the arbitration evidence of facts from witnesses whom neither party is able or willing to call. However, this power is clearly subject to the component of fairness expressed as an objective of arbitration in Rule 1.1 in reflection of section 1(a) of the 1996 Act. Rule 7(e) therefore has to be operated with great care if an Arbitrator makes direct contact with a potential witness in the absence of either or both parties. Each party must be given the opportunity of questioning the witness. If the Arbitrator decides not to make use of the witness's evidence, or if the witness declines to give evidence at the hearing, the Arbitrator ought still to make an accurate record of the witness's remarks which he should then show to both parties. In this connection, it should be clearly appreciated by any competent Arbitrator operating these rules that fairness under rule 1 demands transparency under Rule 7(e). The reason for this is very clear. An Arbitrator in contact with a factual witness in the absence of one or both parties may be exposed to information which consciously or unconsciously influences his judgment on a matter in dispute. It is therefore absolutely axiomatic that the parties should at the very least have the opportunity of access to what the witness or potential witness has said to the Arbitrator so as to enable that party to refute any statement adverse to its case or to rely upon any statement supportive of its case. Whereas, it would in theory be possible for both parties to waive that requirement by an agreement to that effect, Rule 7(e) is not such an agreement. Nor does the reference to the 'economic' resolution of disputes in Rule 1 have the effect of causing the component of fairness to yield to economic expediency.

140. The need for this principled construction of Rule 7.4(e) could be no better illustrated than by two sentences in the Arbitrator's first witness statement quoted earlier in this judgment which I repeat here for convenience:

'Both Pia Mountford and Robert Colussi stated that they were not willing to assist or to provide witness statements and so I decided to disregard any comments that they had made to me .... They had both left Norbrook under difficult circumstances but I did not allow this to bias my view of Norbrook'.

141. This statement obviously raises the question what comments did they make and what was said which might have led the Arbitrator to be biased against Norbrook such that he needed to put it out of his mind. No record of these conversations has been provided to the parties and it must be inferred that no such record exists. The reference to the risk of bias, however, strongly suggests that whatever was said, if not put out of the mind of the Arbitrator, might influence his judgment on matters relevant to his decision.

142. The Arbitrator having directly contacted the witnesses, but having failed to make any exact record of what they said or to disclose such record to the parties, has thus both failed to conduct the proceedings fairly in accordance with s.33(1)(a) and (2) and therefore 'properly' within s.24(1)(d) and has, in this respect, therefore also created a procedural irregularity within s.68.

143. Has that failure caused substantial injustice or will it do so? ...
145. ... Where there is a sole Arbitrator whose impartiality is shown to have been impaired to the effect that a fair minded and properly informed independent observer would perceive that there existed a real possibility of bias in any award already made, substantial injustice will normally be inferred and where an award has yet to be made substantial injustice will normally be anticipated. In the former case the award would normally be set aside under s.68 and in the latter case the Arbitrator would normally be removed before he could make an award, under s.24."

One area where the tribunal can, does and must take the lead using an inquisitorial approach is in the two modern techniques of (i) "hot-tubbing", and (ii) witness conferencing where the witnesses from both parties are put together "on the stand" so it is obvious that neither party can lead the questioning. In brief:
  (i) "hot-tubbing" involves putting the parties' respective expert witnesses of like discipline "on the stand" together to be examined by the tribunal;
  (ii) "witness conferencing" involves putting all of each side's witnesses of fact "on the stand" together to be examined by the tribunal.

Rule 28(2)(f)(i)

Some arbitrations can be, and are, conducted on a documents-only basis, e.g. where the role of witnesses is of lesser importance; there is an increasing trend in international arbitration for smaller cases to be dealt with this way since the costs of convening a hearing can significantly outweigh the advantages (if any) of holding a hearing.

There used to be a presumption that parties were entitled to a hearing and some arbitrators feared being challenged under ss.33 and 68 of the 1996 Act if they did not grant one. However, some arbitrations do not warrant an oral hearing and it would arguably be a breach of s.1(a) and r.24(1)(c) of the Act to grant a hearing where none was merited. Further, some common law lawyers appear to view the main purpose of hearings as being to destroy, in cross-examination, the other side's witnesses, hence see the hearing as essential for that purpose. The civil law approach is not destructive at all and can be a great deal more productive and we in Scotland can learn from this, not least because of the closer relationship of our law to the civil law than is, for example, English law.

Any lingering presumption of a hearing in England was disposed of in *O'Donoghue v Enterprise Inns Plc* [2008] EWHC 2273 (Ch), a rent review case, where Mr O'Donoghue's claim (under s.68(2)(a) of the 1996 Act, i.e. failure by the arbitrator to comply with the general duty under s.33 of the Act), was that the award should be set aside or the rent review remitted to the arbitrator for reconsideration after an oral hearing, during which Mr O'Donoghue should be able to cross-examine Enterprise's expert witness. A serious irregularity had, so he claimed, occurred by reason of the arbitrator's failure to have held an oral hearing and to have allowed cross-examination. Section 34(2)(h) of the 1996 Act (i.e. the direct equivalent of the present r.28(2)(f)(i)) gives the arbitrator discretion whether and to what extent there should be oral evidence and submissions. His Honour Judge Behrens, relying on the judgment of H.H. Judge Coulson QC in *Sinclair v Woods of Winchester* [2005] EWHC 1631, said this:

"46. To my mind there are a number of answers to [the claimant's] submissions. First, the fact that the Arbitrator might have come to a different conclusion if there had been an oral hearing does not begin to establish that the Arbitrator was not acting fairly and impartially as between the parties. Second, as already noted, the Act expressly gives the Arbitrator a discretion on whether to hold an oral hearing. Third, the Arbitrator in his letter of 22nd November invited Mr O'Donoghue to set out his case as to why he wanted an oral hearing. Mr O'Donoghue failed to do this. It is plain from the correspondence I have summarised above that the Arbitrator has been conspicuously fair in giving the parties the opportunity to put their case before coming to a decision. It is true, of course, that the Arbitrator had provisionally decided to hold an oral hearing in the form he set out in his letter of 31st July 2007. However this proposal was not accepted by Mr O'Donoghue and it was in any event open to the Arbitrator to change his mind after receiving Mr O'Donoghue's Counter-Submissions and viewing the premises. Importantly he gave the parties an opportunity to make representations on the point before reaching his conclusion on 8th January 2008. ...

48. Fourth the Arbitrator gave reasons for his decision not to hold an oral hearing. Whether or not I would have exercised my discretion in that way is not a matter I need to decide. In my view the decision he made was one that was open to him on the material before him. He gave both sides the opportunity to make submissions before he made it. He gave reasons for the exercise of his discretion. In those circumstances it is, to my mind, difficult to see that there was any irregularity at all in the failure to hold an oral hearing. ...

51. It follows in my view that there was no serious irregularity on either the original or the amended basis of the claim and the claim accordingly fails. ...

53. [The claimant] submitted that the substantial injustice arose because of the possibility that the Arbitrator would have reached a different result if there had been an oral hearing. ... Whilst I accept that it is possible that there might have been a different result if there had been an oral hearing I do not accept that submission. In particular I do not accept that the possibility of a different result amounts to substantial injustice within s.68. I prefer the views of Judge Coulson QC. Adopting the test formulated in paragraph 23(a) of the judgment it cannot be said that in all the circumstances of this case on any view the Arbitrator's decision not to hold an oral hearing was an unacceptable consequence of the parties' decision to arbitrate the rent review."

We submit that equivalent logic must apply in Scotland.

However, arbitrators must be careful since prudence will normally dictate that, having taken all factors into account, if there is reasonable uncertainty about whether or not a hearing should be held, it is likely to be appropriate to hold one. Section 1(a) and r.24(1)(b) and (c) are paramount. Further, art.24(1) of the Model Law gives a presumption of a hearing:

"However, unless the parties have agreed that no hearings shall be held, the arbitral tribunal shall hold such hearings at an appropriate stage of the proceedings, if so requested by a party."

Rule 28(2)(f)(ii)

See art.24(1) of the Model Law.

Section 1(a) and r.24(1)(b) and (c) are the key here: in each arbitration (treated individually on its merits) how can the various competing requirements be balanced?

In many civil law jurisdictions, arbitral proceedings are dominated by written submissions with only a short oral phase; the tribunal comes to the hearing having fully mastered the written submissions, and the hearing is for the tribunal to ask any clarificatory questions (and, of course, to examine the witnesses). This has the advantage that hearings are generally very short (in Germany, few run more than one week) and the 10/12/16 week hearings common in common law jurisdictions are unknown.

For the tribunal, written submissions offer one very significant practical advantage in that the necessity (tedious, concentration-destroying, time-wasting and wholly inefficient) to take notes or oral submissions is removed. It is clearly undesirable for any tribunal both to listen to detailed oral submissions on complex matters, especially of law, and take detailed notes. Although in many cases in practice a transcript is taken with the text usually available late on the same day, this can mean working far into the night.

Written submissions are, we submit, greatly to be preferred.

Rule 28(2)(f)(iii)

This is self-explanatory.

Rule 28(2)(f)(iv)

This is self-explanatory.

Rule 28(2)(g)

See art.22 of the Model law; the rule tracks s.34(2)(b) of the 1996 Act.

Rule 28(2)(h)

It was unclear under the common law to what extent, if at all, issues relating to evidence were governed by rules of court and associate judicial decisions. In particular, there was an apparent contradiction between (a) the proposition that that an award could not be reduced solely on the grounds that the arbiter had relied on evidence which would have been excluded in court, and (b) s.9 of the the Civil Evidence (Scotland) Act 1988 which appears to imply that court rules are or may be applicable in arbitrations.

See s.34(2)(f) of the 1996 Act.

Rule 29: Place of arbitration **D**

29. The tribunal may meet, and otherwise conduct the arbitration, anywhere it chooses (in or outwith Scotland).

DEFINITIONS
"arbitration": s.2(1)
"tribunal": s.2(1)

STATUS

This is a default rule so it is open to the parties to modify it, agree something different or disapply it completely (see s.9).

All sets of arbitral rules known to the authors contain equivalent provisions.

MODEL LAW
Articles 20 is similar in principle.

COMMENTARY
While this may appear self-explanatory, it was unclear under the common law what the status was of a Scottish arbitration where part or all of the proceedings was held outside Scotland. While Ouagadougou, Wuhan, Nome or Easter Island, or even Paris, might seem sufficiently unlikely candidates to be ignored, it is easily possible to envisage proceedings taking place in Berwick-upon-Tweed, Newcastle or Carlisle as half-way points between English and Scottish parties.

The words "seat", "venue", "place" and "location" are a source of confusion even among jurisdictions where English is the principal language; under this Act, the 1996 Act and others, "seat" means the juridical seat and the other words are synonymous with each other but in some Model Law-related circumstances, the word "place" is used where we would use "seat". It is, therefore, essential to be clear what is in fact meant, particularly if the arbitration is international or involves Scottish subsidiaries of foreign companies.

In this context an anomalous situation arose in *Braes of Doune Wind Farm (Scotland) Ltd v Alfred McAlpine Business Services Ltd* [2008] EWHC 426 (TCC); [2008] 1 Lloyd's Rep. 608, where cl.20.2.2(c) of the contract between the parties provided that:

"This arbitration agreement is subject to English Law and the seat of the arbitration shall be Glasgow, Scotland. Any such reference to arbitration shall be deemed to be a reference to arbitration within the meaning of the Arbitration Act 1996 or any statutory re-enactment."

What did this mean by "seat"? Akenhead J. concluded that "seat" in this context meant "location". Inter alia, he said this:

"15 I must determine what the parties agreed was the 'seat' of the arbitration for the purposes of Section 2 of the Arbitration Act 1996. This means by Section 3 what the parties agreed was the 'juridical' seat. The word 'juridical' is not an irrelevant word or a word to be ignored in ascertaining what the 'seat' is. It means and connotes the administration of justice so far as the arbitration is concerned. It implies that there must be a country whose job it is to administer, control or decide what control there is to be over an arbitration. ...

17 ... (e) Looked at in this light, the parties' express agreement that the 'seat' of arbitration was to be Glasgow, Scotland must relate to the place in which the parties agreed that the hearings should take place. However, by all the other references the parties were agreeing that the curial law or law which governed the arbitral proceedings was that of England and Wales. Although authorities establish that, prima facie and in the absence of agreement otherwise, the selection of a place or seat for an arbitration will determine what the curial law or 'lex fori' or 'lex arbitri' will be, I consider that, where in substance the parties agree that the laws of one country will govern and control a given arbitration, the place where the arbitration is to be heard will not dictate what the governing or controlling law will be.

(f) In the context of this particular case, the fact that, as both parties seemed to accept in front of me, the Scottish courts would have no real control or interest in the arbitral proceedings other than in a criminal context, suggests that they cannot have intended that the arbitral proceedings were to be conducted as an effectively 'delocalised' arbitration or in a 'transnational firmament', to borrow Lord Justice Kerr's words in the *Naviera Amazonica* case."

Rule 52 provides that an award is to be treated as having been made in Scotland even if it is signed at, or delivered to or from, a place outwith Scotland; this is necessary to prevent recurrence of the anomalous decision by the House of Lords in *Hiscox v Outhwaite (No.1)* [1991] 3 All E.R. 641 that an award executed in Paris in relation to a London arbitration between English parties and concerning liabilities arising in England was held to be a French award.

The same principle as r.52 applies to this r.29, i.e. to prevent the arbitration becoming English (or Mauritanian, Chinese, etc.) by reason of some part of it being held outwith Scotland.

However, in *Bay Hotel and Resort Ltd v Cavalier Construction Co Ltd* [2001] UKPC 34, the Judicial Committee of the Privy Council held that a Turks and Caicos arbitration, despite being seated there, was governed by US domestic arbitration practices (specifically the nature and extent of reasons given in the award) because the arbitration had been conducted in accordance with the Construction Industry Arbitration Rules of the AAA and took place in Miami before a panel of three US arbitrators selected from a list supplied by the AAA.

There is another significance of the location of arbitral proceedings in that certain aspects of the law of that location will apply, e.g. (i) if a crime is committed by one of those involved in the proceedings, the law applicable at that location will apply, not the law of Scotland; (ii) if the location is in England, then s.2(2), (3) and (4) of the 1996 Act will or may apply, thereby importing ss.9–11 and 66 and, subject to the discretion of the English court, ss.43 and 44 of that Act. Many other jurisdictions (but, curiously, not this Act) have similar provisions but it is, for obvious reasons, wholly impracticable to list them all here.

Rule 30: Tribunal decisions **D**

30.—(1) Where the tribunal is unable to make a decision unanimously (including any decision on an award), a decision made by the majority of the arbitrators is sufficient.

(2) Where there is neither unanimity nor a majority in favour of or opposed to making any decision—
  (a) the decision is to be made by the arbitrator nominated to chair the tribunal, or
  (b) where no person has been so nominated, the decision is to be made—
     (i) where the tribunal consists of 3 or more arbitrators, by the last arbitrator to be appointed, or
     (ii) where the tribunal consists of 2 arbitrators, by an umpire appointed by the tribunal or, where the tribunal fails to make an appointment within 14 days of being requested to do so by either party or any arbitrator, by an arbitral appointments referee (at the request of a party or an arbitrator).

DEFINITIONS
"arbitration": s.2(1)
"arbitrator": s.2(1)

STATUS

This is a default rule so it is open to the parties to modify it, agree something different or disapply it completely (see s.9).

MODEL LAW

Article 29 refers but it does not address the circumstances envisaged by r.30(2) above.

COMMENTARY

Rule 30(1)

In principle, this is axiomatic and all sets of arbitral rules known to the authors contain equivalent provisions, e.g. art.25(1) of the ICC Rules, art.26(3) of the LCIA Rules and art.31 of the Swiss Rules.

Rule 30(2)(a)

See above at r.30(1); the ICC, LCIA and Swiss Rules all provide an equivalent to r.30(2)(a) above.

Conventionally, the third arbitrator, whether chosen by the two co-arbitrators or by the administering institution, shall chair the tribunal—see art.7.1 of the UNCITRAL Rules, art.5.6 of the LCIA Rules and art.8.4 of the ICC Rules; in any event, a chairman is appointed whereas r.6(b) does not so provide; in the view of the authors, this is a curious and unnecessary lacuna.

Rule 30(2)(b)

Each of art.7.1 of the UNCITRAL Rules, art.5.6 of the LCIA Rules, art.8.4 of the ICC Rules and art.8.2 of the Swiss Rules expressly provide for the appointment of a chairman but neither r.6(b) nor r.30 do so; consequently, none of the ICC, LCIA and Swiss Rules address the circumstances of r.30(2)(b) which is necessary only because of the lacuna in r.6(b).

Rule 30(2)(b)(i)

This was inserted at a late stage in the development of the Bill, originating in a suggestion from the judiciary. In the conventional model, whether UNCITRAL Rules or r.6(b) above, there will always be a last-appointed arbitrator but, where, in any set of rules similar to the LCIA's where the institution appoints all three arbitrators simultaneously, this provision will evidently not work. However, since the LCIA Rules expressly provide for the appointment of a chairman, they will give rise to no difficulty but others may do so.

Rule 30(2)(b)(ii)

Section 22 and r.7 apply.

Rule 31: Tribunal directions **D**

31.—(1) The tribunal may give such directions to the parties as it considers appropriate for the purposes of conducting the arbitration.

(2) A party must comply with such a direction by such time as the tribunal specifies.

DEFINITIONS
"arbitration": s.2(1)
"tribunal": s.2(1)

STATUS
This is a default rule so it is open to the parties to modify it, agree something different or disapply it completely (see s.9).

MODEL LAW
Article 19(2) refers but it does not expressly address the giving of directions but this is self-evident.

COMMENTARY

Rule 31(1)

This is self-explanatory since if the tribunal does not tell the parties what to do, the arbitration can hardly make progress sufficient to meet the overriding obligations imposed by the trio of s.1(a) and rr.24(1)(c)(i) and 25(a). Modern arbitration relies on the tribunal adopting a proactive approach to case management and this in turn requires that appropriate directions be issued as and when applicable; leaving matters to drift along, relying on the initiative (or lack) of the parties, is no longer an option.

Typically, one of the authors was sole arbitrator in an English arbitration but was travelling on business in South East Asia, i.e. at GMT + 7 hours; all times in this paragraph are GMT. A procedural issue arose at 08.30 requiring urgent resolution; the arbitrator issued a procedural order within an hour ordering party A to make any representations it wished on the issue by 11.00, with party B to respond, if it wished, by 17.00. Having considered both sets of representations overnight, the arbitrator issued a new procedural order (in fact, a clarificatory revision of an earlier one) by 09.00 the next day.

Rule 31(2)

This is self-explanatory: s.1(a) and rr.24(1)(c)(i) and 25 apply.

Rule 32: Power to appoint clerk, agents or employees etc. **D**

32.—(1) The tribunal may appoint a clerk (and such other agents, employees or other persons as it thinks fit) to assist it in conducting the arbitration.

(2) But the parties' consent is required for any appointment in respect of which significant expenses are likely to arise.

DEFINITIONS
"arbitration": s.2(1)
"tribunal": s.2(1)

STATUS
This is a default rule so it is open to the parties to modify it, agree something different or disapply it completely (see s.9).

MODEL LAW
There is no equivalent in the Model Law.

COMMENTARY

Given the absence hitherto of a modern codified arbitration law and the consequent difficulty of ascertaining what the law in fact was, Scottish arbiters have in the past often sat with a qualified solicitor in attendance as clerk. This practice is seen by non-Scottish arbitrators as being not too far removed from David Beckham hiring someone to kick the football for him, or Tiger Woods hiring someone to hit his golf ball for him. Further, such practice was at one time so much the norm that some commentators have thought it necessary to cite authority for the proposition that the arbiter has a discretion *not* to appoint a clerk (*Mowbray v Dickson* (1848) 10 D. 1102 at 1125). Whether one attributes this to nervousness about the uncertain state of the law or to some other reason, the cost of a clerk is often cited as a deterrent to parties wishing to submit a dispute to arbitration. It is understood that the practice has become less common in recent years.

Rule 32 does not address the issue of the extent (if any) to which an arbitrator may delegate his/her duties and responsibilities so the issue remains governed by the common law which suggests that an arbitrator may delegate executive, but not judicial functions (*Caledonian Railway Co v Lockhart* (1860) 22 D. (HL) 8).

However, the implication of r.3 (above) is that the concept of personal appointment has an important implication in that arbitrators may be obliged to carry out their duties and fulfil their responsibilities themselves; for the sole practitioner arbitrator this is the norm but arbitrators who are partners in firms of solicitors, chartered accountants, surveyors, engineers, architects and others are effectively barred by r.3 from delegating decision-making responsibilities to associates or other staff. Handing the entire case over to an associate (or pupil-arbitrator) is clearly prohibited and, conversely, employing a secretary to type an award is, equally clearly, permitted but there is a grey area in between where arbitrators must tread carefully, in the event of any doubt erring on the side of caution. In this context, r.7.3 of the CIArb, *Code of Ethics*, is relevant:

"A Member shall not delegate any duty to decide to any other person unless permitted to do so by the parties or applicable law."

Delegation of decision-making by a tribunal to its clerk would represent a serious irregularity in English law: in *Brandeis Brokers Ltd v Black* [2001] 2 Lloyd's Rep. 359, Toulson J. said at [68]:

"To show that an expert witness said things which he would not have been permitted to say in a court of law comes nowhere near to establishing that there was irregularity, let alone serious irregularity, within the meaning of section 68. It would be a different matter if Brandeis could establish, as it asserts, that the arbitrators effectively delegated their decision making on important questions to [the expert]. That criticism, if substantiated, would amount to serious irregularity, but I reject it."

An international internet debate in early 2009 focused on the question of delegation, particularly in the context of busy leading arbitrators with a significant caseload prima facie not capable of being 100 per cent handled by one individual. The consensus was broadly "market choice" in that the international arbitration market knows who are the sole practitioner arbitrators carrying out the entirety of their own work and those who have, and rely on, back office support.

The question of delegation arose in *Agrimex Ltd v Tradigrain SA & Ors* [2003] EWHC 1656 (Comm) (the "others" were GAFTA itself and the five individual members of the tribunal), in the context of an application to reduce alledgly excessive fees but where Thomas J. had some pertinent observations concerning delegation. In that case, 48 per cent of the costs of the arbitration (excluding the parties' own legal and other costs) was represented by the fees charged by a qualified solicitor from an external law firm employed to draft the award, in part because GAFTA arbitrators are "commercial men" (i.e. usually commodity traders) and GAFTA normally excludes lawyers from its panels. The chairman of the tribunal had decided that he required the appointment of a legal draftsman:

"... to ensure as far as possible that the award reflected the opinions of the [tribunal] members, produced an appropriate and clear legal explanation for the award and provided justice to the parties."

At the hearing the solicitor was introduced to the parties and it was explained that he would be the draftsman for the award. The evidence was that it was made clear to him that his role was to be restricted to that of a draftsman and he was not instructed to advise the tribunal on any legal issues; he understood his instructions to be to consider the documentation, attend the appeal hearings, write such notes as were necessary and prepare an award that reflected the tribunal's findings. He was also present when the board subsequently deliberated on the issues and, subsequently, he was provided with the further views of the tribunal members and produced a draft award. He did not comment on any findings but, in his view, simply did his best to reproduce the findings made by the tribunal in the draft award that he prepared.

Thomas J. had this to say:

"32. For some time, and certainly since the enactment of the Arbitration Act 1996, it has been part of the skill ordinarily to be expected of a competent arbitrator that he should produce his own reasoned award. It is commonplace for decision-makers to explain the reasoning for their decision; it is commonly acknowledged that the quality of decisions is improved by requiring the decision-maker to go through the process of expressing those reasons himself. There is no reason why in general a person who takes on the responsibility and duty of an arbitrator should not be able to discharge the function of providing a reasoned explanation for the decision he has reached; for example, awards made by arbitrators of the London Maritime Arbitrators Association who are not legally qualified set out in clear terms their reasoning in disputes that are often far more complex than the matters in this award. It is also clear from the evidence of GAFTA that they recognise that if a person is to sit as an arbitrator, he should be capable of drafting an award; that is one of the objectives of their training."

A different but highly controversial issue concerning a clerk arose in Singapore in *Luzon Hydro Corp v Transfield Philippines Inc* [2004] S.G.H.C. 204; [2004] 4 S.L.R. 705: the case concerns aspects of the role of a tribunal-appointed expert (a qualified engineer) in an ICC arbitration whose role was downgraded to that of administrative assistant. However, the engineer not only attended the hearing on liability but questioned the parties' respective expert engineering witnesses during it. Subsequently, the tribunal relied on his assistance in "administrative matters" concerning the technical issues in dispute—these included collating evidence on technical issues. However, post-hearing the tribunal wrote to the parties stating inter alia (i) that it had decided not to seek any written expert's report from the engineer, and (ii) outlining the administrative assistance he had rendered; this included, "identifying expert evidence, technical matters referred to by witnesses ... technical issues in submissions etc" and, "responding to technical queries of the Tribunal". The engineer was also to review the draft award to ensure the correct use of technical terminology. Neither of the parties raised any objection to the engineer's proposed tasks.

However, post-hearing the engineer expended 486 hours on the case and his timesheet descriptions of his activities led Luzon's solicitors to request copies of all correspondence between the engineer and the tribunal—this disclosure was refused. Luzon applied to set aside the tribunal's award (on liability) on the grounds, inter alia, that: (i) the proceedings had not accorded with the agreement of the parties; (ii) there had been a breach of the rules of natural justice in that the engineer had been permitted by the tribunal an involvement substantially beyond that agreed by the parties; (iii) the engineer had assumed the task of reviewing and determining the relevance of the evidence; (iv) since it had not been provided with copies of the engineer/tribunal correspondence it had been deprived of any opportunity to comment thereon, as required by both ICC Rules and the Model Law.

Remarkably, the court dismissed Luzon's application in a judgment which was strongly attacked by one leading commentator on numerous grounds, including the principle restated by Thomas J. in *Hussman (Europe) Ltd v Al Ameen Development & Trade Co* [2000] 2 Lloyd's Rep. 83 at [46]:

> "I agree with the observation of Professor Merkin in his work [*Arbitration Law*] at paragraph 13.46(e):
>> '... consultation with the experts should not take place after the close of the hearing or otherwise in the absence of the parties as this deprives the parties of their right to comment'.
>
> The point was taken that in the meeting with [the expert], the tribunal was not taking evidence and so the provisions of s37(1)(b) did not apply; *I do not agree* [author's emphasis]. They were plainly discussing with him the [subject matter of his expert opinion] and the content of his report; in my judgment the provisions of the section were applicable to this meeting at which his evidence was discussed."

While there is no suggestion that the tribunal in *Luzon Hydro Corp v Transfield Philippines Inc* [2004] S.G.H.C. 204; [2004] 4 S.L.R. 705 did delegate any part of the decision making to the expert, there is no way of answering any question as to whether it might have done so (i.e. a "serious irregularity", applying English terminology) without disclosure to the parties of the engineer/tribunal communications.

To summarise, there are issues, some serious, concerning the delegation, actual or apparent, of an arbitrator's responsibilities (as opposed to the non-delegable decision-making responsibility) and such delegation (other than the most basic) should be done with considerable care.

While, in the authors' view, the justification hitherto for employing a solicitor as clerk was, at its best, highly questionable, we submit that there can be no justification under this Act.

Rule 33: Party representatives **D**

33.—(1) A party may be represented in the arbitration by a lawyer or any other person.

(2) But the party must, before representation begins, give notice of the representative—
    (a) to the tribunal, and
    (b) to the other party.

DEFINITIONS
    "arbitration": s.2(1)
    "tribunal": s.2(1)

STATUS
This is a default rule so it is open to the parties to modify it, agree something different or disapply it completely (see s.9).

MODEL LAW
There is no equivalent in the Model Law.

COMMENTARY
Article 4 of the UNCITRAL Rules is in equivalent terms to r.33, as are s.36 of the 1996 Act, art.21(4) of the ICC Rules and art.18 of the LCIA Rules.

Article 18 of the LCIA Rules incorporates an extra feature in that the tribunal is empowered to require from any party proof of authority granted to its representative(s). One of the authors has in fact had to use this power in a circumstance where it was unclear which of two law firms was in fact representing one party.

The giving of notice is a consequence of the fairness obligation of s.1(a) and r.24(1)(b); there would be an obvious unfairness if, in a case *Small Business Ltd v Big Multinational Plc*, the former arrived at a hearing accompanied by a small-town solicitor to find itself confronted by a pair of QCs and an army of solicitors from a large law firm.

However, the requirement to give notice might go further than that example: in an ICSID arbitration in 2008, *Hrvatska Elektroprivreda dd v the Republic of Slovenia* (ICSID case no.ARBl05124), the latter's legal representatives notified the tribunal 10 days before the hearing that a Mr M QC would participate as part of their team. There were two issues (i) Mr M QC was a barrister at E Chambers of which the president of the tribunal was a door tenant, and (ii) the lateness of the notification. Further, Slovenia refused to disclose either when Mr M had been retained (it later became clear that Mr M had been on the Slovenian team for at least two months) or what role he was expected to play at the hearing. Hrvatska relied on ICSID Arbitration Rules r.18(1) which obliges a party to notify the secretary general of the identity of counsel and for the secretary general to, "promptly inform the Tribunal and the other party" and sought an order by the tribunal removing Mr M from the case.

The tribunal considered that it was obliged as guardian of the legitimacy of the arbitral process to make every effort to ensure that the award was not affected by procedural imperfection. If it granted the order sought, Slovenia might later contend that there had been a serious departure from a fundamental rule of procedure, i.e. the right to representation (ICSID Arbitration Rules r.19) and the right of being given a full opportunity to present a case. Conversely, if the order were refused, Hrvatska might later assert unfairness. In a key passage ([31] of its ruling), the tribunal said this:

"... The justifiability of an apprehension of partiality depends on all relevant circumstances. Here, those circumstances include ... second, [Slovenia's] conscious decision *not* to inform the Claimant or the Tribunal of Mr M's involvement in the case, following his engagement [two months earlier]; third, the tardiness of [Slovenia's] announcement of Mr M's involvement and, finally, Slovenia's subsequent insistent refusal to disclose the scope of Mr M's involvement, a matter of days before the commencement of the hearing on the merits. The last three matters were errors of judgment on [Slovenia's] part and have created an atmosphere of apprehension and mistrust which it is important to dispel."

The tribunal concluded that, in the light of the fundamental rule enshrined in art.56(1) of the ICSID Convention and given its inherent procedural powers confirmed by art.44, Mr M's participation would be inappropriate and improper.

The DAC Report made some helpful observations in respect of the equivalent s.36 of the 1996 Act and these are relevant to this r.33.

> "184. In the draft produced in July we used the phrase 'a lawyer or other person of his choice'. We have changed this, because we felt that it might give the impression that a party could stubbornly insist on a particular lawyer or other person, in circumstances where that individual could not attend for a long time, thus giving a recalcitrant party a good means of delaying the arbitral process. This should not happen. 'A lawyer or other person chosen by him' does not give this impression: if a party's first choice is not available, his second choice will still be 'a lawyer or other person chosen by him'. The right to be represented exists but must not be abused. Furthermore the right must be read with the first principle of Clause 1, as well as Clauses 33 and 40. If this is done then we trust that attempts to abuse the right will fail.
>
> 185. It has been suggested to the DAC that there should be some provision requiring a party to give advance notice to all other parties if he intends to be represented at a hearing. Whilst in some ways an attractive proposal, this would be difficult to stipulate as a statutory provision, given that it may be impossible in some circumstances, or simply unnecessary in others. Further, different sanctions may be appropriate depending on the particular case. It is clearly desirable that, as a general rule, such notice be given. If it is not, one sanction may be for the tribunal to adjourn a hearing at the defaulting party's cost. In the end, however, this must be a matter for the tribunal's discretion in each particular case.
>
> 186. It has been suggested that this Clause provides an opportunity of extending by statute the privilege enjoyed by legal advisers to non-legal advisers or representatives. We have not adopted this suggestion. It seems to us that it would be necessary to define with great precision which nonlegal advisers or representatives are to be included (e.g. what relationship they must have to the arbitration and its conduct), and the precise classes of privilege which should be extended to them. Further, any such provision would necessarily have an impact on the position beyond arbitration. In short, it seems to us that this question cannot be confined to arbitrations and raises matters of general principle far beyond those of our remit."

Rule 34: Experts **D**

34.—(1) The tribunal may obtain an expert opinion on any matter arising in the arbitration.

(2) The parties must be given a reasonable opportunity—
  (a) to make representations about any written expert opinion, and
  (b) to hear any oral expert opinion and to ask questions of the expert giving it.

DEFINITIONS
  "arbitration": s.2(1)
  "tribunal": s.2(1)

STATUS

This is a default rule so it is open to the parties to modify it, agree something different or disapply it completely (see s.9).

MODEL LAW

Article 26 of the Model Law is in equivalent terms and is on an, "unless otherwise agreed by the parties" basis.

COMMENTARY

The concept of a tribunal-appointed expert ("TAE") was relatively unknown in the common law world until the Civil Procedure Rules introduced it in 1999 (Pt 35) in an effort to reduce the costs of litigation by reducing the tendency, in some classes of litigation, for the proceedings to become a "battle of the experts". In contrast, a court-appointed expert is the norm in civil law jurisdictions and some such do not permit the parties to employ their own experts. However, one of the advantages of arbitration over litigation is being able to choose arbitrators with relevant expertise so there should be less need for any TAE and, in some sectors, employment of such an expert is rare (the authors have never had any case in practice where a TAE was employed).

Section 37 of the 1996 Act, art.20(4) of the ICC Rules, art.21 of the LCIA Rules and art.27 of the Swiss Rules are in equivalent terms to r.34. Note that none of this Act, the 1996 Act, the ICC Rules, the LCIA Rules or the Swiss Rules contain any express power for parties to appoint their own experts but the language of relevant parts of the respective rules assumes that such have been appointed.

A different but highly controversial issue concerning a clerk arose in Singapore in *Luzon Hydro Corp v Transfield Philippines Inc* [2004] SGHC 204; [2004] 4 SLR 705, the case concerns aspects of the role of a tribunal-appointed expert (a qualified engineer) in an ICC arbitration whose role was downgraded to that of administrative assistant. However, the engineer not only attended the hearing on liability but questioned the parties' respective engineering witnesses during it. Subsequently, the tribunal relied on his assistance in "administrative matters" concerning the technical issues in dispute—these included collating evidence on technical issues. However, post-hearing the tribunal wrote to the parties stating inter alia (i) that it had decided not to seek any written expert's report from the engineer, and (ii) outlining the administrative assistance he had rendered; this included "identifying expert evidence, technical matters referred to by witnesses ... technical issues in submissions etc" and, "responding to technical queries of the Tribunal". The engineer was also to review the draft award to ensure the correct use of technical terminology. Neither of the parties raised any objection to the engineer's proposed tasks.

However, post-hearing the engineer expended 486 hours on the case and his timesheet descriptions of his activities led Luzon's solicitors to request copies of all correspondence between the engineer and the tribunal—this disclosure was refused. Luzon applied to set aside the subsequent award in liability on the grounds, inter alia, that (i) the proceedings had not accorded with the agreement of the parties; (ii) there had been a breach of the rules of natural justice in that the engineer had been permitted by the tribunal an involvement substantially beyond that agreed by the parties; (iii) the engineer had assumed the task of reviewing and determining the relevance of the evidence; (iv) since it had not been provided with copies of the expert/tribunal correspondence it had been deprived of any opportunity to comment thereon, as required by both ICC Rules and the Model Law.

Remarkably, the court dismissed Luzon's application in a judgment which was strongly attacked by one leading commentator on numerous grounds, including the principle restated by Thomas J. in *Hussman (Europe) Ltd v Al Ameen Development & Trade Co* [2000] 2 Lloyd's Rep. 83 at [46]):

"I agree with the observation of Professor Merkin in his work [*Arbitration Law*] at paragraph 13.46(e):

'... consultation with the experts should not take place after the close of the hearing or otherwise in the absence of the parties as this deprives the parties of their right to comment'.

The point was taken that in the meeting with [the Expert], the tribunal was not taking evidence and so the provisions of s37(1)(b) did not apply; *I do not agree* [author's emphasis]. They were plainly discussing with him the [subject matter of his expert opinion] and the content of his report; in my judgment the provisions of the section were applicable to this meeting at which his evidence was discussed."

While there is no suggestion that the tribunal in *Luzon Hydro Corp v Transfield Philippines Inc* [2004] S.G.H.C. 204; [2004] 4 S.L.R. 705 did delegate any part of the decision making to the expert, there is no way of answering any question as to whether it might have done so (i.e. a "serious irregularity", applying English terminology) without disclosure to the parties of the expert/tribunal communications.

See also r.60(1)(b)(ii) (below) concerning the reimbursement of the fees of a tribunal-appointed expert (this is a mandatory rule, so giving the same position as s.37(2) of the 1996 Act thereby avoiding the risk of the parties agreeing otherwise and thus disabling the tribunal from recovering from the parties expenses properly incurred); see also r.75 (below) concerning the immunity of experts.

Rule 35: Powers relating to property **D**

35. The tribunal may direct a party—
    (a) to allow the tribunal, an expert or another party—
        (i) to inspect, photograph, preserve or take custody of any property which that party owns or possesses which is the subject of the arbitration (or as to which any question arises in the arbitration), or
        (ii) to take samples from, or conduct an experiment on, any such property, or
    (b) to preserve any document or other evidence which the party possesses or controls.

DEFINITIONS
"arbitration": s.2(1)
"tribunal": s.2(1)

STATUS
This is a default rule so it is open to the parties to modify it, agree something different or disapply it completely (see s.9).

MODEL LAW
Article 17 of the 1985 Model Law covered all interim measures, not merely the items listed in this r.35. However, the 2006 revisions very substantially expanded (from 67 to 1,500 words) that article to cover a wide

range of other measures; it is on an "unless otherwise agreed by the parties" basis.

COMMENTARY

Section 38(4) of the 1996 Act is in equivalent terms but art.23(1) of the ICC Rules, art.25.1 of the LCIA Rules and art.26 of the Swiss Rules follow the 1985 version of the Model Law in being very broadly drafted without these specific references to property.

See also r.46 below.

Rule 36: Oaths or affirmations **D**

36. The tribunal may—
   (a) direct that a party or witness is to be examined on oath or affirmation, and
   (b) administer an oath or affirmation for that purpose.

DEFINITIONS
"tribunal": s.2(1)

STATUS

This is a default rule so it is open to the parties to modify it, agree something different or disapply it completely (see s.9).

MODEL LAW

There is no equivalent provision in the Model Law.

COMMENTARY

Section 38(5) of the 1996 Act is in equivalent terms. In many civil law jurisdictions, the administering of a oath by a mere arbitrator would either be ineffective or void or even an offence in law, such administering being restricted to notaries and the like.

As a practical matter, the administration of an oath is fraught with difficulty given the several different arms of the Christian Church with different versions of the Bible, let alone all the complications of other religions and cultures; in particular, in certain religions it would be highly offensive to a believer to use the equivalent holy book to swear an oath and, in others, it would be offensive for a non-believer to hand the relevant holy book to a believer. One well-known English arbitrator used to travel with a briefcase full of different holy books but that is no longer appropriate. Affirmation gives a far easier solution.

In any event, good practice requires that the tribunal establish at an early date, e.g. in a procedural order, what is to be done in this context.

Rule 37: Failure to submit claim or defence timeously **D**

37.—(1) Where—
   (a) a party unnecessarily delays in submitting or in otherwise pursuing a claim,
   (b) the tribunal considers that there is no good reason for the delay, and
   (c) the tribunal is satisfied that the delay—
      (i) gives, or is likely to give, rise to a substantial risk that it will not be possible to resolve the issues in that claim fairly, or
      (ii) has caused, or is likely to cause, serious prejudice to the other party,

the tribunal must end the arbitration in so far as it relates to the subject-matter of the claim and may make such award (including an award on expenses) as it considers appropriate in consequence of the claim.

(2) Where—
  (a) a party unnecessarily delays in submitting a defence to the tribunal, and
  (b) the tribunal considers that there is no good reason for the delay,
the tribunal must proceed with the arbitration (but the delay is not, in itself, to be treated as an admission of anything).

DEFINITIONS
"claim": s.31(1)
"tribunal": s.2(1)

STATUS
This is a default rule so it is open to the parties to modify it, agree something different or disapply it completely (see s.9).

MODEL LAW
Article 25 of the Model Law is in equivalent terms.

COMMENTARY
Article 28 of the UNCITRAL Rules, art.15.8 of the LCIA Rules and art.28 of the Swiss Rules are in equivalent terms as to principle but r.37 is in more detail and is consistent with s.41(3) of the 1996 Act. Curiously, the ICC Rules include no such equivalent provision.

The 1996 Act introduced a very useful additional feature, the concept of a "peremptory order"; see r.38 below.

Rule 37(1)

Two key points must be noted: first, all three legs of r.37 ((a), (b) and (c)) must be satisfied before the tribunal can act in this regard and, secondly, if so, then the tribunal is obliged to end the arbitration and it has no discretion in the matter.

If the tribunal does indeed end the arbitration via r.37(1), then, provided that the prescription period has not expired, it is open to the claimant to start a fresh claim on the same subject matter. Given that option, the status of an award as envisaged is uncertain although Rix J. (as he then was) had suggested that some form of estoppel might apply (see *James Lazenby & Co v McNicholas Construction Co Ltd* [1995] 2 Lloyd's Rep. 30).

In the later case *Charles M Willie & Co (Shipping) Ltd v Ocean Laser Shipping Ltd* [1999] 1 Lloyd's Rep 225 (a case arising under the 1950 and 1979 Acts), the same judge said this:

  "There is no statutory or common law definition of what constitutes an 'award'. The matter was considered in *Cargill v. Kadinopoulos* [1992] 1 Lloyd's Rep 1. The arbitration in that case was governed by a sophisticated code known as the GAFTA Arbitration Rules. Those Rules provided for a two tier arbitration procedure with a right of appeal to a Board of Appeal from any 'award' of the first tier arbitrator. The Rules also contained detailed limitation provisions together with an overriding discretion in the first tier arbitrator to allow a claim to proceed despite its lateness. A first tier arbitrator found that Kadinopoulos's claim was time-barred and refused in his discretion to allow it to proceed. It followed that the claim, in the words of the Rules, was 'deemed to have been withdrawn and abandoned'. The arbitrator wrote up his decision in the form of an 'interim award'. The House of Lords had to say whether that was an award properly so-called in terms of the Rules so as to permit appeal to the Board of Appeal, which had reversed the arbitrator's decision. Lord Goff of Chieveley, with whose speech the other members of the House agreed, pointed out that the arbitrator's decision had involved both findings of fact, as to whether circumstances had arisen as to whether he was called upon to exercise his discretion, and a decision as to how he should exercise that discretion. Lord Goff then continued (at 4/5):

'Like the Judge and the Court of Appeal, I am of the opinion that this decision was properly made the subject of an award. It is enough for me to say (subject to any right of appeal) it conclusively determined that the arbitration was at an end and so finally disposed of the relevant matters which had been submitted to arbitration; such a determination is properly the subject matter of an award, carrying with it the usual consequences which flow from an award — in particular, it renders the arbitrator functus officio and prevents the unsuccessful claimant from rearbitrating or litigating the identical claim in the future (see generally *Mustill and Boyd on Commercial Arbitration*, 2nd ed., pp 404–405 and 409–413, and cases there cited). It is, in my opinion, unnecessary in the present case to attempt an exhaustive definition of the precise nature of an arbitration award, because I am in no doubt that in the present case the arbitrator's decision was properly made the subject matter of an award. Indeed, as Lord Justice Leggatt pointed out in the Court of Appeal, it would be unrealistic to hold otherwise.

'It was suggested by the buyers that, in the arbitration rules, the expression "award" was, as a matter of construction, to be confined to decisions on jurisdiction or on the merits of a dispute. This would in the present context impose an artificial limit upon the meaning of the word "award", which I would be unwilling to accept without good reason. As it is, there is certainly no express provision to this effect, and I cannot discover an acceptable basis for an implication displacing the ordinary understanding of what is meant by an award. *In the present case the determination of the arbitrator, although it did not amount to a decision of the merits of the sellers' claim, nevertheless did finally dispose of the relevant matters in dispute because it finally determined that the sellers' claim was deemed to have been withdrawn and abandoned and so could no longer be pursued against the buyers. Such a determination is, in my opinion, properly made the subject matter of an award.* In reaching this conclusion, I draw comfort from the fact that the new s.13A of the Arbitration Act, 1950 will, when brought into force, confer upon an arbitrator or umpire the power to make an award dismissing the claim for what, in the context of litigation, is called want of prosecution (see s.102 of the Courts and Legal Services Act, 1990)'"
(emphasis added by the authors).

In fn.3 to this judgment, Rix J. said:

"It seems to me that this passage from Lord Goff's speech in *Cargill v. Kadinopoulos* may support the view that I had tentatively expressed in *James Lazenby & Co v. McNicholas Construction Co Ltd* [1995] 1 WLR 615 at 630/1 to the effect that an award striking out a claim for want of prosecution under section 13A of the Arbitration Act 1950 would be a final determination of the claim."

The authors would phrase this more strongly in that it appears to us that Lord Goff in the emphasised passage is squarely on the issue.

The question of whether unnecessary delay in submitting or in otherwise pursuing a claim can empower a court to strike out the claim has exercised the House of Lords on several occasions, notably in *Grovit v Doctor* [1997] 2 All E.R. 417; [1997] 1 W.L.R. 640. Lord Woolf, giving the only judgment (with which his colleagues, including Lord Clyde, agreed) said this:

> "3. The approach which is adopted at the present time by courts on an application to dismiss an action for want of prosecution is set out by Lord Diplock in *Birkett v. James* [1978] A.C. 297, 318F–G. Lord Diplock basing himself upon a note in the *Supreme Court Practice* (1976) to RSC, Ord. 25.r.1, said:
>> 'The power should be exercised only where the court is satisfied either (1) ... ; or (2)(a) that there has been inordinate and inexcusable delay on the part of the plaintiff or his lawyers, and (b) that such delay will give rise to a substantial risk that it is not possible to have a fair trial of the issues in the action or is such as is likely to cause or to have caused serious prejudice to the defendants either as between themselves and the plaintiff or between each other or between them and a third party.'
>
> 4. In *Birkett v. James* their Lordships were concerned only with the application of principle (2). In this case the courts below have been concerned with both principles (1) and (2). On this appeal Mr Isaac Jacob on behalf of the appellant identifies the primary issue to be determined as being:
>> 'Can inexcusable and inordinate delay (if stigmatised as an abuse of process) constitute or be treated as, prejudice without the need for the defendant to show actual prejudice or a substantial risk that a fair trail of the actual would be impossible? Alternatively is it permissible to take elements which might (but are not sufficient on their own to) amount to a ground for striking out for abuse of process, combine them with delay and treat the combination as an additional and hybrid ground for striking out?' ...
>
> 30. ... I am satisfied that both the deputy judge and the Court of Appeal were entitled to come to the conclusion which they did as to the reason for the appellant's inactivity in the libel action for a period of over two years. This conduct on the part of the appellant constituted an abuse of process. The courts exist to enable parties to have their disputes resolved. To commence and to continue litigation which you have no intention to bring to conclusion can amount to an abuse of process. Where this is the situation the party against whom the proceedings is brought is entitled to apply to have the action struck out and if justice so requires (which will frequently be the case) the courts will dismiss the action. The evidence which was relied upon to establish the abuse of process may be the plaintiff's inactivity. The same evidence will then no doubt be capable of supporting an application to dismiss for want of prosecution. However, if there is an abuse of process, it is not strictly necessary to establish want of prosecution under either of the limbs identified by Lord Diplock in *Birkett v. James* [1978] AC 297. In this case once the conclusion was reached that the reason for the delay was one which involved abusing the process of the court in maintaining proceedings when there was no intention of carrying the case to trial the court was entitled to dismiss the proceedings."

We should, as always, be cautious about applying authority covering judicial striking-out to arbitration but in this case there is no distinction.

Remarkably, there was no 1996 Act authority on dismissal of a claim for claimant's inordinate and inexcusable delay until *TAG Wealth Management v West* [2008] EWHC 1466 (Comm) (Aikens J.). However, in the 1981 case of *The Bremer Vulkan* (*Bremer Vulkan Schiffbau und Maschinenfabrik v South India Shipping Corp Ltd* [1981] A.C. 909), it was held that a claimant's inactivity did not amount either to an offer to terminate the arbitration proceedings or as a repudiation of the arbitration agreement, so that the tribunal had no jurisdiction to strike out the claim for want of prosecution. The actual effect of that decision was reversed by the insertion (by the Courts and Legal Services Act 1990 s.102) into the Arbitration Act 1950 of a new section, s.13A, re-enacted in substance as s.41(3) of the 1996 Act.

TAG was a financial and investment advisor which engaged Mr West as an associate in the period 1996–99 in relation to the sale of both regulated and non-regulated financial products, the arranging of mortgages and the provision of fee-based financial advice; he was paid on the basis of fees or commissions. During 2000, disputes arose between TAG and Mr West and an arbitrator was appointed in January 2002, ordering (inter alia) certain disclosures with which TAG failed to comply. Inter alia, it claimed in May 2007 that it was experiencing great difficulties since its relevant storage facilities had been flooded and documents most likely destroyed. In July 2007, Mr West put TAG on notice that he intended to make a s.41(3) application and he subsequently did so and a one day hearing took place in January 2008. No oral evidence was given and the hearing was taken up with submissions from counsel.

The arbitrator subsequently held that Mr West's s.41(3) application succeeded, and he therefore ordered that TAG's claim against Mr West be dismissed. The arbitrator gave full reasons for his decision, concluding that the delay in the case had been almost entirely the fault of TAG, although he held that there had been some minor delay by Mr West. He also concluded that this delay had been both inordinate and inexcusable; inter alia, some of TAG's commission statements had been destroyed by flooding, others had been destroyed because TAG saw itself being under no obligation to keep such statements longer than six years. Consequently data concerning more than 70 per cent of the policies which Mr West wrote, and on which he claimed commission, were no longer available and it was apparent that it was impossible to have a fair trial. The arbitrator dealt in detail with the issue of limitation, referring to the leading cases of *Birkett v James* [1978] A.C. 297 and *James Lazenby & Co v McNicholas Construction Co Ltd* [1995] 2 Lloyd's Rep. 30. He accepted the proposition that it would be wrong for an arbitrator to dismiss a claim for want of prosecution where the limitation period had not expired. The arbitrator concluded that TAG's claims had all become statute-barred between September 2005 and December 2007. The arbitrator also rejected TAG's submission that, "this is a Trust case to which no period of limitation applies". TAG appealed under both s.68(2)(a) and (d) and s.69, the principal ground being that the arbitrator had failed to comply with s.33 of the Act, and/or that he had failed to deal with all the issues put to him.

TAG's application contained five grounds of serious irregularity, all trenchantly rejected by Aikens J.: in particular, in the present context, ground 1 was that the claim had been struck out only six months after the close of pleadings, which, TAG argued, was bizarre and unprecedented. The judge rejected this characterisation of the procedure as unwarranted. The disclosure process had taken the best part of five years and was even then still incomplete, that delay being almost entirely TAG's fault. Ground 4 was that the arbitrator had allegedly failed completely to have identified the period or periods of inordinate delay for which TAG was said to have been responsible. The judge did not accept that there had been any failure by the arbitrator in this respect, his findings being that the vast majority of the delay had been caused by TAG and that this had been inordinate and inexcusable; that was a rational and reasonable finding. However, even if there had been any failing by the arbitrator to particularise further his findings, such would not constitute an irregularity within either s.68(2)(a) or (d). It did not constitute a failure to act fairly or a failure to deal with one of the issues put to him. Aikens J. concluded that none of TAG's complaints established serious irregularity that affected either the arbitrator or the proceedings or the award. He could find no relevant irregularity at all, let alone any that either had caused or would cause substantial injustice to TAG. Accordingly, the s.68 appeal must be dismissed.

TAG fared no better with its s.69 application, also made on five grounds. Ground 1 was that the arbitrator had allegedly failed to address properly the question of whether there had been inordinate and inexcusable delay by TAG and whether such delay had given rise, or was likely to give rise, to a substantial risk that it was not possible to have a fair resolution of the issues concerning TAG's claim. TAG argued that, instead, the arbitrator had linked the question of whether a fair hearing was possible to the absence of allegedly disclosable documents. Aikens J. would have been prepared to accept that, if the arbitrator had indeed done this, it might reveal an error of law but he had not done so as was clear on the face of the award. Ground 2 was misconceived: s.41(3) provided two ways in which inordinate and inexcusable delay on the part of a claimant could give rise to the issue of an award dismissing the claim. In this case, the arbitrator had found that both tests had been satisfied and there was no error of law in so doing. Ground 4 was that the arbitrator had allegedly failed to identify the features required to find that there was a substantial risk to a fair resolution of the issues in the claim that was caused by inordinate and inexcusable delay. The judge was satisfied that the reasons in the award did conclude, as a matter of fact, that the delay and the loss of relevant documents gave rise to this risk. Contrary to ground 5, the arbitrator had recognised that the application he was dealing with was, "whether TAG has been guilty of inordinate and inexcusable delay, and if so, whether the requirements of section 41(3) of the Arbitration Act 1996 are satisfied". There was entirely correct and there was no error of law in this. Accordingly, Aikens J. held that there had been no error of law on the part of the arbitrator so that s.69 was not applicable at all in this case; the application for leave to appeal must be dismissed.

This case clearly identifies the correct approach to be adopted by arbitrators in r.37(1) circumstances; detailed analysis can be found in Hew R. Dundas, "Dismissal of a Claim for Claimant's Inordinate and Inexcusable Delay: *TAG Wealth Management v West"* (2008) 74 *Arbitration* 467.

Rule 37(2)

This rule substantially follows art.25(b) of the Model Law. There are two key points, first that the tribunal must proceed with the arbitration in the absence of a defence and, secondly, the delay is not, per se and in isolation, to be treated as an admission of anything.

Section 1(a) and r.24 are paramount.

Rule 38: Failure to attend hearing or provide evidence **D**

38. Where—
 (a) a party fails—
  (i) to attend a hearing which the tribunal requested the party to attend a reasonable period in advance of the hearing, or
  (ii) to produce any document or other evidence requested by the tribunal, and
 (b) the tribunal considers that there is no good reason for the failure, the tribunal may proceed with the arbitration, and make its award, on the basis of the evidence (if any) before it.

DEFINITIONS
"arbitration": s.2(1)
"tribunal": s.2(1)

STATUS
This is a default rule so it is open to the parties to modify it, agree something different or disapply it completely (see s.9).

MODEL LAW
Article 25(c) of the Model Law is in substantially equivalent terms.

COMMENTARY
Articles 28(2) and (3) of the UNCITRAL Rules and arts 28(2) and (3) of the Swiss Rules are in equivalent terms; art.21(2) of the ICC Rules mirrors r.38(a)(i) and art.15.8 of the LCIA Rules is sufficiently widely drafted to cover both (i) and (ii).

There is a key point, in distinction to r.37, in that the tribunal *may* proceed with the arbitration but is not *obliged* to do so. In practice, absent obvious reasons such as insuperable transport delays, death, incapacity or serious ill health of one of the parties, a tribunal should normally proceed, inter alia because of its obligations under s.1(a) and r.24(1)(c)(i).

The circumstances of r.38(a)(i) are common especially in the maritime and commodity sectors where wholly uncontestable actions for payment occur frequently.

However, before concluding proceedings by issuing an award, the tribunal will have to consider very carefully whether "due process" has been properly and fully observed; if not, the award is not only open to challenge under r.68 but also, in an international case, open to refusal of enforcement (refer art.V(1)(b) of the New York Convention).

It is important to note that a no-show by the respondent is not, in isolation, a ground for accepting the claimant's claim; the latter still has to meet the ordinary burden of proof. One of the authors has sat in a hearing with a no-show respondent and the tribunal (of three, the other two being civil lawyers well used to proactive judges) tested the claimant's case thoroughly in a very inquisitorial style.

Rule 39: Failure to comply with tribunal direction or arbitration agreement **D**

39.—(1) Where a party fails to comply with—
 (a) any direction made by the tribunal, or
 (b) any obligation imposed by—
  (i) the arbitration agreement,
  (ii) these rules (in so far as they apply), or

(iii) any other agreement by the parties relating to conduct of the arbitration,

the tribunal may order the party to so comply.

(2) Where a party fails to comply with an order made under this rule, the tribunal may do any of the following—
  (a) direct that the party is not entitled to rely on any allegation or material which was the subject-matter of the order,
  (b) draw adverse inferences from the non-compliance,
  (c) proceed with the arbitration and make its award,
  (d) make such provisional award (including an award on expenses) as it considers appropriate in consequence of the non-compliance.

DEFINITIONS
"arbitration agreement": s.4
"tribunal": s.2(1)

STATUS
This is a default rule so it is open to the parties to modify it, agree something different or disapply it completely (see s.9).

MODEL LAW
There is no equivalent in the Model Law.

COMMENTARY
Scots arbitrators, until this Act, had no powers and, prior to the 1996 Act, English arbitrators had inadequate, if any, powers to ensure that a party complied with the procedures governing the arbitration or, in fact, prosecuted its claim with adequate vigour; this was partially rectified in England by s.5 Arbitration Act 1979 but in a manner which proved too complex. The 1996 Act recognises two distinct circumstances (a) the dormant arbitration where the claimant has failed to pursue its claim, and (b) cases where one or other of the parties has failed to comply with orders or directions of the tribunal. The first issue is covered by r.37(1) and the second is the subject of this rule, the equivalent of which is termed a "peremptory order" in England (see s.41(5) of the 1996 Act).

The rule is a default rule; it it noteworthy that exclusion of s.41(3)–(7) of the 1996 Act appears unknown in England.

Rule 39(1)

The 1996 Act inserts "without sufficient cause" here: it is submitted that s.1(a) and r.24(2) in effect require that there be "sufficient cause" despite the omission of the phrase.

Further it has been suggested that it is necessary both to allow the affected party to make representations and to allow the other party to respond; however we submit that since r.38(a) covers only those things which the affected party had either already agreed to do or had already been told to do (assuming always that that was r.23 compliant), the suggestion is one to be considered but does not follow from the Act or the rules.

As regards "fails to comply", there has to be a clear failure to comply with some previous order; inter alia, this requires that the preceding order had both (a) incorporated an appropriate deadline, and (b) been drafted such that "fail" could be objectively assessed; partial failures can give rise to difficulty since these rules do not expressly allow for a partial failure but Professor Merkin's, *Arbitration Law*, at para.16.30, takes the view (as regards England) that a partial failure is sufficient to activate s.41(5); the authors submit that that is so here since a party complies with an order only when it has complied with all of it.

Note the use of "may order" not "shall order"; the element of discretion inherent here is not capable of challenge, other than in extreme circumstances such as infringement of s.1(a) and r.24 obligations.

Rule 39 omits the language, "... prescribing such time for compliance ... appropriate" provided in s.41(5) of the 1996 Act but we submit that this is self-evident; without a clear deadline, it will often be impossible to reach a position of non-compliance, e.g. "I order you to complete your tax return" can be met with, "tomorrow/next month/next year" but "I order you ... by midnight on October 31, 2009" cannot. A stated deadline should always be given "5pm on Friday 31 [Month] [Year]"; as a practical measure, arbitrators should always wait a short time thereafter before taking further action: mail does go astray, fax machines can break down, emails can get temporarily mislaid in cyberspace, etc.

Note that there is no express power to withdraw a r.39 order absent compliance and, since it is likely that it will have been issued pursuant to an application from the other party, it will normally be appropriate to seek representations on any proposed withdrawal.

Careful consideration must be given to the means of service of the r.39 order, particularly on non-UK parties.

Section 42 of the 1996 Act provides for application to the court for an order requiring compliance with a peremptory order; these rules have no express equivalent provision but r.46(1)(g) and (2) arrive at the same point.

Rule 39(1)(a)

As regards, "any direction made ...": a r.39(1) order is ineffective unless it follows an existing, earlier order and therefore cannot introduce anything substantive and new; in practice the drafting should track the earlier order carefully and one of the authors uses a style where the recitals to the r.39(1) order repeat the earlier order so that the actual r.39(1) order becomes very short:

IT IS HEREBY ORDERED PURSUANT TO RULE 39(1) THAT:

1. Respondent [perform some act] in accordance with Procedural Order #XX on or before midday GMT on [date stated].
2. Save as expressly amended herein, the provisions of Procedural Order #XX shall continue in full force and effect.
3. The expenses of this Order shall be costs in the arbitration.

Rule 39(1)(b)

We submit that this is self-explanatory.

Rule 39(2)

This mirrors s.41(7) of the 1996 Act with some drafting differences which, we submit, are inconsequential.

As a matter of practical common sense, arbitrators should beware overreaction to non-compliance and should not rush into r.39(2)—it would be easy to take (unconscious) umbrage at having one's magisterial orders ignored.

The tribunal has four exhaustively-listed remedies open to it and these are expected to cover most eventualities without recourse to the court under s.46; while these four remedies are self-evidentlly non-exclusive, tribunals should be wary of double-penalty; it is submitted that these remedies are potentially very powerful (e.g. failure to disclose documents might bar part or all of the defence) whereas passing the baton to the courts may be less so in many cases.

Rule 39(2)(a)

Proportionality and relevance are the keys, e.g. a failure to disclose documents relating to a particular part of a case, or to give further information of that part of the case, the tribunal might consider the weight (possibly zero in many practical instances) it places on the affected parts of the claim; sometimes that can mean that in effect a claim must fail, or (if the respondent is the defaulter) that it must succeed, but usually only part of the overall case is affected. However, art.V(1)(d) of the New York Convention may be rellevant here.

Rule 39(2)(b)

The "adverse inferences" must be limited to whatever was the subject of the peremptory order and does not permit the tribunal any wider discretion.

Rule 39(2)(c)

This includes possibly dismissing the claim but this is a drastic measure not to be imposed lightly; common sense suggests issuing appropriate warnings and taking in appropriate representations.

A common order in these circumstances is for service of defence submissions, the sanction for non-compliance being that the tribunal will proceed to its award on the basis of the submissions and documentary evidence then available. However, one particular problem that arises quite regularly is that the claimant has not in fact exhibited with its claim all the evidence on which it wished to rely with the consequence that, following the respondent's failure to comply with the r.39 order, the claimant then asks to put in further evidence, while expecting the tribunal simply to proceed with that new evidence without giving the respondent a chance to comment. The tribunal should, in these circumstances, give the respondent the chance to comment and, perhaps, a chance to put in further evidence itself.

Rule 39(2)(d)

The key phrase is, "consequences of the non-compliance": inter alia, the costs consequences must also be limited to whatever was the subject of the peremptory order and do not permit the tribunal any wider discretion.

Rule 40: Consolidation of proceedings **D**

40.—(1) Parties may agree—
    (a) to consolidate the arbitration with another arbitration, or
    (b) to hold concurrent hearings.
(2) But the tribunal may not order such consolidation, or the holding of concurrent hearings, on its own initiative.

DEFINITIONS
  "arbitration": ss.2(1), (2), 31(1)
  "tribunal": ss.2(1), 31(1)

STATUS
This is a default rule so it is open to the parties to modify it, agree something different or disapply it completely (see s.9).

MODEL LAW
The Model Law makes no reference to consolidation.

COMMENTARY
None of the UNCITRAL, ICC nor LCIA Rules address consolidation or concurrent hearings but the Swiss Rules do (art.4) with the curious feature that the decision concerning consolidation will made by the chambers (i.e. the Chambers of Commerce of the six cantons), not by the tribunal, after full consultation with all parties. This means that the relevant cantonal chamber will be the decision-making body, not a committee of all six.

Both the LCIA (art.22.1(h)) and Swiss Rules (art.4(2)) provide for the joining of third parties to the arbitration, a separate matter from that covered by r.40. However, joinder is very rare in practice since it requires all parties to agree. These rules do not address joinder at all, there having been no interest shown in the matter during the consultation process.

There are two main types of consolidation (a) where an employer is in dispute with a main contractor and the latter is in dispute with a sub-contractor on a construction project and the subject matter of the dispute is the same, and (b) commodity "string" contracts where A sells a parcel of goods to B who sells it to C ... and Y sells it to Z who takes delivery.

In the first type, a single arbitration *Employer v Main Contractor v Sub Contractor* might appear logical so that there is one hearing with one roomful of witnesses and so on. However, in practice this almost never happens either because the parties cannot agree to proceed this way and/or because the two disputes are not in fact identical despite superficial appearances to the contrary and/or because MC might envisage itself being sandwiched between E and SC and losing out to both.

In the second, the rules of the main commodity trading associations provide that, within certain limitations, the 25 arbitrations $A\ v\ B, B\ v\ C, \ldots Y\ v\ Z$ shall be consolidated into one single arbitration, effectively $A\ v\ Z$.

A highly impressive example of concurrent arbitrations was seen in a recent LMAA case (*Bunge SA v Adm Do Brasil Ltda* [2009] EWHC 845 (Comm)) where there were nine arbitrations arising out of the same shipment of soybean meal and the arbitrations were heard together, with, in the words of Tomlinson J., "sensible co-operation as to representation and evidence". Two arbitrators sat on all nine tribunals, a third sat on seven and the eighth and ninth arbitration had different third arbitrators. The five arbitrators issued one set of reasons which were common to all nine references. It would, of course, have been simpler with three arbitrators, not five.

When arbitrations cannot be consolidated or run concurrently, one alternative sometimes seen in practice is to run one arbitration in the morning, the other in the afternoon, with the intention of matching the two sets of proceedings. This can be assisted by having the same tribunal.

In such cases, if the arbitrations are not to be consolidated or conducted concurrently, r.26 applies so that everything in each arbitration is strictly confidential from the other, which might present significant practical difficulties where one party is common to both and/or one or more arbitrators is common.

Construction arbitrators preach the consolidation gospel energetically at conferences and the like but they rarely happen in practice for the reasons given above (and others).

Rule 40

We submit that this is self-explanatory.

Part 5

Powers of court in relation to arbitral proceedings

Rule 41: Referral of point of law **D**

41. The Outer House may, on an application by any party, determine any point of Scots law arising in the arbitration.

DEFINITIONS
"arbitration": ss.2(1), 31(1)
"Outer House": s.31(1)
"party": ss.2(1), 31 (1), (2)

STATUS
This is a default rule so it is open to the parties to modify it, agree something different or disapply it completely (see s.9).

An arbitration agreement made before the commencement of the Act which disapplied the now repealed default provision in s.3 of the Administration of Justice (Scotland) Act 1972 is deemed to be an agreement to disapply r.41 unless the parties otherwise agree (s.36(8)). Given that many arbitration clauses excluded the unpopular s.3 it is important to note that these clauses will still be effective to exclude r.41, unless the parties agree that r.41 should apply. Equally, art.18.5 of SAC07 will be effective to exclude r.41 unless disapplied.

MODEL LAW
There is no equivalent provision of the Model Law.

COMMENTARY
This rule replaces the existing stated case procedure under s.3 of the Administration of Justice (Scotland) Act 1972. Under that procedure a party could at any time during the arbitration until the issue of the final award, ask the tribunal to state a case to the Inner House of the Court of Session asking it to give a binding opinion on any question of law which had arisen. The tribunal could decline to do so only on very narrow grounds and any refusal by the tribunal to do so could be reviewed by the court. It was widely believed that the procedure was open to abuse through parties seeking referrals to the court on dubious points of law in order to delay a final award or put financial pressure on the other party (See *ERDC Construction Ltd v HM Love & Co (No.2)*, 1996 S.C. 523, per Lord Hope at 528). The Dervaird Committee Report (1996) (para.5.22) had advised its abolition.

However there can be merit in the obtaining from a court of a binding opinion on a point of law of general importance (see DAC Report, para.218). Equally a preliminary ruling on a point of law may prevent an appeal against the final award on the basis of that point of law. Accordingly the framers of the legislation were persuaded not to throw the baby out with the bathwater but instead to provide a mechanism to allow the tribunal to seek a binding opinion on a point of Scots law but with safeguards against the potential for abuse which previously existed. Those safeguards are contained in r.42 which is mandatory if parties have not excluded r.41.

Rule 41

In contrast to the old s.3, an application is made to the Outer House of the Court of Session and not the Inner House. Given that it is quicker to secure the services of a single Outer House judge rather than a three judge Inner House court, this will speed up the procedure. It is hoped that if the application concerns a point of commercial law the court will allocate the application to a commercial judge even though strictly speaking an application in a commercial matter would not be a "commercial action" in terms of the Rules of the Court of Session 1994.

The use of the word "may" indicates that the court has a residual discretion to refuse to determine the point of law. That discretion might be exercised where for example, the parties have agreed that an issue be referred, but the court regards the matter as unimportant or not properly arising in the arbitration (under s.45 of the 1996 Act the court must be satisfied that the question substantially affects the rights of one or more of the parties). It is however difficult to imagine the court declining to determine the point of law if the validity conditions in r.42(2) have been met. In *Taylor Woodrow Holdings Ltd v Barnes* [2006] EWHC 1693 (TCC); [2006] 2 All E.R. (Comm) 735; [2006] B.L.R. 377, the equivalent to the condition in r.42(2)(a) (consent of all parties) had been met, but it was argued by the claimants in the arbitration that the court should exercise its discretion to refuse to determine the point of law on the grounds that (i) the point should be decided by the arbitrator who was very experienced and who had been chosen by the parties; (ii) the proposed question of law was entangled with the facts which were for him to determine; and (iii) that there would be no saving in cost as the evidential hearing to take place four or five months later in any event. Jackson J. rejected the argument observing (i) that in that case the parties had expressly consented to the making of the application; (ii) there was no dispute over the facts relevant to the question of law which was one of the interpretation of the contract; and (iii) if the respondents in the arbitration were correct on that point of law it would decide the whole arbitration and that this would save substantial sums of money in the evidential hearing.

Only a point of Scots law may be determined. This follows from the position under Scots law that the content of foreign laws are issues of fact to be proved by expert evidence. The Court of Session would not presume to give a binding opinion on the content of a foreign law. With regard to Scots law there is no reason why the point of law could not cover both substantive and procedural law, including the Scots law of arbitration and the meaning of the Act itself, apart from any question as to the tribunal's jurisdiction which is dealt with by rr.22 and 23.

On what is a "point of law" as opposed to a point of fact, the classic explanation is contained in *Edwards v Bairstow* [1956] A.C. 14 at 34–36.

The following have been recognised to be "points of law":
- the meaning of a rule of substantive law;
- the meaning of a contractual document (*Halfdan Grieg & Co A/S v Sterling Coal & Navigation Corp (The Lysland)* [1973] Q.B. 843, per Lord Denning M.R. at 863)
- the meaning of a rule of procedural arbitral law, e.g. the duty to act fairly *ERDC Construction Ltd v HM Love & Co (No.2)*, 1996 S.C. 523 at 527–528;

- whether any concluded finding in fact contained in an award is based on evidence before the arbitrator or is one which no reasonable arbitrator would have reached—but not merely whether the finding in fact is correct—that being a question of fact and not law.

The exercise or proposed exercise by the arbitrator of a discretion where it is not alleged that he has misunderstood any rule of law or contractual document or that he has exercised it or proposes to exercise it in a way in which no reasonable arbitrator would exercise it is not a "question of law", e.g. in an award of expenses (*ERDC Construction Ltd v HM Love & Co (No.2)*, 1996 S.C. 523 at 531).

Rule 42: Point of law referral: procedure etc. M

42.—(1) This rule applies only where an application is made under rule 41.
(2) Such an application is valid only if—
 (a) the parties have agreed that it may be made, or
 (b) the tribunal has consented to it being made and the court is satisfied—
  (i) that determining the question is likely to produce substantial savings in expenses,
  (ii) that the application was made without delay, and
  (iii) that there is a good reason why the question should be determined by the court.
(3) The tribunal may continue with the arbitration pending determination of the application.
(4) The Outer House's determination of the question is final (as is any decision by the Outer House as to whether an application is valid).

DEFINITIONS
"arbitration": ss.2(1), 31(1)
"court": s.31(1)
"Outer House": s.31(1)
"party": ss.2(1), 31(1), (2)

STATUS
Rule 42 is a mandatory rule. This is to ensure that if the parties have not excluded the referral procedure by excluding the application of r.41, they cannot through their agreement force the tribunal to effectively sist (or stay) the arbitral proceedings (although the tribunal has a discretion to do so). The aim is to ensure that the delay caused through the previous s.3 of the Administration of Justice (Scotland) Act 1972 can be avoided as far as possible.

MODEL LAW
There is no equivalent provision of the Model Law.

COMMENTARY
In contrast with the old s.3 of the 1972 Act, r.42 has been designed to promote the speed and reduce the cost of arbitration. In particular:
- if both parties do not agree to the reference, the consent of the tribunal is now essential and cannot be overruled by the court, whereas under the old s.3 the refusal of the tribunal to make the stated case to the court could be overruled by the court itself;

- a refusal by the tribunal to consent is no longer subject to judicial review which could further delay the arbitral process (s.13(1)(b));
- there is specific provision that the tribunal may continue with the arbitration pending resolution of the reference to the court;
- the application is made by a party using a straightforward petition rather than the clumsy and time consuming stated case procedure which involved written input from both the arbitrator and the parties.

Expenses of the application will not be included in the "arbitration expenses" (see commentary to r.59) but will fall to be dealt with by the court rather than the tribunal but, on an analogy with the preparation of the former stated case, the expenses of obtaining the consent of the tribunal fall to be dealt with by the tribunal in terms of r.62 (*Thomson v Earl of Galloway*, 1919 S.C. 611; 1919 2 S.L.T. 80).

Rule 42(1) and (2)

The court can only consider the application if it is valid. Accordingly before taking any steps to consider the merits of the application, the court must satisfy itself that the application meets the test of validity set out in r.42(2). There are two ways in which an application may be valid: (a) that all of the parties have consented to it being made; or (b) that the tribunal has consented to it being made and the court is satisfied on all three of the sub-criteria in r.42(2)(b).

The consent to the application being made can exist in the arbitration agreement itself (*Taylor Woodrow Holdings Ltd v Barnes* [2006] EWHC 1693 (TCC); [2006] 2 All E.R. (Comm) 725; [2006] B.L.R. 377).

The criteria are the same as those in r.23 which allows a similar application to be made in respect of jurisdiction. The sub-criteria are stringent and are intended to preserve a useful tool for the parties where a particular point of law is critical to the dispute and an early decision from the court would be determinative, while at the same time guarding against abuse by a party seeking to cause delay for its own interests.

The requirement for the tribunal to consent serves as a safeguard against the abuse of delay and additional expense identified in *ERDC Construction Ltd v HM Love & Co (No.2)*, 1996 S.C. 523. In deciding whether to give consent the tribunal will have to comply with its duty in r.24 to conduct the arbitration without unnecessary delay and without incurring unnecessary expense. This suggests that a tribunal will not consent to a referral unless it takes the view that the application will promote speed and economy.

Even if the tribunal consents, the court must still be satisfied on all three sub-criteria in r.42(2)(b). "Likely" for the purposes of r.42(2)(b)(i) echoes s.45(2)(b)(i) of the 1996 Act. The use of "likely" in the 1996 Act as opposed to the use of "might" in the previous English 1979 Act was intended to raise the bar for the demonstration of "substantial savings". Equally "substantial savings" seems to be intended to indicate large savings rather than de minimis savings. "Delay" for the purposes of r.42(2)(b)(ii) is likely to be measured from the point when the need to have the point of law determined became evident. In short, the court might be satisfied where it is clear that a contested point of law lies at the heart of the dispute, which if it was not resolved at the outset would result in the lengthening of any evidential hearing due to both legal propositions requiring to be considered and an appeal under r.69.

Rule 42(1) and (2)—Procedure

The application is made by petition in the style contained in RCS Form 14.4 (RCS rr.14.2(h), 14.4) or, if there are undisposed of Outer House proceedings, by note (RCS r.99.5). If both parties consent to the application, it is sensible for them to agree, if possible, the terms of the petition, in order to save time and the expense of answers. The requirements for the petition are set out in RCS r.14.4 and Ch.99 (r.15.2 and Ch.99 for notes), together with the need to:
  (i) aver the giving of consent of the other party or parties to the making of the application; or
  (ii) aver the consent of the arbitrators making up the tribunal to the application being made and the circumstances in which the pre-requisites for an application in r.42(2)(b) (i.e. the substantial savings in expense, etc.) are satisfied;
  (iii) identify the point of law to be determined; the Outer House will not have the power that the English High Court has of on its own initiative amending the wording of the point of law concerned (cf. *HOK Sport Ltd v Aintree Racecourse Co Ltd* [2003] B.L.R. 155 at [39]);
  (iv) require service or intimation on any non-applicant parties to the arbitration and the members of the tribunal and anyone interested in the arbitration.

Together with the petition the applicant should lodge with the Court of Session:
  (i) as productions any written consent of the other party or parties to the making of the application, any written consent of the tribunal to the application being made, and any documentary evidence in support of the matters in r.42(2)(b) as averred in the petition;
  (ii) as productions any documents which are necessary for the determination of the point of law, including the written statements of claim and defence (the pleadings) and any documents lodged in the arbitration which are necessary for the determination of the point of law;
  (iii) the bundle of court documents known as the process (see RCS rr.4.3, 4.4).

Inventories of any productions should be intimated to the other parties and members of the tribunal. On the lodging of the above, the applicant must move for a first order for service on the other party or parties to the arbitration or their representatives in the arbitration, and the members of the tribunal and anyone else who has an interest to allow such persons to lodge answers opposing the petition if they wish (RCS r.99.5).

If the consent of the court is required in order to validate the petition, then after the end of the period for answers, whether answers have been lodged or not, the petitioner should enrol a motion to have the court determine the petition as valid under r.42(2)(b). It seems appropriate for that preliminary matter to be decided before the court and the parties devote themselves to the point of law in issue.

Once the petition is validated, then whether answers are lodged or not, (and there may be scope for a joint petition), the petitioner must apply by motion for further procedure (RCS r.14.8) to have the point of law determined.

If the petitioner is not proactive in pursuing the petition, the respondent can enrol a motion to have the case put out for a hearing to allow the petitioner to explain his delay. Typically a hearing will be required to resolve the point of law but it might not be necessary for the validation issue, if the arguments are clear from the petition and any answers or documents. However the court may make such order for further procedure as it thinks fit (RCS r.99.5). What is written above applies to notes in the same way as it does to petitions.

Rule 42(3)

Notwithstanding the making of an application the tribunal has a power to continue with the arbitration and this must be exercised in the light of the tribunal's duty under r.24. In this context an issue for the tribunal may be whether there is an aspect of the case which can be dealt with without the need for the court's decision on the referral. If there is such an issue, then it might seem reasonable for the tribunal to dispose of that issue while the court is deciding the referral.

Rule 42(4)

The interests of speed make it appropriate that there should be no delay in an appeal to the Inner House. If it is thought that an appeal to the Inner House might be necessary for the point to be resolved, then the course to follow is to prepare to attempt to make a legal error appeal after the making of the award should it go against one.

The tribunal is bound to follow and apply the decision of the court on the referral (*Mitchell-Gill v Buchan*, 1921 S.C. 390; 1921 1 S.L.T. 197). Failure to do so would amount to serious irregularity in terms of r.68 and inevitably lead to an appeal on that ground. However if the decision on the referral forms part of the reasoning for an award it may be possible to have the decision on the referral reviewed by means of an appeal under r.69 (see *Babanaft International Co SA v Avanti Petroleum Inc (The Oltenia)* [1982] 2 Lloyd's Rep. 99, per Donaldson L.J. at 107, in relation to the similar provisions in the former English Arbitration Act 1979).

Rule 43: Variation of time limits set by parties **D**

43. The court may, on an application by the tribunal or any party, vary any time limit relating to the arbitration which is imposed—
    (a) in the arbitration agreement, or
    (b) by virtue of any other agreement between the parties.

DEFINITIONS
    "arbitration agreement": ss.4, 31(1)
    "court": s.31(1)
    "party": ss.2(1), 31(1), (2)
    "tribunal": ss.2(1), 31(1)

STATUS
This is a default rule so it is open to the parties to modify it, agree something different or disapply it completely (see s.9).

MODEL LAW
This rule has no equivalent in the Model Law.

COMMENTARY
This rule allows a party or the tribunal to seek variation of any time limit which is imposed either (a) in the arbitration agreement itself; or (b) "by

virtue of" any other agreement between the parties. The time limits which are the subject of this rule are ones such as a limitation on the period for commencing an arbitration or a time limit in institutional rules that the parties have agreed to adopt. The object of the rule is to provide some leeway for the prevention of "substantial injustice" through the existence of a time limit that is too tight for the circumstances in question. The ability to seek variation of time limits exists in Scottish litigation, known as the ability to seek "prorogation" of a time limit. This rule provides the equivalent for arbitration.

The rule does not however apply to time limits for the taking of steps of procedure imposed by the arbitrator himself. Such time limits are mandatory and if they are not complied with the situation is dealt with by rr.37, 38, and 39 as appropriate.

One example of the use of r.43 is where the agreement requires the tribunal to make a decision within a particular time and there are practical difficulties in achieving that time limit.

The variation is of any time limit relating to the arbitration which is imposed either (a) in the arbitration agreement; or (b) "by virtue of" any other agreement between the parties. The reference to "arbitration agreement" is straightforward enough (see s.4). Are the time limits imposed under the rules themselves, e.g. in rr.6 and 7 in relation to the appointment of an arbitrator, covered by this rule? On one view of this rule such rules are not rules imposed in the arbitration agreement itself. They are imposed in the rules. Therefore they cannot be varied under r.43. The view has some support from the heading of r.43. On another view the object of r.43 is to provide some flexibility for the parties in relation to time limits relating to the arbitration which they themselves have agreed to impose. By agreeing that the arbitration should have a Scottish seat they have agreed to impose the Scottish Arbitration Rules except in so far as competently varied by them. It would moreover seem odd that a party should have a right to seek variation of a time limit that was expressly mentioned it the arbitration agreement but not have the right in relation to a time limit that was by implication imported into the arbitration agreement and which was, like the express terms of the agreement, open to variation by agreement of the parties.

Clearly, ideally an application should be made before the time limit has expired. The rule could be read as only permitting applications before the expiry of the time limit. However a more flexible reading would allow a retrospective variation.

An application may be made to either the Outer House of the Court of Session (RCS r.14.2(h)) or to the sheriff court of the sheriffdom determined under s.6 of the Sheriff Courts (Scotland) Act 1907. Section 6 applies because r.43 appears to fall within s.21(1)(a) of the Civil Jurisdiction and Judgments Act 1982 which excludes the jurisdictional rules in Sch.8 to the 1982 Act. The test for a variation of time limit and details of procedure are set out in r.44 and its commentary.

Rule 44: Time limit variation: procedure etc. **M**

44.—(1) This rule applies only where an application for variation of time limit is made under rule 43.

(2) Such a variation may be made only if the court is satisfied—
    (a) that no arbitral process for varying the time limit is available, and
    (b) that someone would suffer a substantial injustice if no variation was made.

(3) It is for the court to determine the extent of any variation.
(4) The tribunal may continue with the arbitration pending determination of an application.
(5) The court's decision on whether to make a variation (and, if so, on the extent of the variation) is final.

DEFINITIONS
"court": s.31(1)
"party": ss.2(1), 31(1), (2)
"rule": s.31(1)
"tribunal": ss.2(1), 31(1)

STATUS
This is a mandatory rule.

MODEL LAW
This rule has no equivalent in the Model Law.

COMMENTARY

Rule 44(1)–(3)

The court will only consider the application if there is no arbitral process for varying the time limit. This is consistent with the approach throughout the rules that an approach to the court is a step of last resort. This is also reflected in the requirement that the non-making of the variation would result in "substantial injustice". That is a high requirement and it is set high because the underlying policy is that variation of the time limits covered by r.43 should be for the parties themselves or the parties and the tribunal to resolve by agreement.

The court has a discretion to decide not merely whether there should be a variation but as to what the variation should be. It is therefore not restricted to either granting the variation sought or refusing the application.

If the application is made to the Outer House it is made by petition in the style contained in RCS Form 14.4 (RCS rr.14.2(h), 14.4) or, if there are undisposed of Outer House proceedings, by note (RCS r.99.5). The requirements for the petition are set out in RCS r.14.4 and Ch.99 (r.15.2 and Ch.99 for notes), together with the need to:
  (i) aver the time limit in question;
  (ii) aver the circumstances in which the prerequisites for an application in r.44(2) are satisfied;
  (iii) aver the reasons why the usual period of 21 days for answers should be dispensed with (if that is necessary);
  (iv) require service or intimation on the other parties to the arbitration and the members of the tribunal.
If a shorter period of notice is required, then this should also be craved in the petition.

Together with the petition the applicant should lodge with the Court of Session:
  (i) as a production, any written arbitration agreement in which or other agreement or other document by virtue of which, the time limit is imposed;
  (ii) the bundle of court documents known as the process (see RCS rr.4.3, 4.4).
Inventories of any productions should be intimated to the other parties and members of the tribunal.

On the lodging of the above, the applicant must move for a first order for service on the other party or parties to the arbitration or their representatives in the arbitration, and the members of the tribunal and anyone else who has an interest to allow such persons to lodge answers opposing the petition if they wish within 21 days (RCS r.99.5). Therefore it is advised that if a shorter period is required a motion for that shorter period should be sought.

After the end of the period for answers, whether answers have been lodged or not, the petitioner should enrol a motion to have the court determine the petition, with or without a hearing as may be appropriate in the circumstances. What is written above applies to notes in the same way as it does to petitions.

If the application is made to the sheriff court it is made by summary application in the style contained in Form 1 of Sch.1 to the Act of Sederunt (Summary Applications, Statutory Applications and Appeals etc. Rules) 1999 (SI 1999/929) ("SASAR") (SASAR r.2.4). The requirements for the summary application are broadly the same as for the petition described above. Detailed reference should be made to the SASAR.

Expenses of the application will not be included in the "arbitration expenses" (see the commentary to r.59 below) but will fall to be dealt with by the court rather than the tribunal.

Rule 44(4)

The tribunal has a discretion to continue with the arbitration whilst the court is determining the application. The best resolution of this issue is to have the parties agree on the procedure whilst the application is ongoing. If parties cannot agree, then whilst the tribunal has a duty to conduct the arbitration without unnecessary delay (under r.24) it also has a duty to treat the parties fairly (under r.24). If the conduct of the arbitration whilst a time limit variation application is pending could result in unfairness to the applicant, then the tribunal will have to be wary in continuing with the arbitration during what should be a fairly short period during which the court is considering the application. Of course unfairness to the applicant will have to be weighed against unfairness to the respondent party who will not wish to be prejudiced by any delay in the process, particularly if the application could reasonably have been made at an earlier stage. The matter will be for the tribunal which will seek to avoid any substantial injustice which could conceivably result in a challenge to the award for serious irregularity (see r.68 below)

Rule 44(5)

The decision of the "court" is clearly final. Where the court is the Outer House, the position is clear. Where the court is the "sheriff" it is not as clear given that in terms of Sch.1 to the Interpretation Act 1978 "sheriff" includes "sheriff principal" unless the contrary intention appears. Might there be an appeal to the sheriff principal? Two factors suggest not. First, the rule contemplates only one decision which is final. This would appear to exclude the possibility of a review on appeal by the sheriff principal. Secondly, the existence of an appeal would be inconsistent with the founding principle in s.1 that the object of arbitration is to resolve disputes inter alia without unnecessary delay or expense.

Rule 45: Court's power to order attendance of witnesses and disclosure of evidence **M**

45.—(1) The court may, on an application by the tribunal or any party, order any person—
(a) to attend a hearing for the purposes of giving evidence to the tribunal, or
(b) to disclose documents or other material evidence to the tribunal.

(2) But the court may not order a person to give any evidence, or to disclose anything, which the person would be entitled to refuse to give or disclose in civil proceedings.

(3) The tribunal may continue with the arbitration pending determination of an application.

(4) The court's decision on whether to make an order is final.

DEFINITIONS
"court": s.31(1)
"party": ss.2(1), 31(1), (2)
"tribunal": ss.2(1), 31(1)

STATUS
This rule is mandatory. Parties cannot exclude the ability of each other to obtain witness attendance or document or other tangible evidence production orders.

MODEL LAW
Article 27 of the Model Law provides that the arbitral tribunal or a party with the approval of the arbitral tribunal may request from a competent court of the state where the Model Law applies, assistance in taking evidence and that the court may execute the request within its competence and according to its rules on taking evidence. Rule 45 is in line with art.27, except that it allows a party to seek assistance from the court even without the approval of the tribunal. In practice, however as noted in the commentary to r.45, it will be advisable for parties to exhaust any arbitral remedies before seeking the assistance of the court.

COMMENTARY
It is for a party to secure the attendance of a witness or witnesses to a hearing which is concerned with the establishment of the facts of the dispute. Equally it is for a party to obtain whatever documents it may wish to rely upon in the presentation of its case to the tribunal. This rule provides for either the Court of Session or the sheriff court to assist a party or the tribunal in ordering the attendance of witnesses and the disclosure of documents or other material evidence.

Rule 45 widens the scope for recovery to tangible evidence other than documents. It also enables the recovery of documents other than those merely written by or passing to and from the parties. Rule 45 expedites the procedure for recovery by omitting the need for the initial application to the arbitrator and by omitting the need for a commissioner to be appointed to receive the documentary evidence on behalf of the tribunal.

Under the pre-Act common law, if there was any doubt about whether a witness would attend a hearing, a party could apply to the arbitrator to certify that there was good reason for the witness to be ordered to be present at the hearing and then armed with the certificate apply to the Court of Session or sheriff for a warrant for citation of that witness before the arbitrator at the hearing. Failure by a cited witness to attend would then amount to contempt of court. A warrant for citation to attend cannot however be enforced outwith Scotland. For that reason under the common law the court refused to grant a warrant to cite a witness resident outwith Scotland and accepted an argument that the party requiring the witness should seek the appointment of a commissioner from both the arbitrator and the Court of Session to take the evidence of the witness which commission could be enforced under the now repealed Evidence by Commission Act 1843 (*Highland Railway Co. v Mitchell* (1868) 6 M. 896). If the witness is outwith Scotland, then steps to bring him before the tribunal will have to be taken in the territory where the witness is. Where the witness is outwith Scotland and is unwilling to travel to Scotland another option was to apply to the arbitrator for the certificate of good reason for an order together with a recommendation for the appointment of a particular person to act as a commissioner of the arbitrator to take the evidence of the witness. Then, having obtained the certificate and recommendation the party could petition the Court of Session to grant warrant for the commissioner to take the evidence of the witness in question and to report it to the arbitrator. However the commission, like the warrant for citation could not be enforced outwith Scotland. Unfortunately the Evidence by Commission Act 1843 has not been re-enacted in relation to commissions for use in arbitrations by the Evidence (Proceedings in Other Jurisdictions) Act 1975 (*Commerce and Industry Insurance Co. of Canada v Certain Underwriters of Lloyd's of London* [2001] 1 W.L.R. 1323).

Similarly it is for a party to obtain the documents that it needs in order to establish its case. At common law if a party was having difficulties in recovering relevant documents the remedy was similar to that relating to witnesses described above. The party had to draft a document known as a "specification of documents" setting out in paragraphs known as "calls" the documents sought to be recovered with reference to the issues of fact in his pleadings (statements of case) to which they were supposed to relate. The specification was then presented to the arbitrator with an application for a commissioner to be appointed to receive the documents set out in the specification from any person in possession of the documents, i.e. the "haver" of the documents. The arbitrator would decide the application on the basis of the relevancy of the documents in relation to a party's existing case and matters such as privilege. An application to recover documents tending to show a fact not already in issue in terms of the pleadings would be seen as a "fishing diligence" and would be refused. In this respect Scots law is more restrictive in relation to recovery than the law of England and Wales and many other "common law" jurisdictions. If the arbitrator granted the application he would approve the specification of documents and appoint the commissioner to receive the documents within the scope of the approved specification of documents from any haver to whom he was directed by the recovering party. Once he was aware of the identity and address of the haver, the commissioner would then request the haver to produce the documents. If the haver refused, the party seeking recovery could apply to the court for a warrant for citation of the haver to produce the documents to the court's commissioner who might or might not be the same as that appointed by the arbitrator (as in *Crudens Ltd, Petitioners*, 1971 S.C. 64). The court could grant the warrant in relation to a haver even if he was outwith Scotland. However as with the attendance of witnesses, the order of the court was not enforceable by a Scottish court against a haver who was outwith Scotland and the commissioner would have to apply to court or appropriate authority of the country where the haver was present (*John Nimmo & Son Ltd, Petitioners* (1905) 8 F. 173; (1905) 13 S.L.T. 539).

Rule 45(1)

Rule 45 (1) gives the court power to order (a) any person to attend a hearing for the purpose of giving evidence or (b) any person to disclose, "documents or other material evidence" to the tribunal. These powers may be exercised not merely on the application of a party but also the tribunal itself. It is suggested that the rule must be interpreted in the light of two of the founding principles of the Act namely that the object of arbitration is to resolve disputes fairly, impartially and without unnecessary delay or expense, and that the court should not intervene in an arbitration except as provided by the Act (see s.1 above).

Where the application is by a party, it is suggested that where practicable any arbitral remedy be exhausted before a party makes an application to the court. For example it is suggested that where it is thought that the tangible evidence is in the hands of the other party, a recovering party should, if possible, first seek a direction from the arbitrator ordering disclosure under rr.35, 31 and 28(2)(c). Rule 45 gives the court a discretion on whether to grant the order. If a party has not first made an application to the arbitrator, then it is conceivable that the court might, if there was no particular urgency, refuse the application as unnecessary or refuse to award the expenses of the application to the successful applicant.

An application may be made by the tribunal itself. This could arise either where the tribunal's orders were being disregarded and the tribunal wished to obtain the evidence rather than decide the case without it, or where the tribunal decided to exercise an inquisitorial role as it may do under r.28(2)(e).

An order requiring a person to attend a hearing to give evidence is directly effective on the witness once he is aware of it. A separate citation of the witness as under the former common law is not appropriate. There is no restriction on the order being made against a witness who is outwith Scotland although as with the common law enforcement will depend on the witness entering Scotland or the law of the territory where the witness is.

The order for disclosure is effective against any haver of the evidence named in the order and is not restricted to the parties. The order may cover not merely documents but, "other material evidence" regardless of who was the author. In these respects recovery under r.45 is wider than the common law rule for recovery of documents in an approved specification of documents, which was restricted to documents written or sent by or received by a party. The key issue in an application under r.45 will be whether the tangible evidence sought (whether documentary or otherwise) is "material" to the issues in dispute before the tribunal. This should prevent the abuse of r.45 for the purpose of fishing for evidence to allow a case to be made which is not currently made.

Rule 45(1)—Procedure

An application may be made to either the Outer House of the Court of Session (RCS r.14.2(h)) or to a sheriff court of the appropriate sheriffdom determined under s.6 of the Sheriff Courts (Scotland) Act 1907. Section 6 applies because r.45 appears to fall within s.21(1)(a) of the Civil Jurisdiction and Judgments Act 1982 which excludes the jurisdictional rules in Sch.8 to the 1982 Act.

If the application is made to the Outer House it is made by petition in the style contained in RCS Form 14.4 (RCS rr.14.2(h), 14.4) or, if there are undisposed of Outer House proceedings, by note (RCS r.99.5). The requirements for the petition are set out in RCS r.14.4 and Ch.99 (r.15.2 and Ch.99 for notes), together with the need to:
- (i) aver why the order against the witness or haver is necessary;
- (ii) aver the circumstances in which the prerequisites for an application in r.45(1) are satisfied.

If a shorter or no period of notice is required, then this should also be craved in the petition. Any documents or material evidence to be disclosed in terms of the order should be listed in a schedule to the petition, preferably in the form of "calls" as one would find in a specification of documents. It may be helpful for the court to narrate in the schedule next to the evidence in question, its relevancy to the issues in the arbitration.

Together with the petition the applicant should lodge with the Court of Session:
- (i) as a production, any written arbitration agreement in which or other agreement or other document by virtue of which, the time limit is imposed;
- (ii) the written statements of case and defence in the arbitration (the pleadings);
- (iii) the bundle of court documents known as the process (see RCS r.4.3 and 4.4).

Inventories of any productions should be intimated to the other parties on whom the petition is served.

On the lodging of the above, the petitioner should enrol a motion to have the court determine the petition, with or without a hearing as may be appropriate in the circumstances. What is written above applies to notes in the same way as it does to petitions.

If the application is made to the sheriff court it is made by summary application in the style contained in SASAR Sch.1 Form 1 (SASAR r.2.4). The requirements for the summary application are broadly the same as for the petition described above. Detailed reference should be made to the SASAR.

Expenses of the application will not be included in the "arbitration expenses" (see the commentary to r.57 below) but will fall to be dealt with by the court rather than the tribunal.

Rule 45(2)

In considering whether to grant the order the court must apply the rules of privileged confidentiality as they exist in the Scots law of evidence whether under common law or statute. The reader is referred to the standard works on the law of evidence in Scotland. There is also a useful statement of the various categories in *Greens Annotated Rules of the Court of Session* (Edinburgh: W. Green), para.35.2.7. The recognised categories of communications which attract privileged confidentiality are:
- (1) solicitor (or other lawyer) and client;
- (2) communications *post litem motam* (for the purposes of or in anticipation of litigation);
- (3) communications with a view to achieving settlement ("without prejudice" communications);
- (4) public interest immunity;
- (5) communications between spouses;
- (6) self-incrimination; and

(7) communications made as a matter of moral duty, e.g. complaints to an appropriate body.

Confidentiality and privilege of a document or communication may be waived in whole or in part. Documents may be privileged and confidential or merely confidential. Thus documents or communications which are confidential pursuant to a contractual duty not to disclose their content, e.g. commercially confidential documents, journalists' sources, pursuant to a delictual duty of non-disclosure, e.g. doctors, or pursuant to a moral duty of non-disclosure, e.g. clergymen, are not on that basis privileged and immune from disclosure. For the document or communication to be immune from disclosure it must be not merely confidential but also fall acceptably within one of the above categories. In this context if a document or communication falls within one of the above categories it may still be liable to be disclosed if it forms part of the res gestae of the dispute, i.e. the communication is an integral part of the disputed issue for which its recovery is sought (*Kid v Bunyan* (1842) 5 D. 193).

If a haver or a party claims privileged confidentiality for a document, then it should be produced to the court in a sealed packet to allow the court to assess the validity of the claim.

Rule 45(3)

The tribunal has a discretion to continue with the arbitration whilst the court is determining the application. The best resolution of this issue is to have the parties agree on the procedure whilst the application is ongoing. If parties cannot agree, then whilst the tribunal has a duty to conduct the arbitration without unnecessary delay (under r.24) it also has a duty to treat the parties fairly (under r.24). Everything will depend on the subject matter of the application to the court, the stage which the arbitration has reached and the nature of any prejudice that might be caused through the delay in not progressing with the arbitration whilst, for example documents are sought to be recovered. It is clearly in the interests of the arbitral process that any recovery of material documents take place as early as possible so their importance can be assessed at an early stage and there is no delay in any evidential hearing that might have to take place through, in particular, the process of recovery of documents. Ultimately the question of whether and how the arbitration should proceed whilst an application under r.45 has been made but not yet determined, will be a matter for the tribunal. In applying its duties under r.4 the tribunal which will seek to avoid any substantial injustice which could conceivably result in a challenge to the award for serious irregularity (see r.68).

Rule 45(4)

The decision of the "court" is clearly final. Where the court is the Outer House, the position is clear. Where the court is the "sheriff" it is not as clear given that in terms of Sch.1 to the Interpretation Act 1978 "sheriff" includes "sheriff principal" unless the contrary intention appears. Might there be an appeal to the sheriff principal? Two factors suggest not. First, the rule contemplates only one decision which is final. This would appear to exclude the possibility of a review on appeal by the sheriff principal. Secondly, the existence of an appeal would be inconsistent with the founding principle in s.1 that the object of arbitration is to resolve disputes inter alia without unnecessary delay or expense.

Rule 46: Court's other powers in relation to arbitration **D**

46.—(1) The court has the same power in an arbitration as it has in civil proceedings—
    (a) to appoint a person to safeguard the interests of any party lacking capacity,
    (b) to order the sale of any property in dispute in the arbitration,
    (c) to make an order securing any amount in dispute in the arbitration,
    (d) to make an order under section 1 of the Administration of Justice (Scotland) Act 1972 (c. 59),
    (e) to grant warrant for arrestment or inhibition,
    (f) to grant interdict (or interim interdict), or
    (g) to grant any other interim or permanent order.
(2) But the court may take such action only—
    (a) on an application by any party, and
    (b) if the arbitration has begun—
        (i) with the consent of the tribunal, or
        (ii) where the court is satisfied that the case is one of urgency.
(3) The tribunal may continue with the arbitration pending determination of the application.
(4) This rule applies—
    (a) to arbitrations which have begun,
    (b) where the court is satisfied—
        (i) that a dispute has arisen or might arise, and
        (ii) that an arbitration agreement provides that such a dispute is to be resolved by arbitration.
(5) This rule does not affect—
    (a) any other powers which the court has under any enactment or rule of law in relation to arbitrations, or
    (b) the tribunal's powers.

DEFINITIONS
"arbitration": ss.2(1), 31(1)
"court": s.31(1)
"party": ss.2(1), 31(1), (2)
"tribunal": ss.2(1), 31(1)

STATUS
This is a default rule so it is open to the parties to modify it, agree something different or disapply it completely (see s.9).

MODEL LAW
The Model Law, following its amendment by UNCITRAL on July 7, 2006, provides for "interim measures" which are defined in art.17(2) (as amended) as:
"... any temporary measure, whether in the form of an award or in another form, by which at any time prior to the issuance of the award by which the dispute is finally decided, the arbitral tribunal orders a party to:
    (a) maintain or restore the status quo pending determination of the dispute;
    (b) take action that would prevent, or refrain from taking action that is likely to cause, current or imminent harm or prejudice the arbitral process itself;

(c) provide a means of preserving assets out of which a subsequent award may be satisfied; or
   (d) preserve evidence that may be relevant and material to the resolution of the dispute."

Under art.17(1) unless the parties otherwise agree, the tribunal is given power, at the request of a party, to grant such interim measures. Article 17E(1) provides that the tribunal may require the applicant for an interim measure to provide appropriate security in connection with that measure. Article 17F(2) gives power to the tribunal to require any party to promptly disclose any material change in the circumstances on the basis of which the measure was requested or granted.

Having provided power to the tribunal in relation to the interim measures, in art.17H the Model Law provides for the recognition and enforcement of interim measures by a competent court, irrespective of the country in which the interim measure was issued, subject to the provisions of art.17I. Article 17I gives limited defences to the recognition and enforcement by a court of interim measures. These are essentially the same as in relation to the recognition and enforcement of foreign arbitral awards under the New York Convention and s.20 with the addition of the following:

- that the tribunal's decision with respect to the provision of security in connection with the interim measure has not been complied with;
- that the interim measure has been terminated or suspended by the tribunal or where so empowered by the court of the state where the arbitration takes place or where the measure was granted;
- that the interim measure is incompatible with the powers conferred upon the ocurt unless the court decides to reformulate the interim measure to the extent necessary to adapt it to its own powers and procedures for the purposes of enforcing it but without modifying its substance.

As with the enforcement of foreign arbitral awards, art.17I(2) prohibits any review of the substance of the tribunal's decision on the interim measure.

Finally art.17J provides that the court should have the same power of issuing an interim measure in relation to arbitration proceedings within its state as it has in relation to litigation before it. Article 17J requires the court to "exercise such power in accordance with its own procedures in consideration of the specific feature of international arbitration."

A number of these features of the Model Law are reflected in r.46. However because r.46 applies only to arbitrations seated in Scotland, it does not give power to the courts in relation to what is defined in s.2(1) as, "arbitration between parties residing, or carrying on business, anywhere in the United Kingdom" or, "international arbitration". That is a pity. The only remedy would appear to be to seek to raise court proceedings in Scotland seeking the same remedies as in the arbitration, apply for the interim measures at the outset of those proceedings and then to apply for a sist of proceedings (*Mendok BV v Cumberland Maritime Corp*, 1989 S.L.T. 192). Jurisdiction would have to be established for such court proceedings.

COMMENTARY

Rule 46 provides important further powers for the sheriff court and the Court of Session to support Scottish seated arbitrations. It also provides powers to these courts where such arbitral proceedings have not begun but there is or there might become a dispute which in terms of an arbitration agreement is to be resolved by arbitration.

In relation to continuing arbitrations r.46(2)(b) provides that a court can exercise the powers mentioned in r.46(1) only with the consent of the tribunal unless the case is one of "urgency". This structure appears to originate from s.44(4) of the 1996 Act which itself implements the proposal of the DAC Report (para.215). This indicates that a party who wishes the powers to be exercised must first apply to the tribunal for its consent unless the case is one of urgency. It is unclear what a tribunal requires to be satisfied with before it gives its consent. Does the rule require it to in effect second guess what the court is likely to do if the court hears the application? The rule is unclear but given that the consent of the tribunal is necessary except in urgency, this suggests that the tribunal should in effect have to consider for itself whether the court should grant the remedy for which the party seeks consent to apply to the court. This approach gives primacy to the views of the tribunal which accords with the principle, purpose and spirit of arbitration which is that if the parties have entrusted the resolution of their dispute to an arbitral tribunal rather than merely to leave it to the courts, the views of the arbitral tribunal should be paramount. This approach is also consistent with the approach of the DAC which insisted on the requirement of consent, "in order to prevent any suggestion that the court might be used to interfere with or usurp the arbitral process or indeed any attempt to do so" (para.215). Further support comes from *Emmott v Michael Wilson & Partners Ltd* [2009] EWHC 1 (Comm); [2009] 1 Lloyd's Rep. 233, where under the 1996 Act equivalent of r.35 the tribunal directed a shareholding which was the subject matter of the dispute to be placed into its name pending the resolution of the dispute. When the tribunal's order was not complied with an application was made to the court for an order requiring compliance and an order under the equivalent of r.46 for freezing the shareholding. The tribunal had consented to the freezing order and the court took the view that the freezing order should be granted in order to help the arbitral process operate effectively.

If a party is discontent with the tribunal's refusal to consent to the application, judicial review is excluded (s.13(1)(b)) and the only potential remedies are:

- if the refusal related to an application concerning the merits of the arbitration, e.g. interim interdict, to treat the refusal as a provisional award and to seek to appeal it under rr.68 or 69;
- to seek to make a reference to the court under r.41 in relation to a point of law, probably with the consent of the other party.

If a party is discontent with the tribunal's grant of consent to the application its remedy is to challenge the substance of the consent in the hearing before the court.

Rule 46(3) also allows a party in a situation where a dispute has arisen or might arise and there is an arbitration agreement covering that dispute, but the arbitration has not yet begun (see r.1 above), to apply to the court for the exercise of a r.46(1) power as if the arbitration clause did not exist. In practice this is what occurred at common law whereby if a party to a contract required to obtain an interim interdict against the other party in a contract where there was an arbitration clause, the claimant would raise an action and seek interim interdict. The court would grant the interim interdict, quite possibly on an ex parte (without notice) basis which order would then be served on the defender who might seek to have it recalled. After the court had disposed of the interim order the action would be sisted to allow the arbitration to be begun. A similar outcome could ensue if a party required to obtain an interim order of specific implement, although this had to be sought in the Outer House of the Court of Session.

For some reason, unlike rr.41–45 there is no provision that the decision of the court is to be final. Nor is there provision that appeal is to be with leave of the court.

Rule 46(1)(a)—Appointment of safeguarder

Both the Court of Session and the sheriff court have power, if necessary on their own initiative, to appoint a guardian (or tutor or curator) ad litem to a party in a litigation who has no legal capacity and either has no guardian or whose guardian cannot act, e.g. because of a conflict of interest (*Ward v Walker*, 1920 S.C. 80—a workman's compensation arbitration where it was held that the arbitrator had the power to appoint a tutor ad litem to a child claimant whose mother had died and to whom no guardian had yet been appointed). The role of the guardian ad litem is to ensure that the case on behalf of the party lacking capacity is properly conducted. The appointment can be made in relation to a pursuer or defender at any time after the litigation has been raised (*Drummond's Trustees v Peel's Trustees*, 1929 S.C. 484). A guardian ad litem cannot be liable for the expenses of the litigation (*Fraser v Pattie* (1847) 9 D. 303). His entitlement to remuneration for his services may be recovered either from his ward's estate or the estate of the unsuccesful party to the litigation. Where the guardian ad litem requires funds to allow him to perform his duties he is entitled to apply to the court to order an appropriate party to put him in funds and to sist the litigation until he is put in funds (*Studd v Cook* (1883) 10 R. (HL) 53).

Rule 46(1)(b)—Sale of property

The power is to order the sale of any property in dispute in the arbitration. It is unclear what power of the court the originators of this provision had in mind.

Rule 46(1)(c)—Order securing any amount in dispute

In court proceedings in Scotland a court in general does not make an order securing any amount in dispute, except where it orders a party, generally the pursuer (claimant) to provide caution (a guarantee) for the expenses of the defender (respondent). Only where it is clear from the pleadings that a sum (e.g. the price of goods) will ultimately be due to the pursuer (claimant) does the court have a discretionary power to order some or part of the amount claimed to be lodged (consigned) with it (*George Cohen Sons & Co Ltd v Jamieson & Paterson*, 1963 S.C. 289). Instead, where a pursuer (claimant) fears that the defender (respondent) will dissipate assets or become insolvent in order to prevent effective enforcement of the decree (judgment) to be obtained in the proceedings, he will apply to the court for a warrant to enable him to execute "diligence on the dependence" which has the effect of freezing assets which could satisfy the court decree. Almost always the court's role is therefore not to make the order for the provision of security itself, but rather to grant a warrant to enable the pursuer to secure the assets himself.

The execution of a warrant to secure assets in order to meet any amount in dispute is known as "diligence on the dependence". The forms of diligence on the dependence differ depending on whether the amount in dispute is to be secured in the form of moveable or heritable (immoveable) property of the defender (respondent). The diligences on the dependence against moveable property of the defender are:

- arrestment on the dependence of moveable property (including

- incorporeal (intangible) property, e.g. debts) of the defender held, owed or to be owed by third parties;
- interim attachment of the corporeal (tangible) moveable property of the defender held by him.

The principal diligence on the dependence against heritable (immoveable) property of the defender is inhibition on the dependence which gives the claimant a right to "reduce" or quash any transfer of or the granting of any real right (jus in rem) by the defender in, the heritable property. It is also possible to register a notice of litigiosity under s.159 of the Titles to Land Consolidation (Scotland) Act 1868 against heritable property where the pursuer (claimant) seeks reduction (annulment) of a deed transferring rights over heritable property. Strictly speaking a notice of litigiosity does not require a warrant from the court and is not a "diligence on the dependence". However it performs the function of preventing the disposal of heritable property while there is an ongoing action to recover it through court proceedings to reduce the deed of transfer (usually a disposition or standard security (mortgage)).

Rule 46(1)(e) covers the granting of warrants for arrestment or inhibition on the dependence. If therefore r.46(1)(c) covers any diligence on the dependence at all, it covers interim attachment. This commentary proceeds on the basis that interim attachment is covered by r.46(1)(c). If that is incorrect, the alternative basis for an application for a warrant for interim attachment would be r.46(1)(g).

The test for the obtaining of a warrant for interim attachment is set out in ss.9D(2) (in relation to an urgent order without a hearing) and 9E(3) (in relation to an order at a hearing) of the Debt Arrangement and Attachment (Scotland) Act 2002 (as amended). The warrant will be granted where:
  (a) the claimant has a prima facie case on the merits; and
  (b) there is a real and substantial risk enforcement of any award for the claimant would be defeated or prejudiced by reason of:
      (i) the respondent being insolvent or verging on insolvency; or
      (ii) the likelihood of the respondent removing, disposing of, burdening, concealing or otherwise dealing with some or all of his assets; and
  (c) it is reasonable in all the circumstances, including the effect on any person interested.

If the warrant is to be granted without notice to the respondent, then the court must be persuaded that the insolvency or verging on insolvency or the likelihood of removal, etc. arises immediately or would arise before a hearing could take place.

Warrants can be granted before the raising of a litigation provided that the litigation is raised within a certain period of time (see s.15G of the 1987 Act (as amended) and s.9G of the 2002 Act (as amended)). This indicates that a similar process could be followed in relation to arbitration as anticipated by r.46(3) where the court is satisfied that a dispute has arisen or might arise and an arbitration agreement provides that such a dispute is to be resolved by arbitration.

Warrants for, and subsequent executions of interim attachment can be recalled or restricted by the court under s.9M of the 2002 Act (as amended). The court may recall the warrant and any subsequent execution (a) if the claimant does not satisfy the test for the diligence on the dependence in question—the onus of persuasion being on the claimant; or (b) the respondent offers suitable and sufficient alternative security, often in the form of caution (typically a bond from an appropriate insurance company) or consignation of sums with the court. In recalling or restricting the warrant to inhibit the court may impose such conditions as it thinks fit, having regard to the interests of both parties. Section 9N of the 2002 Act provides for variation of orders to recall or restrict and their conditions.

The only power which a court has to actually order provision of security is to order a party, typically a pursuer (claimant) to find caution (a guarantee) for the payment of the defender's (respondent's) expenses in the event of the defender's success. However that is a power which is unlikely to be invoked by parties to an arbitration given that the tribunal itself has the power under r.64 to make such an order and the power to make an award dismissing the claim if the security for expenses was not given.

Rule 46(1)(d)—Order under s.1 of the Administration of Justice (Scotland) Act 1972

Under s.1 of the Administration of Justice (Scotland) Act 1972 a court has power, subject to the law of privileged documents or oral evidence and to recovery of documents from the Crown, to order:
  (1) the inspection, photographing, preservation, custody and detention of documents and other property (including where appropriate, land) which appear to the court to be property as to which any question may relevantly arise in any existing civil proceedings before it or in civil proceedings likely to be brought;
  (2) the production and recovery of any such property, the taking of samples thereof and the carrying out of any experiment thereon or therewith;
  (3) any person to disclose such information as he has as to the identity of any persons who:
     (a) might be witnesses in any existing civil proceedings before it or which are likely to be brought; or
     (b) might be defenders in any civil proceedings likely to be brought.

The powers under s.1 of the 1972 Act can be used before civil proceedings are actually brought. In relation to their application under r.46 if the arbitration has not "begun" then the court must separately be satisfied in terms of r.46(3) that a dispute has arisen or might arise and that an arbitration agreement provides that such a dispute is to be resolved by arbitration. It is worth noting, however that the phrase "civil proceedings" in terms of s.1 has already been interpreted in the Outer House as meaning proceedings of a civil character irrespective of the court or tribunal before which they may be raised and therefore including arbitral proceedings (*Anderson v Gibb*, 1993 S.L.T. 726 at 729). If *Anderson* is correct, then technically the petition or application can be made directly under s.1 without the need to use r.46(1)(d).

The procedure for obtaining orders under s.1 of the 1972 Act is similar to that for obtaining an order for recovery of documents in a specification of documents at common law. This is described in the general commentary to r.45.

The powers under s.1 of the 1972 Act do not apply to the taking of oral evidence. The power of the court to allow the taking of oral evidence of a witness by a commissioner is covered in the commentary to r.46(1)(g). In extraordinary circumstances, the Inner House of the Court of Session may exercise its nobile officium to grant a commission to take evidence of a witness where there was not an arbitration or action before it or an arbitration or action immediately pending (*Galloway Water Power Co v Carmichael*, 1937 S.C. 135 at 140)—see the commentary to r.46(4) below.

Rule 46(1)(e)—Warrant to arrest or inhibit on the dependence

Arrestment on the dependence or inhibition on the dependence are means by which a claimant who fears that the respondent will dissipate assets or become insolvent in order to prevent effective enforcement of an award freezes assets of the respondent which could satisfy the award. Arrestment on the dependence and inhibition on the dependence are known collectively as "diligence on the dependence". The forms of diligence on the dependence differ depending on the nature of the asset to be frozen. The diligences on the dependence against moveable property of the respondent are:

- arrestment on the dependence of moveable property (including incorporeal (intangible) property, e.g. debts) of the respondent held by, owed or to be owed by third parties;
- interim attachment of the corporeal (tangible) moveable property of the respondent held by him.

Warrants for interim attachment are dealt with under r.46(1)(c) or 46(1)(g).

The principal diligence on the dependence against heritable (immoveable) property of the respondent is inhibition on the dependence which gives the claimant a right to "reduce" or quash any transfer of or the granting of any real right (jus in rem) by the respondent in, the heritable property owned by him at the date of inhibition. The inhibition on the dependence takes effect generally upon registration of the executed "schedule on inhibition" and certificate of execution in the Register of Inhibitions but if a preliminary notice of registration is registered before execution, the inhibition can in certain circumstances take effect from the date of the execution. The reader is referred to s.155 of the Titles to Land Consolidation (Scotland) Act 1868 (as introduced by s.149 of the Bankruptcy and Diligence etc. (Scotland) Act 2007). An inhibition on the dependence attaches to all heritable property of the respondent in Scotland regardless of its value. For this reason if more than one item of heritable property is covered respondents often apply to the court for restriction of the inhibition to the property sufficient to cover the sum sought by the claimant and a reasonable figure for expenses. If only one item of heritable property is covered, and there is no ground of challenge to the inhibition in relation to whether the test for obtaining it was satisfied, a respondent may apply to the court for recall of the inhibition and instead offer security in some other form, e.g. through caution or the lodging of a sum with the court (known as "consignation").

The test for the obtaining of a warrant for arrestment on the dependence or inhibition on the dependence is set out in ss.15E(2) (in relation to an urgent order without a hearing) and 15F(3) (in relation to an order at a hearing) of the Debtors (Scotland) Act 1987 (as amended by the Bankruptcy and Diligence etc. (Scotland) Act 2007). The warrant will be granted where:

(a) the claimant has a prima facie case on the merits;
(b) there is a real and substantial risk enforcement of any award for the claimant would be defeated or prejudiced by reason of:
   (i) the respondent being insolvent or verging on insolvency; or
   (ii) the likelihood of the respondent removing, disposing of, burdening, concealing or otherwise dealing with some or all of his assets; and
(c) it is reasonable in all the circumstances, including the effect on any person interested.

If the warrant is to be granted without notice to the respondent and therefore a "hearing", then the court must be persuaded that the insolvency or verging on insolvency or the likelihood of removal, etc. arises immediately or would arise before a hearing could take place.

Warrants can be granted before the raising of a litigation provided that the litigation is raised within a certain period of time (see s.15G of the 1987 Act (as amended)). This indicates that a similar process could be followed in relation to arbitration as anticipated by r.46(3) where the court is satisfied that a dispute has arisen or might arise and an arbitration agreement provides that such a dispute is to be resolved by arbitration.

Warrants for, and subsequent executions of arrestment and inhibition on the dependence can be recalled or restricted by the court under s.15K of the 1987 Act (as amended). The court may recall the warrant and any subsequent execution (a) if the claimant does not satisfy the test for the diligence on the dependence in question—the onus of persuasion being on the claimant; or (b) the respondent offers suitable and sufficient alternative security, often in the form of caution (typically a bond from an appropriate insurance company) or consignation of sums with the court. In recalling or restricting the warrant to inhibit the court may impose such conditions as it thinks fit, having regard to the interests of both parties. Section 15L of the 1987 Act provides for variation of orders to recall or restrict and their conditions.

It is also possible to register a notice of litigiosity against heritable property where the pursuer (claimant) seeks reduction (annulment) of a deed transferring rights over heritable property. Strictly speaking this does not require a warrant from the court and is not a "diligence on the dependence". However it performs the function of preventing the disposal of heritable property while there is an ongoing action to recover it through court proceedings to reduce the deed of transfer (usually a disposition or standard security).

Rule 46(1)(f)—Interdict or interim interdict

The court is given the same power in an arbitration as it has in civil proceedings to grant interdict or interim interdict. An interdict is an order restraining an ongoing or reasonably anticipated future breach of legal duty owed by the respondent to the claimant (*Inverurie Magistrates v Sorrie*, 1956 S.C. 175). An interdict may be interim or permanent. An interim interdict preserves the status quo until the court decides whether to grant a permanent interdict in its final decree (judgment). Rule 49(b) provides that unless the parties agree otherwise, the tribunal may make an award ordering a party to refrain from doing something. Having regard to the principle in s.1 that the court should not intervene in an arbitration except in as provided for in the Act, it cannot have been intended that the court could usurp the jurisdiction of the tribunal to grant a permanent interdict in a dispute governed by an arbitration agreement in which an arbitration had begun. The utility of r.46(1)(f) would therefore appear to be to enable an order of interim interdict to be made to preserve the status quo until the tribunal makes its award on the issue of permanent interdict. With regard to an award of permanent interdict see the commentary to r.49(b) below.

At common law a tribunal had power to grant interim interdict (*Gray v Brown* (1833) 11 S. 353) and by implication permanent interdict. This is restated in r.49(b) as read with r.53. A claimant seeking interim interdict may be in a number of different situations. First, the arbitration may not have begun. If it has not begun the claimant will have to satisfy the court that it may hear the application under r.46(b). Secondly, the arbitration may have begun but the case is one of urgency where the consent of the tribunal is not necessary. Thirdly the arbitration may have begun but the case is not one of urgency. If the arbitration has begun and the case is not of urgency then the claimant should first seek a provisional award of (interim) interdict from the tribunal. However breach of that award will not allow the tribunal to hold the respondent in contempt of court as breach of a court order would allow. For that reason there may be advantage for a claimant holding a provisional award of interim interdict to seek the authority of the court to be added with the court's own order.

In whichever of these situations interim interdict is sought, either the tribunal will make a provisional award or the court will grant it only where the claimant seeks an award under r.49(b) ordering a party to refrain from doing something where the claimant can demonstrate (a) a prima facie case for such an order, and (b) that the balance of convenience favours him rather than the respondent (*WAC Ltd v Whillock*, 1989 S.C. 397, per Lord Justice-Clerk Ross at 410). At the stage of granting interim interdict the tribunal or court is not concerned with whether the respondent disputes the facts put forward by the claimant provided that there is prima facie evidence of some kind to support the claimant's factual position.

In considering the balance of convenience the tribunal or court must weigh the inconvenience to the pursuer if the interim order is not granted with the inconvenience to the defender if the interim order is granted. The factors in relation to balance of convenience include:

- irreparable nature of apprehended wrong;
- offering of caution, consignation or other security or an undertaking to the court by the respondent;
- weakness of the prima facie case;
- financial effect of an interim order on the respondent;
- ease of quantification of putative damages if the respondent breached his duty in the future;
- adequacy of putative damages;
- safety implications;
- public interest;
- undue delay in making the application.

Further detail on balance of convenience with reference to illustrative case law can be obtained from the commentary to RCS r.60.3 in *Greens Annotated Rules of the Court of Session 1994* also contained in *The Parliament House Book* (Edinburgh: W. Green), Vol.2.

Interim interdict is often granted by a court ex parte, that is without notice of the application or indeed the commencement of legal proceedings themselves being given to the defender. The only way in which a person who fears he may be sued for interdict can obtain notice is by lodging a document known as a "caveat" with the court where he thinks that the legal proceedings may be raised. Before hearing an applicant on an application for interim interdict where proceedings have not been raised, the court will check whether the defender has lodged a caveat and if he has, will intimate the application to the defender. However the defender may have little time to prepare for the hearing if the matter is particularly urgent. If the court grants interim interdict ex parte then the defender may apply for recall of the interim interdict on the grounds of the absence of a prima facie case or the balance of convenience favouring him.

There seems to be no good reason why an order of interim interdict could not be made ex parte on the beginning of the arbitration either in terms of r.1 or other agreement of the parties as to commencement. Unfortunately there are conflicting authorities on whether a sheriff court has jurisdiction under s.6 of the Sheriff Courts (Scotland) Act 1907 to grant interim interdict restraining conduct outwith its sheriffdom. This suggests that if there is any possibility of the conduct to be restrained taking place over more than one sheriffdom within Scotland, or even outwith Scotland, the application under r.46(2) should be made by petition to the Outer House of the Court of Session.

An order of interim interdict comes into operation when the defender becomes aware of its content (*Clark v Stirling* (1839) 1 D. 955) whether or not there has been formal service and knowledge by the defender's solicitor may raise a presumption of knowledge by the defender (*Henderson v Maclellan* (1874) 1 R. 920, per Lord President Inglis at 923).

Rule 46(1)(g)—Any other interim or permanent order

Other interim orders which may be covered include:
- (a) a permanent order of specific implement (an order *ad factum praestandum*) for the performance of a "positive" obligation to do something—see the commentary to r.49(b) below;
- (b) an order under s.46 of the Court of Session Act 1988 for the performance of any act by the respondent necessary for reinstating the claimant in a possessory right or for granting other specific relief where the respondent has done any act which the court could have but did not prohibit by interdict;
- (c) an order under s.47(2) of the Court of Session Act 1988 as the court thinks fit regarding interim possession of any property to which the cause relate or regarding the subject matter of the cause—this can involve the making of an interim order of specific implement. This is an important power which could have been used by the court had the situation in *Cetelem SA v Roust Holdings Ltd* [2005] 2 Lloyd's Rep. 494 arisen in Scotland;
- (d) an order under s.10 of the Court of Session Act 1988 to (a) take and report on the depositions of havers of documents; or (b) take and report in writing on the evidence of any witness who is resident beyond the jurisdiction of the court or who by reason of age, infirmity or sickness is unable to attend the proof or trial.

It has already been noted that an application for a warrant for interim attachment could be covered by r.46(1)(g). Reference is made to the commentary for r.46(1)(c) in relation to applications for warrants for interim attachment.

It is unclear whether an order to find caution (pronounced "kayshun") or to consign money with the court covering a party's expenses as a condition precedent to proceeding with or defending a claim, is covered by r.46(1)(g). Equally it is unclear whether an order on a party resident outwith Scotland to sist (in the sense of "add") a mandatory is covered by r.46(1)(g). Sisting a mandatory involves the court ordering a party to add a person resident in Scotland into the action as his "mandatory" and thus potentially liable for all of the expenses of the litigation including those before his addition. The mandatory is responsible to the court for the direction of the action, although he cannot settle his principal's claim. An order to sist a mandatory can be made in a Scottish litigation where the pursuer (claimant) is resident abroad in a country that is not within the European Union or party to the Brussels or Lugano Conventions on jurisdiction and enforcement of judgments. In deciding whether to grant the order, the court exercises its discretion in the interests of justice. Unless there is some difficulty with the directing of the action from abroad, the court may be slow to order the sisting of a mandatory if it can use its powers to make an order for caution or consignation of money instead.

Both of these court powers are concerned with a party being able to recover arbitration expenses from the other party in the event of success. In addition the sisting of a mandatory is concerned with a party resident abroad being able to properly manage the Scottish proceedings. At common law the writers have discovered no case in which the court has used these powers in relation to an arbitration and no case in which an arbitral tribunal purported to exercise these powers. It is unclear whether they would have been implied into an arbitration agreement at common law in a manner similar to the power to award expenses.

The question is whether such orders of the court in relation to caution and sist of a mandatory fall within the catch-all phrase, "any other interim or permanent order". Viewed in the context of r.46 alone, there is nothing to suggest that the court is not entitled to make such orders in relation to an arbitration as it would in relation to a litigation, and that the tribunal, in deciding whether to grant consent to an application should apply the test which the court would apply. However at the same time the Act provides in r.64 that the tribunal should have power to order "security" for the arbitration expenses with a test that is more stringent than the court test in relation to a litigation. If a tribunal should be faced with an application for consent for the making of an application to the court for an order for caution which criteria is it to apply? Should it be the criteria in r.64—with the restriction in r.64(2) in relation to foreign parties—or should it be the criteria applicable by a court in a litigation, without such a restriction (at least in relation to non-EU or non- Brussels or Lugano Convention countries)? It would seem odd that a party could bypass the provisions of r.64 by seeking to invoke r.46(1)(g). All of this suggests that despite the orders in question apparently falling within r.46(1)(g) the true legislative intent was that their subject matter be dealt with by the tribunal under r.62 and that despite the catch-all wording of r.46(1)(g) orders in relation to security for expenses fall to the tribunal under r.64 and not to the tribunal and court under r.46(1)(g). Such a conclusion would also be beneficial from the point of view of attracting international arbitrations to a Scottish seat which was one of the aims of the Act

Rule 46(2)—Procedure

An application may be made to either the Outer House of the Court of Session (RCS r.14.2(h)) or to a sheriff court of the sheriffdom determined under s.6 of the Sheriff Courts (Scotland) Act 1907. Section 6 applies because r.46 appears to fall within s.21(1)(a) of the Civil Jurisdiction and Judgments Act 1982 which excludes the jurisdictional rules in Sch.8 to the 1982 Act.

From a procedural point of view it is important to bear in mind that the application is made under the appropriate part of r.46 which gives the court its jurisdiction in relation to the arbitration, rather than under the provision which would give the court its jurisdiction in relation to a litigation. Having said that, the petition or summary application will have to follow closely any substantive requirements for the equivalent application for a litigation. So for example in relation to seeking diligence on the dependence, the petition or summary application should follow the requirements of s.15D of the Debtors (Scotland) Act 1987 (arrestment or inhibition) or s.9C of the Debt Arrangement and Attachment (Scotland) Act 2002 (attachment).

If the application is made to the Outer House it is made by petition in the style contained in RCS Form 14.4 (RCS rr.14.2(h), 14.4) or, if there are undisposed of Outer House proceedings, by note (RCS r.99.5). The requirements for the petition are set out in RCS r.14.4 and Ch.99 (r.15.2 and Ch.99 for notes), together with the need to:

(i) aver why the order is necessary;
(ii) aver the circumstances in which the prerequisites for an application in terms of the relevant part of r.46 are satisfied;
(iii) aver the consent of the tribunal (unless the arbitration has not begun or the case is one of urgency, in which case that should be averred);
(iv) aver the reasons why the usual period of 21 days for answers should be dispensed with (if that is necessary);
(v) require service or intimation on the other parties to the arbitration, and, if appropriate, to the members of the tribunal, and the haver or witness in question.

If a shorter period of notice is required, then this should also be craved in the petition.

Together with the petition the applicant should lodge with the Court of Session:
(i) as a production, any written arbitration agreement in which or other agreement or other document by virtue of which, the time limit is imposed;
(ii) any written statements of case and defence in the arbitration (the pleadings), if appropriate;
(iii) the bundle of court documents known as the process (see RCS rr.4.3, 4.4).

Inventories of any productions should be intimated to the other parties and members of the tribunal.

If the petition is one where an urgent ex parte order is required, the court will proceed to immediately consider the petition. Regardless of whether such an order is sought or made, the applicant must move for a first order for service on the other party or parties to the arbitration or their representatives in the arbitration, and the members of the tribunal and anyone else who has an interest to allow such persons to lodge answers opposing the petition if they wish within 21 days (RCS r.99.5). Therefore it is advised that if a shorter period is required a motion for that shorter period should be sought.

After the end of the period for answers, whether answers have been lodged or not, the petitioner should enrol a motion to have the court determine the petition, with or without a hearing as may be appropriate in the circumstances.

If the application is made to the sheriff court it is made by summary application in the style contained in SASAR Sch.1 Form 1 (SASAR r.2.4). The requirements for the summary application are broadly the same as for the petition described above. Detailed reference should be made to the SASAR.

Expenses of the application will not be included in the "arbitration expenses" (see the commentary to r.59 below) but will fall to be dealt with by the court rather than the tribunal but, on an analogy with the preparation of the former stated case, the expenses of obtaining the consent of the tribunal fall to be dealt with by the tribunal in terms of r.60 (*Thomson v Earl of Galloway*, 1919 S.C. 611).

Rule 46(3)

The tribunal has a discretion to continue with the arbitration whilst the court is determining the application. The best resolution of this issue is to have the parties agree on the procedure whilst the application is ongoing. If parties cannot agree, then whilst the tribunal has a duty to conduct the arbitration without unnecessary delay (under r.24) it also has a duty to treat the parties fairly (under r.24). Everything will depend on the subject matter of the application to the court, the stage which the arbitration has reached and the nature of any prejudice that might be caused through the delay in not progressing with the arbitration balanced with any prejudice which might be caused through progressing with the arbitration. It is suggested that given the provisional or interim nature of many of the court orders which would be made pursuant to applications under r.46, in most instances the tribunal will wish to progress with the arbitration. Ultimately the question of whether and if so how the arbitration should proceed will be a matter for the tribunal. In applying its duties under r.24 the tribunal which will seek to avoid any substantial injustice which could conceivably result in a challenge to the award for serious irregularity (see r.68).

Rule 46(4)

Rule 46 does not affect other powers which a court may have, regardless of the rule, in relation to arbitrations or the powers of the tribunal. Thus as noted in the commentary, the apparent power of the court to grant an order under s.1 of the Administration of Justice (Scotland) Act 1972 in respect of an arbitration remains unaffected.

In circumstances of a very exceptional kind, the Inner House of the Court of Session will exercise its nobile officium to grant a commission to take evidence of a witness where there is not an action before it or an action immediately pending (*Galloway Water Power Co v Carmichael*, 1937 S.C. 135 at 140—where a witness was departing for Australia where he was likely to be for several years and for which evidence on commission or on interrogatories would be inappropriate; this might not now be followed with video conferencing). In such a case the petition would be to the Inner House of the Court of Session and not under r.46.

For when an arbitration is said to have begun see r.1 (above).

PART 6

AWARDS

Rule 47: Rules applicable to the substance of the dispute **D**

47.—(1) The tribunal must decide the dispute in accordance with—
   (a) the law chosen by the parties as applicable to the substance of the dispute, or
   (b) if no such choice is made (or where a purported choice is unlawful), the law determined by the conflict of law rules which the tribunal considers applicable.

(2) Accordingly, the tribunal must not decide the dispute on the basis of general considerations of justice, fairness or equity unless—
   (a) they form part of the law concerned, or
   (b) the parties otherwise agree.

(3) When deciding the dispute, the tribunal must have regard to—
   (a) the provisions of any contract relating to the substance of the dispute,
   (b) the normal commercial or trade usage of any undefined terms in the provisions of any such contract,
   (c) any established commercial or trade customs or practices relevant to the substance of the dispute, and

(d) any other matter which the parties agree is relevant in the circumstances.

DEFINITIONS
"dispute": ss.2(1), 31(1)
"party": ss.2(1), 31(1), (2)
"tribunal": ss.2(1), 31(1)

COMMENTARY
This is an interesting provision. Although it is peremptory in form, it is a default rule, which means that the parties may ask the tribunal to decide the dispute in accordance with whatever norms the parties agree upon. Thus the parties could direct that the dispute be decided not according to strict law, but according to what might be just, fair or equitable. Alternatively, they could invoke bodies of rules which are not part of any national law, but which have been devised especially to be used by arbitral tribunals in international commercial arbitration, such as the Principles of European Contract Law or the UNIDROIT Principles of International Commercial Contracts. Similarly, they might invoke international conventions even if they have not yet become part of the law of any state, or principles common to two or more legal systems. They might even refer to standards the content of which is of questionable certainty such as *lex mercatoria*, general principles of law, international law, transnational commercial law and the like, or they might ask that a particular national law be applied, but as it stood at a given point in time, or indeed agree that different national laws be applied to different aspects of the dispute, e.g. to the question of whether there has been a breach of contract, to issues such as frustration and to the question of remedies. It has even been known for parties to invoke the principles of law created by arbitral tribunals.

Might the parties validly invite the tribunal to act as *amiable compositeur*, a concept known in certain civilian systems, and recognised by the Model Law, whereby the tribunal can actually readjust the contract between the parties? Section 46(1)(b) of the 1996 Act specifically allows the parties to authorise the tribunal to decide the dispute, "in accordance with such other considerations as are agreed by them or determined by the tribunal", thus expressly permitting decisions according to a system other than national law or according to non-legal criteria (see also DAC Report, para.224). It can be seen that the Act would allow the parties to give the tribunal discretion to select such criteria. Although r.47 is silent on this point, the fact that it is a default rule means that the parties can agree to any arrangement they wish, including empowering tribunals to make their own decisions as to the criteria they will employ. Would the parties be entitled to empower a third party, such as an arbitral institution, to decide what system of law or other criteria the tribunal must apply, an option which does not appear to be possible under the 1996 Act? It might be noted that while party autonomy under the Model Law generally embraces the power to entrust decisions to third parties under art.2(d) (art.2(i) in the version adopted in Scotland), the single exception is the power to determine the law to govern the substance, the representative from the Hague Conference on Private International Law having persuaded the drafters that this would offend a key principle of private international law (see *Summary Record of the 327th meeting on the preparation of the UNCITRAL Model Law on International Commercial Arbitration*, UN A/CN.9/SR.327, paras 320–327). Yet under s.9(4)(a)(iii) of the 2010 Act parties may modify a default rule via anything done with their agreement, which would seem to validate such a choice.

The above view is premised on the courts agreeing that by rendering r.47 a default rule the parties are accorded complete freedom, and this appears to be the view taken by the explanatory notes at paras 153–154. An alternative view is that by not explicitly providing that the parties can invoke considerations such as those mentioned above the Act has left the matter to be governed by the common law. It is difficult to say where Scots common law stands on the matter, but the traditional view of English law, now of course overtaken by the 1996 Act, was that a-national or extra-legal standards could not validly be invoked (see Megaw J. in *Orion Compania Espanola de Seguros v Belfort Maatschappij Voor Alegemene Verzekgringeen* [1962] 2 Lloyd's Rep. 257 at 264; Parker L.J. in *Home and Overseas Insurance Co v Mentor Insurance Co (UK)* [1989] 3 All E.R. 74 at 80). Yet r.47(2)(b) expressly provides that the tribunal can be authorised to decide the dispute on the basis of justice, etc. rather than law, so it would seem to follow that any reference to quasi-legal principles would also be possible, and that the common law, if indeed it would stand against such a choice, is overridden.

In so far as the parties have not made the sort of exotic choice described above, the provisions of r.47 apply.

Rule 47(1)(a)

Choice of law: If the parties have chosen a specific system of law to apply to the substance of the dispute, the tribunal must apply that law. The parties may, of course, have explicitly indicated that a particular law will apply to the substance of the dispute. However, the fact that they have chosen a particular law to govern their contract will amount to an implied choice of law in this context (see Lord Diplock in *Compagnie d'Armement Maritime SA v Compania Tunisienne de Navigation SA* [1971] A.C. 572 at 604). It is sometimes the case that the fact that the parties have chosen to arbitrate in State X amounts to an implied choice of the law of that state to govern their contract and hence the substance of the dispute, but this is far from invariably so (*Compagnie d'Armement Maritime SA v Compania Tunisienne de Navigation SA* [1971] A.C. 572, per Lord Morris at 588; and see *Mitsubishi Corp v Castletown Navigation (The Castle Alpha)* [1989] 2 Lloyd's Rep. 383). A failure to abide by the choice of the parties will surely amount to serious irregularity in terms of r.68, allowing the award to be challenged. Section 46(2) of the 1996 Act makes it clear that a choice of law refers to the substantive law of the state in question rather than its conflict of law rules. This is designed to deal with the problem of *renvoi* whereby the law of a given country is chosen, only to find that its conflict of law rules direct that the law of an entirely different legal system should govern the dispute (see DAC Report, para.224). It is submitted that, despite the absence of a provision equivalent to s.46(2), the terms of r.47 are sufficiently clear to indicate that the choice of the parties relates to substantive law. The idea of *renvoi* is in any case excluded by art.15 of the 1980 Rome Convention on the Law Applicable to Contractual Obligations.

Rule 47(1)(b)

Law determined by applicable conflict of law rules: If the parties have not chosen such a system or their choice is unlawful, the law to be applied must be that determined by the conflict of law rules which the tribunal considers applicable.

Unlawful choice of law: First of all, when might a purported choice of law be unlawful? One example which springs to mind is s.27(2) and (3) of the Unfair Contract Terms Act 1977 which indicates that where a contract is made in the UK, and one party is a consumer who is habitually resident there, the terms of the Act cannot be excluded by a choice of law other than that of the UK. More fundamentally, under art.3 of the Rome Convention, which receives effect in the UK through the Contracts (Applicable Law) Act 1990, if a contract is clearly connected only with one country, the choice of a foreign law to govern the substance clearly cannot override the mandatory rules of the country in question. Thus if, for example, the arbitral tribunal were asked to adjudicate upon a dispute arising out of a contract between two parties incorporated in State X, concerning a project within State X, but found that the parties had sought to invoke the law of State Y to govern their dispute, essentially because the contract would be illegal under the law of State X, it would have to ignore that choice of law. In the context of court proceedings the Court of Appeal in *Shamil Bank of Bahrain EC v Beximco Pharmaceuticals Ltd* [2004] 2 Lloyd's Rep. 1, held that it is not open under the Rome Convention to the parties to choose an extra national system of law—in this case the Sharia. However, this is of no consequence in the context of arbitral proceedings, given that r.47 authorises such choices.

Tribunal applies conflict of law rules: The idea that the default position in the absence of choice by the parties is that the governing law is to be determined by the conflict of law rules which the tribunal considers applicable is to be found in art.28(2) of the Model Law and s.46(3) of the 1996 Act.

It may be noted that the tribunal is not required to apply the law determined by the applicable conflict of law rules, but the law determined by the conflict of law rules which the tribunal *considers* applicable. How wide a discretion is accorded by this formula? The drafters of the Model Law thought that the discretion was considerable, acknowledging that a tribunal might first decide which substantive law it wishes to apply to the dispute, only thereafter looking for a set of conflict of law rules which would allow that choice (see *Report of the UNCITRAL on the work of its eighteenth session*, UN A/40/17, para.237). Thus if the tribunal wishes to apply the law of State X, it is only if no set of conflict of law rules can be found which would allow that choice that it is prevented from doing so. Indeed, the drafters of the Model Law seemed to concede that there would be no practical restriction on the tribunal applying the law of State X in the above circumstances, since no recourse was provided for the erroneous application of art.28 (see UN A/40/17, paras 236, 238). Yet it would seem remarkable that a tribunal could flout the law on such an important issue with impunity. It is submitted that if a tribunal applied a law which was not authorised by any choice of law rule, or a fortiori if it ignored the law chosen by the parties, that should amount to serious irregularity in terms of r.68, allowing the award to be challenged. In *Peterson Farms Inc v C & M Farming Ltd* [2004] 1 Lloyd's Rep. 603, a tribunal which was required to apply the law of Arkansas held not only one of the parties but every company in its group liable to the other party, applying a doctrine not found in the law of Arkansas. The award was set aside on the basis of excess of jurisdiction under s.67 of the 1996 Act. It can be seen how that approach might have seemed appropriate in the facts of that particular case, but it is suggested that serious irregularity will generally be the preferable ground of challenge.

Were the tribunal to apply the Rome Convention to the question of applicable law, art.4(1) would direct that the governing law would be that of the country to which the contract has the closest connection. Article 4(2) then recites that, subject to a number of exceptions, this will be the country where the party who is to perform the contract is habitually resident or in the case of a body has its central administration. Nonetheless, if the contract is entered into in the course of that party's trade or profession, the country shall be where the principal place of business is situated, or where under the contract performance is to be effected through another place of business, the country shall be where that place of business is situated. Were the tribunal to decide that Scots conflict of law rules should be applied to determine the substantive law, it would then have to apply the Rome Convention. Accordingly, if it failed to apply the Convention or misapplied it with the result that it did not apply the rules of the appropriate system to the substance of the dispute, then it is submitted that the award might be challengeable under r.69 on the basis that the tribunal erred on a point of Scots law. (This view is rather tentatively advanced, since a court might take the view that r.69 only applies when Scots law applies to the substance of the dispute.) The same result would probably not follow if the tribunal properly selected another set of conflict of law rules but erred in their application, as this would not be an error on a point of *Scots* law. A court might, however, see this as serious irregularity in terms of r.68.

Rule 47(2)

Decision according to fairness, etc.: The main merit of this provision is that by emphasising that the parties may agree that the dispute may be decided by reference to considerations such as equity, it serves to stress that this is the intended effect of casting r.47 in the form of a default provision. Effectively, if the parties authorise the tribunal to decide the dispute according to equity rather than strict law then r.47(1) is disapplied. The reference to considerations such as justice forming part of the law concerned may seem unfamiliar to those used to common law systems, where such considerations tend to be reflected in particular rules and principles, and where equitable exceptions tend to be part of the fabric of such rules. However, in some systems, e.g. the Sharia, it is sometimes possible for arbitrators to abandon the formal rules and decide according to equity. This provision recognises that possibility.

Rule 47(3)

Considerations to which tribunal should have regard: This to some degree echoes the terms of art.28(4) of the Model Law, which is in turn is modelled on art.33(3) of the UNCITRAL Arbitration Rules (see also ICC Arbitration Rules art.17.2), and is quite similar to art.7(1) of the European Arbitration Convention 1961 (which has never been adopted by the UK). Article 28(4) provides that the tribunal, "shall decide in accordance with the terms of the contract and shall take into account the usages of trade applicable to the transaction". The 1996 Act refers to no such factors, and the view of the DAC Report, para.222 was that:

"... if the applicable law allows this to be done, then the provision is not necessary; while if it does not, then it could be said that such a direction overrides that law, which to our minds would be incorrect."

The framers of the Model Law themselves were not uniformly convinced of the value of art.28(4), which was indeed at one point discarded because of:

"... the many questions and concerns it raised. For example, the reference to the terms of the contract could be misleading where such terms were in conflict with mandatory provisions of law or did not express the true intent of the parties Also, this reference did not belong in an Article dealing with the law applicable to the substance of the dispute, although appropriate in arbitration rules. As regards the reference to trade usages, the concerns related to the fact that their legal effect and qualification was not uniform in all legal systems" (UN A/CN.9/245, para.99).

Yet the provision was ultimately restored because (*Analytical Compilation of Comments on Article 28*, UN A/CN.9/263, para.12):

"... the parties, not without good reasons, expect from the arbitrators that they will, above all, base their decisions on the wording and history of the contract and usages of trade."

It may be added that certain types of arbitration, e.g. GAFTA arbitrations, tend to lean heavily on trade usages.

It may also be observed that the Model Law is not alone in referring to applicable trade usages, as art.1054.4 of the Netherlands Code of Civil Procedure is in similar terms. It could even be argued that the reminder that trade usages are important is very useful in international commercial law, since it has long been sought to promote uniformity of interpretation of commonly used trade terms, and the ICC has even developed the International Rules for the Interpretation of Trade Terms "Incoterms". Nonetheless, there is no easy answer to the question of what the tribunal should do when the law chosen by the parties to govern the dispute prohibits reference to trade usages. Perhaps a choice of such a law counts as a disapplication of r.47(3)(b).

Given that the tribunal must decide as directed by the parties in any case, it is arguable that r.47(3)(a) and (d) are redundant. The meaning of r.47(3)(c) may appear obscure. However, trade customs and practices are commonly invoked in arbitrations in certain industries, e.g. the oil industry, and one of the authors has experience of acting as an expert witness in that regard.

While a failure to have regard to any of these factors may amount to a serious irregularity, it may be difficult to establish that the tribunal has contravened r.47(b) or (c). Where the governing law is Scots law, if such a failure led to an erroneous interpretation of the contract, the award might be challenged on the basis of an error of law.

Rule 48: Power to award payment and damages **M**

48.—(1) The tribunal's award may order the payment of a sum of money (including a sum in respect of damages).
  (2) Such a sum must be specified—
    (a) in any currency agreed by the parties, or
    (b) the absence of such agreement, in such currency as the tribunal considers appropriate.

COMMENTARY

In the version of the Bill originally laid before the Scottish Parliament this was part of r.49, dealing with remedies in general just like s.48 of the 1996 Act. However, r.49 like s.48 is a default rule, and it was decided that these powers were so fundamental that the parties should not be able to exclude them. The Law Society of Scotland, in particular, argued that if the rule was default stronger parties such as main contractors and large retailers would abuse their position in respect of sub-contractors and suppliers in order to insist that the power was routinely excluded. Thus this rule is mandatory. There is no corresponding provision of the Model Law.

Rule 48(1)

Most commonly the remedy sought will be the payment of money. Thus the tribunal might direct that one party should pay the other a sum which is owed under the contract or order the payment of monetary compensation (damages) for breach of contract. (In England there is authority that an award cannot order that money be paid to someone who is not a party, save perhaps where it can be shown that the order is for the benefit of a party—see, e.g. *Wood v Adcock* (1852) 7 Ex. 468.) It is important that r.48 establishes the principle that a tribunal ordinarily has the power to award damages, since one of the notorious deficiencies of Scots common law is that a tribunal has no implied power to award damages, which power must thus be expressly conferred by the parties. This was established by the House of Lords in *Aberdeen Railway Co v Blaikie Bothers* (1853) 15 D. (HL) 20 and the rule has been followed ever since (see, e.g. *Whatlings (Foundations) Ltd v Shanks & McEwan (Contractors) Ltd*, 1989 S.C. 253).

May the tribunal award penal or exemplary damages despite such remedies being unavailable under Scots law? This is not made clear. It is not even clear, given that the provision is mandatory, whether the parties could confer that power by invoking a foreign law. Yet it might be argued that this is really an issue of substantive law, so that if such remedies are permitted by the law chosen to govern the substance, then they will be competent. If the arbitration is entirely Scottish, then things become more difficult and it would surely be assumed that a tribunal would not have that power. Indeed, even though party autonomy is a founding principle of the Act, it might be supposed that power to grant such remedies could not be conferred by the parties in a purely Scottish arbitration, since this would offend public policy (see ICC case 5946 (1991) XVI YCA 97). Even in those cases where it might be possible to award such remedies, there may be difficulties at the enforcement stage if the enforcing state does not countenance remedies of that kind. Thus the German Supreme Court declined to enforce that part of a US award which awarded punitive damages (decision of June 4, 1992 BGHZ 118 at 312).

Rule 48(2)

If money is ordered to be paid the currency must be specified. Prima facie, this will be the currency agreed by the parties, but in the absence of agreement it will be in such currency as the tribunal considers appropriate. Presumably the order might specify a variety of currencies where that would be apt. This would mirror the position at common law (*Commerzbank AG v Large*, 1977 S.L.T. 219). Although the tribunal appears, subject to the agreement of the parties, to be given complete discretion here, in a decision under the 1996 Act the House of Lords in *Lesotho Highlands Development Authority v Impregilo SpA* [2005] 2 Lloyd's Rep. 310, held that it cannot make a quixotic choice of currency which would not be open to the court in a similar situation. Their Lordships further held that a failure by the tribunal to render the award in the currency impliedly selected by the parties was only challengeable as an error of law. Applying that approach in a Scottish context that would mean that the error could not be challenged under r.69 where the law governing the substance was not Scots Law, nor where the parties had disapplied r.69.

Rule 49: Other remedies available to tribunal D

49. The tribunal's award may—

(a) be of a declaratory nature,
(b) order a party to do or refrain from doing something (including ordering the performance of a contractual obligation), or
(c) order the rectification or reduction of any deed or other document (other than a decree of court) to the extent permitted by the law governing the deed or document.

DEFINITIONS
"party": ss.2(1), 31(1), (2)
"tribunal": ss.2(1), 31(1)

COMMENTARY
This provision is also clearly inspired by s.48 of the 1996 Act. There is no corresponding provision of the Model Law. Like s.48 it is a default rule. Unlike s.48(1), it does not explicitly state that the parties are free to agree upon the powers of the tribunal as regards remedies, but that appears to be the intention. Thus the parties may restrict or remove the power of the tribunal to grant certain of these remedies or all of them. Equally, they might look to extend the available remedies (see DAC Report, para.234), and they may do so by invoking a set of arbitral rules or a foreign procedural law which contemplates such remedies (see *Kastner v Jason* [2004] EWHC 592).

Prior to the 1996 Act it was established in England that arbitrators had implied authority to grant any remedy available to a court, save those which obviously only lay in the competence of the court (*President of India v La Pintada Compania Navigacion SA (La Pintada)* [1985] A.C. 104). The question arose whether, following the 1996 Act, arbitrators were confined to granting the remedies specified in s.48, unless the parties extended their competence. It was ultimately confirmed by *Wealans v CLC Contractors Ltd* [1999] 2 Lloyd's Rep. 739 that s.48 had not been intended to restrict the range of remedies available to arbitrators, so that tribunals might, for example, grant special remedies created by statutory provisions in situations where this would be available to a court. The question whether arbitrators have similar powers under Scots law has never arisen, but it is to be hoped that the courts would not take a more restrictive line, and would take the view that r.49 is not intended to restrict those powers.

Rule 49(a)

Declarator: A party may not be seeking compensation for an alleged wrong, but the determination of a contested issue such as the true meaning of a particular term of the contract, or which of the parties is the true owner of a copyright or patent. In such a situation the tribunal might issue a declaration as to the rights of the parties.

Rule 49(b)

Interdict and specific implement: The tribunal may order a party not to do something—an order known as an interdict in Scots law—and a power which already existed under Scots common law (*Gray v Brown* (1833) 11 S. 353). The version of the Bill originally laid before the Scottish Parliament featured a default rule which would have restricted tribunals to granting only those remedies which would have been available to the Court of Session in the same circumstances. As a default rule, it could have been overridden by the parties, but if it was not so overridden, then it would have restricted the circumstances in which the tribunal could have granted this remedy (see Lord President Hope in *Hill v Council of the Law Society of Scotland*, 2000 S.C. 582 at 657). Since this provision has been discarded, then there seems to be nothing to restrict the discretion of the parties here other than the agreement of the parties. Nonetheless, the Crown Proceedings Act 1947 ss.21 and 43 indicate that the Crown cannot be interdicted, and it is very doubtful whether the rule intends to alter that. It is submitted that an interim interdict—the equivalent of an interlocutory injunction—would also lie within the power of the tribunal to grant since a tribunal may make a provisional award under r.53 unless the parties have agreed otherwise. It may be noted that in *Welex AG v Rosa Maritime Ltd (The Epsilon Rosa)* [2003] 2 Lloyd's Rep. 509, the similar power under the 1996 Act has been held to entitle a tribunal to order a party to an arbitration agreement not to seek to litigate in breach of that agreement.

The tribunal might also order a party to do something and this might include ordering the performance of a contractual obligation. This would be known as an order for specific implement, the equivalent of an order for specific performance in England. Again, the discarding of the rule referred to in the previous paragraph means that the power to make such an order is not restricted to those cases where the Court of Session might competently order specific implement, although the power may be restricted by the parties. Once more, however, it is doubtful whether the rule alters the position that an order for specific implement is not competent against the Crown (Crown Proceedings Act 1947 s.21). It may be noted that while under s.48(5)(b) of the 1996 Act (as under s.15 of the Arbitration Act 1950 before it) a court cannot order specific performance of a contract related to land, there is no such restriction under r.49.

Specific implement might be ordered in situations where monetary compensation would not be an adequate remedy for breach of contract, or where, for example, a party is refusing to deliver a commodity as required by the contract, which commodity would be hard to source elsewhere. It is usually not an appropriate remedy to enforce the performance of obligations of some complexity, since the order would require to have a high degree of specificity and performance might thereafter have to be policed by the tribunal (see CIMAR r.12.7). Moreover, in international arbitrations it is often not safe to assume that a court in another jurisdiction will be prepared to enforce an award which does anything other than orders the payment of money, and courts may be particularly reluctant to enforce awards which call on them to supervise the behaviour of a party (see Troy E. Elder, "The Case Against Arbitral Awards of Specific Performance in Transnational Commercial Disputes" (1997) 13 Arbitration Int. 1). Many would also see this as an argument for not empowering tribunals to award such remedies in domestic arbitrations.

Rule 49(c)

Rectification/reduction: Reduction of a deed or document occurs where it is established that it does not properly embody the will of the granter or the agreement of the parties, or perhaps that such will or agreement was unlawfully obtained. It serves to deprive the deed or document of legal effect. Rectification of a deed or document occurs where it is established that it does not properly embody the will of the granter or the agreement of the parties, and its effect is to rectify the deed or document so that it properly expresses that will or agreement (see art.22.1(g) of the LCIA Rules of Arbitration).

Not every system permits arbitrators to reduce or a fortiori to rectify a formal deed or document, so tribunals are only accorded this power to the extent allowed by the law governing the deed or document. Of course, since r.49 is a default provision, the parties might seek to give the tribunal these powers irrespective of the stance of the governing law, but difficulties might then arise at the enforcement stage. A number of systems are simply unfamiliar with the concept of rectification, so what is the effect of r.49(c) in that context? It is suggested that most such systems would permit such a remedy to be resorted to if the parties so agreed. Does the rule then only allow rectification if the parties have expressly agreed to it? It is suggested that a better interpretation would be that, however misguidedly, the rule authorises rectification unless the governing law actually forbids it.

At stage 2 the limitation was imposed that a decree of court cannot be rectified. This is surely axiomatic and it is difficult to think of any legal system where such rectification can be countenanced. Moreover, it is submitted that the fact that this is a default provision does not allow the parties to confer that power.

Where does Scots Law stand on rectification? Such a power was not truly possessed by the courts at common law (see Davidson, *Evidence*, 2007, paras 6.84, 6.85), and had to be conferred by statute (the Law Reform (Miscellaneous Provisions) (Scotland) Act 1985 s.8, discussed in Davidson, *Evidence*, 2007, paras 6.86–6.89). Thus it is unlikely that arbitrators possessed an inherent power of rectification. But what if the parties agree that the tribunal should possess that power? It has been held in England that at common law it is competent for parties to confer such a power (*Asheville Investments Ltd v Elmer Contractors Ltd* [1989] Q.B. 488), and there is no reason to suppose that the Scots courts would take a different view. Since Scots law therefore probably does not prohibit rectification, r.49(c) might be taken to authorise it, subject to the contrary agreement of the parties. That being said, it is doubtful whether an arbitrator could be empowered to rectify a deed or document which is registered in any of the public registers. In terms of the contrary agreement of the parties, a question arises as to whether the tribunal is given inherent power to rectify a document unless that is clearly excluded, or whether the fact that the parties seem to have empowered the tribunal to deal only with breach of contract issues would prevent it dealing with rectification (compare *Cane v Hegeman-Harris Co Ltd* [1993] 4 All E.R. 68 CA, with *Macepark (Whittlebury) Ltd v Sargeant* Unreported July 18, 2002 Ch). Such authorities may now have to be read in light of the decision of the House of Lords in *Premium Nafta Products Ltd v Fili Shipping Co Ltd* [2008] 1 Lloyd's Rep. 254.

In any case r.49(c) must be read in the context of s.11(2) which indicates that an award which purports to rectify or reduce a deed or document is of no effect in so far as it would adversely affect the interests of any third party acting in good faith—see the commentary to that provision above.

Rule 50: Interest **M**

50.—(1) The tribunal's award may order that interest is to be paid on—
  (a) the whole or part of any amount which the award orders to be paid (or which is payable in consequence of a declaratory award), in respect of any period up to the date of the award,
  (b) the whole or part of any amount which is—
    (i) claimed in the arbitration and outstanding when the arbitration began, but

(ii) paid before the tribunal made its award,
in respect of any period up to the date of payment,
(c) the outstanding amount of any amounts awarded (including any award of arbitration expenses or pre-award interest under paragraph (a) or (b)) in respect of any period from the date of the award up to the date of payment.
(2) An award ordering payment of interest may, in particular, specify—
(a) the interest rate,
(b) the period for which interest is payable (including any rests which the tribunal considers appropriate).
(3) An award may make different interest provision in respect of different amounts.
(4) Interest is to be calculated—
(a) in the manner agreed by the parties, or
(b) failing such agreement, in such manner as the tribunal determines.
(5) This rule does not affect any other power of the tribunal to award interest.

DEFINITIONS
"arbitration": ss.2(1), (2), 31(1)
"tribunal": ss.2(1), 31(1)

COMMENTARY
This provision is clearly modelled on s.49 of the 1996 Act. Again it has no counterpart in the Model Law. It represents a considerable advance on the common law, as an arbitrator at common law has no implied power to award interest on sums due prior to the date of the award (see Lord Dunpark in *John G McGregor (Contractors) Ltd v Grampian Regional Council*, 1991 S.L.T. 136 at 137L). This was originally a default rule like s.49, but is now cast in mandatory form, primarily because the Law Society of Scotland argued that stronger parties would routinely insist on depriving the tribunal of this power. The fact that this rule is mandatory may deter parties from certain states from arbitrating in Scotland, due to concerns regarding the enforceability of awards which contain interest. Yet a measure of discretion is restored by r.50(4) and the question of the extent to which this undermines the mandatory nature of the rule is considered in the commentary to that provision. It may be noted as a preliminary matter that the use of the word "may" inevitably suggests that the tribunal is not obliged to award interest, despite the mandatory nature of the provision.

Rule 50(1)(a)

As under s.49(3)(a) of the 1996 Act, the tribunal may award interest on the whole or part of the amount awarded for any period up to the date of the award, e.g. from the date of breach. Despite the discretion accorded to the tribunal interest could surely not be awarded by reference to an earlier date (see *BP Chemicals Ltd v Kingdom Engineering (Fife) Ltd* [1994] 2 Lloyd's Rep. 373; *Durham County Council v Darlington Borough Council* [2003] N.P.C. 136). As under s.49(5) of the 1996 Act, it is also made clear that such interest may also be ordered to be paid on a sum which is not actually awarded but is nonetheless payable because the tribunal has issued a declarator to that effect. It has been held in England that if a sum has been found to be payable, it is not necessary for the tribunal to believe that the respondent acted wrongfully for it to be able to award interest (*Amec Building Ltd v Cadmus Investment Co Ltd* [1997] C.L.Y. 262). A discretion to award interest obviously entails a discretion not to award it, and this discretion will be very difficult to challenge (but see Lord Denning M.R. in *Panchaud Freres SA v R Pagnan & Fratelli* [1974] 1 Lloyd's Rep. 394 at 411; and compare *Anticlizo Shipping Corp v Food Corp of India (The Anticlizo)* [1991] 2 Lloyd's Rep. 485).

Rule 50(1)(b)

If a party claims a sum in the arbitration which is still outstanding when the arbitration begins, but that sum or any part thereof is paid by the time the award is made, clearly that amount may no longer be awarded. However, the tribunal is still entitled to award interest on any such amount up to the date of payment. For example, a sum of £1 million may be claimed, and when it is clear during the course of the proceedings that his defence is bound to fail, the defender may simply decide to pay that sum. However, this does not serve to terminate the proceedings. Since if the tribunal had awarded the payment of that sum it could also have awarded interest thereon from the date of breach, it continues to have jurisdiction to award such interest up to the date of payment. Of course interest cannot be awarded on an amount which is claimed but which has already been paid when the arbitration begins.

Rule 50(1)(c)

The tribunal may also award interest on any amount awarded but not paid from the date of the award up to the date of payment, it being made clear that the amount awarded can include any expenses awarded or indeed any interest in respect of a period prior to the award. In other words, if the tribunal orders the losing party to pay £1,150,000, comprising damages of £1 million, expenses of £50,000 and interest from the date of breach of £100,000, it has discretion to order that post-award interest should be payable on the whole of that sum.

Rule 50(2) and (3)

The award may specify the rate(s) of interest, the period for which it is payable, and whether any rests apply, i.e. periods during which interest should not be payable. It may treat different amounts quite differently here, for example applying different rates to pre and post award interest, or to expenses or damages.

If an award directs that an amount should be paid, for example, within one month of the date of the award and that interest at a particular rate should be payable if the amount is not paid, if the amount awarded is not paid by that date, is interest payable from that date or the date of the award? The tribunal's power to determine the periods for which interest is payable, allows it to choose either date, but if this is not made clear, it is suggested that the rule contemplates that interest is payable from the date of the award.

However, the discretion conferred by r.50(2) and (3) must be considered in the light of r.50(4)

Rule 50(4)

Interest is to be calculated as agreed by the parties or is at the discretion of the tribunal in the absence of such agreement.

Is there any restriction on the power of the parties in this regard? They cannot exclude the power to award interest, but would the mandatory nature of r.50 preclude them from agreeing that interest should be levied at 0 per cent? If so, then presumably agreeing to an infinitesimally low rate of interest would be valid. What if the parties agreed that an exorbitantly high rate should apply? The previous version of r.46 made it clear that compound interest, i.e. interest on interest, might be payable. This is not mentioned in the current version, but given that parties may competently confer such a power at common law, then it must be assumed that they retain this power. The fact that the rule is now mandatory would seem to prevent the parties agreeing that the issue of interest should be governed by a foreign law. But if there was such agreement, could the provisions of that law be invoked by the parties to determine how interest is to be calculated? Is the same true of particular arbitral rules invoked by the parties in so far as those rules address the issue of interest (see, e.g. art.26 of the LCIA Rules)? Can the parties agree that the tribunal should not be able to order rests?

If the parties have not reached agreement on this issue, is there any restriction on the discretion of the tribunal in this context? As noted in the commentary to r.49, the version of the Bill originally laid before the Scottish Parliament featured a default rule which would have restricted tribunals to granting only those remedies which would have been available to the Court of Session in the same circumstances. As a default rule, it could have been overridden by the parties, but if it was not so overridden, then it would have severely restricted the discretion of the tribunal to award interest (and in England the House of Lords has held that the issue of interest is a matter of procedural rather than substantive law, and thus governed not by the law of the contract, but by the 1996 Act—*Lesotho Highlands Development Authority v Impregilo SpA* [2005] 2 Lloyd's Rep. 310). However, the discarding of the rule suggests that the tribunal's discretion here is subject to no fetters other than imposed by the parties, although any implied restriction on the power of the parties re interest must also apply to the tribunal.

Would the tribunal's discretion extend to awarding compound interest? The approach of Scots law is that it cannot be awarded unless the contract specifically authorises it (see Lord Gifford in *Baird's Trustees v Baird & Co* (1877) 4 R. 1005 at 1015). Under s.49 of the 1996 Act the tribunal is expressly empowered to do so unless the parties have withheld that power. The DAC Report, paras 235–238 felt that this power should be made explicit, since the English courts similarly have no inherent power to award compound interest (*Westdeutsche Landesbank Girozentrale v Islington London Borough Council* [1996] A.C. 669). Entrusting this power to tribunals was justified on the basis that most of its respondents favoured such a power, while it felt that fears that it might be abused were groundless. It is submitted that the tribunal's discretion under r.50 would so extend, but it is unfortunate that this has not been made clear.

An award which saw the tribunal exceed its powers regarding the award of interest or ignore the agreement of the parties would presumably be challengeable in the usual way under rr.67–69 (and see *Lesotho Highlands Development Authority v Impregilo SpA* [2005] 2 Lloyd's Rep. 310). If the award were simply silent on interest it would remain to be seen whether it might be challengeable under r.68(2)(c) on the basis that the tribunal had failed to deal with all the issues that were put to it. Such a challenge would surely only be possible if the claimant had raised the issue of interest (*Pirtek (UK) Ltd v Deanswood Ltd* [2005] 2 Lloyd's Rep. 728). English authority to the effect that the tribunal has no jurisdiction to award interest where it has not been invited to consider the issue (*Westland Helicopters Ltd v Al-Hajailan* [2004] 2 Lloyd's Rep. 523) surely cannot be relevant in light of the mandatory nature of the provision.

Rule 50(5)

It is not clear what purpose this provision serves, although it echoes s.49(6) of the 1996 Act. It may be that it is drafted with statutory arbitrations in mind. In *Lesotho Highlands Authority v Impregilo SpA* [2005] 2 Lloyd's Rep. 310 the House of Lords held that s.49(6) was merely a saving provision, which did not oust any other power to award interest conferred by the parties or the Act.

Rule 51: Form of award **D**

51.—(1) The tribunal's award must be signed by all arbitrators or all those assenting to the award.
 (2) The tribunal's award must state—
  (a) the seat of the arbitration,
  (b) when the award is made and when it takes effect,
  (c) the tribunal's reasons for the award, and
  (d) whether any previous provisional or part award has been made (and the extent to which any previous provisional award is superseded or confirmed).
 (3) The tribunal's award is made by delivering it to each of the parties in accordance with rule 83.

DEFINITIONS
 "party": ss.2(1), 31(1), (2)
 "rules": ss.7, 31(1)

COMMENTARY
This rule carries echoes of s.52 of the 1996 Act and art.31 of the Model Law, although it is closer in form to the former. Like the former it is a default rule, whereas art.31 is mandatory in part. The explanatory notes, para.159 suggest that if the award is not in proper form it may be set aside, without suggesting the grounds on which this might be done. It is probable that casting the award in improper form would be a serious irregularity in terms of r.68(2)(a)(ii), but an alternative view is that it does not fall to be regarded as an award at all.

Rule 51(1)

Award must be signed: The award must be signed by all the arbitrators or all those assenting to the award. Were it not so, then a dissenting arbitrator could effectively undermine the proceedings by refusing to sign. Of course, since this is a default rule the parties might decide that all arbitrators should sign, whether assenting or not, thus running the above risk. That would be the practical effect if the parties agreed to arbitration under certain arbitration rules, e.g. the GAFTA Arbitration Rules art.9.1. An arbitrator who refused to sign might well be in breach of contract, and if that refusal were in bad faith, he might forfeit his immunity under r.73 (see *Cargill International SA Antigue (Geneva Branch) v Sociedad Iberica de Molturacion SA* [1998] 1 Lloyd's Rep. 489). Under the Model Law it is enough that the majority of the arbitrators should sign, whether there is dissent or not, provided the reason for the missing signature is stated. As the Model Law is mandatory on this point, it would override the agreement of the parties that all arbitrators must sign. The approach of the Model Law may seem preferable in this regard.

It must be presumed that the arbitrators who do sign may do so at different times and in different places. There has never been any suggestion that Scotland follows the old English common law rule—now almost certainly defunct (see *Bank Mellat v GAA Development Construction Co Ltd* [1988] 2 Lloyd's Rep. 44)—that the arbitrators had to sign the award at the same time and in the same place (see, e.g. *Peterson v Ayre* (1855) 15 C.B. 724). It might be quite a different matter, however, if an arbitrator simply signed a blank piece of paper on the basis that he would be prepared to concur with whatever award were produced (see, e.g. *European Grain & Shipping Ltd v Johnston* [1982] 3 All E.R. 989). Such a signature would surely not be valid, and the same would be true of the award if that signature were necessary. It might also be added that the idea of majority signature presupposes that all the arbitrators were permitted to participate in the decision, so that if one of the arbitrators was excluded from the tribunal's deliberations by the others, then the award might be challenged on the basis of serious procedural irregularity (see the decision in *Czech Republic v CME* Unreported May 15, 2003 Swedish Court of Appeal). This would be the position at common law (*McCallum v Robertson* (1825) 4 S. 66) and under the Model Law (*Report of the Working Group on International Contract Practices on the work of its fourth session*, UN A/CN.9/232, para.18).

Of course the parties may go in the opposite direction and agree that only one arbitrator need sign—perhaps the presiding arbitrator. It should be borne in mind that the question of how many arbitrators must sign the award is different from the question of how many need agree to it. It will be recalled that although the assumption of the Act under r.30 is that majority rule prevails, the parties may agree otherwise. Thus if they have agreed that all decisions must be reached unanimously, but say nothing about the form of the award, while the award will meet the requirements of form in terms of r.51 if signed by those arbitrators who agree with, it will still not be a valid award if one of the arbitrators disagrees with it. In this context it should be noted that in those instances where majority rule does apply a dissenting arbitrator may wish to issue a separate opinion. National laws and institutional rules are generally silent on whether this is permissible. Only the ICSID Arbitration Rules r.47.3—which of course is a very particular form of a-national arbitration—actually sanction such a practice. The issue of dissenting opinions is generally to be discouraged, although in practical terms it may be impossible to prevent a dissenting arbitrator from issuing such an opinion, and indeed some may argue that they may prove useful if a party is considering whether the award might be challenged on the basis of error of law. Such opinions are in no sense part of the award (see *Stinnes Interoil GmbH v A Halcoussis & Co (The Yanxilas)* [1982] 2 Lloyd's Rep. 445), and the tribunal would be well advised to ensure that they are not issued along with the award. It is a different matter if the dissenting party wishes to sign the award, while simply indicating that he dissents from it (See further the articles by Refern, "Dissenting Opinions in International Commercial Arbitration: The Good, the Bad and the Ugly" (2004) 20 Arbitration Int. 223 and Dundas, "F Ltd v M Ltd: The Implications of Dissenting Opinion on Serious Irregularity in Arbitration" (2009) 75 *Arbitration* 454.)

Unlike the 1996 Act and the Model Law, r.51 does not actually demand that the award should be in writing, although the insistence on signatures surely implies this. At common law awards required to be in probative writing unless they were agricultural awards or references *in re mercatoria* which could be in informal writing (see Lord Justice-Clerk Aitchison in *McLaren v Aikman*, 1939 S.C. 222 at 227). However, the Requirements of

Writing (Scotland) Act 1995 seemed to remove any requirement that an award had to be in writing, subject perhaps to the possibility of it being an implied term in the contract between the arbitrator and the parties that the award must be in the same form as the reference (see Lord Neaves in *Dykes v Roy* (1869) 7 M. 357 at 360). The issue is of course now governed by r.51.

Theoretically, the parties could agree to dispense with the need for writing or signatures altogether, but that would court formidable difficulties in terms of enforcement, especially in international arbitration where art.IV.1 of the New York Convention demands a duly authenticated original award or a duly certified copy.

Rule 51(2)(a)

Award must state seat: Since, by virtue of s.7, r.48 only applies to arbitrations seated in Scotland, the effect of this provision is that the award must indicate that Scotland is the seat of the arbitration, except where the parties agree that it should not. They might perhaps do so by invoking institutional rules which suggest that it should take a different form. It might be expected that parties to entirely domestic arbitrations would usually wish to disapply this rule.

Of course the fact that the tribunal improperly omits to include this statement or even indicates an erroneous seat will not mean that Scotland is no longer the seat of the arbitration where it clearly has been so designated in terms of s.3, although such a step may be of more significance where the issue of the seat is debatable. Whether such a failure or error would amount to a serious irregularity justifying a challenge under r.68 is very dubious, since it is not clear how that failure or error could cause substantial injustice to the challenging party. This was indeed the view of the DAC Report, para.250 at least as far as a purely domestic arbitration is concerned. In relation to an international arbitration problems could potentially arise if the award had to be enforced in another jurisdiction and a court in that country took the failure to state a seat or the statement of the wrong seat at face value. This is because an award which is not "made" in a Convention state usually cannot be enforced under the New York Convention. Equally, a number of the grounds for refusing enforcement under the New York Convention refer to the law of the seat, so that a statement of the wrong seat could unexpectedly jeopardise enforcement.

The terms of s.52(5) of the 1996 Act are quite similar, while art.31(3) of the Model Law demands that the award, "shall state the place of arbitration as determined in accordance with Article 20", i.e. the seat. It is clear that a failure to comply with this provision does not render an award invalid in terms of the Model Law (see *Report of the Working Group on International Contract Practices on the work of its third session*, UN A/CN.9/216, para.79).

Rule 51(2)(b)

Award must state when it is made and when it takes effect: Unless the parties agree otherwise, the award must state the date when it is made and the date when it takes effect. Those dates may of course be the same, but the implication is that they might on occasion be different. Certain other rules specify time limits by reference to the award being "made", e.g. r.58(6)(a), while others simply speak of application having to be made within a certain period "of the award", e.g. r.58(4), while r.50 (interest) makes reference to the date of the award. The 1996 Act is clear that the tribunal has discretion as to the date of the award. Does this rule confer similar discretion on the tribunal, or are there specific dates when the rules envisage awards being made or taking effect? If discretion is given, is it subject to any limits? Presumably the tribunal would not be permitted to indicate without good reason that the award takes effect from a point in the remote future? Moreover, it must surely be a logical impossibility for an award to take effect before it is made.

Suppose however, the tribunal indicates that the award takes effect from a date significantly earlier than when it is communicated to the parties in an attempt to render challenge difficult or impossible because of the relevant time limits? Here one must consider the relationship between this provision and r.51(3), which indicates that the award is "made" by delivering it to each of the parties. If the award cannot take effect before it is made, then the date of taking effect cannot precede the date of delivery. Is that date of delivery then the date the award should bear? Rule 51(3) speaks of delivery in accordance with r.83, which seems to suggest—see r.83(5)(b) below—that if an award is posted it would be treated as "made" on the day on which it would be delivered in the ordinary course of post. That would tend to mean that even if the award were despatched to the parties at the same time, if one party were based in the same country as the sender of the award (which may not be Scotland), and the other were based at the other side of the world, the award would almost certainly arrive on different dates in respect of the two parties. When thus is that award "made", and what date should it bear? An alternative and more supportable interpretation is that it is the fact of delivery to each party which serves to make an award, so that the date of delivery is the date when the award is "made" irrespective of when it is actually received by a party. On that construction, the award is not made until delivery is made to every party.

Perhaps the most sensible approach is that the award should bear the date when it is actually signed. When there is only one arbitrator, then this is straightforward, but matters may be more complex if there are a number. In this context it may be observed that s.52(5) of the 1996 Act also demands that the award should state the date when it is made (though not the date when it takes effect), and while, subject to the agreement of the parties the tribunal may decide what is taken to be that date—s.54(1), in the absence of such decision, s.54(2) dictates that the date shall be the date when it is to be signed, or when more than one arbitrator signs the award the date when the last signs. That approach is not itself free from difficulty, since if it is not clear whether a dissenting arbitrator is prepared to sign, the date of the award is rather uncertain. It can be appreciated, however, that the "actual" date of the award under the 1996 Act may be different from the date it bears. Probably then the key issue under the rules is usually when the award is actually made, irrespective of the date which it bears. However, it may still be a ground for setting aside an award that it bears no date or an inappropriate date, since there are key provisions which refer to the date of the award. Again, it will certainly be a ground for setting aside an award that it fails to indicate when it takes effect, since that is a key date and the rules contain no provision deeming a particular date to be the point at which the award takes effect in the absence of a statement in the award. Of course, where an award does not state its date or fails to say when it takes effect either party may ask that this be rectified under r.58(1)(a), and it may be that all legal consequences flow from the point when this is done (see *Weldon Plant Ltd v Commission for the New Towns* [2000] B.L.R. 496).

Generally the relationship between the concepts of the date of the award, the date when it is made and the date it takes effect appears not to have been thought through, and r.51 contains much scope for confusion unless courts adopt a bold and purposive approach to interpretation. The Model Law, on the face of it, is even less helpful, with art.31(3) simply demanding that the award shall state its date, without indicating how that might be determined. At one point, the Model Law indicated that it was made when signed by the tribunal (see *Note by UNCITRAL Secretariat on draft articles 25–36*, UN A/CN.9/WG.II/WP.38, art.27(2)) and at another point that it was deemed to be made on the date that it bore (*Note by UNCITRAL Secretariat on draft articles 1–26*, UN A/CN.9/WG.II/WP.40, art.22(3)), but both those provisions were ultimately discarded. Yet it is perhaps of no consequence that the Model Law gives no guidance on such questions, since nothing important turns on the date of the award or when it can be regarded as made, as time limits regarding such matters as challenge are expressed by reference to the question of when a copy of the award is received by either party. This might have been a preferable approach to adopt, albeit that it raises issues of proof.

It should be remembered that r.51 only applies if the parties do not provide otherwise, so that a clear statement by the parties on how such matters should be resolved would remove any uncertainties. As to how institutional rules might deal with the matter, quite a few such rules equally indicate that the award must state its date. In so far as this is different from the date when the award is made, it remains to be seen whether this would supplant or supplement r.51(2)(b). However, art.18.2 of the Scottish Arbitration Code states that the date the award is made is the date of signature by the arbitrator, which would seem to exclude r.51(3). Article 25.3 of the ICC Rules indicates that the award is to be deemed to be made on the date which it states, which would also exclude r.51(3).

Rule 51(2)(c)

Award must contain reasons: Unless the parties agree otherwise, the award must contain reasons. This is not the position at common law, but most institutional rules demand reasons as do the 1996 Act and the Model Law. Prior to the 1996 Act the position of English law was similarly that reasons did not have to be provided unless the parties had required them. However, the DAC Report, para.247 stated that:

"... it is a basic rule of justice that those charged with making a binding decision affecting the rights and obligations of others should (unless those others agree) explain the reasons for making this decision".

The reasons for an award are of course the reasons of the majority of the tribunal in cases of dissent (see *Cargill International SA Antigua (Geneva Branch) v Sociedad Iberica de Molturacion SA* [1998] 1 Lloyd's Rep. 489).

Rule 57(4) makes it clear that where the award reflects the terms of a settlement between the parties, reasons are not required (since there are none), while r.69(2) provides that an agreement by the parties to dispense with reasons will be taken as an agreement to exclude the right to challenge an award on the basis of an error of Scots law. If the parties agreed to arbitrate under a set of rules which contemplated that reasons should not be given, then that would surely suffice to exclude the need for reasons. It is submitted that rules which give the arbitrator discretion to provide reasons (see, e.g. Law Society of Scotland Arbitration Rules, para.25.6) would have a similar effect. In terms of s.8(4)(b), so would an agreement to arbitrate in Scotland under a procedural law which did not demand a reasoned award, e.g. U.S. law (see *United Steelworkers of America v Enterprise Wheel & Car Corp*, 363 U.S. 593 (1960)), equally impliedly disapply the rule. Institutional rules might also sanction the provision of very limited reasons. In *Bay Hotel and Resort Ltd v Cavalier Construction Co Ltd* [2001] UKPC 34, an arbitration seated in the Turks and Caicos Islands was conducted under the rules of the American Arbitration Association, which required only a "written explanation" of the award. The tribunal ordered the payment of a sum of compensation on the basis that it had found the losing party liable. The Privy Council recognised that while this would not meet the requirement of providing reasons under the relevant legislation, it was within what was contemplated by the AAA rules (see article by Dundas, "Joinder, Reasons and Seat: the Privy Council Decides: *Bay Hotel and Resort Ltd v. Cavalier Construction Co. Ltd*" (2002) 68 *Arbitration* 184).

Some forms of arbitration appear to be inimical to the provision of reasons, e.g. commodity quality arbitrations of the "look-sniff" variety (now increasingly rare in practice), but unless the parties might be said to have impliedly agreed to forgo reasons by electing for such an arbitration, r.51(2)(c) would appear to demand that such awards should be reasoned. Nonetheless, it might be noted that the *travaux preparatoires* to the Model Law suggested that such an implied exclusion might arise in relation to arbitrations where customarily no reasons were given (see *Analytical Commentary on Article 31*, UN A/CN.9/264, para.3).

Of course, the fact that an award is reasoned may be of small comfort to a party who can see that the reasoning is clearly erroneous. An award may not be challenged on the basis that the tribunal has obviously misunderstood the facts or evidence, unless this amounts to an error of law. Moreover, it is only an error of Scots law which is capable of being challenged, so if the reasons demonstrate misapplication of foreign law, no challenge is competent however gross the error is. The same is true even if Scots law applies should the parties have contracted out of the right to challenge an award on the basis of an error of Scots law.

Form of reasons: In terms of how reasons might be given, English authority recognises that if an award is being written by arbitrators who are not lawyers, it might be rather different in form from a judgment. Thus Donaldson L.J. in *Bremer Handelsgesellschaft mbH v Westzucker GmbH (No.2)* [1981] 2 Lloyd's Rep. 130 at 132 (see also the Model Law case of *Navigation Somanar Inc v Algoma Steamships Ltd* (1994) XIX YCA 256 Quebec Supreme Court) suggests that:

> "All that is necessary is that the arbitrators should set out what, on their view of the evidence, did or did not happen and should explain succinctly why, in the light of what happened, they have reached their decision and what that decision is. Where [an] ... award differs from a judgment is that the arbitrators will not be expected to analyse the law and the authorities. It will be quite sufficient that they should explain how they reached their conclusion."

It has also been suggested that there is no need to recite the reasons for rejecting the losing party's arguments as long as it is clear why the arbitrators reached their award (see *Finelvet AG v Vinava Shipping Co Ltd (The Chrysalis)* [1983] 1 Lloyd's Rep. 503).

Power to order reasons: In this context, the reader is also referred to the commentary to r.71(8)(a). This appears to be modelled on s.70(4) of the 1996 Act and relates to awards which are being appealed. It allows the Outer House to order the tribunal to state its reasons for the award being appealed in sufficient detail to enable the Outer House to deal with the appeal properly. The most obvious situation in which the Outer House might exercise this power is where a party wishes to challenge the tribunal's decision on the basis of a suspected error of law, but the tribunal has provided inadequately explained reasons, or has perhaps failed to provide any reasons at all. Nonetheless, there is no suggestion that the power of the Outer House is thus confined, so that it may sometimes feel that it is appropriate to seek fuller reasons in the context of a jurisdictional appeal under r.67 and conceivably even a serious irregularity appeal under art.68. Thus while one might ordinarily suppose that the power under r.71(8)(a) would not be exercised where the award was not based on Scots law, since then it would not be challengeable on the basis of error of law under r.69, that restriction may not apply. Indeed, even where the parties have agreed that the award should not contain reasons, the Outer House may wish to learn the tribunal's reasons in order to be sure that no ground of appeal exists on the basis of excess of jurisdiction or serious irregularity (see Webster J. in *Atlantic Lines & Navigation Co Inc v Italmare SpA (The Appollon)* [1985] 1 Lloyd's Rep. 597 at 601).

It has been held in the context of the 1996 Act that where the parties had agreed that there were to be no reasons given in the award, but that in terms of the then current LMAA Rules reasons were to be provided in a separate document expressly on the basis that no reference should be made to them in subsequent proceedings, s.70(4) permitted the court to insist that the puportedly confidential reasons be revealed to it in order to determine whether there had been a serious irregularity (*Tame Shipping Ltd v Easy Navigation Ltd (The Easy Rider)* [2004] 2 Lloyd's Rep. 626). The same case suggests that the power of the court overrides any agreement by the parties that the award is to remain confidential. In the same context it has also been held that a clear failure to deal with an issue in an award cannot be cured by asking the tribunal to elaborate on its reasons (see *Hussmann (Europe) Ltd v Al Ameen Development Trade Co* [2000] 2 Lloyd's Rep. 83).

It should also be noted that under r.71(2) no appeal is competent unless a party has exhausted any recourse under r.58. This allows a tribunal to correct or clarify an award. These provisions echo ss.57 and 70(2) of the 1996 Act and in that context *Al-Hadha Trading Co v Tradegrain SA* [2002] 2 Lloyd's Rep. 512 held that a party would first be expected to invite the tribunal to provide reasons where none had been given or clarify its reasoning where this was ambiguous or inadequate, before bringing an appeal.

What would happen if an award stated no reasons in circumstances where neither excess of jurisdiction nor serious irregularity were suspected? If the substance of the award was not based on Scots law, the answer might be nothing. Since the award could not be appealed on the basis of an error of foreign law, then while the failure to state reasons would probably itself amount to a serious irregularity, it would be difficult to argue that the irregularity could cause substantial injustice to the appellant (but see *Benaim (UK) Ltd v Davies, Middleton & Davies Ltd (No.2)* [2005] EWHC 1370 (TCC) at [82]).

Rule 51(2)(d)

Award must state whether any previous award was made: Unless the parties agree otherwise, the award must state whether any previous provisional or part award has been made, and the extent to which such provisional or part award has been superseded or confirmed. Contrary agreement might take the form of institutional rules which direct that the award take a different form.

This is a provision which has no parallel in either the 1996 Act or the Model Law, but may be helpful in certain situations. A provisional award (see the commentary to r.53 below) is an award which deals with a particular issue or set of issues on an interim basis. Thus there might be merit in the final award making clear what effect it has on the earlier award. A part award (see the commentary to r.54 below), by contrast deals once and for all with certain of the matters before the tribunal. It cannot be affected by the final award, so that it is not clear what benefit is sought to be gained by insisting that the latter award should refer to it. It should nonetheless be noted that this reflects standard arbitral practice under which awards tend to recite details of all previous awards of whatever nature.

Failure to comply with this provision might amount to a serious irregularity, but it would be difficult to see how that irregularity could cause substantial injustice to a party so as to allow a successful challenge.

Rule 51(3)

Award made by delivery to parties: It should be remembered that this, like the rest of r.51 is a default rule and so may be excluded by the parties. Thus, as noted above, it would be excluded by the parties arbitrating under the Scottish Arbitration Code, art.18.2 of which states that the date the award is made is the date of signature by the arbitrator, or under the ICC Rules, art.25.3 of which indicates that the award is to be deemed to be made on the date which it states.

Otherwise, however, the award is made by delivering it to each of the parties. It is not intended to cover the detail of r.83, for which see the commentary on that rule, but it has already been noted above that it is possible on one construction of this provision for the award to be made at different times in respect of each party. It is submitted that if the parties stipulate that the award must be made by a certain date or within a certain period, the tribunal cannot cure their failure to meet that deadline by stating an erroneous date on the award, since it is delivery of the award rather than the date it bears which determines when an award is made. If the Scottish Arbitration Code is applied, it is suggested that it is the actual date the arbitrator signs which would determine when they award was made, rather than the date the award bears. Since art.25.3 of the ICC Rules provides that the award is to be deemed to be made on the date which it states, that presents more of a challenge, but the ICC Court would never permit a tribunal thus to flout contractually stipulated time limits.

Rule 52: Award treated as made in Scotland **D**

52. An award is to be treated as having been made in Scotland even if it is signed at, or delivered to or from, a place outwith Scotland.

COMMENTARY

This is the equivalent of s.53 of the 1996 Act, which makes it clear that this result follows where England is the seat of the arbitration. While r.52 omits these key words, the intended effect is the same, since the crucial feature which secures the application of the 2010 Act is that the arbitration is seated in Scotland in terms of s.3. As regard arbitrations held outwith the UK, s.18(2) provides than an award seeking enforcement under the New York Convention is to be treated as made at the seat of the arbitration.

This reverses the effect of the remarkable decision of the House of Lords in *Hiscox v Outhwaite* [1992] 1 A.C. 562 (see Fraser P. Davidson, "Where is an Arbitral Award Made?—*Hiscox v Outhwaite*" (1992) 41 I.C.L.Q. 637) that an award in an arbitration between two English parties, conducted in London by an English arbitrator under English substantive and procedural law was to be treated as a French award because the arbitrator indicated that he had signed it while in Paris. The logic of that decision was that the award was "made" wherever the arbitrator happened to be when he signed the award, or presumably where the final arbitrator happened to be when he signed the award if there were several arbitrators. Their Lordships were influenced in reaching their decision by ancient English authority on where an award might be made, while practically no reference was made to the New York Convention. Several grounds for refusing enforcement of an award under the Convention make reference to the law of the country where the award was made. This can only make sense if that place is taken to be the seat of the arbitration, since it cannot be imagined that the framers of the Convention would have put the enforceability of the award in jeopardy by making it depend on the law of a country which might have no connection with the arbitration at all just because of the accidental fact that the arbitrator signed it there. While the *Hiscox* decision no longer applied in England after the 1996 Act, it remained good law in Scotland, being a decision of the House of Lords on a UK statute—the Arbitration Act 1975. It is pleasing to see it finally laid to rest.

It remains common practice for arbitrators to indicate the place where the award is signed. However, in such cases it is the fact that the seat of the arbitration is in Scotland which determines where the award is made. As suggested in the discussion of r.51(2)(a), while the award should ordinarily state that Scotland is the seat of the arbitration, the fact that the award fails to do so, or erroneously states that another country is the seat of the arbitration, will not prevent the award from being regarded as made in Scotland as far as the 2010 Act is concerned. (Other states might choose to regard it as made elsewhere, but this is unlikely.)

Since this is a very important provision, it is curious that, like s.53 of the 1996 Act, it is non-mandatory. However, circumstances may sometimes arise which drive the parties to decide that the award should be made somewhere other than the seat, e.g. if Scotland were to gain independence and were not to adhere to the New York Convention, or if hostilities broke out between the UK and the state where it was hoped that the award would be enforced. That being said, the rule could not bind courts in such other states.

Rule 53: Provisional awards **D**

53. The tribunal may make a provisional award granting any relief on a provisional basis which it has the power to grant permanently.

DEFINITIONS
 "tribunal": ss.2(1), 31(1)

COMMENTARY
 At common law while the parties could certainly confer power on the tribunal to make an interim award—an award which dealt with an issue for the time being only—it was not conclusively settled that a tribunal would have an inherent power to make such awards in the absence of such agreement. Lord President Boyle in *Lyle v Falconer* (1842) 5 D. 236 at 239 seemed to assume that there was such a power, while Lord Cameron in *Taylor Woodrow Construction (Scotland) Ltd v Sears Investment Trust Ltd*, 1992 S.L.T. 609 at 611 appeared to believe that there was not. Most recently, while Lord Malcolm held that there was such a power in *Apollo Engineering Ltd v James Scott Ltd*, 2008 S.L.T. 472, the Inner House ([2009] CSIH 39; 2009 S.C. 525) seemed more dubious, but ultimately ruled that the matter

did not arise for decision in the case. Now a tribunal clearly has that power, albeit the term provisional award is employed, since it is thought to be more in tune with international practice. The Model Law, by referring in art.32 to the tribunal making a final award, seems to imply that other sorts of awards might be possible. Yet a proposal (see *Report of the Secretary General on the possible features of a Model Law on International Commercial Arbitration*, UN A/CN.9/207, para.82) to empower tribunals to make, "interim, interlocutory and partial awards" (as under art.32.1 of the UNCITRAL Arbitration Rules) was rejected on the basis that there was no clear consensus on what those terms meant in international practice (see UN A/CN.9/207, para.73). This then was not an issue addressed by the Model Law, and certain jurisdictions (e.g. British Columbia) in adopting the Model Law explicitly conferred on tribunals power to make such awards. Scotland of course did not follow this lead when it adopted the Model Law.

Power to make provisional awards

Originally r.53 was mandatory. This was apparently designed to protect parties in cases where there is "inequality of arms" and prevent stronger parties routinely excluding the power to make provisional awards (see paras 127, 128 of the consultation paper). This seemed an unlikely scenario and it is surely more sensible that, like cl.23 of Lord Dervaird's draft Bill, the provision is now default. It might be observed that its counterpart in the 1996 Act—s.39—states that the power to make such awards is only conferred when the parties expressly so agree. The DAC deliberately altered the draft of s.39 so that it would take this form because (see DAC Report, para.201):

"... enormous care has to be taken to avoid turning what can be a useful judicial tool into an instrument of injustice [and] we received responses from a number of practising arbitrators to the effect that they would be unhappy with such powers and saw no need for them."

While the original version of this provision would have followed the example of s.39 and given examples of the sort of thing a provisional award might order—the payment of money or the transfer of property to another party, an interim payment towards the arbitration expenses—r.53 omits any such examples, presumably on the basis that the power of the tribunal in this regard is limited by the range of remedies which the parties have empowered it to exercise. However, this is the sort of thing which a tribunal might be expected to do under r.53. It can be appreciated that such a power should be exercised with care. It is a very bold step for a tribunal to order the payment of a substantial sum of money to a party in advance of the actual determination of liability, and one would hope that it would only be taken if the risk that the party concerned might seek to frustrate the outcome of the proceedings was very real indeed. That being said, the tribunal is unfettered as to the circumstances in which it might employ this power. Of course the countervailing risk is that the tribunal orders the payment of money to which it transpires that the other party was not entitled, but which that other party proves unable to repay—something which sensible arbitrators should also bear in mind. It seems that the tribunal would not under r.53 have the power to order a party to provide security for the amount claimed (but see *Kastner v Jason* [2005] 1 Lloyd's Rep. 397), since that is not a relief which it has power to grant permanently, although the court could be asked to do so under r.46(1)(c)—but see the qualifications applied by r.46(2). It should be recalled that the range of remedies open to the tribunal could be wider than might be supposed, since although remedies are specified by r.49, that is a default rule. Thus the parties might expand on those remedies either explicitly, or by invoking a particular set of rules or a particular foreign law to govern the matter.

It might be added that in all of this it has been assumed that such an award would only be made where there is a danger that a party would seek to defeat the proceedings. However, that is not necessarily the case. A situation might arise, for example, where a party is clearly going to be found to be liable, although the extent of that liability remains to be determined. A provisional award in the other party's favour might well be appropriate in those circumstances, especially where the latter would otherwise face financial difficulties (see *Edinburgh and Glasgow Railway v Hill* (1840) 2 D. 468; *BMBF (No.12) v Harland & Wolff Shipbuilding & Heavy Industries Ltd* [2001] 2 Lloyd's Rep. 227). Such situations are commonplace in the construction industry, and standard arbitration rules in that industry have long conferred power on tribunals to order provisional relief (see, e.g. ICE Arbitration Procedure r.19.3, CIMAR Rules r.10).

While s.39 of the 1996 Act is headed "power to make provisional awards", it is clear that in exercising that power the tribunal is only making an order. By contrast, a provisional award under r.53 seems intended to operate as an award. This invites the question to what extent it must comply with the requirements as to form, and to what extent it is challengeable. It might be suggested that it is better not to regard it as an award in these respects, and indeed r.71(3) indicates that no appeal may be made against a provisional award. Yet it seems strange that an award which sought to grant on a provisional basis a remedy which the tribunal would be unable to grant in a final award should not be open to a jurisdictional challenge. Rule 71(3) also appears to imply that if the tribunal were to make a provisional award at the invitation of one party without hearing the other on the question, this could not be challenged on the basis of serious procedural irregularity. Pre-1996 Act authority in England suggests that the decision *not* to make a provisional order is not capable of challenge (*Japan Line Ltd v Aggeliki Charis Compania Maritima SA (The Angelic Grace)* [1980] 1 Lloyd's Rep. 288).

There also remains the question whether such an "award" would be recognised as such under the New York Convention in terms of being enforced abroad.

Rule 54: Part awards **M**

54.—(1) The tribunal may make more than one award at different times on different aspects of the matters to be determined.

(2) A "part award" is an award which decides some (but not all) of the matters which the tribunal is to decide in the arbitration.

(3) A part award must specify the matters to which it relates.

DEFINITIONS
  "arbitration": ss.2(1), (2), 31(1)
  "tribunal": ss.2(1), 31(1)

COMMENTARY

Rule 54(1) and (2)

As with provisional awards, at common law while the parties could certainly confer power on the tribunal to make a part award, it was uncertain whether a tribunal had an inherent power to make such awards in the absence of such agreement (compare Lord Jeffrey in *Lyle v Falconer* (1842) 5

D. 236 at 240 with Lord Cameron in *Taylor Woodrow Construction (Scotland) Ltd v Sears Investment Trust Ltd*, 1992 S.L.T. 609 at 611). Rule 54 now confers that power. Unlike r.53, it is a default rule. Thus the parties may disapply it, either explicitly or by invoking arbitral rules or a foreign law (e.g. that of Gibraltar) which do not permit the making of part awards, although the authors are not aware of any rules which have this effect. It would surely be rare for the power to be excluded by implication, but such was the view taken in *Minerals and Metals Trading Corp of India Ltd v Encounter Bay Shipping Co Ltd (The Samos Glory) (No.2)* [1988] 1 Lloyd's Rep. 51, a case decided under s.14 of the 1950 Act (see now s.47 of the 1996 Act), the court deciding that that the issues in that case were indivisible.

A part award deals conclusively with a particular issue or set of issues, so that unlike a provisional award such matters need not be revisited in the final award (see DAC Report, para.202), and cannot be since they are res judicata. Indeed, while in terms of r.51(1)(d) a final award must note that a previous part award has been made, the tribunal has no power to reconsider any matter dealt with in that part award (*Charles M Willie & Co (Shipping) Ltd v Ocean Laser Shipping Ltd (The Smaro)* [1999] 1 Lloyd's Rep. 225). There is absolutely no doubt that it must be treated like an award in all respects, including requirements of form and susceptibility to challenge. Such an award might be made if there are a number of issues before the tribunal and some may be conveniently dealt with before others. Thus, for example, part awards may serve to dispose of at different times a variety of claims before the tribunal in a given arbitration (see DAC Report, para.227), or perhaps to dispose of the issue of liability prior to quantum (see *Trans Trust SPRL v Danubian Trading Co Ltd* [1952] 2 Q.B. 297), or to deal with every issue save that of expenses (see *Exmar BV v National Iranian Tanker Co (The Trade Fortitude)* [1992] 1 Lloyd's Rep. 169). Exercising this power might indeed assist the tribunal in its duty under r.24(1)(c) to conduct the arbitration without unnecessary delay and avoiding unnecessary expense (see DAC Report, para.227). Subject to its general duties a tribunal would have discretion whether or not to make such an award (see *The Trade Fortitude* [1992] 1 Lloyd's Rep. 169). In England a tribunal has occasionally found it more convenient to make an award on a claim before considering a counterclaim (*SL Sethia Liners v Naviagro Maritme Corp (The Kostas Melas)* [1981] 1 Lloyd's Rep. 18, where the tribunal took the view that the counterclaim was not made in good faith). Again, the power to make part awards was not a matter addressed by the Model Law, and the reader is referred to the discussion of r.53 in this regard.

Such awards would qualify to be regarded as awards under the New York Convention, and thus could be expected to be enforced, assuming that there was anything to enforce (see Robert B. von Mehren, "The Enforcement of Arbitral Awards under Conventions and United States Law" (1985) 9 Yale J. World Pub. Ord. 343). Thus a part award which ordered the payment of money should be enforced, but an award which dealt with liability but not quantum or which was merely declaratory could not be (see *FCLG Enterprises v Golden Margarine Ltd* [2004] O.J. 3804).

Rule 54(3)

Like most of the provision, this may seem to state the obvious. However, a part award would be expected not only to state that it was a part award, but to indicate clearly the issues with which it deals. Thus, for example, an award which stated itself to be a part award and then simply awarded a sum to one party with no further explanation would be inept. A party would thus be entitled to ask the tribunal for a clarification of the award under r.58(1)(b), and if such a step failed, to challenge the award on the basis of a serious irregularity in terms of r.68(2)(a)(ii) (see *Leach v Haringey London Borough Council, The Times*, March 23, 1977).

Rule 55: Draft awards **D**

55. Before making an award, the tribunal—
   (a) may send a draft of its proposed award to the parties, and
   (b) if it does so, must consider any representations from the parties about the draft which the tribunal receives by such time as it specifies.

DEFINITIONS
"party": ss.2(1), 31(1), (2)
"tribunal": ss.2(1), 31(1)

COMMENTARY

This is an issue which is not addressed by either the 1996 Act or the Model Law. At common law while arbitrators had a discretion to issue draft awards, they were under no obligation to do so (see Lord Gifford in *McCallum v Robertson* (1826) 2 W. & S. 344 at 352), except presumably where the parties had agreed that a draft award would be issued (as would be the case if, for example, they agreed to arbitrate under the Law Society of Scotland Arbitration Rules—see r.25.5.). Due to the drafting of s.3 of the Administration of Justice (Scotland) Act 1972 which prevented a final award being challenged on the basis of error of law under the now-repealed stated case procedure (*Fairlie Yacht Slip v Lumsden*, 1977 S.L.T. (Notes) 41), such a challenge was only possible if the tribunal issued a draft award (see Lord President Emslie at 42; *City of Aberdeen Council v Bredero Aberdeen Centre Ltd*, 1998 S.C. 269). While the issuing of draft awards is unknown in many jurisdictions, in domestic arbitration the practice long predates the introduction of the stated case procedure, so that its demise does not undermine the usefulness of such awards. The parties, on seeing such an award may point out clerical, computational and other similar errors, or errors of law, or flaws in the tribunal's reasoning, or points where it has misapprehended a party's case or misunderstood the evidence. If the tribunal takes such points on board, this may obviate the need to seek to have the tribunal correct the award under r.58 or the need to appeal against the award under rr.67, 68 or 69. Critics of the practice, however, would suggest that it is an invitation to the parties to debate the contents, leading to unnecessary, time-consuming and expensive complications.

Rule 55 casts the common law power in statutory form. It is a default rule, so it must bow to any agreement, whether explicit or via the adoption of arbitral rules, that no draft award should be made or that a draft award must be made. Rule 12.10. of CIMAR gives the tribunal a discretion to make a draft award. Article 27 of the ICC Rules of course insists that the award must be scrutinised by the ICC Court, but this does not seem to preclude the showing of draft findings to the parties. Subject to the above, the tribunal seems to have complete discretion whether or not to make such an award. If it does so, it must send a draft to both parties and consider any representations they wish to make about the award. It seems to be entitled to reject such representations, but to refuse to entertain them would be a serious irregularity. It would similarly be a serious irregularity to send the draft only to one of the parties or to consider representations from only one of the parties. Similarly, while the tribunal seems to have discretion as to the period within which such representations might be made, if it were to specify an unreasonably short period, then it would not be treating the parties fairly in terms of r.24(1)(b), and that would also amount to a serious irregularity. Whether an appeal against the final award on such a basis would succeed must of course depend on whether the tribunal's behaviour has caused substantial injustice to the party concerned. In this context it might do so if there had been no further opportunity to challenge or correct the award. This might happen where, for instance, a party has not been allowed to point out an error of law in the award and the award falls into one of the categories of award which may not be challenged by the parties.

If an "award" clearly indicates that it is a draft or proposed award, then it is not an award at all, and has no legal status. Thus it need not comply with any requirements as to form, is not open to challenge, and cannot be enforced.

A final point must be whether the provision sets a trap for an unwary party. Suppose that it is clear from a draft award that the tribunal has exceeded its jurisdiction. Should a party fail to make any representations about this, he would surely be regarded as having lost his right to object by virtue of r.76, and thus be precluded from challenging the final award.

Rule 56: Power to withhold award on non-payment of fees or expenses **M**

56.—(1) The tribunal may refuse to deliver or send its award to the parties if any fees and expenses for which they are liable under rule 60 have not been paid in full.

(2) Where the tribunal so refuses, the court may (on an application by any party) order—
- (a) that the tribunal must deliver the award on the applicant paying into the court an amount equal to the fees and expenses demanded (or such lesser amount as may be specified in the order),
- (b) that the amount paid into the court is to be used to pay the fees and expenses which the court determines as being properly payable, and
- (c) that the balance (if any) of the amount paid into the court is to be repaid to the applicant.

(3) The court may make such an order only if the applicant has exhausted any available arbitral process of appeal or review of the amount of the fees and expenses demanded.

(4) The court's decision on an application under this rule is final.

DEFINITIONS
 "court": s.31(1)
 "party": ss.2(1), 31(1), (2)
 "tribunal": ss.2(1), 31(1)

COMMENTARY

Rule 56(1)

This rule is based on s.56 of the 1996 Act, which in turn was based on s.19 of the 1950 Act. It has no counterpart in the Model Law. It allows the tribunal to refuse to send or deliver the award to the parties if any fees or expenses for which they are liable under r.58 remain unpaid. The term "deliver" was added at stage 2, presumably because under r.51(3) an award is made through delivery to the parties in terms of r.83. The issue of when an award is made and when it takes effect, and whether those two dates might be different is discussed in the context of r.51(2)(b). It is not proposed to rehearse that discussion here. Suffice it to say then that since in terms of r.71(4)(a) an award is generally open to appeal only within 28 days of it taking effect, parties may have an incentive to pay all fees and expenses fairly promptly, just in case the court takes the view that the award takes effect from the date stated thereon (see *International Petroleum Refining & Supply Sdad v Elpis Finance SA (The Faith)* [1993] 2 Lloyd's Rep. 408). It must be wondered whether that 28 day period is suspended where a party makes an application under r.58(2).

Arbitration expenses are defined by r.59 and the parties are under r.60 severally (i.e. separately) liable for all the fees and expenses of the arbitration, including the fees of anyone engaged by the tribunal and any expert from whom it might seek an opinion. In terms of r.60(2) the parties are also severally liable for all the fees and expenses of any arbitral appointments referee and any other third party to whom the parties have given power in relation to the arbitration, e.g. a contractually stipulated appointing authority. This last category might embrace the ICC in an ICC administered arbitration, but even if it does not r.56 surely does not prevent the operation of art.28.1 of the ICC Rules by virtue of which the ICC Secretariat may refuse to issue the award to the parties in an ICC arbitration unless they have paid all expenses including those of the ICC itself.

It can be appreciated that the tribunal may thus decline to deliver the award even if all its own fees and expenses have been paid, if the fees and expenses of any arbitral appointments referee remain unpaid. Of course, it need not decline to deliver the award in those circumstances. If it does not, then the parties are still liable to the arbitral appointments referee, but the latter cannot rely on this lever to encourage payment. It is indeed entirely within the discretion of the tribunal whether it will decline to deliver the award even if its own fees and expenses have not been paid, and tribunals may choose to trust parties in this regard. It is clear that the fees and expenses of the arbitration include those of an umpire—see r.82—but there is nothing in r.56 equivalent to s.56(5) of the 1996 Act, which makes it plain that the reference to arbitrators includes any arbitrator who has ceased to act. Thus it is not certain whether the award might be withheld because the fees and expenses of a former member of the tribunal have not been paid.

Previously, authority from a period when arbitration was usually undertaken on a gratuitous basis suggested that where an arbitrator had refused to release an award unless he was paid a fee rendered that award susceptible to being set aside under art.25 of the Articles of Regulation 1695 on the basis that it was procured by "bribery" (see *Blair v Gibb* (1738) Mor. 664). More recent authority (*Fraser v Wright* (1838) 16 S. 1049) declined to follow this line, although falling short of unambiguously stating that the practice was entirely proper. The practice of withholding an award until fees and expenses were paid was, however, commonplace and sanctioned by various sets of arbitration rules. These are of course now unnecessary, since the practice is now supported by a statutory rule. The rule is of course mandatory, since there is no point conferring such a power on the tribunal if the parties are allowed to withdraw it.

It is the case of course that any party aggrieved by the exercise of this power may ask the court to intervene under r.56(2).

Finally, although any party may pay the relevant fees and expenses in order to obtain the award, the award itself should determine the liability of the parties to meet those fees and expenses as between themselves. Rule 62 governs this issue and indicates what the position is to be when the award fails to address this matter.

Rule 56(2)

Where a tribunal thus refuses to release the award, any party to the arbitration may make an application to the court (the sheriff court or Outer House, but the Inner House when the arbitrator or one of the arbitrators is a judge). Unlike the position under s.56(2) of the 1996 Act, that party need not give notice of that application to the tribunal and other parties, but such a requirement may appear in subsequent rules of court. The court may then order first that the award should be delivered on the applicant paying into court the amount demanded, or such lesser sum as the court may specify. While it is the applicant who has to pay this sum into court, he may in practice seek a contribution from the other party. A court may perhaps exercise its discretion to order delivery on payment of a lesser sum where the applicant is struggling to find the whole sum himself, or where the amount demanded seems obviously excessive. Indeed in this context the DAC Report, para.259 says in relation to the corresponding provision in the 1996 Act that if the power to order payment into court of a lesser sum were not there, "an arbitrator could demand an extortionate amount, in effect preventing a party from taking advantage of the mechanism provided for here". The court then determines the amount which is properly payable and orders that it should be used to pay the fees and expenses, with any balance being repaid to the applicant. The court of course has a discretion under this rule, so that it may not make any order at all. Nonetheless, if it thinks the tribunal is being reasonable and that the full amount demanded is properly payable, the simplest course of action is to order the release of the award on payment of that amount into court, with that amount being used to pay the fees and expenses, and no balance being repayable.

This rule provides recourse for a party who thinks that the amount demanded for the release of the award is or may be excessive. It does not assist a party who has already paid the fees and expenses demanded, but considers them to be excessive (see in this context the decision of the Swedish Supreme Court in *Hober, Kraus ND Melis v Soyak International Construction & Investment Inc, Mealey's International Arbitration Report*, Vol.24 No.3 (March, 2009)). Any recourse for such a party lies through applying to the Auditor of Court under r.60(5). It is clear under ss.56(5) and 28 of the 1996 Act that fees and expenses properly payable are either those fees and expenses which may have been agreed, or those which are fixed by the tribunal as long as in the latter case they are not excessive. In other words only those fees and expenses which are fixed by the tribunal may be challenged under the 1996 Act (*Agrimex Ltd v Tradigrain SA* [2003] 2 Lloyd's Rep. 537). If fees have been agreed, they cannot be challenged. It is not clear whether the court under r.56(2)(b) could decide that agreed fees are not properly payable, but that would be a remarkable position for any court to adopt.

The relationship between this rule and r.60 is similarly unclear. The latter rule contemplates that fees and expenses are to be settled by agreement or determined by the Auditor of Court. Will a party be expected to apply to the Auditor for the determination of fees and expenses prior to making an application to the court under r.56? Presumably not. But suppose the Auditor has already issued such a determination. Does that circumscribe the discretion of the court to decide what fees and expenses and "properly payable"?

In *Agrimex Ltd v Tradigrain SA* [2003] 2 Lloyd's Rep. 537, Thomas J. reduced the fees charged because they included an amount charged by a solicitor employed by the tribunal to draft the award in legally appropriate form, which charge Thomas J. considered to be excessive. He pointed out that he had no power under the Act to determine issues of liability as between the arbitrators and draftsman. However, if the situation were replicated in Scotland, as a matter of contract it might appear that the arbitrators might be liable to make up the draftsman's fee. The lesson must therefore be that the tribunal would be wise to seek the agreement of the parties before incurring such expense. Indeed, while, unless the parties have agreed otherwise, the tribunal has power under r.32(1) to employ agents, r.32(2) directs that the consent of the parties is required for any appointment in respect of which significant expenses are likely to arise. The logic of that rule might appear to be that if such consent has not been obtained, such expenses cannot be recovered from the parties.

It should be added that there may be practical difficulties in enforcing an order under r.56 on an arbitrator who does not live in the UK.

Rule 56(3)

As under s.56(4) of the 1996 Act, the court may not make such an order if there is any available arbitral process of review of the amount demanded.

Rule 56(4)

While under s.56(7) of the 1996 Act leave of the court is required for any appeal from its decision on such a matter, no appeal is possible under r.56. This is sensible since such issues do not appear to be an appropriate subject for an appeal.

Rule 57: Arbitration to end on last award or early settlement **D**

57.—(1) An arbitration ends when the last award to be made in the arbitration is made (and no claim, including any claim for expenses or interest, is outstanding).

(2) But this does not prevent the tribunal from ending the arbitration before then under rule 20(3) or 37(1).

(3) The parties may end the arbitration at any time by notifying the tribunal that they have settled the dispute.

(4) On the request of the parties, the tribunal may make an award reflecting the terms of the settlement and these rules (except for rule 51(2)(c) and Part 8) apply to such an award as they apply to any other award.

(5) The fact that the arbitration has ended does not affect the operation of these rules (in so far as they apply) in relation to matters connected with the arbitration.

DEFINITIONS
 "arbitration": ss.2(1), (2), 31(1)
 "party": ss.2(1), 31(1), (2)
 "rules": ss.7, 31(1)
 "tribunal": ss.2(1), 31(1)

COMMENTARY
This is another curious provision in that it deals with two separate, but related, issues—termination of proceedings and settlements taking the form of an award.

Rule 57(1)

The 1996 Act does not deal explicitly with termination (except with regard to settlement), but art.32 of the Model Law does, since it was thought useful to indicate that a final award terminated the proceedings for three reasons: first, simply to indicate when the proceedings did indeed terminate; secondly, to make it clear that the tribunal was then functus officio; and thirdly to provide a clear point for the running of time limits (see *Report of the Secretary General on the analytical commentary on the draft text of the Model Law on International Commercial Arbitration*, UN A/CN.9/264, paras 1, 2). Since time limits under the 2010 Act generally operate by reference to the date when the award takes effect rather than the date it is made, which might not be the same, this last reason would not seem to be applicable. The rule makes it clear that no award is a final award unless all claims have been disposed of, including any claim for interest or expenses. An expenses award may under r.66 be made either together with or separately from an award on the substance, so it may be that an expenses award is the final award in an arbitration. An award of interest would normally be made as part of an award on the substance, and the fact that the tribunal decides not to award interest would not mean that the matter remained outstanding.

While the rule states that an arbitration ends with the final award, this is subject to the power of the tribunal to correct an award under r.58 and the power of the court to order the tribunal to reconsider an award under r.71. (See art.32(4) of the Model Law, which explicitly acknowledges this.) It may also be open to some other person or body to ask a tribunal to revise an award under institutional rules, e.g. under art.27 of the ICC Rules. That last example suggests how the parties might vary the effect of r.57, which is of course a default rule. Otherwise, it is not clear how the parties could disapply the logical conclusion that a tribunal which has dealt with all issues is functus. Certainly, art.32 of the Model Law is mandatory in this respect.

Rule 57(2)

Rule 57(1) is subject to the qualification that the tribunal may already have ended the arbitration, either under r.20(3) by ruling that it does not have jurisdiction, or under r.37 where it decides that the claimant has delayed unnecessarily in pursuing or submitting a claim. In the former case, the arbitration would revive if under r.21(1) a court ruled that the tribunal did have jurisdiction.

Rule 57(3)

Rule 57(1) is subject to the qualification that the parties may end the arbitration by notifying the tribunal that they have settled the dispute. Presumably the same result would ensue if the parties simply agreed to revoke the authority of the tribunal. Does notification amount to "notice" in terms of r.83? If so, it is a formal communication and must be in writing and delivered as contemplated by that rule. Under art.30(1) of the Model Law it is up to the tribunal to terminate the proceedings when a settlement is reached, which raises the question of what the position might be if the tribunal failed to do so. The approach of r.57(3) is preferable in this regard, but it must be queried whether the provision is strictly necessary.

Rule 57(4)

Settlement in the form of an award: The parties may wish their settlement to be recorded in the form of an award, since the matter is then res judicata, while an award is immediately enforceable, which is a particular advantage in international arbitrations. Most legal systems now recognise this possibility, and this is certainly the position under s.51 of the 1996 Act and art.30(1) of the Model Law. The position under Scots common law was obscure, but there was authority to suggest that, since the status of an award derived from it being a considered judgment on a legal issue, an award on agreed terms was incompetent (*Maule v Maule* (1816) 4 Dow 363). Rule 57(4) is thus to be welcomed in allowing such an award to be made. It had originally been suggested that the Model Law should empower the tribunal to record a settlement in the form of an award unless the parties had provided otherwise (see *Report of the Working Group on International Contract Practices on the work of its third session*, UN A/CN.9/216, para.96), but since the parties may not always wish this to happen, the more sensible view prevailed that the parties should have to request this step. It was also suggested that it should be enough that one party should request that their settlement be recorded in the form of an award, given that only the party seeking enforcement had an incentive to take this step (*Report of the Working Group on International Contract Practices on the work of its fourth session*, UN A/CN.9/232, para.174). Once again, however, this view did not prevail, since, "a settlement may be ambiguous or subject to conditions that may not be apparent to the arbitral tribunal", so that there were, "fewer dangers of injustice by requiring both parties to request [such] an award" (*Report of the Working Group on International Contract Practices on the work of its fourth session*, UN A/CN.9/232, para.174). A similar philosophy seems to underpin r.57(4). The *travaux preparatoires* nonetheless record that the formal request for a settlement to be rendered as an award need only be made by one party, provided it is clear that the request expresses the will of both parties (*Report of the UNCITRAL on the work of its eighteenth session*, UN A/40/17, para.250). It remains to be seen whether a similar approach will be adopted under r.57(4).

Tribunal discretion: The tribunal "may" make such an award, which indicates that it has a discretion in this matter. There may be good reasons why it may wish to decline to do so, e.g. where the settlement seems to be in restraint of trade, or otherwise illegal or contrary to public policy. Originally, under the Model Law the tribunal was only to be permitted to decline to make such an award if it had good reasons for doing so (*Note by UNCITRAL Secretariat on draft articles 25–36*, UN A/CN.9/WG.II/WP.38, art.33, alternative B), but it was recognised that such a qualification would be difficult to interpret and even more difficult to make effective (*Report of the UNCITRAL on the work of its eighteenth session*, UN A/40/17, para.249), so that the tribunal was left with complete discretion. The same position prevails under r.57(4) (and s.51(2) of the 1996 Act). The tribunal may refuse to make such an award for any reason or none. Since this is a default rule, can the parties agree that, should they reach a settlement, the tribunal is to be bound to issue an award on those terms? While such an agreement would, prima facie, not bind the tribunal, if the arbitrator(s) clearly enter the arbitration on that basis, there is no obvious reason why they could not be thus bound. Practically, they might still decline to make such an award, but would then be in breach of contract. Of course it is always open to the parties to seek to dismiss the arbitral tribunal and appoint another who would be willing to render an award on agreed terms.

Tribunal promoting settlement: One situation where a tribunal would no doubt be happy to record a settlement in the form of an award is where it has actively promoted that settlement (see Christopher Newmark and Richard Hill, "Can a Mediated Settlement Become an Enforceable Arbitral

Award?" (2000) 16 Arbitration Int. 81 and the Centre for Effective Dispute Resolution's ("CEDR"), *Rules for Facilitating Settlement in International Arbitration*). It is not proposed to enter into a discussion here of the difficult question of whether this would be an appropriate role for a tribunal to adopt, but such an award would not seem to be open to challenge—see below—and would be unlikely to be denied enforcement. In this context one may note the English case of *W and S v BB* Unreported June 8, 2001 TCC. There the arbitrator, having encouraged the parties to settle, sought to issue directions to the effect that the settlement had to be approved by him and had to contain provisions regarding the payment of his fees and expenses. This was held to justify his removal under s.24(1)(d) of the 1996 Act (see r.12 above) on the basis that he had failed to conduct the proceedings properly.

An award under r.57(4) is like any other award in terms of form and effect, save that it will obviously not state reasons as would otherwise be required by r.51(2)(c). There is no need for it otherwise to indicate that it is an award on agreed terms (see DAC Report, para.244), unless the parties have agreed that it should (as under r.26.8 of the LCIA Rules). However, in England the Civil Procedure Rules direct that where enforcement of an agreed award is sought, the enforcement form must state that it is such an award (CPR r.62.18.5). This might be of significance to third parties such as insurers, who may be bound to compensate a party if he is found liable in litigation or arbitration but not if his liability is effectively self-admitted.

More importantly, such an award is not open to challenge under Pt 8. It is useful that r.57(4) addresses this point, since the matter having been raised during the drafting of the Model Law (see *Report of the Working Group on International Contract Practices on the work of its sixth session*, UN A/CN.9/ 245, para.107), no provision was ultimately adopted, leaving the issue hanging in the air. Although the position under r.57(4) has the merit of certainty, it means of course that such an award is unchallengeable even if it deals with matters which are not arbitrable under Scots law, or if it is illegal or contrary to public policy. This means that the focus then shifts on to whether such awards are enforceable (see DAC Report, paras 373, 374).

Like the Model Law and the 1996 Act, this rule appears to contemplate only a final settlement of the dispute, and does not provide for a part settlement to be expressed as an award. What would happen if a tribunal responded to the parties' invitation to do just that? One view is that, since this is not a matter governed by the 2010 Act, it is subject to Scots common law, under which the status of such awards is at best dubious. The preferable view is that, since this is a default rule, the parties are free to make such arrangements as they like. Thus, since the enforcement of a part award on agreed terms is not hostile to the philosophy of r.57, it should be regarded as supported by the rule.

Rule 57(5)

Even though the arbitration has ended the rules must remain in force to govern such issues as recourse against the award, liability of fees and expenses, etc. The 1996 Act simply directs that the award must have the same form and effect as a normal awards and states that the provisions as to costs remain in force in so far as costs have not been dealt with by the settlement. The 1996 Act is perhaps more straightforward in this respect, since it may be difficult to work out which rules can sensibly apply after settlement. It is particularly useful in making explicit the fact that the tribunal retains the power to make an award regarding expenses if this is not part of the settlement.

Rule 58· Correcting an award **D**

58.—(1) The tribunal may correct an award so as to—
 (a) correct a clerical, typographical or other error in the award arising by virtue of accident or omission, or
 (b) clarify or remove any ambiguity in the award.
(2) The tribunal may make such a correction—
 (a) on its own initiative, or
 (b) on an application by any party.
(3) A party making an application under this rule must send a copy of the application to the other party at the same time as the application is made.
(4) Such an application is valid only if made—
 (a) within 28 days of the award concerned, or
 (b) by such later date as the Outer House or the sheriff may, on an application by the party, specify (with any determination by the Outer House or the sheriff being final).
(5) The tribunal must, before deciding whether to correct an award, give—
 (a) where the tribunal proposed the correction, each of the parties,
 (b) where a party application is made, the other party,
a reasonable opportunity to make representations about the proposed correction.
(6) A correction may be made under this rule only—
 (a) where the tribunal proposed the correction, within 28 days of the award concerned being made, or
 (b) where a party application is made, within 28 days of the application being made.
(7) Where a correction affects—
 (a) another part of the corrected award, or
 (b) any other award made by the tribunal (relating to the substance of the dispute, expenses, interest or any other matter),
the tribunal may make such consequential correction of that other part or award as it considers appropriate.
(8) A corrected award is to be treated as if it was made in its corrected form on the day the award was made.

DEFINITIONS
 "Outer House": s.31(1)
 "party": ss.2(1), 31(1), (2)
 "tribunal": ss.2(1), 31(1)

COMMENTARY

At common law authorities were divided as to whether a tribunal did or did not have power to correct clerical errors and errors of calculation in its award (compare *Simpson v Strachan* (1736) Mor. 17007; *MacBryde v Macrae's Executors* (1748) Mor. 657; *Nasmyth v Magistrates of Glasgow* (1777) 5 Br. Supp. 427), but certainly there was no strong authority in favour of such a power. Of course, such a power could be granted by agreement or through the adoption of suitable institutional rules (see art.23 of the Scottish Arbitration Code, art.29 of the ICC Rules), but the creation of an explicit statutory power is nonetheless welcome. Equally welcome is the power to clarify an award, which was certainly lacking at common law, so that if an award could not be saved by a court imposing a commonsense construction (see Lord Cowan in *Patrick v McCall* (1867) 4 S.L.R. 12 at 13), it would have to be held to be void from uncertainty (*McKenzie v Aberdeen and Inverness Junction Railway Co* (1866) 4 M. 810). These powers of correction would extend to part and provisional awards. Rule 58 is a default provision and thus can be excluded by the parties. This may happen implicitly, as where they invoke a foreign procedural law which does not contemplate such powers.

Similar powers exist under art.33 of the Model Law and s.57 of the 1996 Act (compare s.17 of the 1950 Act). Both those provisions, however, also empower the tribunal to make an additional award to cover any matter submitted to the tribunal but omitted from the award. Such a power is not granted to the tribunal under the 2010 Act. Instead, a party must challenge such an award on the basis of serious irregularity under r.68(2)(c), mirroring the approach taken at common law (see Lord President Dunedin in *Pollich v Heatley*, 1910 S.C. 469 at 481, 482). While that may lead to the court asking the tribunal to reconsider the award rather than setting it aside under r.68, it must be wondered whether this is the most sensible approach and whether the lack of such a power in the tribunal itself is a serious omission. That being said, the parties could no doubt confer such a power on the tribunal by agreement, and will impliedly do so if they adopted certain arbitration rules (e.g. LCIA Rules art.27.3, AAA Rules art.30).

Is the tribunal entitled to charge further fees for the making of such corrections or clarifications? While one might hope that this would never arise in practice, given that the tribunal is responsible for the extra work arising, there would seem to be nothing to prevent it unless the arbitration has been carried out under rules which make it plain that such work attracts no further charges (e.g. UNCITRAL Arbitration Rules art.40(4)).

Finally, the award does not cease to be binding merely because a party has sought a correction or clarification, and the other party is not prevented from seeking to enforce the award. Still, the fact that such a request is under consideration may persuade the court to defer any decision on enforcement until the issue is disposed of.

Rule 58(1)(a)

Correcting errors: A tribunal may correct a clerical or typographical error arising from accident or omission. Section 57(3) of the 1996 Act speaks of just a clerical error, while art.33(1)(a) of the Model Law refers to, "errors in computation, any clerical or typographical errors or any errors of a similar nature". It is clear, nonetheless, that s.57(3) would embrace any computational or typographical error (see *Omnibridge Consulting Ltd v Clearsprings (Management) Ltd* Unreported 2004). Rule 58(1)(a) would no doubt extend to a computational error, but how wide is the concept of "other" error, given that there is no suggestion that this error should be of the same kind as a clerical or typographical error? It is suggested that the phrase should be construed ejusdem generis so that more fundamental errors are not being capable of being cured under this provision. Thus while it might allow the tribunal to deal with an error caused by the inadvertent transposition of the parties (see Sir Roger Ormrod in *Mutual Shipping Corp v Bayshore Shipping Co (The Montan)* [1985] 1 Lloyd's Rep. 189 at 198), it might not permit the tribunal to alter an award on the basis that it had failed to express what the arbitrator had really intended to say (see Goff L.J. in *The Montan* [1989] 1 Lloyd's Rep. 189 at 195, 196), or a fortiori that it did express what the tribunal intended to say, albeit that the tribunal had reached those views on the basis of flawed reasoning or a mistaken understanding of the facts or the evidence (see *Fuga AG v Bunge AG* [1975] 2 Lloyd's Rep. 192; *Al Hadha Trading Co v Tradigrain SA* [2002] 2 Lloyd's Rep. 512). Lloyd L.J. suggests in *The Trade Fortitude* [1987] 1 W.L.R. 134 at 147 that, "it must be an error affecting the expression of the tribunal's thought, not an error in the thought process itself". In *Pancommerce SA v Veecheema BV* [1983] 2 Lloyd's Rep. 304, a decision under s.17 of the 1950 Act, an arbitrator was permitted to "correct" an award in order to deal with a failure to award interest, but this seems a rather dubious authority.

It should always be remembered that, since r.58 is a default provision, the parties could confer wider powers of correction if they so chose. It may also be borne in mind that even if the error is not one which may be corrected by the tribunal, should the tribunal acknowledge the error, the award may be challenged under r.68(2)(k)(i) on the basis that there has been an irregularity in the award that is admitted by the tribunal, and the tribunal may be ordered to reconsider the award under r.68(3)(b).

Rule 58(1)(b)

Clarifying award: A tribunal may also clarify or remove any ambiguity in the award. The terms of s.57(3)(a) of the 1996 Act are identical. This approach is preferable to art.33(1)(b) of the Model Law under which a party may request the tribunal to interpret a specific point of the award, but only if the parties agreed to the tribunal having this power. Under the 1996 Act, it has been held appropriate for parties to seek clarification of the reasons for the award (*Torch Offshore LLC v Cable Shipping Inc* [2004] 2 All E.R. (Comm) 365) and indeed even to seek reasons where none have been provided (*Groundshire v VHE Construction* [2001] B.L.R. 395), but not to challenge the reasons provided where these are quite clear (see *World Trade Corp Ltd v Czarnikow Sugar Ltd* [2005] 1 Lloyd's Rep. 422).

Rule 58(2)

The tribunal may make such a correction or clarification on its own initiative, or on the application by any party. This again echoes the position under s.57(3)(a) of the 1996 Act, but in each case further conditions require to be met. A tribunal may make a correction on its own initiative where, for example, it realises that an error has been made, or where a party informally queries an award and it becomes evident that there has been an error. If both parties agree that there has been an error and insist that it should be corrected, the tribunal may do so on its own initiative, but it is submitted that it cannot be compelled to do so—see the commentary to r.58(4) below.

Rule 58(3)

A party making an application must at the same time as making the application send a copy thereof to the other party or parties. It is submitted that failure in this obligation will of itself have no consequences, but consequences might ensure if the disadvantaged party is thus deprived of a reasonable opportunity to make representations regarding the proposed correction (see the discussion of a similar requirement under the Model Law at *Report of the Working Group on International Contract Practices on the work of its seventh session*, UN A/CN.9/246, para.124).

Rule 58(4)

A party application must be prima facie made within 28 days of the award, but the sheriff or Outer House may extend that period on application by a party. Since this is a default rule, the parties may agree upon a longer or shorter period, and/or exclude the power of the court. If they arbitrate under certain arbitration rules, they will impliedly agree on a longer period (see, e.g. Arbitration Rules of the Stockholm Chamber of Commerce r.20). At a late stage of the drafting process, it was decided to indicate that the court's decision on this issue would be final. If the parties do not exclude the power of the court under this rule, are they permitted to agree that such decision should not be final? That is the logic of the provision being designated as default, but this result would surely not have been intended by the drafters who have otherwise been assiduous in reordering the provisions of the Act to make it clear that the parties may not vary the powers of the court.

What is meant by 28 days "of" the award? Does the period run from the date of the award, or when it is made? In the context of the 1996 Act it has been held that if the application has been made timeously, the tribunal should consider all potential errors or ambiguities drawn to its attention even if some are not raised until after the expiry of this period (*RC Pillar & Sons v Edwards* [2002] C.I.L.L. 1799). Obviously in such a case the tribunal should give the other party a proper opportunity to make representations regarding such matters

Rule 58(5)

A tribunal may decide that a correction is appropriate or that no correction is necessary at all, but before reaching such a decision it must give the parties, or the other party when one has applied for a correction, a reasonable opportunity to make representations about the proposed correction. Obviously, for this to happen the parties must be made aware of the proposed correction, and it is suggested that parties would not be treated fairly in terms of r.68(2)(h) if this was not properly done, or the parties were given insufficient time in which to make representations. The same would of course be true if this was the effect of a party failing to copy the application for a correction to the other. It would appear, however, that as long as the parties are afforded the opportunity to make representations, the tribunal has complete discretion whether or not to make a correction, and if it chooses not to do so, that decision is not subject to challenge no matter how glaring an error may appear to be. Nonetheless, there is English authority (*Danae Air Transport SA v Air Canada* [1999] 2 Lloyd's Rep. 547) to suggest that if a tribunal refused to correct an obvious error, the award would be open to challenge—perhaps on the basis that it had not treated the parties fairly in terms of r.68(2)(h).

The tribunal would have a similar discretion as to whether to make a clarification, and if it declines to do so, a party's only recourse is to challenge the award under r.68(2)(e) on the basis that it is uncertain or ambiguous in its effect. It has been held in England that a party should not challenge the award under the 1996 Act equivalent of r.68(2)(e) without first seeking a clarification from the tribunal (*Gbangola v Smith and Sheriff Ltd* [1998] 3 All E.R. 730), unless the award is plainly "unsalvageable" (*Sinclair v Woods of Winchester Ltd*, 109 Con. L.R. 14), and indeed r.71 in indicating that an appeal under rr.67–69 is only competent where an appellant has exhausted any available arbitral process of appeal or review, specifically includes any recourse available under r.58. While in terms of r.71(4)(a) an appeal must be made no later than 28 days after the award takes effect, under r.71(4)(b) if there has been an arbitral process of appeal or review, the 28 day period only runs from the date when the appellant is notified of the result of that process. Thus should the correction of the award itself create a ground of appeal, a party's position is protected.

Rule 58(6)

The time limit for making such a correction is fairly tight, given the need to allow representations to be made—28 days of the award if the correction is made on the tribunal's own initiative, otherwise 28 days of the application being made. The parties may agree on a different period (see *Home of Homes Ltd v Hammersmith and Fulham London Borough Council*, 92 Con. L.R 48), and will do if they arbitrate under certain arbitration rules (e.g. UNCITRAL Arbitration Rules art.36), while other rules see the tribunal being accorded discretion to extend the period (e.g. LMAA Terms para.25). No provision is made for the sheriff or Outer House to extend this period, by contrast with s.79 of the 1996 Act which confers a general power on the court to extend time limits imposed by the Act or the parties, while art.33(4) of the Model Law gives the tribunal itself power to extend the time limit for making a correction "if necessary". The framers of the Model Law thought that it was particularly important for this power to exist in the context of international arbitration since it might occasionally be difficult to comply with the 30 day time limit which the Model Law would otherwise impose (see *Analytical Commentary on Article 33*, UN A/CN.9/264, para.4).

This provision is very similar to s.57(5) of the 1996 Act, and was practically identical until at stage 2 the 28 day time limit under r.58(6)(b) was altered from running from the date when the tribunal received the application to running from the date when the application was made. This fits rather better with the scheme of the Act, especially r.83, dealing with formal communications, including applications. Rule 83(5)(b) indicates that where a formal communication is posted it is treated as having been served on the day on which it would be delivered in the ordinary course of post and says nothing about when such a communication is treated as having been "received"—an issue which has caused difficulty in England (see *RC Pillar & Sons v Edwards* [2002] C.I.L.L. 1799). The current approach allows the 28 day period to be measured with a degree of certainty, albeit that it might make the 28 day period rather tight, especially where, as in the *Pillar* case, the arbitrator is out of the office for a significant period.

Rule 58(7)

This is a provision with no counterpart in either the 1996 Act or the Model Law. It recognises that a correction may entail consequential corrections elsewhere in the award or in an earlier award and empowers the tribunal to make such corrections. Thus, for example, the tribunal might correct the way in which the award deals with expenses so as better to reflect the corrected award, and in *Gannet Shipping Ltd v Eastrade Commodities Inc* [2002] 1 Lloyd's Rep. 713 a decision under the 1996 Act, it was suggested that a tribunal who failed to do so would be guilty of a serious irregularity. Presumably, the parties are entitled to be made aware of these proposed consequential corrections and to have a reasonable opportunity to make representations about the proposed corrections.

Rule 58(8)

Any correction is to have retrospective effect and to be treated as part of the award from the day the award was made.

PART 7

ARBITRATION EXPENSES

Rule 59: Arbitration expenses **D**

59. "Arbitration expenses" means—
   (a) the arbitrators' fees and expenses for which the parties are liable under rule 60,
   (b) any expenses incurred by the tribunal when conducting the arbitration for which the parties are liable under rule 60,
   (c) the parties' legal and other expenses, and
   (d) the fees and expenses of—
      (i) any arbitral appointments referee, and
      (ii) any other third party to whom the parties give powers in relation to the arbitration,
for which the parties are liable under rule 60.

DEFINITIONS
"arbitral appointments referee": ss.22, 31(1), r.7
"arbitrator": ss.2(1), 31(1)
"party": ss.2(1), 31(1), (2)
"tribunal": ss.2(1), 31

STATUS
This is a default rule so it is open to the parties to modify it, agree something different or disapply it completely (see s.9).

This appears to be because the term "arbitration expenses" is used in rr.61, 62 and 64–66 which are all default rules. It might also be possible for the parties to agree some different definition of "arbitration expenses". For example if the parties adopted the UNCITRAL Rules (not Model Law), art.38 provides a definition of "costs", and arts 39–41 provide specific rules in relation to expenses.

MODEL LAW
There is no provision in the Model Law dealing with expenses. This is principally because no consensus could be reached in 1985 on how to handle expenses, the "winner takes all" approach common (but not universal) in common law jurisdictions being rejected by most civil law jurisdictions. In the USA, the parties' costs in arbitration fall where they lie since US litigation does not normally award costs in either direction. In the Philippines, anything other than a 50/50 split is unlawful.

COMMENTARY
Rule 59 defines the critical concept of "arbitration expenses". In short "arbitration expenses" are the whole costs of the persons carrying out functions in connection with the arbitration other than the courts, those being the parties, the tribunal, any arbitral appointments referee and any other third party empowered by the parties in relation to the arbitration.

A question may arise as to the scope of the phrase, "parties' legal and other expenses". In particular does it include the expenses of any court proceedings ancillary to the arbitration? In *McQuater v Fergusson*, 1911 S.C. 640 it was held that the phrase, "the expenses of and incidental to the arbitration" did not include the expenses of a stated case to the court under an equivalent of r.41 on the basis that Parliament did not indicate that the usual rule that the expenses of a court process should be determined by the court should be departed from. It is suggested that the words, "incidental to the arbitration" fall to be implied in the phrase, "parties' legal and other expenses" and that the rationale of *McQuater* applies to exclude the expenses of court proceedings from the concept of "parties' legal and other expenses" and thus from the concept of "arbitration expenses" as a whole, at least unless the parties are able to modify r.59(c) to include court expenses which are incidental to the arbitration.

Parties' "other expenses" may include witness costs, fees of professional witnesses, travelling and accommodation costs of parties, witnesses, lawyers, administrative costs such as copying charges, telephone and other communication media charges, recording of evidence charges and so forth. They may be substantial. For an early example of a claim for the time of non-professional witnesses in an arbitration being disallowed see *Younger v Caledonian Railway Co* (1847) 10 D. 133.

Rule 60 Arbitrators' fees and expenses **M**

60.—(1) The parties are severally liable to pay to the arbitrators—
  (a) the arbitrators' fees and expenses, including—
    (i) the arbitrators' fees for conducting the arbitration,
    (ii) expenses incurred personally by the arbitrators when conducting the arbitration, and
  (b) expenses incurred by the tribunal when conducting the arbitration, including—
    (i) the fees and expenses of any clerk, agent, employee or other person appointed by the tribunal to assist it in conducting the arbitration,
    (ii) the fees and expenses of any expert from whom the tribunal obtains an opinion,
    (iii) any expenses in respect of meeting and hearing facilities, and
    (iv) any expenses incurred in determining recoverable arbitration expenses.
(2) The parties are also severally liable to pay the fees and expenses of—
  (a) any arbitral appointments referee, and
  (b) any other third party to whom the parties give powers in relation to the arbitration.
(3) The amount of fees and expenses payable under this rule and the payment terms are—
  (a) to be agreed by the parties and the arbitrators or, as the case may be, the arbitral appointments referee or other third party, or
  (b) failing such agreement, to be determined by the Auditor of the Court of Session.
(4) Unless the Auditor of the Court of Session decides otherwise—
  (a) the amount of any fee is to be determined by the Auditor on the basis of a reasonable commercial rate of charge, and
  (b) the amount of any expenses is to be determined by the Auditor on the basis that a reasonable amount is to be allowed in respect of all reasonably incurred expenses.

(5) The Auditor of the Court of Session may, when determining the amount of fees and expenses, order the repayment of any fees or expenses already paid which the Auditor considers excessive (and such an order has effect as if it was made by the court).

(6) This rule does not affect—
  (a) the parties' liability as between themselves for fees and expenses covered by this rule (see rules 62 and 65), or
  (b) the Outer House's power to make an order under rule 16 (order relating to expenses in cases of arbitrator's resignation or removal).

DEFINITIONS
"arbitral appointments referee": ss.22, 31(1), r.7
"arbitrator": ss.2(1), 31(1)
"Outer House": s.31(1)
"party": ss.2(1), 31(1), (2)
"tribunal": ss.2(1), 31(1)

STATUS
This is a mandatory rule (see s.8). This means that the parties cannot disapply or modify it on their own. Furthermore, the provision in s.8 prohibiting disapplication or modification "by any other means" might be seen as preventing parties and arbitrators (arbitral appointments referee or other third party) from disapplying or modifying r.60 by agreement or waiver. It is suggested, however, that s.8 should not be seen as preventing arbitrators and parties from agreeing to add to (but not to detract from) the provisions of r.60 terms and conditions which legally bind both arbitrators and parties. The reason for r.60 being mandatory is to protect the interests of arbitrators, and any agreed addition to r.60 which does not detract from the protection given by the rule is entirely in accordance with the spirit of the rule.

Guideline 3 of the Chartered Institute of Arbitrators Practice Guidelines (available at *http://www.ciarb.org/information-and-resources* [Accessed February 24, 2010]) provides guidelines for arbitrators on how to formulate their terms and conditions and what should be covered in an agreement between the parties and the tribunal. It is recognised practice for arbitrators to require security for their fees and expenses, often by means of a cash sum to be lodged in the hands of an interest bearing account in trust for the parties. See, e.g. UNCITRAL Rules art.41.

MODEL LAW
There is no provision in the Model Law dealing with expenses.

COMMENTARY
Rule 60 is concerned with the liability of the parties to the arbitration to pay for the fees and outlays of the arbitral tribunal, any arbitral appointments referee and any other third party to whom the parties gave powers in relation to the arbitration. Conversely it is concerned with the rights of the arbitrators, etc. to remuneration and reimbursement. At one time, under the common law, there was no implied right of an arbitral tribunal for remuneration, the presumption being that the work was done gratuitously. However by the time of *Macintyre Brothers v Smith*, 1913 S.C. 129, that had been modified and the common law rule came to be that there was an implied term in the contract between the arbitrators and the parties that where the arbitrator was a professional man he was entitled to remuneration from the parties jointly and severally.

Liability under the rule will arise in every arbitration unless the arbitrator or other person with an entitlement under this rule waives that entitlement in whole or in part or agrees with the parties that it should not in some respect apply. In the case of arbitrators this may involve agreement to their terms and conditions. Similarly an arbitral appointments referee may charge a fee for the appointment service provided with terms and conditions attached.

Rule 60(1) and (2)

The liability of the parties to an arbitrator is "several" rather than "joint and several". It is unclear why r.60 does not simply provide for the liability to be joint and several as was the case under the common law (*Macintyre Brothers v Smith*, 1913 S.C. 129). "Several" liability means that the arbitrator can claim the whole of his fee from any one of the parties (*Fleming v Gemmill*, 1908 S.C. 340 at 345) but that the paying party must pay the whole amount without a right of relief against any other party unless or until the arbitrator makes an award under r.62(1) or the equivalent institutional rule, making the other party partly liable for his fee. Fortunately r.62(3) provides that until or unless an award is made under r.62(1) the parties are as between themselves liable for an equal share of any expenses for which they are liable under r.60. This somewhat circuitous drafting has the effect of making the liability under r.60 joint and several.

Rule 60(3)

Rule 60(3) expresses the important principle that the quantum of fees and expenses and the payment terms payable to the arbitrators, etc. are as agreed contractually by the parties and the arbitrators, etc. before they are incurred, failing which not merely the quantum but also the payment terms will be determined by the Auditor of the Court of Session. From the point of view of all concerned, but especially the arbitrators it is highly desirable to agree quantum of fees and terms of payment and all other matters between the parties and the arbitrators beforehand.

The jurisdiction of the Auditor applies only if the fees and expenses have not been contractually agreed (*Hussman (Europe) Ltd v Al Ameen Development and Trade Co* [2000] 2 Lloyd's Rep. 83 at 99 [71]—in relation to s.28(5) of the 1996 Act). In that case it was held that the mere fact that the fees were paid through the medium of an arbitral institution did not mean that they had been contractually agreed with the arbitrators and therefore the court had the jurisdiction given to it under the equivalent provision of the 1996 Act to adjust the fees.

Rule 60(4) and (5)

Rule 60(4) and (5) provide for the situation where the fees and expenses or payment terms have not been agreed between the parties and the arbitrators. Rule 60(5) is one for arbitrators to watch since on the face of it, it would appear to allow the auditor to reopen a payment of expenses which has been made with the agreement of both the parties and the arbitrator. It is suggested that if such both parties and the arbitrator have agreed a payment of fees and expenses which has been made, the Auditor should be slow to order the arbitrator to repay that amount, unless the payment was made by the parties under such error as to make it clearly equitable for such an amount to be repaid.

There does not appear to be any remedy of appeal against the Auditor's decision under r.60(4) and (5) in which event the only possible remedy for either a party or an arbitrator is a petition to the Outer House of the Court of Session for judicial review of the decision.

Rule 61: Recoverable arbitration expenses **D**

61.—(1) The following arbitration expenses are recoverable—
  (a) the arbitrators' fees and expenses for which the parties are liable under rule 60,
  (b) any expenses incurred by the tribunal when conducting the arbitration for which the parties are liable under rule 60, and
  (c) the fees and expenses of any arbitral appointments referee (or any other third party to whom the parties give powers in relation to the arbitration) for which the parties are liable under rule 60.
(2) It is for the tribunal to—
  (a) determine the amount of the other arbitration expenses which are recoverable, or
  (b) arrange for the Auditor of the Court of Session to determine that amount.
(3) Unless the tribunal or, as the case may be, the Auditor decides otherwise—
  (a) the amount of the other arbitration expenses which are recoverable must be determined on the basis that a reasonable amount is to be allowed in respect of all reasonably incurred expenses, and
  (b) any doubt as to whether expenses were reasonably incurred or are reasonable in amount is to be resolved in favour of the person liable to pay the expenses.

DEFINITIONS
"arbitration expenses": r.59
"Outer House": s.31(1)
"party": ss.2(1), 31(1), (2)
"tribunal": ss.2(1), 31(1)

STATUS
This is a default rule so it is open to the parties to modify it, agree something different or disapply it completely (see s.9).
Many institutional rules contain detailed provisions on expenses. These include SAC 07 art.20, the ICC Rules art.31, LCIA Rules art.28, and UNCITRAL Rules arts 38–41. In assessing the effect of these rules on r.61, the starting point is, as with all default rules, to begin with r.61 and then to assess the extent to which the parties' agreement of institutional rules has disapplied or modified r.61.

MODEL LAW
There is no provision in the Model Law dealing with expenses. See the commentary to r.59 above.

COMMENTARY
Rule 61 is important because it defines the quantum of expenses one party to the arbitration might recover from the other in terms of an award of the tribunal under r.62. The phraseology of r.61 is a little misleading in that on an initial reading of r.61(1) one might think that parties' legal and other expenses in connection with the arbitration are not recoverable. Fortunately r.61(2) obliquely includes these as "other arbitration expenses" which a tribunal may find recoverable. This is a reference back to head (c) of the

definition of "arbitration expenses" in r.59 which covers parties' legal and other expenses.

Rule 61(1) and (2)

Read together, r.61(1) and (2) provide that all of the arbitration expenses mentioned in r.59 are recoverable but that the quantum of legal and other expenses of the parties is to be either (a) determined by the tribunal, or (b) referred by the tribunal to the Auditor of the Court of Session. It is rare in England and Wales for the tribunal to make a reference to the court under the equivalent s.63(4) of the 1996 Act and it is suggested that having regard to its duty under r.24 it should be slow to make a reference to the Auditor unless it could be justified under r.24. A reference to the Auditor should not be routine.

Rule 61(2) represents a reform of the common law under which if the tribunal made an award of expenses it had to quantify those expenses in the award (*Younger v Caledonian Railway Co* (1847) 10 D. 133) or at least fix a means of those determining those expenses (*Paterson v Sanderson* (1829) 7 S. 616; *Deko Scotland Ltd v Edinburgh Royal Joint Venture*, 2003 S.L.T. 727 at 730). If the tribunal did not quantify the expenses or fix a means for their ascertainment, they were not recoverable unless in the proceedings for recovery the unsuccessful party waived their right to plead incompetency of recovery, in which event the court would remit the account of expenses sought to be recovered to its auditor of court for taxation (assessment). That is what occurred in the *Younger* case.

It has always been open for the parties to agree to remit an account of expenses to taxation by an auditor of court. However, subject to r.24, r.61(2) specifically empowers the tribunal to make the reference to the Auditor of the Court of Session in relation to the taxation of the "legal and other expenses" of a party. The expense incurred by the tribunal in the making of the reference is itself a recoverable arbitration expense under r.61(1)(b) incorporating r.60(1)(b)(iv). If the tribunal arranges for the Auditor to quantify the quantum of the legal and other expenses of a party which is recoverable, then that quantification would be unappealable if it was not incorporated into the tribunal's award. This suggests that good practice will be for the Auditor's determination to be incorporated into the tribunal's award so that it can be appealed under the general appeal provisions relating to awards. Even if good practice is not followed, it seems to be logical to take the Auditor's determination as being part of the award of the tribunal in relation to expenses, given that the power of the Auditor derives from the reference made to him by the tribunal.

Rule 61(3)

Both the tribunal and the Auditor of the Court of Session are given a discretion as to how to assess and quantify the legal and other expenses of a party. They can either follow the default provisions of paras (a) and (b) of r.61(3) or they can choose some other method of assessment or quantification. Fairness and good practice suggests that if either the tribunal or the Auditor are minded to choose another method of assessment or quantification, for example by reference to a "party-party" litigation basis, they should invite parties to make representations on the appropriateness of that basis. A failure to do so might render the subsequent award appealable under r.68 on the grounds of serious irregularity. Equally, if a party wishes assessment or quantification on a basis other the default basis, then they should apply to the tribunal (or Auditor) for assessment or quantification on their proposed basis. A decision on the basis of assessment and quantification will also allow parties to be able to estimate the quantum of expenses and assist them in reaching agreement as to quantification which in itself may save the expense of the tribunal or the Auditor carrying out the task themselves.

Under the Scots common law there was little authority on how legal and other expenses of a party should be quantified. James Campbell Irons and R.D. Melville, *Arbitration* (Edinburgh: W. Green, 1903) took the view (at p.228) that assessment and quantification should be carried out on the same principles as litigation, that is to say that it should be carried out on the basis of restricted recovery by reference to a party-party scale, rather than on an indemnity (agent-client) basis. That view was followed by Lord Drummond Young in *Deko Scotland Ltd v Edinburgh Royal Joint Venture*, 2003 S.L.T. 727. However neither Irons and Melville nor the court in *Deko* noticed that in *Younger v Caledonian Railway Co* (1847) 10 D. 133, the Inner House of the Court of Session had observed, in relation to an arbitration on the extent of compensation payable for compulsory purchase, that the phrase, "all the expenses of the arbitration and incident thereto" could cover a good deal of expense preparatory to the arbitration which would not be recoverable in an ordinary (party-party) account of expenses in a litigation (*Younger v Caledonian Railway Co* (1847) 10 D. 133, per Lord Justice-Clerk Hope at 137). This suggests that quantification of expenses in an arbitration at common law was not restricted by the rules relating to litigation, although it was clearly influenced by them.

With regard to the basis of assessment in r.61(3)(a) and (b) neither the tribunal nor the Auditor of the Court of Session are given any guidance on how reasonableness is to be assessed. Everything will depend upon circumstances. However the reasonableness of any claim for an item of expense or for the quantum of that item must exist beyond any doubt, that being the effect of r.61(3)(b). That is not a test applied to the taxation of accounts of expenses in Scottish litigations. It appears to originate from s.63(5)(b) of the 1996 Act which in turn originates from r.44.4(2) and (3) of the English Civil Procedure Rules 1998. That said it is also the case that the test of reasonableness is one that features in art.31.1 of the ICC Rules, art.38(c) of the UNCITRAL Rules and one which is recognised in international arbitration. Thus it has been said in an international context in a case before the Iran-US Claims Tribunal governed by art.38(c) of the UNCITRAL Rules:

"A test of reasonableness is not, however an invitation to mere subjectivity. Objective tests of reasonableness of lawyers' fees are well known. Such tests typically assign weight primarily to the time spent and complexity of the case. In modern practice the amount of time required to be spent is often a gauge of the extent of the complexities involved. When the Tribunal is presented with copies of bills for services, or other appropriate evidence, indicating the time spent, the hourly billing rate, and a general description of the professional services rendered, its task need be neither onerous nor mysterious. The range of typical hourly billing rates is generally known and, as evidence before the Tribunal in various cases including this one indicates, it does not greatly differ between the US and countries of Western Europe, where both claimants and respondents before the Tribunal typically hire their outside counsel. Just how much time any lawyer reasonably needs to accomplish a task can be measured by the number of issues involved in a case and the amount of evidence requiring analysis and presentation. While legal fees are not to be calculated on the basis of the pounds of paper involved, the Tribunal by the end of a case is able to have a fair idea, on the basis of submissions made by both sides, of the approximate extent of the effort that was reasonably required. Nor should the Tribunal neglect to consider the reality that legal bills are usually first submitted to businessmen. The pragmatic fact that a businessman has agreed to pay a bill, not knowing whether or not the Tribunal would reimburse the expenses, is a strong indication that the amount billed was considered reasonable by a reasonable man spending his own money or the money of the corporation he serves. That is a classic test of reasonableness." (Separate opinion of Judge Holtzmann, reported in *Iranian Assets Litigation Reporter* 10860 at 10863; 8 Iran-US C.T.R. 329 at 332–333.)

It is suggested that the basis of "reasonableness beyond doubt" should not be used to bring in a party-party litigation basis by the back door. Thus, in principle there is no reason why a winning party cannot recover 100 per cent of his legal and other expenses.

It may be difficult to challenge the tribunal's award on assessment and quantification of recoverable expenses. The two possible routes are a serious irregularity appeal under r.68(2) perhaps under heads (a) (failure to follow r.61 or arbitration agreement), (h) (failure to treat the parties fairly) or a legal error appeal under r.69. It is unclear whether these heads, which refer to irregularities of the tribunal, are applicable to the conduct of the Auditor. Appeal under r.69 is likely to be difficult given that for such an appeal the tribunal must have been asked to decide the point of law, e.g. the reasonableness of a particular item of expenses, and the tribunal's decision was obviously wrong or the court considers the point to be of general importance. Issues of assessment or quantification of expenses are unlikely to be of general importance.

Rule 62: Liability for recoverable arbitration expenses **D**

62.—(1) The tribunal may make an award allocating the parties' liability between themselves for the recoverable arbitration expenses (or any part of those expenses).

(2) When making an award under this rule, the tribunal must have regard to the principle that expenses should follow a decision made in favour of a party except where this would be inappropriate in the circumstances.

(3) Until such an award is made (or where the tribunal chooses not to make such an award) in respect of recoverable arbitration expenses (or any part of them), the parties are, as between themselves, each liable—
　(a) for an equal share of any such expenses for which the parties are liable under rule 60, and
　(b) for their own legal and other expenses.

(4) This rule does not affect—
　(a) the parties' several liability for fees and expenses under rule 60, or
　(b) the liability of any party to any other third party.

DEFINITIONS
"arbitration expenses": r.59
"party": ss.2(1), 31(1), (2)
"tribunal": ss.2(1), 31(1)

STATUS
This is a default rule so it is open to the parties to modify it, agree something different or disapply it completely (see s.9).

Many institutional rules contain detailed provisions on expenses. These include the SAC 07 art.20, the ICC Rules art.31, the LCIA Rules art.28 and the UNCITRAL Rules arts 38–41. In assessing the effect of these rules on r.62 the starting point is, as with all default rules, to begin with r.62 and then to assess the extent to which the parties' agreement of institutional rules has disapplied or modified r.62.

MODEL LAW

This is no equivalent to this rule in the Model Law. See the commentary to r.59 above.

COMMENTARY

Different countries have different provisions in relation to who is to bear the expenses of an arbitration. Under Scots common law a tribunal had an inherent power to award the expenses of the arbitration (*Pollich v Heatley*, 1910 S.C. 469 at 482) except as modified by agreement of the parties in their joint submission or reference to the tribunal.

The award of the tribunal allocating liability for expenses may take place at the same time as or before the award quantifying the expenses under r.61.

Rule 62 does not contain any provisions in relation to appeals. An award of expenses under r.62 whether it be a part award or an award dealing with the whole of the recoverable arbitration expenses is appealable under rr.68 and 69, at least in theory. At common law the setting aside of an award in relation to expenses was not possible at all in relation to errors of law and there had to be some procedural irregularity or lack of jurisdiction or fundamental unreasonableness which rendered the award ultra vires. Where there was a statutory right to state a case to a court in relation to awards of expenses in workmens' compensation arbitrations, the Inner House of the Court of Session held that an arbitrator had a right to go wrong and that the court would interfere only where it was plain that the tribunal had failed to apply the judicial principle in the award of expenses (see below) (*McArdle v J&R Howie Ltd*, 1927 S.C. 779; 1927 S.L.T. 521—appeal unsuccessful; contrasted with *O'Neill v Giffnock Collieries Ltd*, 1924 S.C. 376; 1924 S.L.T. 325—appeal successful).

Rule 62(1)

Rule 62(1) enables a tribunal to make an award allocating the parties' liability for the whole or part of the recoverable arbitration expenses, as specified in r.61. While r.62 is worded in the singular, it must be read with r.54 which appears to allow a part award on some of the matters to be decided in the arbitration. These matters will include liability for expenses. There would appear to be nothing to stop a tribunal from making a part award in relation to some specific aspect of the recoverable arbitration expenses. That was the case under the old Scots common law (*Apollo Engineering Ltd v James Scott Ltd*, 2008 S.L.T. 472). That part award would be subject to quantification and enforcement or appeal in the same way as an award dealing with all of the recoverable arbitration expenses in the arbitration.

An award of expenses may be made together with or separately from an award on the merits of the dispute (r.66).

There is a question of whether in the light of r.62(1) the tribunal must deal with expenses in order to exhaust the reference to it. At common law, in *Pollich v Heatley*, 1910 S.C. 469, an award was sought to be set aside on the ground that it did not deal with expenses but the Inner House of the Court of Session rejected the application on the grounds that while the tribunal had an inherent power to deal with expenses, as expenses were not sought in the parties' submission to the tribunal, the tribunal did not have to deal with expenses in order to exhaust the reference. In *Grampian Regional Council v John G McGregor (Contractors) Ltd*, 1994 S.L.T 133 at 138, Lord President Hope noted that whether the tribunal was obliged to deal with expenses depended on a construction of the submission being made to the tribunal. Looking to the new statutory scheme, r.62(1) should be read with r.68(2)(c) which provides for the tribunal failing to deal with all the issues that were put to it as being a qualifying irregularity, which if causing substantial injustice could give rise to an appeal. Rule 62(1) should also be read with r.57(1) which provides that an arbitration ends when no claim, including any claim for expenses, is outstanding. Taking these three rules into account leads to the conclusion that the tribunal has an obligation to make an award of expenses if that matter is put to it whether in the original submission or reference or pleadings or in a request during the course of the arbitral proceedings. Only if there is no mention of expenses at all could a tribunal be justified in not dealing with expenses without the risk of an appeal under r.68 on the grounds of serious irregularity.

This means that if parties settle the dispute they should take care to deal with issues of expenses as if expenses have not been sought up to that point, an award of consent could be made without any reference to expenses.

Rule 62(2)—test for awards of expenses

Rule 62(2) reflects the principle for the award of expenses in a Scots litigation. That judicial principle was stated as follows:

"The principle upon which the Court proceeds in awarding expenses is that the cost of litigation should fall on him who has caused it. The general rule for applying this principle is that costs follow the event, the ratio being that the rights of parties are to be taken to have been all along such as the ultimate decree declares them to be, and that whosoever has resisted the vindication of those rights, whether by action or by defence is *prima facie* to blame. In some cases, however, the application of the general rule would not carry out the principle and the Court has always, on cause shewn, considered whether the conduct of the successful party, either during the litigation or in the matters giving rise to the litigation, has not either caused or contributed to bring about the law suit" (*Shepherd v Elliot* (1896) 23 R. 695, per Lord President Robertson at 696).

That principle lays stress on who caused the litigation or steps of procedure within it. This principle was also reflected in the Scots common law approach to expenses in an arbitration. Thus it was held that where one party was entirely successful in the arbitral proceedings, then the tribunal ought to award him the expenses unless there was something in his conduct to disentitle him to expenses or unless there was some other stateable ground which rendered a departure from the ordinary rule desirable (*Feeney v Fife Coal Co*, 1918 S.C. 197 at 201).

Rule 62(2) sets out the general rule which is that expenses should follow a decision made in favour of a party except where it would be inappropriate in the circumstances. The question is, in what circumstances would it be "inappropriate" that expenses should follow success? Applying the general principle relating to expenses, the circumstances will be ones where the unsuccessful party has not wholly caused the arbitration or certain steps of it, or in certain circumstances, where the successful party has caused the arbitration. This has been illustrated in cases where the unsuccessful party has made an offer to the successful party which has not been bettered by the award made to the successful party.

One way in which a respondent can protect itself against an award of expenses is to make an offer to the claimant in the hope that any ultimate award to the claimant will not exceed it and the claimant can thus be held to have caused the arbitral procedure after the date of the offer. This is akin to what is in Scots litigation known as a "judicial tender" or "tender" where a defender offers to a pursuer a sum (inclusive of interest) plus expenses to date. The offer is lodged with the court in a sealed envelope. If at the end of the litigation the ultimate judgment is equal to or less than the amount offered (making due allowance for interest between the date of the offer and the date of the judgment), the defender is entitled to expenses from the date of the offer. While it has been observed that there is no normal or general rule of practice in arbitrations relating to tenders (*Carnegie v Nature Conservancy Council*, 1992 S.L.T. 342), there is no reason in principle why tenders cannot be made in arbitrations with results similar to those in litigations. Indeed it may not be in all circumstances necessary for the respondent to offer expenses to date. In *Mikuta v William Baird & Co*, 1916 S.C. 194; 1915 2 S.L.T. 396, during the arbitration the respondent offered a sum to the claimant but without an offer of expenses to date which (if accepted) would have left the tribunal to decide the question of expenses. The claimant did not accept the offer and after obtaining from the tribunal a sum less than the sum offered, the tribunal awarded expenses to the claimant up to the date of the offer and to the respondent from the date of the offer. The basis of the award to the respondent was that it was likely that had the offer been accepted the tribunal would have awarded the claimant the expenses and that being the case it could be said, fairly, that the claimant had caused the procedure in the arbitration after that date.

Circumstances inappropriate for the general rule to apply have included, where before the arbitration the respondent offered to the claimant more than the claimant ultimately obtained and the unsuccessful respondent was awarded the expenses (*Murphy v Farme Coal Co Ltd*, 1918 S.C. 659; 1918 2 S.L.T. 8). They might also include hearings which have been caused or in which time has been taken up by arguments in which both sides have enjoyed significant success where an award of no expenses might be appropriate.

It is important to remember that if a party wishes to found on "inappropriate circumstances" or to rely on an offer in connection with a request for an award of expenses, it should bring the offer and the circumstances to the attention of the tribunal. In *Carnegie v Nature Conservancy Council*, 1992 S.L.T. 342 the petitioner failed to draw to the tribunal's attention the terms of the tender which was below the award and ended up with an award of no expenses due in relation to his legal costs).

Rule 62(3) and (4)

Rule 62(3)(a) is necessary to allow for parties' liabilities for the tribunal's fees and expenses to be joint and several. It is therefore a consequence of the drafting in r.60(1) imposing the unusual "several" liability. Rule 62(4)(a) cannot be read as taking away the effect of r.62(3)(a). The reader is referred to the commentary to r.60 above.

That parties must bear their own legal and other expenses until an award transferring that liability or part of it to another party appears self-evident but for the avoidance of doubt this is restated in r.62(3)(b).

Rule 63: Ban on pre-dispute agreements about liability for arbitration expenses **M**

63. Any agreement allocating the parties' liability between themselves for any or all of the arbitration expenses has no effect if entered into before the dispute being arbitrated has arisen.

DEFINITIONS
"arbitration expenses": r.59
"party": ss.2(1), 31(1), (2)
"tribunal": ss.2(1), 31(1)

STATUS
This is a mandatory rule which cannot be disapplied by the parties.

MODEL LAW
This is no equivalent to this rule in the Model Law.

COMMENTARY
Rule 63 appears to be a straightforward import from English and Welsh law in the shape of s.60 of the 1996 Act. There was no such rule under the Scots common law. The rationale behind the English rule appears to be that there exist or existed many standard form contracts which provided, in one way or another that a precondition of going to arbitration was that the claimant had to bear all of his costs irrespective of the outcome. In effect s.60, and now r.63, exclude reliance on any such unfair contractual provision.

Rule 64: Security for expenses **D**

64.—(1) The tribunal may—
    (a) order a party making a claim to provide security for the recoverable arbitration expenses or any part of them, and
    (b) if that order is not complied with, make an award dismissing any claim made by that party.

(2) But such an order may not be made only on the ground that the party—
    (a) is an individual who ordinarily resides outwith the United Kingdom, or
    (b) is a body which is—
        (i) incorporated or formed under the law of a country outwith the United Kingdom, or
        (ii) managed or controlled from outwith the United Kingdom.

DEFINITIONS
"party": ss.2(1), 31(1), (2)
"tribunal": ss.2(1), 31(1)
"United Kingdom": s.5 and Interpretation Act 1978 Sch.1

STATUS
This is a default rule so it is open to the parties to modify it, agree something different or disapply it completely (see s.9).

Some institutional rules provide for security for expenses but it is not a universal clause. The LCIA Rules art.25.2 provide for security for costs. In assessing the effect of these rules on r.64, the starting point is, as with all default rules, to begin with r.64 and then to assess the extent to which the parties' agreement of institutional rules has disapplied or modified r.64.

MODEL LAW

The Model Law, following its amendment by UNCITRAL on July 7, 2006, provides for "interim measures" which are defined in art.17(2) (as amended) as:

"... any temporary measure, whether in the form of an award or in another form, by which at any time prior to the issuance of the award by which the dispute is finally decided, the arbitral tribunal orders a party to ... (c) provide a means of preserving assets out of which a subsequent award may be satisfied".

Under art.17(1) unless the parties otherwise agree, the tribunal is given power, at the request of a party, to grant such interim measures. Article 17E(1) provides that the tribunal may require the applicant for an interim measure to provide appropriate security in connection with that measure. Article 17F(2) gives power to the tribunal to require any party to promptly disclose any material change in the circumstances on the basis of which the measure was requested or granted.

The Model Law provisions appear to be limited to the provision of security by the applicant in connection with an application for an interim measure, e.g. where the applicant seeks the production of relevant evidence the production of which might entail some prejudice to the producing party, or where the applicant seeks an interim interdict which may turn out to be wrongful having regard to the final outcome. Rule 64 has a different focus. It is concerned with providing a remedy to respondents in relation to impecunious claimants. In the language of a Scottish litigation it is the equivalent of an order for caution for expenses as a condition precedent to further procedure.

COMMENTARY

Rule 64 represents an increase in the powers of the tribunal compared to the previous common law. In effect the tribunal is given a power similar to that of the court to order a party (usually a pursuer/claimant) to find caution for expenses. Unlike the court order, the tribunal's order, being for the "recoverable arbitration expenses" can include, for example the fees and expenses of the tribunal itself and the other elements set out in r.59.

The tribunal may not make the order on the sole ground that the party from whom security is sought is an individual who ordinarily resides outwith the UK or is a body which is formed under the law of a country outwith the UK or is managed or controlled from outwith the UK. The tribunal's power is in this way more restrictive than that of a court in a Scottish litigation, where the party in question is resident outwith the EU or a country which is party to the Brussels or Lugano Conventions on jurisdiction and the enforcement of judgments. The court may require security (in the form of the sisting of a mandatory or the obtaining of caution for expenses) on that sole ground whereas the tribunal may not. On one view the court, with the consent of the tribunal, has that power under r.45(1)(g) in relation to an arbitration but it is suggested that the better view is that the powers of the tribunal are as set out in r.64 and that the tribunal has no power under r.45(2) to consent to the court granting an order for caution for expenses or to sist a mandatory as it would in ordinary court litigation. See also the commentary to r.45(1)(g) above.

Rule 64 does not set out the test which has to be met by a party, typically a respondent, seeking security for recoverable arbitration expenses. In Scots litigation the court applies a number of factors and weighs them against each other to assess the requirements of justice in the matter. In deciding where the interests of justice lie a court will weigh up:

- the impecuniosity of the pursuer (impecuniosity alone may not be sufficient);
- the nature of the case being made by pursuer and whether it has prima facie merit;
- the conduct of the litigation by the pursuer;
- other factors which are not exhaustive but which bear upon whether it is unfair in the circumstances for the defender to have to take the risk of not recovering his expenses if he is successful.

Each case will turn on its own facts. There are however some well established situations where courts have ordered the lodging of caution. Where the pursuer is insolvent in the sense that liabilities exceed assets (though not necessarily sequestrated by formal order) the court will order the lodging of caution (security). Where the pursuer is resident abroad in a country not in the EU or party to the Brussels or Lugano Conventions, the court will order the lodging of caution in place of a mandatory (a Scottish agent who is liable for expenses) being required. Subject to the proviso in r.64(2) the approach of a court in a Scottish litigation may offer some guidance to parties and tribunals. For further information the reader is referred to the commentary in Ch.33 of *Greens' Annotated Rules of the Court of Session* (Edinburgh: W. Green).

Rule 64(1)

The tribunal will have to take care to specify in its order the form of the security and how it is to be provided.

Rule 65: Limitation of recoverable arbitration expenses **D**

65.— (1) A provisional or part award may cap a party's liability for the recoverable arbitration expenses at an amount specified in the award.

(2) But an award imposing such a cap must be made sufficiently in advance of the expenses to which the cap relates being incurred, or the taking of any steps in the arbitration which may be affected by the cap, for the parties to take account of it.

DEFINITIONS
"arbitration expenses": r.59
"party": ss.2(1), 31(1), (2)
"tribunal": ss.2(1), 31(1)

STATUS
This is a default rule so it is open to the parties to modify it, agree something different or disapply it completely (see s.9).

Institutional rules such as the LMAA's SCP include a cost cap as do the about-to-be published CIArb Scottish Short Form Arbitration Rules. In such situations, the starting point will be to consider the extent to which r.65 is inconsistent with or disapplied by any institutional rule.

MODEL LAW
There is no equivalent provision in the Model Law. See the commentary to r.59 above.

COMMENTARY
This rule had no equivalent in Scots common law. It appears to be a straightforward import from English and Welsh law in the shape of s.65 of

the 1996 Act. Section 65 had its origin in the DAC Report, para.272 which states:

> "We consider that such a power [in cl.65, equivalent to that contained in r.65], properly used, could prove to be extremely valuable as an aid to reducing unnecessary expenditure. It also represents a facet of the duty of the tribunal as set out in Clause 33 [equivalent to that contained in r.24]. The Clause enables the tribunal to put a ceiling on the costs so that while a party can continue to spend as much as it likes on an arbitration it will not be able to recover more than the ceiling amount from the other party. This will have the added virtue of discouraging those who wish to use their financial muscle to intimidate their opponents into giving up through fear that by going on they might be subject to a costs order which they could not sustain."

The purpose is to offer some protection to a financially weak party facing financially stronger opponents. The duty referred to in r.24 is presumably that of conducting the arbitration without incurring unnecessary expense. Section 65 of the 1996 Act has been used infrequently, although this may be due to some doubt as to how it is to be applied. Other ways of achieving (at least in part) the same outcome include (i) limiting each party to a single expert; and (ii) disallowing unnecessary or unreasonably expensive legal representation in the assessment and quantification of expenses.

Clearly a party may request the tribunal to make an expenses-capping award. It may also be the case that the tribunal could raise the issue with the parties and ask to be addressed on it, as part of the tribunal's duty under r.24. The issue of the likely cost of the arbitration can be addressed by the tribunal at the preliminary hearing with parties being directed under r.28 to give and exchange estimates as to their likely expenses. This may itself trigger an application under r.65 if there is a material disparity in the estimates. It may also stir the tribunal into raising the issue of expense and a possible r.65 award if the tribunal takes the view that the expenses are wholly excessive or disproportionate to what is at stake in the arbitration. In relation to the making of a r.65 award the questions for parties and tribunals, are:

- what test requires to be satisfied for the making of an award capping liability for recoverable expenses?
- what form would the r.65 award take?

No guidance as to the test is given by either the DAC or the rule itself. An order must be made sufficiently in advance of the taking of steps in the arbitration which may be affected by the order. It is suggested that it must be shown that there is a risk that one party may incur unreasonable expense in relation to its conduct of the arbitration. That may be difficult to show, but one can figure circumstances for example where senior lawyers are being retained for a simple claim, experts are being instructed at large, unascertained or unjustifiable expense relative to the issues at stake or where it can be shown that unnecessary work has been or is being carried out which gives rise to an inference that this may continue into or take place in the future. The tribunal will have to decide whether the items of expense are reasonable and if so whether the quantum of that expense is reasonable, and if not what would be a reasonable cap. Essentially the tribunal will have to carry out an exercise in determining the recoverable expenses under r.61 in advance of them being incurred. The tribunal will have to be supplied with figures with which it can justify the cap sought. Clearly a tribunal will have to act carefully having regard to its various duties under r.24.

A r.65 award may be a part award or a provisional award. A provisional award can be varied later on a change of circumstances but is not subject to appeal during the course of the arbitration (see r.71(3)) until it is incorporated into or confirmed in a permanent part or final award. A part award will be final and will be subject to appeal under rr.68, 69, and 70.

The r.65 award, whether part or provisional will have to be clear and precise in its specification of the recoverable arbitration expenses in particular and the monetary caps which it imposes, so that there is little room for argument as to what it means.

Rule 66: Awards on recoverable arbitration expenses **D**

66. An expenses award (under rule 62 or 65) may be made together with or separately from an award on the substance of the dispute (and these rules apply in relation to an expenses award as they apply to an award on the substance of the dispute).

DEFINITIONS
"rules": s.31(1)

STATUS
This is a default rule so it is open to the parties to modify it, agree something different or disapply it completely (see s.9).

MODEL LAW
There is no equivalent provision in the Model Law. See the commentary to r.59 above.

COMMENTARY
The purpose of r.66 is to emphasise that part awards of expenses can be made and that both part awards and final awards of expenses can be appealed in the same way as an appeal against an award on the merits. In practice, it may however be more difficult to appeal an award in relation to expenses particularly in relation to errors of law.

PART 8

CHALLENGING AWARDS

Rule 67: Challenging an award: substantive jurisdiction **M**

67.—(1) A party may appeal to the Outer House against the tribunal's award on the ground that the tribunal did not have jurisdiction to make the award (a "jurisdictional appeal").

(2) The Outer House may decide a jurisdictional appeal by—
    (a) confirming the award,
    (b) varying the award (or part of it), or
    (c) setting aside the award (or part of it).

(3) Any variation by the Outer House has effect as part of the tribunal's award.

(4) An appeal may be made to the Inner House against the Outer House's decision on a jurisdictional appeal (but only with the leave of the Outer House).

(5) Leave may be given by the Outer House only where it considers—
    (a) that the proposed appeal would raise an important point of principle or practice, or
    (b) that there is another compelling reason for the Inner House to consider the appeal.

(6) The Outer House's decision on whether to grant such leave is final.
(7) The Inner House's decision on such an appeal is final.

DEFINITIONS
"Outer House": s.31(1)
"party": ss.2(1), 31(1), (2)
"tribunal": ss.2(1), 31(1)

STATUS
Rule 67 is a mandatory rule.

MODEL LAW
Article 34 provides that an arbitral award may be set aside if the party applying for the setting aside furnishes proof inter alia that:
> (a) a party to the arbitration agreement was under some incapacity; or the said agreement is not valid under the law to which the parties have subjected it or, failing any indication thereon, under the law of the state whose court is to decide the application; or
> (b) the award deals with a dispute not contemplated by or not falling within the terms of the submission to arbitration, or contains decisions on matters beyond the scope of the submission to arbitration, provided that, if the decisions on matters submitted to arbitration can be separated from those not so submitted, only that part of the award which contains decisions on matters not submitted to arbitration may be set aside; or
> (c) the composition of the arbitral tribunal was not in accordance with the agreement of the parties, unless such agreement was in conflict with a provision of the law of the state whose court is to decide the application from which the parties cannot derogate, or, failing such agreement, was not in accordance with such a law.

Rule 67 is partly based on art.34 of the Model Law. Article 34 contains other grounds for setting aside some of which are contained in r.68.

COMMENTARY
Rule 67 provides the first of the three avenues of challenge to an arbitral award. The first is a challenge to jurisdiction under r.67. The second is a challenge under r.68 to the manner in which or process by which the tribunal reached its award. The third is a challenge under rr.69 and 70 to the merits of the award on the basis of an obviously wrong or seriously doubtful application of Scots law.

The Act does not define what is meant by the tribunal "not having jurisdiction". However r.19 sets out the matters on which a tribunal may rule as to its own jurisdiction and it seems reasonable, on the basis of r.19 to understand a tribunal as not having jurisdiction where:
- there is no valid arbitration agreement providing for the resolution of the dispute (or in the case of a statutory arbitration, the dispute is not covered by the enactment providing for arbitration);
- the tribunal has not been properly constituted; or
- the tribunal deals with or decides matters which have not been submitted to arbitration in accordance with the arbitration agreement.

The reader is referred to the commentary on r.19 above in relation to these grounds of lack of jurisdiction. More detailed commentary is also contained above in the commentaries to ss.4 and 5 (in relation to valid arbitration agreements) and rr.2–7 (in relation the proper constitution of the tribunal).

The general rule is that an appeal has to be made within 28 days of the date when the award is "made". There are exceptions to this and the reader is referred to the commentary to r.71(4) below for more detail in relation to time limits. Before making an appeal the appellant must exhaust any available arbitral process of appeal or review, including any recourse under r.58 (r.71(2)). An appeal is made by a petition in the style contained in RCS Form 14.4 (RCS rr.99.5, 14.4) or, if there are undisposed of Outer House proceedings, by note (RCS rr.99.5, 15.2). The petition or note must set out the grounds of appeal and any other relevant matters required by Ch.99 of the RCS. The petition or note must be lodged with the relevant documents referred to in the commentary to r.42(2).

The Act does not set out whether an appeal against jurisdiction should entail a de novo hearing where the court reconsiders the whole issue afresh, including the possible leading of evidence, or whether the appeal should be limited to errors of law of the tribunal. It is suggested that given that the tribunal has the power and the duty to rule on its own jurisdiction (see discussion of r.19 above), it is not for the court to reconsider the whole issue afresh but to concentrate on whether there has been any error in law on the part of the tribunal in the decision reached by the tribunal. This approach finds support in the practice of various states including France and Germany. It accords with the greater respect given to tribunals in modern international arbitral practice.

Rule 67(1)

The entitlement to make a jurisdictional appeal under r.67 must be seen against the background of other rules relating to jurisdiction of the arbitral tribunal. Rule 19 gives power to the tribunal to rule on its own jurisdiction. Rule 76 provides that a party who participates in an arbitration without making a timeous objection (as defined in r.76(2)) on the ground that the tribunal does not have jurisdiction may not raise the objection later before the tribunal or the court. A party who wishes to contest jurisdiction has two options through which to make a timeous objection. It may use r.20 and make the objection to the tribunal directly. Alternatively it may use r.22 and apply directly to the Outer House of the Court of Session for an order that the tribunal lacks jurisdiction. If a party applies directly to the Outer House then the decision of the Outer House is final (r.23(4)) and it is suggested that an appeal on the same basis cannot be made under r.67 at a later date.

If a party makes the objection to the tribunal under r.20, and the other party does not also insist that the tribunal decide the matter immediately, the tribunal has a discretion to decide whether it should decide the objection now or delay a decision until its final award (r.20(4)). Rule 67 does not permit an appeal against the tribunal's exercise of its discretion on whether it should decide an objection immediately or delay until its final award (*AOOT Kalmneft v Glencore International AG* [2002] 1 Lloyd's Rep. 128 at 139).

If the tribunal does decide the objection immediately and the objecting party is dissatisfied with the tribunal's decision, it has two choices. The first is to appeal the part award to the Outer House within 14 days under r.21 while the arbitration is ongoing. If that route is followed then the decision of the Outer House is final (r.21(3)) and we submit that a further appeal on the same basis cannot be made under r.67 at a later date. The second option is to wait until the tribunal makes its final award and then to appeal the final award under r.67. There are advantages and disadvantages in both options. In the first option there is the advantage of the early disposal of the arbitration proceedings if the appeal is successful and the arbitration proceedings have not yet concluded at the time that the court allows the appeal. However there is not the possibility of a further appeal, with leave, to the Inner House. In the second option, there is the possibility of further appeal to the Inner House (if the Outer House grants leave) but in the meantime the tribunal will have required to decide the merits of the claim. Another risk with the second option is that while a r.67 appeal is ongoing the award might be capable of being enforced in France or New York State in the United States or the sum awarded might be required to be paid into court or otherwise secured under r.71(12).

Except where an appeal is made by a party who claims to have had no notice of the arbitration (as in *The Eastern Navigator* [2006] 1 Lloyd's Rep. 537) the award being appealed against under r.67 must deal in some way—at least in substance if not in form—with an objection on the ground of lack of jurisdiction (*Vee Networks Ltd v Econet Wireless International Ltd* [2005] 1 Lloyd's Rep. 192 at 198). That case also suggests that parties may contract out of the possibility of an appeal from a tribunal's decision on jurisdiction (*Vee Networks* [2005] 1 Lloyd's Rep. 192 at [26]) but it is doubted whether this is possible since it would circumvent the mandatory nature of r.67.

There is English authority, based on the English equivalent of Rule 76 that an appeal on the ground of lack of jurisdiction may not be based on any argument not made before the tribunal unless the appellant shows that it did not know of the argument and could not with reasonable diligence have discovered that ground (*JSC Zestafoni G. Nikoladze Ferroalloy Plant v Ronly Holdings Ltd* [2004] 2 Lloyd's Rep. 335 at 345). For further discussion see commentary to r.76. Whether an argument made at appeal was within the ground of objection made to the tribunal is a matter of degree (See *Primegrade AG v Ythan Ltd* [2006] 1 Lloyd's Rep. 457 at 474). This suggests that a party making an objection to jurisdiction that could give rise to an appeal should frame their grounds of objection to a tribunal broadly so as to allow some flexibility at an appeal, but not so broad as not to give fair notice of the ground to the respondent.

An example of a lack of jurisdiction is where the tribunal makes an award in favour of a person who was not a party to the arbitration agreement, e.g. *Hussman (Europe) Ltd v Al Ameen Development and Trade Co* [2000] 2 Lloyd's Rep. 83.

In deciding a jurisdictional appeal the Outer House has full power to rehear the submissions and any relevant evidence relating to the issue of the jurisdiction of the tribunal (*Azov Shipping Co v Baltic Shipping Co (No.1)* [1999] 1 Lloyd's Rep. 68, per Rix J.). The hearing by the Outer House of a jurisdictional appeal may therefore involve the hearing of oral evidence, if this cannot be agreed. If this is the intention, parties should be clear on whether oral evidence will be necessary by the time that the appellant applies under RCS 99.5 for an order as to further procedure or an order for a hearing. If oral evidence will be necessary the order should include a warrant to the parties to cite witnesses and havers of documents.

Rule 67(2) and (3)

The remedies for an appellant under r.67 are variation or setting aside of the award or part of it. The setting aside of the award corresponds to the former remedy at common law which was to have the award "reduced". In both instances the effect is that the part or whole of the award which is set aside is rendered null and void. The provision for part of the award being set aside is to allow for an award which contains a part which the tribunal had jurisdiction to make and a part where it lacked jurisdiction. In such a situation the court would set aside only the part where the tribunal lacked jurisdiction.

Rule 67(2) also allows the court to vary the award or part of it. It is suggested that the purpose of this power is to allow the court some flexibility in setting aside part of an award, so that if in substance the award is separable into parts where the tribunal had and where it lacked jurisdiction, the court can vary a few words in order to set aside part of an award. However it cannot have been intended to allow the court to vary the substantive terms of the award as that would be to usurp the jurisdiction of the tribunal given to it by the parties. Rule 67(3) is a consequential provision which deems the variations consequential to a separation of the award, to have been part of the tribunal's award.

Rule 67(4)–(6)—further appeals

These provisions provide limits to the right of appeal in order that the finality of the arbitration process be compromised as little as possible compatible with avoiding substantial injustice to a party. Thus appeals from the first instance court (the Outer House of the Court of Session) to the court of appeal in Scotland (the Inner House of the Court of Session), can only be with leave of the first instance court. Appeal up to the Supreme Court in London under s.40 of the Court of Session Act 1988 is excluded.

For the time limit for seeking leave see r.71(5) below and the commentary to that rule. See also RCS r.38.5 in relation to applications for leave to appeal (reclaim).

A requirement that leave be obtained for a further appeal is not incompatible with the right to a fair trial under art.6 of the ECHR (*Kazakhstan v Istil Group Ltd* [2007] 2 Lloyd's Rep. 548).

If leave is refused, can the refusal to grant leave be appealed to the Inner House on the ground that the refusal followed action of the Outer House which was incompatible with the appellant's right under art.6 of the ECHR? See the commentary to r.70(9), (10) and (11) below.

Rule 68: Challenging an award: serious irregularity **M**

68.—(1) A party may appeal to the Outer House against the tribunal's award on the ground of serious irregularity (a "serious irregularity appeal").

(2) "Serious irregularity" means an irregularity of any of the following kinds which has caused, or will cause, substantial injustice to the appellant—
- (a) the tribunal failing to conduct the arbitration in accordance with—
    - (i) the arbitration agreement,
    - (ii) these rules (in so far as they apply), or
    - (iii) any other agreement by the parties relating to conduct of the arbitration,
- (b) the tribunal acting outwith its powers (other than by exceeding its jurisdiction),
- (c) the tribunal failing to deal with all the issues that were put to it,
- (d) any arbitral appointments referee or other third party to whom the parties give powers in relation to the arbitration acting outwith powers,
- (e) uncertainty or ambiguity as to the award's effect,
- (f) the award being—

(i) contrary to public policy, or
(ii) obtained by fraud or in a way which is contrary to public policy,
(g) an arbitrator having not been impartial and independent,
(h) an arbitrator having not treated the parties fairly,
(i) an arbitrator having been incapable of acting as an arbitrator in the arbitration (or there being justifiable doubts about an arbitrator's ability to so act),
(j) an arbitrator not having a qualification which the parties agreed (before the arbitrator's appointment) that the arbitrator must have, or
(k) any other irregularity in the conduct of the arbitration or in the award which is admitted by—
(i) the tribunal, or
(ii) any arbitral appointments referee or other third party to whom the parties give powers in relation to the arbitration.

(3) The Outer House may decide a serious irregularity appeal by—
(a) confirming the award,
(b) ordering the tribunal to reconsider the award (or part of it), or
(c) if it considers reconsideration inappropriate, setting aside the award (or part of it).

(4) Where the Outer House decides a serious irregularity appeal (otherwise than by confirming the award) on the ground—
(a) that the tribunal failed to conduct the arbitration in accordance with—
(i) the arbitration agreement,
(ii) these rules (in so far as they apply), or
(iii) any other agreement by the parties relating to conduct of the arbitration,
(b) that an arbitrator has not been impartial and independent, or
(c) that an arbitrator has not treated the parties fairly,
it may also make such order as it thinks fit about any arbitrator's entitlement (if any) to fees and expenses (and such an order may provide for the repayment of fees or expenses already paid to the arbitrator).

(5) An appeal may be made to the Inner House against the Outer House's decision on a serious irregularity appeal (but only with the leave of the Outer House).

(6) Leave may be given by the Outer House only where it considers—
(a) that the proposed appeal would raise an important point of principle or practice, or
(b) that there is another compelling reason for the Inner House to consider the appeal.

(7) The Outer House's decision on whether to grant such leave is final.
(8) The Inner House's decision on such an appeal is final.

DEFINITIONS
"arbitration agreement": ss.4, 31(1)
"Outer House": s.31(1)
"party": ss.2(1), 31(1), (2)
"rule": s.31(1)
"tribunal": ss.2(1), 31(1)

STATUS
It is mandatory (s.8). Parties cannot exclude its application.

MODEL LAW

Article 34 provides that an arbitral award may be set aside if the party applying for the setting aside furnishes proof inter alia that:
  (a) the party making the application was not given proper notice of the appointment of an arbitrator or of the arbitral proceedings or was otherwise unable to present his case; or
  (b) the arbitral procedure was not in accordance with the agreement of the parties, unless such agreement was in conflict with a provision of the law of the state whose court is to decide the application from which the parties cannot derogate, or, failing such agreement, was not in accordance with such a law; or
  (c) (i) the subject matter of the dispute is not capable of settlement by arbitration under the law of that state; or
      (ii) the award is in conflict with the public policy of that state.

Rule 68 reflects the grounds for setting aside contained in the Model Law and contains further grounds for setting aside which relate to the manner in which or process by which the tribunal reached its award.

COMMENTARY

Rule 68 provides the second of the three avenues of challenge to an arbitral award. The first is a jurisdictional challenge under r.67. The second is a challenge under r.68 to the manner in which or process by which the tribunal reached its award. The third is a challenge under rr.69 and 70 to the merits of the award on the basis of an obviously wrong or seriously doubtful decision under Scots law.

Rule 68 is a crucial provision in the new regime for arbitration. For that reason it is mandatory. The purpose of the provision is to provide a measure of quality control of the arbitration process. No code of arbitration law would be complete without some such provision. The list of grounds seeks to strike a balance between the aim of finality of an arbitral award and the aim of ensuring that arbitrators meet the highest standards. The emphasis in most of the grounds is on defects in the process rather than the result. Some of these grounds were in existence as grounds of reduction at common law. Others are new. So far as a complaint about the result is concerned, the remedy, if one exists, lies in r.69.

The general rule is that an appeal has to be made within 28 days of the date when the award is "made". There are exceptions to this and the reader is referred to the commentary to r.71(4) below for more detail in relation to time limits. Before making an appeal the appellant must exhaust any available arbitral process of appeal or review including any recourse under r.58 (r.71(2)). An appeal is made by a petition in the style contained in RCS Form 14.4 (RCS rr.99.5, 14.4) or, if there are undisposed of Outer House proceedings, by note (RCS rr.99.5, 15.2). The petition or note must set out the grounds of appeal and any other relevant matters required by Ch.99 of the RCS. The petition or note must be lodged with the relevant documents referred to in the commentary to r.42(2).

Rule 68 discards the previous common law remedy of the setting aside of an award through either a defence of setting aside in court proceedings for implement of an award (reduction of the award *ope exceptionis*) or court proceedings, typically judicial review, for setting aside of an award (reduction of the award). Section 13 makes it clear that legal proceedings are competent in respect of a tribunal's award or any other act or omission by a tribunal when conducting an arbitration only as provided for in the rules and that in particular a tribunal's award is not subject to review in any legal proceedings except as provided for in Pt 8 of the rules (rr.67–72).

Rule 68(1)

The ground of appeal under r.68 has the overall title "serious irregularity". That is defined in r.68(2) but the overall title emphasises that the focus is on limited irregularities of the arbitration process and that for the appeal to succeed the irregularity in question must be serious.

Rule 68(2)—qualifying irregularity and "substantial injustice"

A "serious irregularity" requires two elements. First, there must be one of the qualifying and exhaustive irregularities specified in r.68(2). Secondly, that irregularity must have caused or will cause "substantial injustice" to the party appealing.

Where a qualifying irregularity has been established the court cannot allow the appeal unless it is also satisfied that the irregularity in question has caused or will cause "substantial injustice" to the appealing party. "Substantial injustice" has not been defined further. Parliament has thereby indicated that the court must assess the issue on a case by case basis. The word "substantial" has often been seen as having two different meanings, namely (1) large or big; or (2) anything having content which is more than de minimis. Which should apply? The word must be read in the context of the need for a "serious" irregularity. It must also be seen against the background of being one of the three exceptions to the finality of an arbitral award, which is one of the cornerstones of arbitration. If it was applied to any injustice other than a negligible one, then it would risk undermining the finality of an award and of prolonging the proceedings which would be contrary to the general policy of the Act and of arbitration as a whole. A further clue to the approach to "substantial injustice" is given in para.58 of the DAC Report which inspired the equivalent s.68 of the 1996 Act. There the DAC stated:

"We have listed the specific cases where a challenge can be made under this Clause. The test of "substantial injustice" is intended to be applied by way of support for the arbitral process, not by way of interference with that process. Thus it is only in those cases where it can be said that what has happened is *so far removed from what could reasonably be expected of the arbitral process* that we would expect the Court to take action" (emphasis added).

For all of these reasons it is suggested that the word "substantial" should be given the meaning of "large" or "big". This also means that in relation to the issue of "substantial injustice" the focus is on the effect of the irregularity on the appellant's position.

In considering whether the qualifying irregularity has caused substantial injustice to the appellant the court should try to assess how the appellant would have conducted his case but for the procedural irregularity (*Checkpoint Ltd v Strathclyde Pension Fund* [2003] EWCA Civ 84; [2003] L. & T.R. 22, per Ward L.J. at [58]). Where but for the irregularity the appellant would still have failed will make it very difficult to demonstrate that he suffered substantial prejudice as a result of the irregularity (*Margulead Ltd v Exide Technologies* [2005] 1 Lloyd's Rep. 324 at 330 [36]). Whilst each case must be looked at on its own merit, some—but not all—of the English and Welsh case law provides guidance on what has been seen as "substantial injustice". Where, had the irregularity not occurred, it is clear that the decision of the tribunal would have been the reverse of the decision actually made, there will be substantial injustice (*Newfield Construction Ltd v Tomlinson* [2004] EWHC 3051 (TCC); 97 Con. L.R. 148, per H.H. Judge Coulson QC at [44]). Similarly it has been suggested, in passing, that if the duty to give reasons has not been excluded and no or insufficient reasons were given then the substantial injustice would be automatic (*Benaim (UK) Ltd v Davies Middleton & Davies Ltd (No.2)* [2005] EWHC 1370 (TCC); 102 Con. L.R. 1 at [95]). Where a tribunal awarded interest at a rate which neither party had asked for, and on which neither had been invited to make submissions, and which resulted in an extra payment of nearly €1 million, it was held that the tribunal's irregularity had caused substantial injustice (*Van der Giessen-de Noord Shipbuilding Division BV v Imtech Marine & Offshore BV* [2009] 1 Lloyd's Rep. 273 at 280).

However where the tribunal met with an expert without informing the parties and breached the equivalent of its general duty under r.24, but the meeting did not prejudice either party, the irregularity did not cause injustice to the appellant and there was therefore no serious irregularity (*Hussman (Europe) Ltd v Al Ameen Development & Trade Co* [2000] 2 Lloyd's Rep. 83, per Thomas J. at 95). For an example of a breach of the equivalent of r.24 in failing to give an opportunity to cross examine which did not give rise to substantial injustice see *Compania Sud-Americana De Vapores SA v Nippon Yusen Kaisha* [2009] EWHC 1606 (Comm).

Mere loss of confidence in the arbitrator where there has not been substantial injustice caused by a qualifying irregularity will not satisfy the requirements of r.68 (*Benaim (UK) Ltd v Davies Middleton & Davies Ltd (No.2)* [2005] EWHC 1370 (TCC); 102 Con. L.R. 1 at [60])

Rule 68(2)(a)—failure to conduct in accordance with agreement, etc.

This irregularity is defined as having three branches, namely:
(a) failure to conduct the arbitration in accordance with the arbitration agreement;
(b) failure to conduct the arbitration in accordance with the Scottish Arbitration Rules contained in the Act itself;
(c) failure to conduct the arbitration in accordance with any other agreement by the parties relating to the conduct of the arbitration.

The arbitration agreement is the agreement under which the tribunal has its jurisdiction (see s.4 above). A challenge to the jurisdiction of the tribunal, for example that it decided matters which were not referred to it under the arbitration agreement would be made under rr.20, 22 or 67. A challenge under r.68(2)(a) would presumably relate to a failure by the tribunal to follow a procedure set out in the arbitration agreement.

A failure by the tribunal to follow the Scottish Arbitration Rules is an irregularity in itself. This includes in particular a failure to comply with rr.24 and 26. In England and Wales a high hurdle has been placed for appellants seeking to rely on a breach of the equivalent of r.24 as an irregularity giving rise to substantial injustice (*Bandwidth Shipping Corp v Intaari (A Firm) (The Magdalena Oldendorff)* [2008] 1 Lloyd's Rep. 7, per Waller L.J. at 13). So only clear breaches by the tribunal of its statutory duties have resulted in successful appeals. Thus giving a higher award due to an arithmetical error (*Gannet Shipping Ltd v Eastrade Commodities Inc* [2002] 1 Lloyd's Rep. 713), and making an award on a basis contrary to the common position of the parties without giving them an opportunity to make submissions on it (*Omnibridge Consulting Ltd v Clearsprings (Management) Ltd* [2004] EWHC 2276 (Comm)) have been failures to comply with the equivalent of r.24 which have been found to be qualifying irregularities under this head. The failure of the tribunal to give reasons for its award would be a breach of r.48(2)(c) and thus a qualifying irregularity under this head (see *Norbrook Laboratories Ltd v Tank* [2006] 2 Lloyd's Rep. 485, per Colman J. at 505).

For a situation where the tribunal's appointment of an expert on its own initiative was not the breach of the equivalent of r.24 see *Hussman (Europe) Ltd v Al Ameen Development & Trade Co* [2000] 2 Lloyd's Rep. 83.

The parties may have reached agreement to conduct the arbitration in an agreement quite separate from the original arbitration agreement. This might involve agreement on procedure, whether ad hoc or through the adoption of institutional rules. It might involve agreement contained in the pleadings as to the arguments to be submitted to the tribunal, e.g. *Newfield Construction Ltd v Tomlinson*, 97 Con. L.R. 148 at [43] where an arbitrator did not base his decision on expenses on success in terms of the pleadings of the parties and was held to have failed to conduct the arbitration in accordance with the agreement of the parties, that agreement being contained in the procedure agreed by the parties requesting a decision on the cases presented in the written pleadings and not other matters.

Article 34 of the Model Law allows the setting aside of an award where:
- a party was not given proper notice of the appointment of an arbitrator;
- a party was not given proper notice of the arbitral proceedings;
- a party was otherwise unable to present his case;
- the arbitral procedure was not in accordance with the agreement of the parties unless the parties' agreement was in conflict with a provision of the Model Law.

All of these categories can be seen as falling within r.68(2)(a). In effect the Scottish Arbitration Rules can be seen as forming part of the parties' agreement except in so far as they have disapplied or modified a default rule.

Rule 68(2)(b)—acting outwith its powers

This paragraph is intended to cover situations where the tribunal makes an order, other than the making of an award where it lacks jurisdiction, for which it lacks power, e.g. where it appoints an expert under r.34 to report to it but the parties have excluded that default power. This paragraph requires the court to address the question whether the tribunal purported to exercise a power which it did not have or whether it erroneously exercised a power that it did have. If it is merely a case of the latter no excess of power under the equivalent provision in s.68(2)(b) of the 1996 Act is involved (*Lesotho Highlands Development Authority v Impregilo SpA* [2006] 1 A.C. 221, per Lord Steyn at 233 [24]) This provision cannot be used to complain that an award is wrong as a matter of fact and law (*Lesotho Highlands Development Authority* [2006] 1 A.C. 221, per Lord Steyn at 231 [31]).

An example of where a tribunal lacks power to decide an issue is where the subject matter of the reference to it is not arbitrable, e.g. if it is *contra bonos mores* (Irons and Melville, *Arbitration*, 1903, p.22).

Article 34 of the Model Law allows the setting aside of an award which:
- deals with a dispute not contemplated by or not falling within the terms of the submission to arbitration;
- contains decisions on matters beyond the scope of the submission to arbitration.

Both of these categories can be seen as falling within r.68(2)(b).

Rule 68(2)(c)—not dealing with all the issues

"Issues" in this provision mean the issues the determination of which is essential to a decision on the claim or defence raised in the course of the reference (*World Trade Corp Ltd v C Czarnikow Sugar Ltd* [2005] 1 Lloyd's Rep. 422, per Coleman J.). Not every matter that is raised during the course of the arbitration proceedings is therefore an "issue". The issue must therefore be a fundamental issue which had been put to the tribunal for it to decide as only such an issue could be capable of causing substantial injustice to the party putting it (*Fidelity Management SA v Myriad International Holdings Ltd BV* [2005] 2 Lloyd's Rep. 508 at 510). Thus subsidiary issues which are not critical to the primary issues are not "issues" for the purpose of r.66(2)(c) (*Benaim (UK) Ltd v Davies Middleton & Davies (No.2)*, 102 Con. L.R. 1 at [51]–[53]). The distinction between a primary issue which must be dealt with and a subsidiary issue can be difficult to draw (*Van der Giessen-de Noord Shipbuilding Division BV v Imtech Marine & Offshore BV* [2009] 1 Lloyd's Rep. 273 at 282) but the test appears to be whether the primary issue could be fairly decided without the need to decide the subsidiary issue (see *Van der Giessen-de Noord* [2009] 1 Lloyd's Rep. 273).

In this context "dealing with an issue" is a different matter from giving clear or adequate reasons. If parties have agreed that no reasons should be given then there is no duty to give reasons and no irregularity if they are not given. If the court cannot deal with the appeal properly without the tribunal giving reasons or further detailed reasons, then it has the power to order the tribunal to give such reasons (see the commentary to r.71(7) below). A failure to set out each step by which a conclusion was reached or a failure to deal with each point raised by a party under an issue will not amount to a failure to "deal with all the issues put" to the tribunal (*Hussman (Europe) Ltd v Al Ameen Development & Trade Co* [2000] 2 Lloyd's Rep. 83, per Thomas J. at 97). If there is a failure to give clear reasons then this may amount to an irregularity under para.(2)(a)(ii) being a failure to conduct the arbitration in accordance with r.48(2)(c) which requires a tribunal to give reasons.

If a tribunal has in some way been expressly asked to deal with the expenses of an arbitration, its failure to do so would amount to a qualifying irregularity; and see the commentary to r.62 above.

Rule 68(2)(d)—arbitral appointments referee or third party

This deals with an arbitral appointments referee or third party to whom powers were given by the parties acting outwith its powers. This type of irregularity has a close affinity with that of the tribunal itself exceeding its powers (*Lesotho Highlands Development Authority v Impregilo SpA* [2006] 1 A.C. 221 at 236 [29]). The same approach should be followed to ascertain whether the referee or third party has acted outwith its powers as to whether the tribunal has done so. Thus for example where an arbitral appointments referee appointed a tribunal of three persons where the arbitration agreement specified a sole arbitrator, that would amount to an action outwith its powers.

Rule 68(2)(e)—uncertainty or ambiguity as to award's effect

When an award is issued its terms must be carefully scrutinised by all parties so that they understand clearly the meaning of the award. If a party takes the view that the effect of an award is uncertain or ambiguous, it must apply to the tribunal under r.58 for the correction of the award so as to clarify or remove any ambiguity. See the discussion under r.58. Only if the tribunal's decision on the application is unsatisfactory is there a right of appeal under r.68 in respect of the uncertainty or ambiguity of effect of the award (r.71(2)). For the appeal to be successful, there must not merely be uncertainty or ambiguity as to the effect of the award but such uncertainty or ambiguity must cause substantial injustice to the appellant, something which is not required under r.58.

In *Tongyuan (USA) International Trading Group v Uni-Clan Ltd* Unreported January 19, 2001 QB, in connection with opposition to the enforcement of a foreign award on the grounds of uncertainty or ambiguity, Moore-Bick J. said:

"The court should not, in my view, be astute to find difficulties of construction of awards or, for that matter, judgments, where none really exist."

If an award directs a party to pay a sum of money or perform some act, while it is advisable that the award give a time limit for the implement of the payment or the act, the absence of a time limit will leave an implied term that the payment or performance be within a reasonable time (Irons and Melville, *Arbitration*, 1903, p.210). The effect of a successful appeal on this ground may result in an order to the tribunal to reconsider the award or part of it. See the commentary to rr.68(3) and 69 below.

Rule 68(2)(f)—contrary to public policy, obtained by fraud

This paragraph contains three possible irregularities, namely:
 (a) the award being contrary to public policy;
 (b) the award being obtained by fraud;
 (c) the award being obtained in a way contrary to public policy.

This commentary considers the first of these before considering the second and third.

That an award in itself, as opposed to the means by which it was obtained from a tribunal, was contrary to public policy was something never invoked as a discrete ground for setting aside of an award either under the common law or under the 25th Act of the Articles of Regulation 1695 (disapplied by s.26). If the court had been faced with, for example enforcement proceedings for an award on a contract involving smuggling or illegal or immoral activity, the court would have set aside the award on the grounds of the tribunal acting outwith its powers in making an award on an illegal and therefore unarbitrable contract. This common law approach remains open to the court under r.68(2)(b) whereby a tribunal acting outwith its powers is a qualifying irregularity. The concept of "public policy" as a ground for setting aside a Scottish award is something new introduced by the Act. Its origin lies in s.68(2)(g) of the 1996 Act. In turn the origin of that term in the 1996 Act appears to originate from a combination of the Model Law and the Arbitration Act 1975 which implemented the New York Convention for the enforcement of foreign arbitral awards. Interestingly "public policy" did feature as a ground in Scots common law for the refusal of recognition of foreign arbitral awards (see *Hamlyn v Talisker Distillery Co* (1894) 21 R. (HL) 21).

The award being in conflict with "the public policy of the State" is a ground for setting aside under art.34(2)(b)(ii) of the Model Law. That in turn reflects reflects the defence to enforcement of a foreign award under art.V2(b) of the New York Convention. Whilst the rule does not express that it is the public policy of Scots law, given that the rule (unlike its New York Convention equivalent—see s.20(4)(b) above) is being applied in an arbitration with a Scots seat, it is difficult to see what other public policy could be covered. Such an interpretation would be consistent with the Model Law.

However there is reason to believe that "public policy" in terms of r.68 is narrower than "public policy" in terms of the Model Law or the New York

Convention (s.20(4)(b)) on which the Model Law is based. This is because "public policy" under the Model Law was intended to be a broader concept than that under r.68. In the final report leading up to the enactment of the Model Law, the UN Commission observed, that in the Model Law as well as the New York Convention the term "public policy" ("ordre public" in French) in the French sense, was not the equivalent to the political stance or international policies of a state but comprised the fundamental notions and principles of justice, which in France and some civil law jurisdictions included fundamental procedural justice (*Report of the UN Commission on International Trade Law on its work in its 18th Session* (A/40/17), paras 296, 297). It also noted that instances such as corruption, bribery or fraud and similar serious cases would be covered by the concept and in that connection, that the wording, "the award is in conflict with the public policy of this State", was not to be interpreted as excluding instances or events relating to the manner in which an award was arrived at. Given that procedural injustice is covered by paras (2)(a), (g), and (h) at least, of r.68, "public policy" in terms of this rule is intended to have a narrower meaning than its use in the Model Law.

Under the previous common law "public policy" was held to be, "a deeply rooted and important consideration of local policy" (*Hamlyn v Talisker Distillery Co* (1894) 21 R. (HL) 21, per Lord Watson at 27) or, "a fundamental principle of the law of Scotland founded on considerations of public policy" (*Hamlyn* (1894) 21 R. (HL) 21, per Lord Herschell at 23). Contracts *contra bonos mores* have always been regarded as void or unenforceable and therefore not giving rise to arbitrable disputes. In England and Wales it has been held that an award in an English arbitration following a dispute on a contract which would be illegal under English law, was itself contrary to public policy and an appeal against it was allowed (*Soleimany v Soleimany* [1999] Q.B. 785, per Court of Appeal at 799). By contrast in *R v V* [2009] 1 Lloyd's Rep. 97 the court found that the contract was not illegal under and not contrary to public policy and the appeal against the arbitrator's award was refused. It appears to be the position that the English or Welsh court will not question an award on this ground unless it takes the view that the award contravened the public policy of England and Wales which is of worldwide, universal application. It is suggested that in Scotland such an approach should also apply. If a situation such as that in *Soleimany* arose in Scotland it would be dealt with not under public policy but under the issue of arbitrability and the powers of the tribunal (r.68(2)(b)).

The second and third irregularities concern the obtaining of the award by fraud or in a way contrary to public policy. The obtaining of an award through the fraud of a party was always a ground for the setting aside of an award under the Scots common law (see, e.g. the case law cited in Irons and Melville, *Arbitration*, 1903, pp.407–408). In *Boyd & Forrest v Glasgow & South Western Railway Co (No.1)*, 1912 S.C. (H.L.) 93 at 99, Lord Atkinson quoted with approval Lord Herschell's classic definition of fraud in *Derry v Peek* (1889) 14 App. Cas. 337, as follows:

"... fraud is proved where it is shown that a false representation has been made (1) knowingly, or (2) without belief in its truth, or (3) recklessly, careless whether it be true or false. Although I have treated the second and third as distinct cases, I think the third is but an instance of the second, for one who makes a statement under such circumstances can have no real belief in the truth of what he states. To prevent a false statement being fraudulent, there must, I think, always be an honest belief in its truth. And this probably covers the whole ground for one who knowingly alleges that which is false has obviously no such honest belief ... if fraud be proved, the motive of the person guilty of it is immaterial. It matters not that there was no intention to cheat or injure the person to whom the statement was made."

In the context of obtaining an award by fraud the onus on the person alleging this is to make good the allegation by cogent evidence (*Double K Oil Products 1996 Ltd v Neste Oil OYJ* [2009] EWHC 3380 (Comm), per Blair J. at [33]). Mere inadvertent misleading of a party or an innocent production of false evidence will not suffice. In addition to the making of the false representation it must be shown that it had a causal effect on the terms of the award. Thus it has been said that it must be shown that the new evidence being relied on to demonstrate the fraud was not available at the time of the arbitration and would have had an important influence on the award (*Westacre Investments Inc v Jugoimport SDPR Holding Co Ltd* [1999] 2 Lloyd's Rep. 65, per Waller L.J. at 76–77, quoting Colman J. at first instance). Finally, although r.68(2)(f) provides merely states, "obtained by fraud" leaving it open by whose fraud the award might have been obtained it has been observed that it should be read as referring to the fraud of a party to the arbitration or the fraud of some other person to which a party was privy (see *Double K Oil Products* [2009] EWHC 3380 (Comm) at [35], following Aikens J. in *Elektrim SA v Vivendi Universal SA* [2007] EWHC 11 (Comm); [2007] 1 Lloyd's Rep. 693 at [79]). Where the allegation is that the award was obtained by perjury the appellant must produce evidence which with reasonable diligence could not have been produced at the hearing on evidence and would have probably affected the result and it must be sufficiently strong that it could be expected to be decisive at the rehearing (*DDT Trucks of North America Ltd v DDT Holdings Ltd* [2007] EWHC 1542 (Comm); [2007] 2 Lloyd's Rep. 213, per Cooke J. at [22]).

Prior to the Act, the obtaining of an award from arbitrators who were guilty of "corruption, bribery, or falsehood" was a ground for the setting aside of an award under the now disapplied 25th Act of the Articles of Regulation 1695 (see s.28). In place of the disapplied Articles of Regulation comes the broader new concept of the obtaining of an award in a way contrary to public policy. This concept has been held to normally require the demonstration of some form of reprehensible or unconscionable conduct which has contributed in a substantial way to the obtaining of the award (see *Double K Oil Products* [2009] EWHC 3380 (Comm); *Protech Projects Construction (Pty) Ltd v Al-Kharafi & Sons* [2005] 2 Lloyd's Rep. 779; and the commentary to s.20 above). The cases under the equivalent provision in the 1996 Act indicate that reprehensible or unconscionable conduct is not something which the court should be quick to find.

Rule 68(2)(g)—arbitrator not impartial and independent

See the commentary to r.24(1)(a) above.

Rule 68(2)(h)—arbitrator not having treated the parties fairly

See the commentary to r.24(1)(b) above.

Rule 68(2)(i)—arbitrator incapable or justifiable doubts about capability

See the commentary to r.12(c) above.

Rule 68(2)(j)—arbitrator lacking agreed qualification

See the commentary to rr.10(2)(a)(iii) and 12(d) above.

Rule 68(2)(k)—admitted irregularity

This provision is self-explanatory.

Rule 68(3)—remedies

Rule 68(3) sets out the possible outcomes of a serious irregularity appeal. The first, confirmation of the award, is another way of expressing the refusal of the appeal. If the appeal is to any extent successful, the question for the court will lie between the second and third outcomes.

The first issue for the court is whether an order requiring the arbitrator to reconsider the award or any part of it is appropriate. Only if that is inappropriate is it open to the court to set aside the award or part of it. "Reconsideration" implies the same arbitrator using the existing evidence which has been presented to him for the purposes of the award plus any supplementary submissions which are consequential upon the successful appeal (*Ascot Commodities NV v Olam International Ltd* [2002] C.L.C. 277, per Toulson J. at 286). Appeals which are successful under r.68(2)(c) and (e) may well result in a remit for reconsideration. Delay in time between the court's decision and the original award may cause difficulties for the existing arbitrators and this may point towards setting aside being appropriate (see *Ascot Commodities* [2002] C.L.C. 277). However if an appeal is successful under say r.68(2)(g), (h) or (i) a remit for reconsideration may be inappropriate and the setting aside of the award is the proper course to follow. Appeals under r.68(2)(a) may fall into this category also. This may have an impact on the arbitrator's entitlement to his fees.

If the court orders the tribunal to reconsider the award or any part of it, the reconsidered award must be made by no later than three months after the date of the court's order unless the court specifies a different deadline (r.72(1)). For the effects of remission see the commentary to r.72 below.

Rule 68(4)—arbitrator's fees and expenses

Rule 68(4) deals with successful appeals under r.68(2)(a) and (g). In such appeals it is possible that the personal conduct of the arbitrator, rather than that of the parties may have caused the appeal procedure upon the defective award, and indeed may, in the case of setting aside, have caused substantial abortive arbitral procedure. Yet the arbitrator will not be a party to the appeal and so the court will not have any power to find him liable for any expenses arising as a result of the appeal or abortive procedure. This rule gives the court power to abate the fees charged or chargeable by the arbitrator.

The power is stated to be as the court "thinks fit". It is suggested, however that this does not mean that the court has an unfettered discretion in the exercise of its power. Rather the power should be exercised to give effect to the principle that the arbitrator should not be entitled to fees and expenses for procedure caused by or rendered abortive through his failure under r.68(2)(a) or (g). As a matter of natural justice and a right to a fair trial the arbitrator should be given an opportunity to address the court on any proposal to exercise the power.

Rule 68(5), (6), (7) and (8)—further appeals

These provisions provide a limit to the right of appeal in order that the finality of the arbitration process be compromised as little as possible compatible with avoiding substantial injustice to a party. Thus appeals from the first instance court (the Outer House of the Court of Session) to the court of appeal in Scotland (the Inner House of the Court of Session), can only be with leave of the first instance court. Appeal up to the Supreme Court in London under s.40 of the Court of Session Act 1988 is excluded.

For the time limit for seeking leave see r.71(5) below and the commentary to that rule. See also RCS r.38.5 in relation to applications for leave to appeal (reclaim).

A requirement that leave be obtained for a further appeal is not incompatible with the right to a fair trial under art.6 of the ECHR (*Kazakhstan v Istil Group Ltd* [2007] 2 Lloyd's Rep. 548).

If leave is refused, can the refusal to grant leave be appealed to the Inner House on the ground that the refusal followed action of the Outer House which was incompatible with the appellant's right under art.6 of the ECHR? See the commentary to r.70(9), (10) and (11) below.

Rule 69: Challenging an award: legal error **D**

69.—(1) A party may appeal to the Outer House against the tribunal's award on the ground that the tribunal erred on a point of Scots law (a "legal error appeal").

(2) An agreement between the parties to disapply rule 51(2)(c) by dispensing with the tribunal's duty to state its reasons for its award is to be treated as an agreement to exclude the court's jurisdiction to consider a legal error appeal.

DEFINITIONS
"Outer House": s.31(1)
"legal error appeal": r.69(1)
"party": ss.2(1), 31(1), (2)
"rule": s.31(1)
"tribunal": ss.2(1), 31(1)

STATUS

This is a default rule so it is open to the parties to modify it, agree something different or disapply it completely (see s.9).

If parties have agreed to adopt institutional rules, if r.69 is inconsistent with or disapplied by an institutional rule then parties will be treated as having agreed to modify or disapply r.69 (with r.70). In such situations, the starting point will be to consider the extent to which rr.69 and 70 are inconsistent with or disapplied by the institutional rule. Thus in art.28.6 of the ICC Rules the parties are deemed to have waived their right to any form of recourse against the award. A similar provision is contained in art.28.6 of the LCIA rules. Rule 69 appears to be inconsistent with such an institutional rule. The mere provision in an institutional rule, or an arbitration agreement (whether it is part of a larger contract or is a joint submission or reference independent of or consequential to the larger contract) that the arbitrator's decision is to be "final and binding" is likely to be insufficient to exclude a legal error appeal (for a review of English, Canadian and Australian case law see *Essex County Council v Premier Recycling Ltd* [2006] EWHC 3594 (TCC)). This is because it is not inconsistent with r.69 nor does it amount to an express agreement to modify or disapply r.69. The same can be said for a rule that an award is to be, "final conclusive and binding on the parties". The use of the word "conclusive" in that phrase has been held to be insufficient to amount to an agreement to disapply the similar s.69 of the 1996 Act, it being a mere emphasis of the position that an arbitral award is res judicata (*Shell Egypt West Manzala GmbH v Dana Gas Egypt Ltd* [2009]

EWHC 2097 (Comm)). If r.69 has been disapplied then the issue is likely to be raised at the stage of the application for leave to appeal.

An arbitration agreement made before the commencement of the Act which disapplied the now repealed default provision in s.3 of the Administration of Justice (Scotland) Act 1972 is deemed to be an agreement to disapply r.69 unless the parties otherwise agree (s.36(8)). Given that many arbitration clauses excluded the unpopular s.3 it is important to note that these clauses will still be effective to exclude r.69, unless the parties agree that r.69 should apply. An agreement between the parties to disapply r.51(2)(c) requiring the arbitrator to give reasons for his award will be treated as having excluded legal error appeals.

If the parties have chosen a law other than Scots law as the applicable law to decide their dispute, or have required the arbitrator to take non-legal matters of equity into account and to act as an "*amicable compositeur*", the parties have not so much disapplied r.69 as taken the arbitration beyond the scope of r.69 in that the tribunal will not be making its award through the application of Scots law, an error in which could give rise to an appeal. See also the commentary below.

MODEL LAW
There is no equivalent provision in the Model Law.

COMMENTARY
Rule 69 provides the third of the three avenues of challenge to an arbitral award. The first is a challenge under r.67 to jurisdiction. The second is a challenge under r.68 to the manner in which or process by which the tribunal reached its award (serious irregularity). The third is a challenge to the merits of the award on the basis of an obviously wrong or seriously doubtful decision under Scottish law. If the law applicable to the substance of the dispute is not Scots law, then this third avenue will not be available.

Rule 69 can be seen as being applicable in arbitrations (seated in Scotland) where the tribunal has decided the dispute by applying Scots law to the facts, that is to say in Scottish arbitrations (see the commentary to r.47 above). If, under r.47, the tribunal requires to decide the dispute in accordance with a non-Scots law, but is not provided with satisfactory evidence of the relevant rules of that non-Scots law, it requires to apply rules of Scots law on the basis that the rules of the non-Scots law are presumed to be the same as Scots law (*Bonnor v Balfour Kilpatrick Ltd*, 1974 S.C. 223). In such a situation, could an error on a point of Scots law give rise to an appeal under r.69? While on the face of it r.69 would seem to apply to such a situation, it must be remembered that when a tribunal applies rules of Scots law as a presumed non-Scots law, it does so in terms of findings in fact as to the rules of a non-Scots law which are not appealable. It is therefore suggested that r.69 does not extend to appeals on points of Scots law arising when Scots law is used as a presumed non-Scots law.

In enacting rr.69 and 70 Scots law has departed from the common law position which did not allow any appeal against an arbitral award on the merits of the award even if the arbitrator had erred in law. The common law position had been the subject of criticism in the early 1970s which had resulted in the enactment of a default rule (in s.3 of the Administration of Justice (Scotland) Act 1972) whereby a party could apply at any stage of the arbitration up to the making of the award to the Court of Session for a binding opinion of the court on any question of law whatever. This had the effect of significantly slowing down the arbitral process. Rules 69 and 41 can be seen as providing a compromise between the Scots common law/Model

Law situation and that under the former s.3. Fundamentally r.69 seeks to reflect the presumed wishes of the parties that they wish to have the merits of the dispute decided by Scots law and that where the arbitrator has seriously failed to understand that law they should not be bound by such a fundamental failure. An appeal on the grounds of error of law from an arbitral tribunal is however significantly more restricted than such an appeal from any other statutory tribunal or from a court decision in a litigation at first instance. In particular, as under the pre-Act position, the facts found by the tribunal cannot be questioned (see the commentary to r.70(4)(c) below). This is in line with the advantage of finality given to parties choosing to resolve their dispute by arbitration.

Finally respondents will be aware of the possibilities of seeking caution for expenses and also seeking payment of the sum awarded into the court as a condition precedent to an appeal or application proceeding (see r.71(10)–(12) below).

Rule 69(1)

The right to appeal depends on the granting of an application for leave to allow the appeal to proceed (see r.70(2) and (3) below).

Both the application for leave and the appeal itself must be made within short time limits (see r.71(4) and (5) below). Before making an application a party must exhaust any available arbitral process of appeal or review (r.71(2)). For further detail on the procedure for applications for leave to appeal and appeals themselves see below.

Rule 69(2)

If the parties choose to disapply r.51(2)(c) requiring the arbitrator to give reasons for his award they will be treated as having excluded legal error appeals.

Rule 70: Legal error appeals: procedure etc. **M**

70.—(1) This rule applies only where rule 69 applies.
(2) A legal error appeal may be made only—
    (a) with the agreement of the parties, or
    (b) with the leave of the Outer House.
(3) Leave to make a legal error appeal may be given only if the Outer House is satisfied—
    (a) that deciding the point will substantially affect a party's rights,
    (b) that the tribunal was asked to decide the point, and
    (c) that, on the basis of the findings of fact in the award (including any facts which the tribunal treated as established for the purpose of deciding the point), the tribunal's decision on the point—
        (i) was obviously wrong, or
        (ii) where the court considers the point to be of general importance, is open to serious doubt.
(4) An application for leave is valid only if it—
    (a) identifies the point of law concerned, and
    (b) states why the applicant considers that leave should be granted.
(5) The Outer House must determine an application for leave without a hearing (unless satisfied that a hearing is required).
(6) The Outer House's determination of an application for leave is final.

(7) Any leave to appeal expires 7 days after it is granted (and so any legal error appeal made after then is accordingly invalid unless made with the agreement of the parties).
(8) The Outer House may decide a legal error appeal by—
  (a) confirming the award,
  (b) ordering the tribunal to reconsider the award (or part of it), or
  (c) if it considers reconsideration inappropriate, setting aside the award (or part of it).
(9) An appeal may be made to the Inner House against the Outer House's decision on a legal error appeal (but only with the leave of the Outer House).
(10) Leave may be given by the Outer House only where it considers—
  (a) that the proposed appeal would raise an important point of principle or practice, or
  (b) that there is another compelling reason for the Inner House to consider the appeal.
(11) The Outer House's decision on whether to grant such leave is final.
(12) The Inner House's decision on such an appeal is final.

DEFINITIONS
"Outer House": s.31(1)
"legal error appeal": r.69(1)
"party": ss.2(1), 31(1), (2)
"rule": s.31(1)
"tribunal": ss.2(1), 31(1)

STATUS
It is a mandatory rule. This is to ensure that if the default r.69 applies, the parties cannot alter the binding conditions upon which the Scottish Parliament has agreed to allow legal error appeals.

MODEL LAW
There is no equivalent provision in the Model Law.

COMMENTARY

Rule 70(2) and (4)—application to allow legal error appeal to proceed

A legal error appeal may proceed only with the leave of the Outer House, or with the agreement of the parties. The result of the somewhat circuitous drafting in r.70 and r.71(4) means that the general rule is that an application for leave has to be made within 28 days of the date when the award is "made". There are exceptions to this and the reader is referred to the commentary to r.71(4) below for more detail in relation to time limits. In the unusual circumstances of an appeal by agreement, no leave is necessary and the appeal itself has to be made within 28 days of the date when the award is "made". See again the commentary to r.71(4) below.

It has until relatively recently been unusual for an appeal to be made from any court or tribunal to the Outer House of the Court of Session. The Outer House is the first instance aspect of the Court of Session, comprising of a single judge. By contrast the Inner House is the appellate aspect of the Court of Session, sitting typically in "Divisions" of three judges although the Inner House can sit with five or more judges in exceptional circumstances where an otherwise binding precedent requires to be reviewed. Usually appeals are to the Inner House and the provisions in the rules of court reflect this. As a result there are no pre-existing rules in the Rules of the Court of Session 1994 dealing with applications for leave to the Outer House for an appeal to it. The rules relating to leave to appeal to the Inner House have not been applied to Outer House appeals. It is expected that rules of court will be enacted to fill this procedural gap and the reader is referred to the most up to date version of the *Greens Annotated Rules of the Court of Session* (Edinburgh: W. Green) which are also contained in Vol.2 of *The Parliament House Book* (Edinburgh: W. Green). In the absence of amending rules of court, a petition for leave to appeal under RCS r.14.2 would be required but the procedure for petitions is ill suited to applications for leave to appeal.

If leave is granted the appeal must be made within seven days of the granting of leave. See the commentary to r.70(7) and (8) below.

Rule 70(3)—preconditions for legal error appeal

This paragraph sets out the three preconditions which must be satisfied before the Outer House will allow the appeal to proceed. These conditions have largely been taken from s.69 of the 1996 Act.

Rule 70(3)(a)—"substantially affect" parties' rights

The first precondition is that a decision on the point of Scots law in question will "substantially affect" a party's rights. The "rights" in question must be the rights or liabilities under the award itself since it is the award which gives rise to the wish to appeal. In this context given the founding principles in s.1 of the resolution of disputes without unnecessary delay or expense, and that the court should not intervene except as provided for, it is suggested that "substantially" should be interpreted as meaning "greatly" or "essentially". This has been the approach in England and Wales. For example where the tribunal may have erred on two grounds of its decision but on the third ground was not asked to make a decision on the point of law being applied, a decision by the court on the points of law in the two grounds relied upon could not substantially affect the appellant's rights, and on that basis permission to appeal was properly refused (*CMA CGM SA v Beteiligungs KG MS Northern Pioneer Schiffahrtsgesellschaft mbH & Co* [2003] 1 W.L.R. 1015, per Court of Appeal at 1023 [25]–[27]).

This provision has been derived from s.1(4) of the now repealed Arbitration Act 1979 for England and Wales. The case law concerning whether under that section an appellant's rights would be "substantially affected" by the point of law in question may be relevant. In *Coal Authority v Trustees of the Nostell Trust* [2005] EWHC 154 (TCC) an appeal was sought by a public authority in respect of an award against it of (1) £191,000 and (2) £12,500. It was held that in the context of the award as a whole the £12,500 element was not something which substantially affected the rights of the parties.

Rule 70(3)(b)—tribunal "asked to decide" the point of law

The second precondition is that the tribunal was "asked to decide" the point of Scots law on which the tribunal allegedly erred. In England and Wales this has been held to include the raising of the point before the tribunal without conceding that it should be decided a certain way (*CMA CGM SA* [2003] 1 W.L.R. 1015, per Court of Appeal at 1030–1032 [32]–[36]). If the point has not been expressly raised with the tribunal it is difficult to see how it can have been asked to decide the point.

Rule 70(3)(c)—findings in fact (actual or deemed) unalterable

The third precondition has two possible limbs. Both proceed on the basis that the findings of fact are not open to challenge. This indicates the intention of the Scottish Parliament to exclude any challenge to the findings in fact whether or not they proceeded on the basis of an error of law by the tribunal, e.g. lack of evidence or perverse interpretation of the evidence. This accords with the approach under s.69 of the 1996 Act (*Demco Investments & Commercial SA v SE Banken Forsakring Holding AB* [2005] 2 Lloyd's Rep. 650, per Cooke J. at [35]–[45]). It again indicates the limitation of the court's role in relation to review of the merits of the tribunal's decision. Even if permitted appeal on error of law is therefore more restricted than appeal in a litigation from the decision of a court at first instance.

The tribunal may make an award on the basis that even if the claimant's factual allegations are treated as established, i.e. taken *pro veritate*, the law does not entitle him to the remedy which he seeks. If such an award is made then the deemed facts are treated as established in relation to any legal error appeal.

Rule 70(3)(c)(i)—decision on point of law "obviously wrong"

The first possible limb is that based on the findings in fact, the tribunal's decision on the point of law which it was asked to decide was "obviously wrong". If the decision on the point of law, on the application of complex correct legal analysis, was wrong, then it will not be "obviously wrong" and so will not be reviewable on this basis. Merely that the decision was wrong or that another tribunal might have reached the opposite decision will not make the decision "obviously wrong", nor is there any threshold of the length of time taken by the judge to understand the alleged wrongfulness (*Braes of Doune Wind Farm (Scotland) Ltd v Alfred McAlpine Business Services Ltd* [2008] 1 Lloyd's Rep. 608, per Akenhead J. at 615 [28]). It has been said recently that:

> "The "obviously wrong" test is, self-evidently, a stringent one which will seldom be satisfied. It carries with it the implication that the error should normally be demonstrable on the face of the award itself, and that it should not require too close a scrutiny to expose it" (*National Trust for Places of Historic Interest or Natural Beauty v Fleming* [2009] EWHC 1789 (Ch), per Henderson J. at [12]).

Rule 70(3)(c)(ii)—decision of "general importance" and "open to serious doubt"

If the court takes the view that the tribunal's decision was not obviously wrong, the next issue is whether the point of law is "of general importance". In s.69 of the 1996 Act there is a similar provision albeit that it requires the point of law to be of, "general public importance". The reason for the difference appears to flow from the purpose of the provision not requiring the public as a whole to have an interest but merely a section of the public. The interpretation of a clause in a charter party that was said to be "common" without any indication that the market needed a resolution of the interpretation issue or the extent of its use or the existence of other cases where the interpretation issue had arisen has been held not to be a point of law of "general public importance" (*Bottiglieri di Navigazione SpA v Cosco Qingdao Ocean Shipping Co (The Bunga Saga Lima)* [2005] 2 Lloyd's Rep. 1, per Gloster J. at 8 [18]). If, and only if, the court takes the view that the point of law is of general importance does it have to ask itself whether the tribunal's decision on it was, "open to serious doubt". A difference between arbitrators in a tribunal of three experienced and senior arbitrators on whether the Kosovo conflict amounted to a "war" under a contract with a war cancellation clause used as a standard clause in charterparties has been held to be a matter of general public importance where the tribunal's decision was open to serious doubt (*CMA CGM SA* [2003] 1 W.L.R. 1015, per Court of Appeal at 1039–1040 [61]–[64]). The proper interpretation of s.19 of Coal Mining Subsidence Act 1991 relating to the assessment and quantification of remedial work caused by subsidence to listed buildings was said to have been in issue in some 36 claims in the period before the appeal and occurred with reasonable regularity such that it was of, "general public importance" (*Coal Authority v Trustees of the Nostell Trust* [2005] EWHC 154 (TCC), per H.H. Judge Coulson Q.C. at [13])

Rule 70(5)—decision on application without a hearing

The purpose of this rule is to expedite the process relating to appeals. The parties should be informed as soon as possible whether the appeal is to go ahead. The question may arise whether this is compatible with art.6 of the ECHR. The answer to such a question is that in reality the parties have chosen to have their dispute dealt with by arbitration rather than in a court, and so must have tacitly accepted that their appeal rights, including the right to have a hearing on the application for leave to make a legal error appeal, might be curtailed in the interests of the advantages of the arbitral process.

Rule 70(6)—finality of decision on allowance of making of legal appeal

The Outer House's decision on whether a legal error appeal may proceed is final and the right for review by the Inner House under s.18 of the Court of Session Act 1988 has been excluded. In *BLCT (13096) Ltd v J Sainsbury Plc* [2004] 2 P & C.R. 3, it was held by the English Court of Appeal at [33] that statutory provisions limiting the right of appeal from an arbitral award do not offend art.6 of the ECHR. This was because the parties had chosen that course, and (by implication) it was open to parties to agree to waive the protection of a public hearing to which they would otherwise be entitled under art.6.

Rule 70(7) and (8)—legal error appeal: form and remedies

No doubt with a view to expediting procedure, the leave to appeal has a time limit attached to it of seven days after its grant. This means that an appeal (with leave) must be lodged within seven days of the grant of leave. For the method of appeal the reader is referred to Ch.99 of the RCS.

There are a number of possible outcomes for a legal error appeal. The first, confirmation of the award, is another way of expressing the refusal of the appeal. If the appeal is to any extent successful, the question for the court will lie between the second and third outcomes.

The first issue for the court is whether an order requiring the arbitrator to reconsider the award or any part of it is appropriate. Only if that is inappropriate is it open to the court to set aside the award or part of it. "Reconsideration" implies the same arbitrator using the existing evidence which has been presented to him for the purposes of the award plus any supplementary submissions which are consequential upon the successful appeal (*Ascot Commodities NV v Olam International Ltd* [2002] C.L.C. 277, per Toulson J. at 286). Delay in time between the court's decision and the original award may cause difficulties for the existing arbitrators and this may point towards setting aside being appropriate (see *Ascot Commodities* [2002] C.L.C. 277). However if an appeal is successful and the point of law properly applied would inevitably lead to an award in favour of the appellant, a remit for reconsideration may be inappropriate and the setting aside of the award is the proper course to follow.

If the court orders the tribunal to reconsider the award or any part of it, the reconsidered award must be made by no later than three months after the date of the court's order unless the court specifies a different deadline (r.72(1)). For the effects of remission see the commentary to r.72 below.

Rule 70(9), (10), and (11)—further appeals

These paragraphs must be read together. They apply to the decision of the Outer House on the appeal itself rather than the prior decision of the Outer House on whether it should proceed to decide the appeal.

The Outer House's decision on a legal error appeal can only be appealed with its leave. Leave must be sought within 28 days (r.71(5)). The appeal must be made, by reclaiming motion within seven days of leave being granted (r.71(5)). If leave is refused, can the refusal to grant leave be appealed to the Inner House on the ground that the refusal followed action of the Outer House which was incompatible with the appellant's right under art.6 of the ECHR?

With regard to the position in England and Wales under the Arbitration Act 1996 it has been held that there may be an appeal against a refusal to grant leave to appeal to the Court of Appeal on the ground that the refusal followed action of the first instance court which was incompatible with the appellant's art.6 right (*CGU International Insurance Plc v AstraZeneca Insurance Co Ltd* [2007] 1 Lloyd's Rep. 142, per Rix L.J. at 155, 156 [73], following *North Range Shipping Ltd v Seatrans Shipping Corp (The Western Triumph)* [2002] 2 Lloyd's Rep. 1). This rests on the residual jurisdiction of the English Court of Appeal to hear appeals from any court or judgment of the English High Court (Supreme Court Act 1981 s.16) combined with the existence of a remedy under s.9(1) of the Human Rights Act 1998 against an act of a court which is incompatible with Convention rights.

In Scotland the Outer House and the Inner House are part of the same court, namely the Court of Session. Every order of the single judge in the Outer House is subject to review of the Inner House in accordance with the Court of Session Act 1988 (s.18). Review is by means of a "reclaiming" motion against the interlocutor (order) of the Outer House (RCS r.38.2). If the interlocutor refuses leave (as in *CGU International Insurance Plc* [2007] 1 Lloyd's Rep. 142), then such an interlocutor cannot be appealed (RCS r.38.5(6)). In relation to the seeking of leave it appears that the Inner House's residual jurisdiction under the 1988 Act has been excluded by RCS r.38.5(6). It is a question whether RCS r.39.5(6) can be construed (under s.3 of the Human Rights Act 1998) compatibly with art.6 of the ECHR or whether it is incompatible with art.6 in prohibiting any review of the refusal of leave.

A requirement that leave be obtained for a further appeal is not incompatible with the right to a fair trial under art.6 of the ECHR (*Kazakhstan v Istil Group Ltd* [2007] 2 Lloyd's Rep. 548).

Rule 70(12)—appeal to the Supreme Court excluded

This paragraph excludes any further right of appeal to the Supreme Court under s.40 of the Court of Session Act 1988.

Rule 71: Challenging an award: supplementary **M**

71.—(1) This rule applies to—

(a) jurisdictional appeals,
(b) serious irregularity appeals, and
(c) where rule 69 applies to the arbitration, legal error appeals,

and references to "appeal" are to be construed accordingly.

(2) An appeal is competent only if the appellant has exhausted any available arbitral process of appeal or review (including any recourse available under rule 58).

(3) No appeal may be made against a provisional award.

(4) An appeal must be made no later than 28 days after the later of the following dates—
> (a) the date on which the award being appealed against is made,
> (b) if the award is subject to a process of correction under rule 58, the date on which the tribunal decides whether to correct the award, or
> (c) if there has been an arbitral process of appeal or review, the date on which the appellant was notified of the result of that process.

A legal error appeal is to be treated as having being made for the purposes of this rule if an application for leave is made.

(5) An application for leave to appeal against the Outer House's decision on an appeal must be made no later than 28 days after the date on which the decision is made (and any such leave expires 7 days after it is granted).

(6) An appellant must give notice of an appeal to the other party and the tribunal.

(7) The tribunal may continue with the arbitration pending determination of an appeal against a part award.

(8) The Outer House (or the Inner House in the case of an appeal against the Outer House's decision) may—
> (a) order the tribunal to state its reasons for the award being appealed in sufficient detail to enable the Outer House (or Inner House) to deal with the appeal properly, and
> (b) make any other order it thinks fit with respect to any additional expenses arising from that order.

(9) Where the Outer House (or the Inner House in the case of an appeal against the Outer House's decision) decides an appeal by setting aside the award (or any part of it), it may also order that any provision in an arbitration agreement which prevents the bringing of legal proceedings in relation to the subject-matter of the award (or that part of it) is void.

(10) The Outer House (or the Inner House in the case of an appeal against the Outer House's decision) may—
> (a) order an appellant (or an applicant for leave to appeal) to provide security for the expenses of the appeal (or application), and
> (b) dismiss the appeal (or application) if the order is not complied with.

(11) But such an order may not be made only on the ground that the appellant (or applicant)—
> (a) is an individual who ordinarily resides outwith the United Kingdom, or
> (b) is a body which is—
>> (i) incorporated or formed under the law of a country outwith the United Kingdom, or
>> (ii) managed or controlled from outwith the United Kingdom.

(12) The Outer House (or the Inner House in the case of an appeal against the Outer House's decision) may—
> (a) order that any amount due under an award being appealed (or any associated provisional award) must be paid into court or otherwise secured pending its decision on the appeal (or the application for leave to appeal), and

(b) dismiss the appeal (or application) if the order is not complied with.

(13) An appeal to the Inner House against any decision of the Outer House under this rule may be made only with the leave of the Outer House.

(14) An application for leave to appeal against such a decision must be made no later than 28 days after the date on which the decision is made (and any such leave expires 7 days after it is granted).

(15) Leave may be given by the Outer House only where it considers—
  (a) that the proposed appeal would raise an important point of principle or practice, or
  (b) that there is another compelling reason for the Inner House to consider the appeal.

(16) The Outer House's decision on whether to grant such leave is final.

(17) A decision of the Inner House under this rule (including any decision on an appeal against a decision by the Outer House) is final.

DEFINITIONS
"appeal": r.71(1)
"arbitration agreement: ss.4, 31(1)
"jurisdictional appeal": r.67(1)
"legal error appeal": r.69(1)
"notice": r.83
"Outer House": s.31(1)
"party": ss.2(1), 31(1), (2)
"provisional award": r.53
"serious irregularity appeal": r.68(1)
"tribunal": ss.2(1), 31(1)

STATUS

It is a mandatory rule. Rule 71 relates to the court appeal procedures for appeals under rr.67, 68 and 69. Unless r.69 (legal error appeals) is disapplied by the parties, the right to appeal under the conditions specified in those rules exists as a mandatory right and therefore it is logical for the procedures to be mandatory also.

MODEL LAW

This rule is not derived from the Model Law.

COMMENTARY

Rule 71 provides further requirements for the three means of challenge to an arbitral award.

Rule 71(2)—requirement to exhaust other remedies

Given that parties have chosen arbitration over litigation to resolve the dispute, one of the founding principles in s.1 of the Act is that the court should not intervene in an arbitration except as provided in the Act. The requirement on parties to exhaust non-court remedies before appealing or applying for leave to appeal is a consequence of that policy.

The other remedies may include not merely arbitral processes of appeal or review contained in the arbitration agreement or institutional rules incorporated therein but also the correction and clarification process provided under r.58 unless it has been excluded by the parties. In connection with the latter process, a party discontent with an award that might be appealed must first consider if there is a remedy under r.58. The consequence of failing to consider such a remedy is that the appeal or application could be held to be incompetent for failure to exhaust the r.58 remedy but the r.58 remedy may itself be time barred, subject to an application for relief under r.58(4). An example under the 1996 Act where a party's appeal was held to be incompetent for such a reason was *Torch Offshore LLC v Cable Shipping Inc* [2004] 2 Lloyd's. Rep. 446.

Rule 71(3)—no appeal against provisional award

There is no right to appeal against a provisional award, on whatever grounds. This is no doubt to prevent the arbitral process from delay being caused by the appeal process. The absence of a right of appeal can be justified on the basis that the parties have entrusted their dispute to a tribunal of their choice and if they have decided not to exclude provisional awards, they should be bound to comply with such an award.

Rule 71(4), (5) and (6)—time limits

A jurisdictional or serious irregularity appeal or an application for leave to make a legal error appeal must be made within a short time limit of 28 days, the trigger point for which depends on whether there has been an arbitral process of appeal or review or a r.58 process for correction (but apparently not clarification—see r.58). The basic position is where there has been no arbitral appeal or review and no r.58 process. In that situation the trigger point is the date on which the award is made which is the date the award is delivered to each of the parties in accordance with r.83 (see r.51(3)). The first of the 28 days is then the day after the trigger point date. See also the commentary to r.84 below.

The arbitration agreement of the parties may expressly, or by incorporation of separate rules, contain its own arbitral appeal or review process. For the trigger point of the 28 days to be delayed an arbitral process of appeal or review must actually take place. It is not enough for the parties to have provided for such a process if it is not actually used. If there has been an arbitral process of appeal or review the trigger point is the date of notification of the result of that process. The first of the 28 days begins with the day after the date on which the appellant was notified of the result of that process. For what amounts to "notification" see r.83 below.

If there has been a r.58 process for correction the trigger point is the date on which the tribunal decides whether to correct the award. Rule 58 does not provide for the notification of that decision to the parties. That is unsatisfactory. It is suggested that if the decision on a r.58 application is adverse to a party the trigger point for that party should be the date of notification of the adverse decision to that party (for the principle as applied to decisions on entitlement to social security benefits see *R (on the application of Anufrijeva) v Secretary of State for the Home Department* [2003] UKHL 36; [2004] 1 A.C. 604). While a r.58 correction process can be initiated by the tribunal itself, prudence suggests that the possibility of the tribunal initiating the process should not be relied on by parties in deciding whether to appeal.

If there is either an internal arbitral appeal or review process or a r.58 correction process, then the trigger point for the 28 days is the trigger point latest in time under those processes.

If an appeal or application is not lodged within the 28 day period prescribed by r.71(4) an appellant or applicant will also have to lodge a motion with the Outer House to obtain relief under RCS r.2.1 (*Hume v Nursing and Midwifery Council*, 2007 S.C. 644), albeit the ability to seek relief under the RCS has been questioned in *Holmes v Nursing and Midwifery Council* [2009]

CSIH 82). Under RCS r.2.1 the court has a discretion to grant relief if the failure has been due to, "mistake, oversight or other excusable cause" on such conditions, if any, as the court thinks fit. In other words, first the failure must be due to the specified cause. Then, even if the failure is of that type, the court has an overriding discretion in the matter. In relation to late arbitration appeals in English and Welsh law, Colman J. in *AOOT Kalmneft v Glencore International AG* [2002] 1 Lloyd's Rep. 128 at 137 set out the following material factors to be taken into account:

    (i) the length of the delay;
   (ii) whether, in permitting the time limit to expire and the subsequent delay to occur, the appellant was acting reasonably in all the circumstances;
  (iii) whether the respondent to the appeal or the arbitrator caused or contributed to the delay;
  (iv) whether the respondent to the appeal would by reason of the delay suffer irremediable prejudice in addition to the mere loss of time if the appeal were permitted to proceed;
   (v) whether the arbitration has continued during the period of delay (i.e. where the appeal is against a part award) and, if so, what impact on the progress of the arbitration or the costs incurred in respect of it the determination of the appeal by the court might now have;
  (vi) the strength of the appeal;
 (vii) whether in the broadest sense it would be unfair to the appellant for him to be denied the opportunity of having the appeal determined.

This was a case involving international parties. The court is likely to be less sympathetic to appeals by Scottish parties and the factors may be more relevant to the discretion to be exercised by the court. The weight to be given to each of the factors will vary in each case (see, e.g. *Thyssen Canada Ltd v Mariana Maritime SA* [2005] 1 Lloyd's Rep. 640; and *Sinclair v Woods of Winchester Ltd*, 102 Con. L.R. 127—where a delay of one day was fatal).

Rule 71(5) provides for a fairly lengthy period of 28 days to seek leave to appeal to the Inner House against the decision of the Outer House on an appeal. If leave is obtained the appeal (reclaiming motion under RCS r.38.6) must be enrolled within seven days after the obtaining of leave. This overrides the provisions of RCS r.38.3 which provides that a reclaiming motion must be enrolled within 14 days and that leave must be obtained within that time limit (albeit for the possibility of the suspension of that time limit if the judge who made the decision cannot be obtained to consider leave within the 14 days). See also RCS r.38.5 in relation to applications for leave to appeal (reclaim).

Rule 71(6) provides that an appellant must give notice of an appeal to the other party or parties and to the tribunal. This would normally be given after the Outer House makes its order under RCS r.41.21 for service of the appeal on the other parties and such other person as the court thinks fit.

Rule 71(7)—part award appeals

Notwithstanding the making of an appeal against a part award, the tribunal has a power to continue with the arbitration and this must be exercised in the light of the tribunal's duty under r.24. Where there is a part award there may be another aspect of the case which can be dealt with without the need for the court's decision on the part award and if that is the case the tribunal should not cease to act and cause delay in the resolution of such other aspect merely because its part award is being appealed.

Rule 71(8)—order for reasons

The award must contain reasons unless the parties have contracted out of this requirement or the award reflects the terms of a settlement (see the commentary to rr.51(2)(c) and 57(4) above). If parties have not contracted out of this requirement, then usually an order by the court for a statement of reasons should be unnecessary since the award should have reasons. A failure by the award to contain adequate reasons which cause substantial injustice to a party by leaving it in the dark as to a material part of its case, may well amount to a serious irregularity giving rise to an appeal under r.68 and to an order from the court requiring the tribunal to reconsider the award. Alternatively, the appellant or perhaps an applicant may apply to the court for the exercise of its power under r.71(8) to order the tribunal to state its reasons. On the face of it r.71(8) appears to relate only where an appeal has been made and not where a mere application to the Outer House for leave to appeal has been made. It is not wholly clear whether the court may make the order under r.71(8) where there is only an application for leave to make a legal error appeal. The equivalent power in s.70(4) of the 1996 Act exists both when there is an application and an appeal and in relation to an application provides that the power is to enable the court properly to consider the application or appeal. There is no reference to application in r.71(8) but r.71(4) provides that a legal error appeal is to be treated as having been made for the purposes of r.71 if an application is made. It may be that this enables "appeal" in r.71 to be read as "appeal or application" where appropriate.

If the reasons have been given in document separate from the award and which by agreement of the parties is confidential and privileged, the court is nevertheless entitled to look at it to see the reasons of the tribunal if this is necessary to enable it to deal with the appeal properly (*The Easy Rider* [2004] 2 Lloyd's Rep. 626, per Moore-Bick J. at 634).

An application for the exercise of the r.71(8) power is made by motion (RCS r.23.11).

If the court makes an order under r.71(8) it may make such ancillary order as it thinks fit with respect to additional expenses arising from its order. The key words here are, "arising from its order". It is thought that this does not include expenses arising from an unsuccessful opposition to the making of the order. Those expenses would be dealt with by the court applying the standard principles in relation to expenses. Rather the ancillary order is designed to deal with further expense which arises from the need for compliance with its order. The intention behind r.71(8)(b) appears to be that the party—or tribunal—who has caused the need for a statement of reasons to be obtained should bear the expense of the obtaining of that statement. Where there is a possible liability of the tribunal, the court must bear in mind both the need for the tribunal to have an opportunity to make representations and also the tribunal's immunity under r.73 for anything omitted in the performance or purported performance of its functions. Standing r.73, it may be that the tribunal would only be liable in the situations mentioned in r.73(2).

Rule 71(9)

The purpose of this provision is unclear.

Rule 71(10) and (11)

These paragraphs give the court power to order an appellant or an applicant for leave to appeal from a decision of the Outer House, to provide security for the expenses of the appeal, or the application for leave to appeal. These provisions are a mirror image of the provisions of r.64 enabling an arbitrator to order a party to provide security for the arbitration expenses. See the commentary to r.64 above.

An application for the exercise of this power is made by motion setting out the grounds (RCS r.33.2). Where the order is made it will specify the time within which the security is to be provided (RCS r.33.3). The security can be of different forms. Traditionally the security was in the form of a "bond of caution" (pronounced "kayshun") being a guarantee from certain guarantee providing or insurance companies (RCS rr.33.4, 33.5). Another more flexible form is "consignation" being the payment (consignation) of a sum of money into a bank account in the name of the Accountant of Court (RCS r.33.4). Once consigned the money is held under the Court of Session Consignations (Scotland) Act 1895. However the security can be provided by other means if these are approved by the Outer House. These can include a deposit of a sum of money in the joint names of the solicitors of the parties (see RCS r.33.4). For further details of the way in which security is provided and also the common law test for the ordering of security see the commentary in Ch.33 of *Greens' Annotated Rules of the Court of Session* (Edinburgh: W. Green) also available in Vol.2 of *The Parliament House Book* (Edinburgh: W. Green).

There is no formal fetter on the court's discretion except that the order cannot be made on the sole ground that the appellant or applicant resides, is formed, or is managed or controlled from outwith the United Kingdom. In an ordinary litigation in the exercise of its discretion the court has to weigh up a number of factors (see the commentary to r.64 above). In relation to an appeal or application the critical factor will be whether the appellant or applicant has sufficient assets readily available to satisfy any award of expenses against him if his appeal or application is unsuccessful (see *Azov Shipping Co v Baltic Shipping Co (No.2)* [1999] 2 Lloyd's Rep. 39, per Longmore J. at 41). In *Azov Shipping Co* it was commented that the existence of an existing award against the appellant would be a factor only if the evidence as to readily available assets was uncertain. If the motion for the order arises after the court has already upheld an arbitrator's decision, and there is an application for leave to appeal to the Inner House, then it is suggested that the existence of two awards against the applicant may be of greater weight.

Where a party who has been ordered to provide security for expenses has not done so, the court has power to dismiss the appeal or application.

Rule 71(12)

The Outer House also has power to order that the appellant pay the actual sum awarded against him by the award being appealed into the court. No test is given to guide the court in its decision on whether to exercise the power. Two of the founding principles in s.1 of the Act are relevant, namely (a) that the object of arbitration is to resolve disputes fairly, impartially and without unnecessary delay or expense, and (c) that the court should not intervene in an arbitration except as provided by the Act. The purpose of the provision is to support the arbitration process which has found for the claimant and who should not on the face of it be prejudiced in recovering the sum awarded to him by any delay caused in the appeal process. It therefore encourages the attractiveness of arbitration as an expedited method of dispute resolution, in contrast to the ordinary court process where nothing is payable until the appeal process is exhausted. It should therefore be applied in that light rather than in the light of the ordinary court process of appeal.

The power under r.71(12) is similar to that under s.20(6)(b) in relation to applications in foreign jurisdictions to set aside arbitral awards made in those jurisdictions. That power derives from art.VI of the New York Convention (and restated in art.36(2) of the Model Law) which provides that if an application for setting aside, e.g. an appeal, has been made to a competent authority of the law of the seat, the authority where enforcement in sought may if it considers proper adjourn the decision on enforcement and may on the application of the party claiming enforcement of the award, order the other party (the appellant) to give suitable security.

In relation to what is now s.20(6)(b) it was said that there were two important factors to be considered in deciding whether to require the respondent to pay the sum awarded against him into the court as security pending the disposal of the appeal, namely (a) the strength of the argument against the award; and (b) the ease or difficulty of enforcement of the award and whether it would be rendered more difficult, for example through the movement of assets or improvident trading if enforcement was delayed (*Soleh Boneh International Ltd v Government of Uganda* [1993] 2 Lloyd's Rep. 208, per Staughton L.J. at 212). These seem to be relevant factors in relation to r.71(12). The court is not restricted to ordering the payment of the whole amount or nil. Thus in *Soleh Boneh International* the court weighed up the factors and required the respondent to pay into court part of the amount awarded against him. There seems to be no reason why a similar approach should not be followed for a court in deciding whether to make an order under r.71(12). The case law in England and Wales is undeveloped on their equivalent s.70(7) of the Arbitration Act 1996. The purpose of the introduction of s.70(7) was to avoid the risk that while an appeal was pending the ability of the losing party to honour the award was not diminished (DAC Report, para.380—where the proposal was described as a "tool of great value"). In *Peterson Farms Inc v C&M Farming Ltd* [2004] 1 Lloyd's Rep. 614 (not to be confused with the judgment on the merits at [2004] 1 Lloyd's Rep. 603) Tomlinson J. suggested that there should be a difference in the approach to the decision on whether to require payment depending on whether the appeal was to be on jurisdiction, on serious irregularity or on an error of law. That approach seems to be misconceived given that an appeal on any of these is on the face of it capable of otherwise delaying the making of payment as required by the award. In addition Tomlinson J. took account of the fact that the appellant was not likely to be in funds and that he might require to obtain financial support from a third party in order to make the payment as a factor against ordering payment. It is suggested that such a factor is one for the ordering of payment since it tends to suggest that the appellant will indeed be unable to make payment of the award if he is unsuccessful in the appeal.

An application for the exercise of this power is made by motion setting out the grounds (RCS r.33.2). Where the order is made it will specify the time within which the security is to be provided (RCS r.33.3). The presumption is that security must be provided by the payment (consignation) of a sum of money into the court in the name of the Accountant of Court (RCS r.33.4). Once consigned the money is held under the Court of Session Consignations (Scotland) Act 1895. However the security can be provided by other means if these are approved by the Outer House. These can include a deposit of a sum of money in the joint names of the solicitors of the parties (see RCS r.33.4).

Where a party who has been ordered to pay in the whole or part of the payment awarded against him has not done so, the court has power to dismiss the appeal or application

Rule 72: Reconsideration by tribunal **M**

72.—(1) Where the Outer House or, as the case may be, the Inner House decides a serious irregularity appeal or a legal error appeal by ordering the tribunal to reconsider its award (or any part of it), the tribunal must make a new award in respect of the matter concerned (or confirm its original award) by no later than—
    (a) in the case of a decision by the Outer House—
        (i) where the decision is appealed, the day falling 3 months after the appeal (or, as the case may be, the application for leave to appeal) is dismissed or abandoned,
        (ii) where the decision is not appealed, the day falling 3 months after the decision is made, or
        (iii) such other day as the Outer House may specify,
    (b) in the case of a decision by the Inner House—
        (i) the day falling 3 months after the decision is made, or
        (ii) such other day as the Inner House may specify.

(2) These rules apply in relation to the new award as they apply in relation to the appealed award.

DEFINITIONS
  "legal error appeal": r.69(1)
  "Outer House": s.31(1)
  "serious irregularity appeal": r.68(1)
  "tribunal": ss.2(1), 31(1)

STATUS
Rule 72 is a mandatory rule. This is consistent with rr.68 and 70 with which it is closely related.

MODEL LAW
The Model Law provides, in art.34 (4) that the court, when asked to set aside an award, may where appropriate and so requested by a party, suspend the setting aside proceedings for a period of time determined by it.

COMMENTARY
Following remission by the court the part of the award which is to be reconsidered is suspended and no longer binding on any of the matters to be reconsidered unless it is reaffirmed (confirmed) by the tribunal in their reconsidered award (*Huyton SA v Jakil SpA* [1999] 2 Lloyd's Rep. 83, per Brooke L.J. at 87). Once the tribunal deliver their reconsidered award the part of the award which has been remitted falls away and becomes null and void (*Huyton SA* [1999] 2 Lloyd's Rep. 83). Any part of the award which is not to be reconsidered remains in full force and effect. If the remission has been made in order to remove any uncertainty or ambiguity as to the award's effect, this does not affect the substance of the award and the tribunal has no power to alter or revisit any aspect of the substance of the award (*Carter (t/a Michael Carter Partnership) v Harold Simpson Associates (Architects) Ltd* [2004] UKPC 29; [2004] 2 Lloyd's Rep. 512).

The tribunal must make either a new award in respect of the matter remitted to it or confirm the original award having regard to the findings of the court. It has three months in which to make the fresh award, although if the remit is made by the Outer House and is appealed unsuccessfully to the Inner House the three months runs from the dismissal or abandonment of the appeal.

PART 9

MISCELLANEOUS

Rule 73: Immunity of tribunal etc. **M**

73.—(1) Neither the tribunal nor any arbitrator is liable for anything done or omitted in the performance, or purported performance, of the tribunal's functions.
    (2) This rule does not apply—
        (a) if the act or omission is shown to have been in bad faith, or
        (b) to any liability arising from an arbitrator's resignation (but see rule 16(1)(c)).
    (3) This rule applies to any clerk, agent, employee or other person assisting the tribunal to perform its functions as it applies to the tribunal.

DEFINITIONS
    "arbitrator": ss.2(1), 31(1)
    "tribunal": ss.2(1), 31(1)

STATUS
    This rule is mandatory.

MODEL LAW
    There is no provision in the Model Law on the immunity of arbitrators.

COMMENTARY
    Different legal systems have different provisions regarding the immunity of arbitrators. In this rule Scotland has chosen to follow its traditional common law favouring of immunity. The rationale for this approach was stated obiter in *McMillan v Free Church of Scotland* (1862) 24 D. 1282 at 1295 where, in relation to a claim for damages against members of the General Assembly of the Church of Scotland who had exercised a jurisdiction to make a decision against the claimant, Lord Curriehill said:
    "[P]arties upon whom judicial functions are lawfully conferred, and who in the *bona fide* exercise of these functions over parties subject to their authority, fall into errors of judgment, are not liable in damages to their parties in consequence of such errors. *Humanum est errare.* Infallibility of judgment is attainable by no man, however laboriously or conscientiously he may exert his powers to do what is right, and if notwithstanding a judge's best and *bona fide* endeavours to do so, he should be liable in damages for errors into which he might fall, such offices would be shunned by those best qualified for performing their functions. But such functionaries have an immunity from liability for errors in judgment, unless their errors arise from corruption or malice. The law unquestionably confers such an immunity upon judges officiating in the public judicial institutions of the country ... It also extends such immunity to private persons, upon whom parties, by

voluntary agreement, confer authority to adjudicate certain matters among themselves; it being the policy of our law to encourage and support the settlement of disputes by such private arrangements ... Such arbitrators are not liable in damages to the contracting parties for errors of judgment into which they happen to fall in the *bona fide* exercise of the functions so conferred upon them."

There is nothing to prevent parties from agreeing with the tribunal the extent of any immunity at the outset when the arbitrator is appointed. This is what occurs for example when parties adopt various institutional rules. Thus the traditional Scottish approach is reflected in the LCIA Rules which provides for immunity, "save where the act or omission is shown by [the claimant] party to constitute conscious and deliberate wrongdoing committed by the body or person alleged to be liable to that party" (art.31(1)). It is in line with art.8 of the SAC 07.

Rule 73(1)

The immunity applies to liability for breach of the express or implied terms of the arbitration agreement or delictual (tortious or quasi-delictual) wrong during the performance or purported performance of the tribunal's functions. Thus it does not apply to other forms of liability that there may be on the person who is the arbitrator in question. So before the immunity applies, there has to be breach of the arbitration agreement by the arbitrator or delictual wrong by the arbitrator in the fulfilment of his functions as an arbitrator. Whether there has been a breach of the arbitration agreement or there has been a delictual wrong in the performance or purported performance of the tribunal's functions are separate issues of fact and/or law. If there has been such a breach or delictual wrong, the immunity will—or should—apply unless r.73(2) applies.

The immunity exists only in relation to liability for anything done or omitted to be done in the performance or purported performance of functions by the tribunal. If an arbitrator incurs liability when he is not performing or purportedly performing the functions of the tribunal, then the immunity will not cover that liability.

Rule 73(2)

The immunity is based on the understanding that to err is human and that without such an immunity capable persons would be discouraged from accepting arbitral appointments. However where the conduct goes beyond mere error but involves bad faith of the arbitrator, the understanding upon which the immunity is conceived no longer applies. There is no apparent reason why the arbitrator should enjoy immunity if his breach of contract or delictual wrong was in bad faith. Rule 73(2) reflects this.

The act of resignation is a conscious and deliberate refusal to carry out the duty to resolve the dispute that the arbitrator has agreed to resolve. Therefore on the face of it, it involves something which is akin to a breach of the arbitration agreement in bad faith. It is not the performance or purported performance of his functions as an arbitrator. If an arbitrator wishes to resign without incurring the danger of liability in respect of his resignation, he should seek the parties' waiver of any claim arising out of or in connection with his resignation. If the parties are unwilling to agree to this or indeed to the resignation, the arbitrator is well advised to apply to the court under r.15(2) for authorisation to resign together with an order finding him not liable as a result of his resignation (r.16(1)(c)).

Rule 73(3)

The immunity also applies to any clerk to the arbitration or any agent, employee or other person assisting the tribunal to perform its functions.

Rule 74: Immunity of appointing arbitral institution etc. **M**

74.—(1) An arbitral appointments referee, or other third party who the parties ask to appoint or nominate an arbitrator, is not liable—
    (a) for anything done or omitted in the performance, or purported performance, of that function (unless the act or omission is shown to have been in bad faith), or
    (b) for the acts or omissions of—
        (i) any arbitrator whom it nominates or appoints, or
        (ii) the tribunal of which such an arbitrator forms part (or any clerk, agent or employee of that tribunal).

(2) This rule applies to an arbitral appointments referee's, or other third party's, agents and employees as it applies to the referee or other third party.

DEFINITIONS
    "arbitral appointments referee": ss.22, 31(1)
    "arbitrator": ss.2(1), 31(1)
    "tribunal": ss.2(1), 31(1)

STATUS
    Rule 74 is a mandatory rule.

MODEL LAW
    There is no provision in the Model Law on the immunity of appointing arbitral institutions.

COMMENTARY
Rule 7 provides for appointment of an arbitrator by an arbitral appointments referee, failing which by the court. In addition other persons such as the President of the Law Society of Scotland or the Dean of the Faculty of Advocates or other heads of professional bodies or sheriffs principal or sheriffs may have been agreed upon as person who may nominate an arbitrator (arbiter). The purpose of r.74 is to prevent bodies from being discouraged from seeking appointment as and acting as arbitral appointments referees through fear of contractual or delictual liability. Until this Act where parties had agreed on a private arbitral appointments referee, for example the President of the Law Society of Scotland, and he did not make immunity a precondition of the exercise of his powers, there was some uncertainty on whether he could be liable for making an unreasonable appointment. International arbitral institutions regularly exclude their liability in respect of the arbitral appointments which they make. Where the court made the appointment the court was protected by its immunity. It therefore seemed appropriate that the rules provide for the immunity of both arbitral appointment referees as designated under the Act and also "other third parties", that is to say private referees designated in the parties' own agreement.

It also appeared appropriate that the rule exclude any possibility of vicarious liability of the appointers of arbitrators (and their employees and agents) for any liability of the arbitrator.

There is nothing to prevent the appointer of arbitrators to agree with the parties an immunity before exercising his power.

Rule 74(1) and (2)

In this paragraph, "other third party" includes persons such as the President of the Law Society of Scotland, Dean of the Faculty of Advocates or Chairman of the Scottish Branch of the Chartered Institute of Arbitrators or the like whom the parties have nominated in their arbitration agreement to choose the arbitrator. It would also include the court, if there was any doubt over whether the court was entitled to its judicial immunity in exercising its function of appointment.

Rule 75: Immunity of experts, witnesses and legal representatives **M**

75. Every person who participates in an arbitration as an expert, witness or legal representative has the same immunity in respect of acts or omissions as the person would have if the arbitration were civil proceedings.

DEFINITIONS
"legal error appeal": r.69(1)
"Outer House": s.31(1)
"serious irregularity appeal": r.68(1)
"tribunal": ss.2(1), 31(1)

STATUS
Rule 75 is a mandatory rule.

MODEL LAW
There is no provision in the Model Law on the immunity of experts, witnesses and legal representatives.

COMMENTARY
The purpose of this rule is simply to equate arbitral proceedings to civil court proceedings in Scotland for the purpose of any question of the liability of experts, witnesses and legal representatives. Whether liability actually arises against any of these persons will depend on various criteria depending on the ground of liability in question. For the position in Scotland see *Karling v Purdue*, 2004 S.L.T. 1067.

Rule 76: Loss of right to object **M**

76.—(1) A party who participates in an arbitration without making a timeous objection on the ground—
    (a) that an arbitrator is ineligible to act as an arbitrator,
    (b) that an arbitrator is not impartial and independent,
    (c) that an arbitrator has not treated the parties fairly,
    (d) that the tribunal does not have jurisdiction,
    (e) that the arbitration has not been conducted in accordance with—
        (i) the arbitration agreement,
        (ii) these rules (in so far as they apply), or
        (iii) any other agreement by the parties relating to conduct of the arbitration,
    (f) that the arbitration has been affected by any other serious irregularity,
may not raise the objection later before the tribunal or the court.
(2) An objection is timeous if it is made—
    (a) as soon as reasonably practicable after the circumstances giving rise to the ground for objection first arose,

(b) by such later date as may be allowed by—
  (i) the arbitration agreement,
  (ii) these rules (in so far as they apply),
  (iii) the other party, or
(c) where the tribunal considers that circumstances justify a later objection, by such later date as it may allow.

(3) This rule does not apply where the party shows that it did not object timeously because it—
  (a) did not know of the ground for objection, and
  (b) could not with reasonable diligence have discovered that ground.

(4) This rule does not allow a party to raise an objection which it is barred from raising for any reason other than failure to object timeously.

DEFINITIONS
"arbitration agreement": ss.4, 31(1)
"court": s.31(1)
"party": ss.2, 31(1), (2)
"rules": s.31(1)
"timeous objection": r.76(2)
"tribunal": ss.2(1), 31(1)

STATUS
Rule 76 is a mandatory rule.

MODEL LAW
The Model Law provides, in art.4:
"A party who knows that any provision of this Law from which the parties may derogate or any requirement under the arbitration agreement has not been complied with and yet proceeds with the arbitration without stating his objection to such non-compliance without undue delay, or if a time limit is provided therefor, within such period of time, shall be deemed to have waived his right to object."
Rule 76 follows the spirit of the Model Law.

COMMENTARY
The purpose of this rule is to preserve the speed and openness of the arbitral process as a form of dispute resolution. If during the arbitral process one of the qualifying objections set out in the rule, arises, and a party is either aware of it or could with reasonable diligence have discovered it, then it must make the objection at that time and not keep it to itself to be used at a later date as a secret insurance should the decision on the merits appear to be going against it. Early intervention should also enable early cure within the arbitral proceedings if this is possible.

Rule 76(1)—the need for timeous objection

This sets out the types of objection which must be made timeously if they are not to be waived. The common feature of all of these is that they are the type of objection which relates to either the jurisdiction of the tribunal or a qualifying procedural irregularity both of which could give rise to a challenge to an arbitral award under rr.67 and 68.

An "objection" in terms of the rule means a ground of objection in the sense that for example an objection to jurisdiction on one ground need not cover an objection to jurisdiction on an entirely different ground (*Primegrade AG v Ythan Ltd* [2006] 1 Lloyd's Rep. 457 at 474, and the cases cited therein). This stems from the purpose of the provision being to encourage open dealing and to ensure that all arguments are raised at the earliest opportunity. Whether a later argument, e.g. at appeal, was within an earlier ground of objection made to the tribunal is a matter of degree. This suggests that a party making an objection that could give rise to an appeal should frame their grounds of objection to a tribunal broadly so as to allow some flexibility at an appeal, but not so broad as not to give fair notice of the ground to the respondent. In *Athletic Union of Constantinople (AEK) v National Basketball Association* [2002] 1 Lloyd's Rep. 305 at 311, the appellant's ground of appeal on lack of jurisdiction was not within an earlier ground on lack of jurisdiction and the appellant was barred from raising this new ground in an appeal.

For ineligibility to act as an arbitrator see r.4 above. For impartiality and independence see r.24(1)(a) above. For fair treatment of the parties see r.24(1)(b) above. For lack of jurisdiction see r.20 above.

For objections on the grounds that the arbitration has not been conducted in accordance with the arbitration agreement, the rules, or any other agreement of the parties relating to its conduct see r.68 above.

Rule 76(2)(a)—what is "timeous"?

The starting point for making an objection is that it must be made no later than the date at which it became reasonably practicable to make it. Clearly it must be after the circumstances giving rise to the ground for objection first arose. The "reasonably practicable" test sets an objective standard of a reasonable party in the position of the objecting party. The tribunal or court must assess when it would have become not merely practicable but reasonably practicable for that reasonable party to make that objection. It is a test which has been used in other contexts to impose time bars on personal injury claims (*Agnew v Scott Lithgow Ltd (No.2)*, 2003 S.C. 448) and employment tribunal claims (*Royal Bank of Scotland Plc v Theobald* Unreported January 10, 2007 EAT Scotland). The date at which it first became "reasonably practicable" for a party to make an objection will be a question of fact which will vary from case to case.

In *ASM Shipping Ltd of India v TTMI Ltd of England* [2005] EWHC 2238 (Comm); [2006] 1 Lloyd's Rep. 375, the issue of timeous objection was raised in relation to s.73 of the 1996 Act which, unlike r.76, requires objection to be made "forthwith". ASM and TTMI were engaged in a London arbitration arising out of a charterparty where Mr X QC was appointed chairman of the tribunal. ASM's principal witness was Mr M, a shipbroker. In a wholly separate (but relatively recent) arbitration (the "other arbitration") between entirely unrelated parties, M had been a key witness for one of the parties and TTMI's solicitors in the present case, WH, had represented the other side and, for a short time and in respect of one preliminary issue only (which was settled), Mr X QC had been instructed by WH and had drafted certain disclosure applications. M had been the target, so he alleged of an attack by WH in the other arbitration. Mr X QC had had a brief and peripheral involvement in the other arbitration. On the morning before M gave evidence, ASM were made aware of M's allegation. M's evidence started after lunch. Mr X QC had no recollection of meeting M and had not conducted any part of any hearing or other proceeding involving M. M's evidence was not completed that day. ASM's legal team considered the matter overnight. On the following day they objected to Mr X QC's participation in the tribunal at the end of M's evidence under reservation of taking instructions in the course of M's evidence. Having obtained instructions to object ASM's legal team maintained the objection. ASM took up an award and it was held, thereby waived its right to object to the chairman of the tribunal so he was not removed but the judge made it clear that he should have been. The judge rejected a submission that the objection should have been made before M began to give evidence. Applying the reasonable practicability test in r.76 it is suggested that it was not *reasonably* practicable for ASM to object before M began to give evidence.

Rule 76(2)(b) and (c)—timeous objection: later dates

If it is found that the objection was not made by the date of reasonable practicability the tribunal or court must consider whether it was made within any later date that:
- the arbitration agreement allows;
- the rules allow;
- the other party has allowed, other than in the arbitration agreement, for example by waiver of the point, or
- is justified by circumstances.

This last escape route, "justified by circumstances", appears to give the tribunal or court an ultimate discretion

Rule 77: Independence of arbitrator **M**

77. For the purposes of these rules, an arbitrator is not independent in relation to an arbitration if—
   (a) the arbitrator's relationship with any party,
   (b) the arbitrator's financial or other commercial interests, or
   (c) anything else,
gives rise to justifiable doubts as to the arbitrator's impartiality.

DEFINITIONS
"arbitration": ss.2(1), 31(1)
"arbitrator": ss.2(1), 31(1)
"party": ss.2, 31(1), (2)

STATUS
Rule 77 is mandatory given its critical importance.

MODEL LAW
The Model Law in art.12 allows for challenge to an arbitrator if, "circumstances exist that give rise to justifiable doubts as to his impartiality or independence". It therefore distinguishes between "impartiality" and "independence". The rules in the Act use different terminology in the sense that lack of independence is defined by any feature which gives rise to justifiable doubts as to the arbitrator's impartiality. For the purposes of the rules impartiality is equated with actual bias whereas "independence" is equated with justifiably feared bias. The rules do not subdivide lack of independence, or justifiably feared bias further, but simply give examples of where such justifiable fear could emerge from and then finish with a catch all provision of "anything else" which could give rise to the justifiable doubts.

COMMENTARY
The purpose of this rule is to provide a definition of lack of independence for the purposes of rr.8(2), 10(2)(a), 12(a) and 24(1)(a). The reader is referred to the commentary to those rules above.

Rule 78: Consideration where arbitrator judged not to be impartial and independent **D**

78.—(1) This rule applies where—
- (a) an arbitrator is removed by the Outer House under rule 12 on the ground that the arbitrator is not impartial and independent,
- (b) the tribunal is dismissed by the Outer House under rule 13 on the ground that it has failed to comply with its duty to be impartial and independent, or
- (c) the tribunal's award (or any part of it) is returned to the tribunal for reconsideration, or is set aside, on either of those grounds (see rule 68).

(2) Where this rule applies, the Outer House must have particular regard to whether an arbitrator has complied with rule 8 when it is considering whether to make an order under rule 16(1) or 68(4) about—
- (a) the arbitrator's entitlement (if any) to fees or expenses,
- (b) repaying fees or expenses already paid to the arbitrator.

DEFINITIONS
"arbitrator": ss.2(1), 31(1)
"Outer House": s.31(1)
"party": ss.2, 31(1), (2)
"tribunal": ss.2(1), 31(1)

STATUS
This is a default rule so it is open to the parties to modify it, agree something different or disapply it completely (see s.9).
If parties have agreed to adopt institutional rules, the starting point will be to consider what is the position under r.78 and then to see the extent to which r.78 is inconsistent with or disapplied by the institutional rule.

MODEL LAW
There is no equivalent provision in the Model Law.

COMMENTARY
The requirement that an arbitrator be independent and impartial is a fundamental one for any person undertaking that role. So fundamental is it that if an arbitrator breaches that requirement, the Outer House has a power under rr.16(1) and 68(4) to restrict or exclude the arbitrator's entitlement to his fees.
This rule provides that in considering whether and if so how to exercise that power, the court must have particular regard to whether the arbitrator complied with his duty under r.8 to disclose without delay to parties any circumstance known to him or which becomes known to him during the arbitration which might be considered relevant to the question of whether he was independent and impartial. See further the commentary to r.8 above.

Rule 79: Death of arbitrator **M**

79. An arbitrator's authority is personal and ceases on death.

DEFINITIONS
"arbitrator": ss.2(1), 31(1)

STATUS
This rule is mandatory (a) since no arbitrator can fulfil any of his functions after he/she dies, and (b) since an arbitrator's duties are non-delegable so neither his executors nor his partners (if applicable) nor employees can take over.

MODEL LAW
There is no equivalent provision in the Model Law.

COMMENTARY
The purpose of this rule is to make it clear beyond doubt that an arbitrator's appointment has *delectus personae* and falls with his death and does not transmit to his executor. See the commentary to r.3 above.

Rule 80: Death of party **D**

80.—(1) An arbitration agreement is not discharged by the death of a party and may be enforced by or against the executor or other representative of that party.

(2) This rule does not affect the operation of any law by virtue of which a substantive right or obligation is extinguished by death.

DEFINITIONS
"arbitration agreement": ss.4, 31(1)
"party": ss.2, 31(1), (2)

STATUS
This is a default rule so it is open to the parties to modify it, agree something different or disapply it completely (see s.9).

MODEL LAW
There is no equivalent provision in the Model Law.

COMMENTARY
The purpose of this rule is to clarify the position regarding rights and obligations under an arbitration agreement following the death of a party to it. Rule 80 clarifies the situation in relation to arbitration agreements (including clauses). The common law position is that prima facie all contractual rights and obligations pass on to the executors of the deceased party, whose duty it is to ingather the estate, settle the deceased's debts and obligations and distribute the residue to beneficiaries either under a will or under intestacy. The matter is now beyond any doubt in relation to arbitration agreements.

The position expressed above in relation to the common law is preserved by r.80(2).

Rule 81: Unfair treatment **D**

81. A tribunal (or arbitrator) who treats any party unfairly is, for the purposes of these rules, to be deemed not to have treated the parties fairly.

DEFINITIONS
"arbitrator": ss.4, 31(1)
"party": ss.2, 31(1), (2)
"tribunal": ss.2(1), 31(1)

STATUS
This is a default rule so it is open to the parties to modify it, agree something different or disapply it completely (see s.9).

If parties have agreed to adopt institutional rules, the starting point will be to consider what is the position under r.81 and then to see the extent to which r.81 is inconsistent with or disapplied by the institutional rule.

MODEL LAW
There is no equivalent provision in the Model Law

COMMENTARY
The purpose of this rule is unclear. It appears to have a definitional role in deeming the unfair treatment of one party unfair treatment of "the parties".

Rule 82: Rules applicable to umpires **M**

82.—(1) The following rules apply in relation to an umpire appointed under rule 30 (or otherwise with the agreement of the parties) as they apply in relation to an arbitrator or, as the case may be, the tribunal—
rule 4
rule 8
rules 10 to 14
rule 24
rule 26
rules 59, 60 and 61(1)
rule 68
rule 73
rules 76 to 79

(2) But the parties are, in so far as those rules are not mandatory rules, free to modify or disapply the way in which those rules would otherwise apply to an umpire.

DEFINITIONS
"arbitrator: ss.4, 31(1)
"court": s.31(1)
"party": ss.2, 31(1), (2)
"tribunal": ss.2(1), 31(1)

STATUS
This is a mandatory rule.

MODEL LAW
There is no equivalent provision in the Model Law

COMMENTARY
See the commentary to r.30 above in relation to umpires (formerly known under Scots common law as "oversmen"). Essentially the same key rules apply to umpires as they do to arbitrators.

Rule 83: Formal communications **D**

83.—(1) A "formal communication" means any application, award, consent, direction, notice, objection, order, reference, request, requirement or waiver made or given or any document served—
(a) in pursuance of an arbitration agreement,

(b) for the purposes of these rules (in so far as they apply), or
(c) otherwise in relation to an arbitration.
(2) A formal communication must be in writing.
(3) A formal communication is made, given or served if it is—
  (a) hand delivered to the person concerned,
  (b) sent to the person concerned by first class post in a properly addressed envelope or package—
    (i) in the case of an individual, to the individual's principal place of business or usual or last known abode,
    (ii) in the case of a body corporate, to the body's registered or principal office, or
    (iii) in either case, to any postal address designated for the purpose by the intended recipient (such designation to be made by giving notice to the person giving or serving the formal communication), or
  (c) sent to the person concerned in some other way (including by email, fax or other electronic means) which the sender reasonably considers likely to cause it to be delivered on the same or next day.
(4) A formal communication which is sent by email, fax or other electronic means is to be treated as being in writing only if it is legible and capable of being used for subsequent reference.
(5) A formal communication is, unless the contrary is proved, to be treated as having been made, given or served—
  (a) where hand delivered, on the day of delivery,
  (b) where posted, on the day on which it would be delivered in the ordinary course of post, or
  (c) where sent in any other way described above, on the day after it is sent.
(6) The tribunal may determine that a formal communication—
  (a) is to be delivered in such other manner as it may direct, or
  (b) need not be delivered,
but it may do so only if satisfied that it is not reasonably practicable for the formal communication to be made, given or served in accordance with this rule (or, as the case may be, with any contrary agreement between the parties).
(7) This rule does not apply in relation to any application, order, notice, document or other thing which is made, given or served in or for the purposes of legal proceedings.

DEFINITIONS
"arbitration": ss.2(1), 31(1)
"arbitration agreement": ss.4, 31(1)
"party": ss.2, 31(1), (2)
"rules": s.31(1)
"tribunal": ss.2(1), 31(1)

STATUS
This is a default rule so it is open to the parties to modify it, agree something different or disapply it completely (see s.9).
If parties have agreed to adopt institutional rules, those rules will usually have provisions relating to communications between parties. Examples include art.2 of SAC 07, arts 3.1–3.3 of the ICC Rules, art.4 of the LCIA Rules, and art.2 of the UNCITRAL Rules. In such situations, the starting point will be to consider what is the position under r.83 and then to see the

extent to which r.83 is inconsistent with or disapplied by the institutional rule.

In addition, parties can agree to disapply r.83 ad hoc in relation to particular communications (see s.9(3)(b)). For example where a party makes an oral request at a hearing and there is no objection from the other parties to the arbitration, it will be possible to see the parties as having agreed to disapply r.83(2) requiring the request to be in writing, and with it any other rules consequential upon the need for a request to be in writing.

MODEL LAW

Article 3 (1) of the Model Law provides:
"Unless otherwise agreed by the parties:
  (a) any written communication is deemed to have been received if it is delivered to the addressee personally or if it is delivered at his place of business, habitual residence or mailing address; if none of these can be found after making a reasonable inquiry, a written communication is deemed to have been received if it is sent to the addressee's last-known place of business, habitual residence or mailing address by registered letter or any other means which provides a record of the attempt to deliver it;
  (b) the communication is deemed to have been received on the day it is so delivered."

Rule 83 goes beyond the Model Law provisions to make more detailed provision.

COMMENTARY

Essentially r.83 provides a comprehensive code for communications between the parties and the tribunal and between the parties themselves in relation to the arbitration. While the term "formal communication" is used both in the heading for the rule and also in the definition of its subject matter, the term is given a wide definition. In particular it includes any "notice", "objection", "request" or "requirement" made or given in pursuance of the arbitration agreement, for the purposes of the rules or otherwise in relation to an arbitration. Rule 83(7) makes it clear that r.83 does not apply to communications made in or for the purposes of "legal proceedings" by which is presumably meant proceedings before any court.

Rule 83(1), (2), and (4)—requirement of writing

The general rule is that the communication in question must be in writing. With communications such as awards, directions, notices, orders and references this is what one would expect. However r.83 goes further and requires all of the communications covered by the rule to be in writing. Thus any application, notice, objection, request, requirement, or perhaps more controversially, any waiver, must be in writing.

If the communication is sent by email, fax or other electronic means, for it to be treated as being in writing, it must be legible and capable of being used for subsequent reference. Presumably this test for electronic communications is one to be applied by reference to what is received by the recipient. It is therefore conceivable that the sender is under the impression that r.83 has been complied with when because of the failure of the electronic transmission, for whatever reason, a legible and therefore written communication has not been received.

There is no requirement for the written communication to be signed but it is good practice to do so in order that any confusion between drafts and final versions and copies and originals is avoided.

Rule 83(3)(a) and (5)(a)—hand delivery

A formal communication is made if it has been hand delivered to the person concerned. That appears straightforward. But there can be issues as to whether the test has been satisfied. Does it include hand delivery to the address of the person concerned? It is suggested that merely to go to the address of the person concerned and to put the document through the letterbox would not amount to hand delivery to the person concerned. Quite apart from the wording of r.83(3)(a), the purpose of r.83(3) is to ensure that the formal communication is actually communicated. To allow a watering down of r.83(3)(a) to allow mere delivery to the address of the person concerned would thwart the object of the rule.

Can there be hand delivery to a recipient who is a corporate body or other legal person? Rule 83(3)(b) which deals with delivery by post distinguishes between those "persons concerned" who are individuals and those who are bodies corporate. By contrast r.83(3)(a) does not make any such distinction and this suggests that there can be hand delivery to a corporate body or other legal person. This would also accord with a practical approach. There is no good reason why delivery to a sole director of a small company should not count as hand delivery to the company. However with corporate bodies or other legal persons and particularly large organisations there can be a question of whether delivery to an individual within the body who is not authorised to receive it amounts to delivery to the corporate body? It has been held that an email sent to an "info@" email address which was received by a customer service representative but then not forwarded to the relevant individual within the body was served on the body in question (*The Eastern Navigator* [2006] 1 Lloyd's Rep. 537). On the same principle a delivery to an individual employee of that body might amount to delivery to the body. Clearly if the individual in question is authorised to receive post that would be sufficient for hand delivery (*Burt v Kirkcaldy* [1965] 1 W.L.R. 474 applied in *Duffy v Normand*, 1995 S.L.T. 1264). Whether on an analogy with *The Eastern Navigator* delivery to any employee or agent of the body would be sufficient, however unconnected they were from the function of receiving post, is open to question.

Rule 83(5)(a) provides that a formal communication is, unless the contrary is proved, to be treated as having been made given or served where hand delivered, on the day of delivery. From a practical point of view given that there is no presumption of the making of hand delivery and the necessity of proof of hand delivery, r.83(5)(a) does not alter the need for the party making the hand delivery to provide evidence that the delivery was made. If that evidence is present, then the presumption in r.83(5)(a) comes into play and it is for the recipient to disprove it.

Rule 83(3)(b) and (5) (b)—first class post

Another form of communication is the sending of the written communication to the person concerned by first class post. For this form of communication to be effective, sending is sufficient and there is no requirement that it be received. Rule 83(3)(b) and (5)(b) in effect for most purposes supersedes most of s.7 of the Interpretation Act 1978. Apart from its possible applicability in relation to service on Scottish partnerships by post, the only requirement of s.7 which is not reflected in r.83 but which must be read with it is that the postage must be pre-paid.

It is unfortunate that the phrase "body corporate" is used given that Scottish partnerships without limited liability are legal persons in their own right, separate from the individuals (or bodies corporate) who may be their partners but not bodies corporate. Indeed there may be other legal persons who are not "bodies corporate". Unless the phrase "body corporate" can be construed as including a Scottish partnership, the making, giving or serving of a formal communication by post on such a partnership is to be done either under the "other means" head of r.83(3)(c) (see below).

Rule 83(3)(c) and (5)(c)—other means

The only restriction on other methods of transmission of formal communications, not being covered by the earlier parts of r.83(3), is that the sender must reasonably consider the method to be likely to cause the communication to be delivered on the same day as or the next day after sending. Thus the methods can include email, fax, or other electronic means, or by other postal means not involving r.83(3)(b). Thus a private postal service such as document exchange, or in Scotland, Legal Post, would be covered. First class post to legal persons who are not corporate bodies, e.g. the Scottish unlimited liability partnership, would be covered. For both private post and the first class post in this limited sense, s.7 of the Interpretation Act 1978 would appear to apply where there is a gap in r.83. The provisions of s.7 are as follows:

"Where an Act authorises or requires any document to be served by post (whether the expression 'serve' or the expression 'give' or 'send' or any other expression is used) then, unless the contrary intention appears, the service is deemed to be effected by properly addressing, pre-paying and posting a letter containing the document and, unless the contrary is proved, to have been effected at the time at which the letter would be delivered in the ordinary course of post."

Rule 83(6)—communication not reasonably practicable

Rule 83(6) provides for the situation where the tribunal is satisfied that it is not reasonably practicable for r.83 to be complied with. In such a situation the tribunal is given wide powers to provide for the delivery of formal communications in such other manner as it may direct or to dispense with delivery entirely. The purpose of the powers in r.83(6) are to deal with the situation where the location of a party is unknown or a party is evading service such that it is not practicable for that party to be communicated with using the methods of r.83 or other methods agreed by the parties. Given the wide variety of methods in r.83 (and institutional rules) it is unlikely that these powers will often be used.

A common feature of the standard r.83 methods is that the communication must be delivered to the person concerned. If that is not practicable by those methods it is conceivable that the tribunal could determine that the communication should be delivered to some other person where there is reason to believe that in this way the person concerned could become aware of the communication, e.g. a relative of or solicitor or other agent who had recently acted for the person concerned. Another method may be by newspaper advertisement in a newspaper circulating in the area of the last known residence or whereabouts of the person concerned. In any determination of the tribunal under r.83(6) it is important that the tribunal bears in mind its overriding duty under r.24 to be impartial and independent, treat the parties fairly and conduct the arbitration without unnecessary delay and unnecessary expense. Rule 83(6) would also not appear to assist in the giving of a notice of arbitration under r.1 given that a tribunal would not have been appointed at that time.

A determination by the tribunal that a formal communication need not be delivered is one which the tribunal is likely to reach only in extreme circumstances. In effect the tribunal will need to be convinced that if it made such a determination its award would still withstand an appeal on the grounds of serious irregularity or lack of jurisdiction.

Rule 84: Periods of time **D**

84. Periods of time are to be calculated for the purposes of an arbitration as follows—
 (a) where any act requires to be done within a specified period after or from a specified date or event, the period begins immediately after that date or, as the case may be, the date of that event, and
 (b) where the period is a period of 7 days or less, the following days are to be ignored—
   (i) Saturdays and Sundays, and
   (ii) any public holidays in the place where the act concerned is to be done.

DEFINITIONS
"arbitration": ss.2(1), 31(1)

STATUS
This is a default rule so it is open to the parties to modify it, agree something different or disapply it completely (see s.9).

Parties can modify or disapply it completely or in part (see s.9). If parties have agreed to adopt institutional rules, those rules will usually have provisions relating to communications between parties. Examples include art.2 of SAC 07, arts 3.1–3.3 of the ICC Rules, art.4 of the LCIA Rules, and art.2 of the UNCITRAL Rules. In such situations, the starting point will be to consider what is the position under r.84 and then to see the extent to which r.84 is inconsistent with or disapplied by the institutional rule.

COMMENTARY
The purpose of this rule is to set out how time is to be calculated for the purposes of an arbitration. The rule applies not merely to time limits set out in the rules but also to time limits fixed by a tribunal in its directions. It does not apply where time is calculated by the rules of court (RCS or SASAR). In those situations calculation of time is determined by the application of the relevant rule.

The basic rule is that where something has to be done "within" a specified period then the period begins to run immediately after the date of commencement. So for example where on March 1 it was ordered that a document had to be lodged within 14 days, then the period begins to run with March 2 and the last day of the period will be March 15.

The time of an act is always linked to the place where the act in question has to be done. The location of such an act depends on what it is. The place of the making of a formal communication, for example under r.83 will be where the relevant part of r.83 (or the rule displacing it) was satisfied. That place may differ, for example on whether there is hand delivery or posting. This is important where parties and their advisers are located in different time zones. From a practical point of view if the tribunal or parties wish to have a uniform timescale they should specify the time with reference to a particular recognised time zone, e.g. 12 hrs GMT.

Parties and their advisers have to beware of the effect of public holidays and weekends. Rule 84, indicates, by implication, that a period of time is not suspended merely because the last day falls within a public holiday, unless the period in question was seven days or less. So if a period of time happens to end on a holiday Monday, it may in practice require compliance by the previous Friday. A "public holiday" is determined by reference to the place where the act for which the period of time exists is to be done (r.84(b)). Public holidays in Scotland are either bank holidays or local holidays.

Bank holidays are set out in Sch.1 to the Banking and Financial Dealings Act 1971. These are at present January 1, January 2 (or if it is a Sunday, January 3), Good Friday, first Monday in May, first Monday in August, November 30 (or if it is a Saturday or Sunday December 1 or December 2), Christmas Day (or if it is a Sunday, December 26), and any other day that Her Majesty may from time to time appoint by Royal Proclamation. The other days which have in the past been made bank holidays by Royal Proclamation are the English originating last Monday in May (the Whitsun holiday) and December 26 (if it is not a Monday).

Local holidays are popular in Scotland and depend on the locality. Local councils or chambers of commerce should be able to advise on whether a day is a local holiday. Popular local holidays can include Easter Monday, Edinburgh Victoria Day being the third Monday in May, Glasgow Fair, or various "Trades" holidays in July or August, and a Monday in September which varies from locality to locality.

INDEX

The words and other expressions listed in the following index are defined or otherwise explained for the purposes of these rules by the provisions indicated in the index.

Expression	*Interpretation provision*
arbitral appointments referee	section 24
arbitration	section 2
arbitration agreement	section 4
arbitration expenses	rule 59
arbitrator	section 2
claim	section 31(1)
court	section 31(1)
default rule	section 9(1)
dispute	section 2
independent	rule 77
Inner House	section 31(1)
mandatory rule	section 8
Outer House	section 31(1)
part award	rule 54
party	sections 2 and 31(2)
provisional award	rule 53
recoverable arbitration expenses	rule 61
rule	section 2
statutory arbitration	section 16(1)
tribunal	section 2

Arbitration (Scotland) Act 2010

SCHEDULE 2

REPEALS

(introduced by section 29)

Enactment	*Extent of repeal*
Arbitration (Scotland) Act 1894 (c. 13)	The whole Act
Arbitration Act 1950 (c. 27)	The whole Act
Administration of Justice (Scotland) Act 1972 (c. 59)	Section 3
Arbitration Act 1975 (c. 3)	The whole Act
Law Reform (Miscellaneous Provisions) (Scotland) Act 1980 (c. 55)	Section 17
Law Reform (Miscellaneous Provisions) (Scotland) Act 1990 (c. 40)	Section 66 Schedule 7

INDEX

AAR
see **Arbitral appointments referee (AAR)**
Abroad, persons resident
fees and expenses, security for, 286–287
seat of arbitration, 256
sist, 30, 37–38, 233
witnesses, 219–220, 221
Ad factum praestandum
see **Specific Implement**
Additional awards
correction of awards, 270
Adjournments
enforcement of awards, 43, 79–80
Administrative matters
clerks, agents or employees, 193–194
experts, 197–198
Admissibility of evidence
tribunal to determine, 174–176
Advisers
see **Clerks, agents or employees; Experts**
Affirmations and oaths
default rule, 199
Age
eligibility to act as arbitrators, 110
Agents
see **Clerks, agents or employees**
Agreements
see **Arbitration agreements; Contracts**
All issues, failure to deal with,
serious irregularity appeals, 293, 298–299
Ambiguity
see **Clarification or removal of ambiguity in awards**
Amicable compositeurs
contracts, readjustment of, 237
legal error appeal, exclusion of, 305
procedural irregularity, 69
Ancillary provisions
Scottish Ministers, powers of, 96
Annulment
see **Reduction**
Anonymity in legal proceedings
see also **Confidentiality**
appeals, 52
application to court for orders, 48–50
appointment of arbitrators, 50
arbitration agreements, 50
civil proceedings, 49–52
conditions for disclosure, 48–49
confidentiality, 49–52
criminal proceedings, 49
damages, 49
enforcement of awards, 49–50
exceptions, 51–52
finality of court determination, 52
lawful interests, disclosure to protect, 52
public functions exception, 51–52
public interest exception, 52
removal of arbitrators, 50
sist, 50
Appeals
see also **Jurisdictional appeals; Legal error appeals; Serious irregularity appeals**
anonymity in legal proceedings, 52

annulment appeals, 40
appointment of arbitrators or tribunal, 116, 117, 294, 298
arbitral appointments referee, 116
arbitration agreements, 293–294, 297–298, 305, 312
awards, 1, 38, 40–43, 48, 254–255, 272, 289–320
challenges to awards, 42–43, 48, 272, 289–320
clarification or removal of ambiguity in awards, 272
enforcement of awards, 41, 42–43
evidence, 176–178, 223
fees and expenses, 43, 262–263, 265, 277, 281–283
final and binding nature of awards, 38, 40
independence and impartiality, 162
institutional rules, 40
interim measures, 226
judges as arbitrators or umpires, 88, 89
no part in proceedings, persons who take, 47–48
Outer House, 42–43
reasons for awards, 254–255
reconsideration of award by tribunal, 294, 303, 307, 310–311
reconstitution of tribunal, 143
referral of points of law, 215
resignation of arbitrators, 140
Scottish Arbitration Rules, 45
security for expenses of appeal, 43
stated case procedure, 92
tenure, termination of, 141
time limits, 218, 262–263
umpires, 88, 89
witnesses, 223
Appointment of arbitrators or tribunal
see also **Arbitral appointments referee (AAR)**
3-person tribunals, 110–112, 114–115, 124–125, 148, 189
additional arbitrators, 114
anonymity in legal proceedings, 50
appeals, 116, 117, 294, 298
appointing authorities, 112
arbitration agreements, nominations in, 107–108, 144
balance of tribunal, 110–111
bodies corporate, 108–109
burden of proof, 65
chair, 112, 190
challenges to appointments, 121–124, 135, 137
civil law countries, 109
commencement of arbitration, 106–107
confirmation of appointment, 121
conflict of interests, duty to disclose, 117–120, 159
court intervention, 46–47
death of arbitrator, 108
default rules, 28, 107–108, 111–115, 121–124
ethics, 113

337

Index

European Convention on Human Rights, 122
expert determination, 108–109
failure of appointment procedure, 91–92, 115–117, 121
fair hearings, 122
fairness, 121
guidelines on selection, 113–114
immunity, 322–323
independence and impartiality, 113, 117, 121, 123
individual, arbitrator must be an, 89, 108
ineligibility for appointment, 109–110, 139, 323, 325
institutional rules, 107–108, 110–114, 122–123
interviews, 113–114
judges, 86–89
jurisdiction, 148, 157
legal persons, 108–109
limited liability partnerships, 109
location, disclosure of, 114
mandatory rules, 108–110, 117–120
method of appointment, 107–108, 111–115
multi-party arbitrations, 114–115
nationality, 108, 112
natural justice, 122
natural persons, 108–109
nominations in arbitration agreements, 107–108, 144
notice, 65, 294, 298
number of arbitrators, 68, 110–112, 114–115, 124–125, 148, 189
opportunity to respond, 122
partnerships, 108–109
party-appointed arbitrators (PAAs), 113–115, 211
party autonomy, 114
personal appointment, 109
qualifications, 121, 123, 126, 294
reasons for appointment, 87–88
referral of points of law, 211
refusal of recognition or enforcement, 58, 64, 65
resignation, 123, 141–142
revocation of appointment, 120, 121, 125, 139
serious irregularity appeals, 294, 298
simultaneously as judge and arbitrator, sitting, 89
sole arbitrators, 110, 111–112
striking out names, 122
tenure, termination of, 139
time limits, 65, 111, 121, 123, 124, 148, 216
tribunals other than 1 or 3, 111, 148, 189
umpires, 86–92, 111
unincorporated bodies, 108
vicarious liability, 323

Approach of Act
Scottish Arbitration Rules, 5
unique features, 4–5, 25

Arbiter
see **Arbitrators**

Arbitrability
authorisation, 94
employment, 93
fraud, 93
governing law, 94

international arbitration, 93
jurisdiction, 94
New York Convention 1958, 74, 94
property rights, 93
validity, 21–22

Arbitral appointments referee (AAR)
appeals, 116, 293, 294, 299
arbitration agreements, 116
conflicts of interest, 117
default rules, 116
disciplinary procedures, 86
eligibility criteria, 116–117
experience, 86
failure of appointment procedure, 115–117
fees and expenses, 274, 275–276, 277
immunity, 322
individuals, as, 116–117
joint and several liability for fees, 263
ministerial authorisation of AARs, 86
notice of referral, 115
powers, acting outwith, 293, 299
qualifying bodies, 86, 116–117
removal of arbitrators, 125
serious irregularity appeals, 293, 294, 299
training, 86

Arbitral proceedings
amendment of claims or defences, 174
arbitration agreements, failure to comply with, 205–208
attend hearing, failure to, 204
claims,
  exchange, 180
  time for submission of, 174
clerks, agents or employees, power to appoint, 191–194
confidential information, 166
consolidation of proceedings, 208–210
counterclaims, 181
decisions, 189–190
defences,
  delay, 199–200
  exchange, 180
  time for submission of, 174
delay in submission of claim or defence, 199–200
directions, 190–191, 205–208
disclosure, 174, 181–182
discretion, 182
documents-only basis, arbitration on a, 185, 187
evidence, 174–187, 205, 218–223
experts, 196–198
failure to comply, 205–208
foreign procedural law, invoking a, 29
improperly conducted arbitration, 68–69
interim measures, 223–236
irregularities, 184–185
jurisdiction, 155–158
language, 175
legal error appeals, 306–311
oaths or affirmations, 199
party autonomy, 175
party representatives, 194–196
persons who take no part, 47–48
place of arbitration, 174, 187–189
powers of court, 210–236
property, powers relating to, 198–199
reconstitution of tribunal, 142

Index

referral of points of law, 210–215
responses, 181
signing awards, 250
time limits, variation of, 215–218
when arbitration is conducted, tribunal determining, 174
witnesses,
  attendance of, 218–223
  contacting, 184–185
Arbitral tribunals
  see **Appointment of arbitrators or tribunal; Tribunal**
Arbitration agreements
  appeals, 293–294, 297–298, 305, 312
  applicable law, 147–148
  appointment of tribunal, 107–108, 144
  arbitral proceedings, 205–208
  certainty of agreements, 147
  choice of law, 23–25
  commencement of arbitration, 103
  consumer arbitration agreements, 6
  death, 328
  definition, 20
  dismissal of tribunal by court, 132
  existence of agreements, 145–147, 31–32
  failure to comply with agreements, 205–208, 293–294, 297–298
  frustration, 147
  governing law, 22–25, 37, 147–148
  illegality, 22
  immunity, 321
  incapable of being performed, agreements which are, 35–36
  incorporation of agreements, 20–21
  inconvenience, 37
  inoperative, where agreement is, 36–37
  interdicts or interim interdicts, 231
  interim measures, 226
  interpretation, 36
  invalid contracts, effect of, 21–22
  jurisdiction, 40, 145–148, 156–157, 312
  legal error appeals, 305, 312
  main agreements,
    governing law, 23–24
    invalidity, 147
  names of arbitrators, 91–92
  New York Convention 1958, 56–57
  not conducted in accordance with agreement, arbitration, 323, 325
  object, loss of right to, 323, 325
  oral agreements, 21
  original agreements, production of, 80–82
  preconditions for operation of arbitration agreements, 156–157
  referral of points of law, 210, 213
  Scott v *Avery* clauses, 37
  seat of arbitration, 22–23
  separability, 21–22, 24, 147
  serious irregularity appeals, 293, 294, 297–298, 312
  sist, 146
  statutory arbitrations, 20
  time limits, 217, 314
  transitional provisions, 99–101
  translations, 82
  validity, 21–22, 43, 91–92, 145–148, 312
  variation, 215–217

void, voidable or otherwise unenforceable, not, 34–37
writing, 21, 157
Arbitrators
  see also **Appointment of arbitrators or tribunal; Challenge to arbitrator's appointment; Independence and impartiality; Removal of arbitrators by court**
  age, 110
  arbiters, use of term, 101
  capacity, 110, 293
  case management, 163, 164, 191
  Code of Ethics, 113
  conflict of interests, 117–120
  damages and payments, power to award, 241–242
  death, 327–328
  decisions of tribunal, 189
  declarator, 243
  default rules, 110–111, 120–124
  dissenting arbitrators, signatures of, 249–250
  eligibility, 109–110, 139, 323, 325
  ethics, 113
  failure to participate, disclosure of, 173–174
  fees and expenses, 141–142, 263, 273–289, 303
  identity unknown, where, 65
  immunity, 139–140, 249, 320–323
  interdicts or interim interdicts, 231, 243
  judges, as, 86–89
  liability, 135–136, 139–142
  mandatory rules, 109–110
  names, validity of agreements and, 91–92
  number of arbitrators, 68, 110–115, 124–125, 148, 189
  object, loss of right to, 323, 325
  qualifications, 121, 123, 126, 294
  rectification, 244–245
  reduction, 244
  remuneration, 276
  replacements, 140
  resignation, 121, 123, 135–140, 321–323
  signing awards, 249–250
  sole arbitrators, 110, 111–112
  specific implement, 244
  tenure, 120–121, 139–142
  termination of tenure, 139–142
  umpires, 86–89
Arrestment on the dependence of moveable property
  security, 227, 229–231
Attendance at hearings
  failure to attend, 204–205, 219
  ill-health, 205
  reason, lack of good, 205
  sanctions for failure to attend, 219
  witnesses, 218–223
Awards
  see also **Challenges to awards; Enforcement of awards; Part awards; Provisional awards; Reasons for awards; Setting aside awards**
  additional awards, power to make, 270
  ambiguity, 255, 270–274, 293, 299–300, 319–320

339

Index

amiable compositeur, 237
appeals, 1, 289–293, 312–319
arbitration agreements, failure to comply with, 206
authentication of awards, 80–81
calculation of awards, errors in, 260
binding nature of awards, 38–40, 266, 270, 288–289
challenges, 40, 42–43, 48, 146, 179, 261–262, 268, 270–274, 289–320
choice of law, 236, 238–239
clarification or removal of ambiguity in awards, 255, 270–274, 293, 299–300, 319–320
clerical, typographical or other errors arising by accident or omission, 268, 269, 270–271
commercial or trade usages, paying regard to, 236, 240–241
confidentiality, 166, 255, 316
confirmation of awards, 289, 294, 303, 307, 320
conflict of law rules, 236, 238, 239–240
contents of awards, 251–256
contract, paying regard to provisions of any applicable, 236
correction, 42–43, 255, 260, 268–274
court intervention, 45, 46
currency, 241, 242
damages, 241–242
date of awards, 251–253, 256
declaratory awards, 242, 243
default rule, 236–273
defences timeously, failure to lodge, 200–201
delay, 148
delivery to parties,
  award made by, 256
  date of awards, 252, 256
directions, failure to comply with, 206
discretion, 42–43, 251
do or refrain from doing something, orders for parties to, 242, 243–244
draft awards, 192–194, 260–262, 264–265
England is seat of arbitration, where, 256–257
equity, 236–237, 240
failure to lodge claims timeously, 200–201
fairness, 236–237, 240
fees and expenses, 262–265, 270
final and binding, as, 38–40, 266, 270, 288–289
foreign awards, 44
form requirements, 249–256
interdicts, 242, 243–244
interest, 245–248, 270
jurisdictional appeals, 148–152, 289–293, 312–19
justice, 236–238, 240
last award, termination of arbitration on, 265–268
legal error appeals, 304–311, 312–319
mandatory rule, 289–320
new awards, making, 320
New York Convention awards, 300–301
no part in proceedings, persons who take, 47–48
objections to jurisdiction, 148–152

oral hearings, 185
payment and damages, power to award, 241–242
place of arbitration, 251, 256–257
previous award was made, award must state whether, 255–256
public policy, 300–301
reconsideration, 185, 266, 270, 294, 303, 319–320, 327
rectification, 38, 40, 242, 244–245, 266
reduction, 1, 176, 187, 244
registration, 44
relevant matters, paying regard to, 236
remedies other than damages, 242–245
remission of awards, 126
removal of arbitrators, 126, 161–162
representation of parties, 269
rules, invoking bodies of, 237
Scotland, award treated as made in, 256–257
scrutiny of awards under institutional rules, 40
seat, awards must state, 251
security, 227
serious irregularity appeals, 270, 293–304, 312–319
settlements, termination of arbitration on, 265–268
signed, awards must be, 249–251, 252–253, 256
specific implement, 242, 243–244
standards, reference to, 237–238
stated case procedure, 1
substance of dispute, rules applicable to, 236–241
substantive jurisdiction, 289–293
termination of arbitration on last award or early settlement, 265–268
time for taking effect, award must state, 251–253
time limits, 200–201, 251–253, 256, 269
trade usages, 236, 240–241
translations, 82
tribunal should pay regard, considerations to which, 236, 240–241
validity of awards, 251
variation of awards, 289, 292–293
when it is made, award must state, 251–253
withholding award for non-payment of fees or expenses
writing, 250–251

Bank holidays
  time periods, calculation of, 334
Banking
  confidentiality, 51–52, 170–171
Bias
  see **Independence and impartiality**
Binding nature of awards
  see **Final and binding nature of awards**
Bodies corporate
  appointment of arbitrators or tribunal, 108–109
  expert determination, 108–109
Burden of proof
  appointments, notice of, 65
  attend, failure to, 204

Index

referral of points of jurisdiction, 156
refusal of recognition or enforcement, 59–60, 65, 67, 69–70, 74
sist, 34–35, 37

Capacity
corporations, 62
curator ad litem, 223, 226–227
eligibility to act as arbitrators, 110
incapable of being performed, where agreements are, 35–36
public authorities, 62
refusal of recognition or enforcement, 58, 61–63
removal of arbitrators, 125, 131
resignation of arbitrators, 137
safeguarders, appointment of, 226–227
serious irregularity appeals, 293, 294
sist, 35–36
tenure, termination of, 141
void agreements, 35

Case management
delay, 164
directions, 191
fees and expenses, 163

Caution
see also **Security**
appeals, 312–313, 317–318
consent, 234
court's power to order, 227, 228, 233–234
interim measures, 233, 234
legal error appeals, 306
tribunal's power to order, 286–287

Certificated awards
refusal of recognition or enforcement, 80–81

Chair
appointment, 112, 190

Challenges
see **Challenges to arbitrator's appointment; Challenges to awards**

Challenges to arbitrator's appointment
competence of objections, 121
confirmation of appointment, 121
default rule, 121–124
European Convention on Human Rights, 122
factual basis of objection, 121, 123
failure of tribunal to make a decision, 121
fairness, 121, 122
hearings, 185
independence and impartiality, 121, 123, 161–162
institutional rules, 122–123
natural justice, 122
notice to other party, 121
one member of tribunal, to, 123–124
opportunity to respond, 122
party's right to object to appointment, 122
qualifications, lack of specific, 121, 123
resignation, 123, 135, 137
revocation of appointment, 121
striking out names, 122
time limit for lodging objection, 121, 123, 124

Challenges to awards
appeals, 146, 289–293, 304–319
correction of awards, 271

discretion, 42–43
draft awards, 261–162
enforcement of awards, 42–43
error, 101
evidence, 179
final and binding nature of awards, 40
good faith, 91
hiding assets, risk of, 43
jurisdictional appeals, 146, 289–293, 312–319
legal error appeals, 304–311, 312–319
mandatory rule, 289–320
New York Convention 1958, 43, 58
no part in proceedings, persons who take, 47–48
part awards, 260
reasons for awards, 254
refusal of recognition or enforcement, 71–72
serious irregularity appeals, 293–304, 312–319
settlements, 268
sist, 43
stated case procedure, 101
substantive jurisdiction, 289–293

Choice of law
awards, 236, 238–239
conflict of laws, 238
default rules, 29
governing law, 23–25, 239
habitual residence, 238
implied choice of law, 24–25, 238
renvoi, 238
Rome Convention 1980, 238–239
seat of arbitration, 63–64
serious irregularities, 238
unfair contract terms, 238–239
unlawful choice of law, 238–239

Civil law countries
appointment of arbitrators or tribunal, 109
cross-examination, 183–185
oaths or affirmations, 199
oral hearings, 187

Civil proceedings
see also **Sist**
advantages of arbitration, 167–168
anonymity in legal proceedings, 49–52
confidentiality, 166, 167–168

Claims
counterclaims, 96, 181, 260
exchange of claims, 180
failure to lodge claims timeously, 199–204
time for submission, 180, 199–204

Clarification or removal of ambiguity in awards
appeals, 272
challenging refusal, 272
consequential corrections, 273
correction of awards, 255, 268, 270, 271–274
discretion, 272
institutional rules, 273
part awards, 260
parties, request of, 271–272
reasons for awards, 255
reconsideration of awards, 319–320

341

Index

representations, opportunity to make, 271–272
retrospectivity, 273
serious irregularity, 273
time limits, 271–273
tribunal's own initiative, 271, 272–273
Clerical, typographical or other errors arising by accident or omission
correction of awards, 268, 269, 270–271
Clerks, agents or employees
administrative matters, 193–194
appointment, 191–194
arbitral proceedings, 191–194
awards, drafting, 192–194
consent, 191
default rule, 191–194
delegation, extent of, 192–194
discretion, 192
fees and expenses, 193, 275
immunity, 320, 322–323
lawyers, 192–193
natural justice, 194
serious irregularity, 192
technical issues, 193–194
Commencement
see **Commencement of Act; Commencement of arbitration**
Commencement of Act
day appointed by Ministers by order, on, 98
other provisions, entry into force of, 98
Royal Assent, provisions to come into force on, 98, 102
section 36, entry into force of, 102
transitional provisions, 98–101
Commencement of arbitration
agreements on date of commencement, 99–100
arbitration agreements, existence of, 103
constitution of tribunal, 106–107
content of notice, 103
default rules, 99–101, 102–107
email, notice by, 103–104
institutional rules, 103
notice, 102–107
prescription, 84–85
receipt, giving, 102–104
reconstitution of tribunal, 143–144
requests, 99–100
time limits, 84–85
transitional provisions, 99–100
validity of notice, 103–107
Commercial or trade usages
awards, 236, 240–241
Commissioners
appointment, 219–220
witnesses, 219–220, 229, 236
Competence-competence
jurisdiction, 145, 149–150, 157
Competition
EC law, breach of, 78
Concurrent hearings
consolidation, 208–209
Confidentiality
anonymity in legal proceedings, 49–52
another arbitration, disclosing material used in, 169

arbitral proceedings, information relating to, 166
authorisation of disclosure, 166
awards, information relating to, 166
banking confidentiality, 51–52, 170–171
categories of confidential information, 223
civil proceedings under section 15 of Act, 166
common law, 172–173
consent, 170, 171
court orders, 168–169, 171
defamation and absolute privilege, 166
default rule, 166–173
definition of confidential information, 166
disclosure or discovery, court compelling, 168–169
discretion, 169, 171
disputes, information relating to, 166
enactments or rules of law, compliance with, 166
evidence, 222–223
exceptions to actionability, 166–171
fairness, 168–169
general duties of tribunal, 166–173
governing law, 171–172
implied obligation, 170
informing parties of obligations, 166
institutional rules, 166, 170, 172
interests of justice, 166, 171
jurisdiction, 171
lawful interests, disclosure for protection of, 52, 166, 171
litigation, advantage over, 167–168
parties,
  disclosure by, 166
  third parties, 166, 169
privacy,
  common law, 172–173
  discretion, 169
  distinguished from, 168, 169, 171–172
public body or office-holder, proper performance of functions by, 166
public domain, information in the, 166
public functions, disclosure for proper performance of, 166
public interest, 52, 166, 168, 170, 171
reasons for awards, 255, 316
third parties,
  disclosure, by, 166, 173
  parties, disclosure by, 169
trade secrets, 169, 170
tribunal,
  disclosure by the, 166
  general duties of tribunal, 166–173
  required by tribunal where disclosure is, 166
  third parties, prevention of disclosure by, 166
waiver, 222–223
Conflict of laws
awards, 236, 238, 239–240
Conflicts of interest
appointment of arbitrators or tribunal, 117–120, 159
arbitral appointments referee, 117
arbitrators, 117–120, 129–130, 159, 162
categorisation, 118–119

circumstances known or become known to individual, 117
common basis of disclosure, 119–120
disclosure, 117–120, 159, 162
European Convention on Human Rights, 117, 119
excessive disclosure, 119
fair hearings, 117
governing law, 239
guidelines, 118–120
independence and impartiality, 117–119, 159, 162
prospective arbitrators, 117
relevance, 117–120
removal of arbitrators, 129–130
Rome Convention 1980, 239–240
search for disclosable facts, extent of obligation to, 119
trivial associations, 120
Consent
cautions, 234
clerks, agents or employees, 191
confidentiality, 170, 171
interim measures, 225–226, 235
referral of points of jurisdiction, 155
referral of points of law, 211, 212, 213–215
registration of awards, 44
resignation of arbitrators, consent of parties to, 135, 136–137
settlements, 266–268
Consolidation of proceedings
concurrent hearings, 208–209
default rule, 208–210
statutory arbitrations, 54
Contempt of court
interdicts or interim interdicts, 231
witnesses, 219
Contracts
see also **Arbitration agreements**
amicable compositeurs, 237
awards, 236
choice of law, 238–239
fees and expenses, 277
land, 244
readjustment of contracts, 237
resignation of arbitrators, 135–137
Rome Convention 1980, 238–240
specific implement, 244
unfair contract terms, 6, 164
Corporations
bodies corporate, 108–109
capacity, 62
Correction of awards
additional awards, power to make, 270
ambiguity, removal of, 268, 270, 271–274
calculation of awards, errors in, 260
challenging awards, 271
clarification or removal of ambiguity, 268, 270, 271–274
clerical, typographical or other errors arising by accident or omission, 268, 269, 270–271
consequential corrections, 269, 273
draft awards, 261
enforcement of awards, 42–43
fees and expenses, 270
finality of awards, 270

form, awards treated as if made in corrected, 269
institutional rules, 269
interest, 270
other awards made by the tribunal, affecting, 269
part awards, 269
part of corrected award, correction affecting, 269
provisional awards, 269
reconsideration of award, 270
representations of parties, 269
serious irregularity, 270
time limits, 269
tribunal's own initiative, 268–269
validity of applications, 269
Costs
see also **Fees and expenses**
definition, 274
experts, 197
inability to pay, 36
liability of arbitrators, 139
stated case procedure, 92
Counterclaims
arbitral proceedings, 181
claims as including counterclaims, 96
part awards, 260
Court
definition, of, 32
Court dismissal of tribunal
arbitration agreements, failure to act in accordance with, 132
continuation of arbitration pending decision, 133
expenses, 134
finality of Outer House decision, 133
grounds, 133–134
immunity, 133
independence and impartiality, 132–133
institutional rules, 132
mandatory rule, 132–135
misconduct, 132
natural justice, 133
notice, 133–134
petitions, 133–134
preconditions for dismissal, 133–134
representations, opportunity for, 133
right of party to apply for dismissal, 132
substantial injustice, 132
tenure of arbitrators, 121, 140
third parties, recourse to, 133, 134
Court intervention and court powers
see also **Appeals**
anonymity in legal proceedings, 48–52
appointment of arbitrators, 46–47
arbitral proceedings, 210–236
awards, 45, 46, 263–264
breakdown in procedures, 46–47
civil proceedings, definition of, 245
confidentiality, 168–169, 171
default rules, 46
definition of court, 45
delivery of awards, refusal of, 263–264
dismissal of tribunal, 121, 132–135, 140
evidence, 218–223
experts, 197
fees and expenses, 263–264, 275
finality of court's decisions, 231–232

Index

founding principles of Act, 11, 12–13, 33
governing law, 23–24
interim measures, 223–236
jurisdiction, 45, 145, 154–158
limits on intervention, 11–13, 33, 45, 132–134, 157, 221
payments into court, 317–318
reasons for awards, 254–255, 316
referral of point of jurisdiction, 157
referral of point of Scots law, 210–215
removal of arbitrators, 125–132, 142, 161–162, 185
seat of arbitration, 16, 18–19, 25
sist, 32–33
time limit variation, 215–218
witnesses, attendance of, 218–223
Crime
anonymity in legal proceedings, 49
fraud, 93, 293, 300–301
perjury, 36–37, 302
Cross-examination
civil law countries, 183–185
common law countries, 183–184
Crown application
binding the Crown, Act as, 97–98
Her Majesty, representation of, 97–98
Prince and Steward of Scotland, 97
Crown proceedings
interdicts or interim interdicts, 243
specific implement, 244
Currency
awards, 241–242

Damages and payments, power to award
see also **Awards**
anonymity in legal proceedings, 49
awards, 241–242
currency, 241, 242
mandatory rule, 241–242
penal or exemplary damages, 242
serious irregularity appeals, 300
Death
appointment of arbitrators or tribunal, 108
arbitration agreements, 328
arbitrators, of, 108, 327–328
executors, 328
legal persons, 108
mandatory rule, 327–328
parties, of, 54, 328
statutory arbitrations, 54
Decisions of tribunal
arbitrators, 189
chair, appointment of, 190
default rule, 189–190
delegation, 192
evidence, 223
institutional rules, 190
majority decisions, 189
reasons, 193
umpires, 189
unanimity, 189
Decreets or decrees
see also **Awards**
use of term, 101
Declarator
see also **Awards**
arbitrators, power of, 243

awards, 242, 243
default rules, 243
interest, 246
no part in proceedings, persons who take, 47–48
Defamation
absolute privilege, 166
Default rules
appointment of tribunal, 28
arbitration rules, 28
choice of law, 29
disapplication, 27–28
foreign procedural law, invoking a, 29
institutional rules, 5, 29
mandatory rules, 26, 28
modification, 27–28
party autonomy, 27
writing, 27–28
Defences
arbitral proceedings, 174, 180
arbitration agreements, failure to comply with, 208
delay, 199–200
exchange of defences, 180
failure to lodge claims timeously, 199–204
New York Convention 1958, 58
refusal of recognition or enforcement, 61–69
service, 208
time for submission, 174, 199–204
Definition of arbitration
domestic arbitration, 14–15
international arbitration, 14–15
parties, 114–115
valuers, 14
Definitions
arbitration, 14–15, 114–115
court, 32
disputes, 15
final provisions, 95–96
key terms, 13–16
Delay
active case management, 164
appeals, 305, 308, 310–311
arbitral proceedings, 199–200
avoidance of unnecessary delay, 11, 12, 158, 163–164, 165
claims, submission of, 199–200
defences, submission of, 199–200
evidence, 220–221, 223
fairness, 163–164
founding principle, avoiding delay as, 11, 12, 158, 163–164, 165
general duties of tribunal, 158, 163–164, 165
historical background, 1
incapable of being performed, agreements which are, 36
independence and impartiality, 327
inexcusable and inordinate delay, 202–203
interim measures, 235
jurisdiction, 148–149, 152, 154–155, 291
legal error appeals, 305, 308, 310–311
liability of arbitrators, 140
mandatory rule, 26–27, 165
objections, 148, 324
payments into court, 317–318
referral of points of law, 213, 214, 215

Index

representatives, 196
quantum for delay, 140
serious irregularity, 163
termination of arbitration, 266
time limits, 218
want of prosecution, striking out for, 201–203
witnesses, 220–221, 223
Delegation
clerks, agents or employees, 192–194
Delivery of awards to parties
court intervention, 263–264
date of awards, 252, 256
discretion, 263–264
fees and expenses, failure to pay, 262–264
refusal of delivery, 262–264
Depositions, power to take
interim measures, 233
Diligence on the dependence
insolvency, 227
security, 227–228, 229–231
Directions of tribunal
arbitral proceedings, 190–191, 205–208
case management, 191
compliance, 190, 205–208
default rule, 190–191
Disclosure
anonymity in legal proceedings, 48–49
appointment of arbitrators or tribunal, 114
arbitral proceedings, 174, 181–182
arbitrators' failure to participate, 173–174
confidentiality, 52, 166, 168–169, 171
conflicts of interest, 117–120, 159, 162
evidence, 218–223
failure to disclose documents, 208
lawful interests, protection of 52, 166, 171
location, 114
public functions, disclosure for proper performance of, 166
Dismissal of tribunal
see **Court dismissal of tribunal**
Dispute, definition of a
'difference', meaning of, 15
gap-filling by tribunals, 15
Documents
documents-only basis, arbitration on, 185, 187
evidence, 174–175, 181–182
failure to disclose documents, 208
inspection, 174–175, 181–182
presentation, 174–175, 181–182
reduction or rectification, 38, 40, 90–91, 242, 244–245
reviews, 181–182
specification, 220, 221
Domestic arbitration
definition, 14–15
Draft awards
challenging awards, 261–262
clerks, agents or employees, 192–194
common law, 261
corrections, 261
default rule, 260–262
discretion, 261
errors, 261–262
fees and expenses, 264
institutional rules, 261

jurisdiction, excess of, 262
parties, power to send draft award to, 261
representations, obligation to consider, 261
serious irregularity, 261
stated case procedure, 261
time limits, 261–262
Duress
sist, 35

EC law
see **EU law**
ECHR
see **European Convention on Human Rights**
Eligibility to act as arbitrators
age, 110
Arbitration (Scotland) Bill, 110
capacity, 110
mandatory rules, 109–110
qualifications, 121, 123, 126, 294
Email, fax or other electronic means
commencement of arbitration, notice of, 103–104
service and formal communications, 330–333
Employment
see also **Clerks, agents or employees**
arbitrability of disputes, 93
Enforcement of arbitral awards
adjournment, 43, 79–80
anonymity in legal proceedings, 49–50
appeals, 41, 42–43, 291–292
applications, 41–42
authentication, 41
challenge proceedings, 42–43
common law, 42, 43–44
corrections, awards subject to, 42–43
Court of Session, 44
declining enforcement, 41–42
discretion, 41–42, 44
exception, reduction by, 42
final and binding nature of awards, 38
foreign awards, 44, 56–58, 94, 100
governing law, 24–25
incapable of being performed, agreements which are, 36
interim measures, 225
jurisdiction, 41, 43–4, 291–292
no part in proceedings, persons who take, 47–48
notification of proceedings, 42
outside UK, enforcement, 38
part awards, 43, 260
prohibition on enforcement, 41–42
public policy, 42
registration, 41, 43–44
resisting enforcement, 48
scope of application of Act, 44
seat, awards with no, 44
security, 43
setting aside by exception not contemplated, 42
sheriff court, 44
signing awards, 250–251
sist, 43
transitional provisions, 100
warrants, 41

345

Index

Equality
fairness, 164
full opportunity to present case, 164
general duties of tribunal, 158–159, 164–165
inequality of arms, 258
neutrality of arbitrator, 165
professional help, inability to afford, 164–165
provisional awards, 258
resources, differences in, 164–165
unfair contract terms, 164

Equity
awards, 236–237, 240

Errors
see also **Legal error appeals**
clerical, typographical or other errors arising by accident or omission, 268, 269, 270–271
date of awards, 256
draft awards, 261–262
reasons for awards, 254–255
seat of arbitration, 251

Estoppel
claims and defences timeously, failure to lodge, 200
refusal of recognition or enforcement, 60–61
sist, 32, 37

Ethics
appointment of arbitrators or tribunal, 113
Code of Ethics, 113
public policy, 65–76
refusal of recognition or enforcement, 75–76

European Convention on Human Rights (ECHR)
appointment of arbitrators, challenges to, 122
conflicts of interest, 117, 119
independence and impartiality, 158–162

EU law
breach as ground for refusing to enforce award, 78
Brussels Convention, 234, 286
cautions, 234
choice of law, 238–239
Civil Jurisdiction and Judgments Act 1982, 19, 44, 216
competition, 78
foreign awards, enforcement of, 44
Lugano Convention, 19, 234, 286
public policy, 78
Rome Convention 1980, 238–240

Evidence
see also **Experts**
abroad, havers resident, 220
absence of evidence, 177–179
abuse, 221
admissibility, 174–176
appeals, 176–178, 223, 292
arbitral proceedings, 174–187, 205, 218–223
arbitration agreements, failure to comply with, 208
assistance in taking evidence, requests for, 219
awards,
  authentication or certification, 80–81
  challenging, 179
  reduction of, 176, 187
calls, 220, 222
checklist, 180
civil proceedings, definition of, 229
commissioners, appointment of, 219–220, 229
common law, 176, 187, 222
confidentiality, 222–223
continuation of arbitration, 219, 223
court intervention, limiting, 221
cross-examination, 183–185
default rule, 174–187
delay, 220–221, 223
directions, failure to comply with, 208
disclosure, court's power to order, 168–169, 218–223
discretion, 221
documents, review of, 181–182
exhaustion of arbitral remedies, 221
expenses, 220–221, 222, 223
facts, finding of, 176–180
fairness, 220–221, 223
finality of decisions, 223
fishing diligence, 220, 221
fraud, 302
governing law, 177
identity and address of haver, 220
immunity from disclosure, 223
independence and impartiality, 220–221
initiative of tribunal, 174
inquisitorial system, 183–185, 221
inspection or presentation of documents, 174–175, 181–182, 229
inventories, production of, 214
jurisdictional appeals, 282
legal error appeal, 176–178
lodgement of documents, 222
mandatory rule, 218–223
materiality, 174
opportunity to present case, 66–67
oral evidence, 229
orders for disclosure, 218–223
originals, 182
Outer House, 221, 223
preservation of property, 198
privilege, waiver of, 222
procedure, 221–223
process, lodging bundles known as the, 222
production of documents, 20–22
property, 198
questioning parties, 174–175, 183
questions of law, 176–179
recovery of evidence, 218–223, 229
refusal of recognition or enforcement, 80–82
relevance, 174, 182, 197, 220, 222
res gestae, 223
reviews, 223
rules of evidence, 175, 177–178, 187
service or intimation, 221–222
sheriff court, 221, 222, 223
specification of documents, 220, 221
substantial injustice, 223
taking evidence, rules on, 219

textbooks, 222
time limits, 221
tribunal, role of, 174
unawareness of evidence, 66–67
weight, 174, 176
witnesses,
   arbitrators contacting, 183–185
   independence and impartiality, 184
   questioning, 183–184
Executors
   death, 328
Exhaustion of other remedies
   evidence, 221
   jurisdictional appeals, 313–314
   legal error appeals, 313–314
   serious irregularity appeals, 313–314
Expenses
   see **Fees and expenses**
Experts
   administrative matters, 197–198
   appointment, 196–197
   arbitral proceedings, 196–198
   Civil Procedure Rules, 197
   costs, 197
   court-appointed experts, 197
   default rule, 196–198
   expert determination, 14, 108–109
   fees and expenses, 198, 263, 275
   hot-tubbing, 185
   immunity, 323
   inspection of property, 198
   institutional rules, 197
   judges as arbitrators or umpires, 87
   natural justice, 197
   opinions, 196
   preservation, 198
   questioning experts, 196
   representations, opportunity to make, 196
   resignation of arbitrators, 135
   sampling, 198
   serious irregularity appeals, 297
   technical issues, advice on, 197–198
   tribunal-appointed experts (TAE), 197–198
   umpires, 87

Facts, finding of
   evidence, 176–180
   legal error appeals, 308–309
   referral of points of law, 211–212
Failure to attend hearings or provide evidence
   awards, proceeding with, 205
   default rule, 205
   due process, 205
   ill-health, 205
   institutional rules, 205
   reason, lack of good, 205
Failure to lodge claims or defences timeously
   abuse of process, 202
   awards, status of, 200–201
   default rule, 199–204
   delay, 199–200
   discretion, 200–201
   estoppel, 200
   expenses awards, 200
   fairness, 199
   inexcusable and inordinate delay, 202–203
   institutional rules, 200

interim awards, 201
prejudice, causing, 199, 202
reason for the delay, lack of good, 199–200
serious irregularity, 203–204
striking out for want of prosecution, 201–203
substantial risk to fair resolution of issues, 199
termination of arbitration, 200
Failure to comply with tribunal directions or arbitration agreements
   adverse inferences, 206, 208
   awards, making, 206
   cause, without sufficient, 206
   continuing with arbitration, 206
   default rule, 205–208
   defence submissions, service of, 208
   disclose documents, failure to, 208
   discretion, 207, 209
   dismissal of claims, 208
   dormant arbitrations, 206
   evidence, 208
   orders to comply, tribunal's power to make, 206–208
   partial failure, 206–207
   peremptory orders, 206, 207, 208
   provisional awards, 206
   remedies, 208–209
   service of orders, 207
   subject matter of orders to comply, parties not entitled to rely on, 206
   time limits for compliance, 207
Fair hearings
   appointment of arbitrators, challenges to, 122
   conflicts of interest, 117
   independence and impartiality, 159
   legal error appeals, 310, 311
   resignation of arbitrators, 135–136, 140
   serious irregularity appeals, 293, 294
Fairness
   see also **Fair hearings**
   appointment of arbitrators, challenges to, 121
   claims timeously, failure to lodge,199
   confidentiality, 168–169
   default rule, 328–329
   defences timeously, failure to lodge, 199
   definition, 162–163
   delay, 163–164
   equality, 164
   evidence, 220–221, 223
   founding principle of Act, as, 11, 12, 158, 162–163
   general duties of tribunal, 158, 162–163
   institutional rules, 329
   legal representation, 195
   mandatory rules, 26–27
   natural justice, 162–163
   object, loss of right to, 323
   opportunity to present case, 162
   oral hearings, 162, 186
   payments into court, 317–318
   removal of arbitrators, 125, 131
   representatives, 195
   seat of arbitration, 18
   serious irregularity appeals, 163
   service and formal communications, 334

Index

time limits, 218
witnesses, 184–185, 220–221, 223
Fees and expenses
  abroad, security from parties resident 286–287
  allocation between parties, 281
  appeals, 43, 262–263, 265, 277, 281–283, 312, 317
    Auditor of Court of Session, set by, 277
    legal error appeals, 306, 308, 312, 317
    serious irregularity, 281, 294, 298, 299, 303, 312
    time limits, 262–263
  arbitral appointments referee, 263, 274, 275–276, 277
  arbitration expenses, 141–142, 263, 273–289, 303
  Auditor of Court of Session, set by, 275, 277–280
  awards,
    failure to pay, 262–265
    final and binding nature, 266
    reasons, 316
    setting aside, 282
  calculation of amount, 275, 277–282
  capacity, 141
  case management, 163
  caution for expenses, 227, 228, 233, 286–287, 317
  clerks, agents or employees, 193, 275
  commercial rate, 275
  common law, 278–280, 282, 283, 285, 286
  contractual agreement, 277
  correction of awards, 270
  costs, definition of 274
  court intervention, 263–264, 275
  default rule, 273–289
  defences timeously, failure to lodge, 200
  definition of arbitration expenses, 263, 273–274
  delivery of awards, refusal of, 262–264
  deposits, 142
  discretion, 263–264, 279
  dismissal of tribunal by court, 133
  draftsman's fees, 264–265
  estimates, 279
  evidence, 220–221, 222, 223
  excessive amount, 264
  experts, 198, 263, 275
  final awards, 266, 288–289
  financially weak parties, 287–288
  founding principles of Act, 11, 12, 158, 162–165
  general duties of tribunal, 158, 162–163
  guardians ad litem, expenses and remuneration and, 227
  hearing facilities, 275
  indemnity basis, 279
  independence and impartiality, 327
  inoperative, where agreement is, 37
  institutional rules, 278, 281, 285, 287
  interest, 245, 247
  interim interdicts, 286
  interim measures, 233, 235, 285–286
  joint and several liability, 263, 275–277, 284
  judges as arbitrators or umpires, 87, 89
  judicial review, 277
  judicial render, 283–284
  jurisdiction, 152, 155, 156, 157, 312, 317
  legal and other expenses, 274, 278–279
  legal error appeals, 306, 308, 312, 317
  liability for arbitration expenses, 139, 140, 142, 274–278, 281–285
  limitation of recoverable arbitration expenses, 287–289
  mandatory rule, 165, 276, 284–285
  meeting facilities, 275
  non-payment, power to withhold awards for, 262–265
  objections to jurisdiction, 152, 155
  offers, making 283–284
  other expenses, definition of, 274–275
  part awards, 282, 287, 288–289
  party-party basis, 279–280
  payments into court, 262, 317–318
  pre-dispute agreements on liability, ban on, 284–285
  provisional awards, 287, 288
  reasonableness, 280, 282
  reasons for awards, 316
  recoverable arbitration expenses, 275, 277–289
  reduction, 142
  referral of points of law, 211, 212, 213–214
  removal of arbitrators, 124, 142
  remuneration of arbitrator, 276
  repayment, 139, 142, 198, 275, 277
  representations, 279
  resignation of arbitrators, 141–142
  reviews, 262
  seat of arbitration, 18
  security, 43, 142, 227, 228, 233, 276, 285–287, 312, 317
  serious irregularity, 279, 281, 294, 298, 299, 303, 312, 317
  settlements, 268, 283
  several liability, 276–277, 284
  sist, 37, 233
  stated case, 274
  taxation of expenses, 279, 280
  tenure, termination of, 141–142
  test for awards of expenses, 283–284
  third parties, 263, 274, 275–276, 277
  time limits, 200, 218
  umpires, 87, 89
  waiver, 276
  witnesses, 220–221, 222, 223
Final and binding nature of awards
  appeals, 38, 40, 291–292, 295, 304
  assignment, 39
  challenging awards, 40
  correction of awards, 270
  deeds or other documents, rectification or reduction of, 38, 40
  default rule, 38
  enforcement of awards outside UK, 38
  fees and expenses, payment of, 266, 288–289
  informal dispute resolution, 72
  jurisdictional appeals, 152, 158, 291–292
  legal error appeals, 304
  mandatory rules, 39–40
  New York Convention 1958, 57, 71–72
  persons claiming through parties, as binding on, 39

Index

provisional awards, 38, 40
reconsideration of awards, 266
rectification, 38, 40, 266
refusal of recognition or enforcement, 71–72
res judicata, 39
Scottish Arbitration Rules, 38
scrutiny of awards under institutional rules, 40
serious irregularity appeals, 295
third parties, 38, 39–40
trade associations, 39

Final provisions
definitions, 95–96

Finality
see also **Final and binding nature of awards**
anonymity in legal proceedings, 52
court decisions, 135, 139, 306, 220–221
evidence, decisions on, 223
liability of arbitrators, 139
referral of points of jurisdiction, 158
referral of points of law, 212
resignation of arbitrators, 135
time limits, 218
witnesses, 220–221

Financial resources
financially weak parties, 287–288
incapable of being performed, agreements which are, 36

Fishing diligence
evidence, 220, 221

Foreign law
disapplication of foreign law, 254, 255
interest, 247–248
procedural law, 29
reasons for awards, 254, 255
referral of points of law, 211
seat of arbitration, 29

Formal communications
see **Service and formal communications**

Forum, law of the
governing law, 24

Founding principles of Act
see also **Delay; Fairness; Fees and expenses; Independence and impartiality**
arbitration agreements as foundation of jurisdiction, 40
construction of the Act, 11–12
court intervention, limits on, 11, 12–13, 33
general principles, 11
object of arbitration, 12
party autonomy, 11, 12, 33
public interest, safeguards in the, 11
ranking of principles, 11

Fraud
arbitrability of disputes, 93
evidence, 302
serious irregularity appeals, 293, 300–301
setting aside awards, 300

Freezing orders
interim measures, 226

Frustration
arbitration agreements, validity of, 147

Functus officio
termination of arbitration, 265

General duties of tribunal
confidentiality, 166–173
delay, avoiding, 158, 163–164, 165
equal treatment, 158–159, 164–165
expenses, avoiding, 158, 164, 165
fairness, 158, 162–163
independence and impartiality, 158–162
mandatory rules, 158–165
opportunity to put case, giving parties, 158
privacy of deliberations, 173–174

General importance, decisions of
legal error appeals, 309–310

Governing law
arbitrability of disputes, 94
arbitration agreements, 22–25, 37, 147–148
choice of law, 23–25, 239
confidentiality, 171–172
conflicts of interest, 239
court, determination by, 23–24
enforcement, refusal of, 24–25
evidence, 177
forum, law of the, 24
implied choice of law, 24–25
inoperative, where agreement is, 37
international arbitration agreements, 23
main agreements, law governing, 23–24
non-specification of governing law, 23
Scots law, 23
seat of arbitration, 22–23, 29
separability, 24
sist, 34–35, 37

Guardian ad litem
expenses and remuneration, 227

Hearings
see also **Fair hearings; Oral hearings**
attend hearings, failure to, 204
awards, reconsideration of, 185
challenges to arbitrators, 185
concurrent hearings, 208–209
consolidated hearings, 208–210
cross-examination, 185
de novo hearings, 290
entitlement, 185
expenses of hearing facilities, 275
fairness, 186
independence and impartiality, 186
legal error appeals, 310
oral hearings, 144, 185 187
serious irregularity, 186
tribunal's power to determine scope of

Historical background
common law, 1
legislation, 1

Human rights
see **European Convention on Human Rights; Human Rights Act 1998**

Human Rights Act 1998
independence and impartiality, 159

Illegality
competence-competence, 76
public policy, 75–76
refusal of recognition or enforcement, 75–76
separability, 22, 76

Immunity
appointing arbitral institutions, of, 322–323
arbitral appointments referee, 322

349

arbitration agreements, breach of, 321
arbitrators, 139–140, 249, 320–323
  bad faith, 320, 321
  clerks, agents or employees, 320, 322–323
  common law, 320
  dismissal of tribunal by court, 133
  evidence, 223
  experts, witnesses and legal representatives, 323
  institutional rules, 321, 322
  judicial immunity, 323
  mandatory rule, 320–323
  resignation of arbitrators, 135, 321–322
  signing awards, 249
  state or sovereign immunity, 63
  third parties, 323
  tribunal, of, 320–323
  valuers, 14
  vicarious liability, 323
Impartiality
  see **Independence and impartiality**
Impossibility
  incapable of being performed, agreements which are, 35–36
  sist, 37
Improperly conducted arbitration
  composition of tribunal not in agreed form, 68
  procedural irregularity, 68–69
  refusal of recognition or enforcement, 67–69
  time limits, 69
Incapable of being performed, agreements which are
  costs, inability to pay, 36
  delay, 36
  enforcement of awards, doubts over, 36
  financial resources, lack of, 36
  impossibility, 35–36
Incapacity
  see **Capacity**
Independence and impartiality
  appeals, 162, 293, 294
  appointment of arbitrator, 113, 117, 121, 123, 161–162
  challenges to appointments, 122–123
  conflicts of interest, 117–118, 159, 162
  de minimis approach, 159–160
  definition, 117–118, 158–162
  delay, 327
  dismissal of tribunal by court, 131–133
  equality, 164–165
  European Convention on Human Rights, 159, 161–162
  evidence, 220–223
  fair hearings, 159
  fees and expenses, 327
  founding principle, as, 11, 159
  general duty of tribunal, as, 158–162
  Human Rights Act 1998, 159
  institutional rules, 327
  justifiable doubts, 160–161
  mandatory rules, 26–27
  object, loss of right to, 325, 326–327
  oral hearings, 186
  Outer House, 327
  professional help, inability to afford, 164–165

real danger test, 160–161
reasonable apprehension of bias test, 160–161
reasonable likelihood test, 160
reconsideration of awards, 327
removal of arbitrators, 125, 128–131, 161–162, 185
serious irregularity appeals, 162, 293, 294
service and formal communications, 334
witnesses, arbitrators, contacting, 184
Injunctions
  see **Interdicts or interim interdicts; Specific implement**
Inoperative, where agreement is
  governing law, 37
  inconvenience or expense, 37
  interpretation, 36
Inquisitorial system
  evidence, 183–185, 221
Insolvency
  diligence on the dependence, 227
  security, 227, 228, 229
Inspection
  evidence, 174–175, 181–182
Interdicts or interim interdicts
  arbitration agreements, 231
  arbitrator, power of the, 231, 243
  awards, 242–243, 244
  balance of convenience, 231–232
  common law, 231
  contempt of court, 231
  court, power of the, 231–232
  Crown proceedings, 243
  definition, 231
  fees and expenses, 286
  interim measures, 226, 231–232
  provisional interdicts, 231–232, 243–244
  urgent cases, 231
Interest
  awards, 245–248
  calculation, 245–248
  claimed and outstanding when the arbitration began, on whole or part of any amount, 245
  common law, 246, 247
  compound interest, 247
  correction of awards, 270
  declarator, 246
  different provisions in respect of different amounts, 245, 247
  discretion, 245, 247
  expenses, 245, 247
  foreign law, 247–248
  mandatory rule, 245–248
  manner agreed by the parties, in, 246
  no effect on other power to award interest, 246
  outstanding when arbitration begins, sums which are, 246
  parties, power of the, 247–248
  period for which interest is payable, 245
  period from date of award to the date of payment, 247
  period up to the date of the award, in respect of, 245, 246, 247
  post-award interest, 247
  rate of interest, 245, 247–248, 297
  serious irregularity appeals, 297

Index

whole or part of any amount ordered to be paid, 245
Interests of justice
 confidentiality, 52, 166, 171
Interim measures
 appeals, 226
 arbitral proceedings, 223–226
 arbitration agreements, 226
 cautions, 233, 234
 consent of tribunal, 225–226, 235
 continuation of arbitration, 225, 235–236
 court's powers, 225–236
 default rule, 225–236
 delay, 235
 depositions, power to take, 233
 diligence on the dependence, 227–228, 229–231
 fees and expenses, 233, 235, 285–286
 freezing orders, 226
 interdicts or interim interdicts, 226, 231–232
 interim attachment, warrants of, 227–228, 230, 233
 interim possession of property, orders for, 233
 lodgement, 235
 procedure, 234–236
 property, 227, 233
 recognition and enforcement, 225
 reinstatement, orders for, 233
 remedies for refusal of consent, 226
 reviews, 225
 safeguarders, appointment of, 226–227
 sale of property, 227
 security, 225, 227–229
 sheriff court, applications to, 234–235
 sist, 233
 specific implement, 226, 233
 substantial injustice, 236
 time limits, 235
 urgency, 235
 witnesses,
  commission to take evidence, grant of, 236
  powers to take reports on evidence of, 233–234
International arbitration
 definition, 14–15
 sist, 30
Interpretation
 arbitration, 14–15, 114–115
 final provisions, 95–96
 founding principles of Act, 11–12
 inoperative, where agreement is, 36
 key terms, 13–16
Interviews
 appointment of arbitrators or tribunal, 113–114
Interim interdicts
 see **Interdicts or interim interdicts**
Intimation
 see **Service and formal communications**
Irregularity
 see **Procedural irregularity; Serious irregularities**

Joinder
 consolidation, 209
 New York Convention 1958, 58

Joint and several liability
 fees and expenses, 263, 275–277, 284
Judges as arbitrator or umpire
 appeals, 88, 89
 authorisation, 88
 authority in area of law, where judge is, 87–88
 commercial disputes, 86–87, 88
 expertise, 87–88
 fees, 89
 individual, appointment as an, 89
 Inner House, 89
 national security, 88
 power to act as arbitrator or umpire, 86–89
 reasons for appointment, 87–88
 simultaneously as judge and arbitrator, sitting, 89
 Technology and Construction Court, 87, 88
 when a judge may act, 88–89
Judicial involvement in arbitration
 see **Court intervention and court powers**
Judicial review
 exclusion of, 45–46, 232
 fees and expenses decision of Auditor of Court of Session, 277
 replacement by appeal, 232
Jurisdiction of court
 see **Court intervention and court powers**
Jurisdiction of tribunal
 see also **Jurisdictional appeals**
 arbitrability of disputes, 94
 arbitration agreements,
  existence of, 145–147
  extent of, 148
  founding principles of Act, 40
  invalidity of, 43, 145–148
 challenges, 47–48, 146
 competence–competence, 145
 confidentiality, 171
 continuance of arbitration, 155
 court intervention, limits on, 145
 draft awards, 262
 enforcement of awards, 41, 43, 44
 excess of jurisdiction, 43, 71, 148–151, 262
 foreign awards, enforcement of, 44
 founding principles of Act, 40
 lack of jurisdiction, 43, 44, 69–71, 145–148
 legal error appeals, 304, 311
 loss of right to object, 43, 151, 155, 323–326
 mandatory rule, 145–158
 no part in proceedings, persons who take, 47–48
 objections,
  loss of right to raise, 43, 151, 155, 323–326
  mandatory rule, 148–152, 323–324
 part of awards, enforcement of, 43
 party autonomy, 145
 power of tribunal to rule on own jurisdiction, 145–148, 156
 referral by tribunal,
  default rule, 154–155
  delay, 155
  procedure for referrals, 155–158
  saving of expense, 155

351

Index

review of determination by court
referral of points to court, 154–158
refusal of recognition or enforcement, 69–71
reviews of jurisdiction, 146
sist of legal proceedings, 145–146
termination of arbitration, 266
tribunal not properly constituted, 148
ultra petita, 71
validity of arbitration agreements, 43, 145–148

Jurisdictional appeals
appeals, 289–293, 297, 298
arbitration agreements, void, 312
awards,
    challenges, 153, 289–293, 312–319
    making, 154
    provisional awards, 259
challenges to jurisdiction, 47–48, 146, 259, 297, 298
compelling reason for Inner House to consider the appeal
confirmation of awards, 289
continuing with arbitration pending appeal, 152, 154
default rule, 153
delay, avoidance of, 154
discretion, 154
enforcement of awards, 291–292
evidence, 292
exhaustion of other remedies, 313–314
fees and expenses, security for, 312, 317
finality of appellate decisions, 152, 154, 155, 158, 289, 291–293
important point of principle or practice, 289
Inner House, 153–154, 291–292
judicial review, 153
lack of jurisdiction, 292
leave to appeal, 289, 293, 313
mandatory rule, 152–154
no part in proceedings, persons who take, 47–48
notice of appeal, 292, 312
objections to jurisdiction, 48, 151–155, 291–292, 323, 324–325
part awards, 291, 315–316
payment into court, 312–313, 317–319
period for appeal, 153–154
provisional appeals, 312, 314
provisional awards, 259, 312, 314
reasons for appeal, 312, 316
reconsideration of award by tribunal, 319–320
res judicata, 154, 158
reviews of jurisdiction, 146
serious irregularity appeals, 297, 298
setting–aside awards, 289–290, 292–293
substantial injustice, 293
time limits, 152, 153–154, 291, 312, 314–315
variation of awards, 289, 292–293

Justice
awards, 236–238, 240, 253
reasons for awards, 253

Key terms
definitions, 13–16

Land
specific implement, 244
Language
arbitral proceedings, 175
awards, translation of, 82
refusal of recognition or enforcement, 66
Law, points of
see **Referral of points of law**
Lawful interests, protection of
confidentiality, 52, 166, 171
Legal error appeals
arbitration agreements, 305, 312
awards,
    challenges, 304–311, 312–319
    confirmation, 307
cautions for expenses, 306
common law, 305
confirmation of award, 307
default rule 304–311
delay, 305, 308, 310–311
evidence, 176–178
exclusion of, 304–305
exhaustion of other remedies, 313–314
fair hearings, 310, 311
fees and expenses, 306, 308, 312, 317
finality of tribunal decisions, 304–306, 310
findings of fact deemed unalterable, 308–309
form of appeals, 310–311
further appeals, 311
general importance, decisions of, 309–310
hearings, decisions on applications without, 310
identification of points of law in leave applications, 306
institutional rules, 304
jurisdiction, 304, 311
leave to appeal, 304, 306–308, 310–311, 312, 313
notice of appeal, 312
non-Scots law, 305
obviously wrong decisions on points of Scots law, 309
open to serious doubt, decisions which are, 309–310
part awards, 315–316
payment into court, 312–313, 317–319
preconditions, 308–309
procedure, 306–311
provisional awards, 312, 314
reasons, 304, 306, 312, 316
reconsideration of award by tribunal, 306–307, 310–311
referral of points of law, relationship with, 215
remedies, 310–311, 313–314
repeals, 92
rules of court, 307–308
setting–aside of award, 292–293, 306–307, 310–311
substantially effect on party's rights, 306, 308
Supreme Court, exclusion of appeals to, 311
time limits, 306, 307–308, 310–311, 312, 314–315
tribunal asked to decide the point, 308

Index

Legal persons
  appointment of arbitrators or tribunal, 108–109
Legislation
  relationship of 2010 Act to other legislation, 5–6
  repeals, 91–92, 336
Liability of arbitrators
  applications, 139
  arbitrators, applications by, 139
  costs, quantum of additional, 140
  delay, quantum for, 140
  fees and expenses,
    entitlement to, 139, 140
    repayment, 139, 142
  finality of Outer House decision, 139
  immunity, 139–140, 320–322
  mandatory rule, 139–142
  parties, application by, 139
  removal of arbitrators, 127–128, 142
  replacements, 140
  resignation, 135–136, 139, 140, 321–323
  rule 15, applicability of, 139
  tenure, end of, 139–142
  unlimited liability, 142
  vicarious liability, 323
Limitation
  see **Time limits**
Limited liability partnerships (LLPs)
  appointment of arbitrators or tribunal, 109
Litigation
  see **Civil proceedings**
Litigiosity, notice of
  security, 227–228, 231
Location
  appointment of arbitrators or tribunal, 114
  disclosure, 114
  seat of arbitration, 16, 18, 19, 20
Loss of right to object
  appeals, 325
  arbitration agreements, arbitration not conducted in accordance with, 323, 325
  arbitrators, ineligibility of, 323, 325
  definition of objection, 325
  delay, 324
  fairness, 323
  independence and impartiality, 325, 326–327
  jurisdiction, 155, 323, 324–325
  mandatory rule, 323–326
  other agreements, arbitration not conducted in accordance with, 323
  rules, arbitration not conducted in accordance with, 323
  serious irregularity, 324–325
  timeous objections, 324–326

Mandatory rules
  default rules, 26–27
  delay, avoidance of, 26–27
  fairness, 26–27
  impartiality, 26–27
  list of rules, 25–26
  policy memorandum, 26–27

  removal of arbitrators, 26
Mandatory, sist of *see* **Security**
Meeting facilities
  fees and expenses, 275
Multi-party arbitration
  appointment of arbitrators or tribunal, 114–115
  awards, 96
  interpretation, 96
  parties, 114–115

National security
  judges as arbitrators or umpires, 88
Nationality
  appointment of arbitrators or tribunal, 108, 112
Natural justice
  appointment of arbitrators, challenges to, 122
  clerks, agents or employees, 194
  dismissal of tribunal by court, 133
  experts, 197
  fairness, 162–163
  public policy, 64–65, 77
  refusal of recognition or enforcement, 64–65, 77
  removal of arbitrators, 123
  resignation of arbitrators, 140
  serious irregularity appeals, 303
Natural persons
  appointment of arbitrators or tribunal, 108–109
Neutrality
  see **Independence and impartiality**
New York Convention on recognition and enforcement of foreign arbitral awards 1958
  see also **Refusal of recognition or enforcement of New York Convention awards**
  accession, 55
  amendment, 89–90
  arbitrability of disputes, 94
  Arbitration Act 1975, repeal of, 5
  arbitration agreements, 56–57
  binding nature of awards, 57
  challenging awards, 58
  compensation, plea of, 58
  declarations that state is subject to Convention, 56
  defence, 58
  definition of awards, 56
  Geneva Convention 1927, 6
  governing law, 24
  joinder, 58
  part awards, 58, 260
  place of arbitration, 256–257
  provisional awards, 259
  public policy, 300–301
  re-enactment of provisions in 2010 Act, 5–6
  reciprocity reservation, 56
  res judicata, 58
  seat of arbitration, 16, 56, 57, 256
  signing awards, 250–251
  sist, 30, 32–36, 38
  writing, definition of, 56–57

Index

Newspaper advertisements
service and formal communications, 333–334
Notification
see **Service and formal communications**
Number of arbitrators
appointment of arbitrators or tribunal, 68, 110–112, 114–115, 148, 189
default rules, 110–111
institutional rules, 110–111
international arbitration, 110–111
party autonomy, 110–111
removal of arbitrators, 124–125
sole arbitrators, 110, 111–112

Oaths or affirmations
default rule, 199
Objections
see also **Objections to jurisdiction**
appointments, 121–124
competence, 121
factual basis, 121, 123
loss of right to object, 323–32
mandatory rule, 323–326
reconstitution of tribunal, 143
time limits, 121, 123, 124
Objections to jurisdiction
see also **Jurisdictional appeals**
arbitration agreements, arbitration not conducted in accordance with, 323, 325
arbitrators, ineligibility of, 323, 325
awards,
after making of awards, 148
challenges, 149, 151–152
delay until awards made, 148
setting aside, 148, 151
competence-competence, 149–150
constitution of tribunal, after, 150
court, referral of points to, 154–158
default rule, 154–155
definition of objection, 325
delay, 149, 152, 291, 324
discretion, 152, 291
effect of objections, 148–149, 151–152
excess of jurisdiction, 148–151
expense, avoiding unnecessary, 152, 155
fairness, 323
independence and impartiality, 325, 326–327
jurisdiction, lack of, 323, 324–325
late objections, circumstances justifying, 150–151
loss of right to object, 43, 151, 155, 323–326
mandatory rule, 148–152, 155–158, 323–326
other agreements, arbitration not conducted in accordance with, 323
part termination of arbitration, 151–152
partial awards, setting aside, 148, 151–152
parties, by, 148–149
procedure for referral, 155–158
provisional awards, setting aside, 148, 151–152
referrals of points of jurisdiction, 154–158
rules, arbitration not conducted in accordance with, 323

rulings by tribunal, status of, 152
serious irregularity, 324–325
termination of arbitration, 148, 151–152
timeousness, 149–151, 153, 324–326
Online arbitrations
seat of arbitration, 16
Opportunity to present case
appointment of arbitrators, challenges to, 122
equality, 164
evidence, unawareness of, 66–67
fairness, 158, 162
general duties of tribunal, 158
language, 66
refusal of recognition and enforcement, 64, 66–67
removal of arbitrators, 124
representatives, 195
serious irregularity appeals, 298
Oral agreements
common law, 21
Oral hearings
awards, reconsideration of, 185
civil law countries, 187
credibility, assessment of, 144
cross-examination, 185
discretion, 185–186
fairness, 162, 186
independence and impartiality, 186
presumption of entitlement, 185
reconstitution of tribunal, 144
serious irregularity, 186
Orders
Scottish Ministers, powers of, 97
statutory instruments, 97
Oversman
see **Umpires**

Parallel regimes
transitional provisions, 98–101
Part awards
arbitrators, power of, 259–260
challenging awards, 260, 269
clarification, 260
common law, 259–260
counterclaims, 260
definition, 255, 259
different times on different aspects, awards at, 260
discretion, 260
enforcement, 43, 260
fees and expenses, 282, 287, 288–289
jurisdiction, 43, 148, 151–152, 291, 315–316
mandatory rule, 259–260
New York Convention 1958, 260
previous award was made, award must state whether, 255–256
res judicata, 260
serious irregularity appeals, 315–316
setting aside, 148, 151–152, 292–293
specification of matters to which part award relates, 259
Parties
see also **Capacity**
anonymity, 49–52
appointment of arbitrators or tribunal, 110–111, 113–115, 122

354

Index

arbitral proceedings, 194–196
autonomy, 11, 12, 27, 33, 110–111, 114, 145, 175
confidentiality, 166
death, 54, 328
default rules, 27
definition, 114–115
disclosure, 166
dismissal of tribunal, applications for, 132
draft awards, sending, 261
evidence, 174–175, 183
financially weak parties, 287–288
founding principles of Act, 11, 12, 33
interest, 247–248
jurisdiction, 45, 148–149
liability of arbitrators, 139
multi-party arbitrations, 114–115
no part in proceedings, persons who take, 47–48
number of arbitrators, 110–111
objections to jurisdiction, 148–149
questioning parties, 174–175, 183
removal of arbitrators, 124–125, 139
representation, 194–196, 323
seat of arbitration, 16, 17–18

Partnerships
appointment of arbitrators or tribunal, 108–109
limited liability partnerships, 109

Party representatives
default rule, 194–196
delay, 196
fairness, 195
immunity, 323
notice, 195–196
institutional rules, 195
legal privilege, 196
legal representation, 194–196
opportunity to present case, 195

Payments
see **Damages and payments, power to award**

Payments into court
amount, 318
court intervention, 317–318
delay and expenses, 317–318
fairness, 317–318
fees and expenses, 262
independence and impartiality, 317
jurisdictional appeals, 312–313, 317–319
legal error appeals, 312–313, 317–319
serious irregularity appeals, 312–313, 317–319
third parties, 318
time limits, 318–319

Peripatetic arbitrations
seat of arbitration, 16

Perjury
refusal of recognition or enforcement, 76–77
serious irregularity appeals, 302

Place of arbitration
applicable law, 189
arbitral proceedings, 174, 187–189
awards, 251, 256–257
default rules, 187–189
New York Convention, 256–257
seat, 16, 18, 19, 29, 57, 188–189
terminology, 188

Points of law
see **Referral of points of law**

Powers of the Court
see **Court intervention and court powers**

Prescription
commencement of arbitration, 84–85
Consumer Protection Act 1987, 85
default rules, 85
effect of Act on prescription and limitation, 84
interruption by arbitration, 83–85
negative prescription, 83, 85
positive prescription, 83, 84–85

Present case, opportunity to
see **Opportunity to present case**

Privacy
see also **Confidentiality**
arbitrator's failure to participate, disclosure of, 173–174
common law, 172–173
confidentiality, 168, 169, 171–173
default rule, 173
deliberations of tribunal, 173–174
discretion, 169
institutional rules, 173–174

Privilege
defamation, 166
evidence, 222, 229
legal privilege, 196
waiver, 222

Procedural irregularity
see also **Serious irregularity appeals**
amicable compositeurs, 69
improperly conducted arbitration, 68–69
provisional awards, 259
refusal of recognition or enforcement, 68–69
signature of awards, 250
witnesses, 184–185

Procedure
see **Arbitral proceedings; Procedural irregularity**

Professional help, inability to afford
equality, 164–165

Proof
see **Hearings**

Property
arbitrability of disputes, 93
arbitral proceedings, 198–199
arrestment on the dependence of moveable property, 227, 229–231
default rule, 198
evidence, preservation of, 198
inspection, preservation, sampling etc, 198
institutional rules, 199
interim possession, orders for, 233
sale of property, 227
security, 227–228, 229–230
tribunal powers relating to property, 198–199

Provisional awards
appeals, 259, 312, 314
arbitration agreements, failure to comply with, 206
arbitrators, power of, 257–259
common law, 257
correction of awards, 269
definition, 40, 255

Index

default rule, 257–259
directions, failure to comply with, 206
fees and expenses, 287, 288
final and binding nature of awards, 38, 40
inequality of arms, 258
jurisdictional challenge, 148, 151–152, 259, 312, 314
legal error appeals, 312, 314
New York Convention, 259
objections to jurisdiction, 148, 151–152
procedural irregularity, 259
remedies, 258
security, 258
serious irregularity appeals, 259, 293, 312, 314
previous award was made, award must state whether, 255–256

Public bodies or officer–holders
capacity, 62
confidentiality, 166
proper performance of duties, 166
refusal of recognition or enforcement, 62

Public functions
confidentiality, 166
proper performance, 166

Public holidays and weekends
time periods, calculation of, 335

Public interest
anonymity in legal proceedings, 52
confidentiality, 52, 166, 168, 170, 171
founding principles of Act, 11
interests of justice, 52

Public policy
due process, 64–65
enforcement of awards, 42, 59, 64–65, 73–78
EU law, breach of, 78
illegality or immorality, 75–76
improperly obtained awards, 76–77
international public policy, 75
natural justice, 64–65, 77
New York Convention awards, 59, 64–65, 73–78, 300–301
parts of awards, 75
perjury, 76–77
refusal of recognition or enforcement, 59, 64–65, 73–78
serious irregularity appeals, 293, 300–301

Qualifications of arbitrator
appointment of arbitrators, challenges to, 122, 123
removal of arbitrators, 126
serious irregularity appeals, 294

Ranking of principles
founding principles of Act, 11

Reasons for awards
adequacy of awards, 316
appeals, 254–255, 296–297, 299, 304, 306, 312, 316
challenging awards, 254
common law, 253
confidentiality of awards, 255, 316
correction or clarification of awards, 255
court orders, 254–255, 316
decisions of tribunal, 193
discretion, 253

dispensing with reasons, 253, 255
errors, 254–255
fees and expenses, 316
foreign law, misapplication of, 254, 255
form of reasons, 254
institutional rules, 253–255
jurisdictional appeals, 312, 316
justice, 253
legal error appeals, 304, 306, 312, 316
limited reasons, 253–254
majority of tribunal, of, 253
Outer House, 254–255
refusal of recognition or enforcement, 69
separate document, in, 255
serious irregularity, 255 , 296–297, 299, 312, 316
settlements, 268

Recognition of awards
see also **Refusal of recognition or enforcement of New York Convention awards**
interim measures, 225
New York Convention, 56–58, 94

Reconsideration of awards
confirmation of awards, 320
correction of awards, 270
final and binding nature of awards, 266
independence and impartiality, 327
jurisdictional appeals, 319–320
legal error appeals, 310–311, 319–320
mandatory rule, 319–320
new awards, making, 320
serious irregularity appeals, 294, 300, 303, 319–320
time limits, 303
uncertainty and ambiguity, removal of, 319–320

Reconstitution of tribunal
appeals, 143
commencement from beginning, 143–144
default rule, 142–144
discretion, 143–144
institutional rules, 143
objections, 143
oral argument, 144
procedure, 142
re-use of previous work, 144
tenure, termination of, 142–144
witnesses, 144

Recovery of evidence
Administration of Justice (Scotland) Act 1972 section 1, 229
admissibility of evidence , 174–176
civil proceedings, definition of, 229
commission for recovery, 229
confidentiality, 222–223
court's power to assist tribunal or parties, 219
inspection, photographing, preservation etc. of property, 229
mandatory rule, 218–223, 229
oral evidence, taking of, 229
privileged documents, 229
samples, taking of, 229
tribunal's powers, 229
witnesses, identity of, 229

Rectification
see also **Correction of awards**

Index

arbitrator, powers of, 244–245
awards, 38, 40, 242, 244–245, 266
common law, 245
decrees of court, 245
deeds or other documents, registration of reduction of rectification of, 90–91
final and binding nature of awards, 38, 40, 266
public registers, 245
Reduction
arbitrator, powers of, 244
awards, 1, 38, 40, 176, 187, 242, 244–245
deeds or other documents, registration of reduction of rectification of, 90–91
evidence, 176, 187
final and binding nature of awards, 38, 40
Referral of points of jurisdiction
agreement of parties, 156
applications, 155–157
appointment of arbitrators, 157
awards, making, 157
burden of proof, 156
competence-competence, 157
conditions for valid applications, 156–157
consent of parties, 155
continue proceedings, discretion to, 157–158
court intervention, 154–158
delay, avoidance of, 155, 157
discretion, 157–158
documents to be lodged with court, 214
exclusion of, 210
expenses, avoidance of, 155, 156, 157
finality of decisions, 158
good reason to determine the question, court satisfied that there is, 156
institutional rules, 155
loss of right to object, 155
mandatory rule, 155–158
objections, 154–158
point of law, 211–212
preconditions for operation of arbitration agreements, 156–157
procedure, 155–158
sist, 157
written agreements, 156
Referral of points of law
abuse, 210, 213
appeals, 215
arbitral proceedings, 210–215
arbitration agreements, 210, 213
arbitrators chosen by parties, decisions by, 211
binding opinions, 210
commercial actions, 211
consent, 211, 212, 213–215
continuation of arbitration pending determination, 212, 215
default rule, 210–215
delay, 213, 214, 215
discretion, 211–212
documents to be lodged with court, 214
exclusion of, 210
expenses, 211, 212, 213–214
fact, unreasonable findings on, 211–212
finality, 212
foreign law, 211
identification of point of law, 214

inventories of productions, intimation to other parties of, 214
legal error appeals, 215
mandatory rule, as, 212
mandatory safeguards, 210
point of law, 211–212
procedural law, points of, 211
procedure, 212–215
process, lodging bundles known as the, 214
reviews, 215
Scots law, points of, 211
service or intimation, 214
sist, 212
stated case procedure, replacement of, 210–211, 213
substantive law, points of, 211
validity conditions, 211–214
Referrals
see **Referral of points of jurisdiction; Referral of points of law**
Referees
see **Arbitral appointments referee (AAR)**
Reform process
approach of Act, 4–5
background, 4
legislation, relationship of Act to other, 5–6
Refusal of recognition or enforcement of New York Convention awards
adjournments, 79–80
appointment of arbitrators, 68
arbitrability under Scottish law, 74
arbitration agreements, production of original, 80–82
authenticated awards, 80–81
awards,
authentication or certification of, 80–81
grounds relating to, 69–74
translations, 82
binding, awards not yet, 71–72
burden of proof, 59–60, 65, 67, 69–70, 74
certificated awards, 80–81
challenge, awards open to, 71–72
common law, 82–83
composition of tribunal not in agreed form, 68
corporations, capacity of, 62
defences, 61–69
discretion, 60–61, 67, 78
due process, 64–65, 66
estoppel, 60–61
EU, breach of, 78
evidence, 66–67, 80–82
excess of jurisdiction, 71
exclusive grounds, 51
extra petita, 70
finality, 71–72
form, tribunal not in agreed, 68
grounds, 58–69
identity of arbitrators is unknown, where the, 65
illegality, 75–76
immorality, 75–76
improperly conducted arbitration, 67–69
improperly obtained awards, 76–77
incapacity, 58, 61–63
invalidity of agreements, 58, 62, 63–64

357

jurisdiction, lack of, 69–71
language, 66
matters not submitted to arbitration, 59
natural justice, 64–65, 77
notice of process or appointment of tribunals, 58, 64, 65
partial enforcement, 75, 78
perjury, 76–77
present case, inability to, 64, 66–67
procedural irregularity, 68–69
public authorities, capacity of, 62
public policy, 59, 64–65, 73, 74–78
reasons, 69
seat, law of the, 67
security, 59, 79–80
setting aside awards, 72–74
sist, 59, 78–79
state or sovereign immunity, 63
translations of agreements or awards, 82
ultra petita, 71

Registration of awards
preservation, for purposes of, 44

Reinstatement
interim measures, 233

Remedies
see also **Awards; Damages and payments, power to award; Interdicts and interim interdicts; Interest; Rectification; Reduction; Specific implement**
arbitration agreements, failure to comply with, 208–209
declaratory, 47–48, 242, 243, 246
directions, failure to comply with, 208–209
exhaustion of other remedies, 313–314
interim measures, 226
legal error appeals, 310–311, 313–314
provisional awards, 258
serious irregularity appeals, 303, 313–314

Remission of awards
removal of arbitrators, 126

Removal of arbitrators
3 person tribunals, 124–125
anonymity in legal proceedings, 50
arbitral appointment referees, 125
awards, remission of, 126
conflicts of interest, 129–130
court, by, 50, 125–132, 185
default rules, 124–125
fairness, 125, 131
fees and expenses, 124, 142
incapacity of arbitrator in arbitration, 125, 131
independence and impartiality, 125, 128–131, 161–162, 185
institutional rules, 124–126
liability, 127–128, 142
mandatory rules, 125–132
misconduct, 126–131
natural justice, 124
parties, 124–125, 139
representations, opportunity to make, 124
revocation of appointment, 125
qualifications, lack of, 126
substantial injustice, 126–132
tenure of arbitrators, 121, 139
third parties, 124
truncated tribunals, 125
witnesses, direct contact with, 127–128

Remuneration
arbitrators, 276
fees and expenses, 276
guardians ad litem, 227

Renvoi
choice of law, 238

Repeals
list, 91–92, 336

Replacement of arbitrators
liability of arbitrators, 140

Representations
clarification or removal of ambiguity in awards, on, 271–272
correction of awards, 269
dismissal of tribunal by court, 133
draft awards, 261
experts, 196
fees and expenses, 262
removal of arbitrators, 124

Representatives of parties
default rule, 194–196
delay, 196
equality, 164–165
fairness, 195
immunity, 323
institutional rules, 195
legal privilege, 196
legal representation, 194–196
notice, 195–196
opportunity to present case, 195
professional help, inability to afford, 164–165

Res judicata
final and binding nature of awards, 39
jurisdictional appeals, 154, 158
New York Convention 1958, 58
settlements, 266

Resignation of arbitrators
appeals, 140
appointment, challenges to, 121, 123, 135, 137
authorisation, applications for, 138
consent of parties, 135, 136–137
consequences, agreements on, 140
contractual right to resign, 135–137
expert opinions, disapplication or modification of rule on, 135
fair hearings, 135–136, 140
fees and expenses, 141–142
finality of Outer House decision, 135
grounds, 136–137
immunity, 135, 321–322
incapacity to act, 137
institutional rules, 136
legal advice, taking, 137–138
liability, 135–136, 139, 140, 321–322
mandatory rule, 135–139
natural justice, 140
notice, 135, 138
process, 135–136, 138–139
refusal of resignation, 138–139
tenure of arbitrators, 121, 141–142

Resources
differences, in, 164–165
financially weak parties, 287–288
incapable of being performed, agreements which are, 36

Index

Respond, opportunity to
see **Opportunity to present case**
Reviews
  documents, 181–182
  evidence, 223
  final and binding nature of awards, 38, 40
  interim measures, 225
  jurisdiction, 146
  referral of points of law, 215
  time limits, 218
  witnesses, 223
Revocation of appointments
  challenges to appointment, 122
  tenure of arbitrators, 120
Royal Assent
  date, 11, 98, 102

Safeguarders, appointment of
  capacity, 226–227
  guardian ad litem, expenses and remuneration and, 227
  interim measures, 226–227
Sampling
  evidence, 198, 229
Savings
  ancillary provision, 96
***Scott v Avery* clauses**
  sist, 37–38
  statutory arbitrations, 37
Scottish Arbitration Rules
  amendment, 89
  approach of Act, 5
  arbitral appointments referee, 86
  arbitration not conducted in accordance with rules, 323
  challenging awards, 91
  deeds or other documents, registration of reduction of rectification of, 90–91
  default rules, 5, 27–29
  founding principles of Act, 11
  mandatory rules, 25–27
  modification or disapplication, 27–29
  procedural law, 20
  Scottish Arbitration Code, alternative title of, 5
  seat of arbitration, 16, 20
  text, 102–335
Seat of arbitration
  abroad, arbitrations held, 256
  awards must state seat of awards, 251
  choice of law, 63–64
  close connection, 19
  court, designation by, 16, 18–19, 25
  designation of seat, 16–19, 25
  disclosure of location, 114
  enforcement of arbitral awards, 67
  England, seat in, 256–257
  errors, 251
  expenses, avoidance of unnecessary, 18
  fairness, 18
  first seised, court, 19
  foreign procedural law, invoking a, 29
  governing law, 22–23, 29
  implied designation, 17–18
  injunctions, 19
  invalid or ambiguous designation, 18–19
  juridical seat, 188–189
  New York Convention 1958, 16, 56, 57, 256
  no seat, awards with, 44
  online arbitrations, 16
  parties, designation by, 16, 17–18
  peripatetic arbitrations, 16
  physical location of proceedings, 16, 18, 19, 29, 57
  place of arbitration, 188–189
  procedural law, 19–20
  refusal of recognition or enforcement, 67
  Scotland, seat in, 16–20, 22–23, 57, 216, 251
  serious irregularity, 251
  signing, place of, 57, 256–257
  sist, 37
  statutory arbitrations, 17, 53–54
  substantive law, effect on, 16, 19–20
  third parties, designation by, 16, 17, 18, 25
  time for designation, 18
  time limits, 216
  tribunal, designation by, 16, 17, 25
Security
  abroad, persons resident, 286–287
  adjournments, 79–80
  amount, 80
  appeals, 43
  arrestment on the dependence of moveable property, 227, 229–231
  awards,
    enforcement, 43
    provisional awards, 258
    sums claimed in, 227
  Brussels Convention, 286
  caution, provision of a, 227, 228, 233–234, 286–287, 317
  consignation, 230–231
  diligence on the dependence, 227–228, 229–231
  discretion, 227, 317
  enforcement of awards, 43, 59, 79–80
  fees and expenses, 142, 228, 233–234, 276, 285–287, 317
  forms of security, 287, 317
  insolvency, 227, 228, 229
  interim attachment, 227–228, 230
  interim measures, 225, 227–229
  litigiosity, notice of, 227–228, 231
  mandatory, sist of, 233–234
  moveable property, 227–228, 229–230
  property, recovery of, 227–228, 229–230
  provisional awards, 258
  refusal of recognition or enforcement, 59, 79–80
  warrants for arrestment or inhibition on the dependence, 228, 229–231
Separability
  arbitration agreements, 21–22, 147
  governing law, 24
  illegality, 22
Serious irregularities
  see also **Serious irregularity appeals**
  clarification or removal of ambiguity in awards, 273
  clerks, agents or employees, 192
  delay, 163
  draft awards, 261
  fees and expenses, 279, 281

Index

oral hearings, 186
previous award was made, award must state whether, 256
reasons for awards, 255
seat of arbitration, 251
time limits, 218
Serious irregularity appeals
   all issues, failure to deal with, 293, 298–299
   appointment of arbitrators, lack of proper notice of, 294, 298
   arbitral appointments referee
      irregularities, 294
      outwith their powers, acting, 293, 299
   arbitration agreements,
      failure to conduct arbitration in accordance with, 293, 294, 297–298
      void agreements, 312
   awards
      challenges, 293–304, 312–319
      confirmation, 294, 303
      reconsideration, 294, 303
      uncertainty and ambiguity, 293, 299–300
   challenges to awards, 293–304, 312–319
   claims timeously, failure to lodge, 203–204
   conduct arbitration in accordance with other agreements, failure to, 293, 294–295, 297–298
   confirmation of awards, 294, 303
   correction of awards, 270
   defences timeously, failure to lodge, 203–204
   definition of serious irregularity, 293, 295–296
   excess of power, 298
   exhaustion of other remedies, 313–314
   experts, 297
   fair hearings, 303–304
   fairness, 163, 293, 294
   fees and expenses, 281, 294, 298, 299, 303, 312, 317
   finality of awards, 295
   fraud, 293, 300–301
   further appeals, 303–304
   incapacity of arbitrator, 293
   independence and impartiality, 162, 293, 294
   institutional rules, 298
   interest rate, 297
   jurisdictional challenges, 297, 298
   leave to appeal, 294, 303–304, 313
   mandatory rule, 293–304
   natural justice, 303
   no part in proceedings, persons who take, 47–48
   notice of appeal, 294, 312
   part awards, 315–316
   payment into court, 312–313, 317–319
   payment of sums of money, 300
   perjury, 302
   powers, tribunal acting outwith, 298
   present case, opportunity to, 298
   primary issues, 299
   provisional awards, 259, 312, 314
   public policy, 293, 300–301
   qualifications, arbitrator's lack of, 294
   qualifying irregularity, 296–297
   reasons, 296–297, 299, 312, 316
   reconsideration of award by tribunal, 294, 300, 303, 319–320
   remedies, 303, 313–314
   reprehensible or unconscionable conduct, 302
   rules, failure to conduct arbitration in accordance with, 293, 297–298
   setting aside awards, 294–295, 300, 303
   subsidiary issues, 299
   substantial injustice, 296–297, 298–299
   Supreme Court, 303–304
   third parties,
      irregularities, 294
      outwith their powers, acting, 293, 299
   time limits, 295, 300, 303–304, 312, 314–315
   tribunal acting outwith its powers, 293
   uncertainty or ambiguity as to the award's effect, 293, 299–300
Service and formal communications
   arbitration agreements, failure to comply with, 207
   default rule, 330–334
   defence submissions, 208
   directions, failure to comply with, 207
   email, fax or other electronic means, 330–333
   enforcement of awards, 42
   evidence, 221–222
   fairness, 334
   first class post, 332–333
   formal communications, definition of, 330
   hand delivery, 332
   independence and impartiality, 334
   institutional rules, 330–331
   methods, 330
   newspaper advertisements, 333–334
   not reasonably practicable, communications which are not, 333–334
   private postal services, 333
   referral of points of law, 214
   time limits, 217, 334–335
   witnesses, 221–222
   writing, 331–332
Setting aside awards
   competent authority, definition of, 72–73
   enforcement of awards, 42, 72–74
   fees and expenses, 282
   fraud, 300
   jurisdictional appeals, 148, 151, 289–290
   part awards, 148, 151–152, 292–293
   provisional awards, 148, 151–152
   reconsideration, 294
   refusal of recognition or enforcement, 72–74
   serious irregularity appeals, 294–295, 300, 303
Settlements
   awards, 265, 266–268
   challenging awards, 268
   consent awards, 266–268
   discretion to make an award, 267
   early settlement, 265–268
   fees and expenses, 268, 283
   form of award, settlements in, 266–267
   notification, 265, 266

Index

promotion of settlement by tribunal, 267–268
reasons for awards, 268
res judicata, 266
termination of arbitration, 265–268
Several liability
  fees and expenses, 276–277, 284
Signature of awards
  arbitrators, 249–250
  assenting to award, all those, 249–250
  date of award, 252–253
  dissenting arbitrators, 249–250
  enforcement of awards, 250–251
  immunity of arbitrators, 249
  institutional rules, 250
  New York Convention 1958, 57, 250–251
  place of signing, 57
  procedural irregularity, 250
  same time and same place, 249–250
  seat of arbitration, 57, 256–257
Sist
  abroad, orders on parties who are, 30, 37–38, 233
  adjournments, 79
  anonymity in legal proceedings, 50
  applications, 29–32
  arbitration agreements, existence of, 31–32, 146
  arbitration seated outwith Scotland, 30, 37–38
  awards, challenges to, 43
  burden of proof, 34–35, 37
  capacity, 35
  common law, 30, 33
  court, definition of, 32
  court, intervention by the, 32–33
  discretion, 233
  duress, 35
  effect of sist, 32
  enforcement of awards, 43, 59, 78–79
  estoppel, 32, 37
  expenses, 37, 233
  governing law, 34–35, 37
  grounds, 29–34
  impossibility, 37
  incapable of being performed, where agreement is, 35–36
  interim measures, 233
  international arbitration, 30
  jurisdiction, 145–146, 157
  legal proceedings, 29–34
  mandatory orders, 233–234
  New York Convention 1958, 30, 32–36, 38
  non-Scottish arbitrations, 37–38
  notice of proceedings, 32
  prevention of bringing proceedings, 29–30
  referral of points of law, 212
  refusal of recognition or enforcement, 59, 78–79
  Scott v *Avery* clauses, 37–38
  Scottish Advisory Committee on Arbitration Law, 32–33
  seat of arbitration, 37
  statutory arbitrations, 30, 37
  steps taken in legal proceedings, 32–33
  tribunals, legal proceedings before, 32
  validity of arbitration agreements, 31–32, 34–35

void provisions in arbitration agreements, 34–37
waiver of right to arbitrate, 34, 37
where applications should be made, 32
Sole arbitrators
  appointment of arbitrators or tribunal, 110, 111–112
Specific implement
  arbitrator, power of, 244
  awards, 242, 243–244
  Crown proceedings, 244
  interim measures, 226, 233
  land, contracts relating to, 244
  permanent orders, 233
  supervision, 244
Specific performance
  see **Specific implement**
State or sovereign immunity
  refusal of recognition or enforcement, 63
  waiver, 63
Stated case procedure
  abuse, 210
  appeals, 92
  awards, 1, 101
  challenging awards, 101
  costs, 92
  default rules, 101–102
  draft awards, 261
  fees and expenses, 274
  historical background, 1
  legal error appeals, 101
  legislation, relationship of Act to other, 5
  referral of points of law, 210–211, 213
  Scottish Advisory Committee on Arbitration Law, 92
  transitional provisions, 101–102
Statutory arbitrations
  arbitration agreements, 20
  consensual arbitrations, 53, 54
  consolidation of proceedings, 54
  death of parties, 54
  definition, 52
  power to adapt enactments providing for statutory arbitration, 55
  Scott v *Avery* clauses, 37
  seat of arbitration, 17, 53–54
  sist, 30, 37
  special provisions, 52–54
  time limits, extension of, 54
Statutory instruments
  negative procedure, 97
  positive resolutions, 97
Stay of proceedings
  see **Sist**
Striking out
  want of prosecution, 201–203
Submission
  see **Arbitration agreements**
Supreme Court
  appeals, exclusion of, 311
  serious irregularity appeals, 303–304
Suspension of legal proceedings
  see **Sist**

Technology and Construction Court
  judges as arbitrators or umpires, 87, 88
Tenure of arbitrators
  default rule, 120–121

361

Index

dismissal of tribunal, 121
removal, 121
resignation, 121
revocation of appointment, 120
termination, 139–144
Tenure, termination of
appeals, 141
appointment, revocation of, 139
death of arbitrator
dismissal of tribunal, 140
fees and expenses, adjustment of, 141–142
incapacity of arbitrator, 141
ineligible to act, arbitrator becomes, 139
liability, 139–142
mandatory rule, 139–42
methods, 139–140
nomination in arbitration agreements ceasing to have effect, 144
notice, 141
petitions, 140–141
reconstitution of tribunal, 142–144
removal of arbitrators, 139
resignation of arbitrator 140, 141–142
third parties, removal by, 139
Termination
see **Tenure, termination of; Termination of arbitration**
Termination of arbitration
default rule, 265–268
claims and defences timeously, failure to lodge, 200
delay, 266
functus officio, 265
jurisdiction, 148, 151–152, 266
last awards, on, 265–268
objections to jurisdiction, 148, 151–152
partial termination, 151–152
settlement, 265–268
time limits, 265–266
Third parties
confidentiality, 166, 169, 173
disclosure, 166, 173
dismissal of tribunal by court, 133, 134
fees and expenses, 263, 274, 275–276, 277
final and binding nature of awards, 38, 39–40
good faith, 40
immunity, 323
joint and several liability, 263
no part in proceedings, persons who take, 47–48
payments into court, 318
powers, acting outwith, 293, 299
removal of arbitrators, 124, 139
seat of arbitration, 16, 17, 18, 25
serious irregularity appeals, 293, 294, 299
tenure, termination of, 139
Time limits
appeals, 152–154, 218, 262–263, 291, 293, 300, 303–304, 312–315
appointment of arbitrators, 65, 111, 121, 123, 124, 148, 216
arbitral proceedings, 215–218
arbitration agreements or other agreements, 207, 217, 314
awards, 251–253, 256, 303
calculation, 334–335

challenges to arbitrators' appointments, 121, 123, 124
claims, failure to lodge, 174, 199–204
clarification or removal of ambiguity in awards, 271, 272–273
commencement of arbitration, 84–85
continuing with arbitration pending determination of variation application, 216, 218
correction of awards, 269
damages, 84
default rule, 85, 215–216
defences, failure to lodge, 174, 199–204
delay, 218
directions, failure to comply with, 207
discretion, 216, 218
draft awards, 261–262
effect of Act on limitation, 84
evidence, 221
expenses, 218
fairness, 218
finality of decision on variation, 218
improperly conducted arbitration, 68–69
institutional rules, 215
interim measures, 235
interruption by arbitration, 83–85
jurisdictional appeals, 149–154, 291, 312, 314–315
legal error appeals, 306, 307–308, 310–311, 312, 314–315
mandatory rule, 216–218
negative prescription, 83, 85
objections, 121, 123, 124, 149–151, 153, 324–326
Outer House, applications for variation to, 216, 217, 218
payments into court, 318–319
positive prescription, 83, 84–85
prescription, 83–85
procedure for variation, 216–218
prorogation, 216
reconsideration of awards, 303
reviews, 218
seat in Scotland, 18, 216
serious irregularity, 218, 295, 300, 303–304, 312, 314–315
service or intimation, 217, 334–335
sheriff court, applications for variation to, 216, 218
steps in procedure by arbitrators, 216
statutory arbitrations, 54
substantial injustice, 215, 216, 217, 218
termination of arbitration, 265–266
variation, 215–218
Time periods, calculation of
bank holidays, 334
default rules, 334–335
institutional rules, 334
public holidays and weekends, 335
Trade associations
final and binding nature of awards, 39
Trade usages
awards, 236, 240–241
Transitional provisions
arbiters, use of term, 101
arbitration agreements entered into prior to Act, 99–101
commencement of Act, 98–101

362

Index

commencement of arbitration, 99–100
consultation by ministers, 98, 101
decreets or decrees, use of term, 101
enforcement of foreign awards, 100
former regime, existing arbitrations continuing under, 98–100
parallel regimes, 98–101
stated case procedure, contracting out of, 101–102

Tribunal
see **Appointment of arbitrators or tribunal; Arbitrators; Independence and impartiality; Jurisdiction of tribunal**
admissibility of evidence, determinations of, 174–176
agreed form, not in, 68
arbitration agreements, failure to comply with, 206–208
composition, 68, 106–107
confidentiality, 166, 173–174
correction of awards on own initiative, 268–269
decision making, 189–190, 192–193
deliberations, privacy of, 173–174
directions to parties, 190–191, 205–208
disclosure by the tribunal, 166
dismissal by court, 132–134
evidence, 174–176, 229
experts, 197–198
gap-filling, 15
general duties, 158–165, 173–174
immunity, 320–323
inquisitorial power, 183–185, 221
objections to jurisdiction, rulings on, 152
powers, acting outwith, 293
property, powers relating to, 198–199
reconstitution, 142–144
seat of arbitration, 16, 17, 25
serious irregularity appeals, 293
settlements, promotion of, 267–268
truncated tribunals, 125

Umpires
appointment, 91–92, 111
decisions of tribunal, 189
judge as umpire, 86–89
mandatory rule, 329
number, 111
rules applicable to, 329

UNCITRAL Model Law 1985
influence, 2–4
repeal, 82

Unfair contract terms
consumer arbitration agreements, 6
equality, 164
monetary limits, 6

Unfair treatment
see **Fairness**

Unincorporated bodies
appointment of arbitrators or tribunal, 108

Unique features of Act
approach of Act, 4–5, 25

Urgent cases
interdicts or interim interdicts, 231
interim measures, 235

Validity
applicable law, 147–148
arbitrability, 21–22
arbitration agreements, 21–22, 31–36, 43, 58, 62–64, 91–92, 145–148, 312
awards, 251
capacity, 35
certainty of agreements, 147
commencement of arbitration, notice of, 103–107
correction of awards, applications for, 269
duress, 35
existence of agreements, 145–147
frustration, 147
governing law, validity under, 147–148
impossibility, 36
incapable of being performed, agreements which are, 35–36
invalid contracts, effect of, 21–22
jurisdiction, 43, 145–148, 312
main contract, invalidity of, 147
names of arbitrators, 91–92
place of arbitration, 251
referral of points of law, 211–214
refusal of recognition or enforcement, 58, 62, 63–64
seat, law of the, 63–64
separability, 147
serious irregularity appeals, 312
sist, 31–32, 34–35

Valuers
distinguished between valuation and arbitration, 14
expert determination, 14
immunity in negligence, 14

Venue
see **Place of arbitration; Seat of arbitration**

Vicarious liability
immunity, 323

Waiver,
see **Loss of right to object**

Want of prosecution
striking out, 201–203

Warrants
arrestment or inhibition on the dependence, 228, 229–231
citation, for, 219–220, 221
evidence, 220
security, 228, 229–231

Witnesses
abroad, witnesses resident, 219–220, 221
appeals, 223
arbitrators contacting witnesses, 127–128, 183–185
assistance in securing attendance, requests for, 219–220
attendance, court's power to order, 218–223
commissioners, appointment of, 219–220, 229, 236
common law, 219, 221
conferencing, 185
continuation of arbitration, 219, 223
contempt of court, 219
court intervention, limiting, 221
credibility, assessment of, 144

Index

delay, 220–221, 223
evidence, 183–185
expenses, 220–221, 222 , 223
failure to attend, sanctions for, 219
fairness, 184–185, 220–221, 223
finality of decisions, 223
identity of witnesses, 229
immunity, 323
independence and impartiality, 184, 220–221
interim measures, 233–234, 236
mandatory rule, 218–223
orders for attendance, 219, 220–221
procedure, 184–185, 218, 221–223
questioning, 183–184
reconstitution of tribunal, 144
removal of arbitrators, 127–128
reports on evidence, power to take, 233–234
reviews, 223
service or intimation, 221–222
sheriff court, 221, 222, 223
substantial injustice, 223
time limits, 221
warrants for citation, 219–220, 221
warrants to take evidence, 220

Writing
arbitration agreements, 21
default rules, 27–28
referral of points of jurisdiction, 156
service and formal communications, 331–332
signatures on awards, 249–251, 252–253, 256